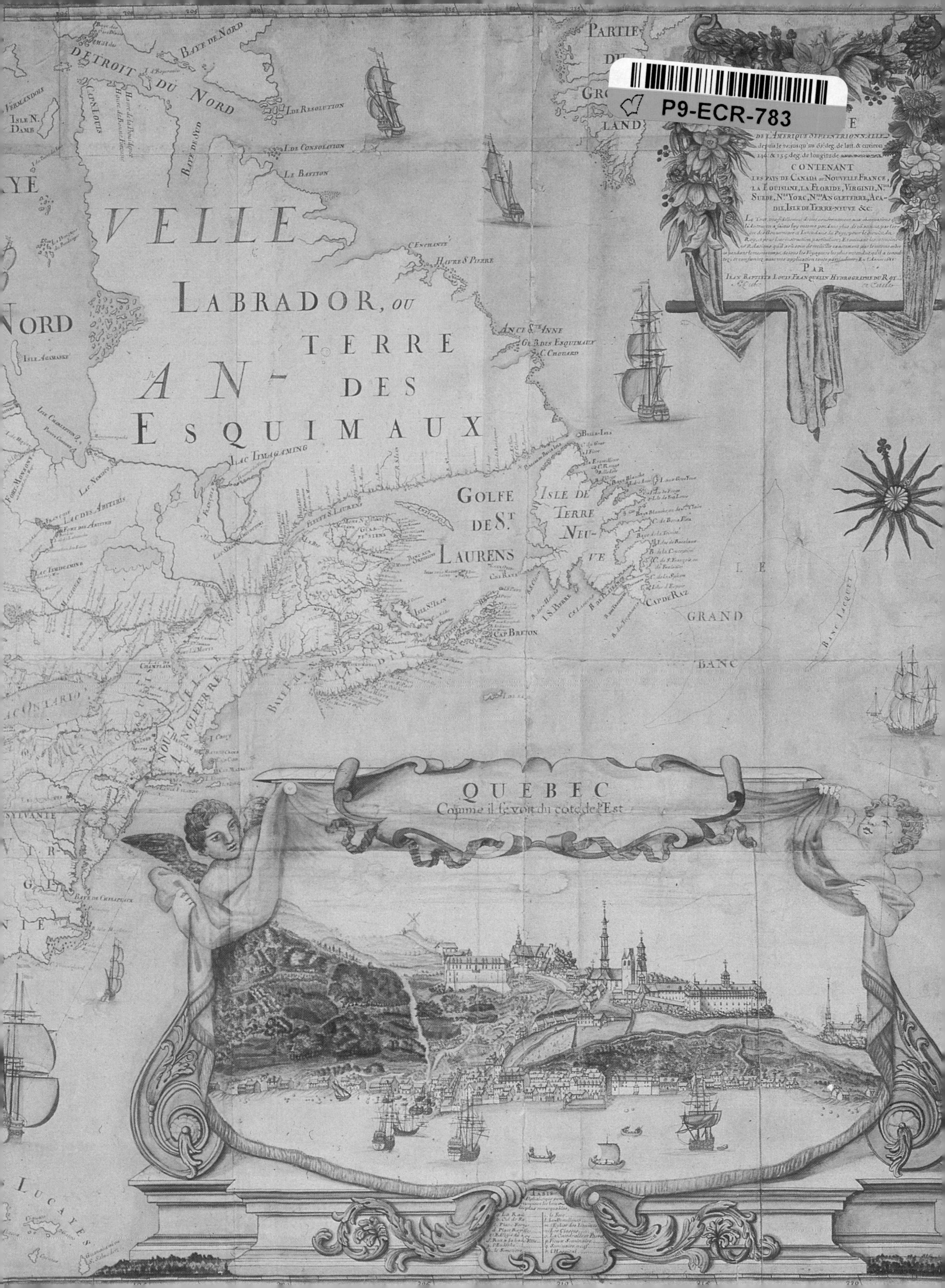

PARTIE
DE L'AMERIQUE SEPTENTRIONNALLE
CONTENANT
LES PAYS DE CANADA OU NOUVELLE FRANCE, LA LOUISIANE, LA FLORIDE, VIRGINIE, N.LLE SUEDE, N.LLE YORC, N.LLE ANGLETERRE, ACADIE, ISLE DE TERRE-NEUVE &C.
PAR
IEAN BAPTISTE LOUIS FRANQUELIN HYDROGRAPHE DU ROY
BAYE DE NORD
DETROIT DU NORD
I. DE RESOLUTION
I. DE CONSOLATION
LE BASTION
VELLE
C. ENCHANTE
HAVRE S. PIERRE
LABRADOR, OU TERRE DES ESQUIMAUX
ANCE S.TE ANNE
C. CHOUARD
NORD
ISLE AGAMASKE
LAC TIMAGAMING
LAC DES ABITIBIS
FORT DES ABITIBIS
LAC TIMISCAMING
GOLFE DE S.T LAURENS
ISLE DE TERRE NEUVE
CAP DE RAZ
CAP BRETON
LE GRAND BANC
BANC IACQUET
LAC ONTARIO
CHAMPLAIN
NOUVELLE ANGLETERRE
BAYE FRANÇOISE
BAYE DE CHESAPEACK
VIRGINIE
SYLVANIE
LUCAYES
QUEBEC
Comme il se voit du coté de l'Est

Records of Our History

Dreams of Empire
Canada before 1700

by André Vachon
of the Royal Society of Canada
in collaboration with
Victorin Chabot and André Desrosiers

Public Archives Canada   Archives publiques Canada

Available in Canada through Authorized Bookstore Agents and other bookstores or by mail from
Canadian Government Publishing Centre
Supply and Services Canada
Ottawa, Canada K1A 0S9

Catalogue No. SA2-129/1-1982E
ISBN 0-660-10977-8
Canada: $24.95
Other Countries: $29.95
Price subject to change without notice

Canadian Cataloguing in Publication Data
Vachon, André, 1933–
Dreams of Empire: Canada before 1700
(Records of Our History)
Issued also in French under title: Rêves d'empire.
Includes index.
DSS cat. no. SA2-129/1-1982E (bound)–DSS cat. no. SA2-129/1-1982-1E (pbk.)
ISBN 0-660-10977-8 (bound): $24.95 ($29.95, foreign)
–ISBN 0-660-11074-1 (pbk.): $14.95 ($17.95, foreign)
1. Canada – History – To 1763 – Archival resources.
I. Chabot, Victorin. II. Desrosiers, André. III. Public Archives Canada.
IV. Title. V. Series.
FC305.V3213   971.01
CIP C82-097002-6   F1030.V3213

Table of Contents

Government
167

Wars
211

Economy
255

Society and Culture
297

Religion
343

Index
383

Foreword

Dreams of Empire is the first volume of a new Public Archives collection entitled *Records of Our History.* Intended for the general public, as well as for students, this collection broadly traces the many facets of Canada's development and presents reproductions of the principal archival documents, the guides to the past that researchers consult when writing on the history of the country. The volumes in this collection are both a memorial to and an illustration of Canadian history, and include several unpublished and little-known documents kept at the Public Archives and in other Canadian and foreign institutions. The books are intended to enrich the general reader's vision of the past and to make the student's contact with original sources more vivid.

Dreams of Empire presents an overview of the history of Canada from the coming of the first explorers up to 1700. The book opens with a short historical survey, which paints a quick portrait of the period under study. The two hundred and fifty documents reproduced come from fifty-two Canadian, American and European institutions, and include maps, engravings, paintings, seals, medals, manuscripts and printed matter. The material is arranged by theme and subtheme, and each section has a short introduction. A caption accompanies each document. It gives a technical description, situates the document in context, indicates the source or provenance, and sometimes reproduces important extracts.

With this structured thematic framework, the reader will be able to leaf casually through the book and to find close at hand all the necessary information about any particular document. For those reading the book from beginning to end, the documents serve to illustrate, confirm or complement the author's assertions.

Well-known historian, archivist and editor André Vachon, a fellow of the Royal Society of Canada, is the author of this book. He drafted the text and made the final choice of documents. However, the publications would not have been possible without the work of Victorin Chabot and André Desrosiers from the French Archives Section of the Public Archives. They were assisted by Françoise Bouvier, Theresa Rowat and Auguste Vachon for the choice of pictures, Normand Saint-Pierre and Lise Perron-Croteau for the printed matter, and Nadia Kazymyra-Dzioba, Edward H. Dahl and Gilles Langelier for the maps and plans. All of them worked on the initial selection of documents and helped find supplementary documents to flesh out certain themes, before the final choice was made. They also prepared the technical description and wrote the historical note for each document. Raymonde Litalien and Mrs. J.M. White located and arranged for the reproduction of several documents housed in foreign institutions.

In addition to ensuring the coordination of the project, Victorin Chabot reviewed the entire text, made useful suggestions to the author and had copies made of the documents from the various institutions. In a word, he followed the project from beginning to end.

For his part, André Desrosiers drafted all the legends and chose the textual extracts from documents that were too long to be reproduced in their entirety.

The editing was done by staff members of Communication Services in the Public Archives. The graphic design was done by Eiko Emori. Translation of the book into English was handled by John F. Flinn, professor of French at the University of Toronto.

Using facsimiles of the same documents that appear in this publication, an exhibition was prepared for display across Canada and abroad.

We wish to express our most sincere gratitude to André Vachon and all those who cooperated in the preparation of this volume, particularly the institutions, which kindly allowed us to reproduce their originals for the book and the exhibition.

Bernard Weilbrenner
Assistant Dominion Archivist

Provenance of documents

Canada

Archives de l'archidiocèse de Québec, Québec
Archives des sœurs de la Congrégation de Notre-Dame, Montréal
Archives des ursulines de Québec, Québec
Archives du Séminaire de Québec, Québec
Archives du Séminaire de Saint-Sulpice, Montréal
Archives nationales du Québec, Centre d'archives de la Capitale, Québec
Archives nationales du Québec, Centre régional de Montréal, Montréal
Bibliothèque de la ville de Montréal, Montréal
Hudson's Bay Company, Winnipeg
Library of Parliament, Ottawa
McGill University, Osler Library, Montréal
Monastère des augustines de l'Hôpital-Général de Québec, Québec
Monastère des augustines de l'Hôtel-Dieu de Québec, Québec
Musée du Séminaire de Québec, Québec
Musée Historial, Sainte-Anne-de-Beaupré
National Library of Canada, Ottawa
New Brunswick Museum, Saint John
Paroisse Notre-Dame, Montréal
Public Archives of Canada, Ottawa
Religieuses hospitalières de Saint-Joseph, Montréal

Other countries

Archives de la Compagnie de Jésus, Chantilly, France
Archives départementales de la Charente-Maritime, La Rochelle, France
Archives départementales de la Gironde, Bordeaux, France
Archives départementales de la Seine-Maritime, Rouen, France
Archives du ministère des Affaires étrangères, Paris, France
Archives nationales, Paris, France
Archivum Romanum Societatis Iesu, Rome, Italy
Biblioteca Apostolica Vaticana, Vatican City
Biblioteca Estense, Modena, Italy
Bibliothèque Mazarine, Paris, France
Bibliothèque municipale, Troyes, France
Bibliothèque nationale, Paris, France
British Library, London, England

British Museum, London, England
Cornell University Library, Ithaca, New York, U.S.A.
Folger Shakespeare Library, Washington, D.C., U.S.A.
John Rylands University Library of Manchester, Manchester, England
Musée du Louvre, Paris, France
Musée national de la Légion d'honneur et des ordres de chevalerie, Paris, France
Museo Naval, Madrid, Spain
National Gallery, London, England
New York Public Library, New York, New York, U.S.A.
Pierpont Morgan Library, New York, New York, U.S.A.
Public Record Office, London, England
Service historique de la Marine, Vincennes, France
Stofnun Árna Magnússonar, Reykjavik, Iceland
Thomas Gilcrease Institute of American History and Art, Tulsa, Oklahoma, U.S.A.
Yale University, Beinecke Rare Book and Manuscript Library, New Haven, Connecticut, U.S.A.

Private Collections

Archives of the Le Moyne de Sérigny family, Bordeaux, France
Mr. Xavier de Rémy de Courcelles, Amiens, France
Mrs. Walter Raleigh Gilbert, Compton Castle, Devon, England
Sir Cennydd Traherne, Coedarhydyglyn, Nr. Cardiff, Wales

America entered into world history with the first great explorations for a passage to Asia. Hardy navigators braved the dangers of this vast uncharted territory in their quest for silk and other luxuries that Europeans had considered indispensable since the Crusades.

However, rivalries soon developed among the Portuguese, the Spanish, the English and the French, who were all seeking to carve out an empire in the New World. North America became a battleground for the French and the English.

In spite of the conflicts, Cartier's hopes and Champlain's plans were followed by Talon's undertakings, and by the end of the seventeenth century a new country, a new France – Canada – emerged in the St. Lawrence lowlands, spreading its influence in all directions.

Introduction

The discoveries

A great number of hypotheses have been put forward concerning the origin of the populations living in the two Americas at the time of Christopher Columbus's discovery. Several of those hypotheses were based upon rather surprising observations: concordances of vocabulary, for example, between certain Australian languages and some Patagonian (South American) languages. None of the theories, however, have resisted thorough examination, and all of them have come up against insuperable difficulties: how – to confine ourselves to the same example – could Australians have travelled from Australia to South America some thousands of years ago? The fact remains that no explanation has yet been found. This is all the more intriguing since the antiquity of man in those regions – thirty thousand years at most, according to archaeological discoveries – cannot account for differences that would let us suppose a much longer evolution.

The question of origins is not the same for North America. The civilizations that are encountered there – at least on the territory that corresponds at the present time to Canada and the northern part of the United States – have existed for scarcely more than ten thousand years, and physical types there, like ways of life, do not vary essentially, except for the Inuit, whose language has no similarity to that of the Indians. Inuit, Indians of the Algonkian family (Micmacs, Montagnais, Attikamegues, Ottawas, Algonkins, Nipissings, Ojibwas, Sioux, etc., nomads all) and Indians of the Iroquoian family (Hurons, Petuns, Neutrals, Iroquois, all of whom were semi-sedentary) are believed to have reached America by way of Behring Strait at a period when Asia and America were joined there by a strip of land. It seems almost certain that that was the main point of entry, if not the only one, for the native populations of the two Americas. In any case anthropology seems to confirm the relationship of the North American Indians with certain Mongolian-type peoples of Asia.

Many theories have also been proposed concerning the discovery of America by the Phoenicians or Egyptians in ancient times, or by St. Brendan's Irish monks at the beginning of our era. None of these theories have been retained by a majority of historians or archaeologists. According to current knowledge it was the Vikings who were the first to land in America, coming around the year 1000 from Greenland, where they had established a colony a short time before. It must be said that their voyages in the northern regions were made much easier by the considerable warming of the climate that was happening at the time. Eric the Red and his fellow countrymen made occasional stays at three points on the continent, which they named Helluland (Flagstoneland), Markland (Woodland), and Vinland (Wineland), and which are believed to be Baffin Island, Labrador, and the northeastern tip of Newfoundland respectively. The site of Vinland, the most famous and, it seems, the most frequently visited by the Viking settlers in North America, has given rise to many conjectures and a great deal of research. According to Icelandic sources, that colony enjoyed a temperate climate; wheat and grapes grew there wild. These pieces of information directed the researchers for a long time towards the south: Cape Cod, Chesapeake Bay, even Florida; however, according to recent archaeological discoveries, Vinland should be located at L'Anse aux Meadows, on the Strait of Belle Isle in Newfoundland. If we keep in mind the warming of the climate at that period, the existence of wild grapes in that region is not improbable. In fact, it was the gradual cooling of the climate that put an end, around the middle of the fourteenth century, to the temporary occupation of our coasts by the Vikings.

There is evidence that in the period between the Vikings' departure and Columbus's discovery, the banks of Newfoundland were frequented by fishermen. A single document that can support that belief, although it does not furnish proof of it, is an agreement reached in December 1514 between the monks of the abbey of Beauport in Brittany and the inhabitants of the island of Bréhat. It is also possible that after Columbus's discovery John Cabot was preceded in North America by a sailor from the Azores, Juan Fernandez; at least this is the contention of a Canadian cartographer who studied the problem of the discoveries some years ago.

Whatever the truth about those possible precursors, John Cabot is believed to have been the first person after the 1492 discovery to head in the direction of the North Atlantic in search of the country of the Great Khan (Asia). He made two voyages in England's name, in 1497 and 1498, and like many others after him, he sailed along the east coast of North America, seeking an opening to the west. However, his exact route is not known; it is not even certain that, having started out farther south, he came as far north as present-day Canada. He was followed by a Portuguese, Gaspar Corte-Real, who probably reached Labrador and the northern part of the island of Newfoundland in 1500 and 1501. Having reached the coast of America, these explorers, like Columbus in 1492, thought that they were on the shores of Asia and within easy reach of the precious spices.

Neither Cabot (1498) nor Corte-Real (1501) returned from their final voyages. Is that why England and Portugal lost interest in North America? For more than twenty years after the arrival of the Bretons, who according to certain sixteenth-century historians had been the first to arrive in North America in 1504, the "New-Found Land" was visited regularly only by cod fishermen. The cod fishermen probably contributed a great deal to the knowledge of this part of America, which, Europe learned thanks to Magellan, was a continent and not an advanced headland of Asia. Thus Francis I sent Giovanni da Verrazzano in 1524 and 1528 to seek a passageway through the continental barrier; in 1524–25 Esteban Gómez applied himself to the same task in the name of Spain. Neither of them found a navigable channel that would have made it possible to sail into the interior of the continent.

In 1534 Francis I entrusted Jacques Cartier with the task of carrying on the exploration that had been begun by Verrazzano. Sailing into the gulf beyond the Strait of Belle Isle, Cartier meticulously went right around the shoreline. On 24 July he erected a cross at Gaspé, fastened to it the Arms of the King of France, and took official possession of the territory. However, he returned to France without having sighted the mouth of the St. Lawrence River. The following year he did reach the great river of Hochelaga (the St. Lawrence) and sailed as far as Stadacona (Québec City). Then he went to visit Hochelaga (Montréal) before spending the winter on the Sainte-Croix River (Saint-Charles). When he returned to France in July 1536, with his men decimated by scurvy, he had discovered the St. Lawrence, explored the interior of the continent as far as Montréal, proven that Anticosti was an island and, by sailing back through Cabot Strait, proven that Newfoundland was also an island. At one go New France had yielded several of her secrets. When Roberval unsuccessfully attempted to found a colony in 1541–42, he added nothing to the information Cartier had acquired.

After Cartier's second voyage there was a respite in actual exploration. With the exception of Roberval's undertaking, Newfoundland was left to the cod fishermen and New France to the fur traders who, following in Cartier's wake, sailed up the St. Lawrence every year to obtain furs in the interior. By the 1550s and 1560s the fur trade was well under way. In 1600–01 Chauvin tried to establish a permanent trading post at Tadoussac, which had already become a meeting place between Indian and white man. Urged on by rivalries, certain prominent persons were soon seeking a monopoly of the fur trade in return for the promise to establish settlers in New France. This was the case with La Roche de Mesgouez, who founded a settlement on Sable Island in 1598, and Du Gua de Monts, who started a colony in Acadia in 1604. Unfortunately, the Sable Island settlement came to a wretched end within five years.

Around 1578 an Englishman, Humphrey Gilbert, vainly sought to found a colony on Newfoundland. During the season the island was visited only by a few fishermen who set up "stages" for drying cod. Many fishermen landed on the island only to take on water, preparing and salting the cod on board their ships. These fishermen were of various nationalities: French, Basque, Spanish, Portuguese and English. England, as we saw through Gilbert's attempt, took a particular interest in Newfoundland.

England had also begun to be interested in a northwest passage that would carry ships towards Asia. Leaving the St. Lawrence route to the French, England headed much farther north. From 1577 to 1631 no fewer than eleven explorers made voyages there; they discovered Frobisher Bay, Davis Strait, Hudson Strait, Baffin Bay, Baffinland, and Hudson Bay (1610). But no trace was found of a passage to the west. If we except the 1620 voyage of Jens Eriksen Munk of Denmark, England had been alone in pursuing this search in the North. She returned to Hudson Bay in the seventeenth century, but did not resume the search for the famous passage for a long time.

Settlement

Pierre Du Gua de Monts, who was appointed lieutenant general of New France in 1603, and Samuel de Champlain, his principal collaborator, gave great impetus to New France. In March 1603 Champlain left for Canada along with François Gravé Du Pont. Champlain explored the St. Lawrence, stopping at Gaspé, while de Monts, the new holder of the trade monopoly, organized a company in France for trading in Canada. In 1604 de Monts decided, apparently on Champlain's advice, to establish his colony in Acadia; as a temporary site they chose Île Sainte-Croix, where they were shut in for the whole winter. By 1604 Champlain had inspected the coastline of Acadia. In the summer of 1605 he continued his exploration with de Monts; they went as far as Mallebare (Nauset Harbour) to the south. In the meantime the colony had been moved to Port-Royal, where the winters of 1605–06 and 1606–07 were spent under more pleasant circumstances. In 1606 Champlain again explored the coast of New England, this time with Poutrincourt. Upon their return to Port-Royal on 14 November they were greeted with a welcoming performance of the *Théâtre de Neptune en Nouvelle France*, a play by Marc Lescarbot, which Champlain referred to as "light entertainment". Since de Mont's monopoly had been taken away from him, the colony returned to France in 1607. In 1610 the French came back to Port-Royal; in the meantime Champlain had gone off towards the St. Lawrence.

On 3 July 1608, in fact, Champlain was arriving at the "point of Quebec". There he had an *Abitation* (habitation) built for himself and the fur-trading clerks. Quebec was founded. Champlain spent the winter in Canada at the habitation, where sixteen of his men died of scurvy. In 1609 Champlain discovered the lake that now bears his name, and at Ticonderoga, in the present-day state of New York, he won his first victory with his Huron and Algonkin allies over the Iroquois. He won another battle in 1610 on the banks of the Richelieu River. In 1613 he went up the Ottawa as far as Allumette Island; in 1615, again following more or less the same route, he went beyond Allumette Island and headed for the Huron Country, where he discovered Lake Attigouantan (Lake Huron). Wounded during an indecisive battle with the Iroquois, Champlain spent the winter among the Hurons. After that, as he was completely taken up by business matters and was constantly being obliged to defend the future of the "colony," Champlain went on no more journeys; nor did he again have to confront the Iroquois, who asked for peace in 1624.

Champlain generally spent the winter in France; he would come back to Québec in the spring for the annual trading. All his life he had to struggle against the merchants, who, despite their commitments, gave little support to his plan for a colony and above all refused to carry settlers to New France. Since 1612, however, Champlain had been lieutenant to prominent people, dukes and princes, who bore in turn the title of viceroy of New France. In addition Champlain had seen his authority increase in 1620, when the king had promoted him, as it were, governor, without the title, of New France. All was to no avail: the program for colonization that he had proposed in 1618 to the king and the *Chambre du commerce* of Paris remained unheeded. The merchants barely provided maintenance for the few Recollets who had gone to Québec in 1615 and the Jesuits who had landed there in 1625. Nearly twenty years after being founded Québec in no way resembled a colony; it was a trading post and was entirely dependent upon the mother country.

It was under these circumstances that the Compagnie de la Nouvelle-France, called the Compagnie des Cent-Associés, was created in 1627 at Richelieu's instigation. The company was granted New France "in full ownership, justice, and seigneury," as well as the monopoly of the fur trade in perpetuity, and of all other trade – codfishing and whaling excepted – for fifteen years. During this period the company would pay no import or export duties; every three years it would propose the commandant (or governor) of the country and the fort commandants, who would be appointed by the king. In return the company was to assume the "expenses of the country," maintain garrisons and ecclesiastics, and above all transport four thousand people to New France before the end of 1643 and maintain them for three years. This spelt the fulfilment of Champlain's dearest wishes.

In 1628 the Cent-Associés sent a small fleet commanded by Claude Roquemont and consisting of four ships bearing settlers and goods to New France. But the English now had designs on New France: the Kirke brothers seized this fleet, inflicting heavy losses from which the company never completely recovered. Since they received no help, Champlain and Gravé Du Pont had to surrender the following year and return to France with most of the French, the missionaries included. From 1629 to 1632 Québec was occupied by the English, who were also masters of Port-Royal – which Samuel Argall had devastated in 1613.

Champlain returned to Canada in 1633. He hastened to raise the habitation from its ruins and had the church of Notre-Dame-de-Recouvrance built. The following year he had a fort built on a small island halfway between Québec and Trois-Rivières; he also sent people to begin a settlement at Trois-Rivières. Having renewed the alliances with the Indians in the St. Lawrence valley, he sent Jean Nicollet to the Great Lakes region with the mission of winning the Indians over to the French cause. Finally, being aware of the obstacles that would be put in the way of the colony by the English on the one hand and by the Iroquois on the other, he asked Richelieu for help to chase the English from Tadoussac and to exterminate the Iroquois if necessary. On 25 December 1635, shortly after making this request, Champlain died at Québec, happy, certainly, to have been present at the arrival of several families the preceding summer.

The Cent-Associés

In 1636 Charles Huault de Montmagny, governor of New France and Champlain's successor, landed at Québec. One of his first concerns was to assure the security of the settlers, who were threatened by the Iroquois. The latter became all the more formidable because from 1639 on the Dutch supplied them with harquebuses in large quantities. Montmagny converted the Château Saint-Louis into a fortress and had a gun-platform fitted out at Trois-Rivières. In 1642 he had Fort Richelieu built on the Richelieu River. The year before, in fact, the Iroquois, who had been making occasional forays into the colony since 1634, had taken to the warpath in earnest. Trois-Rivières and then Montréal received the first attacks. In 1641, Montmagny had tried to dissuade the "Montréalistes" from settling on Montréal Island; Chomedey de Maisonneuve had not been willing to change his plan, and on 18 May 1642 Ville-Marie was founded. In 1645, it is true, the Mohawks signed a peace treaty at Trois-Rivières; but it was only a truce, to which only one Iroquois tribe out of five momentarily submitted.

During the Iroquois war Ville-Marie became the colony's "bastion" and "rampart." Its founders, however, were impelled primarily by religious motives; they wanted to work for the conversion of the Indians. In this regard the founding of Montréal in 1642 entered into the same apostolic movement as the founding of the *réduction* or Indian village at Sillery (1637), and of the Ursuline convent and the Hôtel-Dieu at Québec (1639). In these years all the religious institutions in the colony were intended first of all for the Indians; and in actual fact the colony itself often seems to have been a sort of extension of the mission, so intense were the apostolic concerns and activity.

It must be said that from 1632 on the Jesuits (who had returned to Québec without the Recollets) were the great driving force behind the mission and the colony, both through their activity in Canada and through the publication in France of their annual *Relations*. The Jesuits were propagandists for New France among the French public, missionaries, interpreters, ambassadors to the Indians, explorers and discoverers, leaders of the religious life among the settlers, owners of seigneuries encouraging agriculture, teachers in their college at Québec, supporters of the Nuns Hospitalers and Ursulines, and advisers to the governors; all the Jesuits played an indispensable role in New France up until the 1660s. Though few in number, they nevertheless carried on their work at Québec, Trois-Rivières, Montréal, Tadoussac, Lake Saint-Jean, on the Saint-Maurice and the Ottawa Rivers – everywhere that the settlers or Indians were to be found. In 1634 some of them had gone to re-open the Huron mission, which had been started before the fall of Quebec in 1629. In the 1640s it became the most flourishing mission in New France, but it was completely destroyed by the Iroquois in the period 1647–49. Several Jesuits suffered martyrdom at that time.

Despite the aid of the Compagnie de Beaupré, which owned the seigneuries of Beaupré and Île d'Orléans, and of the Jesuits and seigneurs such as Robert Giffard, who collaborated in the settlement of New France within the framework of the seigneurial régime, the Compagnie des Cent-Associés, which had lost 400,000 livres in 1628, and whose initial momentum was broken by the fall of Québec in 1629, was not the dynamic element that the colony needed. Moreover, by blocking the inland routes for the fur trade and diverting to New Netherland (New York) the furs intended for New France, the Iroquois soon drove the company to the brink of bankruptcy. In 1645 the Cent-Associés, apparently at the insistence of the Jesuits, handed over to the Communauté des Habitants the monopoly on furs, along with financial responsibility for the colony. After a few profitable years, thanks to the precarious peace of 1645, this company, which was made up of prominent people in the colony, in turn ran into difficulties. In 1659, at the height of the Iroquois war, it surrendered its rights to the Compagnie de Rouen. It reclaimed these rights in 1661, but disappeared in 1663 at the same time as the Compagnie des Cent-Associés.

In 1647, after the creation of the Communauté des Habitants, the king installed in the colony a council that was to keep watch on the fur trade. It was first modified in 1648, then again in 1657 and 1659. The role of this council, which at first was interested only in matters concerning the fur trade, was subsequently broadened; this resulted in a certain diminution of the powers of the governor, who up until 1647 had jurisdiction over everything except the running of the fur trade and the financial administration, strictly speaking, of the colony. The governor even dispensed justice in civil and criminal matters. In 1651 two seneschal's courts were instituted, one at Québec, the other at Trois-Rivières, which were responsible for hearing cases coming from the two regions in the first instance, and perhaps appeals emanating from the seigneurial courts in their jurisdictions. The governor, the council, the seneschal's courts, and finally the seigneurial courts of justice – such were the administrative institutions in the colony of Canada up until 1663, when the Compagnie des Cents-Associés submitted its resignation to the king. If all that was still of little importance, it must not be forgotten that the population scarcely exceeded three thousand in 1663; this figure was much greater than that of Acadia, where since 1632 internal quarrels had divided the colony, making it an easy prey for the English, who imposed their law on it from 1654 to 1667.

Jean Talon's work

As the Compagnie des Cents-Associés had resigned at the beginning of 1663 and handed New France over to the king, Louis XIV appointed a new governor, an intendant of justice, public order and finances, and a *Conseil souverain* (sovereign council). The governor became the king's personal representative in the colony. The intendant received very vast powers, since everything came under his authority except war and diplomacy, which were in the governor's jurisdiction, and religious matters, which were governed by the vicar apostolic. The Conseil souverain, which was a court of justice, nevertheless played a certain administrative role, which was increased for some years because the first intendant appointed to New France, the Sieur Robert de Fortel, never arrived.

Now, these institutions were scarcely in place (in the absence of an intendant) when the king and Jean-Baptiste Colbert changed their minds to a certain extent and created the Compagnie des Indes occidentales (the French West Indies Company), to which they handed over ownership and administration of New France, as they had done earlier with the Compagnie des Cents-Associés. At the same time they granted it a monopoly of trade and shipping for a period of forty years. The company's régime was established in Canada on 16 July 1665, a little less than two months before Intendant Jean Talon landed at Québec. Some weeks later Talon informed Colbert of his opposition to the company: if the king wanted the company to become rich, its rights and privileges had to be guaranteed; but if the king wanted the colony to progress, he could not leave the ownership and administration of New France, and even the management of its trade, in any hands other than his own. During his two stays in New France, from 1665 to 1668 and 1670 to 1672, Talon – imitated by Boutroue and Courcelle – endeavoured to impose the king's authority in the colony, often to the detriment of the company, whose charter was revoked in 1674.

In the same year as Talon there landed at Québec the Carignan-Salières regiment, which the king had sent under the command of Lieutenant General Alexandre de Prouville de Tracy to finally quell the Iroquois, who for so long had been hindering development of the colony. In anticipation of the impending campaign the authorities had three wooden forts built on the Richelieu River in the autumn of 1665. In January 1666 Governor Daniel de Rémy de Courcelle set out with little more than five hundred men. Not having Indian guides, he did not reach the Iroquois country and in the spring returned ingloriously. (The Canadian René-Louis Chartier de Lotbinière left a burlesque poem recounting this expedition.) In September M. de Tracy set off in his turn with some thirteen hundred men, including about a hundred Indians. He had to be content with burning the Mohawk villages, whose inhabitants had fled, and taking possession of them officially in the king's name. Frightened by this show of might, the five Iroquois tribes signed peace treaties, the last one in 1667, the year when the Treaty of Breda gave Acadia back to France.

Talon had not waited for peace to set about his work. In 1665 he turned his attention to increasing the population. First, he himself did the first nominal census of the colony in the winter of 1665–66. Then, despite his prejudices against the company, he reached an agreement with it to bring a large number of settlers to New France – families, single men, and *filles du roi* (king's daughters), several hundred of whom found husbands in the days or weeks following their arrival. It must be said that the some five hundred officers and men of the Carignan-Salières regiment who settled in Canada at Talon's invitation increased for a time the numerical imbalance that had always existed between the unmarried men and women. Not satisfied just to bring in settlers, the intendant adopted and had the king's council adopt various social measures intended to encourage marriages and large families. Talon's activity in this sphere assured the permanence of the colony; the major part of the French-speaking population of Québec and Canada came from the families that were settled in the country before 1672, in the seigneuries granted in large measure by the intendant.

Every year, in anticipation of the arrival of new settlers, Talon had a certain number of plots of land made ready; to the new arrivals he distributed provisions and tools to enable them to manage on their own as quickly as possible. In addition, the ships brought a number of domestic animals which the intendant distributed among the habitants, who were encouraged in various ways to increase and diversify their production. The intendant encouraged the setting up of several "manufactories" for producing wool, leather, hemp, tar, in order to furnish an outlet for the development of agriculture and forestry. His great idea, which proved to be profitable throughout his two stays in Canada, was to closely link agriculture, industry, and trade. It was with this in mind that he had a brewery built at Québec "at great expense," to use up surplus grains, in particular barley, and to stimulate the growing of hops. Similarly he created "marine workyards" on the Saint-Charles River for building ships. This industry was effective in encouraging the development of forest products, the growing of hemp, cord making, and even the production of tar, at which several attempts were made. The intendant also dreamed of creating forges for making iron fittings, anchors, and guns intended for the ships that were built in Canada. In turn these ships were to serve, and indeed some did, for exporting the colony's products – wheat, all sorts of cereals, wood (planks, boards, stave wood), beer, salt pork and fish – to Acadia and the West Indies. Talon had in fact conceived the idea of a three-way system of trade between Canada, the West Indies, and France, based in Québec. Canadian products were to be delivered to the West Indies, products from the West Indies were to be shipped to France, and goods intended for the valley of the St. Lawrence were to be loaded in France.

If he was successful in organizing a vast operation oriented towards the export industry and trade, Talon did not succeed, despite the many searches that he had carried out, in finding mines – other than coal – that could be exploited with the means of the period when the difficulties peculiar to the colony, such as the distances, the absence of roads and means of transport, and the lack of specialized workmen, were taken into account. It is in fact significant that every time that he got into a new sector of economic activity, he had to bring the necessary manpower from Europe: shipwrights, a man to make tar, a skilled miner, etc. Talon was already encountering the difficulty which his successors would constantly come up against: the scarcity of specialized workers, and even of labourers, and consequently their excessively high cost, which would become one of the main causes of the weakness of industry in New France.

Despite the company Talon was successful in 1669 in having free trade accorded the inhabitants of New France. Besides, both to set an example and to get economic activity started, Talon, with Colbert's approval, engaged in trade in the colony himself: the brewery in Québec belonged to him; he grew hops on his land at Les Ilets; he sold goods that he brought in from France. Otherwise Talon was rather an exponent of a planned economy, issuing or having the Conseil souverain issue ordinances which were aimed at promoting such and such an activity or protecting others. To ensure the progress of his brewery and make the habitants drink beer, for example, he had importation of wine and spirits reduced. The merchants were somewhat distrustful of him, and it was this distrust, it seems, that prevented him from setting up a company to develop inshore fishing; the merchants, according to Frontenac, were afraid "that they would lose the freedom to do it in their own way, wanting to be the sole masters and directors of their business activities."

During his first term of office Talon had scarcely had time to do more than lay the foundations of a diversified agriculture, of an industry that became the driving force behind the Canadian economy, and of a commerce founded on exporting. In the course of his second term of office, while pursuing the work that he had undertaken in 1665, he wanted to concern himself "with relating New France to its natural, geographical, and economic ties" (Lionel Groulx). First of all, in view of the strategic situation of Acadia, certain of whose ports were more easily and quickly reached than the port of Québec, Talon wanted to establish there the storage areas that Colbert desired. To make communications easier – for economic as well as military purposes – he also wanted to open up a land route from Lévis to Pentagouet. Similarly, to ensure that furs reached the colony he made a very audacious suggestion for harnessing the Ottawa rapids, "which interfere to such an extent with the Indians' travelling by water that sometimes they are discouraged from coming down to us to bring us their pelts." Looking even further and perhaps without knowing it, he took up one of Davaugour's suggestions, which would subsequently be put forward many times again, and recommended to the king that New Netherland be conquered or bought, so as to give the colony a second port of entry farther south and open all year, to bring the Iroquois under French influence, and to contain the English in New England within their territory. Louis XIV rejected this recommendation, which might perhaps have ensured his heirs of possession of most of North America. Talon also proposed that a fort be built on Lake Ontario to put an end to the "acts of piracy" by the Iroquois, who were seizing French furs with impunity to take them to the Dutch or English.

Since he too was obsessed by the idea of the *Mer du Sud* (the Pacific Ocean), and since he wanted to form an alliance with the native tribes of the continent, Talon sent explorers off in all directions, thanks to the St. Lawrence, which led off "towards the West," and the rivers that opened "the route to the North and the South." Given the task of surveying the country, discovering new waterways, and going even as far as the Mer du Sud, these "resolute men" were also to take possession, with all the required formalities, of the territories that they would cover. It was with those aims that Cavelier de La Salle, Dollier de Casson and Bréhant de Galinée, Daumont de Saint-Lusson and Nicolas Perrot, Denys de Saint-Simon and Albanel, set out, as did Jolliet and Marquette shortly after the intendant's departure but at his request. From their travels across the country would be born the grandiose vision – which Talon had often conjured up since 1665 – "of a great country of vast and prodigious extent."

This country with the proportions of an empire suffered, according to Talon, from never having "been regarded [by France] as it ought to have been," and "its whole failure" came from the fact that it had never been turned to account "through farming." For five years Talon as intendant worked with admirable imaginativeness and energy at turning it to account; when he left in 1672, however, the king had already warned him that the war with Holland left little money for Canada and that no more settlers would be sent. Furthermore, Talon was not replaced until 1675, and very quickly the impetus that he had given the colony was almost completely lost.

Church, economy, society

In 1672, both Jean Talon and Bishop François de Laval sailed for France, the former to remain there for good, the latter to work there at his appointment as titular bishop of Québec. Bishop Laval, who had been vicar apostolic of New France since 1658 with the "foreign" title of bishop of Petraea, had arrived in the colony on 16 June 1659. He first had to have his authority recognized ahead of that of the archbishop of Rouen, who claimed jurisdiction over Canada and from whom a Sulpician, Abbé Queylus, had received letters patent as vicar general. The court even had to intervene in favour of Bishop Laval. At Québec, since they did not know exactly what the status of a vicar apostolic was, the women's religious communities themselves had hesitated between Bishop Laval and the archbishop of Rouen. When his authority had finally been established, Bishop Laval went to France on matters concerning the colony, in particular to have trade in spirits forbidden.

On 26 March 1663, through an ordinance published in Paris, he founded the Séminaire de Québec, an institution that, in keeping with the spirit of the Council of Trent, would bring the secular priests who were responsible for the various ministries together in a community under the leadership of the vicar apostolic (and later the bishop). As well as being an institution for training clerics (or Grand Séminaire), the Séminaire de Québec was, in its founder's words, "to serve as clergy for this new Church." The priests would pool all their wealth and revenues in it, and the seminary would support them "in sickness and in health, either in the exercise of their functions or in the community when they were recalled to it." To this end the seminary would collect the tithes, which Bishop Laval had also instituted in 1663, and would distribute them equitably to the priests in charge of or serving the parishes. In 1668 the vicar apostolic, who was still concerned about the training of future priests, founded in addition a Petit Séminaire, whose pupils, candidates for the priesthood, studied at the Jesuit college and boarded at the seminary.

On 26 September 1659, Bishop Laval set up an officialty (ecclesiastical court) at Québec; in 1664 he established the parish of Québec canonically; and in 1666 he consecrated its church. He had, in a missionary spirit, asked for and obtained in 1665 the affiliation of his seminary with the Séminaire des Missions Étrangères in Paris. But the quarrel over the trade in spirits, which had died down in 1663, broke out anew in 1668. The firmness of the bishop of Petraea created enemies for him, who cast into doubt the authority that he exercised as vicar apostolic. Remembering that the king had named him to the bishopric of Québec in 1662, Bishop Laval wanted to obtain confirmation of this appointment from Rome as quickly as possible. Therefore he went to France in 1672. The new governor, Buade de Frontenac, took advantage of his absence to try to subject the clergy to his whims. However, the king's intervention and Bishop Laval's return in 1675 with the title of bishop of Québec, which he had obtained in 1674, put an end to many more or less futile quarrels. The bishop ratified most of the acts of his preceding administration, established several parish charges, and in 1684 completed the organization of his Church by endowing it with a diocesan chapter.

The first bishop of Québec had returned to the colony in the same year that the king resumed possession and entire administration of it. The preceding year (1674) had seen the revocation of the charter of the Compagnie des Indes occidentales. The Conseil souverain was reorganized and a new intendant, Jacques Duscheneau, came – with a three-year delay! – to replace Jean Talon alongside the irascible Frontenac. Unfortunately, from the moment of their first contact the two top civil authorities in New France – the governor and the intendant – clashed head-on. For a period of seven years there resulted endless quarrels, into which were drawn law officers, merchants, secular clergy and members of religious orders, often against their will. While the clans were fighting one another ferociously, the economic reform undertaken by Talon was reaching the final degree of deterioration, to the point that wheat had to be imported, whereas under "the great intendant" Canada had exported it. As a result of the cupidity of the governor and his protégés, anarchy invaded the whole fur-trading network, which was soon out of control. Favouritism, illegality, even smuggling went unchecked. In vain the king and the colonial authorities forbade taking to the woods on pain of the most severe punishments, and in desperation they promised amnesty to those coureurs des bois who returned to the colony. Equally vainly they instituted a system of permits (licences to engage in fur trading) to control access to the hunting grounds. Nothing worked, as a large part of the young men had irrevocably chosen a life of freedom in the woods, far from surveillance, constraints, and the tedium of daily work.

Ten years had sufficed to wipe out Talon's remarkable work. Very quickly furs again became the colony's sole resource, but because the Indian tribes scarcely brought furs to the colony any more, they had to be sought from farther and farther away, hence the increasing number of coureurs des bois. The Indians were more and more tempted to sell furs at Albany, at New York, at Hudson Bay, where the English were offering much better prices than the French. All along the waterways leading to the English factories, trading posts had to be established to stop the Indians. Between those posts and the colony appeared forts such as Fort Frontenac and those at Michilimackinac and Detroit, which served as relays and supply bases. The king was opposed, however, to the expansion of New France; but how could it be prevented, when it had to be recognized as a vital necessity? Besides, the problem of the colony was not at its outermost points, however far away they were, but at its centre, where settlement was weak, agriculture stagnant, and industry just about non-existent, despite a slight revival under Intendants Jacques de Meulles and Jean Bochart de Champigny. It was the heart of the colony that risked failing.

Society at all levels was feeling the effects of the absence of a structured economy. It was under the influence of the free and somewhat insouciant life style that had been adopted by many young men, and even by the sons of good families who had no other means of subsistence than taking to the woods and engaging in the fur trade. The wars themselves damaged the stability of the habitants, all militiamen since 1669, who had to put up with corvées and distant excursions and neglect their land. According to the testimony of the authorities, poverty reigned in the colony in the 1680s; the nobles were "beggars," good-for-nothings, too proud to work the land. Many seigneurs, who were however commoners, pretended to live like the country gentry in France. With a few rare exceptions the merchants were "penniless"; too many settlers were abandoning the land to take to the woods. In short, only those people who worked their land seriously lived relatively comfortably, although many of them were ruined by the Iroquois raids at the beginning of the 1690s. This population readily proved independent, even rebellious. Bishop Saint-Vallier detected "abuses" in it, which he endeavoured to correct, although nothing was very serious. Besides, many of the faults for which this newborn nation was reproached were soon to be considered the very qualities that would ensure its survival.

Eventful years

In 1682 the king recalled Frontenac and Duchesneau. In the same year the Compagnie du Nord was founded to conduct the fur trade in the Hudson Bay area. This company was the Canadian response to the Hudson's Bay Company of London, which through its trading in the region of the bay for the preceding ten years threatened to get possession of the richest furs in the continent, those from the northwest. Le Moyne d'Iberville distinguished himself in fighting for this company, which until 1697 had to carry on trade and war at the same time. Again in 1682 the Iroquois attacked the Illinois, a tribe that was allied with the French. This breach of the peace caused great anxiety in the colony, as did the rumour of other hostile intentions attributed to the Five Nations. At an assembly convoked by the new governor, Le Febvre de La Barre, it was decided that a punitive expedition was necessary. La Barre played for time; in 1684, after an attack by the Senecas on Fort Saint-Louis-des-Illinois, he finally led an expedition as far as Anse de la Famine (Famine Cove) on Lake Ontario, where the Iroquois imposed a shameful peace upon him.

La Barre was recalled, and his successor, René Brisay de Denonville, was ordered to avenge the honour of the French. In the summer of 1687 the governor burned down the Seneca villages; meanwhile, Bochart de Champigny seized a group of Onondagas, some forty of whom were sent to the galleys in France. The Iroquois' reprisal took two years to come; it was the massacre of Lachine. Many other localities were attacked by the Iroquois. In 1693 Champigny spoke of the ruins caused by the "enemies" – that is to say, the Iroquois – "above Trois-Rivières," for example.

During all these years, which were marked by quarrelling between governors and intendants – at least until Champigny's arrival in 1686 – Bishop Laval for his part had not been content with laying the foundations of the Canadian Church, but had successfully begun building it. In 1688, the year in which his successor arrived in the colony, "Monseigneur l'Ancien," as he was henceforth called, could have presented the following statistics: the number of parishes had grown from 5 in 1659 to 35; the number of priests, regular and secular, had increased from 5 to 102, and of nuns from 32 to about 97. Of the 33 secular priests in the colony 13 were Canadian, and 50 of the nuns in the diocese had been born in Canada. In addition, religious and secular clergy were carrying on the missionary work; the Gospel was being preached to more and more distant tribes, still with the same zeal. But if the Canadian Church continued to be a missionary church, it was no longer a mission church. Bishop Laval, its first head, had made it, as we should say today, a national church. And if he had had to resist the civil authority more than once, in particular in the matters concerning the trade in spirits and the parishes, he was none the less respected and esteemed by all, having "great influence [on the population] because of his character and his reputation for saintliness," according to Denonville.

Bishop Saint-Vallier's episcopate was marked from the beginning by the bishop's quarrels with the directors of the Séminaire de Québec. Under Bishop Laval the pastoral charges were attached to the seminary; Bishop Saint-Vallier wanted them to be attached to him directly. The dispute was settled by the king in 1692; from then on the seminary would no longer be anything but an institution for training future priests. Monseigneur l'Ancien accepted with great resignation the king's decision, which altered his dearest work to such a degree as to make it unrecognizable.

Otherwise, Bishop Saint-Vallier showed great pastoral zeal and great charity. In this respect it must be noted that he was the founder of the Hôpital-Général de Québec (1693) and that he contributed to the founding of the Hôpital-Général de Montréal (1694), two institutions that took in the poor, the invalid, the sick or aged of the whole colony. And the poor were more and more numerous in this country "half ruined by the war" which had been raging since 1689. Numerous too were the "habitants crippled by the war," the "poor widows," and the children who "had difficulty in getting something to eat."

Since the massacre of Lachine the Iroquois had resumed their bloody raids into the colony; moreover, the war of the League of Augsburg, which was declared in 1689, gave the English the opportunity to show up in New France after the raids launched on New England by Frontenac at the beginning of 1690. (The old governor had been sent back to the colony the preceding year). In May 1690 Sir William Phips seized Port-Royal; in October he besieged Québec with thirty-four ships. To his call for surrender, Frontenac made a proud reply; Québec remained in French hands. After that, except in the Hudson Bay region, Acadia, and Newfoundland, where Le Moyne d'Iberville upheld the French cause all by himself and carried the war victoriously, the French and English did not confront each other except during an English attempt against La Prairie in 1692. The New England settlers were content to arm the Iroquois and send them against the colony. For their part the French planned two sea-borne expeditions, one against New York (1689), the other against Boston (1697), which were not carried out; however, they did successfully carry out two offensives into Iroquois territory early in 1693 and in the summer of 1696. The Treaty of Ryswick, signed in 1697, put an end to this terrible war, and in 1701 the "Peace of Montréal," signed by the Five Nations Confederacy, ensured for the colony a little badly needed peace.

The war of the League of Augsburg made evident the growing difficulty that the inhabitants of Canada were encountering in defending a territory as vast as New France. Did not d'Iberville's extraordinary journeys, from Hudson Bay to Acadia, from Acadia to Newfoundland, then from Newfoundland to Hudson Bay, make clear the extreme mobility that was needed to ward off dangers everywhere they appeared and to strike the enemy before he struck you? To march on Massachusetts or New York or the Mohawk villages in the middle of the winter; or else, to set off for the Mississippi or Lake Superior... Beyond any doubt, despite the courage and endurance of her soldiers, militiamen, and coureurs des bois, this colony was becoming too big and too fragile. And at that moment, to protect a territory that was already too vast – even though it was no longer possible to protect Acadia properly – another colony, Louisiana, had to be founded (in 1700) to contain the English, it was said, and to prevent them from becoming the masters of all America "sooner or later."

I

The Origins

At the very beginning of our recorded history we encounter a legend (St. Brendan), a falsification (the Zeno brothers), an unconfirmed hypothesis (Irish monks in Newfoundland in the 10th century), and the still very little known odyssey of the Vikings. If we may be certain of the presence of the Vikings on our coasts around the year 1000, much still has to be discovered to solve the mystery surrounding their comings and goings, in particular in the marvellous region that was Vinland.

It was after Christopher Columbus's discovery that the existence of a New World – the American continent – was known in Europe. The Vikings had reached it somewhat accidentally in the course of their sailing from one island to another; for his part Columbus had run up against it as an obstacle between Europe and the Indies, which he thought he could reach by going west.

Besides, it took a certain time to realize even approximately just how big this obstacle was, and above all to be convinced of the existence between Asia and Europe of a hitherto unknown continent. Was there not a passage somewhere through this continent that would give access to Asia, the Indies, and Cathay (China) if one kept pushing on to the West?

It was in an attempt to find that passage that the first expeditions pushed off, in the hope that it would provide European merchants with a faster and safer route towards the trading posts of Asia.

In the name of England John Cabot (Giovanni Caboto) made two voyages, in 1497 and 1498, and inspected part of the northeastern coast of America, although we do not know exactly what his itinerary was in one or the other year nor at what points on the shore he landed. In 1500 and 1501 Portugal in its turn sent an explorer, Gaspar Corte-Real; again it is very difficult to say where he went, except that he seems to have followed the coast of Labrador and put in on the northern part of the island of Newfoundland.

I

After 1501 Europe appears to have lost interest in the New-Found Land, abandoning it to the codfishermen who rushed to its waters every year.

Continuing exploration at the latitude of Newfoundland later became almost exclusively France's business. In 1524, on the order of Francis I, Giovanni da Verrazzano explored the American coast from Florida or North Carolina to Newfoundland; in 1528 he undertook a second voyage of exploration, from which he did not return. France had not found, any more than had England or Portugal, the famous passage to Cathay. Spain too had tried its luck at it in 1524–25 with Estevão Gomes (Esteban Gómez), without any greater success.

The search that had been undertaken by Verrazzano was continued by Jacques Cartier from 1534 to 1536. With him the New-Found Land began to deliver up its secrets: in 1534 Cartier sailed around the gulf and took possession of the country at Gaspé in the name of the king of France; in 1535 he discovered the St. Lawrence and sailed up it as far as Stadacona (Québec) and Hochelaga (Montréal), before spending the winter near Stadacona. The explorer brought back from his two voyages an account that was precise and entertaining, despite its apparent dryness.

Thanks to Cartier more than anyone else, and thanks to his first two voyages much more than to Jean-François de La Rocque de Roberval's attempt at colonization, the lands of Canada, Hochelaga, the Saguenay – in short New France – came into history.

The possibility of finding a passage to Cathay through the American continent continued to preoccupy many European sailors. This time they looked for it up in the Arctic. Two Englishmen, Martin Frobisher and John Davis made two voyages of exploration there, the first in 1577 and 1578, the other in 1585, 1586, and 1587: Frobisher entered the bay that bears his name, as well as Hudson Strait, and Davis entered the strait to which his name is attached.

In the meantime another Englishman, Humphrey Gilbert, who was fascinated by America, wanted to establish a colony there; to that end he had obtained letters patent in 1578 and was preparing a program for colonization in collaboration with some of the leading Catholics in the kingdom. His project was not realized. At the same time a Frenchman, Troilus de La Roche de Mesgouez, provided with letters patent in 1577 and 1578, was also vainly trying to transport settlers to America. In January 1598 he was named lieutenant general of New France; finally, in that same year, he founded on Sable Island a settlement, which in the course of the winter of 1602–03 was rocked by tragic events (sedition, murders); the eleven survivors were repatriated for good in the spring of 1603.

Pierre Du Gua de Monts was ready to take over from La Roche de Mesgouez. Having been named lieutenant general of New France at the end of 1603, he would attempt to establish a colony in Acadia, first on the Île Sainte-Croix (1604–05), then at Port-Royal (1605–07). When they were forced to give up the latter settlement in 1607, Du Gua and Samuel de Champlain turned towards the St. Lawrence. On 3 July 1608 Champlain founded Québec and undertook to build a habitation there.

After much searching and many setbacks the unbroken history of New France began.

I

While waiting for Columbus...

During the seven years that their marvellous voyage lasted, according to legend, St. Brendan and his monks went from one wonder to another, not to say from one miracle to another. The iconography of the late Middle Ages has preserved traces of them in which we can see how easily the popular imagination accepted the simultaneous existence of mythological beings, supernatural forces, and saints with extraordinary powers.

If the Irish monks did not reach America, the Vikings for their part did arrive there around the year 1000, coming from Greenland. Documentary proof remains of their short stay on the Atlantic coast: the "Saga of Erik the Red" and the "Saga of the Greenlanders," two accounts relating their American adventures, to which it will perhaps be necessary one day to add the recently discovered map of Vinland (1440), the authenticity of which has not yet been established.

Except for the Vikings no European seems to have landed in America before Christopher Columbus. The voyage attributed to the Zeno brothers, who are supposed to have gone as far as Nova Scotia around 1380 after putting in at several islands, is a pure fabrication; that did not prevent the map that supposedly recorded their discoveries from being accepted as authoritative for nearly a century and a half, despite its non-existent islands with the fanciful names, and even from inspiring the idea, it seems, of looking for a northwest passage.

~ 1 ~

~ 2 ~

~ 3 ~

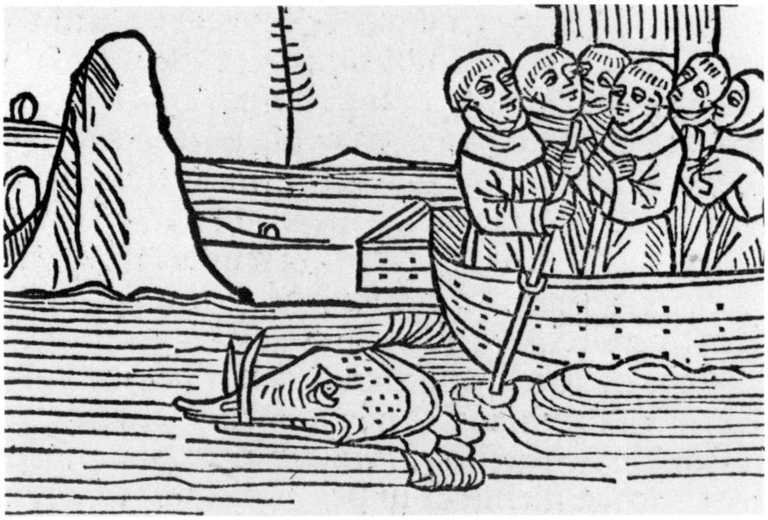

Saint Brendan (circa 484–577) and his Monks at Sea Encounter a Siren, Meet a Holy Man Floating on the Sea, and Their Ship is Attacked by Sea Monsters; woodcuts; 6.1 x 8.8 cm., 6.1 x 8.9 cm., 6 x 8 cm. (images).

In Saint Brendan. Legend. *Sankt Brandos Leben*. Ulm: Johann Zainer, 1499, pp. aiii^{v}, biii, ci^{v} (details).

According to a medieval legend, around the year 560, in the course of a long voyage filled with marvellous and prodigious events, Saint Brendan and some Irish monks were supposed to have visited some astonishing countries in the Atlantic. Some people believed that they had discovered America.

British Library, London, England.

Extract from the "Saga of the Greenlanders," probably written around the year 1200.

In it is told the story of the Vikings who, around the year 1000, under the leadership of Leifr Eiriksson, landed on the east coast of North America. They spent the winter at a place where grapevines grew: "Leifr gave the country a name that was suggested by its natural qualities and called it Vinland (Wineland)."

Stofnun Árna Magnússonar, Reykjavik, Iceland.

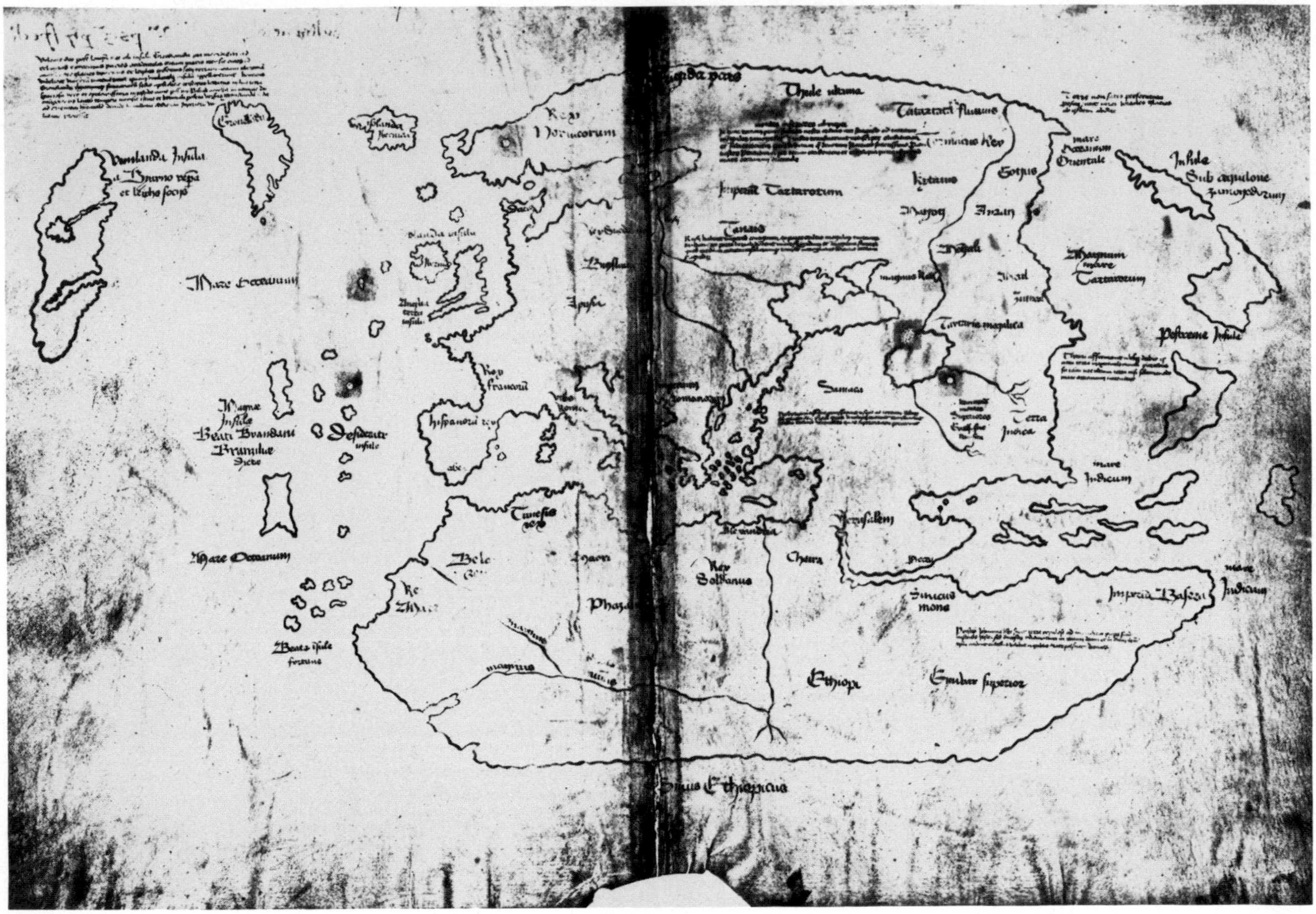

[The Vinland map of the world, circa 1440]; anonymous; col. ms.; 30 x 40 cm.

This is perhaps the oldest cartographic document concerning the New World. Vinland, the region of North America discovered by the Vikings, appears in it in the upper left-hand corner. The authenticity of this document is, however, questioned today by several historians and cartographers.

Yale University, Beinecke Rare Book and Manuscript Library, New Haven, Connecticut, U.S.A.

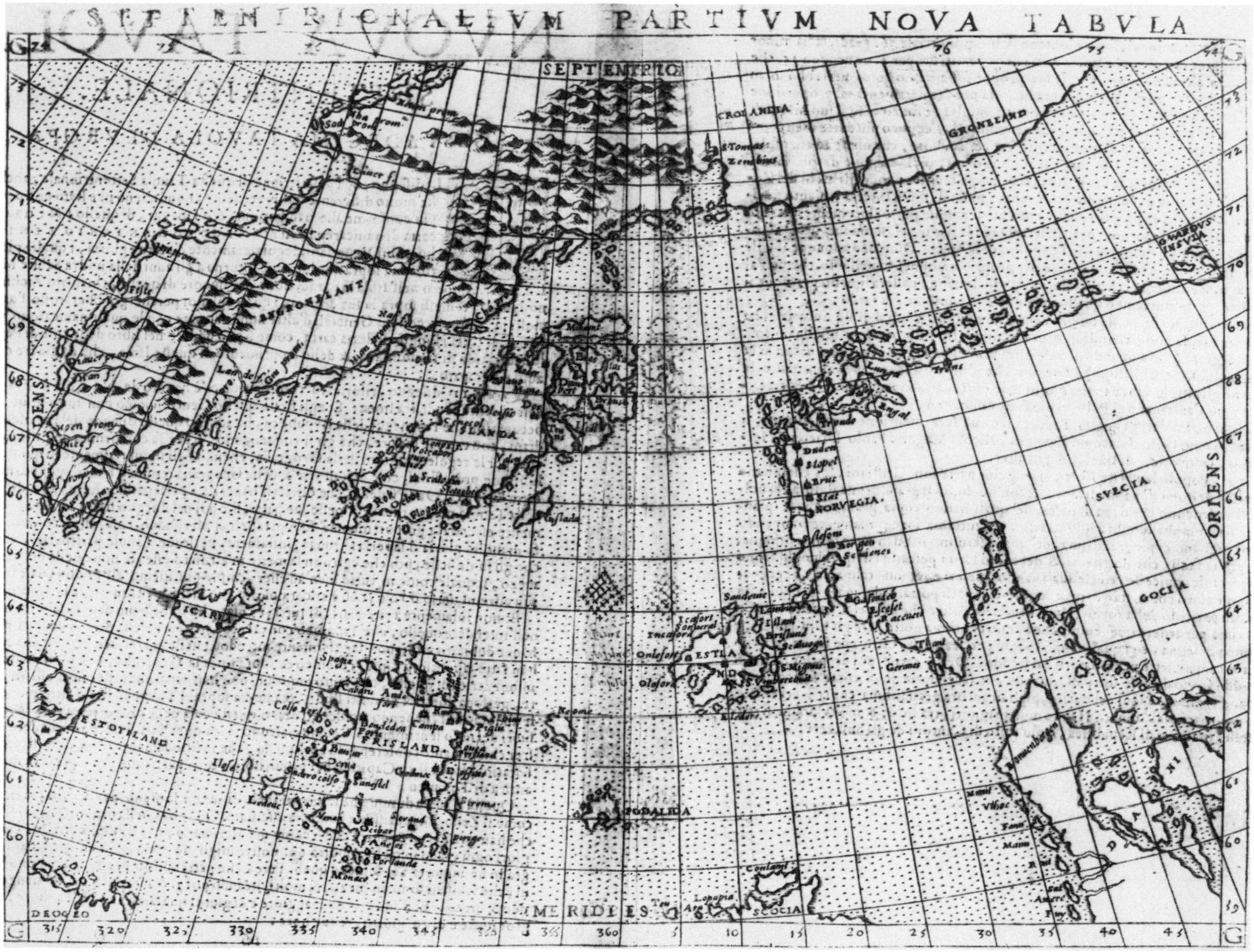

Septentrionalium Partium Nova Tabula, [1574]; Nicolò Zeno; map printed from woodblock; 18.8 x 26.2 cm.

In Claudius Ptolemaus. *La Geografia di Clavdio Tolomeo*.... Venetia: Giordano Ziletti, 1574.

Published in 1558, this map, which relates to the alleged discoveries of the Zeno brothers, misled geographers and sailors for more than a century. The brothers, Nicolò and Antonio Zeno, from Venice, did not visit Nova Scotia and certain other islands in the North Atlantic around 1380, as a book published in 1588 by a member of the Zeno family let it be believed.

Public Archives of Canada, National Map Collection, Ottawa (NMC 10225).

I

England and Portugal

After the discovery of America by Christopher Columbus, John Cabot, an Italian in the service of England, was the first person to explore the northeast coast of the continent. On 5 March 1496 King Henry VII had granted him letters patent authorizing him to take possession in the name of the Crown of the lands that he might discover.

Cabot had drawn up a map of the coast that he had explored. That map is lost, but we have Juan de La Cosa's, which bears the date of 1500 and which is supposed to have been made in part after Cabot's. In any event La Cosa's map is the first known portrayal of the northeast coast of America.

Sebastian Cabot, John's son, was for his part in charge of an expedition that had the mission of discovering a passage to the northwest in 1508 or 1509. Our information about this voyage is rather poor in actual fact, since it comes from some people who wrote several years later. One of them, Pietro d'Anghiera (alias Peter Martyr), was perhaps a friend and table companion of Sebastian, but he is scarcely more explicit because of that.

Meanwhile, in 1500 and 1501, Gaspar Corte-Real had made two voyages of discovery, the memory of which was preserved for a fairly long time: a map from 1520 represented North America as an island, which was called "Terra de Corte-Real"; and in 1502 another map, Cantino's, called Newfoundland "Terra del Rey de Portuguall" ("Country of the King of Portugal").

7

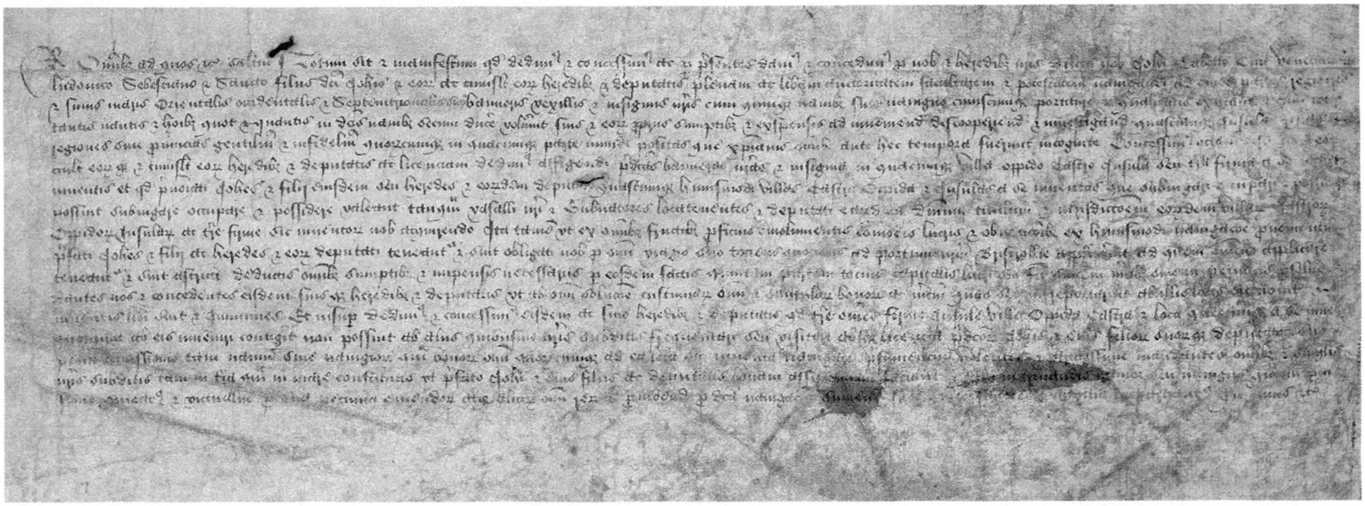

Letters patent for a voyage to discover new lands granted John Cabot and his three sons by the king of England, Henry VII, at Westminster on 5 March 1496.

The following year the Italian John Cabot set out on a voyage during which he explored part of the east coast of North America.

Public Record Office, London, England: Chancery, Warrants for the Great Seal, Series II, C 82/146, no.6.

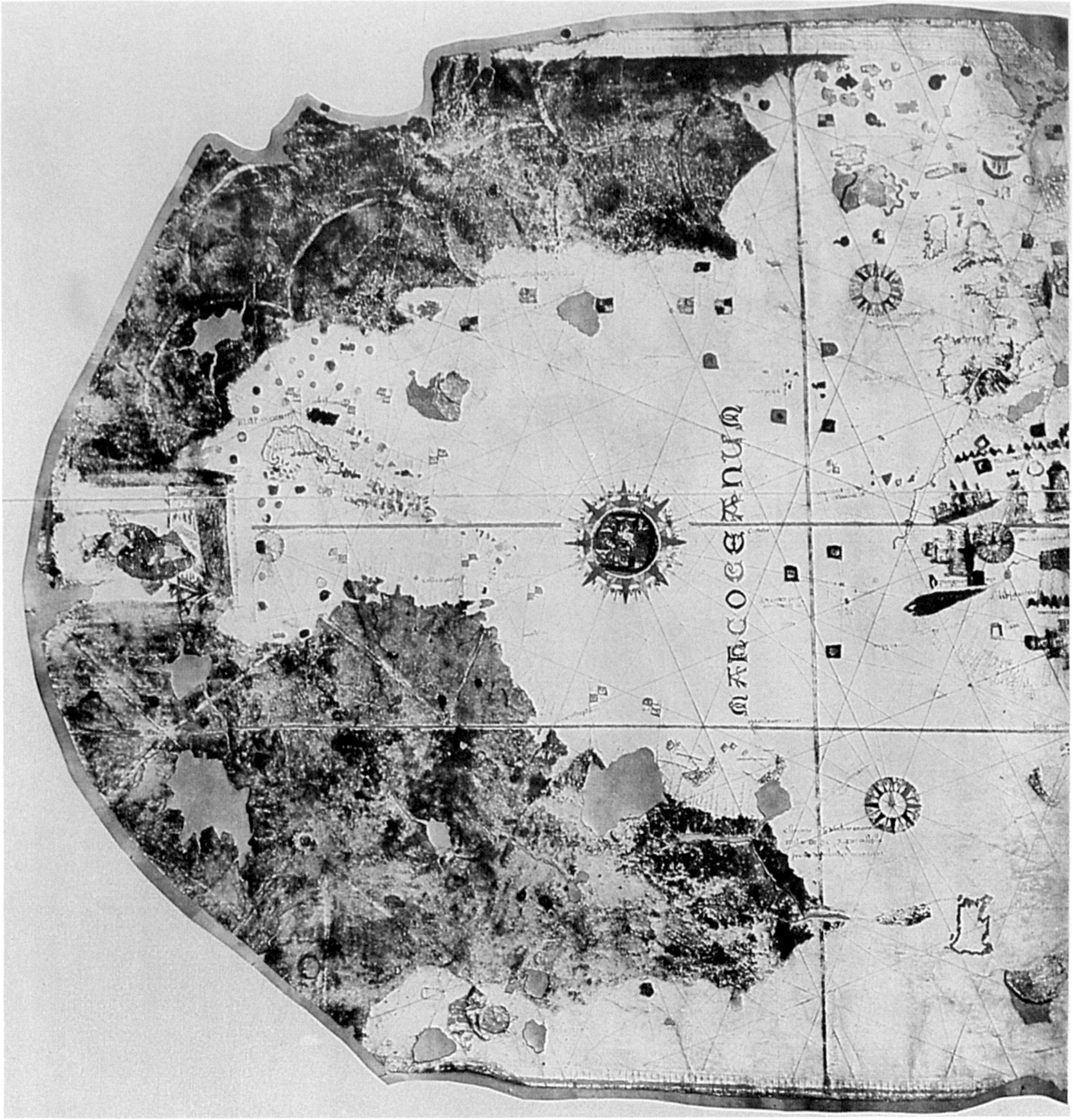

[Map of the world], 1500; Juan de La Cosa; copy; 37.5 x 40.8 cm.

In [Duke of Alba]. *Mapas Españoles de America, Siglos xv-xvii.* Madrid: 1951.

This map, of which only the part relative to North America is reproduced here, is the first known representation of the northeastern coast of America. The part of this coast that was visited by the explorer John Cabot in 1497 is marked on it by English flags and by the phrase "mar descubierto por inglese" (sea discovered by the English).

Public Archives of Canada, National Map Collection, Ottawa. The original is in the Museo Naval, Madrid, Spain.

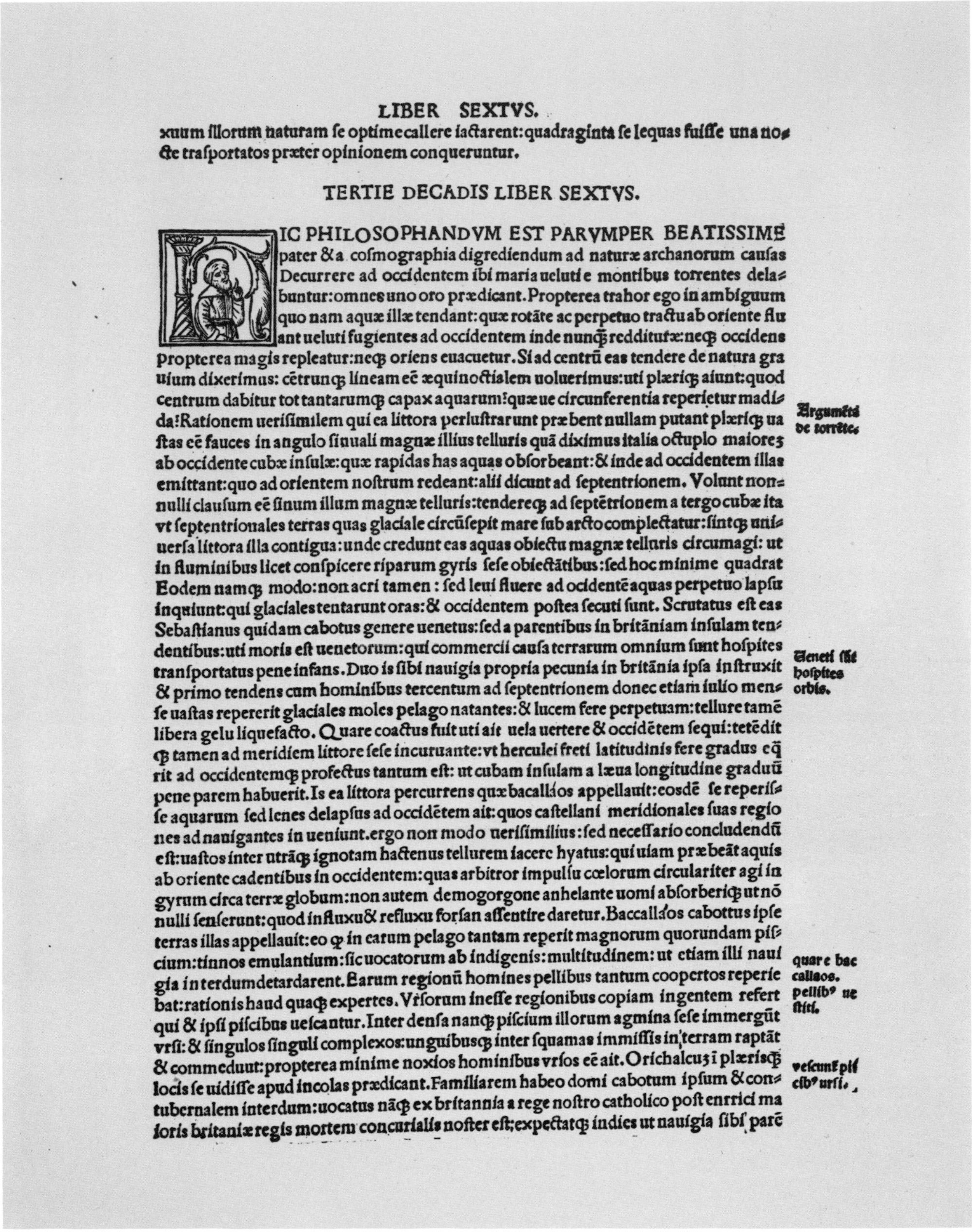

LIBER SEXTVS.

xuum illorum naturam ſe optime callere iactarent: quadraginta ſe leuquas fuiſſe una no-
cte traſportatos præter opinionem conqueruntur.

TERTIE DECADIS LIBER SEXTVS.

HIC PHILOSOPHANDVM EST PARVMPER BEATISSIME
pater & a coſmographia digrediendum ad naturæ archanorum cauſas
Decurrere ad occidentem ibi maria ueluti e montibus torrentes dela-
buntur: omnes uno oro prædicant. Propterea trahor ego in ambiguum
quo nam aquæ illæ tendant: quæ rotãte ac perpetuo tractu ab oriente flu
ant ueluti fugientes ad occidentem inde nunq̃ redditur æ: neq; occidens
propterea magis repleatur: neq; oriens euacuetur. Si ad centrũ eas tendere de natura gra
uium dixerimus: cẽtrunq; lineam eẽ æquinoctialem uoluerimus: uti plæriq; aiunt: quod
centrum dabitur tot tantarumq; capax aquarum? quæ ue circunferentia reperietur madi-
da? Rationem uerisimilem qui ea littora perluſtrarunt præbent nullam putant plæriq; ua
ſtas eẽ fauces in angulo ſinuali magnæ illius telluris quã diximus italia octuplo maiorez
ab occidente cubæ inſulæ: quæ rapidas has aquas obſorbeant: & inde ad occidentem illas
emittant: quo ad orientem noſtrum redeant: alii dicunt ad ſeptentrionem. Volunt non-
nulli clauſum eẽ ſinum illum magnæ telluris: tendereq; ad ſeptẽtrionem a tergo cubæ ita
vt ſeptentrionales terras quas glaciale circũſepit mare ſub arcto complectatur: ſintq; uni-
uerſa littora illa contigua: unde credunt eas aquas obiectu magnæ telluris circumagi: ut
in fluminibus licet conſpicere riparum gyris ſeſe obiectãtibus: ſed hoc minime quadrat
Eodem namq; modo: non acri tamen: ſed leui fluere ad ocidentẽ aquas perpetuo lapſu
inquiunt: qui glaciales tentarunt oras: & occidentem poſtea ſecuti ſunt. Scrutatus eſt eas
Sebaſtianus quidam cabotus genere uenetus: ſed a parentibus in britãniam inſulam ten-
dentibus: uti moris eſt uenetorum: qui commercii cauſa terrarum omnium ſunt hoſpites
tranſportatus pene infans. Duo is ſibi nauigia propria pecunia in britãnia ipſa inſtruxit
& primo tendens cum hominibus tercentum ad ſeptentrionem donec etiam iulio men-
ſe uaſtas repererit glaciales moles pelago natantes: & lucem fere perpetuam: tellure tamẽ
libera gelu liquefacto. Quare coactus fuit uti ait uela uertere & occidẽtem ſequi: tetẽdit
q; tamen ad meridiem littore ſeſe incuruante: vt herculei freti latitudinis fere gradus eq̃
rit ad occidentemq; profectus tantum eſt: ut cubam inſulam a læua longitudine graduũ
pene parem habuerit. Is ea littora percurrens quæ bacallaos appellauit: eoſdẽ ſe reperiſ-
ſe aquarum ſed lenes delapſus ad occidẽtem ait: quos caſtellani meridionales ſuas regio
nes ad nauigantes in ueniunt. ergo non modo uerisimilius: ſed neceſſario concludendũ
eſt: uaſtos inter utrãq; ignotam hactenus tellurem iacere hyatus: qui uiam præbeãt aquis
ab oriente cadentibus in occidentem: quas arbitror impulſu cœlorum circulariter agi in
gyrum circa terræ globum: non autem demogorgone anhelante uomi abſorberiq; ut nõ
nulli ſenſerunt: quod influxu & refluxu forſan aſſentire daretur. Baccallaos cabottus ipſe
terras illas appellauit: eo q; in earum pelago tantam reperit magnorum quorundam piſcium: tinnos emulantium: ſic uocatorum ab indigenis: multitudinem: ut etiam illi naui
gia interdum detardarent. Earum regionũ homines pellibus tantum coopertos reperie
bat: rationis haud quaq; expertes. Vrſorum ineſſe regionibus copiam ingentem refert
qui & ipſi piſcibus ueſcantur. Inter denſa nanq; piſcium illorum agmina ſeſe immergũt
vrſi: & ſingulos ſinguli complexos: unguibusq; inter ſquamas immiſſis in terram raptãt
& commeduut: propterea minime noxios hominibus vrſos eẽ ait. Orichalcuz i plæriſq;
locis ſe uidiſſe apud incolas prædicant. Familiarem habeo domi cabotum ipſum & con-
tubernalem interdum: uocatus nãq; ex britannia a rege noſtro catholico poſt enrrici ma
ioris britaniæ regis mortem concurialis noſter eſt; expectatq; indies ut nauigia ſibi parẽ

Argumẽtũ de torrẽte.

Veneti ſũt hoſpites orbis.

quare baccallaos.

pellib⁹ ueſtiti.

veſcunt piſcib⁹ urſi.

Pietro Martire d'Anghiera. *De orbe nouo Decades*. [Alcala: Impressal in contubernio Arnaldi Guillelmi, 1516], sig g 6 r.

In this passage d'Anghiera mentions the voyage that Sebastian Cabot embarked upon in 1508 or 1509 in the Arctic regions, looking for a passage leading to Asia: "First he sailed sufficiently far to the North that even in the month of July large ice fields could be seen floating on the sea and it was daylight almost continually."

New York Public Library, Rare Books and Manuscripts Division, Astor, Lenox and Tilden Foundations, New York, New York, U.S.A.

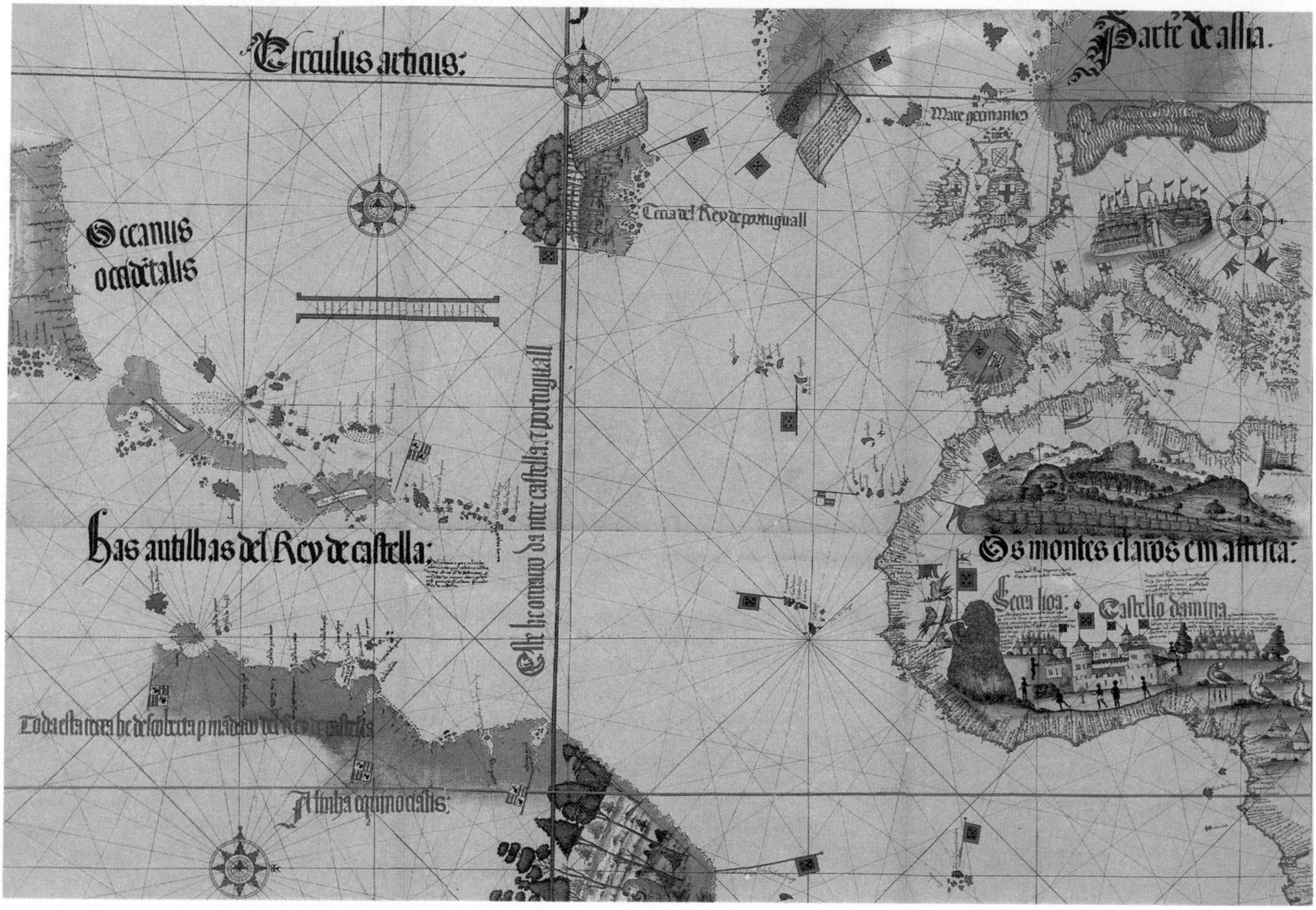

[The "Cantino" map of the world, 1502]; anonymous; copy; 96.7 x 105.6 cm. *In* Henry Harisse. *Les Corte-Real et leurs voyages au Nouveau-Monde.* Paris: E. Leroux, 1883.

This document, which is attributed to Alberto Cantino, represents under the name "Terra del Rey de portuguall"the land discovered in 1500–01 by the Portuguese explorer Gaspar Corte-Real. It is thought to be the island of Newfoundland.

Public Archives of Canada, National Map Collection, Ottawa. The original is in the Biblioteca Estense, Modena, Italy.

I

France and Spain

After England and Portugal it was France's turn to take an interest officially in North America. Francis I had recourse to the Florentine Giovanni da Verrazzano, who explored the coast in 1524 from Florida (or perhaps North Carolina) to Newfoundland. Upon his return Verrazzano submitted a report to the king, a good Italian version of which (the Cèllere manuscript) has been preserved.

In 1526 Verrazzano was preparing a new voyage: on 11 May in anticipation of his absence he chose his brother Gerolamo and Zanobis de Rousselay as his attorneys. The deed, which is written in French, is signed "Janus Verrazanus" – the Latin form of his name.

Verrazzano was not to leave again for America until 1528. In the preceding year Maggiolo had made a map of the coastline that the Florentine had explored in 1524; the placenames on it are in Italian, and the whole area is named "Francesca."

Spain sent an expedition to the north under the leadership of a Portuguese, Esteban Gómez, who was charged with the mission of discovering a passage across the continent somewhere between Florida and Newfoundland. In 1524–25 Gómez made the same voyage of exploration as Verrazzano. Ribero's magnificent map of 1529 shows a "Tiera de Estavã Gomez," which corresponds pretty well to present-day New England and Nova Scotia. This map, moreover, constitutes, as it were, a summary of the voyages of exploration previous to Jacques Cartier's.

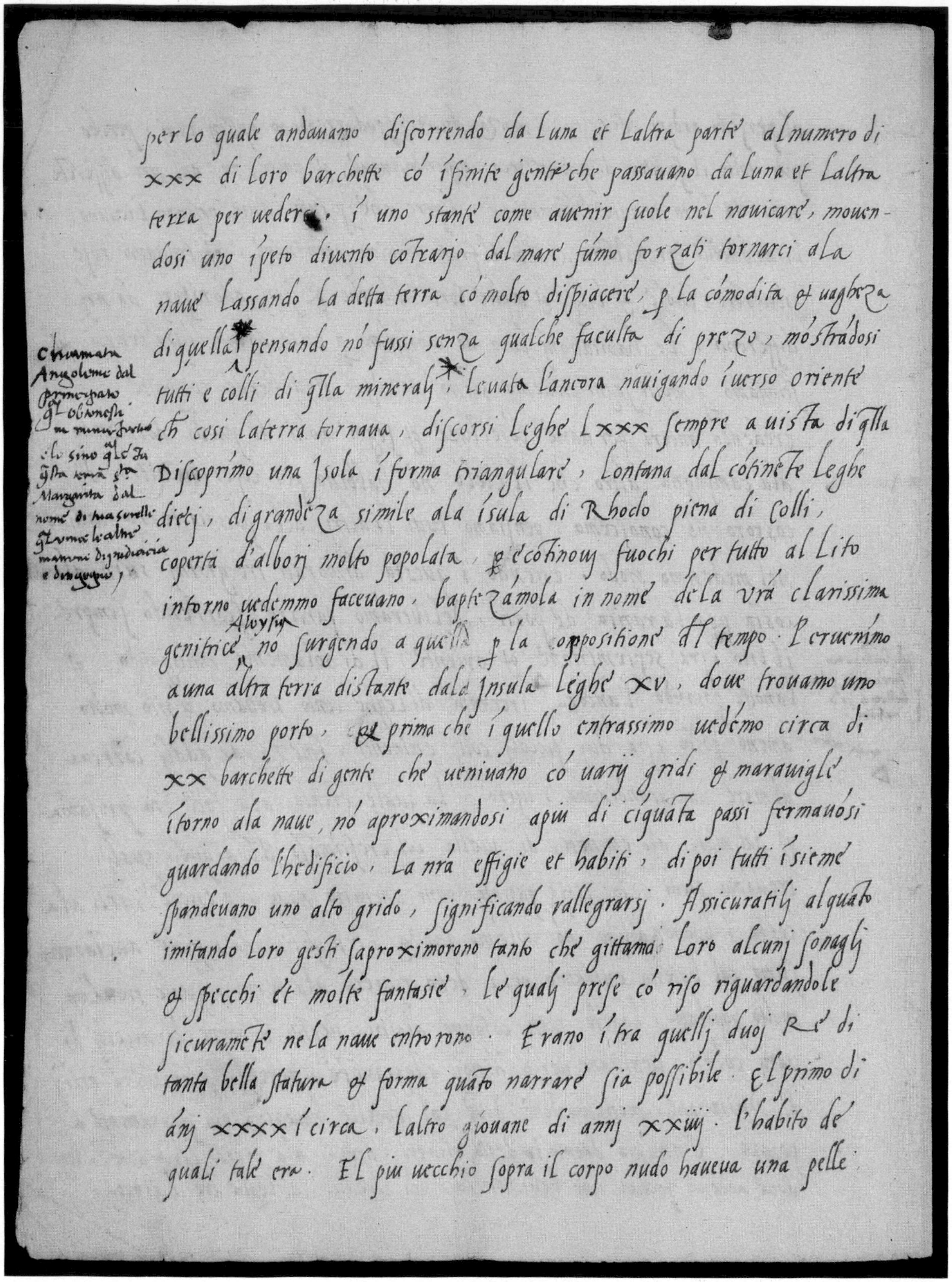

Chiamata Angolemme dal principato ql obtenesti in minor fortuna et il sino ql fa qsta terra s.ta Margarita dal nome di tua sorella ql vince laltre matrone di pudicitia e d'ingegno;

per lo quale andauamo discorrendo da luna et laltra parte al numero di
XXX di loro barchette có isinite gente che passauano da luna et laltra
terra per uederci. i uno stante come auenir suole nel nauicare, mouen-
dosi uno ispeto diuento cótrario dal mare fumo forzati tornarci ala
naue lassando la detta terra có molto dispiacere, p la cómodita et uagheza
di quella * pensando nó fussi senza qualche faculta di prezo, móstrádosi
tutti e colli di qlla minerali. * leuata lancora nauigando iuerso oriente
ch cosi laterra tornaua, discorsi leghe LXXX sempre a uista di qlla
Discoprimo una Isola i forma triangulare, lontana dal cótinēte leghe
diecj, di grandeza simile ala isula di Rhodo piena di colli,
coperti d'alborj molto popolata, p cótinouj fuochi per tutto al lito
intorno uedemmo faceuano. baptezamola in nome dela vrá clarissima
genitrice Aloysia no surgendo a quella p la oppositione dl tempo. Peruenimo
auna altra terra distante dala Insula leghe XV, doue trouamo uno
bellissimo porto, et prima che i quello entrassimo uedémo circa di
XX barchette di gente che ueniuano có uarij gridi et marauiglie
itorno ala naue, nó aproximandosi apiu di ciquata passi fermauósi
guardando lhedificio, la nrá effigie et habiti, di poi tutti isieme
spandeuano uno alto grido, significando rallegrarsj. Assicuratilj alquato
imitando loro gesti saproximorono tanto che gittamo loro alcunj sonaglj
et specchi et molte fantasie, le qualj prese có riso riguardandole
sicuramēte ne la naue entrorono. Erano itra quellj duoj Re di
tanta bella statura et forma quato narrare sia possibile. El primo di
anj XXXX i circa, laltro giouane di annj XXiiij. lhabito de
quali tale era. El piu uecchio sopra il corpo nudo haueua una pelle

Letter from Giovanni da Verrazzano to the king of France, Francis I, relating his voyage to North America, 8 July 1524.

Verrazzano had visited the spot where the city of New York is situated today: "Sire, we named this land Angoulême, from the name that you bore formerly when you were in a less fortunate state."

Pierpont Morgan Library, New York, New York, U.S.A.: Cèllere Manuscript.

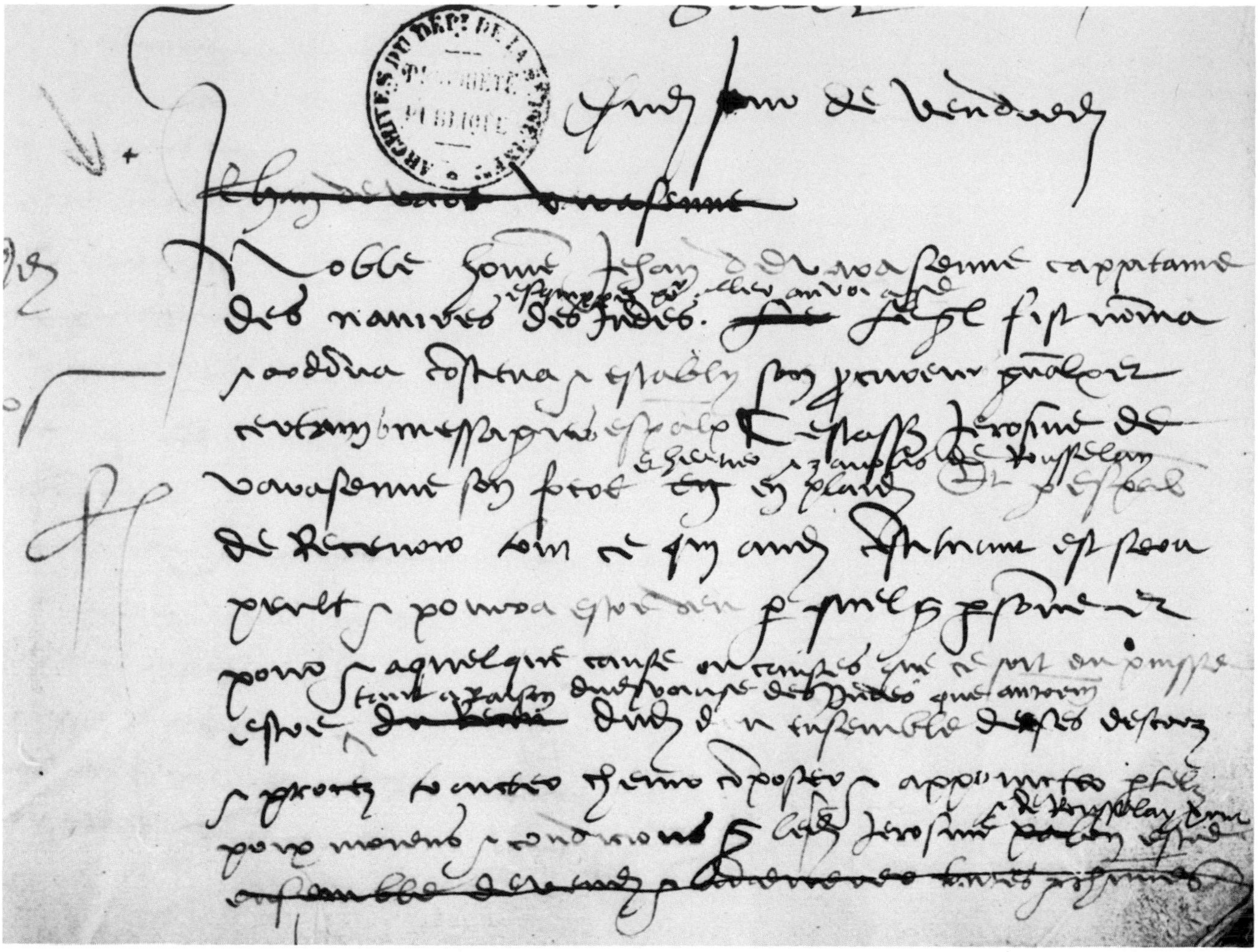

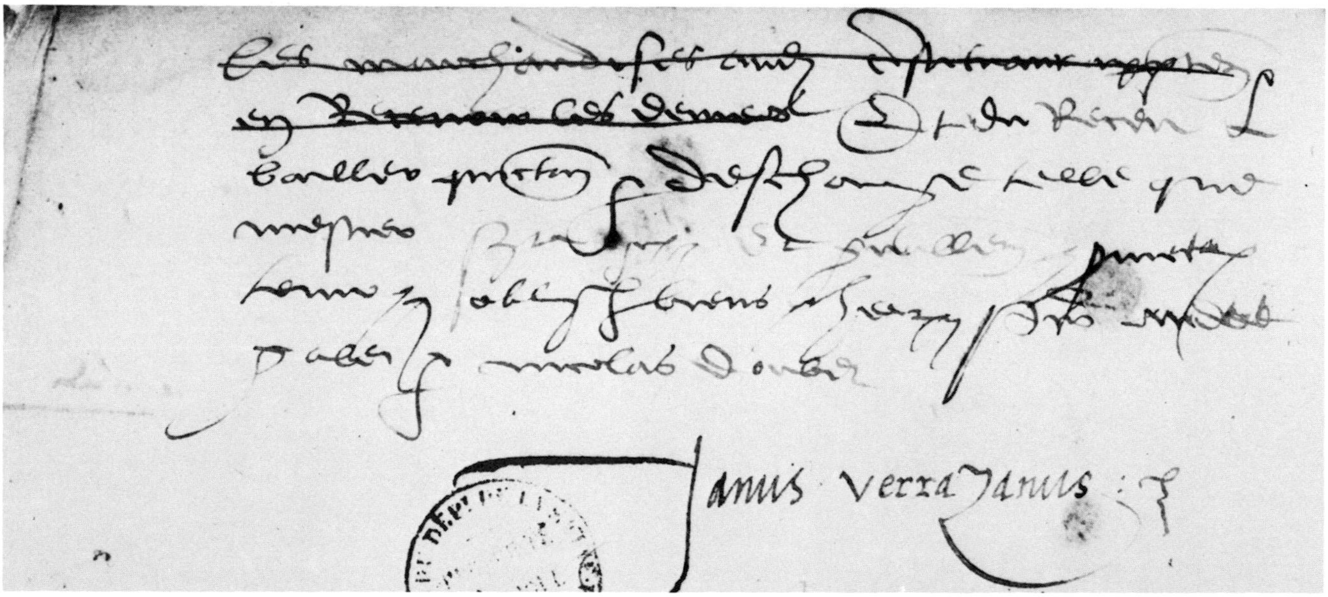

Power of attorney given by Giovanni da Verrazzano to his brother Gerolamo and Zanobis de Rousselay, 11 May 1526.

Verrazzano was the first European to sail along the east coast of North America from Florida to Newfoundland. This voyage was made in 1524 under the official patronage of France.

Archives départementales de la Seine-Maritime, Rouen, France: Série E, tabellionage de Rouen, "meuble," fol. 11–12.

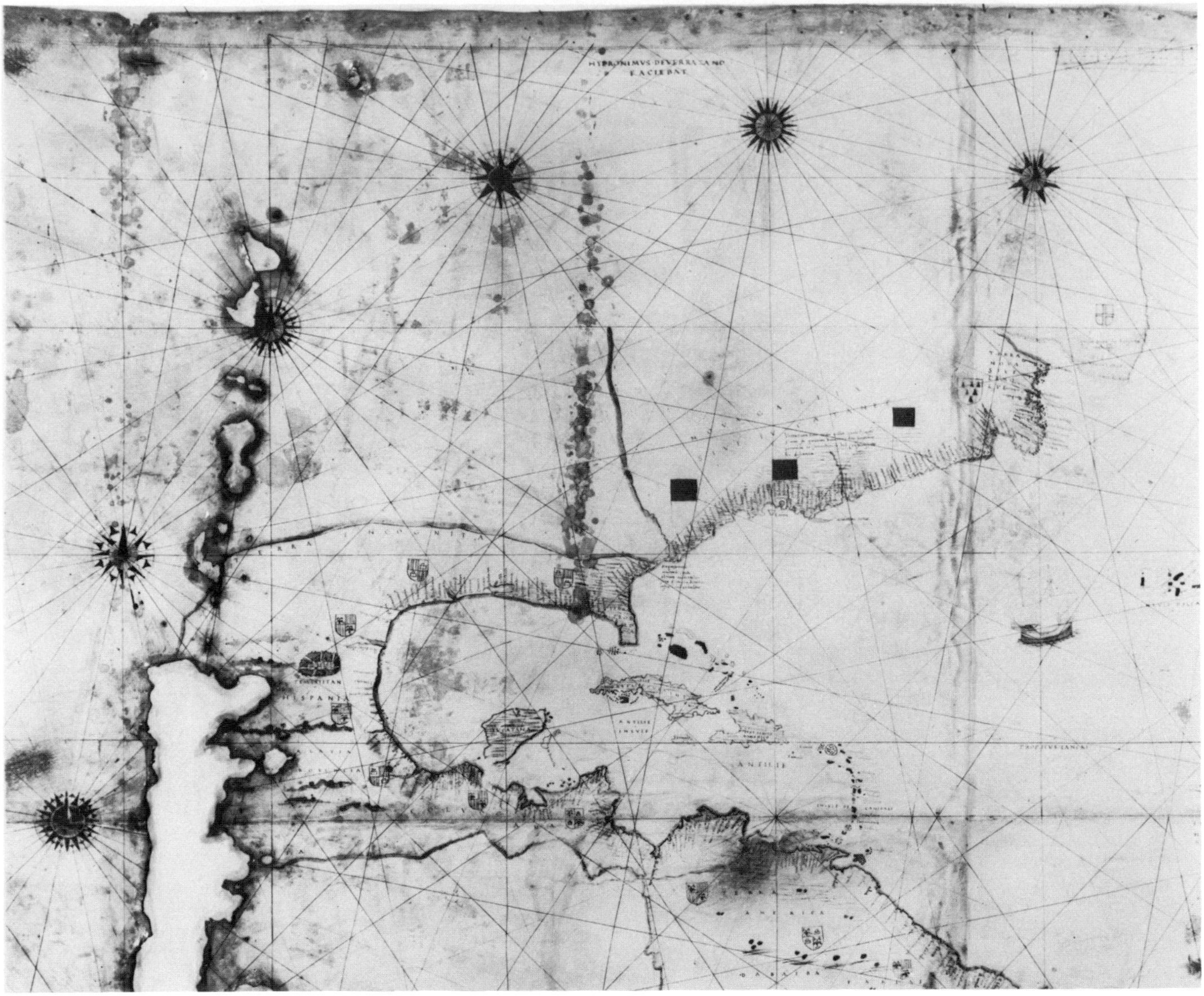

[Map of the world, 1529]; Gerolamo da Verrazzano; ms.; 129.6 x 259.2 cm.

Of the map of the world prepared by Gerolamo da Verrazzano, only the east coast of North America is reproduced here. His brother, Giovanni da Verrazzano, sailed along it in 1524 in the hope of discovering a passage to Asia.

Biblioteca Apostolica Vaticana, Vatican City.

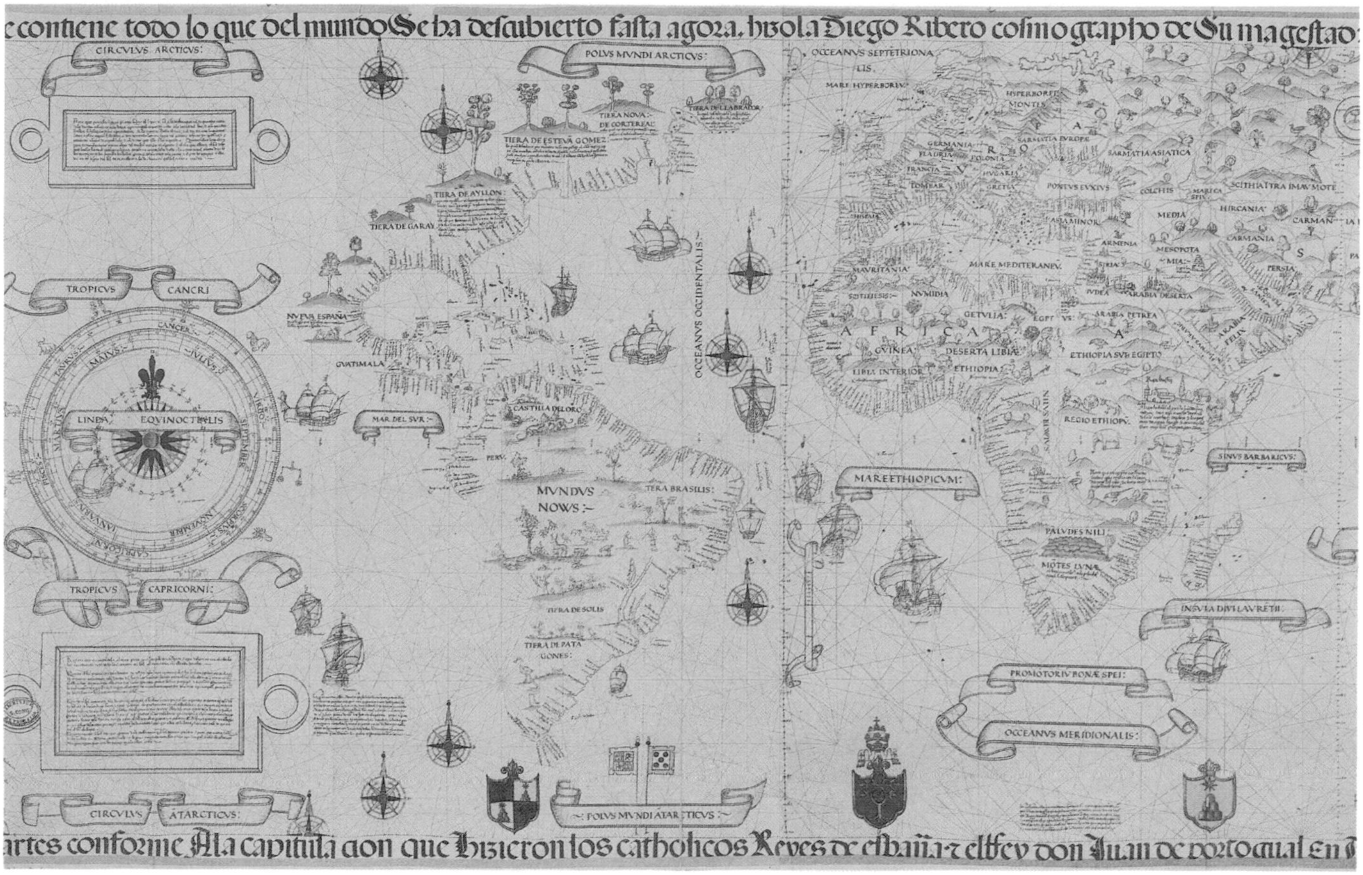

"Carta Universal... 1529 é Seujlla"; Diogo Ribero; copy; 58.2 x 139.4 cm. Reproduced from the original... by W. Griggs, London [1886].

The Spanish cosmographer Ribero took into account the explorations previous to Jacques Cartier's, particularly the expedition led by Esteban Gómez, who sailed along the North American coast from Florida to Cape Race in 1524–25. New England and Nova Scotia are marked on it under the name "Tiera de Estevã Gomez."

Public Archives of Canada, National Map Collection, Ottawa. The original is in the Biblioteca Apostolica Vaticana, Vatican City.

I

The discovery of the St. Lawrence

In 1534 Francis I entrusted Jacques Cartier with continuing the explorations that had been begun by Verrazzano. The commission granted the sailor from Saint-Malo has not been found, but a payment order discloses the objective of his voyage: "to discover certain islands and lands where it is said that there must be great quantities of gold and of other precious things."

In 1535 Cartier again sailed for the "New Lands." Of his first two voyages we are fortunate to possess the *Brief recit, & succincte narration...*, published in Paris in 1545. Indeed, on 17 August Cartier very briefly and very succinctly noted down entering the great river of Hochelaga (the St. Lawrence) – which he had just discovered and which would take him far inland.

At Stadacona (Québec) Cartier left behind the *Grande Hermine* and the *Petite Hermine*, which were probably very much like the ship with which Descelliers decorated his 1546 map. Going up the river on board the *Emérillon*, Cartier and some of his men were very well received at Hochelaga (Montréal) by the Iroquois who were living there at that time.

Cartier had discovered the St. Lawrence and had been the first to penetrate deeply into the interior of the continent; it was not he, however, but Jean-François de La Rocque de Roberval who, on 15 January 1541, was commissioned by the king to found a settlement "in the aforementioned countries of Canada and Ochelaga."

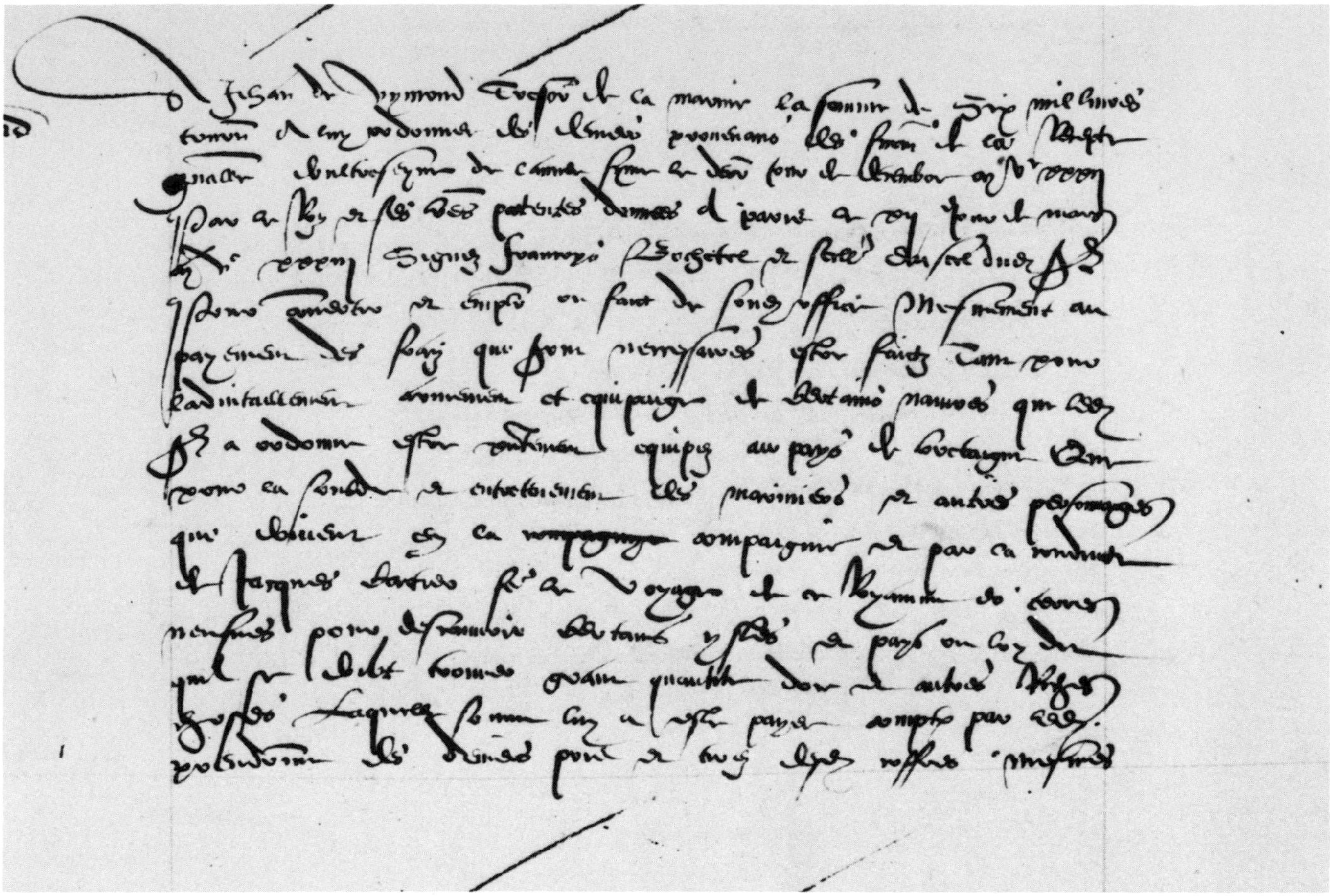

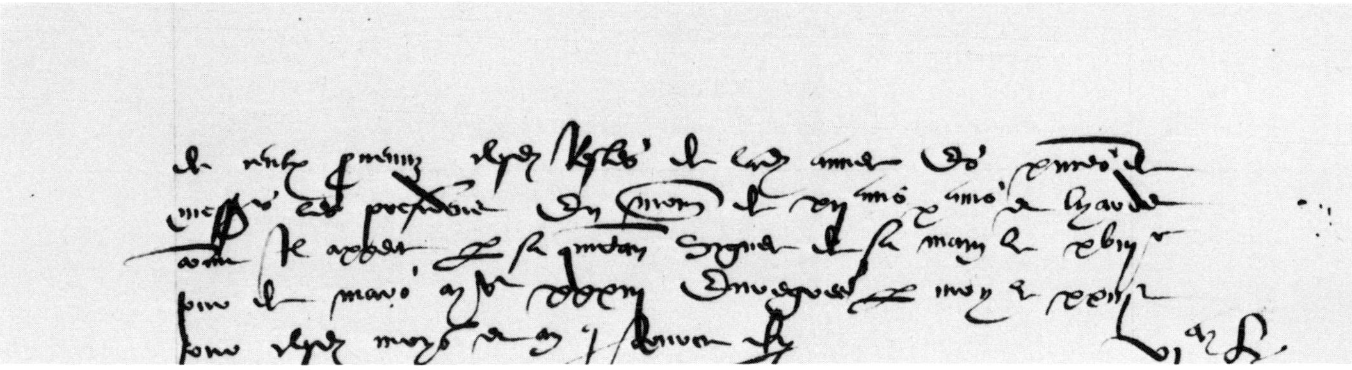

Extract from the "original ledgers of the savings accounts" concerning the payment of the sum of 6,000 livres given to Jacques Cartier by the king of France to enable him to "discover certain islands and lands where it is said that there must be great quantities of gold and of other precious things," March 1533.

Cartier explored the Gulf of St. Lawrence the following year and at Gaspé took possession in the name of the king of France of the newly discovered country.

Bibliothèque nationale, Département des manuscrits, Paris, France: Fonds français, 15628, fol. 213v, 214.

16

BRIEF RECIT, & ſuccincte narration, de la nauigation faicte es yſles de Canada, Hochelage & Saguenay & autres, auec particulieres meurs, langaige, & cerimonies des habitans d'icelles: fort delectable à veoir.

Avec priuilege

On les uend à Paris au ſecond pillier en la grand ſalle du Palais, & en la rue neufue Noſtredame à l'enſeigne de leſcu de frãce, par Ponce Roffet dict Faucheur, & Anthoine le Clerc frères.

1545.

Jacques Cartier. *Brief recit, & succincte narration....* Paris: Librairie Tross, 1863. leaves [xvii], 9 rv.

On 17 August 1535 Cartier noted down his entrance into the great river of Hochelaga (the St. Lawrence), the mouth of which he had just discovered: "The aforesaid Indians have assured us that this is the way to and the beginning of the great river of Hochelaga and the route to Canada."

Cartier sailed up the river to Stadacona (Québec) and Hochelaga (Montréal) before spending the winter near Stadacona.

Nous rāgeaſmes leſdictes terres du Su depuis ledict iour iuſques au mardy que le vent vint Onaiſt, & meiſmes le cap au Nord pour aller querir leſdites haultes terres que voyons, & no^{s} eſtãs là trouuaſmes leſdictes terres vnyes & baſſes vers la mer, & les montaignes deuers le Nort par ſus leſdictes haultes terres giſant icelles terres, Eſt, & Onaiſt vng cart de Sur Onaiſt, Et par les sauuaiges que auions, nous a eſté dict que ceſtoit le commencement du Saguenay & terre habitable. Et que de la ve

b

noit le cuyure rouge qu'ilz appellẽt caignet-daze. Il y a entre les terres du Su & celles du Nort, enuiron trente lieues, & plus de deux cens braſſes de perfond & nous ont leſdictz Sauuaiges certiffié eſtre le chemin, & cõmencement du grãt Silenne de Hochelaga & chemin de Canada : lequel alloit touſiours en eſtroiſſent iuſques à Canada, puis q̃ l'on treuue l'aue doulce qui va ſi loing que iamais hõme n'auroit eſté iuſques au bout qu'ilz euſſent ouy, & que autre paſſaige n'y auoit que par bateaulx. Et voyant leur dire & qu'ilz affermoient n'y auoir autre paſſaige, ne voulut led· cappitaine paſſer oultre iuſques a auoir veu le reſte de ladicte terre & coſte deuers le Nort, qu'il auoit obmis veoir depuis la Baye ſainct Laurens pour aller veoir la terre du Su pour veoir s'il y auoit aucun paſſaige.

Public Archives of Canada, Library, Ottawa (Negatives nos. C 113344 to C 113346).

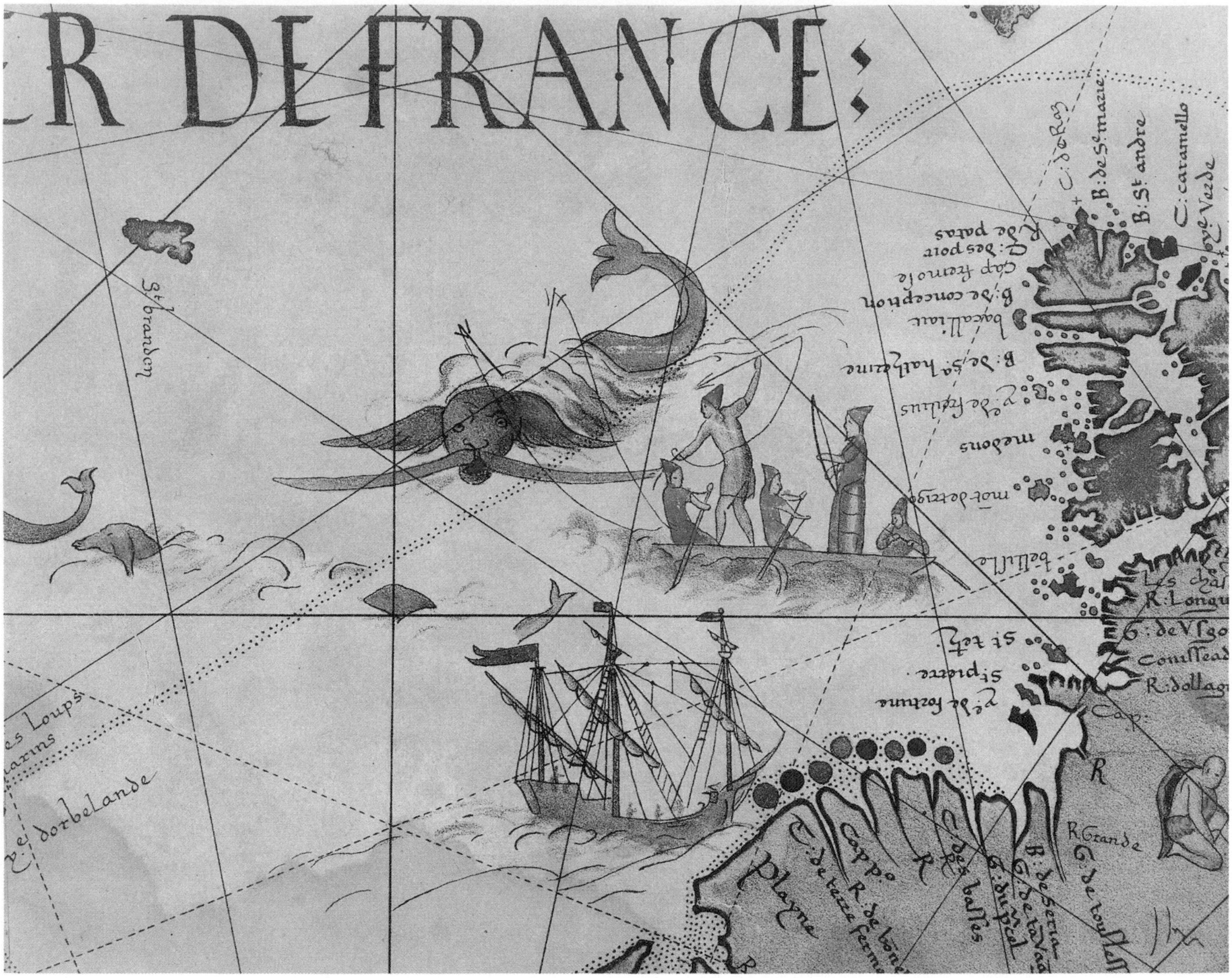

[Map of the world], 1546; Pierre Descelliers; copy; 65.2 x 81.8 cm.

In Edme François Jomard. *Les monuments de la géographie*.... Paris: Kaeppelin Q. Vollaire, 1854.

This extract from Descelliers's map represents a ship which was probably similar to those of the French explorers at the time, particularly to Jacques Cartier's *Grande Hermine*.

Public Archives of Canada, National Map Collection, Ottawa, The original is in the John Rylands University Library of Manchester, Manchester, England.

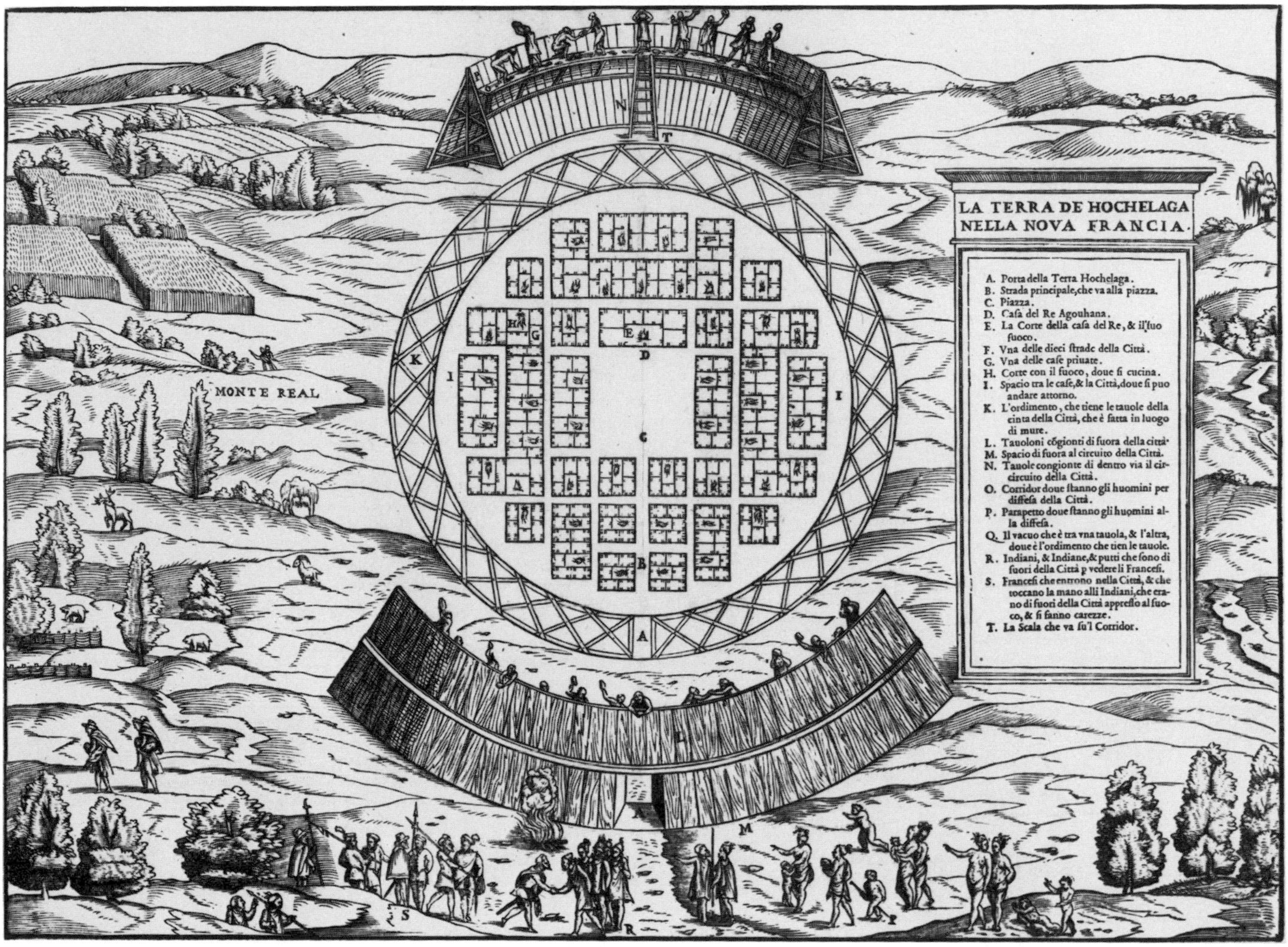

La Terra de Hochelaga Nella Nova Francia, [1556]; Giovanni Battista Ramvsio; map printed from woodblock; 26.7 x 36.7 cm.

In Giovanni Battista Ramvsio. *Terzo volvme delle navigationi et viaggi....* Venetia: Nella stamperia de Givnti, 1565, pp.446–447.

This document shows the warm welcome received by Jacques Cartier and his men at the Iroquois village of Hochelaga (Montréal) at the beginning of October 1535. Cartier named the nearby mountain Mount Royal.

Public Archives of Canada, National Map Collection, Ottawa (NMC 1908).

Commission from King Francis I appointing La Rocque de Roberval "lieutenant general, head, leader and captain" of the undertaking intended for Canada, with authority to "make decisions, enjoin, and order in all matters that he will consider to be good, useful, and fitting," Fontainebleau, 15 January 1541.

In 1542 Roberval built a settlement at Charlesbourg-Royal on Cap-Rouge, but his attempt at establishing a colony lasted only a few months.

Archives nationales, Paris, France: Fonds anciens, série K, 1232, pièce 31.

I

New France in the middle of the sixteenth century

In the middle of the sixteenth century, thanks in large measure to Verrazzano, Cartier, and Roberval, New France – or if one wishes, North America – was relatively well known. Descelliers's 1546 map shows fairly accurately the Gulf of St. Lawrence, Gaspé Peninsula, Chaleur Bay, Anticosti Island, and the St. Lawrence River; on it are also mentioned Canada, Hochelaga, the Saguenay. What progress in less than half a century!

America – and South America still more than North America – henceforth had a large place in the economy of Europe. In all the ports one could witness the departure and the return of the ships which regularly crossed the Atlantic, and already these voyages were no longer perceived as much as they had been previously as superhuman odysseys or perilous exploits.

Despite her great youth New France had made her entry straight into history; is it not true that in his *Histoire universelle du Monde* published in Paris in 1572, the Sieur François de Belleforest devoted a chapter to her entitled: "Des Terres Neufves. De la nouvelle France, contenant Hochelaga, Canada, Saguenai, & la Floride, & des peuples qui y habitent" ("On the New-Found Lands. On New France, including Hochelaga, Canada, Saguenay, and Florida, and on the peoples who live there")?

In 1563 on a map by Bertelli and in 1566 on one by Zaltieri, Acadia herself appeared under the name of "Larcadia."

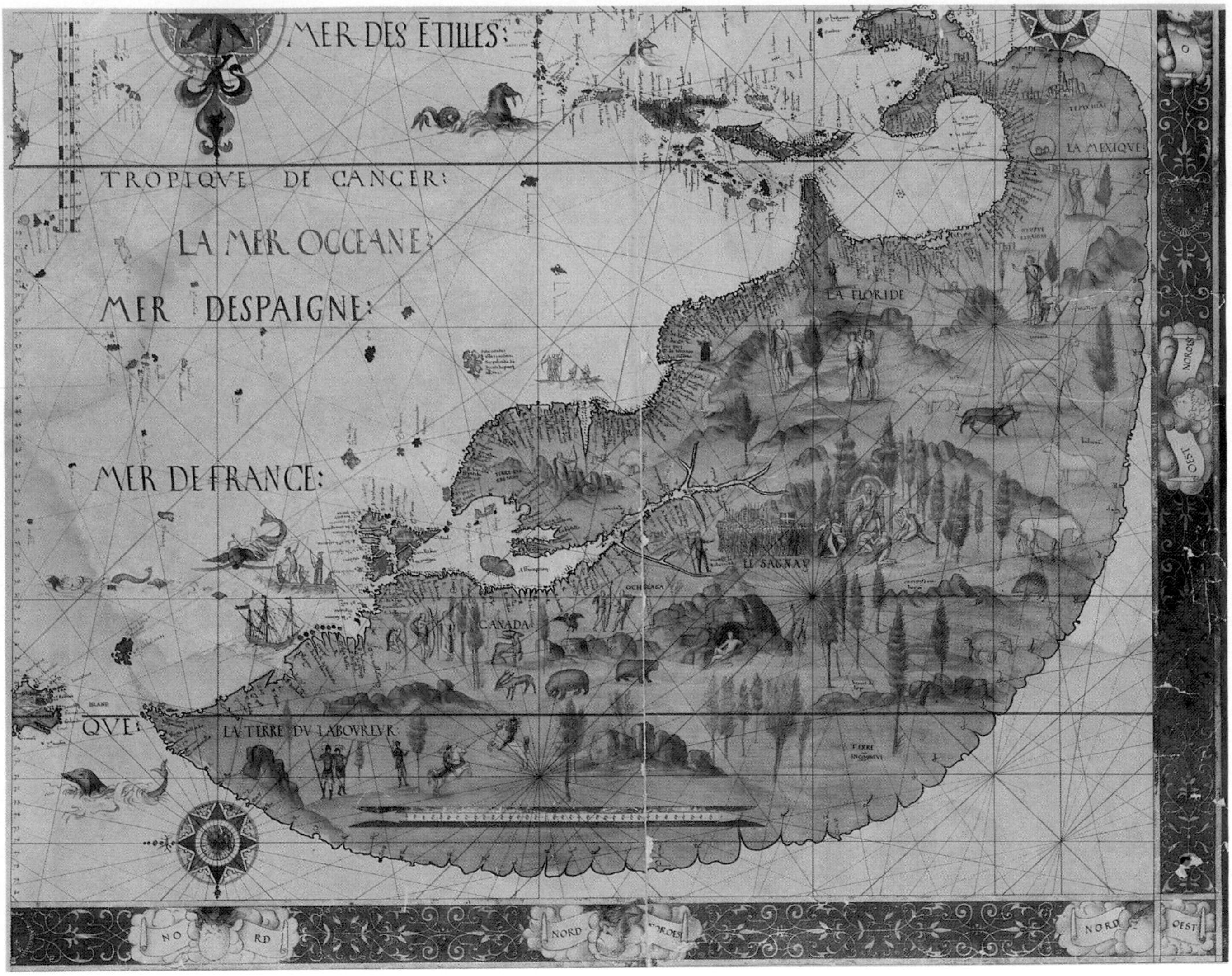

[Map of the world], 1546; Pierre Descelliers; copy; 65.2 x 81.8 cm.

In Edme François Jomard. *Les monuments de la géographie*.... Paris; Kaeppelin Q. Vollaire, 1854.

Extract from Descelliers's map showing the progress made in knowledge of the North American continent in the middle of the sixteenth century. It is one of the earliest representations of Canada, from the Gulf of St. Lawrence to Hochelaga (Montréal), with the details and names (Saguenay, Gaspé, etc.) given by Cartier and Roberval.

Public Archives of Canada, National Map Collection, Ottawa. The original is in the John Rylands University Library of Manchester, Manchester, England.

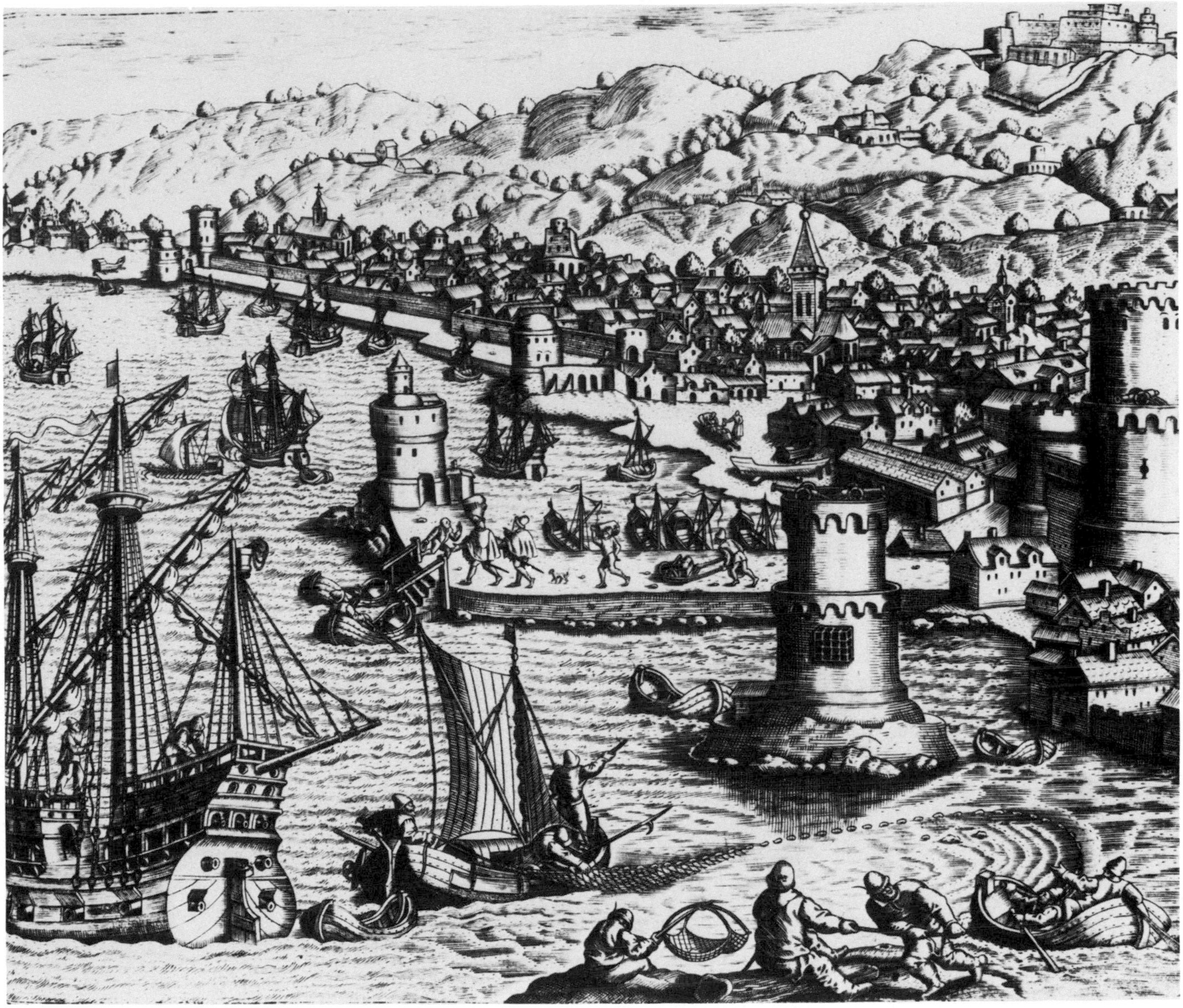

Departure for the New World from a European Port; engraved by Theodor de Bry (1528–98) after Le Moyne; engraving; 16.1 x 19.3 cm. (image).

In Theodor de Bry. [America. pt. 4. Latin]. Americae pars quarta. *Sive, insignis & admiranda historia de reperta primùm Occidentali India....* Francoforti: Typis I. Feyrabend, impensis T. de Bry, 1594. Plate 1.

In the middle of the sixteenth century ships sailed regularly in the direction of America from the European ports on the Atlantic. Some went to Newfoundland to fish for cod. The natural resources and riches of the American continent – chiefly those of South America – were the cause of this sea traffic.

British Library, London, England.

22

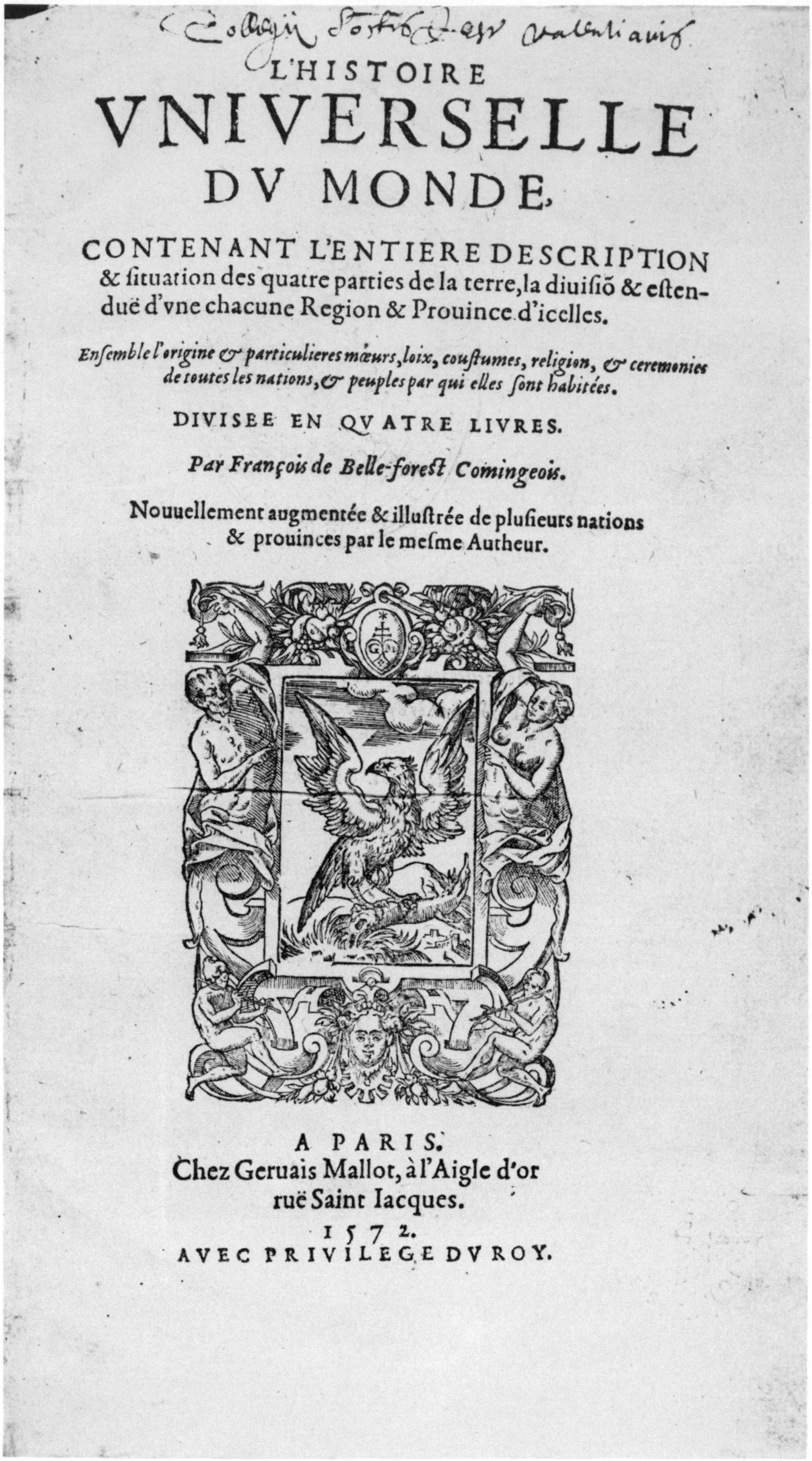
L'HISTOIRE
VNIVERSELLE
DV MONDE,
CONTENANT L'ENTIERE DESCRIPTION
& situation des quatre parties de la terre, la diuisiõ & estenduë d'vne chacune Region & Prouince d'icelles.
Ensemble l'origine & particulieres mœurs, loix, coustumes, religion, & ceremonies de toutes les nations, & peuples par qui elles sont habitées.
DIVISEE EN QVATRE LIVRES.
Par François de Belle-forest Comingeois.
Nouuellement augmentée & illustrée de plusieurs nations & prouinces par le mesme Autheur.
A PARIS.
Chez Geruais Mallot, à l'Aigle d'or ruë Saint Iacques.
1572.
AVEC PRIVILEGE DV ROY.

François de Belleforest. *L'histoire vniverselle dv monde*.... Paris: Chez G. Mallot, 1572, title page, p. 266.

The third chapter of this work deals with "On the New-Found Lands. On New France, including Hochelaga, Canada, Saguenay, & Florida, & on the peoples who live there."

DES TERRES NEVFVES. 266

De la nouuelle France . contenant Hochelagá, Canadá, Saguenai, & la Floride, & des peuples qui y habitent. Chapitre troisieme.

FORT peu d'hommes y a il eu de noſtre temps qui ne ayent ouy parler de ce grand Pilote & expert Capitaine de Mer, Iaques Cartier, qui du temps du grand Roy François, & ſuyuant la trace de Iean Denys Normand (qui comme i'ay dit l'an mil cinq cens huict, auoit voltigé le lõg de Canadá) commença auſſi à raſer les ſillons de la mer pour faire voir à chacun, & la gaillardiſe des François, & leur induſtrie auſſi bien ſur l'Ocean, qu'à manier les combatz, & les affaires en terre ferme. Ceſtuy-cy ſ'eſtant fié à l'inconſtance des ondes eſmeu de ſa propre curioſité, & des ſolicitations de Charles de Mouy ſeigneur de la Milleraye, & lieutenãt de l'Admiral, en l'an de noſtre ſalut mil cinq cens trente quatre prit la route du Ponant, iuſqu'à tant qu'il vint à Cap de Raz, prenant port à Carpont, & Degrad, ſur l'occident, pource que la coſte qui regarde le Leuant eſt baſſe, dangereuſe, & pleine de bancs, & où tout le pays eſt plein d'Iſles telles que ſont celles de ſaincte Catherine, de Breſts, des Oyſeaux, & celle de Blanc Sablon, où les ſauuages ſe tiennent pour y peſcher le long de l'eſté, mais l'hyuer perſonne ne ſ'y arreſte à cauſe des froidures, ains ſe retirent tous en terre ferme, cerchants les pays plus chaults & les moins expoſez aux aſſaults & rigueurs de la Biſe, & ce ſont ceux de Blãc Sablon qui en vſent ainſi, & ceux de l'iſle ſainct Iaques, ainſi nommée par le Pilote Iaques Cartier, qui pẽſant pour le bon port que ce fut quelque bõne terre, n'y trouua rien que des pierres, & rochers, nomplus qu'à celle de blãc Sablon, ou il ne veit que des haliers eſpineux, & les roches toutes reueſtues de mouſſe paliſſante. Or eſt-il choſe merueilleuſe ce que ledict Cartier racompte de certaines iſles eſquelz il ne ſe trouua rien que des oyſeaux, & du nom deſquelz ilz les baptiſerent, le nom deſquelz eſtoient Godetz ainſi dictz de ceux du Pays, & leſquelz ſont de la grandeur d'vn Geay, noirs & blãcs de couleur, & ayans le bec comme vn Corbeau, & fort ayſez à prendre, gras à merueilles, & bons à manger, les autres ſont appellez Margaux, qui ſont plus blancs, & plus grands que les premiers, mais difficiles à prendre, à cauſe qu'ilz ſe deffendent eſtrangement du bec, & mordent preſque cõme vn chien lors qu'on les approche, & ſont de la grandeur d'vn oye, & on dit le nombre eſtre ſi grand que toute la terre en eſtoit couuerte, & que les Ours paſſoiẽt des autres Iſles auant pour ſe venir paiſtre ſur ceſte volaille, Mais laiſſons ces Iſles deſertes pour voir les hommes pour leſquelz noſtre hiſtoire eſt dreſſée plus que pour la ſingularité ny des animaux, ny des païſages, iaçoit que ie ne vueille du tout taire cecy, comme le voyant aſſez neceſſaire à noſtre diſcours, & au Lecteur plaiſant & prouffitable. En terre ferme que Cartier eſt deſcendu, il voit du peuple qui les acoſte & cognoiſt; ce que nous auons dit cy deſſus, à ſçauoir que tout ce

Iaques Cartier excellent Pilote de noſtre temps.

Charles de Mouy ſeign. de la milleraye.

Iſles de la terre Françoiſe.

Iſles S. Iaques nommée par Cartier.

Iaques Cartier, en ſa premiere relatiõ

DDd ij

Public Archives of Canada, Library, Ottawa (Negatives nos. C 99594 and C 113749).

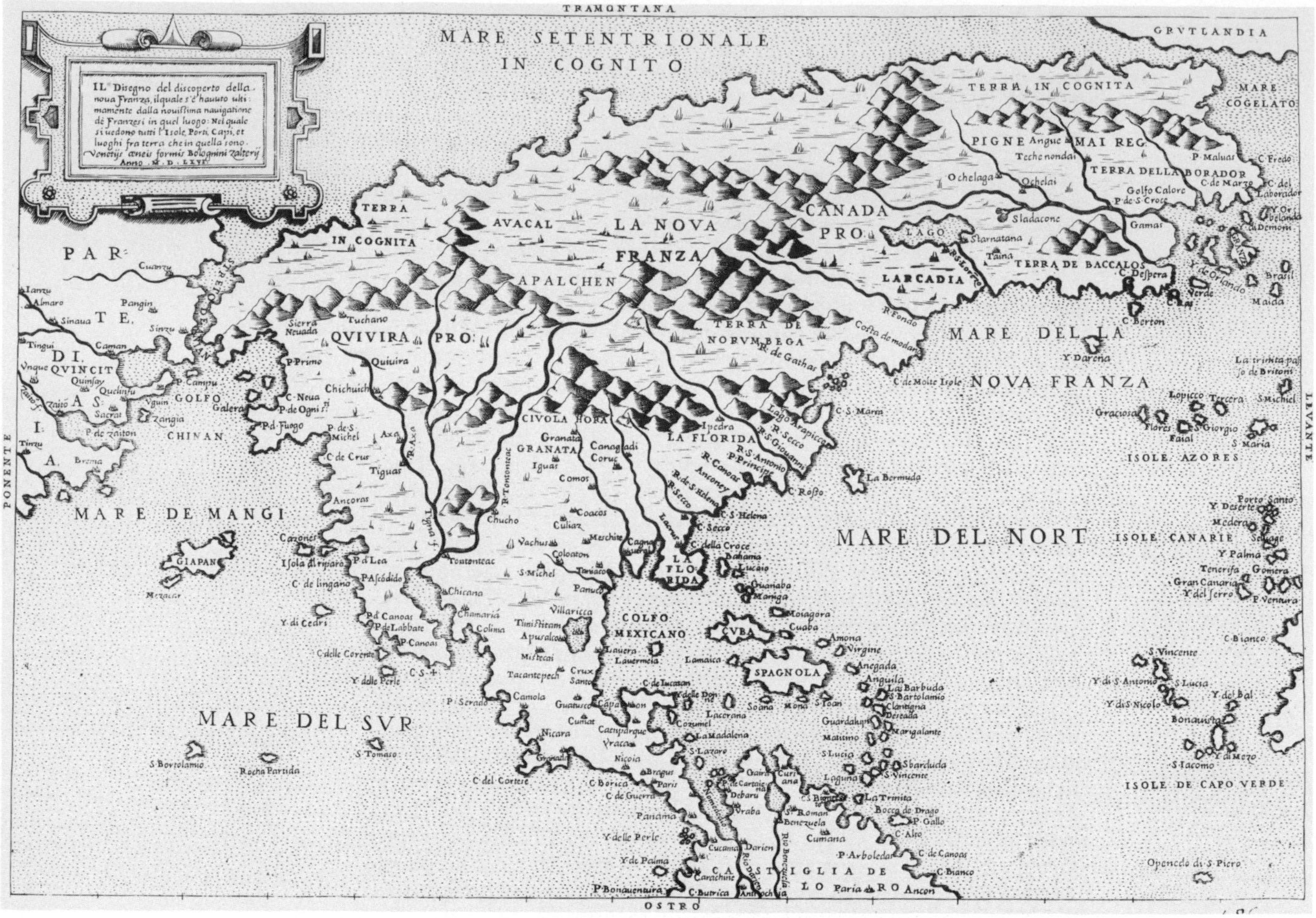

Il Desegno del discoperto della nova Franza.... [Venice], 1566; Bolognino Zaltieri; map printed from copperplate; 25.8 x 38.5 cm.

Acadia began to appear on maps of this period under the name of "Larcadia."

Public Archives of Canada, National Map Collection, Ottawa (NMC 6577).

I

Towards the Arctic

For a long time an Englishman, Martin Frobisher, had wanted to find a passage to Cathay in the Northwest. During his initial voyage in 1576 he discovered a large "strait" (Frobisher Bay). In 1577 and 1578 he made two more voyages, entering Hudson Strait by mistake during the second one. Edward Wright's map (made towards 1600) shows the "Frobusshers Straightes" and part of the Arctic territories ("Meta Incognita"), but detaches them from America to join them to Greenland.

The same map bore mention of Davis Strait. After making three voyages, from 1585 to 1587, in search of a northwest passage, John Davis contributed greatly to spreading information about the geography of this part of the world; by publishing *The Worldes Hydrographical Discription* in 1595 he opened up, as it were, the way for Henry Hudson and William Baffin.

From his first voyage Frobisher had brought back a native and had even brought along his kayak, thus succeeding in amazing all of London and part of the kingdom; for his part, Davis devoted to the Eskimos one of the oldest studies that have come down to us. It must be admitted that for Europe in the sixteenth century the Inuit, as we call them today, were indeed objects of astonishment, both because of their physical appearance and costume and their way of life. Above all else perhaps they were the revelation and at the same time the symbol of a "New World."

Septentrionalium Terrarum descriptio, [1595]; Gerard Mercator; map printed from copperplate, hand col.; 36.4 x 38.6 cm.

In Gerard Mercator. *Atlas sive cosmographicae*.... Duisburg: [1595].

Map of the North Pole, including Davis and Frobisher Straits. The bay shown on the far left seems to be Hudson Bay, even if we have no proof that the Europeans knew of its existence before Henry Hudson's voyages of exploration.

Public Archives of Canada, National Map Collection, Ottawa.

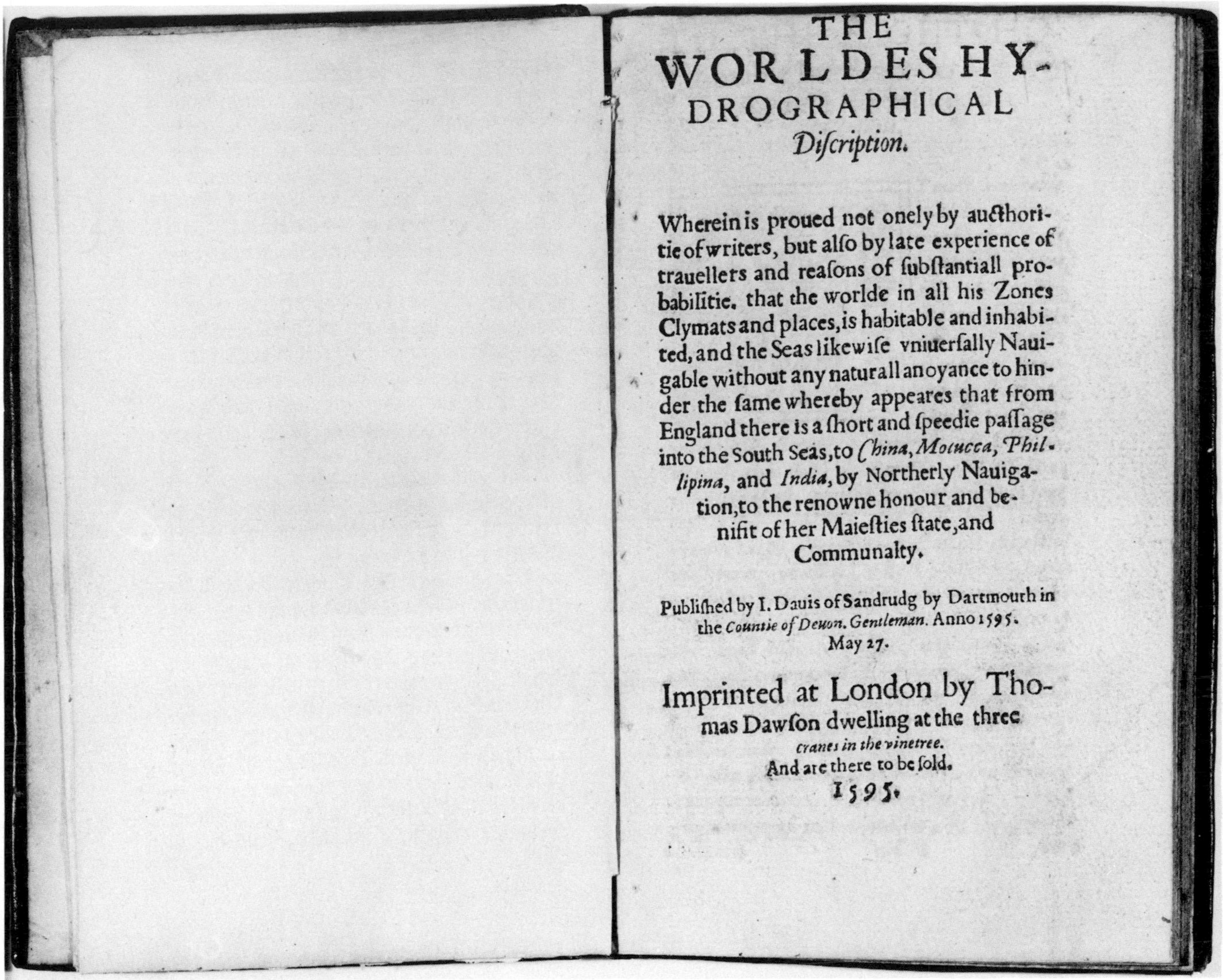

THE
WORLDES HY-
DROGRAPHICAL
Discription.

Wherein is proued not onely by aucthoritie of writers, but also by late experience of trauellers and reasons of substantiall probabilitie, that the worlde in all his Zones Clymats and places, is habitable and inhabited, and the Seas likewise vniuersally Nauigable without any naturall anoyance to hinder the same whereby appeares that from England there is a short and speedie passage into the South Seas, to *China, Molucca, Philipina*, and *India*, by Northerly Nauigation, to the renowne honour and benifit of her Maiesties state, and Communalty.

Published by I. Dauis of Sandrudg by Dartmouth in the *Countie of Deuon. Gentleman.* Anno 1595. May 27.

Imprinted at London by Thomas Dawson dwelling at the three *cranes in the vinetree.* And are there to be sold. 1595.

John Davys. *The Worldes Hydrographical Discription*. Sandrudg: I. Danis, 1595. Excerpts.

After three voyages in the Arctic in the period 1585–87 looking for a northwest passage to Asia, John Davis published this work, which contributed greatly to spreading knowledge about the geography of that part of the world.

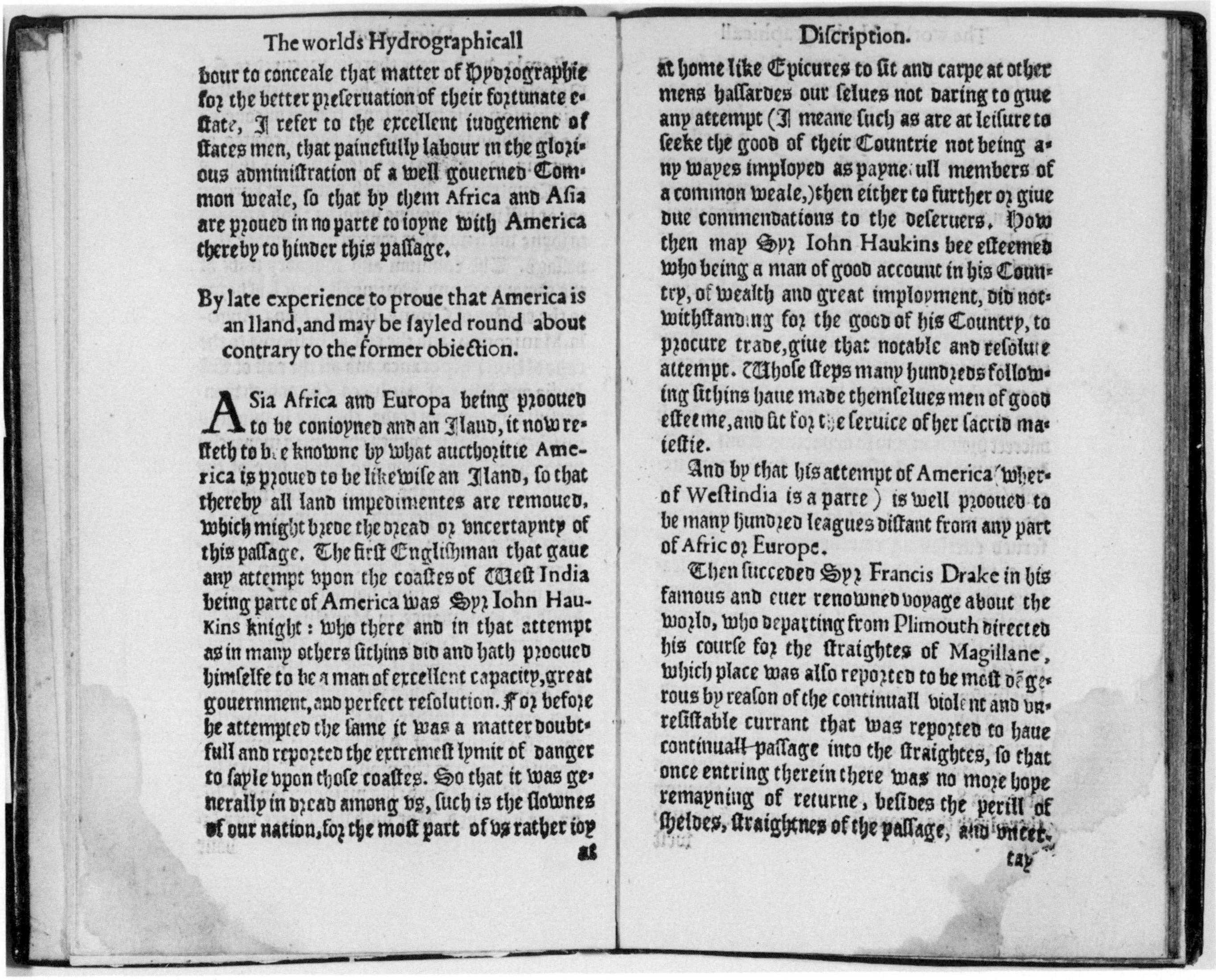

The worlds Hydrographicall

bour to conceale that matter of Hydrographie for the better preseruation of their fortunate estate, I refer to the excellent iudgement of states men, that painefully labour in the glorious administration of a well gouerned Common weale, so that by them Africa and Asia are proued in no parte to ioyne with America thereby to hinder this passage.

By late experience to proue that America is an Iland, and may be sayled round about contrary to the former obiection.

ASia Africa and Europa being prooued to be conioyned and an Ilaud, it now resteth to be knowne by what aucthoritie America is proued to be likewise an Iland, so that thereby all land impedimentes are remoued, which might brede the dread or vncertaynty of this passage. The first Englishman that gaue any attempt vpon the coastes of West India being parte of America was Syr Iohn Haukins knight: who there and in that attempt as in many others sithins did and hath procued himselfe to be a man of excellent capacity, great gouernment, and perfect resolution. For before he attempted the same it was a matter doubtfull and reported the extremest lymit of danger to sayle vpon those coastes. So that it was generally in dread among vs, such is the slownes of our nation, for the most part of vs rather ioy as

Discription.

at home like Epicures to sit and carpe at other mens hassardes our selues not daring to giue any attempt (I meane such as are at leisure to seeke the good of their Countrie not being any wayes imployed as paynefull members of a common weale,) then either to further or giue due commendations to the deseruers. How then may Syr Iohn Haukins bee esteemed who being a man of good account in his Country, of wealth and great imployment, did notwithstanding for the good of his Country, to procure trade, giue that notable and resolute attempt. Whose steps many hundreds following sithins haue made themselues men of good esteeme, and fit for the seruice of her sacrid maiestie.

And by that his attempt of America (whereof Westindia is a parte) is well prooued to be many hundred leagues distant from any part of Afric or Europe.

Then succeded Syr Francis Drake in his famous and euer renowned voyage about the world, who departing from Plimouth directed his course for the straightes of Magillane, which place was also reported to be most dangerous by reason of the continuall violent and vnresistable currant that was reported to haue continuall passage into the straightes, so that once entring therein there was no more hope remayning of returne, besides the perill of sheldes, straightnes of the passage, and vncertay

Folger Shakespeare Library, Washington, D.C., U.S.A.

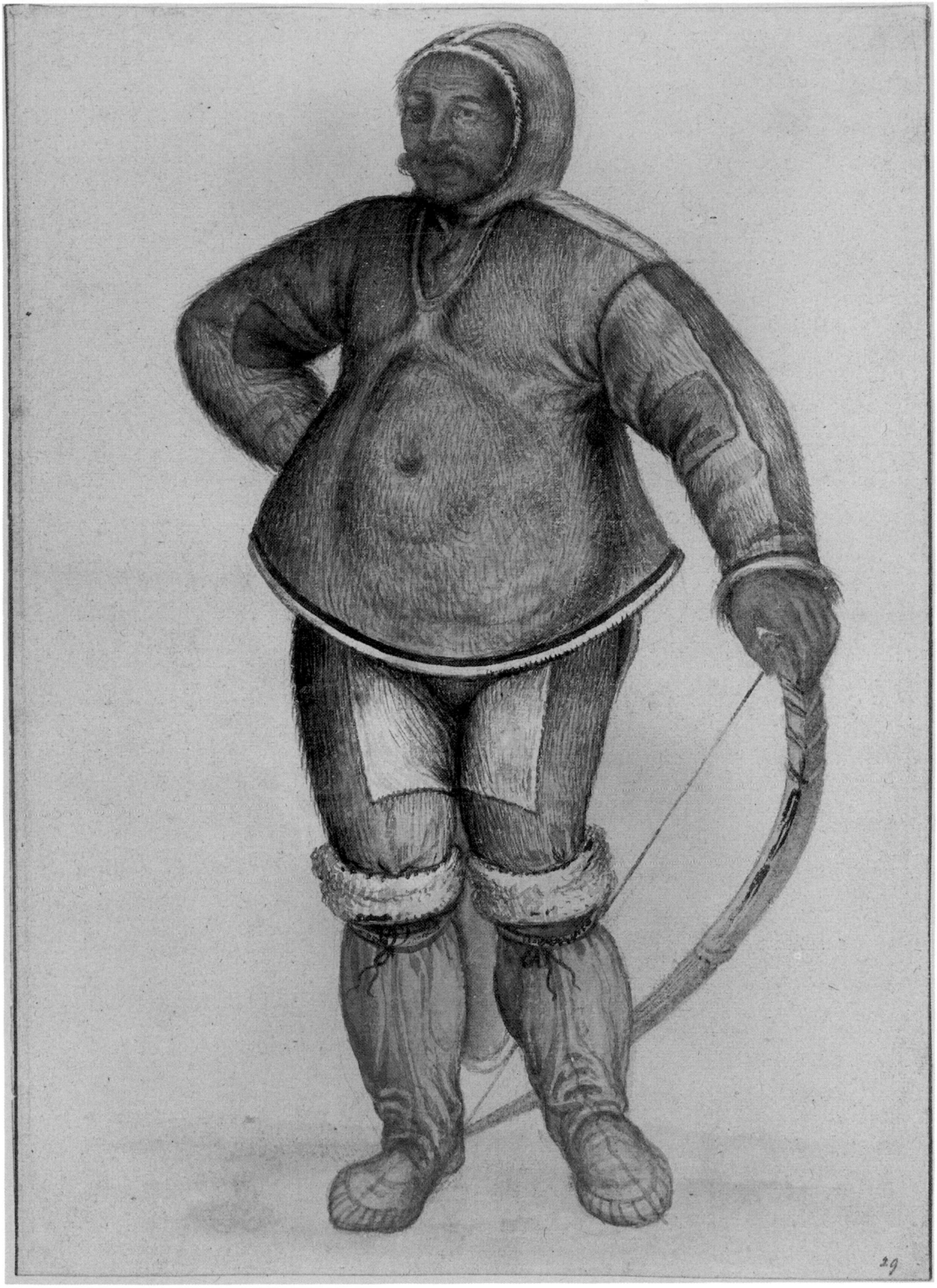

Eskimo Man; John White (known 1585–93); watercolour; 22.7 x 16.4 cm.

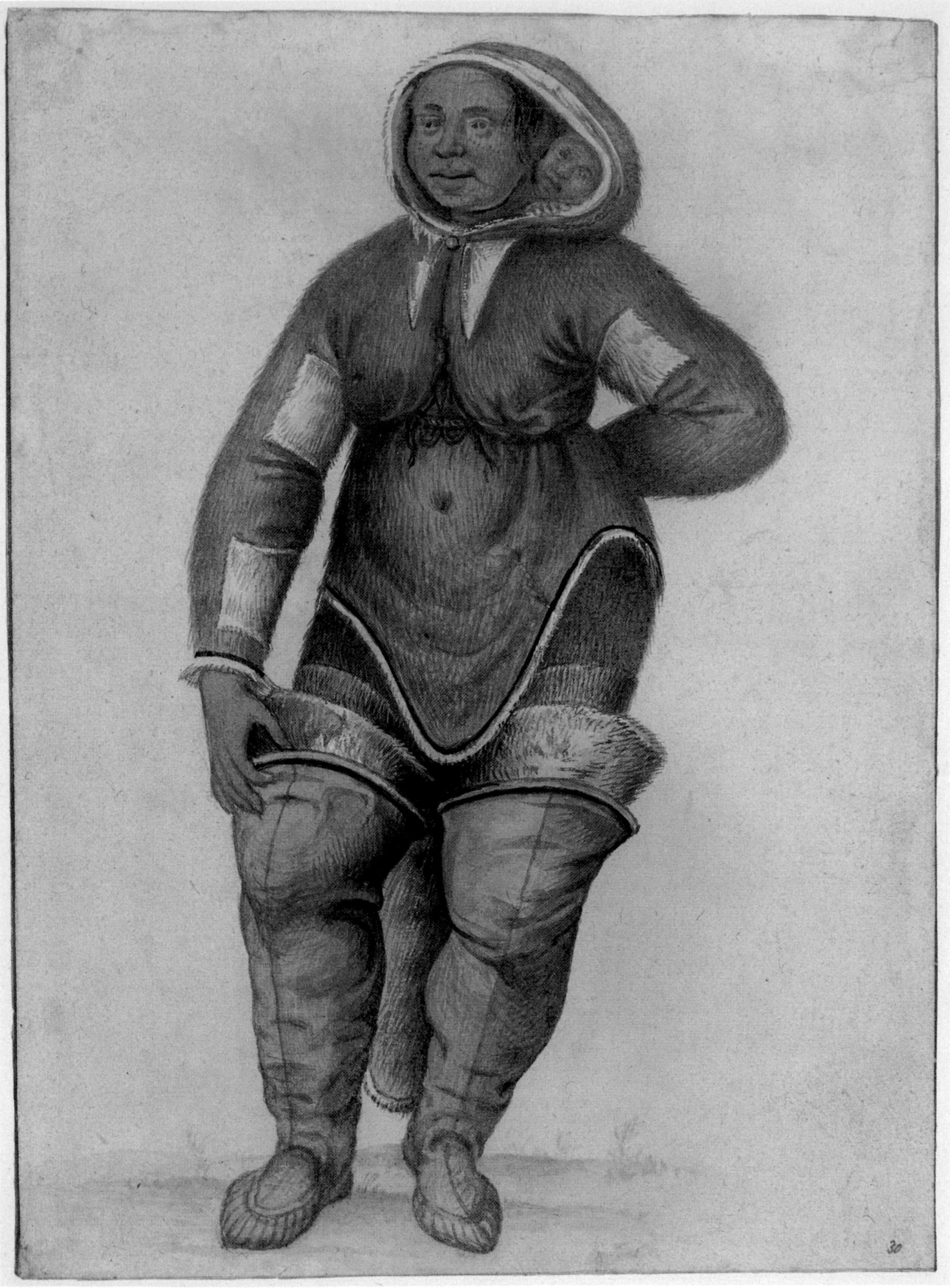

Eskimo Woman and Baby; John White (known 1585–93); watercolour; 22.2 x 16.6 cm.

These two drawings depict fairly faithfully the physical appearance and the costumes of the Eskimos at the period. John White is believed to have seen these natives while taking part in Sir Martin Frobisher's expedition south of Baffinland in 1577.

British Museum, Department of Prints and Drawings, London, England.

I

Plans and attempts at colonization

Humphrey Gilbert dreamed of setting up a colony. Having obtained letters patent on 11 June, 1578, he became the promoter of a settlement on the Atlantic coast and interested several Catholics of the realm in his plans. Among them were Sir Thomas Gerrard and Sir George Peckham, to whom he proposed an understanding in June 1582, which among other arrangements provided for the adoption of measures likely to encourage women to go to the New-Found Lands.

Around the same period Troilus de La Roche de Mesgouez received in successive years, 1577 and 1578, two commissions authorizing him on the one hand to take possession of the territories "of which he could make himself master," and on the other hand to govern the country. Being unable to lead to their destination the two expeditions that he had got ready, then having been prevented by the civil war from carrying out his plan, he received new letters patent on 12 January 1598 and finally founded a settlement on Sable Island.

All attempts at colonization in North America had failed. Now, on 18 December 1603, Henry IV granted Pierre Du Gua de Monts the monopoly of trade with the Indians and the title of lieutenant general of New France, on condition that he set up sixty settlers a year in the country and work at converting the natives.

Under Du Gua's authority an "Abitasion" (habitation), of which Champlain has left us a drawing done by himself, was built at Port-Royal.

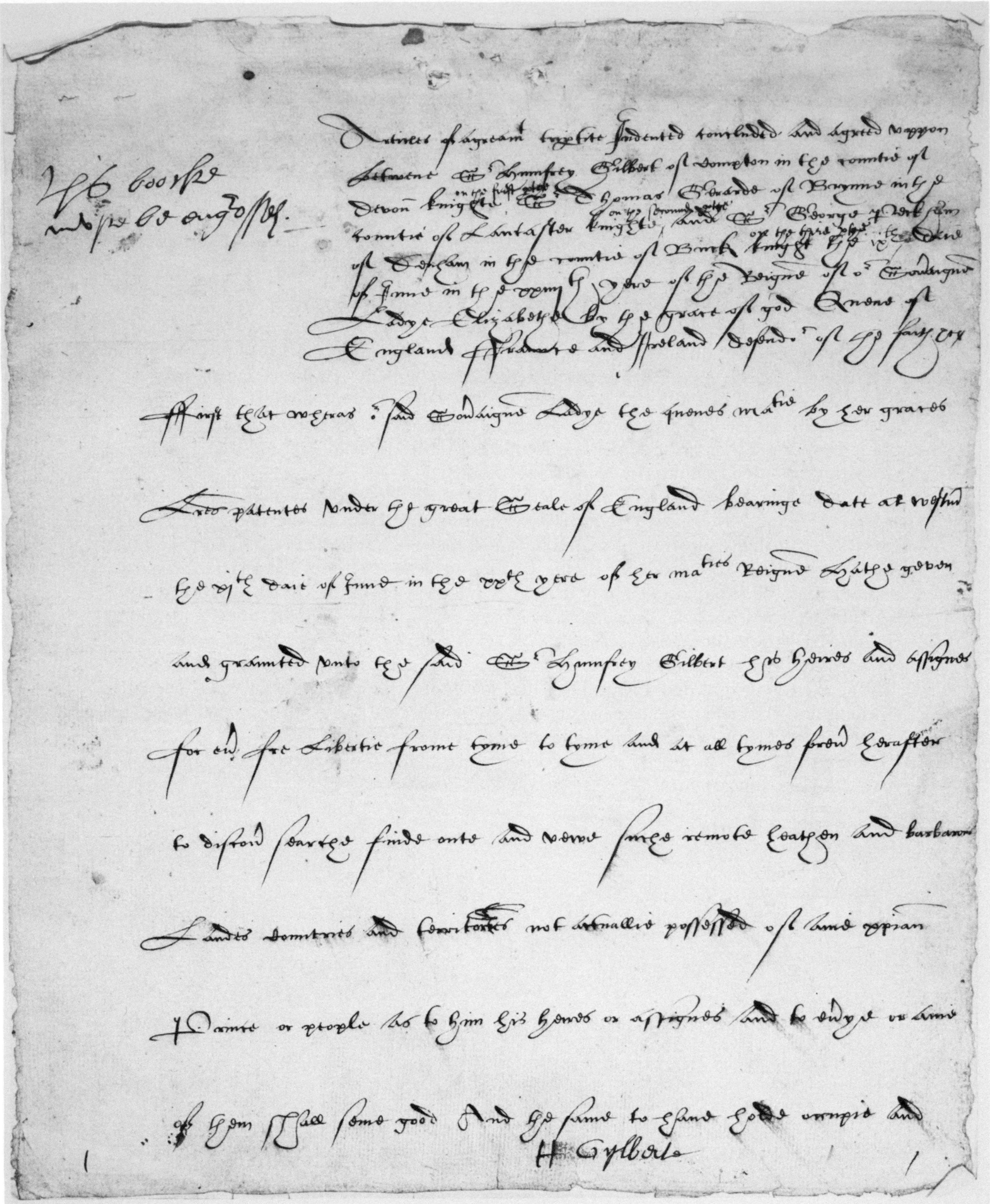

Articles of agreament tripartite indented concluded and agreed uppon betwene Sr Humfrey Gilbert of Compton in the countie of Devon knight in the first parte Sr Thomas Gerrarde of Brynne in the countie of Lancaster knight on the second parte and Sr George Peckham of Denham in the countie of Buck knight on the third parte the vth daie of June in the xxiiijth yere of the Reigne of our Soveraigne Ladye Elizabeth by the grace of god Queene of England Ffraunce and Ireland defendor of the faith etc

Ffirst that whereas our said Soveraigne Ladye the Queenes matie by her gracious lres patentes under the great Seale of England bearinge date at westm the xjth daie of June in the xxth yere of her maties Reigne hathe geven and graunted unto the said Sr Humfrey Gilbert his heires and assignes for ever free libertie from tyme to tyme and at all tymes from hereafter to discover searche finde oute and viewe suche remote heathen and barbarous landes countries and territories not actuallie possessed of anie christian Prince or people as to him his heires or assignes and to everye or anie of them shall seme good And the same to have holde occupie and

H Gylberte

Agreement between Sir Humphrey Gilbert, Sir George Peckham, and Sir Thomas Gerrard, 5 June 1582.

Gilbert concluded various agreements with Catholic compatriots, among them Peckham and Gerrard, with a view to founding a settlement on the east coast of North America. On 5 August 1583 he took possession officially, in the name of the crown of England, of Newfoundland.

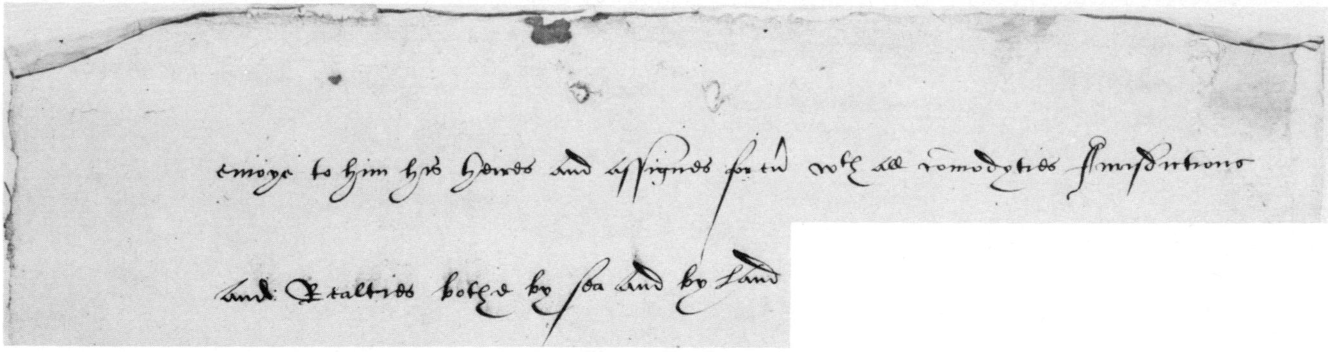
tinewe to him his heires and assignes for ever with all comodities Jurisdictions

and Royalties bothe by Sea and by Land

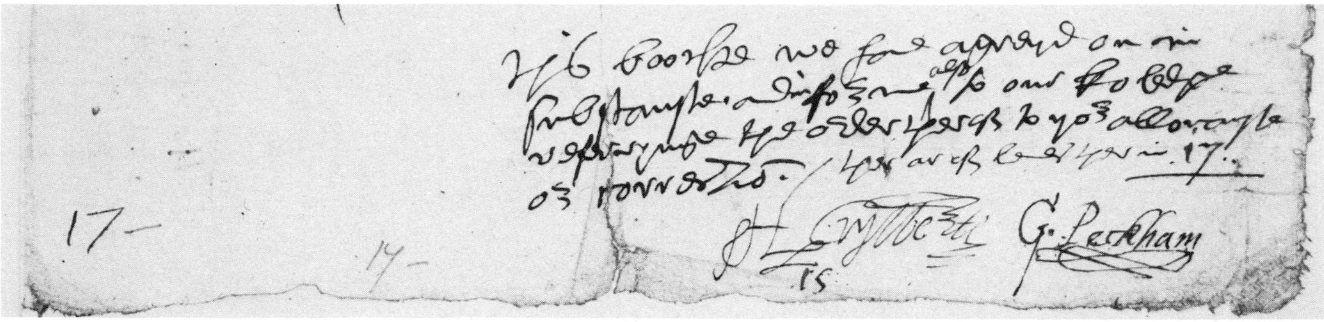
17–

H. Gylberte G. Peckham

Public Archives of Canada, Ottawa: Brudenell Collection, MG 18, B 18, pp. 1, 2, 17.

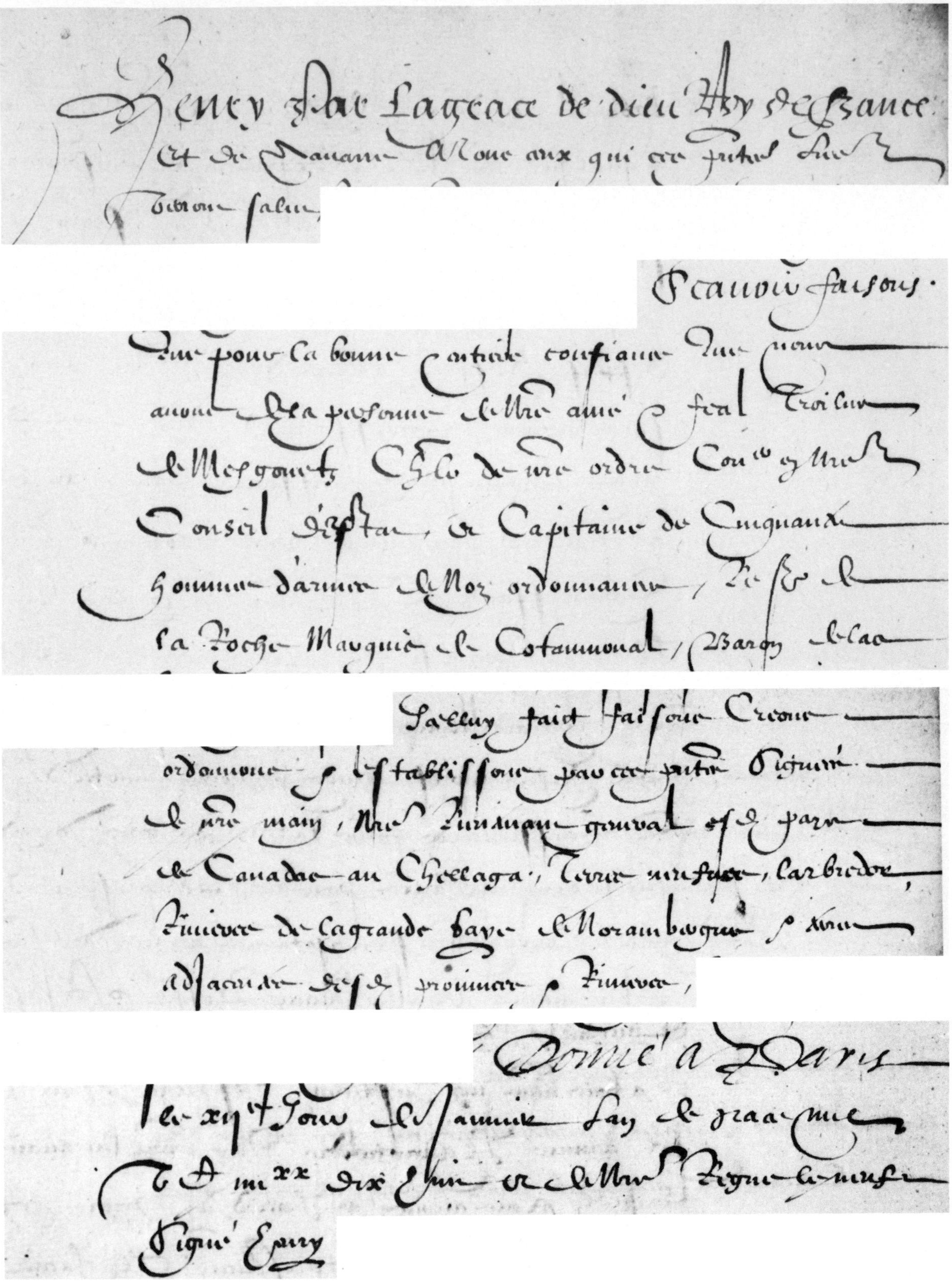
Henry par la grace de dieu Roy de France
Et de Navarre A tous ceux qui ces presentes lettres
verront salut,
Scavoir faisons
que pour la bonne et entiere confiance que nous
avons de la personne de nostre amé et feal le sieur
de Mesgouets Chlr de nostre ordre Con[er] en nostre
Conseil d'Estat, et Capitaine de cinquante
hommes d'armes de noz ordonnances, Sr de
la Roche Marquis de Cotenmonal, Baron de la
Icelluy faict faisons creons
ordonnons et establissons par ces presentes signées
de nostre main, nostre lieutenant general es pays
de Canada, Hochelaga, Terres neufves, Labrador,
riviere de la grande baye de Norambegue et terres
adjacentes desd. provinces et rivieres,
Donné a Paris
le xij jour de Janvier l'an de grace mil
cinq cens iiij^xx dix huit et de nostre regne le neufe
Signé Henry

Letters patent from the king of France, Henry IV, appointing the Marquis de La Roche-Mesgouez "lieutenant general in the aforesaid countries of Canada, Hochelaga, Newfoundland, Labrador, the river of the Great Bay of Norumbega, and the lands adjoining the said provinces and rivers," Paris, 12 January 1598.

In that same year La Roche founded a settlement on Sable Island (to the south-east of Nova Scotia) that lasted five years.

Archives départementales de la Seine-Maritime, Rouen, France: Registre du Parlement de Rouen, mars–avril 1598, fol. 3–10.

19

DEFENSES DV ROY

PREMIERES ET SECONDES

à tous ſes ſubiects, autres que le ſieur de Monts & ſes aſſociez. De traffiquer de Pelleteryes & autres choſes auec les Sauuages, de l'eſtendue du pouuoir par luy donné audit ſieur de Monts, ny de s'aſſocier auecques les Eſtrangers, pour ſoubs leur nom, ou en quelque autre ſorte & maniere que ce ſoit, troubler en icelle traitte ledit ſieur de Monts & ſes aſſociez. Sur grandes peynes.

HENRY par la grace de Dieu Roy de France & de Nauarre. A nos amez & feaulx Conſeillers, les officiers de noſtre Admiraulté, de Normandie, Bretagne, Picardie & Guyenne: Et à chacun d'eux endroit ſoy: & en l'eſtendue de leurs reſſorts & iuriſdictions, Salut. Nous auons pour beaucoup d'importantes occaſions, ordonné, commis & eſtably le ſieur de Monts, gentilhomme ordinaire de noſtre chambre, noſtre Lieutenant general, pour peupler & habituer les terres, coſtes, & pays de Lacadie, & autres circonuoiſins, en l'eſtendue du quarantieſme degré, iuſ-

C ij

Monopoly of trade with the Indians granted Pierre Du Gua de Monts by the king of France, Henry IV, Paris, 18 December 1603.

In 1604 de Monts, who had been appointed lieutenant general of New France, tried to establish a colony in Acadia, first on Île Sainte-Croix (1604–05), then at Port-Royal (1605–07).

ques au quarante ſixieſme . Et là eſtablir noſtre auctorité , & autrement s'y loger & aſſeurer : en ſorte que nos ſubiets deſormais y puiſſent eſtre receuz, y hanter, reſider & trafiquer auec les Sauuages habitãs deſdits lieux . Comme plus expreſſement nous l'auons declaré par nos lettres patentes, expediees & deliurees pour ceſt effect audit ſieur de Monts , le 8 . iour de Nouembre dernier : & ſuiuant les conditions & articles . Moyennant leſquelles il s'eſt chargé de la conduite & execution de ceſte entrepriſe . Pour faciliter laquelle, & à ceux qui s'y ſont ioints auec luy : & leur donner quelque moyen & commodité, d'en ſupporter la deſpence: Nous auons eu agreable de leur permettre, & aſſeurer; Qu'il ne ſeroit permis à aucuns autres nos ſubiets, qu'à ceux qui entreroyent en aſſociation auec luy, pour faire ladite deſpence de traffiquer de Pelleterie, & autres marchandiſes , durant dix annees , és terres, pays, ports, riuieres & aduenues de l'eſtendue de ſa charge . Ce que nous voulons auoir lieu.

Donné à Paris, le 18. Decembre, l'an de grace mil ſix cens trois . Et de noſtre regne le quinzieſme . Ainſi ſigné, HENRY.

Archives du ministère des Affaires étrangères, Paris, France: Mémoires et documents, Amérique, vol. 4, fol. 12–12v, 13v.

31

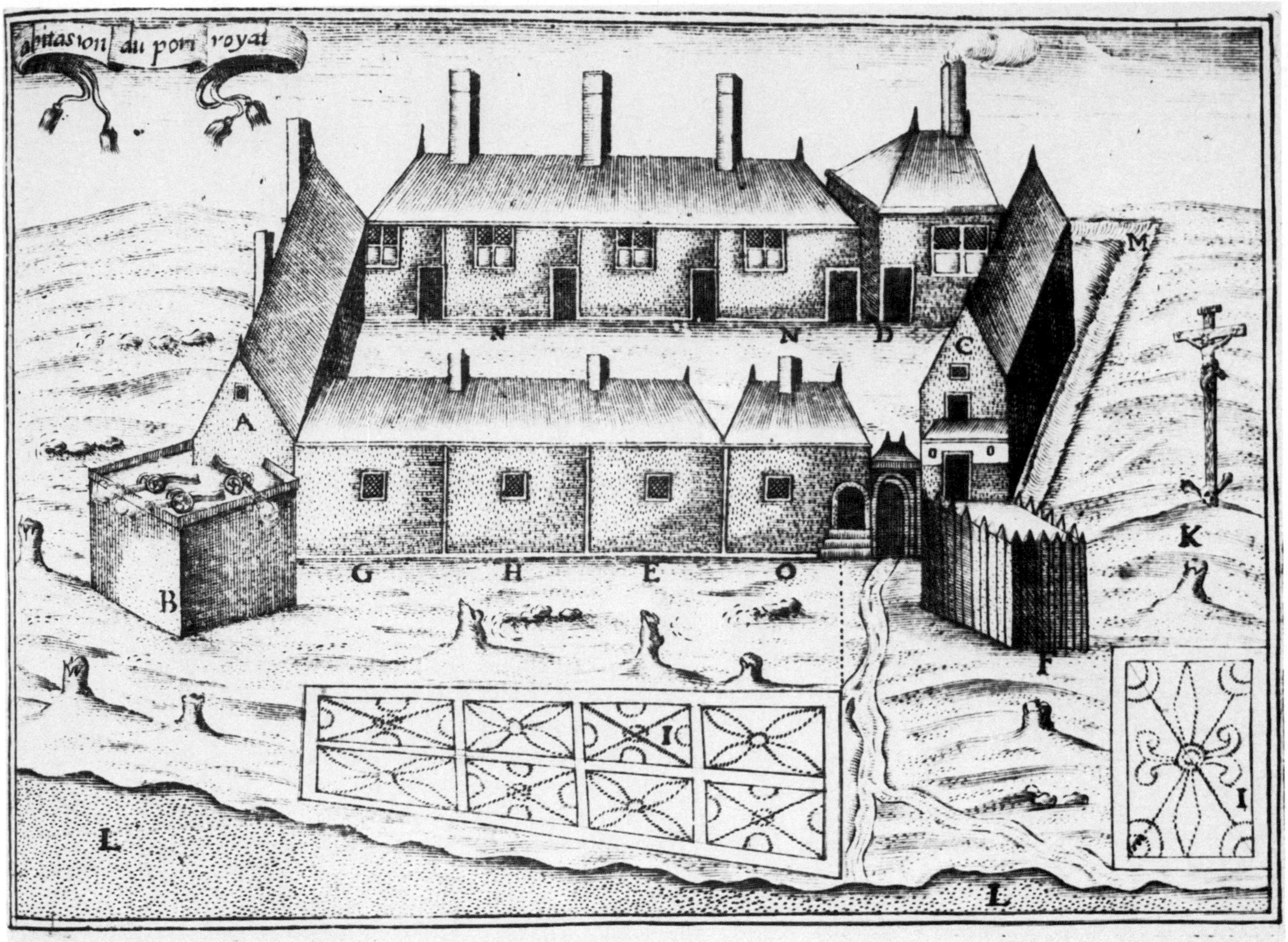

A Logemens des artiſans.
B Plate forme où eſtoit le canon.
C Le magaſin.
D Logemẽt du ſieur de Pont-graué & Champlain.
E La forge.
F Paliſſade de pieux.
G Le four.
H La cuiſine.
O Petite maiſonnette où l'on retiroit les vtanſiles de nos barques; que de puis le ſieur de Poitrincourt fit rebaſtir, & y logea le ſieur Boulay quand le ſieur du Pont s'en reuint en France.
P La porte de l'abitation.
Q Le cemetiere.
R La riuiere.

Habitation at Port-Royal; after a drawing by Samuel de Champlain (1567 [?]–1635); line and stipple engraving; 10.9 x 15.4 cm. (plate).

In Samuel de Champlain. *Les voyages dv sievr de Champlain Xaintongeois, capitaine ordinaire pour le roy, en la marine, divisez en deux livres....* Paris: Chez Jean Berjon, 1613, p. 99.

As the winter spent at Sainte-Croix in 1604–05 had been very difficult because of the severe cold and scurvy, the French decided to leave the place to go to build a settlement at Port-Royal in 1605. The latter settlement was abandoned in 1607, the year in which the Sieur de Monts's monopoly was revoked by the king. Later Port-Royal became the chief centre in Acadia.

National Library of Canada, Rare Books and Manuscripts Division, Ottawa.

I

The founding of Québec

When Port-Royal had to be abandoned in 1607, a search was made in 1608 off towards the St. Lawrence to find a place suitable for founding a permanent colony. Champlain sailed up the river, which he explored in 1603; on 3 July he stopped off the point of Québec, which he chose as the site for a habitation – at once the embryo and the heart of the new colony. As he tells us himself in his *Oeuvres,* Champlain set his men to work without delay.

Québec was founded.

The habitation of Québec served as lodgings, storehouse, and fortress all together; in it were to be found an arms depot, a forge, and even a pigeon-house; on the upper floor the dwelling-quarters were surrounded with galleries that could be useful in case of attack. The habitation was, moreover, surrounded with a stockade and moats; access to it was by a drawbridge; inside it platforms had been prepared for guns.

The habitation stood between the St. Lawrence and the cape, where the Place Royale is today, almost at the foot of the Côte de la Montagne, which links Upper Town and Lower Town. Being situated at the very point where the St. Lawrence suddenly narrows before widening out again, Champlain's fort occupied a strategic position and could theoretically prevent any potential enemy from pushing farther inland.

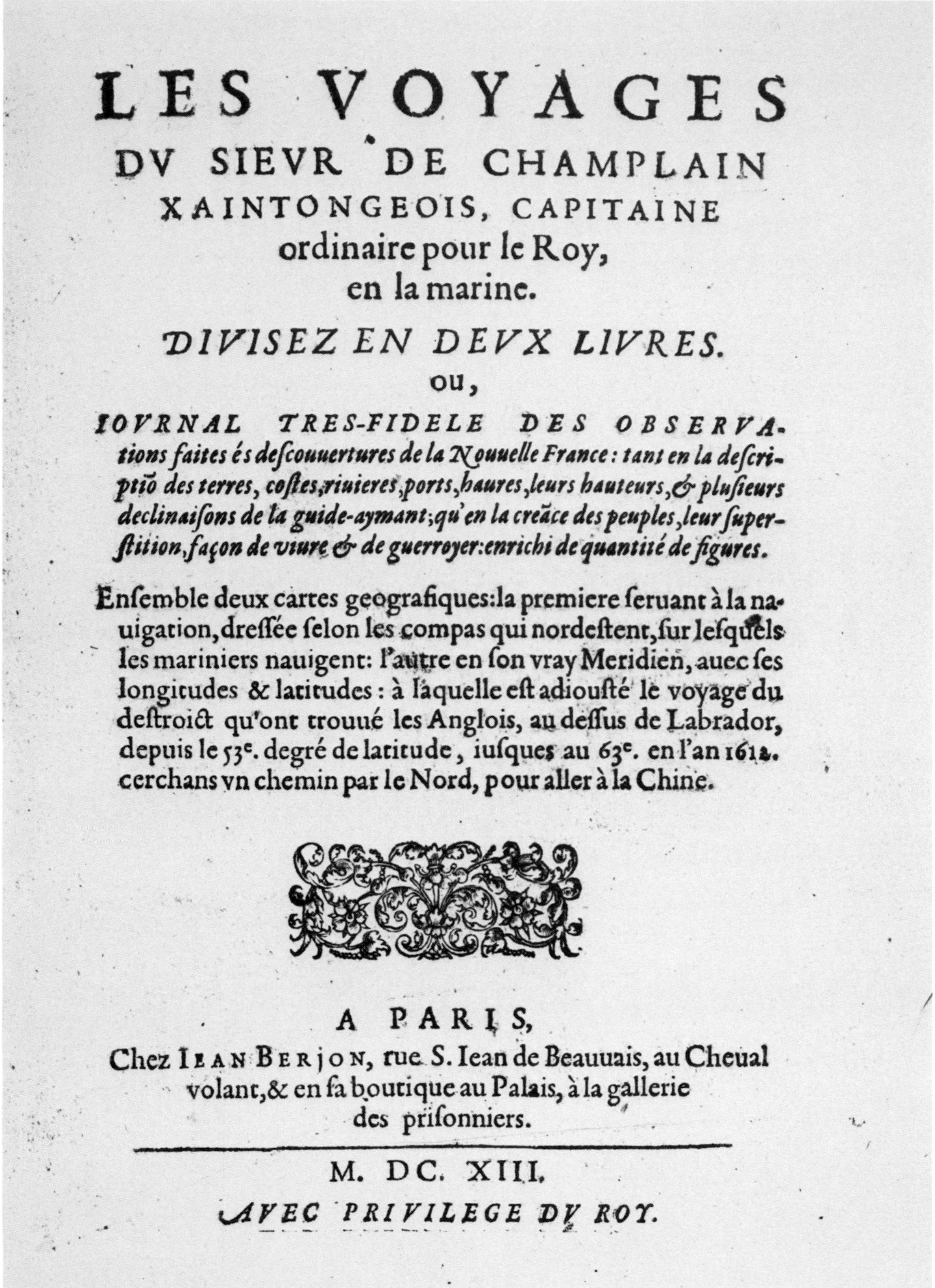

LES VOYAGES
DV SIEVR DE CHAMPLAIN
XAINTONGEOIS, CAPITAINE
ordinaire pour le Roy,
en la marine.

DIVISEZ EN DEVX LIVRES.
ou,

IOVRNAL TRES-FIDELE DES OBSERVATIONS faites és descouuertures de la Nouuelle France: tant en la descriptiõ des terres, costes, riuieres, ports, haures, leurs hauteurs, & plusieurs declinaisons de la guide-aymant; qu'en la creãce des peuples, leur superstition, façon de viure & de guerroyer: enrichi de quantité de figures.

Ensemble deux cartes geografiques: la premiere seruant à la nauigation, dressée selon les compas qui nordestent, sur lesquels les mariniers nauigent: l'autre en son vray Meridien, auec ses longitudes & latitudes: à laquelle est adiousté le voyage du destroict qu'ont trouué les Anglois, au dessus de Labrador, depuis le 53e. degré de latitude, iusques au 63e. en l'an 1612. cerchans vn chemin par le Nord, pour aller à la Chine.

A PARIS,
Chez IEAN BERJON, rue S. Iean de Beauuais, au Cheual volant, & en sa boutique au Palais, à la gallerie des prisonniers.

M. DC. XIII.
AVEC PRIVILEGE DV ROY.

Samuel de Champlain. *Les voyages dv sievr de Champlain Xaintongeois, capitaine ordinaire pour le roy, en la marine, divisez en deux livres....* Paris: Chez Jean Berjon, 1613, title page, pp. 175–176.

Champlain gives an account of the founding of Québec, 3 July 1608.

ARRIVEE A QVEBECQ, OV NOVS FISMES NOS logemens, sa situation. Conspiration contre le seruice du Roy, & ma vie, par aucuns de nos gens. La punition qui en fut faite, & tout ce qui ce passa en cet affaire.

CHAP. III.

DE l'isle d'Orleans iusques à Quebecq, y a vne lieue, & y arriuay le 3. Iuillet: où estãt, ie cherchay lieu propre pour nostre habitatiõ,

mais ie n'en peu trouuer de plus commode, n'y mieux situé que la pointe de Quebecq, ainsi appellé des sauuages, laquelle estoit remplie de noyers. Aussitost i'emploiay vne partie de nos ouuriers à les abbatre pour y faire nostre habitation, l'autre à scier des aix, l'autre fouiller la caue & faire des fossez: & l'autre à aller querir nos commoditez à Tadoussac auec la barque. La premiere chose que nous fismes fut le magazin pour mettre nos viures à couuert, qui fut promptemẽt fait par la diligence d'vn chacun, & le soin que i'en eu.

National Library of Canada, Rare Books and Manuscripts Division, Ottawa.

RETOVR DV PONT-GRAVE EN FRANCE. DEſcriptiõ de noſtre logemẽt & du lieu où ſeiourna Iaques Quartier en l'an 1535.

CHAP. IV.

APrés que toutes ces choſes furent paſſees le Pont partit de Quebecq le 18. Septembre pour s'en retourner en France auec les trois priſonniers. Depuis qu'ils furent hors tout le reſte ſe comporta ſagement en ſon deuoir.

Ie fis continuer noſtre logement, qui eſtoit de trois corps de logis à deux eſtages. Chacun contenoit trois thoiſes de long & deux & demie de large. Le magazin ſix & trois de large, auec vne belle caue de ſix pieds de haut. Tout autour de nos logemens ie fis faire vne galerie par dehors au ſecõd eſtage, qui eſtoit fort commode, auec des foſſés de 15. pieds de large & ſix de profond: & au dehors des foſſés, ie fis pluſieurs pointes d'eſperons qui enfermoient vne partie du logement, là où nous miſmes nos pieces de canon: & deuant le baſtiment y a vne place de quatre thoiſes de large, & ſix ou ſept de lõg, qui dõne ſur le bort de la riuiere. Autour du logement y a des iardins qui ſont tres-bons, & vne place du coſté de Septemptrion qui a quelque cent ou ſix vingts pas de long, 50. ou 60. de large.

Samuel de Champlain. *Les voyages dv sievr de Champlain Xaintongeois, capitaine ordinaire pour le roy, en la marine, divisez en deux livres*.... Paris: Chez Jean Berjon, 1613, pp. 184–185.

Champlain describes the habitation at Québec in 1608.

National Library of Canada, Rare Books and Manuscripts Division, Ottawa.

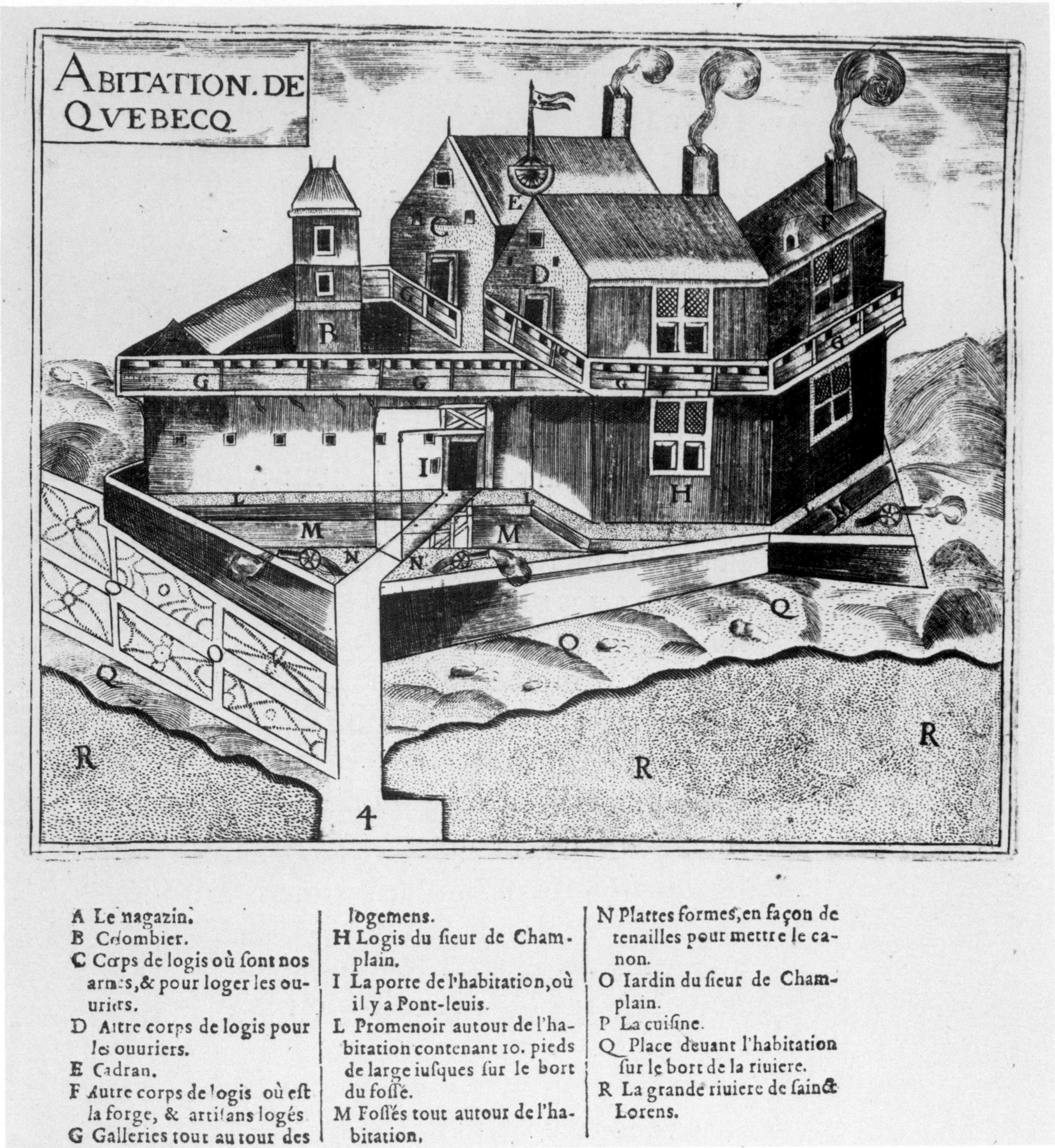

ABITATION. DE QVEBECQ
A
B
C
D
E
F
G
H
I
L
M
N
O
Q
R
4
A Le nagazin.
B Colombier.
C Corps de logis où ſont nos armes,& pour loger les ouuriers.
D Autre corps de logis pour les ouuriers.
E Cadran.
F Autre corps de logis où eſt la forge, & artiſans logés
G Galleries tout au tour des logemens.
H Logis du ſieur de Champlain.
I La porte de l'habitation, où il y a Pont-leuis.
L Promenoir autour de l'habitation contenant 10. pieds de large iuſques ſur le bort du foſſé.
M Foſſés tout autour de l'habitation.
N Plattes formes, en façon de tenailles pour mettre le canon.
O Iardin du ſieur de Champlain.
P La cuiſine.
Q Place deuant l'habitation ſur le bort de la riuiere.
R La grande riuiere de ſainct Lorens.

Habitation at Québec; after a drawing by Samuel de Champlain (1567 [?]–1635); line and stipple engraving; 13.1 x 15.9 cm. (plate).

In Samuel de Champlain. *Les voyages dv sievr de Champlain Xaintongeois, capitaine ordinaire pour le roy, en la marine, divisez en deux livres....* Paris: Chez Jean Berjon, 1613, p. 187.

Upon his arrival at Québec in 1608 Champlain had this habitation built to live in himself, to lodge the workers and craftsmen, and to store arms and provisions in.

National Library of Canada, Rare Books and Manuscripts Division, Ottawa.

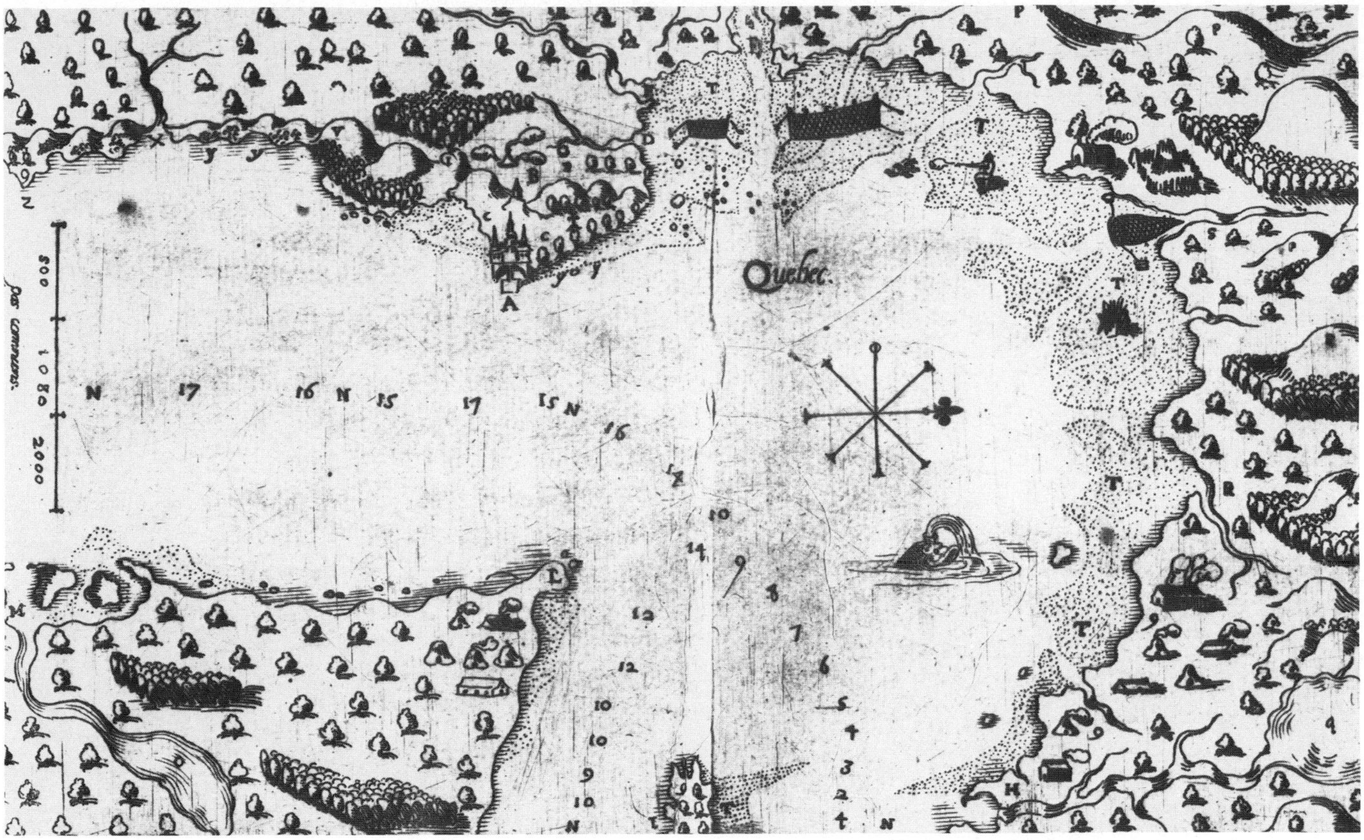

Les chifres montrent les braſſes d'eau.

- A Le lieu ou l'habitation eſt baſtie.
- B Terre deffrichee où l'on ſe-me du bled & autres grains.
- C Les iardinages.
- D Petit ruiſſeau qui vient de dedans des mareſcages.
- E Riuiere ou hyuerna Iaques Quartier, qui de ſon tẽps la nomma ſaincte Croix, que l'on a transferé à 15. lieues audeſſus de Quebec.
- F Ruiſſeau des marais.
- G Le lieu ou l'on amaſſoit les herbages pour le beſtail que l'on y auoit mené.
- H Le grand ſaut de Mont-morency qui deſcent de plus de 25. braſſes de haut dans la riuiere.
- I Bout de l'iſle d'Orlans.
- L Pointe fort eſtroite du coſté de l'orient de Quebecq.
- M Riuiere bruyante, qui va aux Etechemains.
- N La grãde riuiere S. Laurens
- O Lac de la riuiere bruyante.
- P Montaignes qui ſont dans les terres; baye que i'ay nõmé la nouuelle Biſquaye.
- Q Lac du grãd ſaut de Mont morency.
- R Ruiſſeau de loure.
- S Ruiſſeau du Gendre.
- T Prairie qui ſont inondees des eaux a toutes les marees
- V Mont du Gas fort haut, ſur le bort de la riuiere.
- X Ruiſſeau courant, propre à faire toutes ſortes de moulins.
- Y Coſte de grauier, où il ſe trouue quantité de diamants vn peu meilleurs que ceux d'Alanſon.
- Z La pointe aux diamants.
- 9 Lieux où ſouuent cabanent les ſauuages.

[Québec, 1613]; Samuel de Champlain; map printed from copperplate; 15.2 x 24.8 cm.

In Samuel de Champlain. *Les voyages dv sievr de Champlain Xaintongeois, capitaine ordinaire pour le roy, en la marine, divisez en deux livres*.... Paris: Chez Jean Berjon, 1613.

Map drawn by Samuel de Champlain showing Québec, the habitation built in 1608, and the surrounding area.

National Library of Canada, Rare Books and Manuscripts Division, Ottawa.

II

Exploration and Occupation of the Continent

Once the post of Québec had been founded, Champlain undertook only three more exploration trips. In 1609, going up the Rivière des Iroquois (the Richelieu), he discovered the lake that bears his name and went as far as Ticonderoga (Crown Point, New York). In 1613, proceeding via the Ottawa River and a series of lakes he reached Allumette Island (on a level with Petawawa, Ontario). Finally in 1615, going beyond Allumette Island and travelling via the Mattawa River, Lake Nipissing, and the French River, he discovered Lake Huron; he went to Lake Simcoe, crossed the eastern end of Lake Ontario, followed the Oneida River for some time; then he spent the winter in the Huron country and visited Tobacco Nation to the south of Nottawasaga Bay and the Cheveux-Relevez (Ottawas) to the south of Georgian Bay. These were his last exploration trip and his last discoveries.

While Champlain was seeking to get to know the interior of the continent, more attention than ever was being paid to a northwest passage, particularly in England. After the voyages of Frobisher and Davis there were those of George Waymouth (1602) and John Knight (1606); but it was Henry Hudson who in 1610 was successful in making his way into Hudson Bay via the strait that bears his name. Would the passage that was so ardently desired be found on the west coast of this bay? Thomas Button's voyage in 1612–13 led him to have strong hopes of that; but in 1614 William Gibbons did not even succeed in entering Hudson Strait, and in 1615 William Baffin discovered no passage, even if he did discover the bay and the land that bear his name. As for William Hawkridge, he discovered nothing in 1625. In 1631 Thomas James and Luke Fox, each one on his own, explored the west coast of Hudson Bay: there was no passage there. Disappointment was so great in England that for nearly two centuries people ceased to be interested in this search.

Enthusiasm for discoveries was cooling in England just at the moment when New France was launching headlong into exploring the continent. In 1634, in a mad dash,

II

Jean Nicollet plunged deeply into the Great Lakes region. In 1641 the Jesuits Isaac Jogues and Charles Raymbaut discovered Lake Superior. In 1646 Father Gabriel Druillettes followed the Chaudière River to reach the headwaters of the Kennebec, whose whole course he explored as far as the ocean. In 1647, Father Jean de Quen discovered Lake Saint-Jean; in 1651, Father Jacques Buteux and a few Frenchmen went up the Saint-Maurice for a distance of one hundred leagues. In 1655, it would seem, Médard Chouart Des Groseilliers travelled in Wisconsin. In 1661 the Jesuits Gabriel Druillettes and Claude Dablon, who had started out for Hudson Bay, went as far as the watershed at Lac Nicabau. How many others, in the search for souls to be converted or furs to be bartered for, criss-crossed the country, from north to south and east to west, always discovering new routes – rivers, lakes, and portages – to lead them on farther and farther?

These exploration trips had been carried out without any plan or concerted effort, but as circumstances directed. When he arrived, Jean Talon, a man of vision and genius, understood what advantage could be drawn from the discoveries for the future greatness of New France and the honour of France. He undertook to send "resolute men" in all directions, with the mission of exploring and discovering, certainly, but also of taking possession of the territories officially in the king's name.

To the west he sent Simon-François Daumont de Saint-Lusson; to the south, in the direction of Mexico, Robert Cavelier de La Salle; to the southwest, in search of the Mississippi and the Mer du Sud (the Pacific Ocean), Louis Jolliet; to Hudson Bay, Father Charles Albanel and Paul Denys de Saint-Simon, who were the first to arrive there by the overland route. The Sulpicians François Dollier de Casson and René de Bréhant de Galinée for their part explored in minute detail the shores of Lake Ontario, where Talon was already thinking of building a fort to subdue the Iroquois. What is more, Talon was thinking of acquiring New Netherland (New York), which would give New France easy access to the ocean, even in winter, and would permit her to encircle and contain the English in New England, while at the same time bringing the Iroquois under French influence.

The plan to purchase or conquer New Netherland was rejected by the king; but in 1673 Frontenac followed up with the plan for a fort on Lake Ontario. The following year Colbert informed him of Louis XIV's displeasure at seeing the colony extending farther and farther; they had to concentrate in the valley of the St. Lawrence and stick together to defend themselves better against any possible enemy.

But how was the expansion of the colony to be slowed down without at the same time doing harm to the missionaries' apostolic works? And how were fur traders to be prevented from setting up trading posts near the missions? Was expansion not necessary to the colony, which still depended almost entirely on the fur trade? And did not this trade have to be protected in the most distant places by installing garrisons there? In short, if exploration was at first a consequence of the missionary ardour, expansion became little by little an economic necessity, then, because of commercial rivalries, a military necessity.

It was in fact for economic and military reasons that the search for the Mer du Sud was continued, that Pierre Le Moyne d'Iberville, Pierre Allemand, Daniel Greysolon Dulhut and so many others "explored" the continent, that posts – or forts – such as Michilimackinac and Detroit were constructed, that Louisiana was founded, while at the same time the scattering of the vital forces of an underpopulated colony was deplored.

II

Champlain's voyages of discovery

In 1615 Champlain resumed his voyages of discovery: on 1 July he reached Lake Attigouantan, which was, he said, nearly "four hundred leagues in length" and "fifty leagues wide," and which he called "the freshwater sea." It was Lake Huron.

At Lake Attigouantan Champlain and his companions met three hundred Ottawas, whom they called "Cheveux-Relevez" because of the way in which their hair was "arranged" and "combed." Champlain left four drawings of them, which show "the way in which they arm themselves on going to war" and the way the women dressed in summer and the men in winter.

Champlain spent the winter of 1615–16 in the Huron country. There he studied their manners at his leisure and wrote with obvious interest a description of a deer hunt: there was a beat organized in such a way as to drive the animals towards a big "enclosure," a sort of triangle open on one side only, where, once inside, they were at the mercy of the hunters.

In 1632, towards the end of his career, Champlain published his last big map, which was a synthesis of all his explorations since 1603 and of the things that he had learned from the Indians. On the map, for example, are the freshwater sea (Lake Huron), Lake Saint-Louis (Lake Ontario), Lake Champlain, and the Ottawa River. The short letter that Champlain sent from Québec on 15 August 1633 to Richelieu was also a synthesis describing an immense and beautiful country that had to be aided whatever the price.

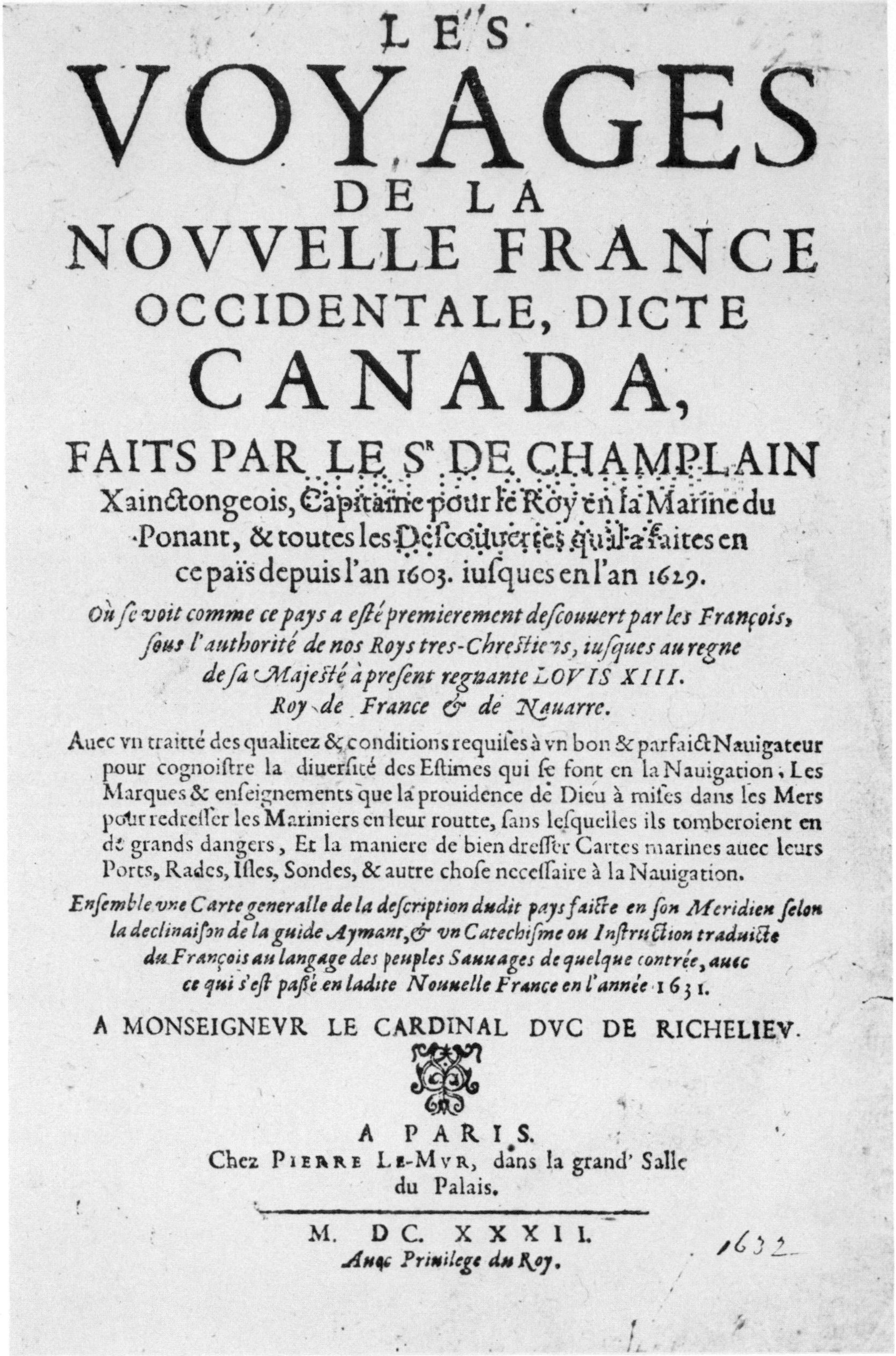

LES

VOYAGES

DE LA

NOVVELLE FRANCE

OCCIDENTALE, DICTE

CANADA,

FAITS PAR LE S^r DE CHAMPLAIN

Xainctongeois, Capitaine pour le Roy en la Marine du Ponant, & toutes les Descouuertes qu'il a faites en ce païs depuis l'an 1603. iusques en l'an 1629.

Où se voit comme ce pays a esté premierement descouuert par les François, sous l'authorité de nos Roys tres-Chrestiens, iusques au regne de sa Majesté à present regnante LOVIS XIII. Roy de France & de Nauarre.

Auec vn traitté des qualitez & conditions requises à vn bon & parfaict Nauigateur pour cognoistre la diuersité des Estimes qui se font en la Nauigation. Les Marques & enseignements que la prouidence de Dieu à mises dans les Mers pour redresser les Mariniers en leur routte, sans lesquelles ils tomberoient en de grands dangers, Et la maniere de bien dresser Cartes marines auec leurs Ports, Rades, Isles, Sondes, & autre chose necessaire à la Nauigation.

Ensemble vne Carte generalle de la description dudit pays faicte en son Meridien selon la declinaison de la guide Aymant, & vn Catechisme ou Instruction traduicte du François au langage des peuples Sauuages de quelque contrée, auec ce qui s'est passé en ladite Nouuelle France en l'année 1631.

A MONSEIGNEVR LE CARDINAL DVC DE RICHELIEV.

A PARIS.

Chez PIERRE LE-MVR, dans la grand' Salle du Palais.

M. DC. XXXII.

Auec Priuilege du Roy.

1632

Samuel de Champlain. *Les voyages de la Nouvelle France occidentale, dicte Canada*.... Paris: Pierre Le-Mur, 1632, title page, pp. 246–247.

In 1615 Champlain discovered Lake Attigouantan (Lake Huron), of which he gave the following description: "It is very large and is nearly four hundred leagues in length from east to west and fifty leagues wide; and because of its great expanse I have called it the freshwater sea."

Le lendemain nous nous feparafmes,& continuafmes noftre chemin le long du riuage de ce lac des Attigouantá,où il y a vn grand nombre d'ifles, & fifmes enuiron 45.lieues,coftoyant toufiours cedit lac. Il eft fort grãd, & aprés de quatre cents lieues de longueũr de l'Orient à l'Occident, & de large cinquante lieues; & à caufe de fa grande eftendue,ie l'ay nommé la mer douce. Il eft fort abondant en plufieurs efpeces de tres-bons poiffons, tant de ceux que nous auons, que de ceux que n'auons pas, & principalement des truittes qui font monftrueufement grandes, en ayant veu qui auoient iufques à quatre pieds & demy de long, & les moindres qui fe voyent font de deux pieds & demy. Comme auffi des brochets au femblable, & certaine maniere d'efturgeon, poiffon fort grand, & d'vne merueilleufe bonté. Le pays qui borne ce lac en partie eft afpre du cofté du nort, & en partie plat, & inhabité de Sauuages, quelque peu couuert de bois,& de chefnes. Puis aprés nous trauerfafmes vne baye, qui fait vne des extremitez du lac, & fifmes enuiron fept lieues, iufques à ce que nous arriuafmes en la cõtrée des Attigouantan, à vn village appellé Otoüacha, qui fut le premier iour d'Aouft, où trouuafmes vn grand changement de pays, ceftuy-cy eftant fort beau,& la plus grande partie deferté,accompagné de force collines,& de plufieurs ruiffeaux,qui rendent ce terroir agreable. Ie fus vifiter leurs bleds d'Inde, qui eftoient lors fort aduancez pour la faifon.

Attigouantan lac de quatre cens lieues de long.

Lac abondant en truites.

Village nõmé Otoua-cha.

Pays deferté.

Public Archives of Canada, Library, Ottawa (Negatives nos. C 113062 to C 113064).

"Cheveux-Relevez" (Algonkins); after a drawing by Samuel de Champlain (1567 [?]–1635); etching; 13.8 x 8.4 cm. (plate).

In Samuel de Champlain. *Les voyages de la Novvelle France occidentale, dicte Canada....* Paris: Pierre Le-Mur, 1632, p. 245.)

At Lake Attigouantan (Lake Huron), Champlain and his companions met three hundred Algonkins whom they called "*Cheveux-Relevez,* because they had [their hair] put up and arranged very carefully, and combed better than our courtiers." A and C show "how they are armed when going off to war." B and D show how the women dressed in summer and the men in winter.

Public Archives of Canada, Library, Ottawa (Negative no. C 113067).

Huron Deer Hunt; after a drawing by Samuel de Champlain (1567[?]–1635); etching; 13.7 x 16.7 cm. (plate).

In Samuel de Champlain. *Les voyages de la Novvelle France occidentale, dicte Canada....* Paris: Pierre Le-Mur, 1632, p. 265.

At certain hunts the Indians used to organize a beat to drive the animals towards a great "enclosure" where, once inside, they were at the hunters' mercy.

Public Archives of Canada, Library, Ottawa (Negative no. C 113066).

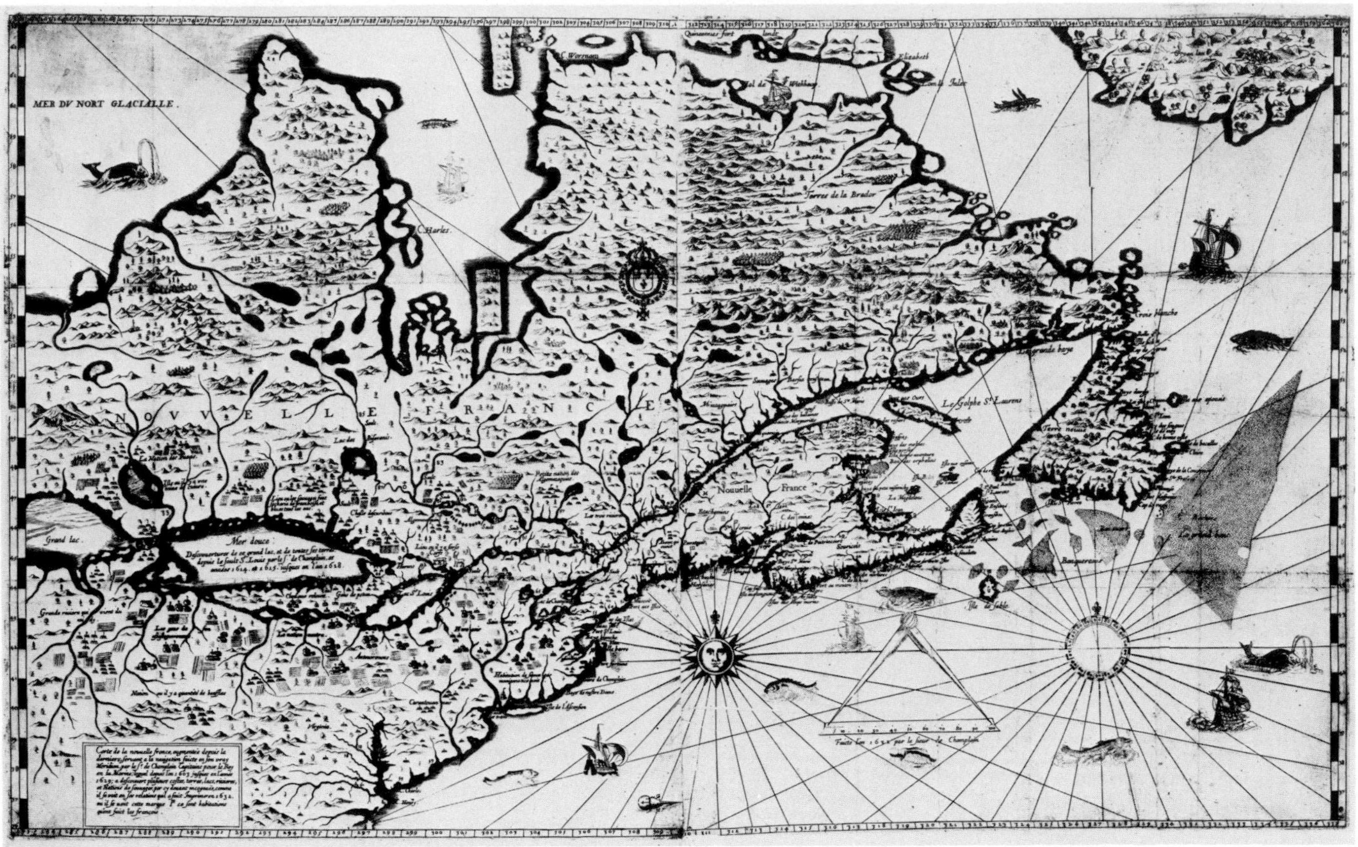

Carte de la nouuelle france...1632...; Samuel de Champlain; map printed from copperplate; 52.7 x 86.4 cm.

In Samuel de Champlain. *Les voyages de la Novvelle France occidentale, dicte Canada....* Paris: Chez Claude Collet, 1632.

This map takes in all that was known at the time of New France, from Acadia to the Great Lake (Lake Superior?), thanks to the explorations of Champlain, Etienne Brulé and Jean Nicollet, and also information supplied by the Indians. On it appear, among other features, the fresh water sea (Lake Huron), Lake Saint-Louis (Lake Ontario), and Lake Champlain. Also shown are the areas where the various Indian tribes known at the period lived.

Public Archives of Canada, National Map Collection, Ottawa (NMC 15661).

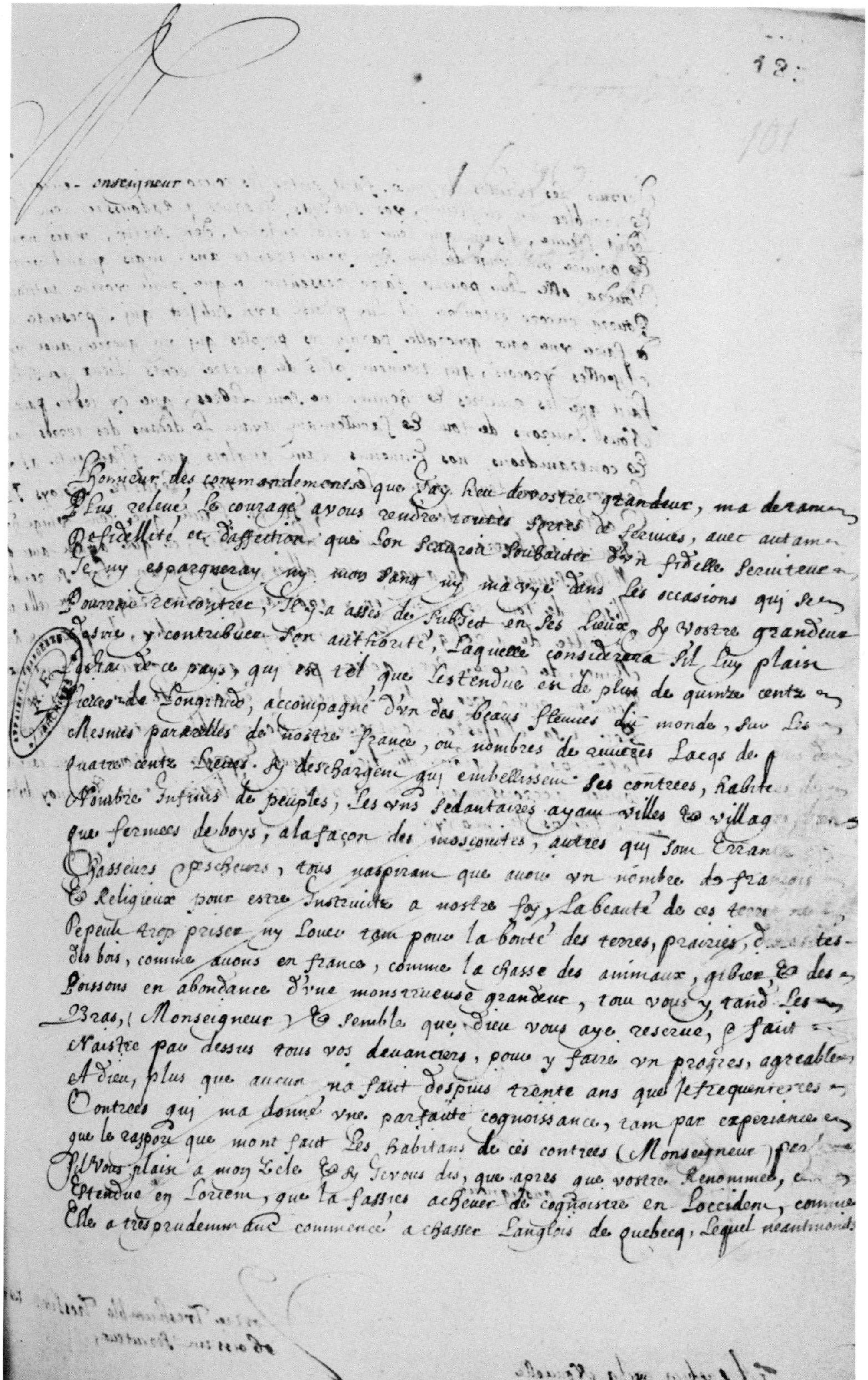

l'honneur des commandements que j'ay receu de vostre grandeur, m'a donné
plus relevé le courage a vous rendre toutes sortes de services, avec autan
de fidellité et d'affection que l'on scauroit souhaitter d'un fidelle serviteur
Je n'y espargneray ny mon sang ny ma vye dans les occasions qui se
pourront rencontrer, il y a assés de subiect en ces lieux, si vostre grandeur
desire y contribuer son authorité, laquelle considerera s'il luy plaist
l'estat de ce pays, qui est tel que l'estendue est de plus de quinze cents
lieues de longitude, accompagné d'un des beaux fleuves du monde, sur les
mesmes paralelles de nostre France, ou nombres de rivieres lacqs de
quatre cents lieues. Et descharger qui embellissent ces contrees, habite
nombre infinis de peuples, les uns sedantaires ayant villes et villag
que fermees de boys, a la façon des moscovites, autres qui sont erran
chasseurs pescheurs, tous n'aspirant que avoir un nombre de françois
et religieux pour estre instruicts a nostre foy, la beauté de ces terres ne
se peult trop priser ny louer tant pour la bonté des terres, prairies, diversités
des bois, comme avons en France, comme la chasse des animaux, gibier, et des
poissons en abondance d'une monstrueuse grandeur, tout vous y tend les
bras, (Monseigneur) et semble que dieu vous aye reservé, et faict
naistre par dessus tous vos devanciers, pour y faire un progres, agreable
a Dieu, plus que aucun n'a faict despuis trente ans que je frequente ces
contrees qui m'a donné une parfaicte cognoissance, tant par experience
que le rapport que m'ont faict les habitans de ces contrees (Monseigneur) s'il
vous plaist a mon zele, et je vous dis, que apres que vostre renommee, a
estendue en l'orient, que la fassiez achever de cognoistre en l'occident, comme
elle a tresprudemment commencé a chasser l'Anglois de quebecq, lequel neantmoins

Letter from Samuel de Champlain to Cardinal Richelieu, Québec, 15 August 1633.

Champlain speaks highly of the vastness and beauty of the territory of Canada: "It is more than fifteen hundred leagues in length from east to west and has one of the most beautiful rivers in the world, ... the beauty of these lands cannot be too highly prized or extolled, both for the excellence of the land and the grasslands, the variety of woods, ... and for animal hunting, with game and fish in abundance."

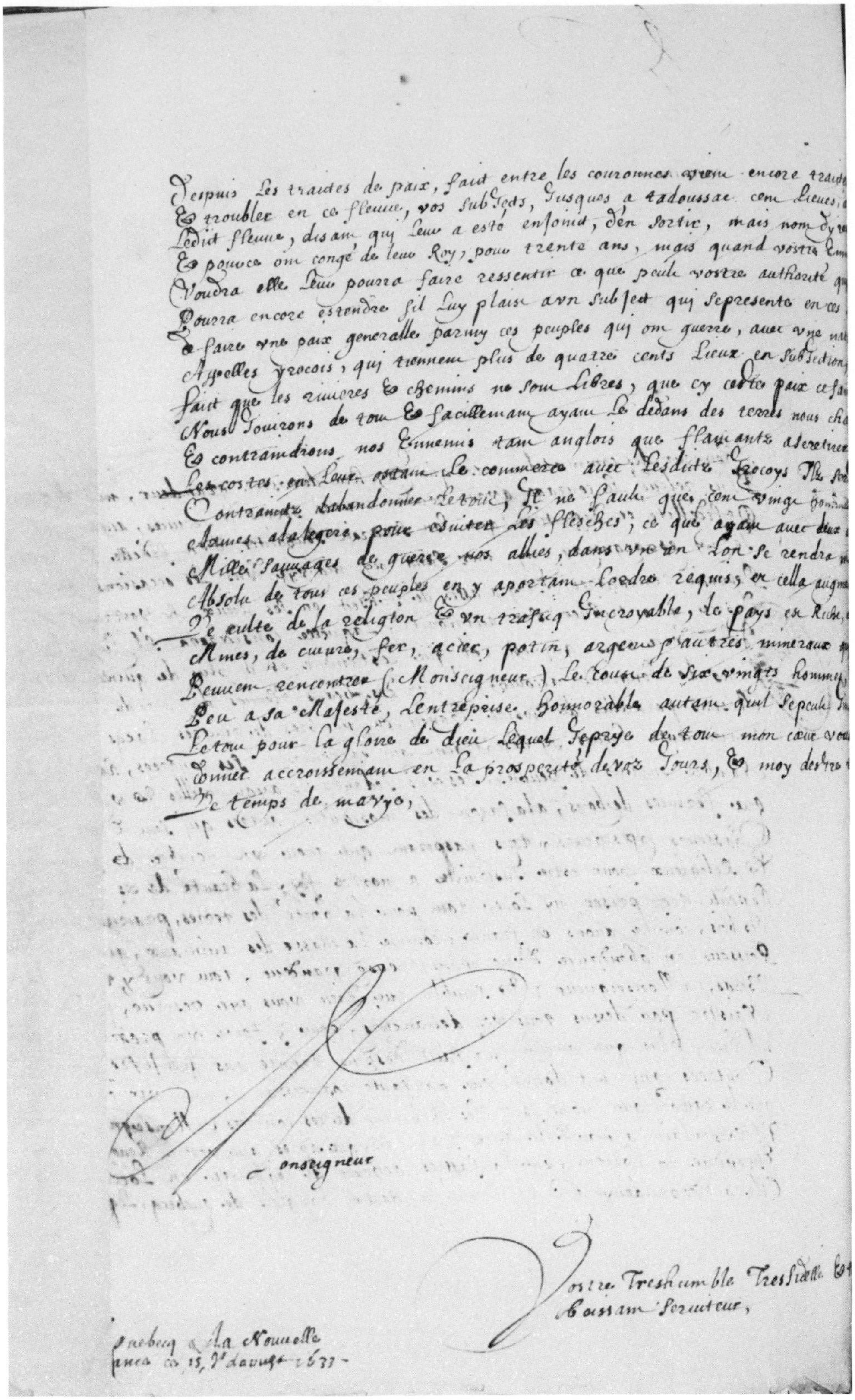

Depuis les traides de paix, faict entre les couronnes ayant encore trait...
Et troubler en ce fleuve, vos subiectz, jusques a tadoussac cent lieues...
Ledit fleuve, disant quy leur a esté enjoinct, d'en sortir, mais non d'y...
Et pource ont congé de leur Roy, pour trente ans, mais quand vostre Em...
Voudra elle leur pourra faire ressentir ce que peult vostre authorité qu...
Pourra encore estendre s'il luy plaist a un subject qui se presente en ces...
a faire une paix generalle parmy ces peuples qui ont guerre, avec une na...
Appellés yrocois, qui tiennent plus de quatre cents lieux en subiection,...
faict que les rivieres & chemins ne sont libres, que cy cette paix ce fai...
Nous jouirons de tout & facillemant ayant le dedans des terres nous cha...
Et contraindrons nos ennemis tant anglois que flamants a se retire...
Les costes en leur ostant le commerce avec lesdits yrocoys ils sero...
Contraintz d'abandonner le tout, Il ne fault que cent vingt hommes...
armés a la legere, pour eviter les flesches; ce que ayant avec deux...
Mille sauvages de guerre nos alliés, dans un an l'on se rendra m...
Absolu de tous ces peuples en y aportant l'ordre requis, et cella augm...
Le culte de la religion & un trafiq incroyable, le pays est riche,...
Mines, de cuivre, fer, acier, potin, argent & autres mineraux q...
Peuvent rencontrer (Monseigneur) le tout de six vingts hommes...
Peu a sa Majesté, l'entreprise honnorable autant qu'il se peult...
Le tout pour la gloire de dieu lequel je prye de tout mon coeur vou...
Donner accroissement en la prosperité de vos jours, Et moy des tres...
De temps de marys,

Monseigneur

Vostre treshumble tresfidelle et obeissant serviteur,

Quebecq en la Nouvelle France ce 15e d'aoust 1633

Archives du ministère des Affaires étrangères, Paris, France: Mémoires et documents, Amérique, vol. 4, fol. 125–125v.

II

The northern ice

Henry Hudson had already made three voyages to America when he set off in 1610 to look for a northwest passage. He sailed into Hudson Strait, and then into the bay of the same name. In October he was in James Bay, where he spent the winter.

In the spring of 1611 Hudson's men met some Eskimos for the first time; when they approached them, they were driven off by a shower of arrows. These inhospitable natives only added to the perils of navigation and wintering in the northern ice.

After the unsuccessful expeditions led by Button, Gibbons, and Hawkridge, Thomas James in his turn explored the west coast of Hudson Bay and James Bay in 1631–32. In 1631 Luke Fox also examined the west coast of Hudson Bay; then he steered north, pushed on beyond Fox Channel, and sailed into the basin of the same name. Until then no one had pushed on so far.

The existence of Hudson Bay had long been known in New France; people there were also interested in the Northern Sea – the "Mer du Nord" – "which adjoins that of China" and to which only "the gateway" – that is to say the passage – remained "to be found." Being interested both in evangelization and the geographical question, the Jesuits Claude Dablon and Gabriel Druillettes decided in 1661 to reach Hudson Bay overland.

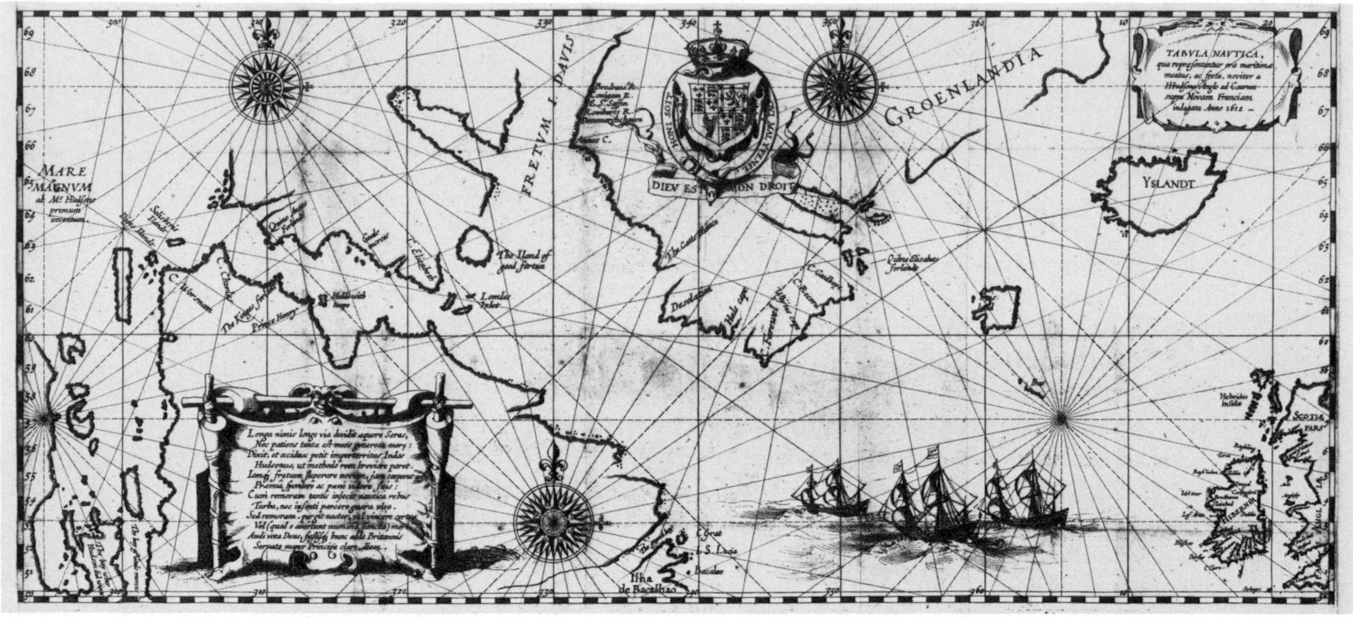

Tabvla Navtica...Anno 1612; [Hessel Gerritsz]; map printed from copperplate; 24.5 x 54.9 cm.

In Hessel Gerritsz. *Descriptio ac delineatio Geographica Detectionis Freti....* Amsterodami: Ex Officina Hesselij Gerardi, Anno 1613.

This map was prepared to illustrate the voyages of exploration by the English in the northern regions of America and principally the discovery of Hudson Bay by Henry Hudson in 1610.

Public Archives of Canada, National Map Collection, Ottawa (NMC 19228).

Englishmen in a Skirmish with Eskimos; John White (known 1585–93) (Sloane copy); watercolour and ink; 31.5 x 26.6 cm.

Attacks by the Eskimos and the ice fields were grave dangers for the English explorers who, like Martin Frobisher (1576–78) and Henry Hudson (1610–11), sought a northwest passage to Asia.

British Museum, Department of Prints and Drawings, London, England.

A Ship Lifted by Pressure Ice; engraving, hand coloured; 14.1 x 20.3 cm. (image).

In Gerrit de Veer. *Waerachtighe Beschrijvinghe van drie seylagien....* Amstelredam: Cornelis Claesz, 1598. After 1 23ᵛ.

British Library, London, England.

Portrait of Admiral Sir Thomas Button (before 1588–1634); artist unknown; oil; 152.4 x 76.2 cm.; early seventeenth century.

In 1612–13 Thomas Button commanded the expedition sent to find out what had become of the explorer Henry Hudson and to complete "the full and perfect discovery of the North-West passage." During this voyage he is believed to have made his way through Hudson Strait and to have crossed Hudson Bay.

Sir Cennydd Traherne, Coedarhydyglyn, Nr. Cardiff, Wales.

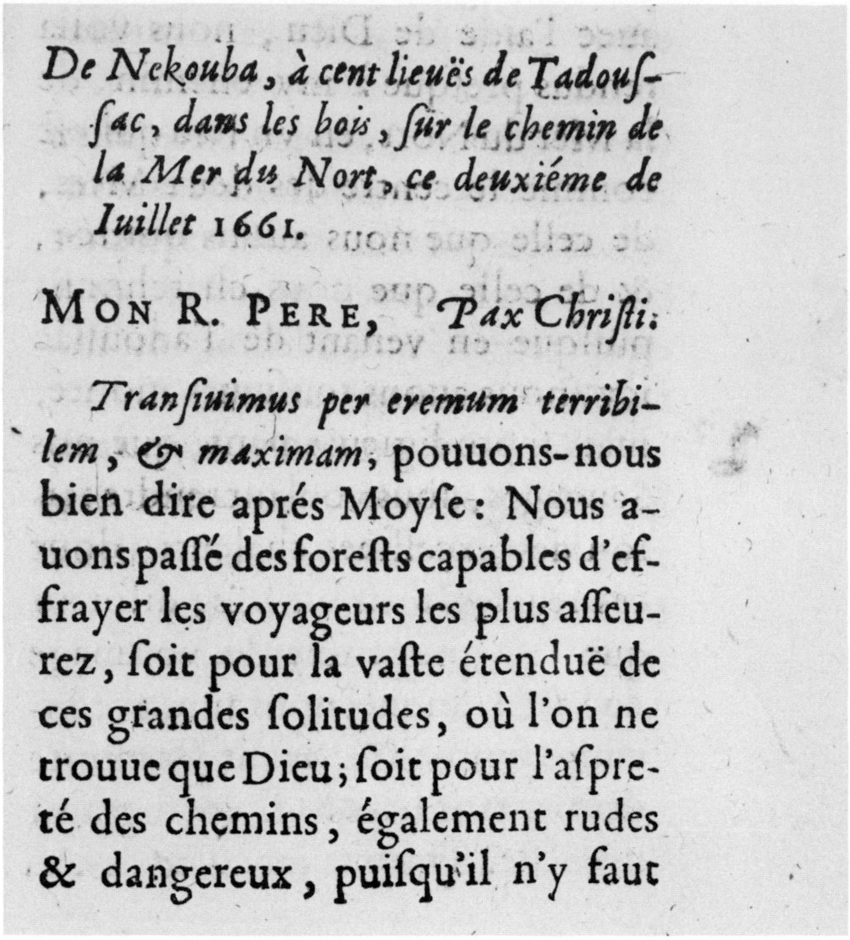

De Nekouba, à cent lieuës de Tadouſſac, dans les bois, ſur le chemin de la Mer du Nort, ce deuxiéme de Iuillet 1661.

MON R. PERE, *Pax Chriſti.*

Tranſiuimus per eremum terribilem, & maximam, pouuons-nous bien dire aprés Moyſe: Nous auons paſſé des foreſts capables d'effrayer les voyageurs les plus aſſeurez, ſoit pour la vaſte étenduë de ces grandes ſolitudes, où l'on ne trouue que Dieu; ſoit pour l'aſpreté des chemins, également rudes & dangereux, puiſqu'il n'y faut

Paul Le Jeune. *Relation de ce qvi s'est passé de plvs remarqvable avx Missions des Pères de la Compagnie de Iesvs, en la Novvelle France, ès années 1660 & 1661....* Paris: Chez Sébastien Cramoisy, 1662, pp. 59–61.

These pages tell us of the voyage undertaken by the Jesuits Gabriel Druillettes and Claude Dablon to try to reach the Northern Sea, which, it was believed, "adjoins that of China."

marcher que ſur des precipices, & voguer par des abyſmes, où l'on diſpute ſa vie ſur vne freſle écorce, contre des boüillons capables de perdre de grands Vaiſſeaux. Enfin, auec l'aide de Dieu, nous voila rendus preſque à my-chemin, de la Mer du Nort, en vn lieu qui eſt comme le centre des deux Mers, de celle que nous auons quittée, & de celle que nous cherchons; puiſque en venant de Tadouſſac icy, nous auons touſiours monté, mais ſi prodigieuſement, que nos Sauuages, nous voulant rendre raiſon des exceſſiues chaleurs, dont ces regions ſont brûlées, diſoient que cela prouenoit du voiſinage du Soleil, duquel nous auons beaucoup approché, ayant ſurmonté des ſaults ſi hauts, & en ſi grand nombre. D'vn autre coſté, nous

n'auons plus deſormais qu'à deſcendre; toutes les riuieres ſur leſquelles nous auons à nauiger, s'allant décharger dans la Mer du Nort, comme toutes celles que nous auons paſſées, ſe vont rendre à Tadouſſac.

Bibliothèque de la ville de Montréal, Salle Gagnon, Montréal.

"Resolute men"

Since Champlain's time there had never been any stop in New France in exploring the interior of the continent. Now, scarcely had he arrived than Intendant Jean Talon had "resolute men" start off in order to "press farther ahead than has ever been done," with the orders to take possession in the name of the king of France of the territories through which they travelled.

The network of rivers in New France permitted relatively easy access to the most distant regions: to the south, where it was believed that Mexico could be reached, Cavelier de La Salle was sent; Daumont de Saint-Lusson was sent to the west, where it was hoped that some way of getting through to the Mer du Sud (the Pacific) would be found; in the meantime the Sulpicians Dollier and Galinée were exploring the region around Lake Ontario.

Saint-Lusson had just returned: the Mer du Sud did not seem to be so far away that it could not soon be reached. While La Salle was continuing his explorations Talon sent the Jesuit Charles Albanel and Paul Denys de Saint-Simon to Hudson Bay, where a great trade in furs was going on to the benefit of the English and where the famous northwest passage was somewhere to be found – two questions that had to be examined more closely.

If the map made by the Jesuit Claude Dablon in 1672 accounts for only part of the discoveries to date, it nevertheless shows how knowledge of the interior was becoming more accurate year by year.

46

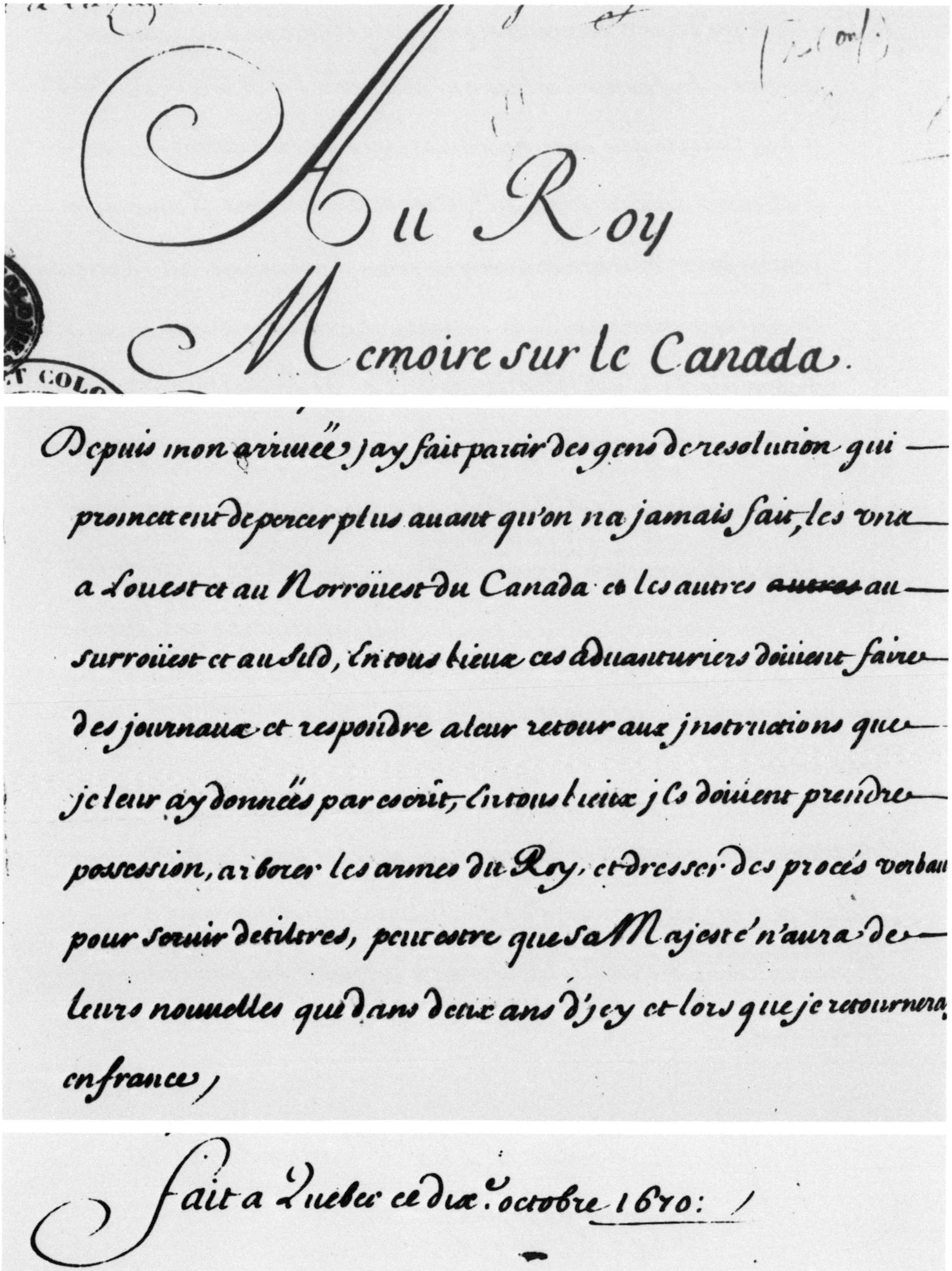

Au Roy

Memoire sur le Canada.

Depuis mon arrivée j'ay fait partir des gens de resolution qui promettent de percer plus auant qu'on n'a jamais fait, les vns a Louest et au Norroüest du Canada et les autres ~~autres~~ au surroüest et au Sud, En tous lieux ces aduanturiers doiuent faire des journaux et respondre a leur retour aux instructions que je leur ay données par escrit, En tous lieux ils doiuent prendre possession, arborer les armes du Roy, et dresser des procés verbaux pour seruir de tiltres, peutestre que Sa Majesté n'aura de leurs nouuelles que dans deux ans d'icy et lors que je retourneray en france,

Fait a Quebec ce dix.e octobre 1670.

Report on Canada sent to the king of France, Louis XIV, by Intendant Jean Talon, Québec, 10 October 1670.

Talon had "resolute men [start off] who promise to press farther ahead than has ever been done" into the distant regions and who were "to take possession of them, raise the king's arms, and draw up reports to be used as title-deeds."

Archives nationales, Paris, France: Fonds des Colonies, série C^{11A}, vol. 3, fol. 94, 96v, 97v.

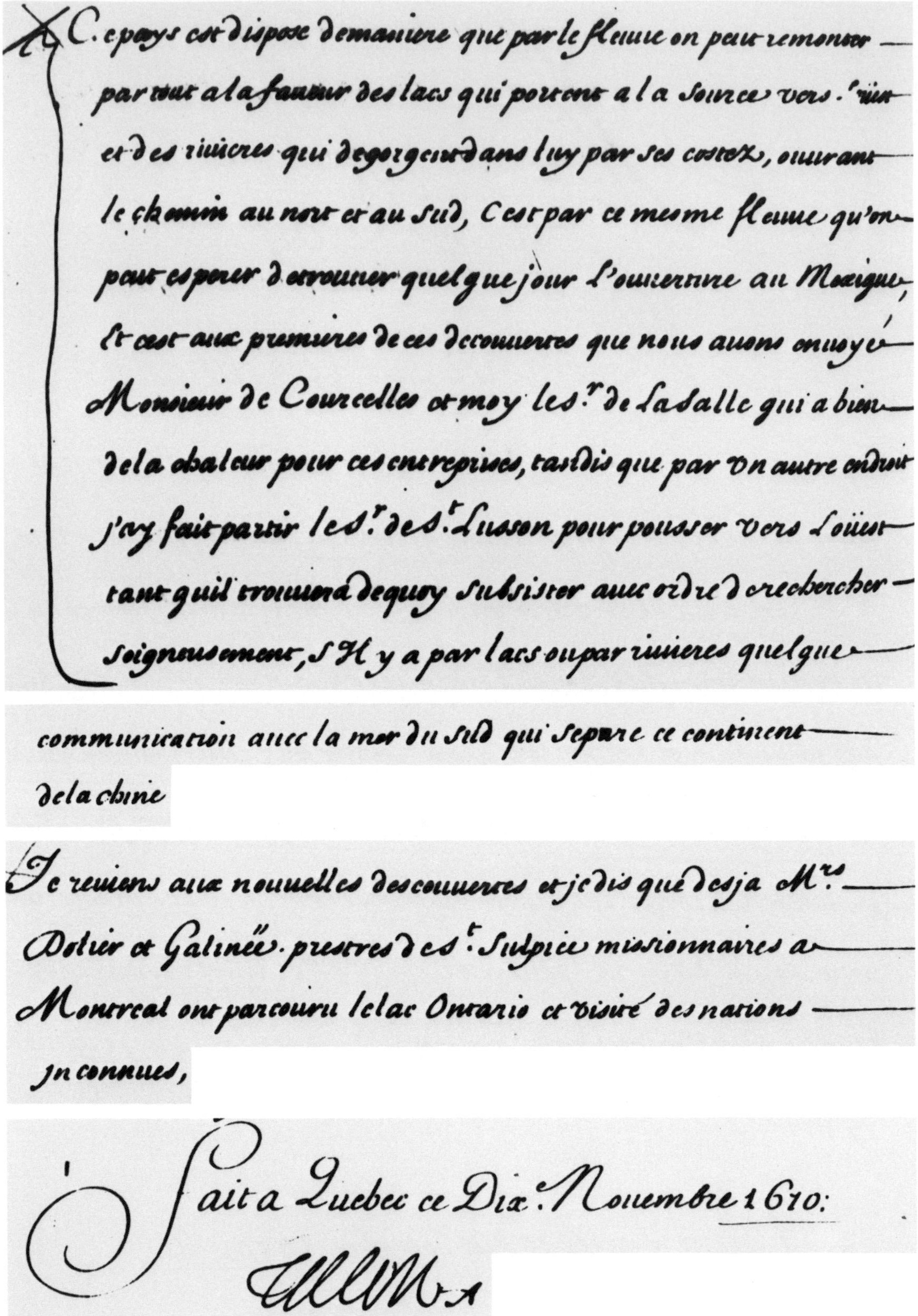

Ce pays est disposé de maniere que par le fleuve on peut remonter
partout a la faveur des lacs qui portent a la source vers l'ouest
et des rivieres qui degorgent dans luy par ses costez, ouvrant
le chemin au nort et au sud, C'est par ce mesme fleuve qu'on
peut esperer de trouver quelque jour l'ouverture au Mexique,
Et c'est aux premieres de ces descouvertes que nous avons envoyé
Monsieur de Courcelles et moy le s.r de La Salle qui a bien
de la chaleur pour ces entreprises, tandis que par un autre endroit
j'ay fait partir le s.r de S.t Lusson pour pousser vers l'ouest
tant qu'il trouvera dequoy subsister avec ordre de rechercher
soigneusement, s'il y a par lacs ou par rivieres quelque
communication avec la mer du sud qui separe ce continent
de la chine

Je reviens aux nouvelles descouvertes et je dis que desja M.rs
Dollier et Galinée prestres de S.t Sulpice missionnaires a
Montreal ont parcouru le lac Ontario et visité des nations
inconnues,

Fait a Quebec ce Dix.e Novembre 1670.

Talon

Report sent to the king of France by Intendant Talon, Québec, 10 November 1670.

Among the "resolute men" who had gone to explore the interior of the continent Talon mentions the following: La Salle, who had been sent to the south in the hope "of one day finding the passage to Mexico"; Saint-Lusson, who had gone westward "with orders to search diligently...for some communication with the Mer du Sud [the Pacific Ocean], which separates this continent from China"; and finally, the Sulpicians Dollier and Galinée, who "have crossed Lake Ontario and visited unknown nations."

Archives nationales, Paris, France: Fonds des Colonies, série C^{11A}, vol. 3, fol. 106v, 107, 111.

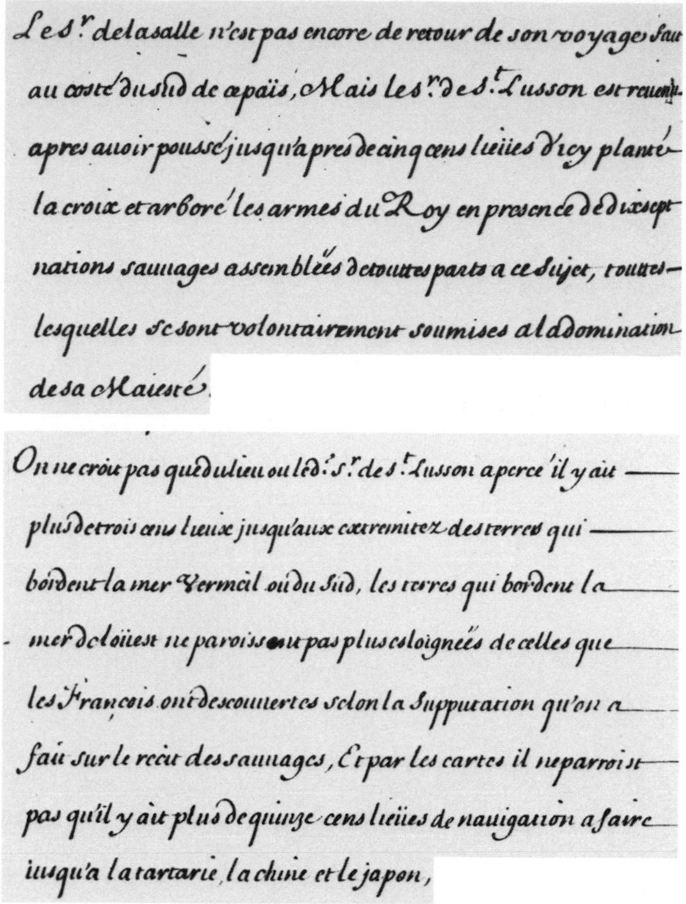

Le sr. delasalle n'est pas encore de retour de son voyage fait au costé du sud de ce païs, Mais le sr. de st. Lusson est revenu apres auoir poussé jusqu'a pres de cinq cens lieües d'icy planté la croix et arboré les armes du Roy en presence de dixsept nations sauuages assemblées de toutes parts a ce sujet, toutes lesquelles se sont volontairement soumises a la domination de sa Maiesté.

On ne croit pas que du lieu ou led. sr. de st. Lusson a percé il y ait plus de trois cens lieües jusqu'aux extremitez des terres qui bordent la mer Vermeil ou du Sud, les terres qui bordent la mer de l'ouest ne paroissent pas plus esloignées de celles que les François ont descouvertes selon la supputation qu'on a fait sur le recit des sauuages, Et par les cartes il ne parroist pas qu'il y ait plus de quinze cens lieües de nauigation a faire jusqu'a la tartarie, la chine et le japon,

Report on Canada sent to the king of France by Intendant Talon, Québec, 2 November 1671.

Talon had sent the Jesuit Albanel and the Sieur de Saint-Simon to Hudson Bay; they were "to take possession of it again in His Majesty's name." At Sault Ste. Marie Saint-Lusson had taken possession of the western territories "and raised the king's arms in the presence of seventeen Indian nations."

Il y a trois mois que i'ay fait partir auec le Pere Albanel
jesuiste le s.r de S.t Simon jeune gentilhomme de Canada
honnoré par le Roy depuis peu de ce tiltre, ils doiuent
pousser jusqu'à la baye d'hudson, faire des memoires sur
tout ce qu'ils descouuriront lier commerce de pelteries auec
les sauuages et surtout reconnoistre s'il y a lieu d'y faire
hiuerner quelques bastiments pour y faire vn entrepost
qui puisse vn jour fournir des rafraichissements aux
Vaisseaux qui pourront cy apres descouurir par cet endroit
la communication des deux mers du nord et du sud, depuis
leur depart i'ay receu trois fois de leurs lettres, les dernieres
apportées de cent lieües d'icy par lesquelles ils me marquent
que des sauuages qu'ils ont trouué sur leur chemin les ont
assuré que deux Vaisseaux anglois et trois barques auoient
hiuerné dans le voisinage de cette baye et y auoient fait grand
amas de castors, si mes lettres en response sont fidellement

rendues aud. pere, cet establissement sera bien examiné
et sa Maiesté en sera bien informée, comme ces terres
ont esté anciennement descouuertes, premierement par
les françois i'ay donné commission aud. s.r de S.t Simon
de prendre possession reiterée au nom de sa Maiesté auec
ordre d'y arborer l'escusson de france dont il est chargé

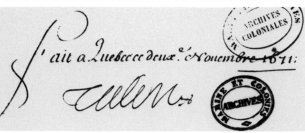

Fait a Quebec ce deux.e Nouembre 1671.

Talon

Archives nationales, Paris, France: Fonds des Colonies, série C^{11A}, vol. 3, fol. 161v, 162, 162v, 163, 171v.

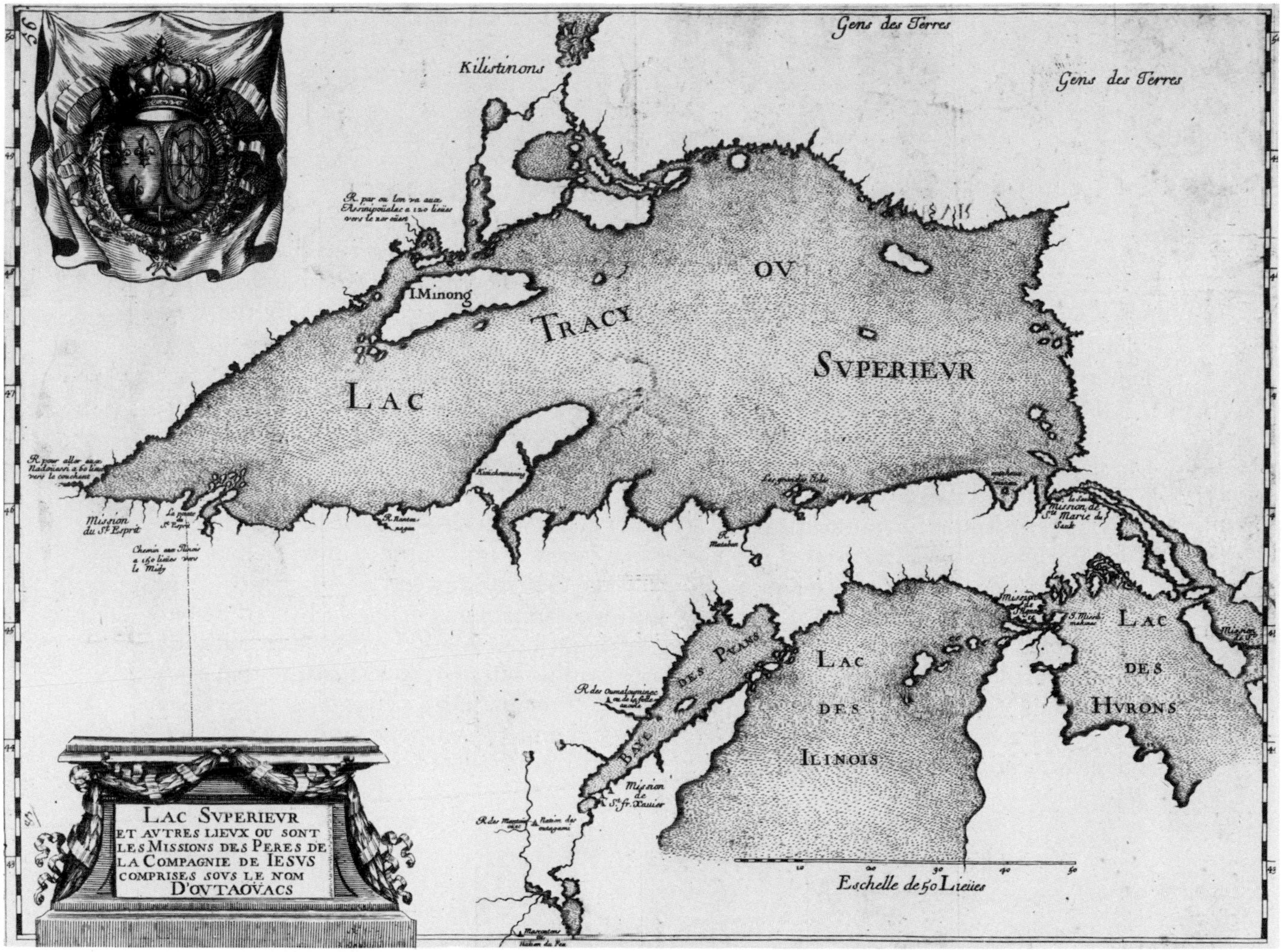

Lac Svperievr et autres lieux ou sont les Missions des Peres de la Compagnie de Iesvs comprises sovs le nom D'Ovtaovacs, [*1673*]; [*Claude Dablon*]; map printed from copperplate; 35.1 x 47.5 cm.

In Claude Dablon. *Relation de ce qui s'est passé de plus remarquable aux missions des pères de la Compagnie de Jésus, en la Nouvelle France les années 1671 et 1672.* A Paris: M. Cramoisy, 1673.

This map of the Jesuit missions in the Great Lakes region reveals the territorial expansion of New France thanks to the undertakings of the missionaries, explorers, and coureurs des bois.

Public Archives of Canada, National Map Collection, Ottawa (NMC 10296).

II

The drive towards the Mer du Sud

In 1672 Talon sent Louis Jolliet to "discover the Mer du Sud, via the country of the Mashoutins [Mascoutens], and to the great river that they call the Michissipi which is believed to flow into the Sea of California." Jolliet, who had been joined by the Jesuit Jacques Marquette, discovered and explored the Mississippi in 1673, stopping just short of the present-day boundary between Arkansas and Louisiana.

Jolliet had come back convinced that the Mississippi (which had been baptized the Rivière Colbert) flowed into the Gulf of Mexico, as his map, which was dedicated to Governor Louis de Buade de Frontenac, clearly mentions.

It belonged to La Salle to discover the mouths of the Mississippi and to verify the accuracy of Jolliet's hypothesis on the orientation of that river. On 9 April 1682 La Salle had drawn up an official deed of "the possession taken by him of the country of Louisiana near the three mouths of the River Colbert in the Gulf of Mexico."

La Salle ended up being murdered by his own companions in 1687. Even if he only completed the discovery begun by Jolliet, he knew how to take care of his reputation, thanks for example to an author such as Hennepin, but also to the magic that those enormous "countries" exercised on people's imaginations, countries where one encountered such great lakes and rivers in such number – without omitting waterfalls like those at Niagara, with which Hennepin illustrated one of his works.

BROTIER vol. 155 1

Relation dela decouverte dela Mer du Sud

faite par les Riuieres dela nouuelle france
Enuoyée de Quebec par le Pere Dablon
Superieur general des missions dela Compagnie
de Jesus le 1er. Jour d'Aoust 1674.

Il y a deux ans que Monsieur le Comte de frontenac nostre gouuerneur et Mr. Talon alors nostre Intendant, jugerent qu'il estoit important de s'appliquer a la decouuerte dela mer du midy, apres celle qui a esté faicte dela mer du Nord, et sur tout de sçauoir dans quelle mer s'alloit decharger la grande Riuiere dont les Sauuages font tant de recit, et qui est a 500 lieües d'icy, au dela des outaoüax. dans ce dessein ils ne purent faire choix de personne qui eust de plus belles qualités que le sieur Jolliet, qui a beaucoup frequenté ce pais la, et qui de fait s'en est acquitté auec toute la generosité, toute l'adresse, et toute la conduite qu'on pouuoit souhaitter.

Estant arriué aux Outaoüax il se joignit au pere Marquette, qui l'attendoit pour cela, et qui depuis long temps premeditoit cette entreprise, l'ayant bien des fois concertée ensemble.

Ils se mirent en chemin auec cinq autres françois vers le commencement de Juin 1673, pour entrer dans des pais, où jamais aucun Europeau n'auoit mis le pied. Estans partis dela Baye des puants par les 43 degrés quarente minuttes d'eleuation, ils nagerent sur vne petite Riuiere fort douce et fort agreable, pres de 60 lieües tirant vers l'ouëst suroüest; ils cherchoient vn portage de demy lieüe qui les deuoit faire passer de cette Riuiere dans vne autre qui venoit du Noroüest, sur laquelle s'estants embarqués, et ayant fait quarente lieües vers le soroüest, Enfin le 15 de Juin, se trouuant a 42 degrés et demy, ils entrerent heureusement dans cette fameuse Riuiere que les sauuages appellent Missisipi, comme qui diroit la grande riuiere, parceque de fait c'est la plus considerable de toutes celles qui sont en ce pais la; Elle vient de fort loing du costé du Nord, au rapport des Sauuages; elle est belle et a pour l'ordinaire vn quart de lieüe de large; Elle a bien plus aux endroits où elle est coupée d'Isles, qui sont neantmoins tres rares, Elle a jusques a dix brasses d'eau, et elle coule fort doucement jusqu'a ce qu'elle reçoiue la decharge d'vne grosse Riuiere qui vient de l'ouëst noroüest, vers le 38 degré de hauteur: car estant enflée de ces deux eaües, elle deuient si rapide, et a vn courant si roide, qu'en remontant on ne peut faire que quatre a 5. lieües par jour voguant depuis le matin jusqu'au soir.

Il y a des bois des deux costés jusques ala mer: les plus puissants des arbres qu'on y voit, sont vne espece de Cottonnier, qui sont extraordinairement gros et hauts, aussy les sauuages s'en seruent ils pour faire des Canots tout d'vne piece, de 50 pieds de long, et trois de large, dans lesquels 30 hommes auec leur equipage peuuent s'embarquer, ils les trauaillent auec bien plus de petitesse que nous ne faisons les nostres; et ils en ont vn si grand -

11

Account of the discovery of the Mississippi River sent from Québec by the Jesuit Father Claude Dablon, Québec, 1 August 1674.

On 15 June 1673 the Sieur Louis Jolliet and the Jesuit Jacques Marquette "successfully entered this famous river that the Indians call Mississippi."

Archives de la Compagnie de Jésus, Chantilly, France: Fonds Brotier, 155, pièce 11.

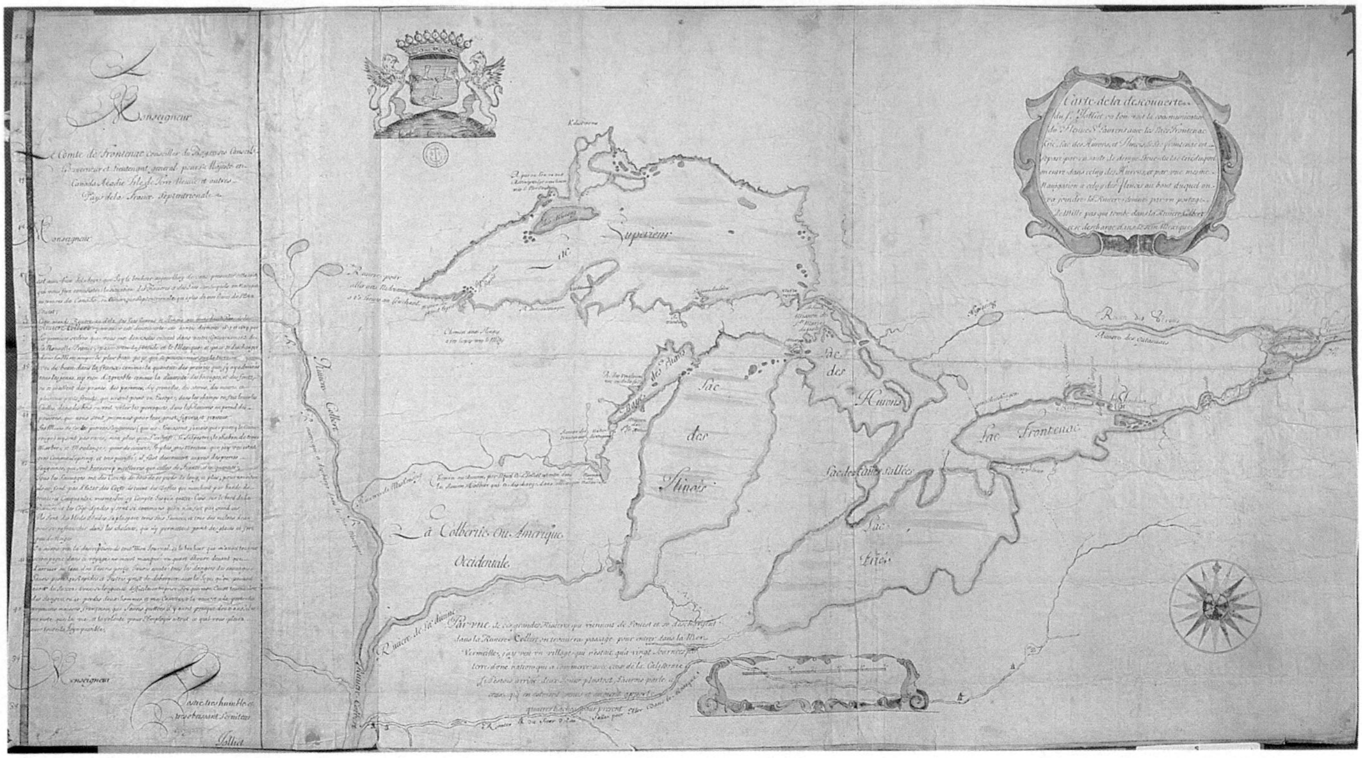

"Carte de la descouverte du Sr Jolliet, où l'on voit la communication du fleuve St Laurens avec les lacs Frontenac, Erié, lacs des Hurons, et Ilinois" [1674–75]; Louis Jolliet and Jean-Baptiste-Louis Franquelin; col. ms.; 37 x 123 cm.

This map relating to the discovery of the Mississippi River shows that considerable progress had been made in knowledge of North American geography. In addition to revealing the existence of the Mississippi River (Rivière Colbert) and the Ohio River, it shows that the Mississippi empties into the Gulf of Mexico.

Service historique de la Marine, Vincennes, France: Recueil 67 (ancien 4044B), no. 37.

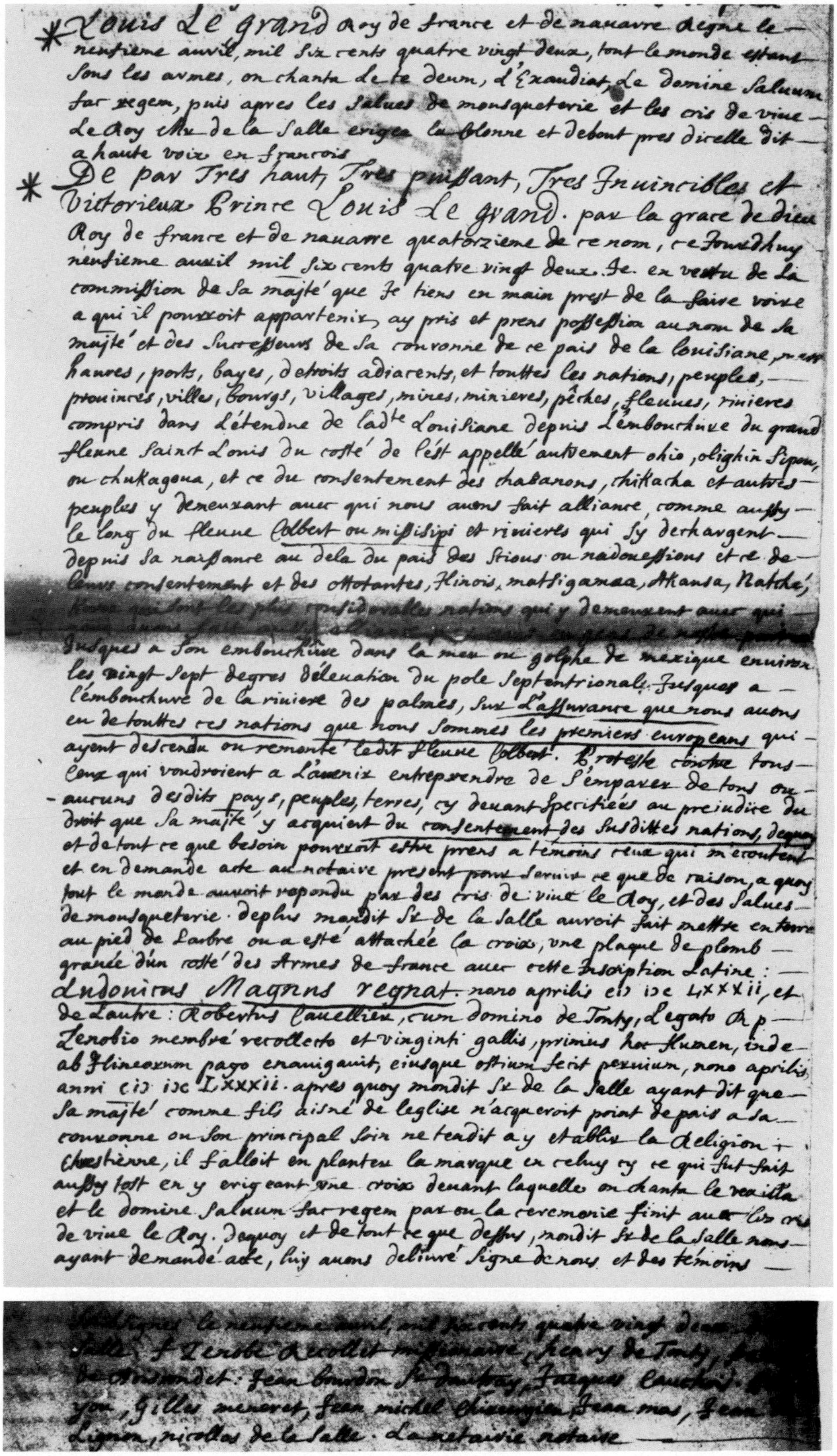
Louis Le grand Roy de france et de nauarre regne le
neufieme auril, mil six cents quatre vingt deux, tout le monde estant
sous les armes, on chanta le te deum, l'Exaudiat, le domine saluum
fac regem, puis apres les salues de mousqueterie et les cris de viue
le Roy Mr de la Salle erigea la colonne et debout pres d'icelle dit
a haute voix en francois
De par Tres haut, Tres puissant, Tres Inuincible et
Victorieux Prince Louis Le grand. par la grace de dieu
Roy de france et de nauarre quatorzieme de ce nom, ce Jourd'huy
neufieme auril mil six cents quatre vingt deux. Je, en vertu de la
commission de sa majté que Je tiens en main prest de la faire voire
a qui il pourroit appartenir, ay pris et prens possession au nom de sa
majté et des successeurs de sa couronne de ce pais de la Louisiane, mers
hauvres, ports, bayes, detroits adiacents, et touttes les nations, peuples,
prouinces, villes, bourgs, villages, mines, minieres, pesches, fleuues, riuieres
compris dans l'étendue de ladte Louisiane depuis l'embouchure du grand
fleuue Saint Louis du costé de l'est appellé autrement ohio, olighin Sipou,
ou chukagoua, et ce du consentement des chaouanons, chikacha et autres
peuples y demeurant auec qui nous auons fait alliance, comme aussy
le long du fleuue Colbert ou mississipi et riuieres qui s'y dechargent
depuis sa naissance au dela du pais des Sioux ou nadouessions et ce de
leurs consentement et des ottotantes, Ilinois, matsigamea, Akansa, Natché,
[illegible]
[illegible]
Jusques a son embouchure dans la mer ou golphe de mexique enuiron
les vingt sept degres d'eleuation du pole Septentrional, Jusques a
l'embouchure de la riuiere des palmes, sur l'assurance que nous auons
eu de touttes ces nations que nous sommes les premiers europeans qui
ayent descendu ou remonté ledit fleuue Colbert. Proteste contre tous
ceux qui voudroient a l'auenir entreprendre de s'emparer de tous ou
aucuns desdits pays, peuples, terres, cy deuant specifiées au preiudice du
droit que sa majté y acquiert du consentement des susdittes nations, dequoy
et de tout ce que besoin pourroit estre prens a temoins ceux qui m'escoutent
et en demande acte au notaire present pour seruir ce que de raison, a quoy
tout le monde auroit repondu par des cris de viue le Roy, et des salues
de mousquetterie. de plus mondit Sr de la Salle auroit fait mettre en terre
au pied de l'arbre ou a esté attachée la croix, une plaque de plomb
gravée d'un costé des Armes de france auec cette Inscription Latine:
Ludouicus Magnus regnat nono aprilis cIↃ IↃC LXXXII, et
de l'autre: Robertus Cauellier, cum domino de Tonty, Legato R. p.
Zenobio membré recollecto et vinginti gallis, primus hoc flumen, inde
ab Ilineorum pago enauigauit, eiusque ostium fecit peruium, nono aprilis
anni cIↃ IↃC LXXXII. apres quoy mondit Sr de la Salle ayant dit que
sa majté comme fils aisné de l'eglise n'acquerroit point de pais a sa
couronne ou son principal soin ne tendit a y establir la Religion
chrestienne, il falloit en planter la marque en celuy cy ce qui fut fait
aussy tost en y erigeant une croix deuant laquelle on chanta le vexilla
et le domine saluum fac regem par ou la ceremonie finit auec les cris
de viue le Roy. dequoy et de tout ce que dessus, mondit Sr de la Salle nous
ayant demandé acte, luy auons deliuré signé de nous et des temoins
soubsignez le neufieme auril, mil six cents quatre vingt deux [illegible]
Salle, f. Zenobe Recollet missionnaire, henry de Tonty, [illegible]
de Boisrondet: Jean bourdon Sr dautray, Jacques Cauchois, [illegible]
you, Gilles meneret, Jean michel chirurgien, Jean mas, Jean
Lignon, nicollas de la Salle. La metairie notaire

Report on the taking possession of Louisiana by Robert Cavelier de La Salle, 9 April 1682.

La Salle "takes possession in the name of His Majesty and of his successors to the crown of this country of Louisiana...from the mouth of the great Saint-Louis River on the East, otherwise called the Ohio...and following the Colbert or Mississippi River...as far as the point where it enters the sea or gulf of Mexico."

Archives nationales, Paris, France: Fonds des Colonies, série C[13C], vol. 3, fol. 29–29v.

The Assassination of Sieur de La Salle;
I. van Vianen (circa 1660 – after 1726);
etching; 18.8 x 14 cm. (page).

In Louis Hennepin. *Nouveau voyage d'un pais plus grand que l'Europe avec les réflections des entreprises du Sieur de la Salle, sur les mines de St. Barbe,...* Utrecht: A. Schouten, 1698, p. 73.

The explorer Robert Cavelier de La Salle had discovered the mouths of the Mississippi River in 1682. On 19 March 1687 he was murdered by members of his expedition near the Rivière aux Canots (Trinity River, Texas).

Public Archives of Canada, Library, Ottawa (Negative no. C 99233).

Niagara Falls; etching; 15.4 x 18.6 cm. (page).

In Louis Hennepin. *Nouvelle découverte d'un très grand pays situé dans l'Amérique entre le Nouveau Mexique, et la Mer Glaciale....* Utrecht: Chez Guillaume Broedelet, 1697. p. 44.

The Recollet Louis Hennepin accompanied Cavelier de La Salle on his voyages of exploration in 1679–80. He described Niagara Falls as follows: "Between Lake Ontario and Lake Erie there is a great and prodigious drop, whose waterfall is quite surprising. It is unequalled in the whole universe....The waters that fall from this great height foam and seeth in the most frightening manner in the world."

Public Archives of Canada, Library, Ottawa (Negative no. C 113049).

II

The temptation of the West

Lake Ontario was of great strategic importance for trade as well as for war. In 1673 Frontenac went there in person and had a fort built where the city of Kingston stands today. This fort (if we think of its military role) or trading post (if we think of its economic role), the first to be built in the West, soon served as a relay station, if not a base, for the explorers and traders who were drawn by the immense stretches of the West and South.

But in 1674 Colbert informed Frontenac that it was not the king's intention that there should be expansion of this sort, far beyond the limits of the populated colony, and that on the contrary it was necessary to concentrate in the valley of the St. Lawrence and in the places "closest to the seacoasts and to communications with France."

The king could not, however, oppose the missionaries' work. In 1671 the *Relation* described "the famous island of Missilimakinac" where during the winter "some foundation work for the Saint-Ignace mission" had been done. It was a place of transit; in less than ten years there was a trading post there, of course, and by 1683 a garrison.

And then, how could one resist the attraction of the Mer du Sud, which explains not only the discovery of America but also, for the French in New France, most of their expeditions into the interior of the continent? The Sieur Dulhut did not hesitate to make use of it in a petition to the minister as an argument on his behalf.

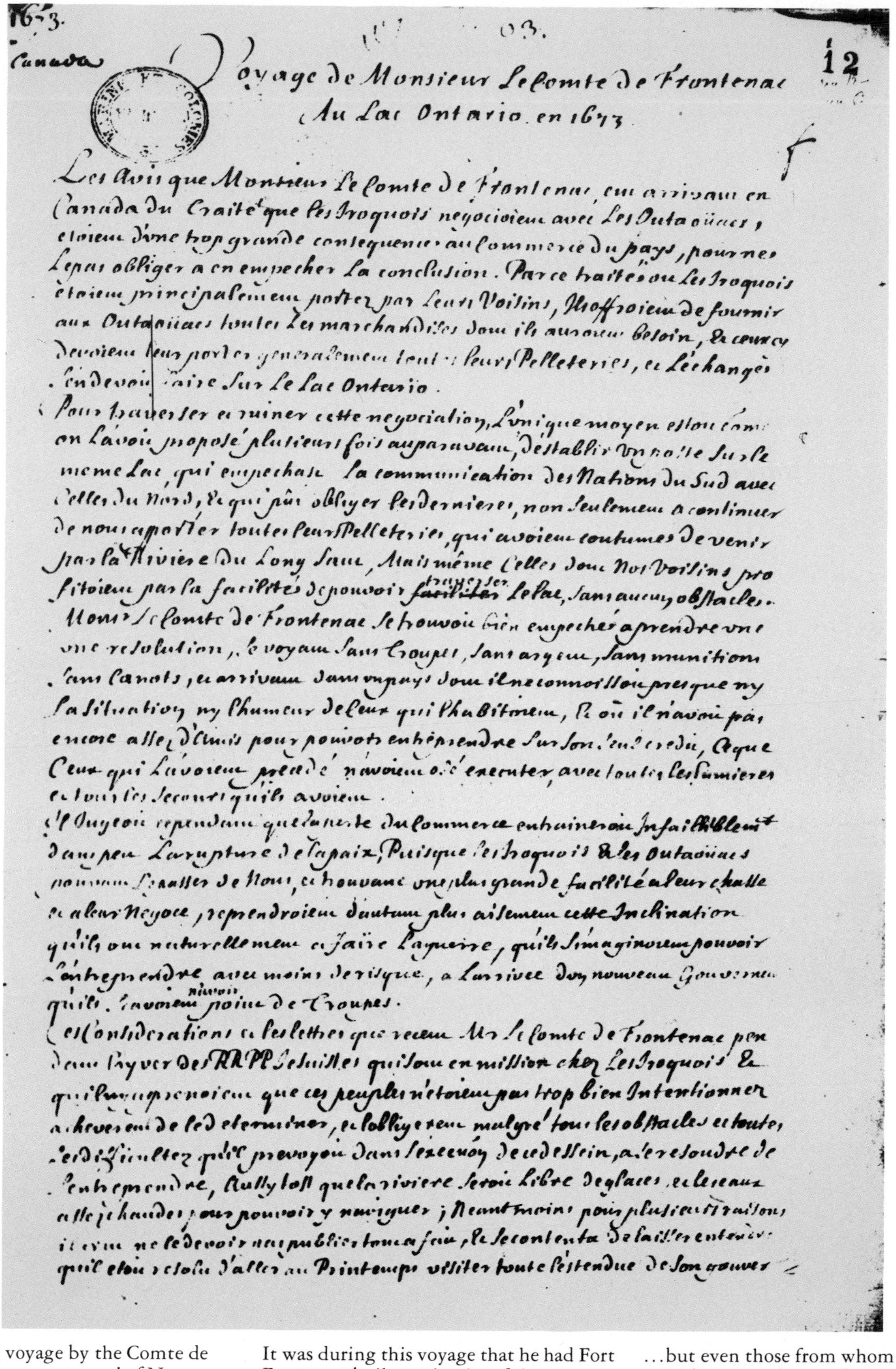
1673.

Canada

12

Voyage de Monsieur le Comte de Frontenac
Au Lac Ontario en 1673.

Les Avis que Monsieur le Comte de Frontenac, eut en arrivant en Canada du Traité que les Iroquois negocioient avec les Outaouacs, estoient d'une trop grande consequence au commerce du pays, pour ne le pas obliger a en empescher la conclusion. Par ce traité ou les Iroquois estoient principalement portez par leurs Voisins, Ils offroient de fournir aux Outaouacs toutes les marchandises dont ils auroient besoin, Et ceux cy devoient leur porter generalement toutes leurs Pelleteries, et l'eschange s'en devoit faire sur le lac Ontario.

Pour traverser et ruiner cette negociation, l'unique moyen estoit comme on l'avoit proposé plusieurs fois auparavant, d'establir un poste sur le meme Lac, qui empeschast la communication des Nations du Sud avec celles du Nord, Et qui pust obliger les dernieres, non seulement a continuer de nous apporter toutes leurs Pelleteries, qui avoient coutumes de venir par la Riviere du Long Saut, Mais méme celles dont nos Voisins profitoient par la facilité de pouvoir traverser le lac, sans aucun obstacle.

Monsieur le Comte de Frontenac se trouvoit bien empesché a prendre une resolution, se voyant sans Troupes, sans argent, sans munitions, sans Canots, et arrivant dans un pays dont il ne connoissoit presque ny la situation ny l'humeur de ceux qui l'habitoient, et où il n'avoit pas encore assez d'amis pour pouvoir entreprendre sur son seul credit, ce que ceux qui l'avoient precedé n'avoient osé executer, avec toutes les lumieres et tous les secours qu'ils avoient.

Il jugeoit cependant que la perte du commerce entraineroit infailliblement dans peu la rupture de la paix, Puisque les Iroquois et les Outaouacs pouvant se passer de Nous, et trouvant une plus grande facilité a leur chasse et a leur Negoce, reprendroient d'autant plus aisement cette Inclination qu'ils ont naturellement a faire la guerre, qu'ils s'imagineroient pouvoir l'entreprendre avec moins de risque, a l'arrivée d'un nouveau Gouverneur qu'ils scavoient n'avoir point de Troupes.

Ces considerations et les lettres que receut Mr le Comte de Frontenac pendant l'hyver des RR. PP. Jesuittes qui sont en mission chez les Iroquois, et qui luy apprenoient que ces peuples n'estoient pas trop bien Intentionnez, acheverent de le determiner, et l'obligerent malgré tous les obstacles et toutes les difficultez qu'il prevoyoit dans l'execution de ce dessein, a se resoudre de l'entreprendre, aussy tost que la riviere seroit libre de glaces, et les eaux asses hautes pour pouvoir y naviguer; Neantmoins pour plusieurs raisons il crut ne le devoir pas publier tout a fait, et se contenta de faire entendre qu'il estoit resolu d'aller au Printemps visiter toute l'estendue de son gouver-

Report on the voyage by the Comte de Frontenac, governor general of New France, to Lake Ontario, 1673.

It was during this voyage that he had Fort Frontenac built on the site of the present-day city of Kingston in order to protect the trade in furs with the distant Indian tribes: "The only means was…to set up a post on the same lake which would prevent the southern tribes from coming into contact with the northern ones and which could oblige the latter not only to continue bringing us all their pelts, …but even those from whom our neighbours used to profit because of the ease with which they could cross the lake, without any obstacle."

Archives nationales, Paris, France: Fonds des Colonies, série C^{11A}, vol. 4, fol. 12.

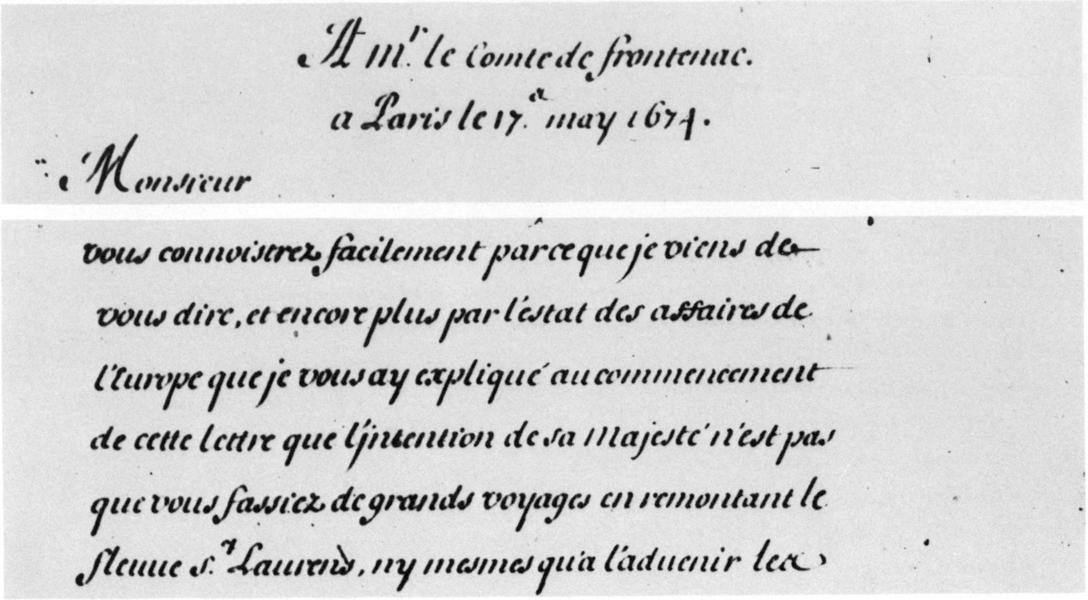
A Mr. le Comte de Frontenac.
a Paris le 17e may 1674.

Monsieur

vous connoistrez facilement par ce que je viens de vous dire, et encore plus par l'estat des affaires de l'Europe que je vous ay expliqué au commencement de cette lettre que l'intention de sa Majesté n'est pas que vous fassiez de grands voyages en remontant le fleuve St Laurens, ny mesmes qu'a l'advenir les

Letter from the minister Colbert to Governor General Frontenac, Paris, 17 May 1674.

Colbert expressed little favour for expanding beyond the inhabited regions: "His Majesty's intention is not...that in future the inhabitants should expand as much as they have done in the past, on the contrary he wishes that you work...at restraining them and bringing them together and creating towns and villages with them...rather than thinking of distant discoveries."

habitans s'estendent autant qu'ilz ont fait par le passé, au contraire Elle veut que vous trauailliez jncessamment, et pendant tout le temps que vous demeurerez en ce païs-là a les resserrer, et a les assem:bler, et en composer des villes, et des villages pour les mettre auec dautant plus de facilité en estat de se bien deffendre, ensorte que quand mesmes l'estat des affaires de l'Europe seroit changé par vne bonne, et aduantageuse paix a la gloire, et a la satisfaction de Sa Majesté, Elle estime bien plus conuenable au bien de son seruice de vous appliquer a bien faire deffri:cher, et bien habiter les endroits les plus fertiles, les plus proches des costes de la mer, et de la communica:tion auec la France, que non pas de penser au loin, des decouuertes au dedans des terres des païs si es:loignez qu'ilz ne peuuent jamais estre habitez ny possedez par des françois.

Cette regle generale peut auoir ses exceptions en deux cas, l'vn si les païs dont vous prendriez possession sont necessaires au commerce, et aux traites des françois, et s'ilz pouuoient estre decouuerts, et pos:sedez par quelque autre nation qui pust troubler le commerce, et les traites des françois; mais come il n'y en a point de cette qualité, Sa Majesté estime tousjours, que vous pouuez, et debuez laisser les

56

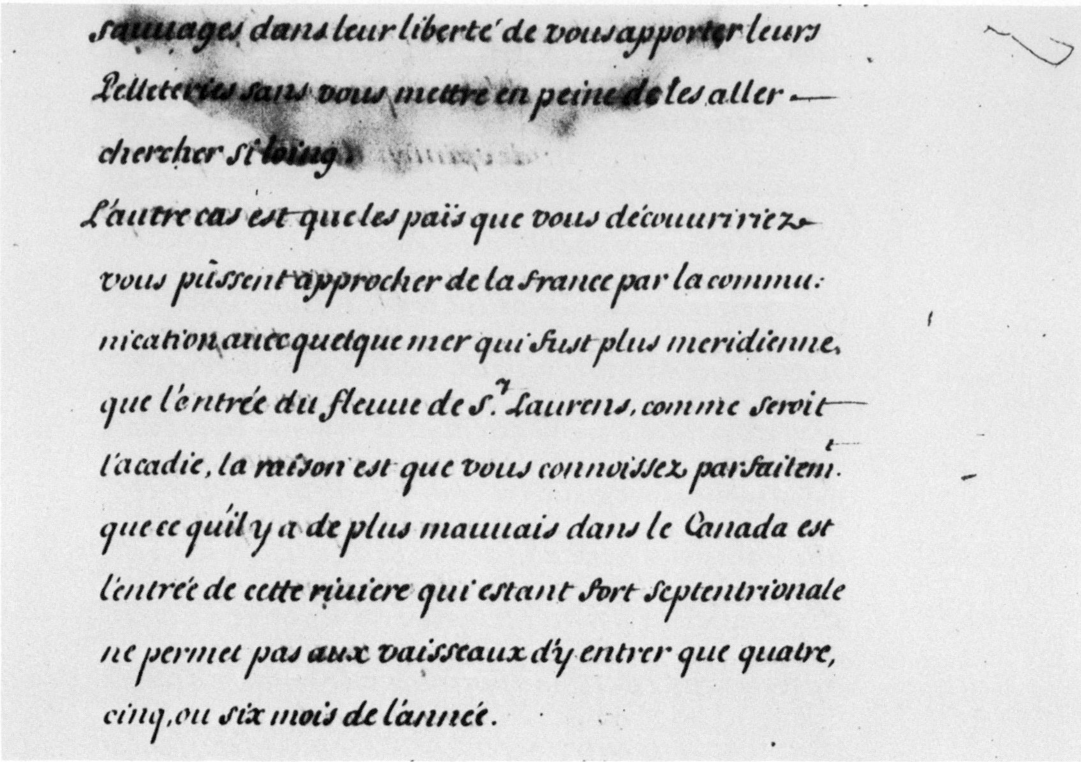
sauuages dans leur liberté de vous apporter leurs
Pelleteries sans vous mettre en peine de les aller
chercher si loing.
L'autre cas est que les païs que vous découurirez
vous puissent approcher de la France par la commu:
nication auecquelque mer qui fust plus meridienne,
que l'entrée du fleuue de St. Laurens, comme seroit
l'acadie, la raison est que vous connoissez parfaitemt.
que ce quil y a de plus mauuais dans le Canada est
l'entrée de cette riuiere qui estant fort Septentrionale
ne permet pas aux vaisseaux d'y entrer que quatre,
cinq, ou six mois de l'année.

Archives nationales, Paris, France: Fonds des Colonies, série B, vol. 6, fol. 28, 32, 32v, 33.

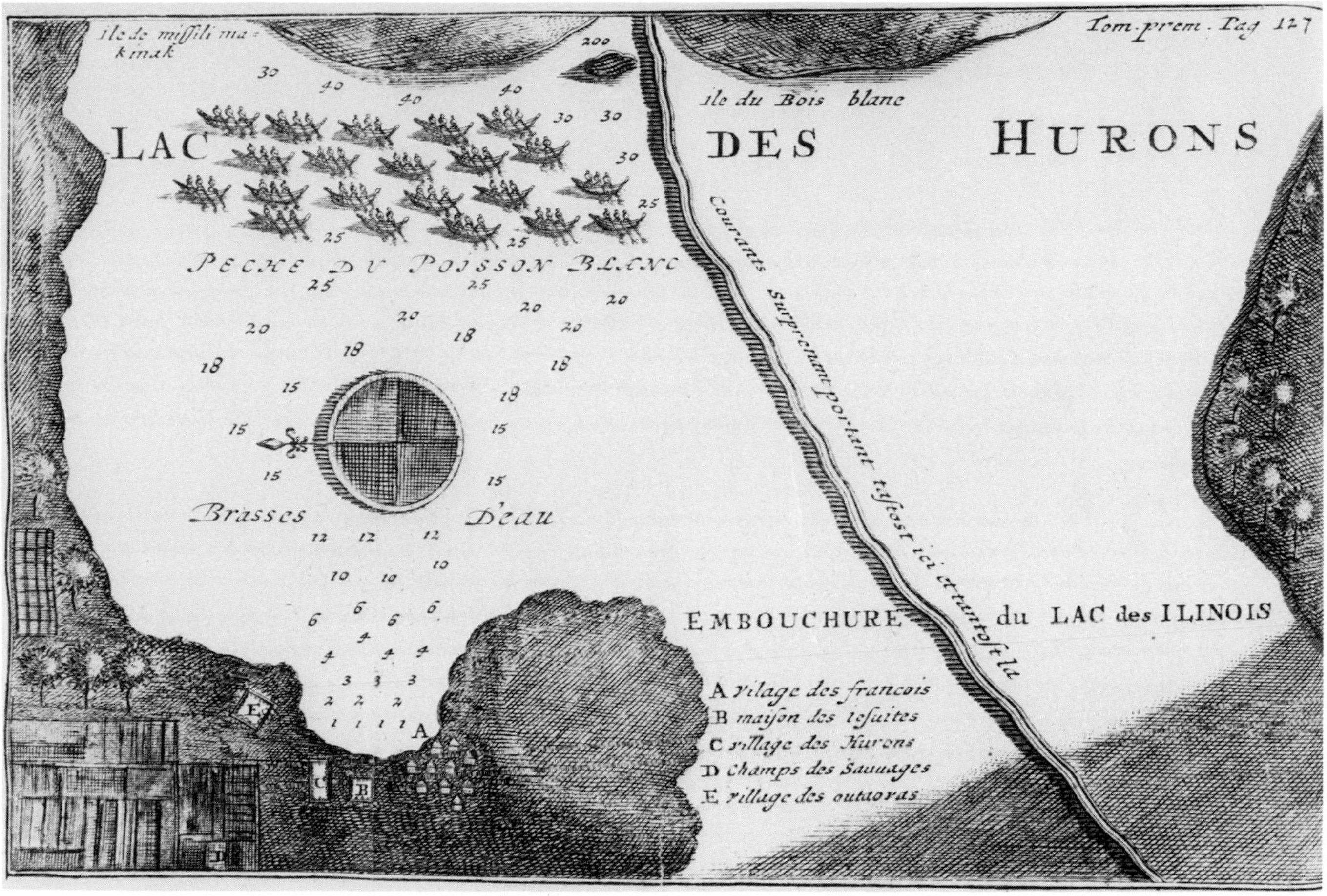

Lake of the Hurons; etching with line engraving; 16.5 x 17 cm. (page).

In Louis Armand de Lom d'Arce, baron de Lahontan. *Voyages du baron de La Hontan dans l'Amérique septentrionale*.... 2e éd. rev., corr. et augm. La Haye: C. Delo, 1706, p. 127.

During the years 1680–1700 the post of Michilimackinac, at the junction of Lake Huron and Lake Michigan, was a very important centre for the western fur trade. A Jesuit mission ministered to the Ottawa and Huron villages. Not far from this mission was built Fort Buade, to which was attached a strong garrison. The military and religious authorities at Michilimackinac saw to it that good relations were maintained with the western tribes so that they would not enter into any alliances with the Iroquois and the English.

Public Archives of Canada, Library, Ottawa (Negative no. C 99256).

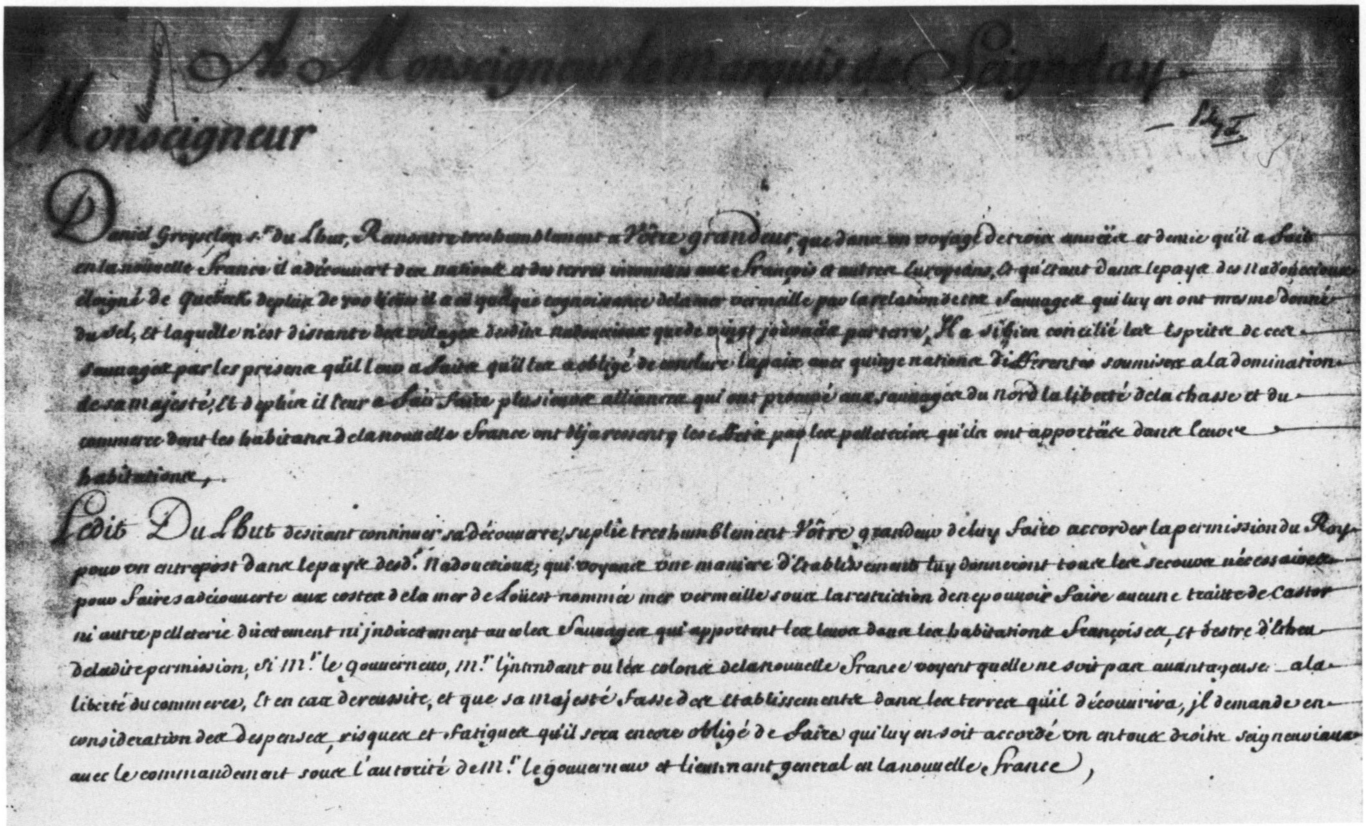

A Monseigneur le Marquis de Seignelay

142

Monseigneur

Daniel Greysolon s.r du Lhut, Remonstre tres humblement a Votre grandeur, que dans un voyage de trois années et demie qu'il a faict en la nouvelle France il a découvert des nations et des terres inconnües aux François et autres Européens, Et qu'estant dans le pays des Nadouecioux éloigné de Quebeck de plus de 700 lieües il a eu quelque connoissance de la mer vermeille par la relation de ces Sauvages qui luy en ont mesme donné du sel, Et laquelle n'est distante des villages desdits Nadouecioux que de vingt journées par terre, Il a si bien concilié les Esprits de ces Sauvages par les presens qu'il leur a faits qu'il les a obligé de conclure la paix avec quinze nations differentes soumises a la domination de sa majesté, Et de plus il leur a fait faire plusieurs alliances qui ont procuré aux sauvages du nord la liberté de la chasse et du commerce dont les habitans de la nouvelle France ont déja ressenty les effets par les pelleteries qu'ils ont apportées dans leurs habitations,

Ledit Du Lhut desirant continuer sa découverte, suplie tres humblement Votre grandeur de luy faire accorder la permission du Roy pour un entrepost dans le pays desd. Nadouecioux; qui voyant une maniere d'Etablissement luy donneroient tous les secours necessaires pour faire sa découverte aux costes de la mer de Sioux nommée mer vermeille sous la restriction de n'y pouvoir faire aucune traitte de Castor ni autre pelleterie directement ni indirectement avec les Sauvages qui apportent leurs [illegible] dans les habitations Françoises, et d'estre déchu de ladite permission, si M.r le gouverneur, M.r l'intendant ou les colons de la nouvelle France voyent qu'elle ne soit pas avantageuse a la liberté du commerce, Et en cas de reussite, et que sa majesté fasse des Etablissements dans les terres qu'il découvrira, il demande en consideration des despenses, risques et fatigues qu'il sera encore obligé de faire qui luy en soit accordé un [illegible] droits seigneuriaux avec le commandement sous l'autorité de M.r le gouverneur et lieutenant general en la nouvelle france,

Request addressed by the explorer Daniel Greysolon Dulhut to the Marquis de Seignelay, the minister of Marine, around 1682.

Dulhut reported that "being in the country of the Sioux, which is more than 700 leagues from Québec, he has had some knowledge of the Mer Vermeille [the Pacific Ocean]...which is at only twenty days' journey by land from the villages of the aforementioned Sioux." He offered to try to find that sea.

Archives nationales, Paris, France: Fonds des Colonies, série C^{11E}, vol. 16, fol. 11.

II

Expansion in spite of everything

Despite the king's desire to prevent the colony from spreading out far and wide, the remote posts were increasing and even more so the number of coureurs des bois. On 21 May 1696 the king did away with all licences or permits "to go to trade with the Indians" and forbade anyone from "going to trade in the interior of the lands" on pain of being sent to the galleys.

On 18 October 1700 the acting governor, Louis-Hector de Callière, and Intendant Jean Bochart de Champigny informed the minister of their highly unsuccessful efforts "to make the Frenchmen living in the depths of the forest come back," all the more so since many of them had gone to take refuge in the direction of the brand-new settlement on the Mississippi.

In fact Pierre Le Moyne d'Iberville had founded the colony of Louisiana in that same year. How could one have resisted the argument in favour of it that he had written the preceding year, showing that unless she took possession of the region of the Gulf of Mexico and contained expansion by the English in that direction, France would sooner or later find herself thrown out of North America?

The necessity of ensuring the colony's security through outposts and also of reducing English influence on the Indians, suppliers of furs and warriors, was at the origin of the official founding of the fort – and the post – of Detroit in 1701.

In spite of everything the fleurs-de-lis were proliferating.

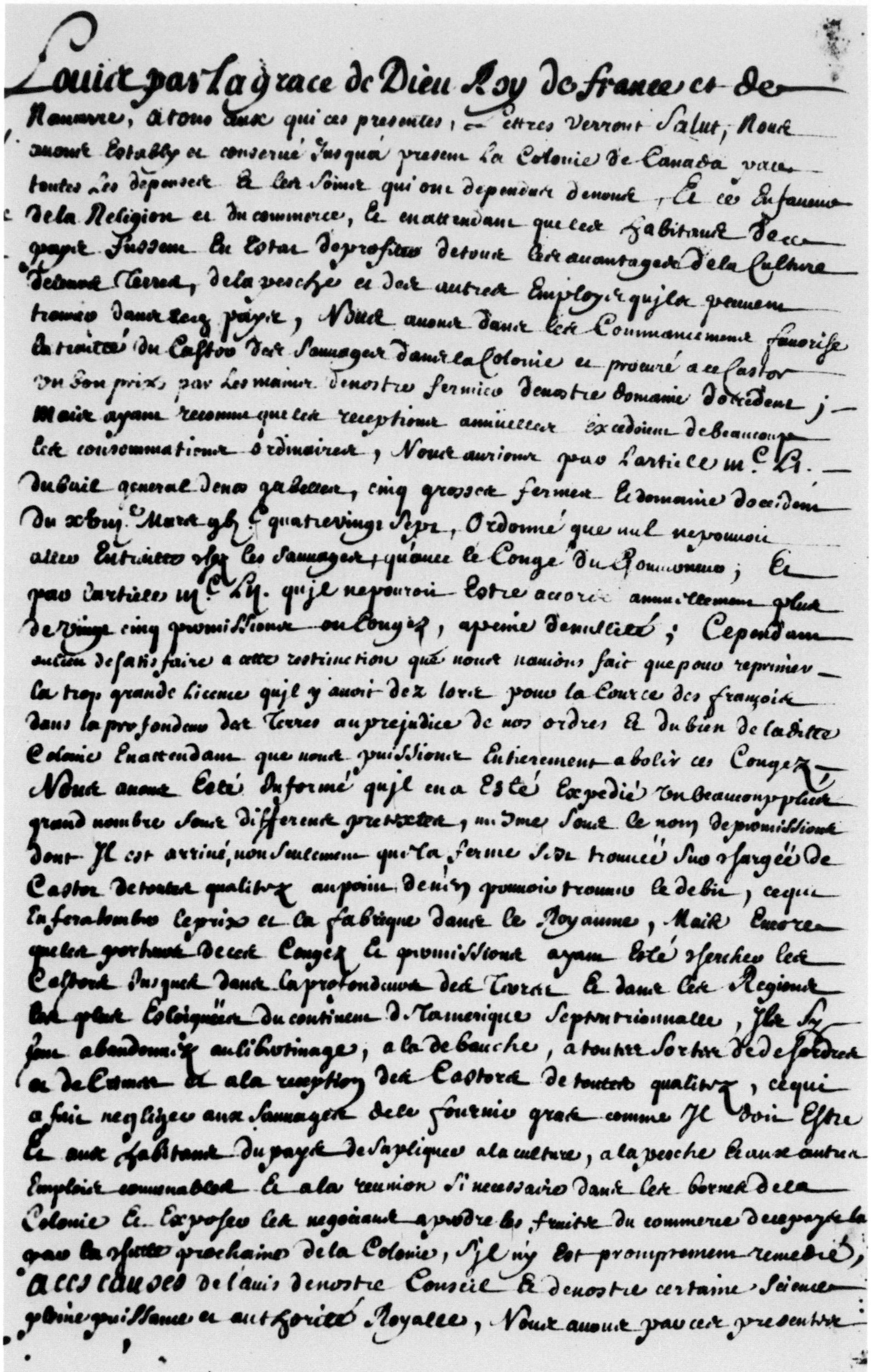

Louis par la grace de Dieu Roy de france et de
Navarre, a tous ceux qui ces presentes Lettres verront Salut; Nous
avons Establi et conservé jusqu'a present la Colonie de Canada par
toutes les depenses et les soins qui ont dependu de nous, Et en faveur
de la Religion et du commerce, et en attendant que les habitans de ce
pays fussent en Estat de profiter de tous les avantages de la Culture
de leurs Terres, de la pesche et des autres Employs qu'ils peuvent
trouver dans leur pays, Nous avons dans les Commancemens favorisé
la traitte du Castor des Sauvages dans la Colonie et procuré a ce Castor
un bon prix par les mains de nostre fermier de nostre domaine d'occident;
Mais ayant reconnu que les receptions annuelles excedoient de beaucoup
les consommations ordinaires, Nous aurions par l'article m.C.LX.
du bail general de nos gabelles, cinq grosses fermes et domaine d'occident
du xbvj.e Mars gbj.c quatrevingt sept, Ordonné que nul ne pourroit
aller Entraiter chez les Sauvages, qu'avec le Congé du Gouverneur; Et
par l'article m.C.LXj. qu'il ne pourroit estre accordé annuellement plus
de vingt cinq permissions ou Congez, a peine de nullité; Cependant
au lieu de satisfaire a cette restriction que nous n'avions fait que pour reprimer
la trop grande licence qu'il y avoit [illegible] pour la Course des françois
dans la profondeur des Terres au prejudice de nos ordres et du bien de ladite
Colonie En attendant que nous puissions Entierement abolir ces Congez,
Nous avons esté informé qu'il en a Esté Expedié un beaucoup plus
grand nombre sous differens pretextes, mesme sous le nom de permissions
dont Il est arrivé non seulement que la ferme s'est trouvée surchargée de
Castor de toutes qualitez au point de n'y pouvoir trouver le debit, ce qui
en fera tomber le prix et la fabrique dans le Royaume, Mais Encore
que les porteurs de ces Congez et permissions ayant esté chercher les
Castors jusques dans la profondeur des Terres et dans les Regions
les plus Eloignées du continent de l'Amerique Septentrionale, Ils se
sont abandonnez au libertinage, a la debauche, a toutes sortes de desordres
et de Crimes et a la reception des Castors de toutes qualitez, ce qui
a fait negliger aux Sauvages de les fournir gras comme Il doit Estre
Et aux habitans du pays de s'appliquer a la culture, a la pesche et aux autres
Emplois convenables Et a la reunion si necessaire dans les bornes de la
Colonie Et Exposé les negocians a perdre les fruits du commerce de ce pays la
par la perte prochaine de la Colonie, s'il n'y est promptement remedié;
A ces causes de l'avis de nostre Conseil Et de nostre certaine Science
pleine puissance et authorité Royalle, Nous avons par ces presentes

Declaration by King Louis XIV putting an end to licences and permits to go to trade with the Indians, Versailles, 21 May 1696.

Such a measure was imperative, because France was at that time "overloaded with beaver of every quality, to the point of not being able to find any sale for them," and also because too many Canadians were taking to the woods and were failing to "apply themselves to farming, fishing, and other fitting occupations."

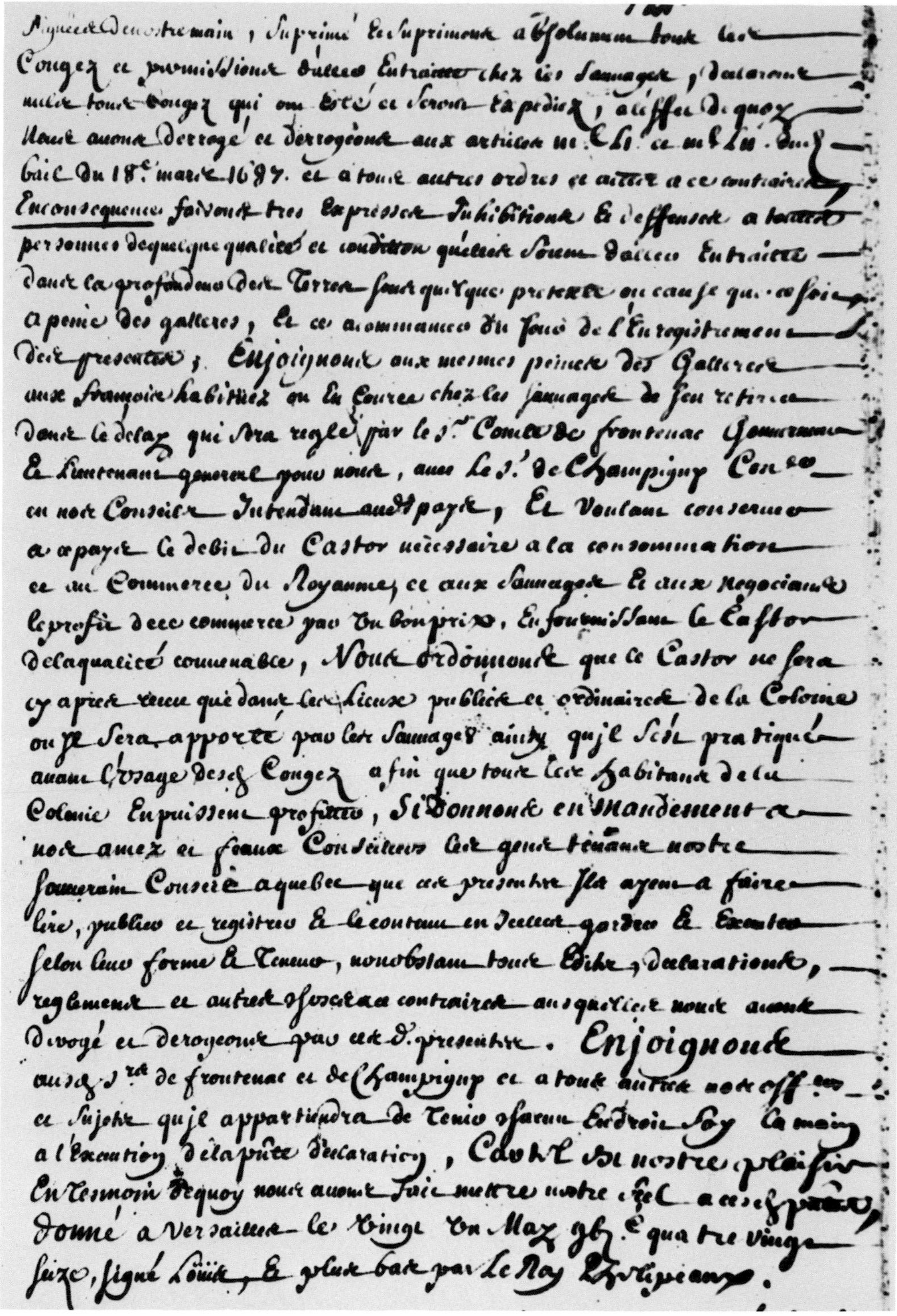

signée de nostre main, supprimé et supprimons absolument tous les
Congez et permissions d'aller en traitte chez les sauvages, declarons
nuls tous congez qui ont esté et seront expediez, a l'effet de quoy
Nous avons derrogé et derrogeons aux articles III. et IIII. de l'Edict du 18e mars 1687. et a tous autres ordres et actes a ce contraires,
En consequence faisons tres expresses Inhibitions et deffenses a toutes
personnes de quelque qualité et condition qu'elles soient d'aller en traitte
dans la profondeur des Terres sous quelque pretexte ou cause que ce soit
a peine des galleres, et ce a commencer du jour de l'Enregistrement
des presentes; Enjoignons aux mesmes peines des Galleres
aux François habituez ou en courses chez les sauvages de s'en retirer
dans le delay qui sera reglé par le Sr Comte de Frontenac Gouverneur
et Lieutenant general pour nous, avec le Sr de Champigny Conser
en nos Conseils Intendant audit pays, Et voulant conserver
a ce pays le debit du Castor necessaire a la consommation
et au commerce du Royaume, et aux sauvages et aux negocians
le profit de ce commerce par un bon prix, en fournissant le Castor
de la qualité convenable, Nous ordonnons que le Castor ne sera
cy apres receu que dans les lieux publics et ordinaires de la Colonie
ou il sera apporté par les sauvages ainsy qu'il se pratiquoit
avant l'usage des congez afin que tous les habitans de la
Colonie en puissent profiter, Si donnons en mandement a
nos amez et feaux Conseillers les gens tenans nostre
souverain Conseil a Quebec que ces presentes ils ayent a faire
lire, publier et registrer et le contenu en icelles garder et executer
selon leur forme et teneur, nonobstant tous Edits, declarations,
reglemens et autres choses a ce contraires auxquelles nous avons
derogé et derogeons par ces d. presentes. Enjoignons
aud. Srs de Frontenac et de Champigny et a tous autres nos off.ers
et sujets qu'il appartiendra de tenir chacun endroit soy la main
a l'execution de la pnte declaration, Car tel est nostre plaisir
En tesmoin de quoy nous avons fait mettre nostre scel a ces presentes
donné a Versailles le vingt un May gbic quatre vingt
seize, signé Louis, et plus bas par le Roy Phelypeaux.

Archives nationales du Québec, Centre d'archives de la Capitale, Québec: Insinuations du Conseil souverain, vol. 2, fol. 120, 120v.

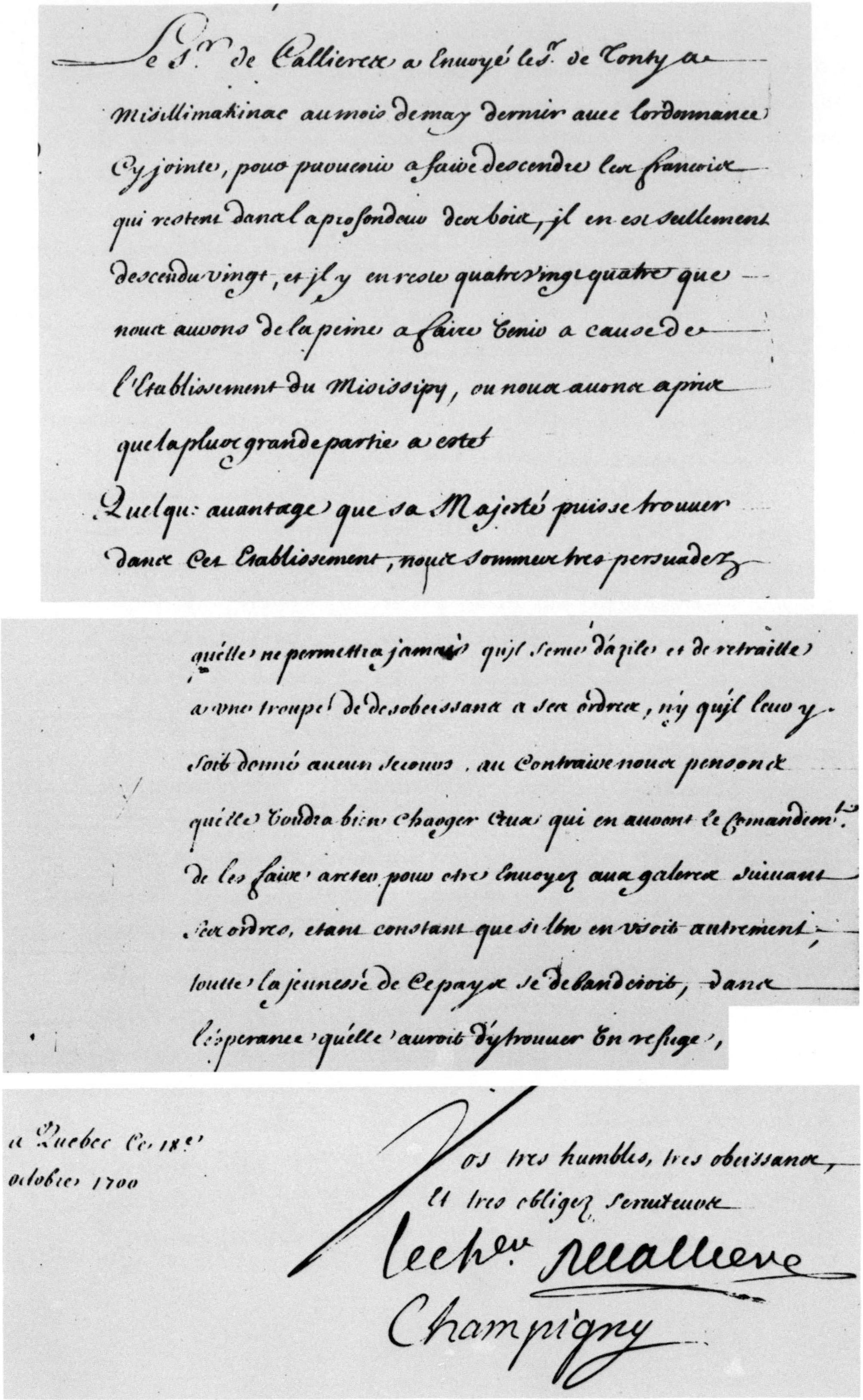
Le Sr. de Callieres a Envoyé le Sr. de Conty a Missilimakinac au mois de may dernier avec lordonnance Cy jointe, pour parvenir a faire descendre les françois qui restent dans la profondeur des bois, il en est seullement descendu vingt, et il y en reste quatre vingt quatre que nous avons de la peine a faire venir a cause de l'Etablissement du Mississipy, ou nous avons apris que la plus grande partie a estée

Quelque avantage que sa Majesté puisse trouver dans Ces Etablissement, nous sommes tres persuadez

qu'elle ne permettra jamais quil serve d'azile et de retraitte a une troupe de desobeissans a ses ordres, ny quil leur y soit donné aucun secours, au Contraire nous pensons qu'elle voudra bien Charger Ceux qui en auront le Comandemt. de les faire arrester pour estre Envoyez aux galeres suivant ses ordres, estant constant que si lon en usoit autrement, toutte la jeunesse de Ce pays se debanderoit, dans l'esperance qu'elle auroit d'y trouver un refuge,

a Quebec Ce 18e octobre 1700

Vos tres humbles, tres obeissans, et tres obligez Serviteurs

Lechev. de Callieres

Champigny

Letter from Governor Callière and Intendant Champigny to the Comte de Pontchartrain, the minister of Marine, Québec, 18 October 1700.

A good many coureurs des bois were refusing to obey orders to come back to the inhabited part of the colony and were going to take refuge in Louisiana: "We have difficulty in making [them] come because of the settlement of the Mississippi, where...the majority have gone."

Archives nationales, Paris, France: Fonds des Colonies, série C^{11A}, vol. 18, fol. 5v, 6, 21.

1699.

Memoire de la Coste de la Floride et d'une Partie du Mexique

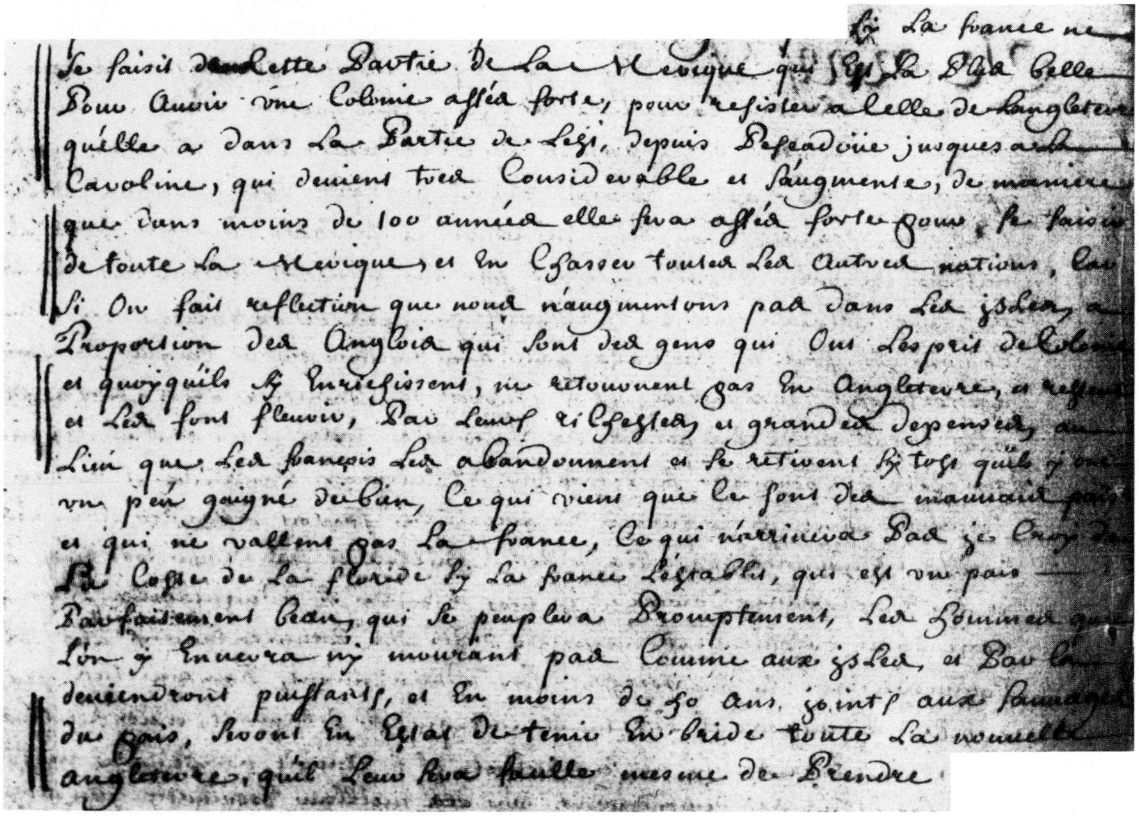

Si La france ne se saisit de cette Partie de l'Amerique qui est la plus belle Pour avoir une Colonie assez forte, pour resister a celle de l'angleterre quelle a dans la Partie de l'Est, depuis Pescadoüe jusques a la Caroline, qui devient tres Considerable et s'augmente, de maniere que dans moins de 100 années elle sera assez forte pour se saisir de toute l'Amerique, et en Chasser toutes les autres nations, car si on fait reflection que nous n'augmentons pas dans les Isles a Proportion des Anglois qui sont des gens qui ont l'esprit de Colonie et quoyqu'ils s'y Enrichissent, ne retournent pas en Angleterre, et restent et les font fleurir, Par leurs richesses et grandes depenses, au Lieu que les françois les abandonnent et se retirent si tost qu'ils y ont un peu gagné de bien, Ce qui vient que ce sont des mauvais pais et qui ne vallent pas la france, Ce qui n'arrivera Pas je Croy de la Coste de la floride si la france s'establit, qui est un pais Parfaitement beau, qui se peuplera Promptement, les hommes que l'on y Envoyera n'y mourant pas Comme aux Isles, et Par la deviendront puissants, et en moins de 50 ans, joints aux sauvages du pais, seront en Estat de tenir en bride toute la nouvelle angleterre, quil leur sera facille mesme de Prendre

"Report on the Florida coast and part of Mexico," by Pierre Le Moyne d'Iberville, 1699.

D'Iberville believed that the French should settle solidly in Louisiana to prevent the British colonies from spreading west of the Appalachians: "If France does not take possession of this part of America, which is the most beautiful, to have a colony strong enough to resist those of England...in less than 100 years" the English colonies would be powerful enough "to take possession of all of America and drive all the other nations out."

Archives nationales, Paris, France: Fonds des Colonies, Série C^{13A}, vol. 1, fol. 167, 176.

62

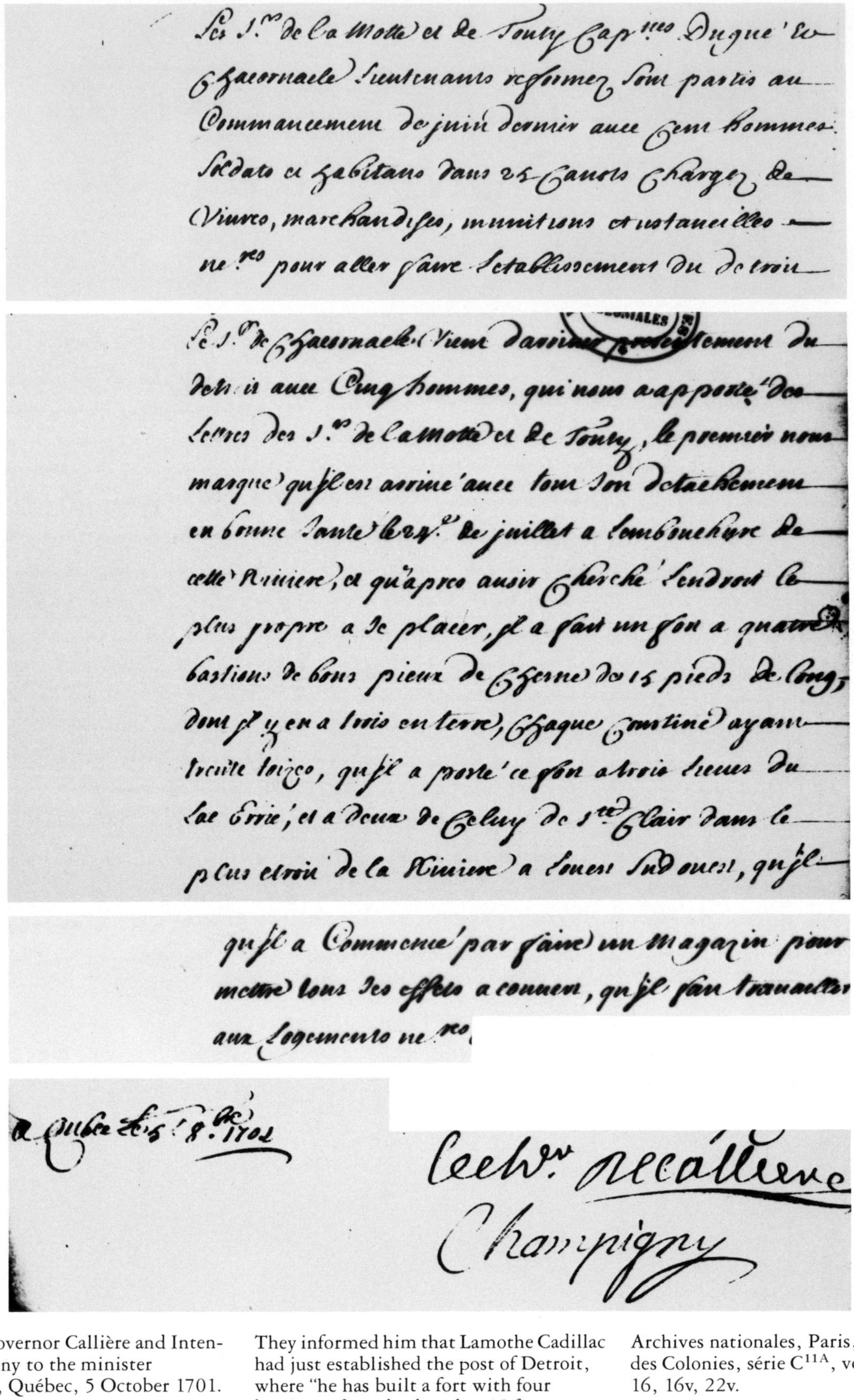
Les Srs de la Motte et de Tonty Capnes Dugué et Chacornacle Lieutenans reformez sont partis au commancement de juin dernier avec cent hommes soldats et habitans dans 25 canots chargez de vivres, marchandises, munitions et ustancilles necres pour aller faire l'establissement du detroit

Le Sr de Chacornacle vient d'arriver presentement du detroit avec cinq hommes, qui nous a apporté des lettres des Srs de Lamotte et de Tonty, le premier nous marque qu'il est arrivé avec tout son detachement en bonne santé le 24e de juillet a lembouchure de cette riviere, et qu'apres avoir cherché l'endroit le plus propre a se placer, il a fait un fort a quatre bastions de bons pieux de chesne de 15 pieds de long, dont il y en a trois en terre, chaque courtine ayant trente toises, qu'il a posté ce fort a trois lieues du lac Errie, et a deux de celuy de Ste Claire dans le plus etroit de la riviere a l'ouest sud ouest, qu'il

qu'il a commencé par faire un magazin pour mettre tous ses effets a couvert, qu'il fait travailler aux logements necres,

a Quebec le 5e 8bre 1701

Le chevr de Callière

Champigny

Letter from Governor Callière and Intendant Champigny to the minister Pontchartrain, Québec, 5 October 1701.

They informed him that Lamothe Cadillac had just established the post of Detroit, where "he has built a fort with four bastions of good oak stakes 15 feet long...that he began by building a storehouse to put all his effects under cover, that he is having the necessary lodgings prepared."

Archives nationales, Paris, France: Fonds des Colonies, série C^{11A}, vol. 19, fol. 14v, 16, 16v, 22v.

63

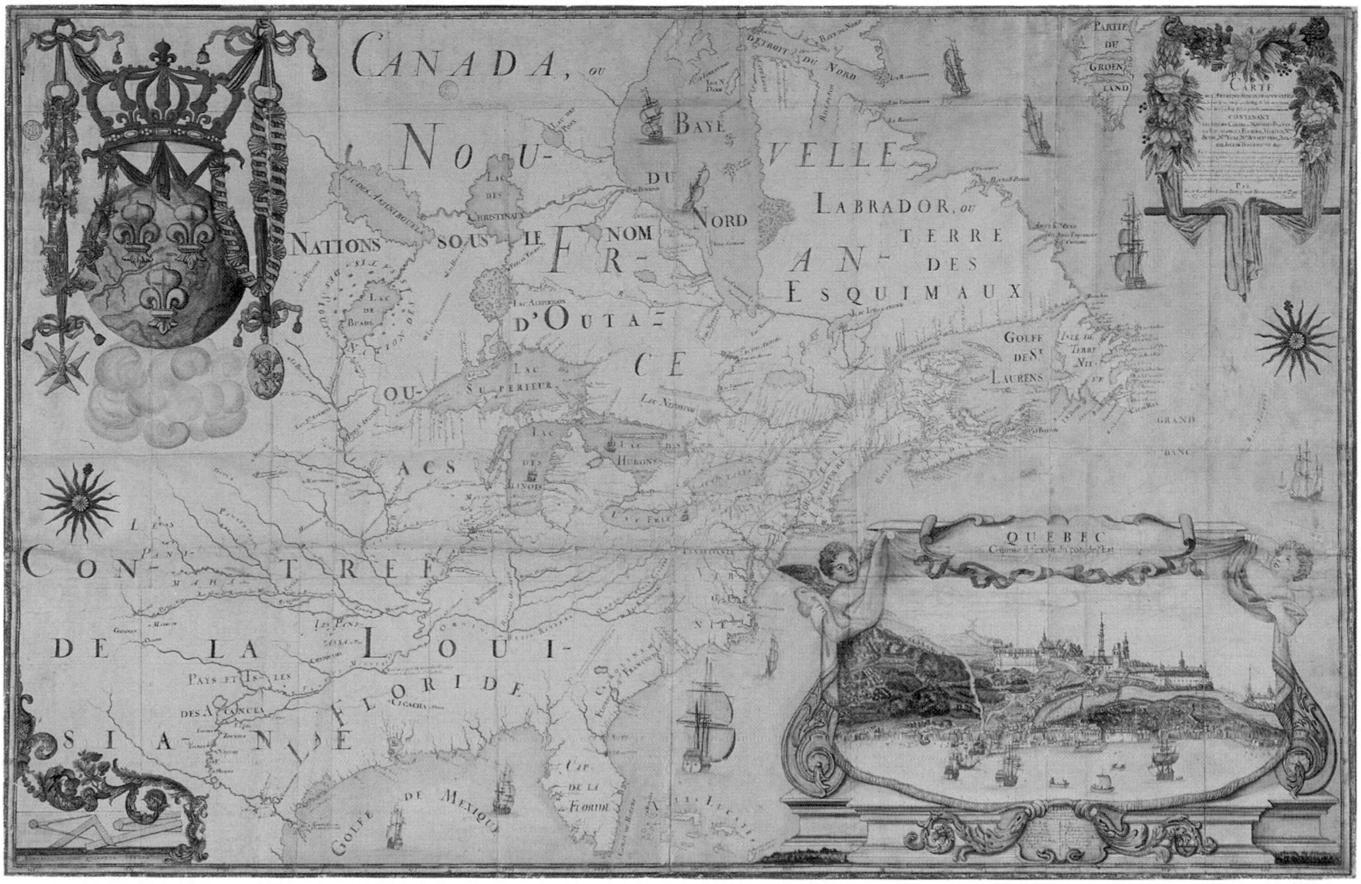

"Carte de l'Amerique Septentrionnalle..., 1688"; Jean-Baptiste-Louis Franquelin; col. ms.; 94.5 x 147.1 cm.

This magnificent map by Franquelin shows all the territory of North America that was known at the period. It reveals that the French had begun to cut out an immense empire for themselves by establishing forts or posts throughout the continent, to the north, the south, the east and the west. On it is also shown a fine view of the town of Québec, the capital of this empire.

Service historique de la Marine, Vincennes, France: Vol. 4040B, no. 6.

III

Population and Settlement

Since 1608 Québec had been simply a trading post – or a trading factory, if one prefers; clerks and a few tradesmen were to be found there, all of them in the merchants' service, but there were no real settlers, unless Louis Hébert's family, which had arrived in 1617, is excepted. On a few occasions merchant societies had promised, in return for trading benefits, to bring settlers to Canada and set them up there. None of them really gave any attention to doing so, or at least had any success at it. It was to correct "these disorders" and establish "a powerful colony" in New France that on 29 April 1627 was created the Compagnie des Cent-Associés, whose first obligation was to bring over and settle in New France, in a period of fifteen years, four thousand people of French nationality and of the Catholic faith. Champlain's plans for settlement seemed destined this time to be realized.

In 1628 the Cent-Associés sent four ships carrying four hundred people and everything that was necessary for settling them. These ships fell into the hands of the English, and the following year, for lack of aid, Champlain had to surrender the post of Québec to the Kirke brothers. It was a very bad start and a very bad economic situation for the large company, which suffered such losses that it seems never to have completely recovered. Under those conditions it is not at all surprising that in 1643 the company was far from having carried to Canada the four thousand persons that it had undertaken to bring. In 1663 the colony counted barely more than three thousand inhabitants.

With the powerful help of the Jesuits, who in their yearly *Relations* made great efforts to make New France known, gather support for the country, and attract settlers to it, the Compagnie des Cent-Associés, whose trade soon suffered from the Iroquois war, did its best to populate the colony. But it had to rely on the initiative of private individuals and the religious communities. Thus, following the example of Robert Giffard, the Jesuits, and the Compagnie de Beaupré, certain holders of seigneuries did recruiting in France. To cope with the lack of manpower the religious communities and ordinary settlers had recourse to the system of indentured servants, most often unmarried, who agreed to come to work for them, generally for a period of three years, in return for having their crossing paid and an annual salary. Now, sometimes these workmen remained in Canada once their engagement was ended, just as did soldiers from the garrison.

In the meantime a system of settlement and land distribution had been thought up and put into operation for New France. Immense tracts of land called seigneuries were granted to private individuals or religious communities; in return the seigneurs had to grant pieces of land (generally measuring three arpents by thirty or forty) to settlers. As a result, to use Rameau de Saint-Père's expression, the seigneur was turned into "a contractor for settling a given tract of land," and the seigneury, which most often coincided with the area of the parish, became an organized living unit in which even justice was sometimes exercised. This system of settlement – the seigneurial régime – gave excellent results in the seventeenth century, and by 1700 the banks of the St. Lawrence and the Richelieu were completely occupied.

The 1660s were the most important years in the history of New France, as far as settlement of the colony is concerned. The numerous appeals launched in the *Relations* and by Bishop Laval and certain inhabitants of Canada – for example Pierre Boucher – led Louis XIV to decide to take the colony in hand after the Cent-Associés resigned in 1663 and to send there to subdue the Iroquois the Carignan-Salières regiment, many of whose officers and soldiers settled down in Canada. During those years a great number of girls of marriageable age ("filles du roi" or "king's daughters"), unmarried men, and families were sent to the colony. The king and Intendant Talon applied themselves to encouraging marriages and large families. The idea was even entertained of frenchifying the Hurons and Algonkins to eventually make out of them and the French "one people and one race." The reason for this was that France was on the point of putting an end to sending settlers and girls of marriageable age; after 1672, the year in which Talon granted forty-six seigneuries, Canada had to find the way to increase its population by itself.

And that was what was done, in fact, without assimilating the Indians and in spite of life in the woods, which was luring more and more young men away from the shores of the St. Lawrence. Thanks to a high birth-rate, and taking into account also the arrival of a certain number of immigrants every year, the population of Canada is believed to have been around 12,000 in 1688 and probably more than 15,000 in 1700. In Acadia, however, things were quite different: fewer than a thousand French people were living there in 1686, many people having preferred to settle down in New England, in the vicinity of Boston. Around the same time Newfoundland counted perhaps about 2,000 English-speaking residents, most of them men, who worked in fishing and trading, so that one can not yet speak of the existence of a true English colony on the island. And the French there were even less numerous: upon his arrival at Plaisance in 1670 the local commandant, La Poippe, counted only 73 people there. In the seventeenth century, around 1685, the population there seems to have reached a peak, with 640 people being counted, 474 of them being indentured servants.

III

Laying the foundations

Champlain was greatly interested in the Indians. He never missed an opportunity to observe them from close up and to describe their external appearance, their customs, and the tools that they used. He also published drawings of them that he did with his own hand to illustrate his texts or embellish his maps – such as that done in 1612, which shows the "figures" of two Montagnais and two "Almouchicois" (Abenakis).

At the rate that things were going, the "colony" risked remaining indefinitely, for lack of settlers, the exclusive territory of the Indian tribes. That was the reason for the creation in 1627 of the Compagnie des Cent-Associés, which undertook to bring to New France before the end of 1643 four thousand people of French nationality and of the Catholic faith.

In 1634, two years after Québec was returned to France, Champlain had a fort built on the Île de Richelieu and the foundations of a post laid at Trois-Rivières. From then on the French had "three habitations on the great St. Lawrence River."

In 1611 Champlain had made a stop at Montréal, seeking "a place there to build." It fell to the Société Notre-Dame de Montréal, however, to found a settlement there. On 17 May 1642 Paul Chomedey de Maisonneuve landed there with a group of settlers to establish a permanent settlement.

Carte Geographiqve De La Novvelle Franse..., 1612; Samuel de Champlain; map printed from copperplate; 44 x 76.5 cm.

In Samuel de Champlain. *Les voyages dv sievr de Champlain Xaintongeois, capitaine ordinaire pour le roy, en la marine, divisez en deux livres*.... Paris: Chez Jean Berjon, 1613.

This drawing from a map by Champlain represents two Montagnais and two "Almouchicois" (Abenaki) Indians. The Montagnais inhabited an immense territory northeast of the valley of the St. Lawrence, and the "Almouchicois" lived on the Atlantic coast (New England). These Indians were on good terms with the French.

National Library of Canada, Rare Books and Manuscripts Division, Ottawa.

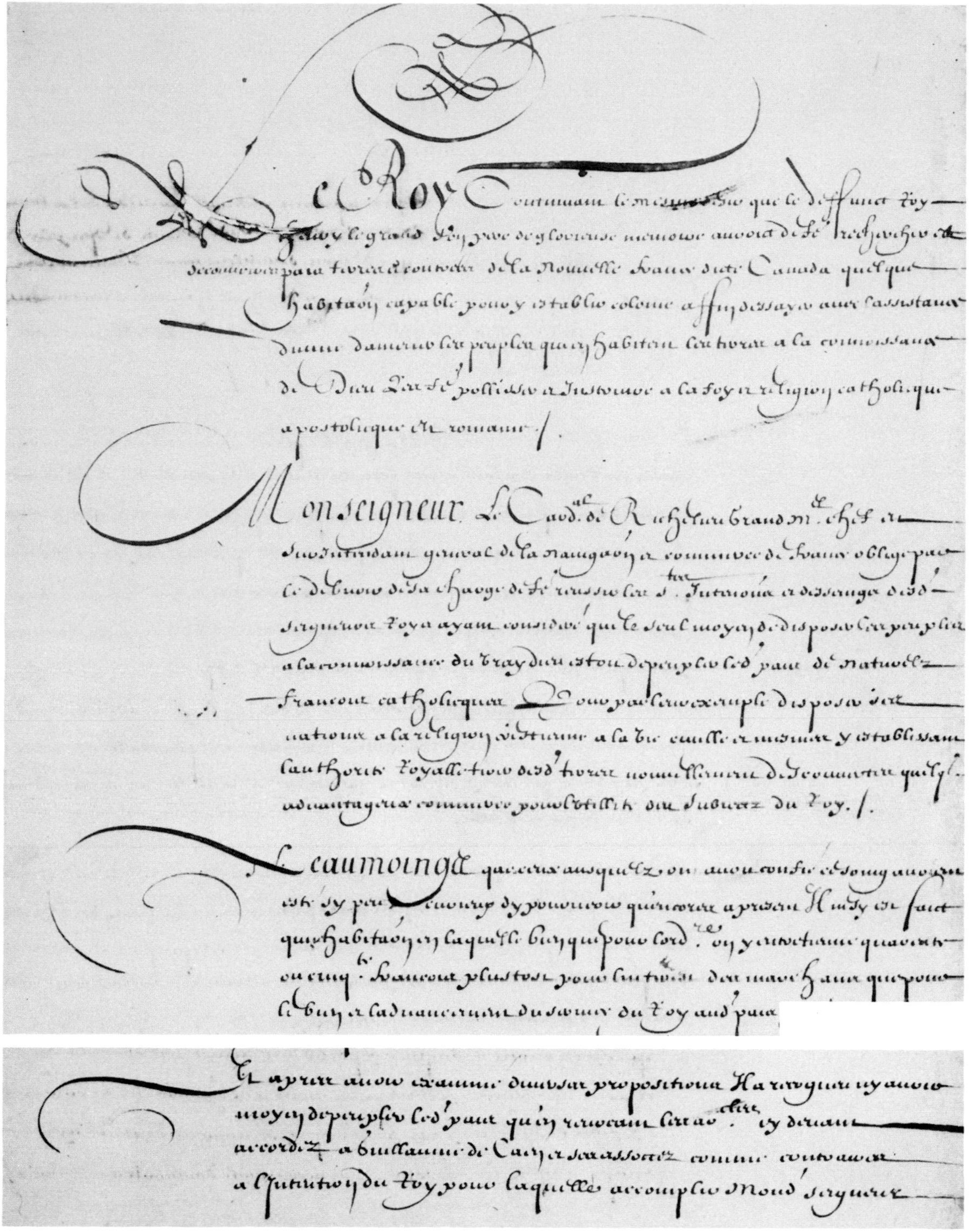

Act establishing the Compagnie de la Nouvelle-France, called the Compagnie des Cent-Associés, Paris, 29 April 1627.

Canada was sparsely populated at the time: "There is only one settlement there [Québec]," consisting of "forty or fifty French people." To remedy this situation Richelieu obliged the new company to "send to the aforementioned country of New France...four thousand [persons] of both sexes in the next fifteen years...thus to populate the aforesaid colony with native French Catholics."

le Card. auroict commis les sieurs de Rocquemont Houel, Lattaignant Dabloy, Duchesne de Castillon, de leur bon sort vouluz pour cest Effect s'assembler avec iceux et leur proposer les moyens et qu'ayant esté par eux effectué Ilz ont promis a Mondict Seigneur le Card. de dresser une compagnie de cent associez et faire tous leurs effortz pour peupler la Nouvelle france dicte Canada suivant les articles cy dessoubz declarez,

C'est assavoir que lesd. Sieurs de Rocquemont Houel Lattaignant Dabloy Duchesne et Castillon, tant pour eulx que pour les autres faisant le nombre de Cent leurs associez promettent faire passer aud. pays de la Nouvelle france deux a trois cens hommes de tous mestiers des l'annee prochaine 1628 et pendant les annees suivantes en augmenter le nombre jusques a quatre mil de l'un et l'autre sexe dans quinze ans prochainement venans et qui finiront en decembre que l'on comptera 1643, les y loger nourrir et entretenir de toutes choses generallement quelconques necessaires a la vie pendant trois ans seullement, et iceux expirez lesd. associez seront deschargez si bon leur semble de leur nourriture et entretenement en leur assignant la quantité des terres deffrichées suffisante pour leur subvenir avec le bled necess.re pour les ensemencer la premiere fois et pour vivre jusques a la recolte lors prochaine ou autrement leur pourvoir en telle sorte qu'ilz puissent de leur industrie et travail subsister aud. pays et s'y entretenir par eux mesmes,

Sans toutteffois qu'il soit loisible aud. associez et autres faire passer aucuns estrangers esd. lieux ains peupler lad. colonie de naturelz françois catholiques

Faict a Paris le vingt neufiesme Avril mil six cens vingt sept. Signé Armand Card. de Richelieu, De Rocquemont, Houel tant pour moy que lesd. Duchesne et Lattaignant Dabloy Seneschal de Dieppe et Castillon,

Public Archives of Canada, Ottawa: Compagnie de la Nouvelle-France, MG 18, C 1, pp. 1–4, 11.

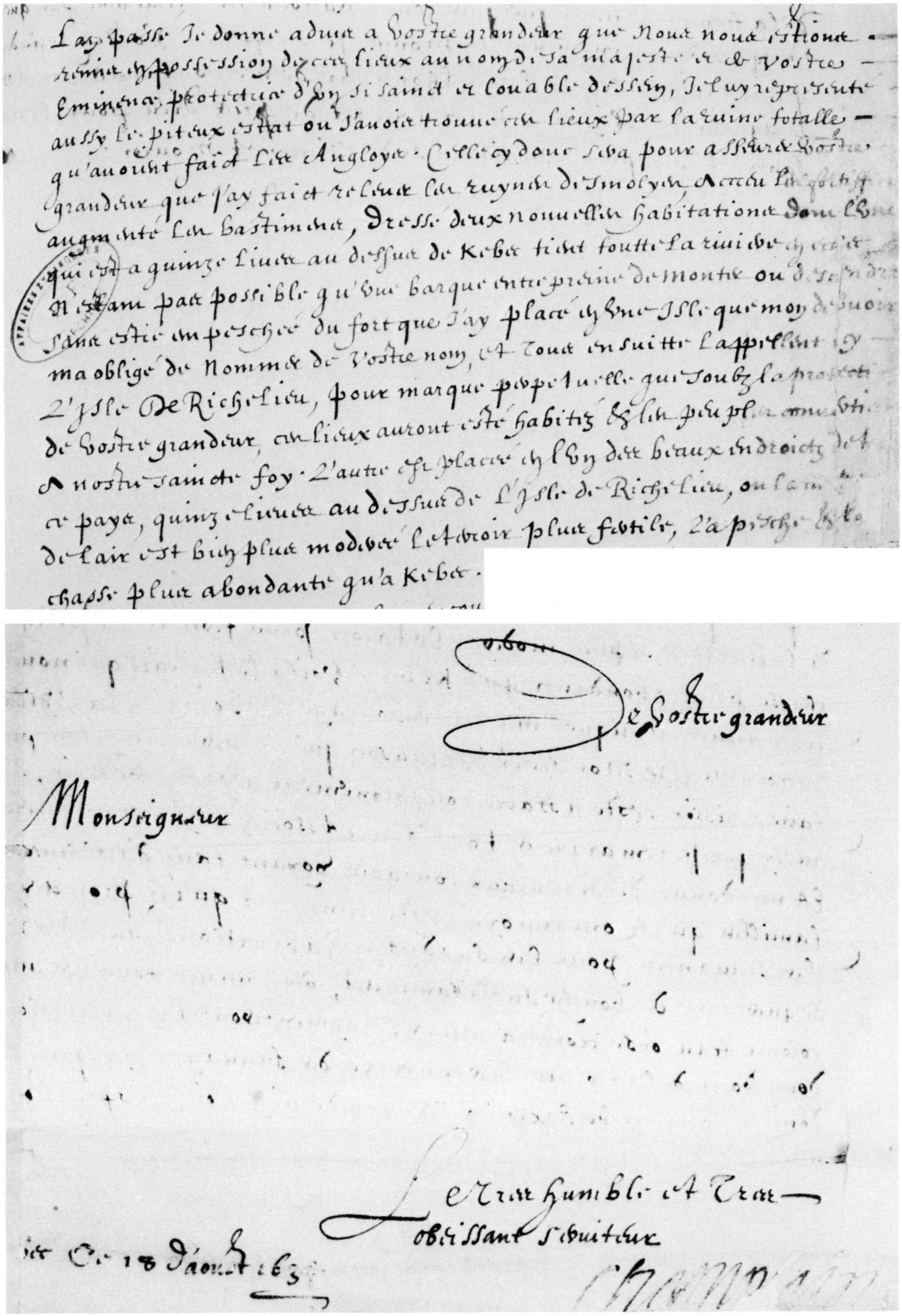

J'ay passé je donne advis a Vostre grandeur que nous nous estions
remis en possession de ces lieux au nom de sa majesté et de Vostre
Eminence protecteur d'un si saint et louable dessein, je luy represente
aussy le piteux estat où j'avois trouvé ces lieux par la ruine totalle
qu'avoient faict les Angloys. Celle cy donc sera pour asseurer Vostre
grandeur que j'ay faict relever les ruynes de [illegible] accreu les fortiff[illegible]
augmenté les bastimens, dressé deux nouvelles habitations dont l'une
qui est a quinze lieues au dessus de Kebec tient toutte la riviere [illegible]
n'estant pas possible qu'une barque entreprenne de monter ou descendre
sans estre empesché du fort que j'ay placé en une Isle que mon devoir
m'a obligé de nommer de Vostre nom, et tout ensuitte l'appellant
L'Isle de Richelieu, pour marque perpetuelle que soubz la protection
de Vostre grandeur ces lieux auront esté habitez & les peuples convertis
a nostre sainte foy. L'autre est placée en l'un des beaux endroictz de
ce pays, quinze lieues au dessus de l'Isle de Richelieu, où la [illegible]
de l'air est bien plus moderée le terroir plus fertile, la pesche & la
chasse plus abondante qu'a Kebec.

De Vostre grandeur

Monseigneur

Le tres humble et tres
obeissant serviteur

[illegible] ce 18 d'aoust 163[illegible]

Champlain

Letter from Samuel de Champlain to Cardinal Richelieu, Québec, 18 August 1634.

Champlain informed Cardinal Richelieu that he had had a fort built on the Île de Richelieu and the foundations laid for a post at Trois-Rivières.

Archives du ministère des Affaires étrangères, Paris, France: Mémoires et documents, Amérique, vol. 4, fol. 131–131v.

RELATION
DE CE QVI S'EST PASSE'
EN LA
NOVVELLE FRANCE,
EN L'ANNE'E 1634.
Enuoyée au
R. PERE PROVINCIAL
de la Compagnie de IESVS
en la Prouince de France.
Coll. Queb. Soc. Jesu Cat. Ins. 1720
Par le P. Paul le Ieune de la mesme Compagnie,
Superieur de la residence de Kebec.

Cat. Inscr. an. 1745.

A PARIS,
Chez SEBASTIEN CRAMOISY, Imprimeur
ordinaire du Roy, ruë S. Iacques, aux Cicognes.
M DC. XXXV.
AVEC PRIVILEGE DV ROY.

Paul Le Jeune. *Relation de ce qui s'est passé en la Novvelle France, en l'année 1634.* Paris: Chez Sébastien Cramoisy, 1635, title page, p. 338.

Father Le Jeune reported that the French "now have three settlements" in the St. Lawrence valley: Québec, Trois-Rivières and Fort Richelieu.

338 *Relation de la Nouuelle France,*

l'allay ſaluër, il me dit qu'il nous amenoit vn petit Sauuage orphelin, nous en faiſant preſent, pour luy ſeruir de pere; ſi toſt qu'on aura moyen de recueillir ces pauures enfans, on en pourra auoir quelque nombre, qui ſeruiront par apres à la conuerſion de leurs Compatriottes. Il nous dit encore qu'on trauailloit fort & ferme au lieu nommé les trois Riuieres, ſi bien que nos François ont maintenant trois habitations ſur le grand fleuue de ſainct Laurens, vne à Kebec fortifiée de nouueau, l'autre à quinze lieuës plus haut dans l'Iſle de ſaincte Croix, où Monſieur de Champlain a faict baſtir le fort de Richelieu. La troiſiéme demeure ſe baſtit aux trois Riuieres, quinze autres lieuës plus haut, c'eſt à dire à trente lieuës de Kebec. Incontinent apres le depart des vaiſſeaux, le Pere Iacques Buteux & moy irons là demeurer pour aſſiſter nos François, les nouuelles habitations eſtant ordinairement dangereuſes, ie n'ay pas veu qu'il fut à propos d'y expoſer le Pere Charles Lallemant, ny autres, le Pere Buteux y vient auec moy

Library of Parliament, Ottawa.

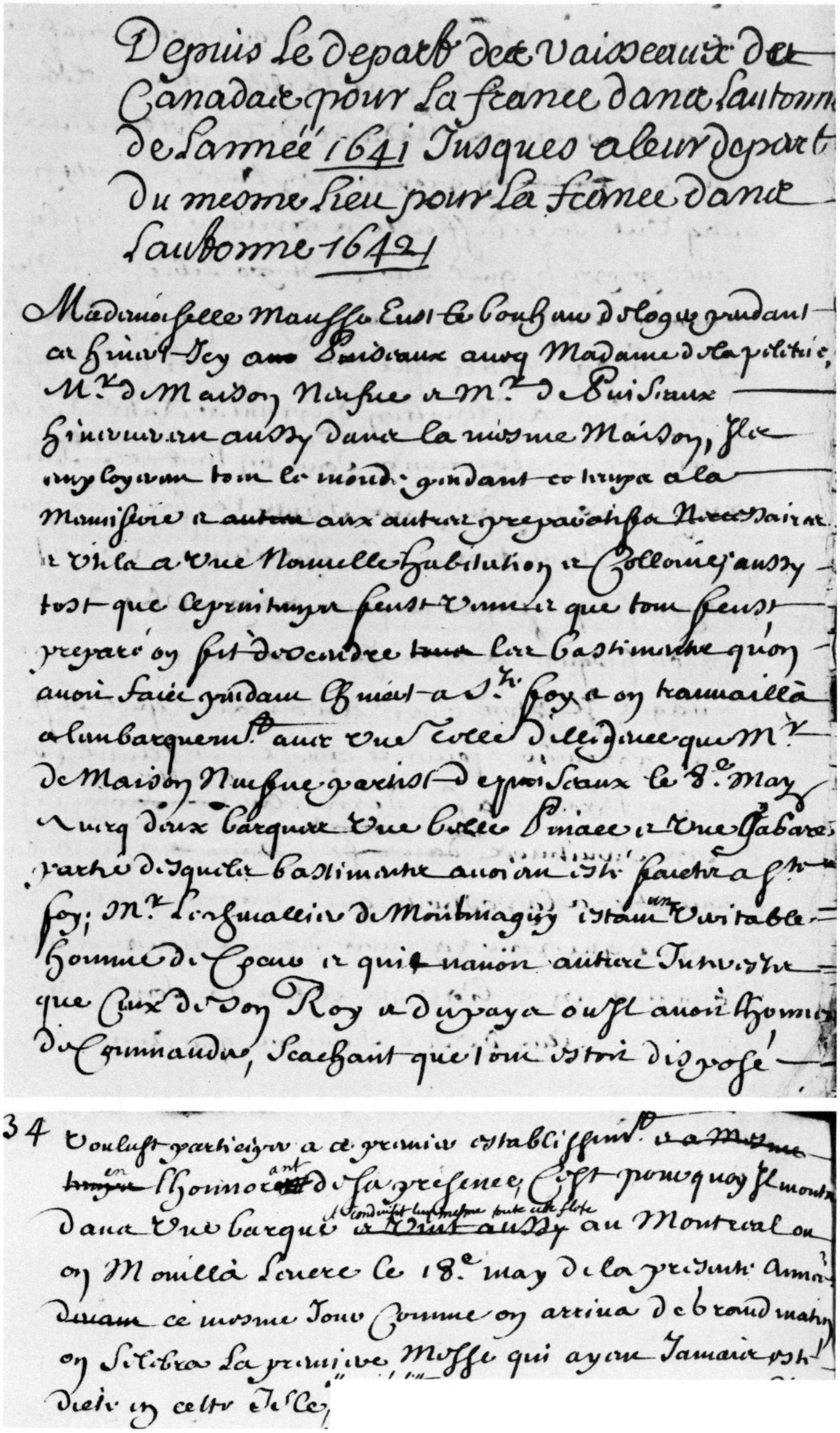
Depuis le depart des vaisseaux de Canada pour la France dans l'automne de l'année 1641 jusques a leur depart du mesme lieu pour la France dans l'automne 1642

Extracts from the *Histoire du Montréal* written by the Sulpician Dollier de Casson, relating the founding of Montréal in 1642.

"M. de Maisonneuve started out from Pizeaux [near Québec] on 8 May with two boats, a fine pinnace and a sailing barge,... M. le Chevalier de Montmagny ...embarked on a boat and led all this fleet in person to Montréal, where they cast anchor on 18 May of this year; on the same day, as thcy arrived early in the day, they celebrated the first mass that had ever been said on this island."

Comme le fist autrement bien voir
le reverend pere Vimont dans la predication quil
fit ce matin la pendant la grande messe quil y
celebra, voyez vous Messieurs, disoit il, ce que vous
voyez n'est qu'un grain de moutarde mais il est
jetté par des mains sy pieuses et animées de lesprit
de la foy et de la Religion que sans doute il faut
que le ciel ayt de grands dessins puis quil
se sert de telles ouvrieres, et donc faut aucune
doute que ce petit grain ne produise un grand arbre,
ne fasse un jour des merveilles, ne soit multiplié
et ne s'estende de toutes partes: comme s'il eust voulu
dire le ciel ne commance son ouvrage presentement
que par une quarantaine d'hommes ~~de quarante hommes~~, mais
scachez quil a bien dautre dessins une les
personnes quil y employe pour le faire reussir Sachez que vos coeurs
ne sont pas suffisants pour annoncer icy les louanges
quil y pretend recevoir mais quil les multiplira
remplissant de peuple toutes ces contrées de ces lieux
dou maintenant nous prenons la possession de sa
part en luy offrant ce sacrifice: toute cette journée

Bibliothèque Mazarine, Paris, France:
Vol. 1963, pp. 33–35.

III

Propaganda and recruiting

In their *Relations* the Jesuits became the propagandists for the colony with both the people at court and the future settlers. While hiding neither the difficulties nor the very real dangers which awaited them in Canada, they pointed out to the latter the advantages, also very real, that they would find there.

To meet the pressing needs in manpower, recourse was had to the system of indenturing, usually for a period of three years. On 9 April 1643, for example, Olivier Le Tardif, the chief clerk of the Cent-Associés, signed a contract at La Rochelle with Jacques Ragot, who undertook to enter the service of the Sieur Guillaume Couillard.

Furthermore, the company made grants of immense tracts of land to private individuals in return for the obligation to establish settlers on them. On 15 January 1634 Robert Giffard was granted in this way the seigneury of Beauport on the condition, along with others, that the people whom he would bring to New France would be "credited to the said Company, to reduce the number that it [was] to send out."

The Société Notre-Dame de Montréal contributed greatly, still under the régime of the Cent-Associés, to establishing settlers at Ville-Marie (Montréal). The "great contingent" in 1653 in particular – which counted more than a hundred men – gained the reputation of having saved that settlement, which was at grips with the Iroquois.

69

Adiouſtez, s'il vous plaiſt, qu'il y a vne infinité d'artiſans en France, qui faute d'employ, ou faute de poſſeder quelque peu de terre, paſſent leur vie dans vne pauureté, & dans vne diſette pitoyable. Vn tres-grand nombre vont mandier leur pain de porte en porte: pluſieurs ſe iettent dedans les vols & dans les brigandages publics; d'autres dans les larçins & tromperies ſecrettes, chacun s'efforçant de tirer à ſoy ce que pluſieurs ne ſçauroient poſſeder. Or comme la Nouuelle France eſt de ſi grande eſtenduë, on y peut enuoyer ſi bon nombre d'habitans, que ceux qui reſteront à l'Ancienne auront dequoy employer leur induſtrie honneſtement, ſans ſe ietter dans des vices qui perdent les Republiques;

Paul Le Jeune. *Relation de ce qvi s'est passé en la Novvelle France en l'année 1635....* Paris: Chez Sébastien Cramoisy, 1636, p. 54.

In their *Relations* the Jesuits became propagandists for settlement of the colony: "There are a great number of craftsmen in France who for lack of work or for lack of owning a little land spend their life in pitiful poverty and want.... Now, as New France is of such great size, such a large number of settlers can be sent there that those who remain in Old France will be able to employ their skill honourably."

Bibliothèque de la ville de Montréal, Salle Gagnon, Montréal.

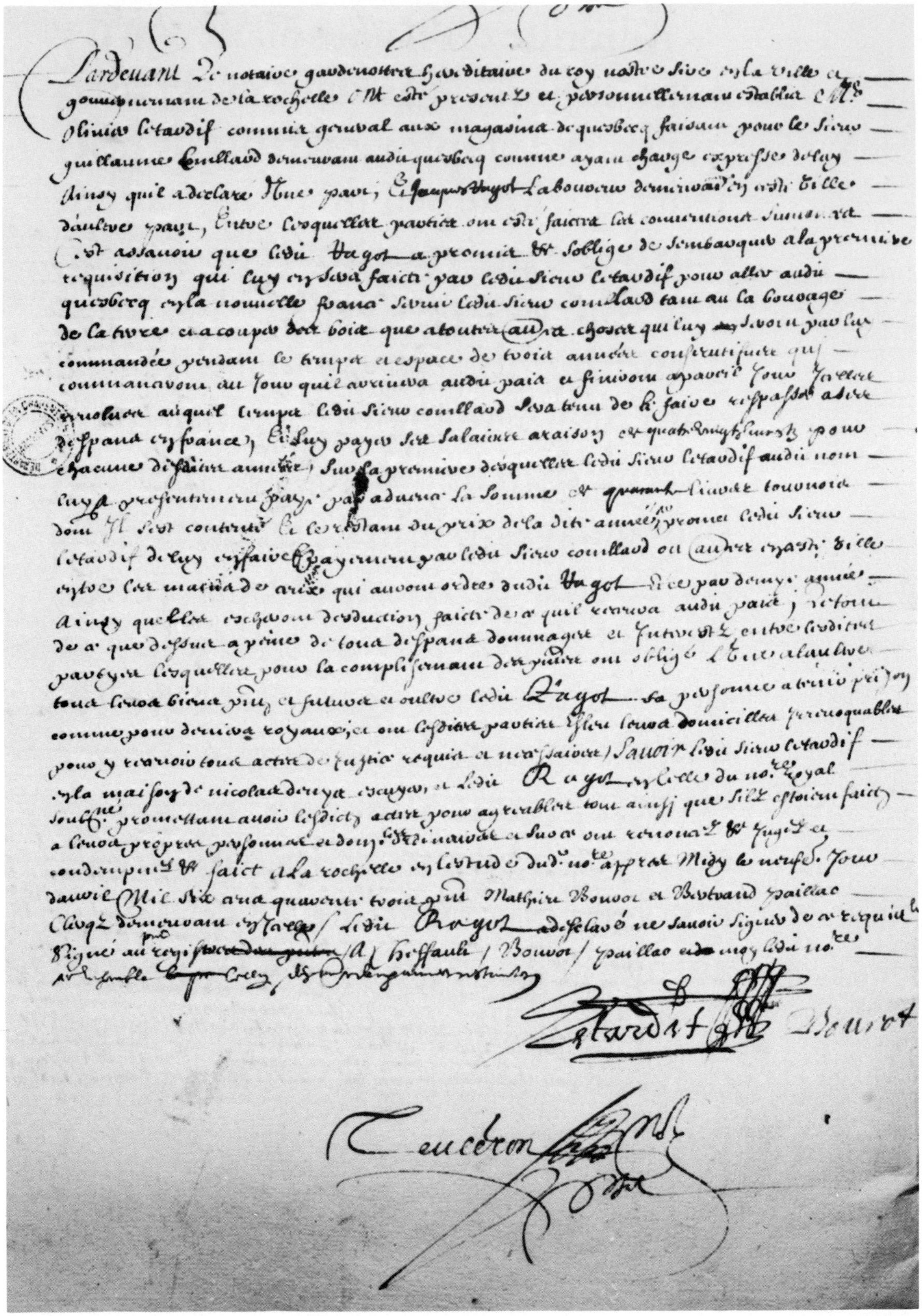

Contract by which Olivier Le Tardif hired Jacques Ragot, La Rochelle, 9 April 1643.

Ragot contracted "to go to the aforesaid Québec in New France to serve the aforesaid Sieur Couillard in ploughing land and cutting wood as well as in all other things that he will be ordered to do for the period of three consecutive years."

Several of these indentured employees decided to settle in the colony once their contract was ended.

Archives départementales de la Charente-Maritime, La Rochelle, France: Série E, minutes du notaire Teuleron, registre 1643–1644, fol. 46v.

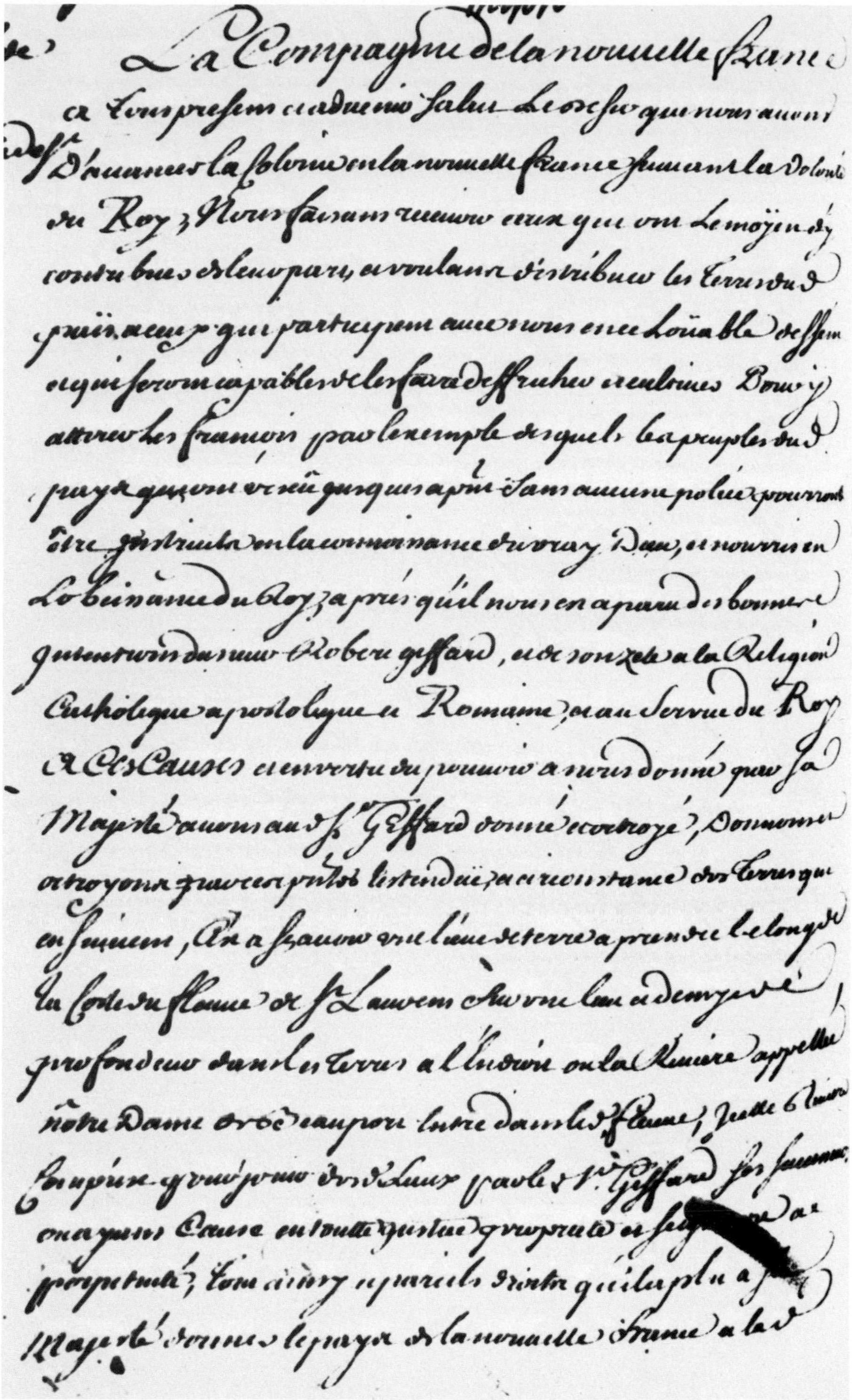

La Compagnie de la nouvelle france
a tous presens et advenir Salut. Le soing que nous avons
d'avancer la Colonie en la nouvelle france suivant la volonté
du Roy, Nous faisant recevoir ceux qui ont le moyen d'y
contribuer de leur part, et voulant distribuer les terres du
pais à ceux qui participent avec nous en ce louable dessein
et qui seront capables de les faire deffricher et cultiver pour y
attirer les François par l'exemple desquels les peuples du
pays qui ont vescu jusques à present sans aucune police pourront
estre instruits en la connoissance du vray Dieu, et nourris en
l'obeissance du Roy, après qu'il nous en a paru des bonnes
qualitez du sieur Robert giffard, et de son zele à la Religion
Catholique apostolique et Romaine, et au service du Roy
A ces causes et en vertu du pouvoir à nous donné par sa
Majesté avons au d. Sr Giffard donné et octroyé, donnons et
octroyons par ces presentes l'estendue et circonstance des terres qui
ensuivent, c'est à scavoir une lieue de terre à prendre le long de
la coste du fleuve de St Laurent sur une lieue et demye de
profondeur dans les terres à l'endroit où la Riviere appellée
Notre Dame de Beauport entre dans le d. fleuve, jusques à la riviere
Comprise, pour jouir de ladite lieue par le d. Sr Giffard ses successeurs
ou ayans cause en toute justice propriété et seigneurie [illegible] à
perpetuité, tout ainsy et pareils droits qu'il a plu à sa
Majesté donner le pays de la nouvelle france à la d.

Act from the Compagnie de la Nouvelle-France granting the seigneury of Beauport to Robert Giffard, Paris, 15 January 1634.

This company granted vast tracts of land to private individuals in exchange for the obligation to bring in settlers for them. Giffard, who was the first colonizing seigneur in New France, was also the promoter of immigration from the Perche, France, to Canada.

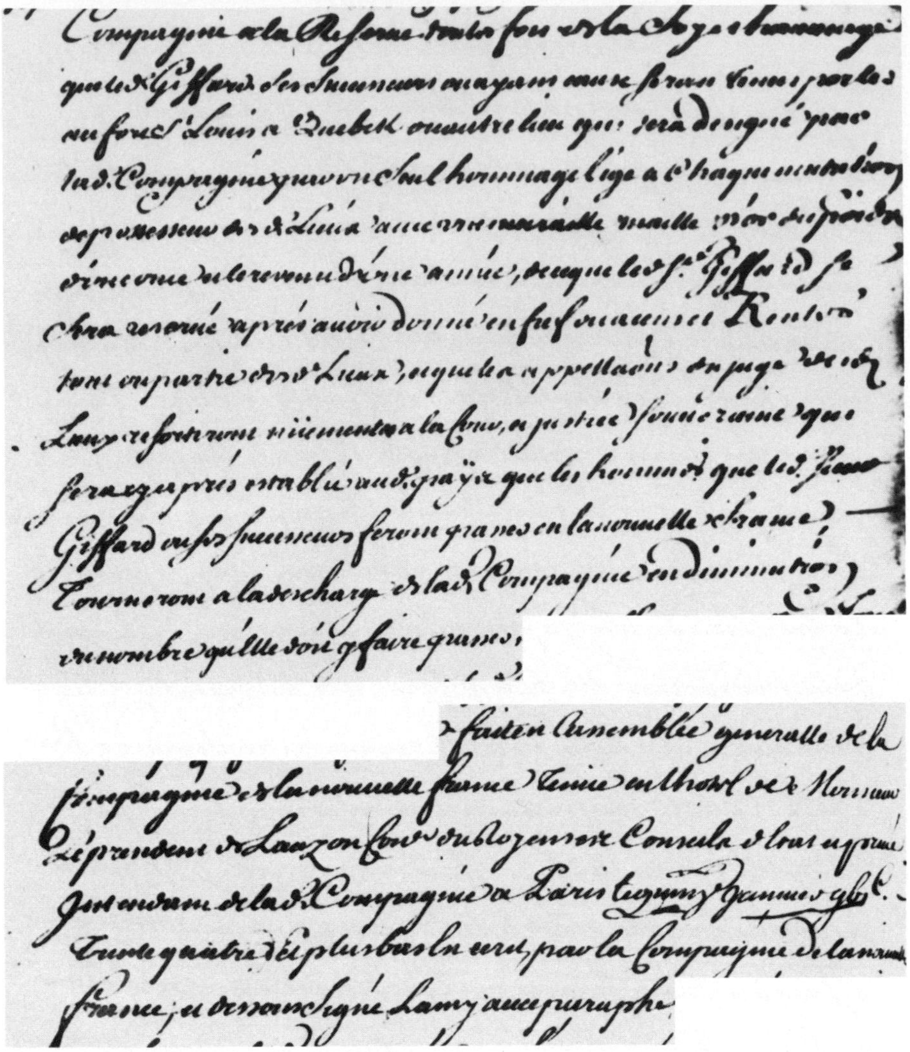

Compagnie de la Reserve toutes fois de la foy et hommage que led. Giffard ses successeurs ou ayans cause seront tenus porter au fort St Louis a Quebecq ou autre lieu qui sera designé par lad. Compagnie qui sont seul hommage lige a chaque mutation de possesseur dud. lieu avec une maille d'or du poids d'une once et le revenu d'une année, ce que led. Sr. Giffard sera tenu après avoir donné en fief aucunes rentes tout en partie dud. lieu, et que les appellations du juge dud. lieu ressortiront nuement a la Cour et justice souveraine qui sera cy après establie aud. pays et que les hommes que led. sieur Giffard ou ses successeurs feront passer en la nouvelle france tourneront a la descharge de lad. Compagnie en diminution du nombre qu'elle doit y faire passer.

… faite en l'assemblée generalle de la Compagnie de la nouvelle france tenue en l'hostel de Monsieur le president de Lauzon Conr du Roy en ses Conseils d'estat et premier Intendant de lad. Compagnie a Paris le quinziesme Janvier gbic trente quatre et plus bas est escrit, par la Compagnie de la nouvelle france, et de rechef signé Lamy avec paraphe.

Archives nationales du Québec, Centre d'archives de la Capitale, Québec: Cahier d'intendance, no 2, fol. 655.

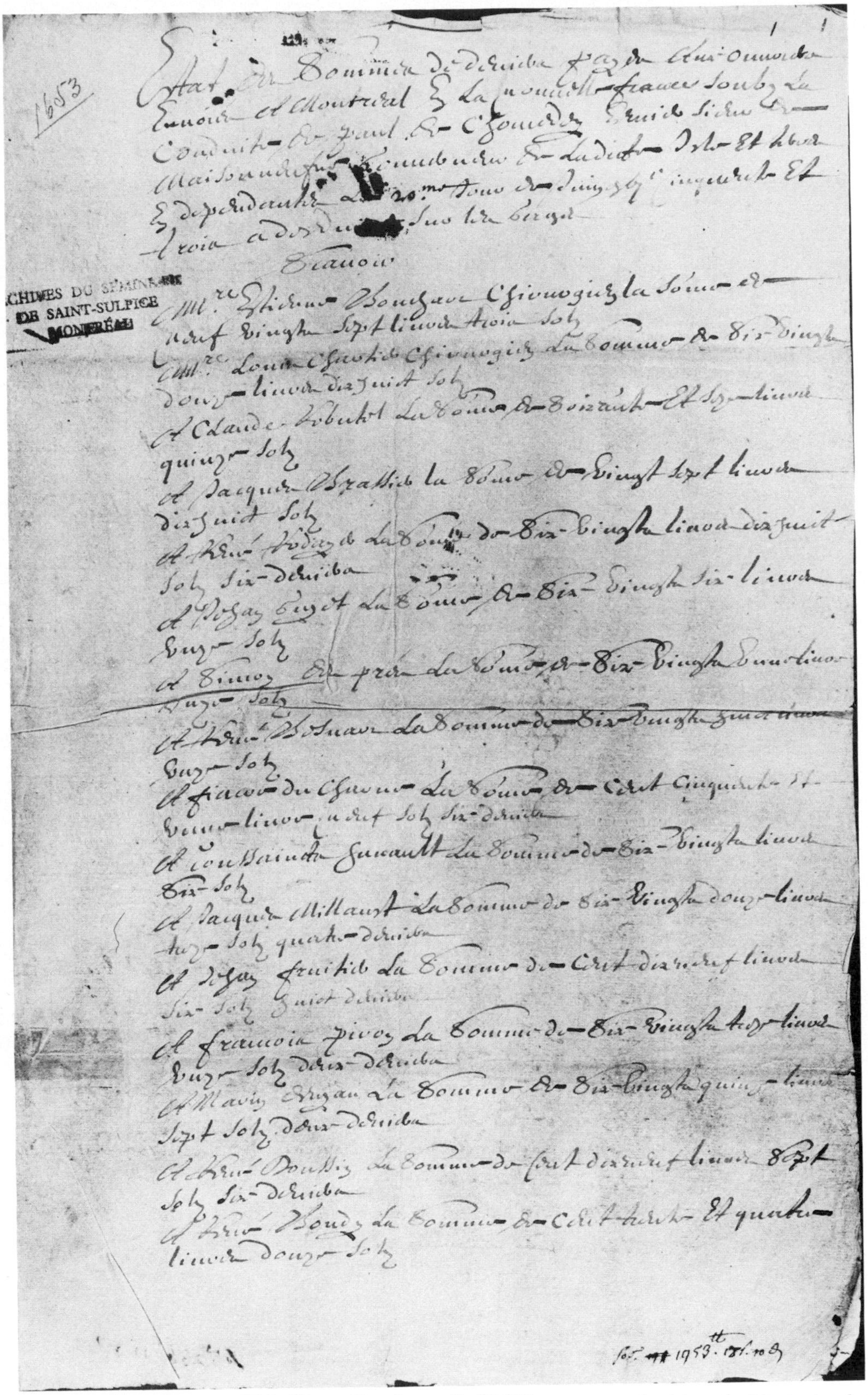

Statements of the amounts paid to the recruits sent to Montréal from France under Maisonneuve's leadership, 20 June 1653.

This "Great Contingent" of 1653, comprising more than a hundred persons, acquired the reputation of having saved Montréal, which was fighting against the Iroquois.

Archives du Séminaire de Saint-Sulpice, Montréal.

Gallia. Nova totius Galliae geographica descriptio..., Amsterdam, 1600; Jodocus Hondius; map printed from copperplate, hand col.; 50 x 38 cm.

The majority of the settlers in New France in the seventeenth century came from the French provinces of Normandy, Brittany, Poitou, Aunis, and Saintonge.

Bibliothèque nationale, Paris, France: Ge DD 627 (I).

III

Immigration and a plan for frenchification

In 1636 the first large group of immigrants arrived at Québec; two families alone, the Repentignys and the La Poteries, counted forty-five persons.

In reality many more unmarried men – indentured servants, clerks, or soldiers – came to New France than did families. Consequently, thought had to be given to sending girls of marriageable age (filles du roi) to the colony. In the summer of 1666, for example, 90 of them arrived; by mid-November 84 of them were married. Similarly in 1669, 102 of the girls who arrived in the summer had found husbands by mid-November. Men and families were also sent out, which sometimes caused Intendant Talon problems.

Several of the filles du roi married officers and men of the Carignan-Salières regiment, who had decided in large numbers to settle down in Canada, much to the king's satisfaction.

Around the same time the king and Colbert strongly urged the civil and religious authorities in New France to frenchify the Indians, especially the Hurons and Algonkins, "so that in due course of time, having the same laws and the same masters," French and Indians "may become only one people and one race." This project failed, so much so that it was the Indians who won the French over to their way of life.

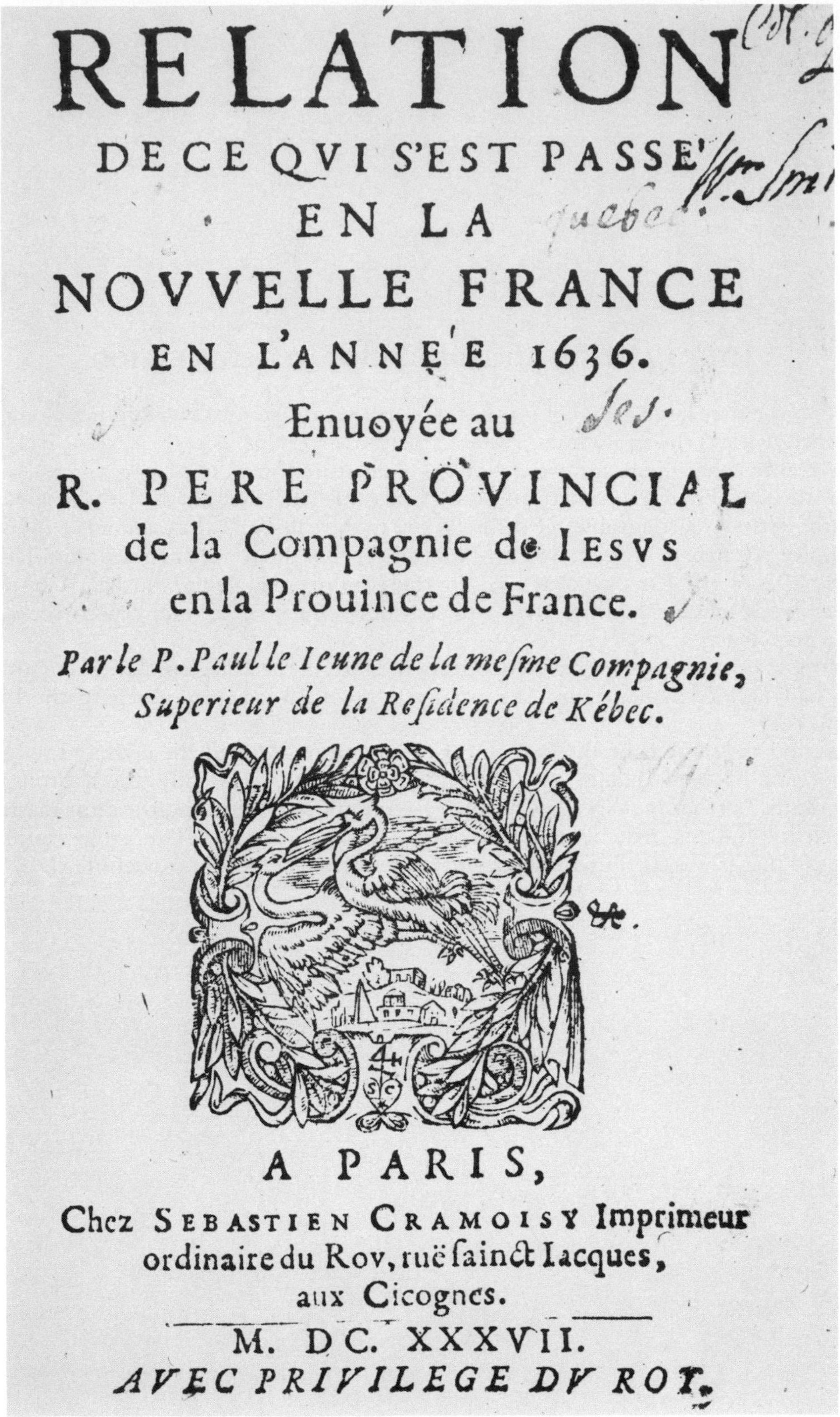
RELATION
DE CE QVI S'EST PASSE'
EN LA
NOVVELLE FRANCE
EN L'ANNE'E 1636.
Enuoyée au
R. PERE PROVINCIAL
de la Compagnie de IESVS
en la Prouince de France.
Par le P. Paul le Ieune de la mesme Compagnie, Superieur de la Residence de Kébec.

A PARIS,
Chez SEBASTIEN CRAMOISY Imprimeur
ordinaire du Roy, ruë sainct Iacques,
aux Cicognes.

M. DC. XXXVII.
AVEC PRIVILEGE DV ROY.

Paul Le Jeune. *Relation de ce qvi s'est passé en la Novvelle France en l'année 1636....* Paris: Chez Sébastien Cramoisy, 1637, title page, pp. 6–7.

The arrival of the first large group of immigrants spread joy in the colony: "It was a reason to praise God, to see very dainty young ladies, little children in their tender youth, in these regions."

ce meſme iour parut vn Vaiſſeau commandé par Monſieur de Courpon, qui nous rendit le P. Nicolas Adam, & noſtre Frere Ambroiſe Cauuet. Ces entreueuës en vn païs ſi éloigné de noſtre Patrie, apres auoir trauerſé tant de mers, ſont ſenſibles par fois aux yeux, auſſi bien qu'au cœur. Noſtre ioye ne ſe tint pas-là, la quantité de familles qui venoient groſſir noſtre Colonie, l'accreut notablement; celles entre autres de Monſieur de Repentigny, & de Monſieur de la Poterie, braues Gentilshommes, compoſées de quarante cinq perſonnes. C'eſtoit vn ſujet où il y auoit à loüer

Dieu, de voir en ces contrées, des Damoiſelles fort delicates, des petits enfans tendrelets ſortir d'vne priſon de bois, comme le iour ſort des tenebres de la nuict, & ioüir apres tout d'vne auſſi douce ſanté, nonobſtant toutes les incommoditez qu'on reçoit dans ces maiſons flotantes, comme ſi on s'eſtoit pourmené au cours dans vn caroſſe. Voila comme ce iour nous fut doublement vn iour de feſte & de réioüiſſance:

Library of Parliament, Ottawa.

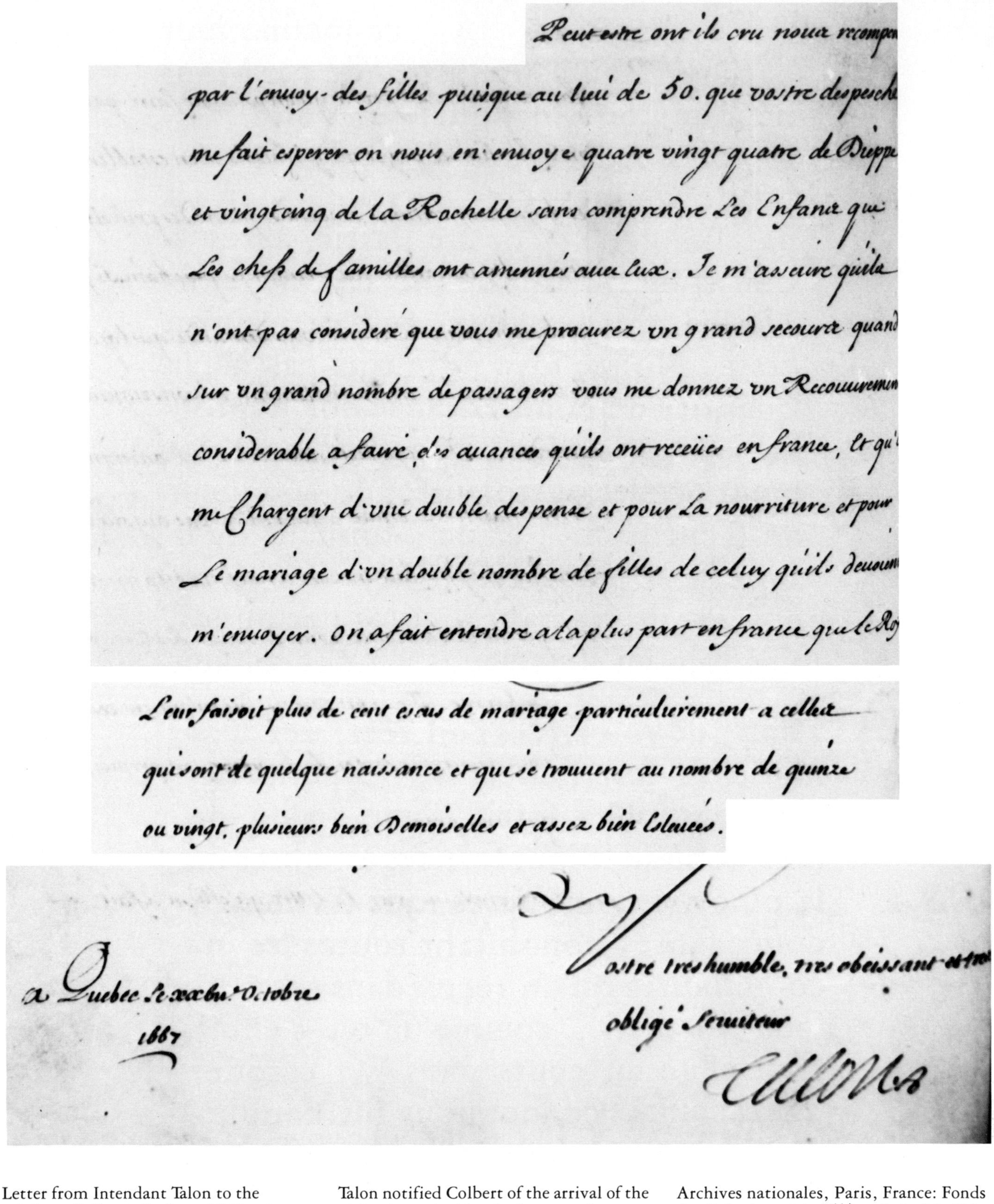

Peut estre ont ils cru nous recompen
par l'envoy des filles puisque au lieu de 50. que vostre despesche
me fait esperer on nous en envoye quatre vingt quatre de Dieppe
et vingtcinq de la Rochelle sans comprendre les Enfans qui
les chefs de familles ont amennés avec eux. Je m'asseure qu'ils
n'ont pas consideré que vous me procurez un grand secours quand
sur un grand nombre de passagers vous me donnez un Recouvremen
considerable a faire des avances qu'ils ont receües en france, et qu'i
me chargent d'une double despense et pour la nourriture et pour
le mariage d'un double nombre de filles de celuy qu'ils devoien
m'envoyer. On a fait entendre a la plus part en france que le Roy
leur faisoit plus de cent escus de mariage particulierement a celles
qui sont de quelque naissance et qui se trouvent au nombre de quinze
ou vingt, plusieurs bien Demoiselles et assez bien Elevées.

A Quebec le xxvii.e Octobre 1667

Vostre treshumble, tres obeissant et tres
obligé Serviteur
Talon

Letter from Intendant Talon to the minister Colbert, Québec, 27 October 1667.

Talon notified Colbert of the arrival of the girls whom the king had sent to the colony to find husbands: "Eighty-four are being sent to us from Dieppe and twenty-five from La Rochelle...several of them definitely young ladies and rather well brought up."

The majority of these "king's daughters" were married shortly after their arrival in Canada.

Archives nationales, Paris, France: Fonds des Colonies, série C^{11A}, vol. 2, fol. 312v–313, 320v.

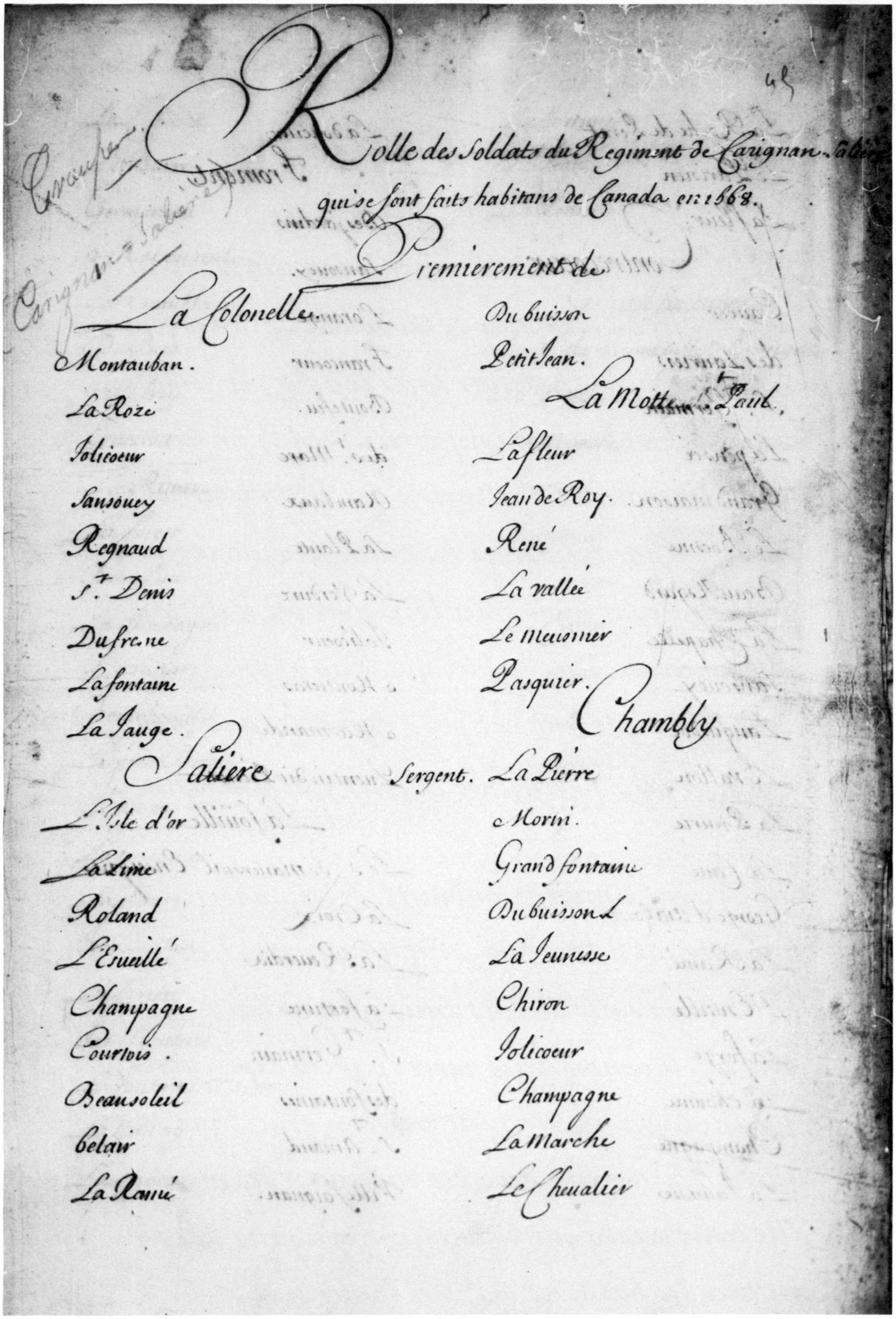

45

Rolle des Soldats du Regiment de Carignan Salières qui se sont faits habitans de Canada en 1668.

Premierement de

La Colonelle

Montauban.
La Rozé
Jolicoeur
Sansoucy
Regnaud
St Denis
Dufresne
Lafontaine
La Jauge.

Salière

L'Isle d'or
La Lime
Roland
L'Esveillé
Champagne
Courtois.
Beausoleil
Belair
La Ramée

Du buisson
Petit Jean.

La Motte St Paul

Lafleur
Jean de Roy.
René
La vallée
Le Meusnier
Pasquier.

Chambly

Sergent. La Pierre
Morin.
Grand fontaine
Dubuisson
La Jeunesse
Chiron
Jolicoeur
Champagne
La Marche
Le Chevalier

List of the soldiers of the Carignan-Salières regiment who became settlers in Canada in 1668.

Hundreds of the soldiers of this regiment decided to settle in the colony. Many married "king's daughters."

Archives nationales, Paris, France: Fonds des Colonies, série D^{2C}, vol. 47.

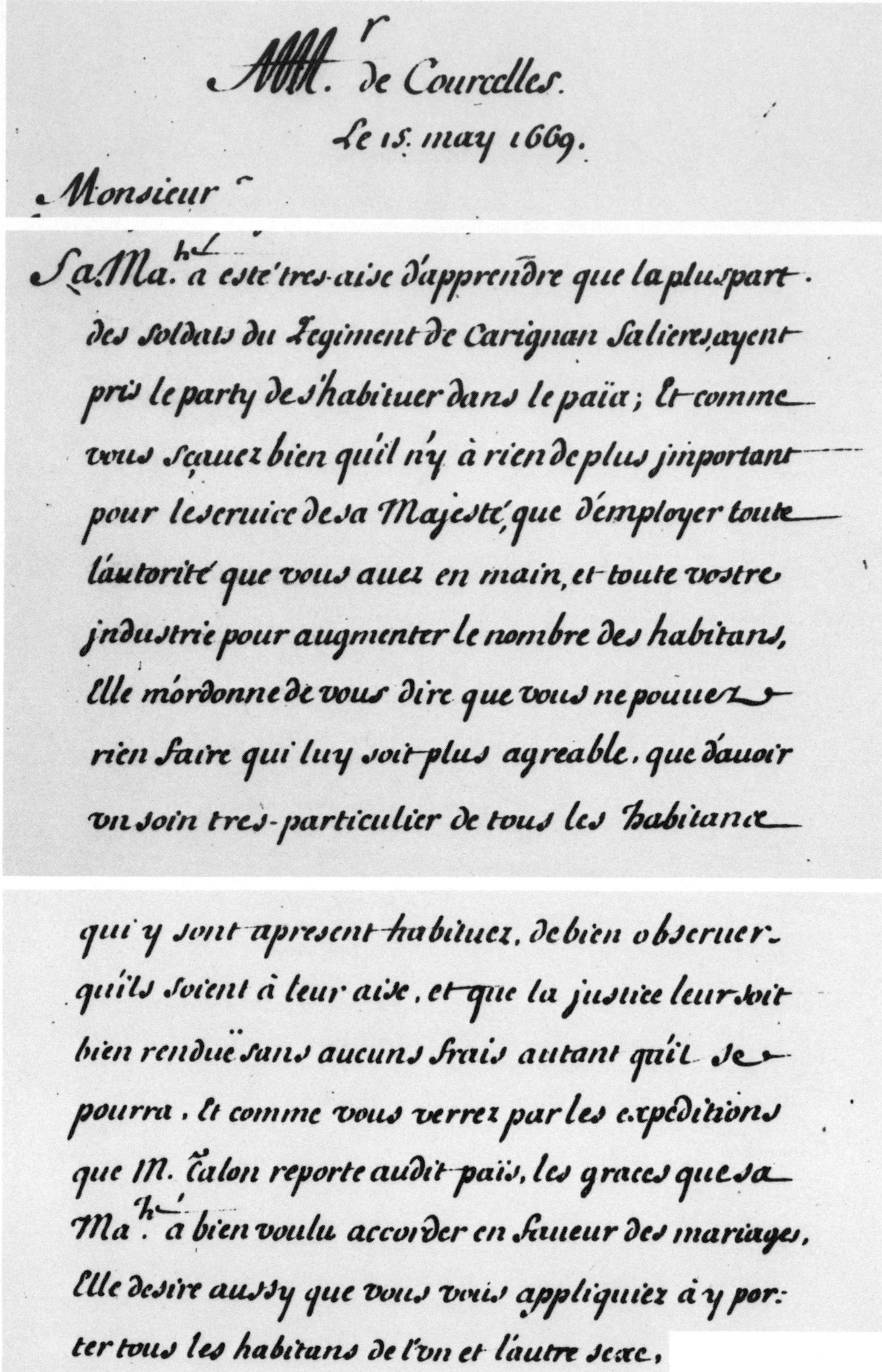

Mr. de Courcelles.
Le 15. may 1669.
Monsieur
Sa Ma.té a esté tres aise d'apprendre que la pluspart
des soldats du Regiment de Carignan Salieres ayent
pris le party de s'habituer dans le païs; Et comme
vous sçauez bien qu'il n'y à rien de plus important
pour le seruice de sa Majesté, que d'employer toute
l'autorité que vous auez en main, et toute vostre
industrie pour augmenter le nombre des habitans,
Elle m'ordonne de vous dire que vous ne pouuez
rien faire qui luy soit plus agreable, que d'auoir
vn soin tres-particulier de tous les habitans
qui y sont apresent habituez, de bien obseruer
qu'ils soient à leur aise, et que la justice leur soit
bien rendüe sans aucuns frais autant qu'il se
pourra. Et comme vous verrez par les expeditions
que M. Talon reporte audit païs, les graces que sa
Ma.té a bien voulu accorder en faueur des mariages,
Elle desire aussy que vous vous appliquiez à y porter tous les habitans de l'vn et l'autre sexe,

Letter from the minister Colbert to Governor General Courcelle, 15 May 1669.

"His Majesty was very pleased to learn that most of the soldiers of the Carignan-Salières regiment have chosen to remain in the country."

Archives nationales, Paris, France: Fonds des Colonies, série B, vol. 1, fol. 141–141v.

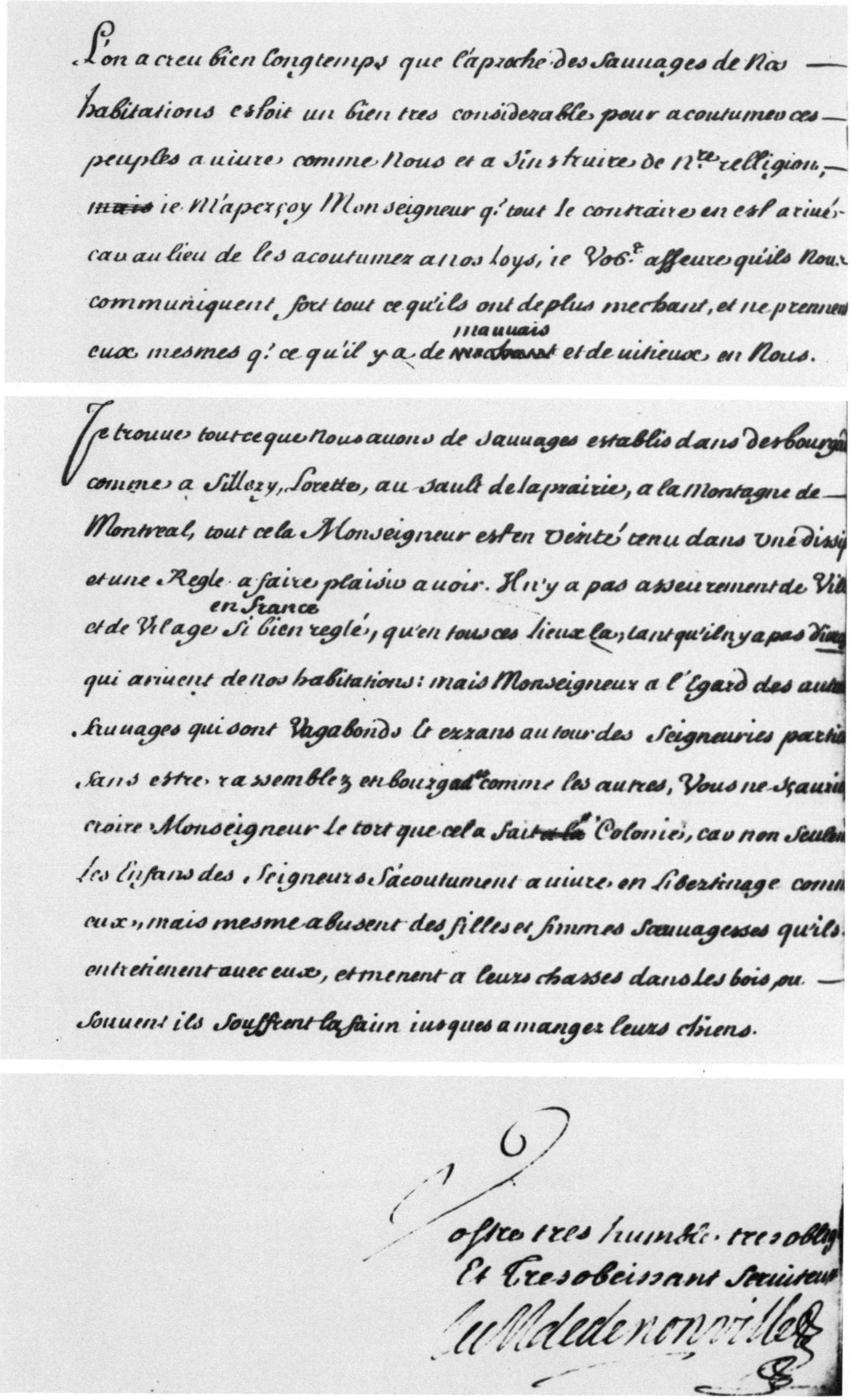

L'on a creu bien longtemps que l'aproche des Sauuages de Nos habitations estoit un bien tres considerable pour acoutumer ces peuples a uiure comme Nous et a s'instruire de N.re relligion, ~~mais~~ ie M'apercoy Monseigneur q. tout le contraire en est arivé car au lieu de les acoutumer a nos loys, ie Vo.s asseure quils Nous communiquent fort tout ce qu'ils ont de plus mechant, et ne prennent eux mesmes q. ce qu'il y a de ~~mechant~~ mauuais et de uitieux en Nous.

Je trouue tout ce que Nous auons de Sauuages establis dans des bourga[des] comme a Sillery, Lorette, au Sault de la prairie, a la Montagne de Montreal, tout cela Monseigneur est en verité tenu dans une dissi[pline] et une Regle a faire plaisir a uoir. Il n'y a pas asseurement de Vil[le] en France et de Vilage si bien reglé, qu'en tous ces lieux la, tant qu'il n'y a pas d'iu[rognes] qui arivent de nos habitations: mais Monseigneur a l'Egard des aut[res] Sauuages qui sont Vagabonds et errans au tour des Seigneuries parti[culières] sans estre rassemblez en bourgad.es comme les autres, Vous ne sçauri[ez] croire Monseigneur le tort que cela fait ~~a la~~ Colonies, car non seulem[ent] les Enfans des Seigneurs s'acoutument a uiure en libertinage comm[e] eux, mais mesme abusent des filles et femmes Sauuagesses quils entretienent auec eux, et menent a leurs chasses dans les bois ou souuent ils souffrent la faim iusques a manger leurs chiens.

Vostre tres humble, tres oblig[é]
Et Tresobeissant Serviteur
Le M. de denonville

Letter from Governor General Denonville to the Marquis de Seignelay, the minister of Marine, Québec, 13 November 1685.

Denonville explained that they were having no success in "frenchifying" the Indians as the French authorities wanted: "Instead of accustoming them to our laws, I assure you that they pass on to us to a great degree what is most malicious in them and take themselves only what is bad and vicious in us."

Archives nationales, Paris, France: Fonds des Colonies, série C[11A], vol. 7, fol. 90v, 106v.

The Indians Settle at La Prairie de la Magdeleine Alongside the French; Father Claude Chauchetière (1645–1709); brown ink; 20 x 15.7 cm., from the manuscript "Narration annuelle de la mission du Sault depuis sa fondation jusques à l'an 1686" (1667–86).

With the aim of familiarizing the Indians with French customs and encouraging their conversion to Christianity, the Jesuits set up a mission in 1667 at Laprairie where Indians (especially Iroquois) and French would live together for a few years.

Archives départementales de la Gironde, Bordeaux, France.

At Work in the Fields; Father Claude Chauchetière (1645–1709); brown ink; 20 x 15.7 cm.; from the manuscript "Narration annuelle de la mission du Sault depuis sa fondation jusques à l'an 1686" (1667–86).

Archives départementales de la Gironde, Bordeaux, France.

III

A mode of settlement

From the beginnings of the colony a mode of settlement was adopted, the seigneurial régime, which was inspired by the French feudal system, but without its abuses, and adapted to Canada. Of the feudal system several principles of jurisprudence were retained, as were part of the vocabulary and a certain ceremonial, such as the rendering of "faith and homage," through which the seigneur, "being without a sword, bareheaded and one knee on the ground," declared himself to be the vassal of the king or of another seigneur whom he recognized as his suzerain.

Similarly the seigneur had regularly to present to the intendant (or to the company's representative) a "recognition of sovereignty and census" ("aveu et dénombrement") of his seigneury, in which he declared for each of his copyholders his land titles, the *cens et rentes* to be paid, the number of arpents cleared and cultivated and the number of buildings (house and outbuildings) on his land.

The seigneur could retain his seigneury only if he established settlers on it, to whom he made a "concession" of land, generally through a notarial deed; for their part the settlers were assured ownership of their land only if they cleared and worked it and took up residence on it.

In the seventeenth century the seigneurial régime proved to be very effective. As early as 1641, for example, the Côte de Beaupré (from Montmorency Falls to Cap Tourmente) counted a good number of pieces of land that had been given in concession and of habitants who were living there.

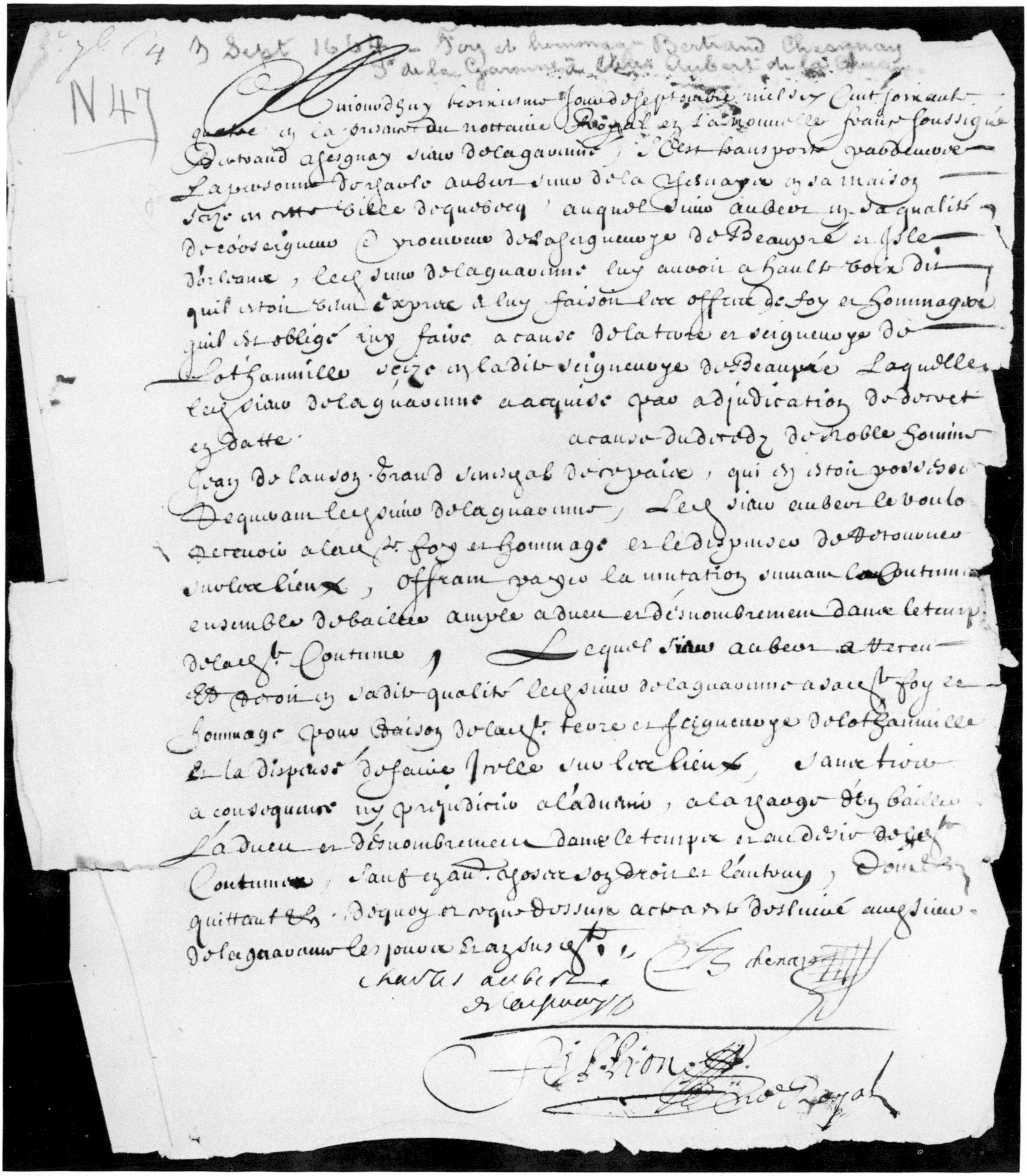

Oath of fealty and act of homage by Bertrand Chenaye, Sieur de La Garenne, to Charles Aubert de La Chesnaye for his fief of Lothainville, Québec, 3 September 1664.

Every seigneur was required to perform the oath of fealty and act of homage by which, "without a sword, bareheaded and on one knee," he declared himself to be vassal of the king or of another seigneur whom he recognized as his suzerain.

Archives nationales du Québec, Centre d'archives de la Capitale, Québec: Minutier de Michel Fillion, pièce 47.

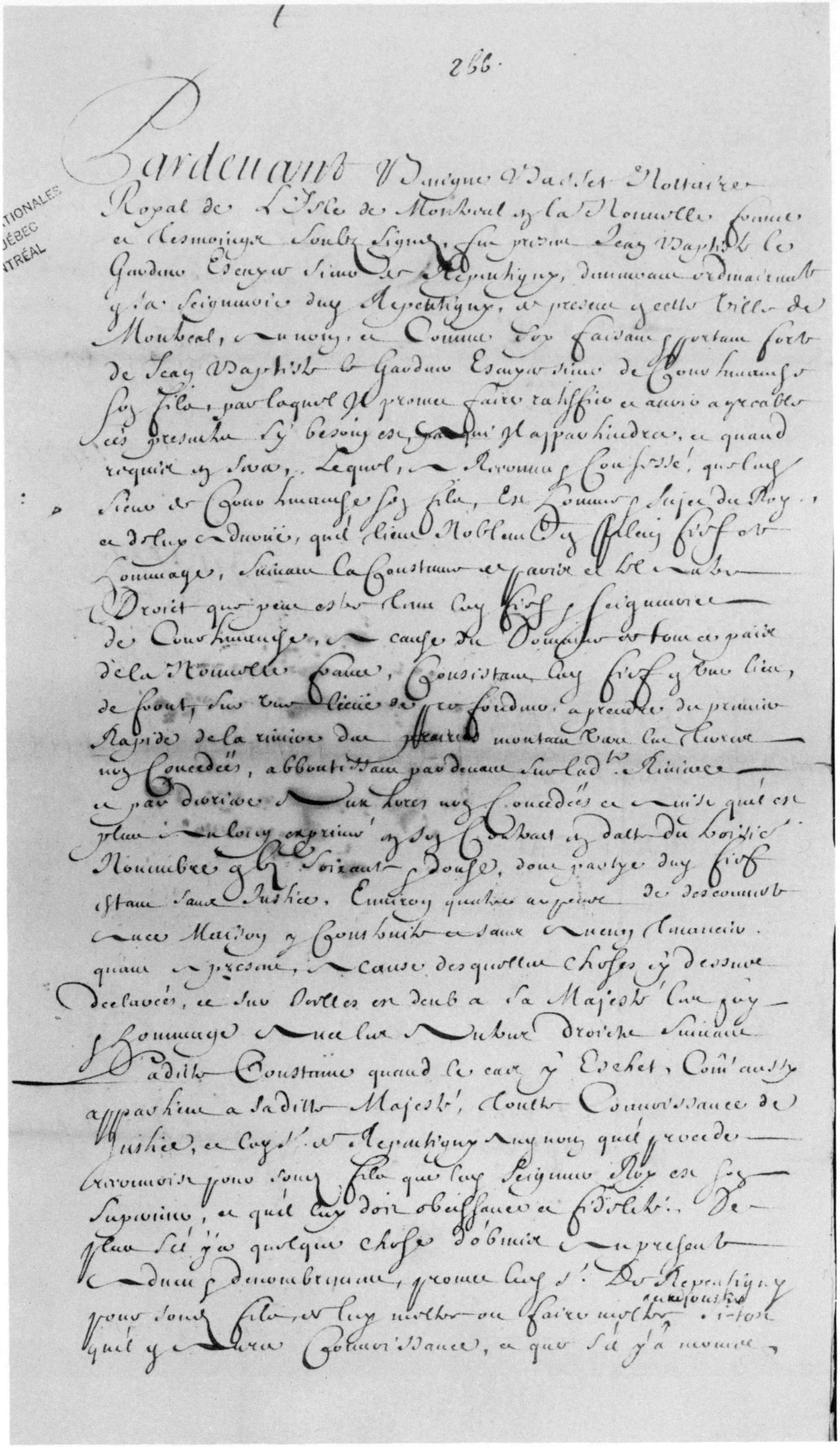

256.

Pardevant Benigne Basset Nottaire Royal de L'Isle de Montreal en la Nouvelle France et tesmoings soubz signez, fut present Jean Baptiste le Gardeur Escuyer sieur de Repentigny, demeurant ordinairement en la Seigneurie dud. Repentigny, et presentement en cette ville de Montreal, au nom et comme soy faisant et portant fort de Jean Baptiste le Gardeur Escuyer sieur de Courtemanche son fils, par lequel il promet faire ratiffier et avoir agreable ces presentes sy besoing est, quand il appartiendra, et quand requis en sera, Lequel a recognu confessé que led. sieur de Courtemanche son fils, est homme sujet du Roy et de luy advoüe, quil tient noblement en fief foy et hommage, suivant la Coustume de paris et les droicts que peut estre dans un fief et seigneurie de Courtemanche, a cause du Domaine de tout ce paiis de la Nouvelle France, Consistant en un fief d'une lieue de front, sur une lieue et demie de profondeur, a prendre du premier Rapide de la riviere des prairies montant vers les terres non concedées, aboutissant par devant sur lad. Riviere et par derriere aux terres non concedées et ainsi quil est plus amplement exprimé au contract en datte du [illegible] Novembre mil six cent soixante douze, dont partye dud. fief estant sans Justice. Environ quatre arpens de desert [illegible] avec Maison et bastiments [illegible] quant a present, a cause desquelles choses cy dessus declarées, et [illegible] est deub a Sa Majesté une foy et hommage avec les autres droicts suivant ladite Coustume quand le cas y escheet, Com. aussy appartient a Sadite Majesté toute connoissance de Justice, et led. sr de Repentigny au nom quil procede recognoist pour son fils que le Seigneur Roy est son souverain, et quil luy doit obeissance et fidelité. De plus sil y a quelque chose d'obmis au present denombrement, promet led. sr de Repentigny pour son fils et luy mettre ou faire mettre aussitost quil en aura connoissance, et que sil y a [illegible]

Recognition of sovereignty and census by Jean-Baptiste Legardeur de Repentigny for the fief of Courtemanche, Montréal, 15 September 1677.

The seigneur was required to submit to the intendant a recognition of sovereignty and census of his fief with a description of each of the pieces of land granted and the names of the copyholders and number of arpents that were cleared and under cultivation.

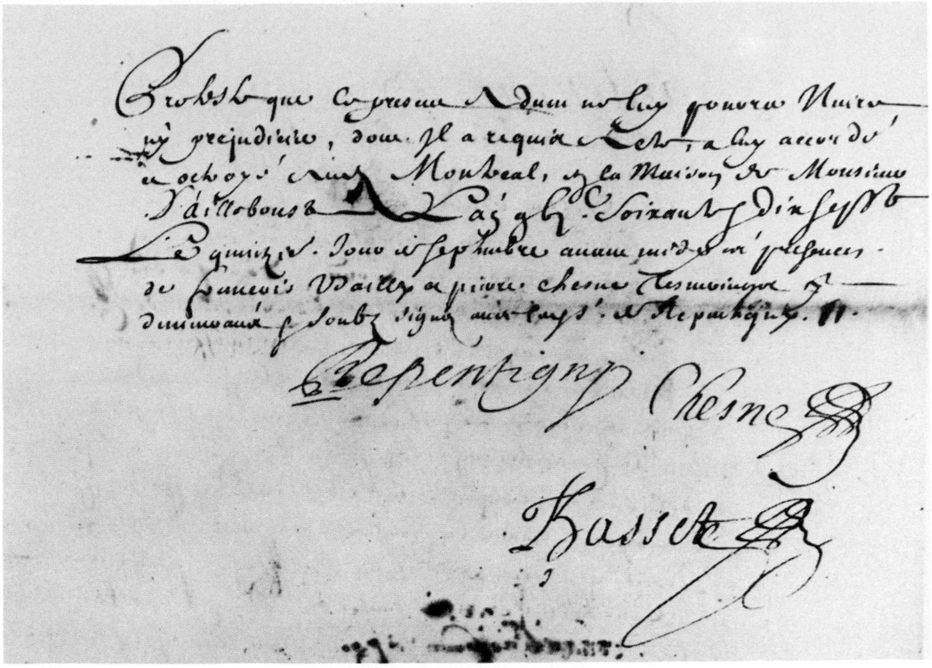
Repentigny
Chesne
Basset

Archives nationales du Québec, Centre régional de Montréal, Montréal: Minutier de Bénigne Basset, pièce 1438.

~ 83 ~

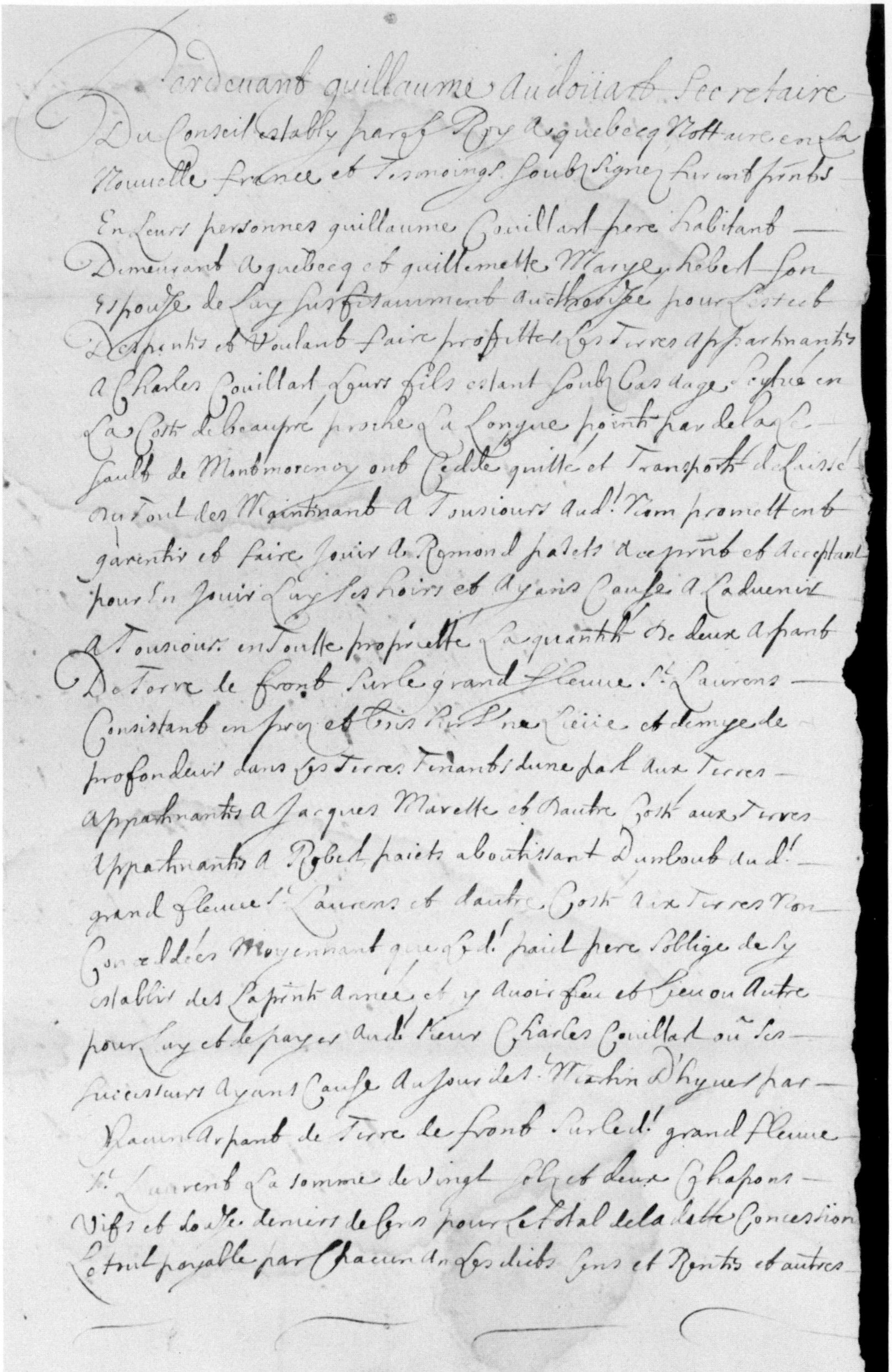
Pardevant guillaume Audouart Secretaire
du Conseil estably par le Roy a quebecq Nottaire en la
Nouvelle france et tesmoings soubsignez furent presens
En leurs personnes guillaume Couillart pere habitant
Demeurant a quebecq et guillemette Marye hebert son
espouse de luy suffisamment authorisée pour l'effect
des presentes et voulant faire proffitter les terres appartenantes
a Charles Couillart leurs fils estant soubs l'aage scituée en
la coste de beaupré proche la Longue pointe par dela le
sault de Montmorency ont Cedde quitte et transporté delaissé
du tout des maintenant a tousiours aud. nom promettent
garentir et faire jouir a Raymond paiets a ce present et acceptant
pour en jouir luy ses hoirs et ayans cause a ladvenir
a tousiours en toutte proprietté la quantité de deux arpans
de terre de front sur le grand fleuve St Laurens
Consistant en [illegible] lieüe et demye de
profondeur dans les terres tenans dune part aux terres
appartenantes a Jacques Marette et d'autre costé aux terres
appartenantes a Robert paiets aboutissant d'un bout aud.
grand fleuve St Laurens et d'autre costé aux terres non
concedées Moyennant que led. paiet pere s'oblige de s'y
establir des la presente année et y avoir feu et lieu ou autre
pour luy et de payer aud. sieur Charles Couillart ou ses
successeurs ayans cause au jour de St Martin d'hyver par
chacun arpant de terre de front sur led. grand fleuve
St Laurent la somme de vingt sols et deux chapons
vifs et douze deniers de cens pour l'estal de la dite concession
le tout payable par chacun an les dicts cens et rentes et autres

Land grant by Guillaume Couillard and his wife to Raymond Paget, Québec, 3 April 1661.

Paget "binds himself to settle there this year and to take up residence there or have someone else do so in his place."

Each settler was assured of keeping his land only if he cultivated it and took up residence on it.

Redebuances deubs aux dicts Seigneurs de Beaupré selon que Led.
Ceddant est Obligé par Le Tiltre de Concession a luy donne et
Outre plus Led. preneur Sera Teneu en faveur de la ditte
Remise de donner par chacun An aud. Ceddant Luy Ses hoirs
ou Ayans Cause a Ladvenir deux Chapons Vifs Lesquels
Chapons tant deubs auxd. its Seigneurs que autres Cens et
Rentes Seigneurialles Led. preneur Soblige Jceux payer et bailler
Aud. Ceddant en sa Maison de quebecq ou Autre Lieu qui Luy
Sera designe au Jour et feste de St. Martin d'hyver par chacun
An Ne pourra Led. preneur faire Chasse ny pesche que Sur
La ditte Concession Sy Ce n'est du gre et Consentement de ses
Voysins A La Charge de Laisser Les Chemins qui Seront
Jugez Necessaires par Les officiers Sera Teneu et Obligé
Led. preneur faire Mouldre Ses grains au Moulin des
dits Seigneurs de Beaupré ainsy que Led. Ceddant est
Obligé Les prez Le Long dud. fleuve Seront Communs Sinon
que Led. preneur Les pourra faire faucher au preiudice de
tous Autres et pour eviter a procest differends Entretenir
paix et Amytye entre ses Voysins Led. preneur Soblige
de Clorre ses Terres au fur et A Mesure qu'il Les desertira
et A faulte de Ce faire Il ne pourra prestendre aucun
dommage ny Jnterrests pour les delicts que pourroyent
faire Les bestiaulx de ses Voysins pour en Jouir par Led.
preneur ses hoirs et ayans Cause a Ladvenir des dittes Terres
Cy dessus Mentionné en toutte propriette faire et disposer
ainsy que bon Luy semblera Luy ses hoirs et ayans
Cause promettants &c. obligeant &c. Chacun endroict Soy
&c. Renonceants &c. faict et passe a quebecq en La Maison

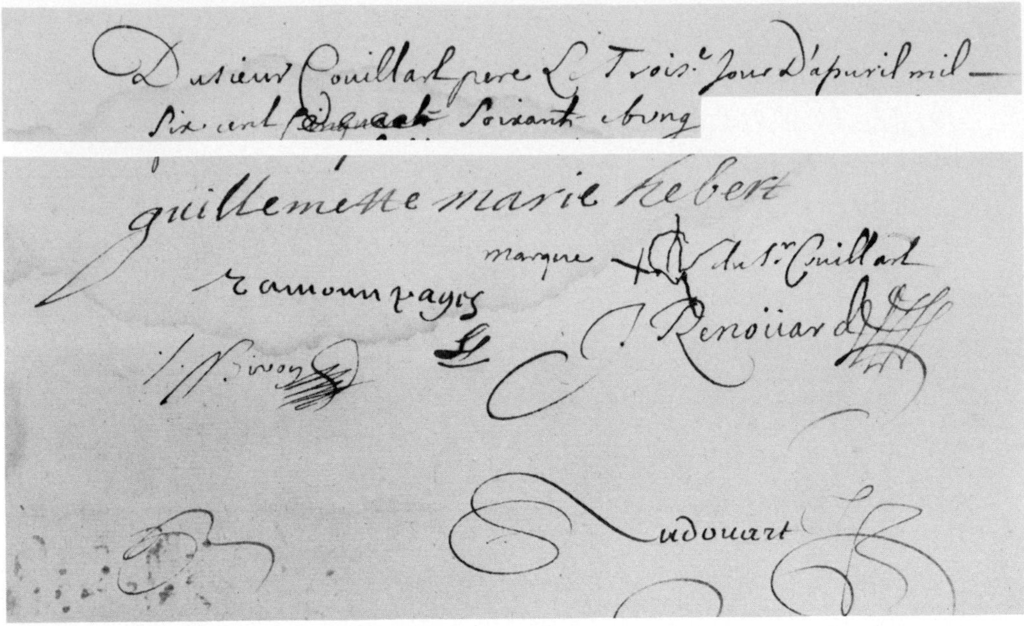
Du sieur Couillart pere Le Trois.e Jour d'apuril mil
Six cent Soixante cinq
guillemette marie hebert
marque du Sr Couillart
ramoun payes
J. Renouard
Audouart

Archives nationales du Québec, Centre d'archives de la Capitale, Québec: Minutier de Guillaume Audouart, pièce 990.

84

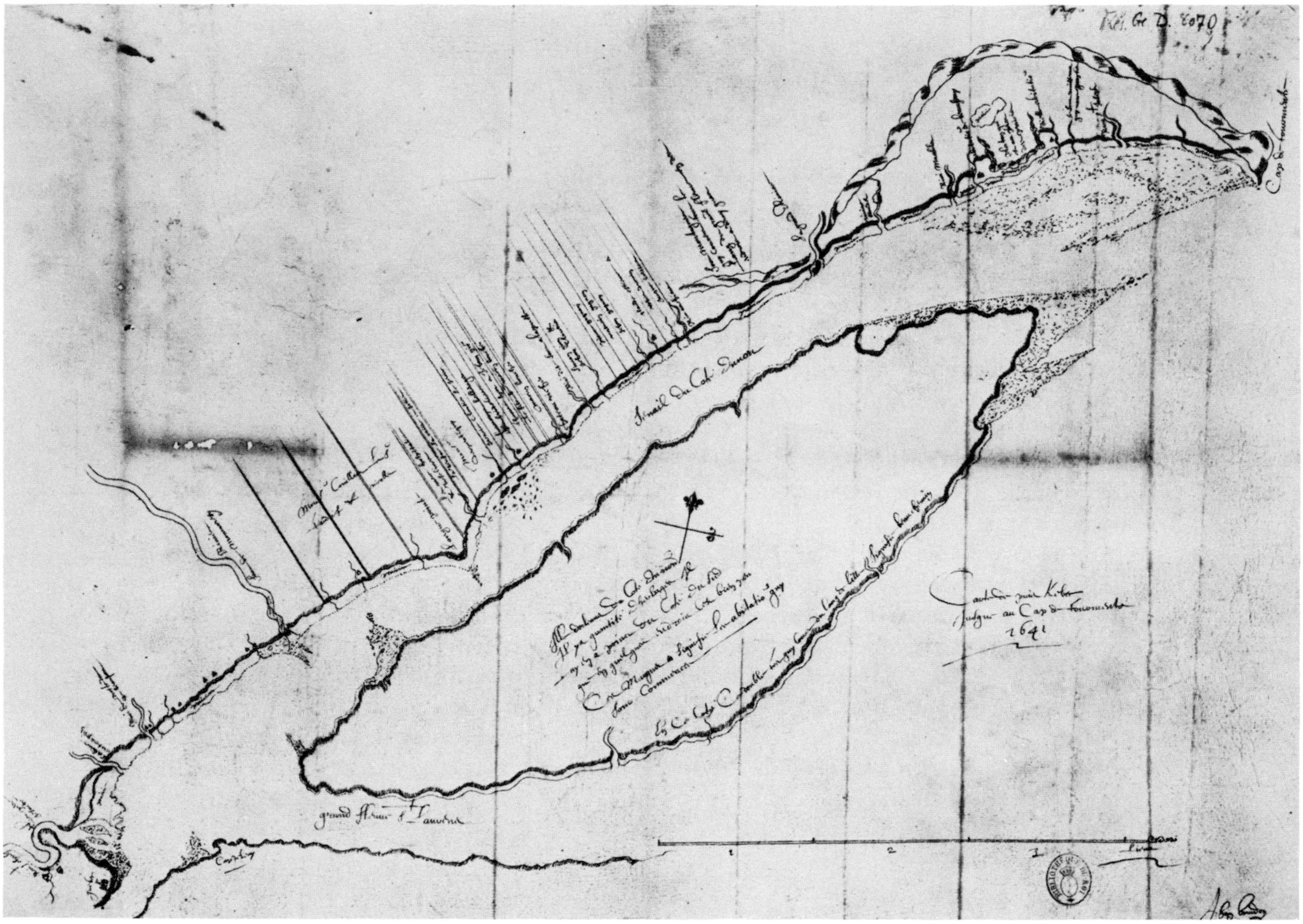

"Carte depuis Kebec jusques au Cap de Tourmente 1641"; Jehan Bourdon; ms.; 39 x 28.3 cm.

This map of the region between Québec and Cap Tourmente mentions the names of the settlers on the Côte de Beaupré. It was in the vicinity of Québec that the first seigneuries (Notre-Dame-des-Anges, Beauport, and Côte de Beaupré) began to develop in the first half of the seventeenth century.

Bibliothèque nationale, Département des cartes et plans, Paris, France: Portefeuille 200, pièce 5233.

Incentives and punitive measures

In 1669 the king's council of State adopted a series of measures: a yearly allocation of three hundred livres to the parents of ten children and four hundred to the parents of twelve; a gift of twenty livres on their wedding day to young men under twenty-one years of age; honours to be paid to the habitants who had the largest number of children; but also fines "against fathers who [did] not marry their children at twenty years of age for the boys and sixteen for the girls."

Since not all the unmarried men felt like getting married so early, Talon issued an ordinance in 1671 forbidding the recalcitrants "the enjoyment of the right to hunt and fish and trade with the Indians and even to go into the Woods." They either had to get married or starve to death!

But how many obstacles had had to be overcome and would still have to be overcome to populate the colony! The Iroquois war had greatly delayed the creation of the seigneuries; once peace had returned, it was the life in the woods that kept the soundest elements among the young men from getting married and working the land.

And then the king himself, as Colbert declared, did not intend "to depopulate his kingdom...to people Canada." From 1672 on that became quite clear; all immigration activity suddenly ceased. This was in the same year that Frontenac was writing of the town of Québec that it could not be better situated "when it should one day become the capital of a great empire..."

Sadite Majesté estant en son
Con.el a ordonné et ordonne qu'a l'avenir tous
les habitans dud. pays qui auront jusques au
nombre de dix enfans vivans nez en legitime
mariage, non prestres, Religieux, ny Religieuses
seront payez des deniers que sa Ma.té envoyera
aud. pays d'une pension de trois cens livres
par chacun an, et ceux qui en auront douze de
quatre cens livres,

Veut de plus Sad. Ma.té qu'il soit payé par les
ordres dud. Intendant a tous les garçons qui se
marieront a vingt ans et au dessoubs vingt
livres pour chacun le jour de leurs nopces ce
qui sera appellé le present du Roy.

Decree from the king's council of State to encourage marriages and large families in Canada, Paris, 3 April 1669.

Among the measures contained in this decree was a yearly allowance to the parents of ten children or more and a gift of twenty livres to those young men who married before they were twenty-one.

qu'il soit reglé quelques honneurs
aux principaux habitans qui prennent soin
des affaires de chacune bourgade et Communauté,
Soit pour leur rang dans l'Eglise, soit ailleurs,
et que ceux des habitans qui auront plus grand
nombre d'enfans Soient tousjours preferez aux
autres, si quelque raison puissante ne l'empesche.
Et qu'il soit estably quelque peine pecuniaire

applicable aux hospitaux des lieux contre
les peres qui ne marieront point leurs enfans
a l'aage de 20 ans pour les garçons, et de 16
pour les filles.

Fait au Conseil
d'Estat du Roy tenu a Paris le troisiesme
avril 1669 signé Colbert.

Archives nationales, Paris, France: Fonds des Colonies, série B, vol. 1, fol. 113–114.

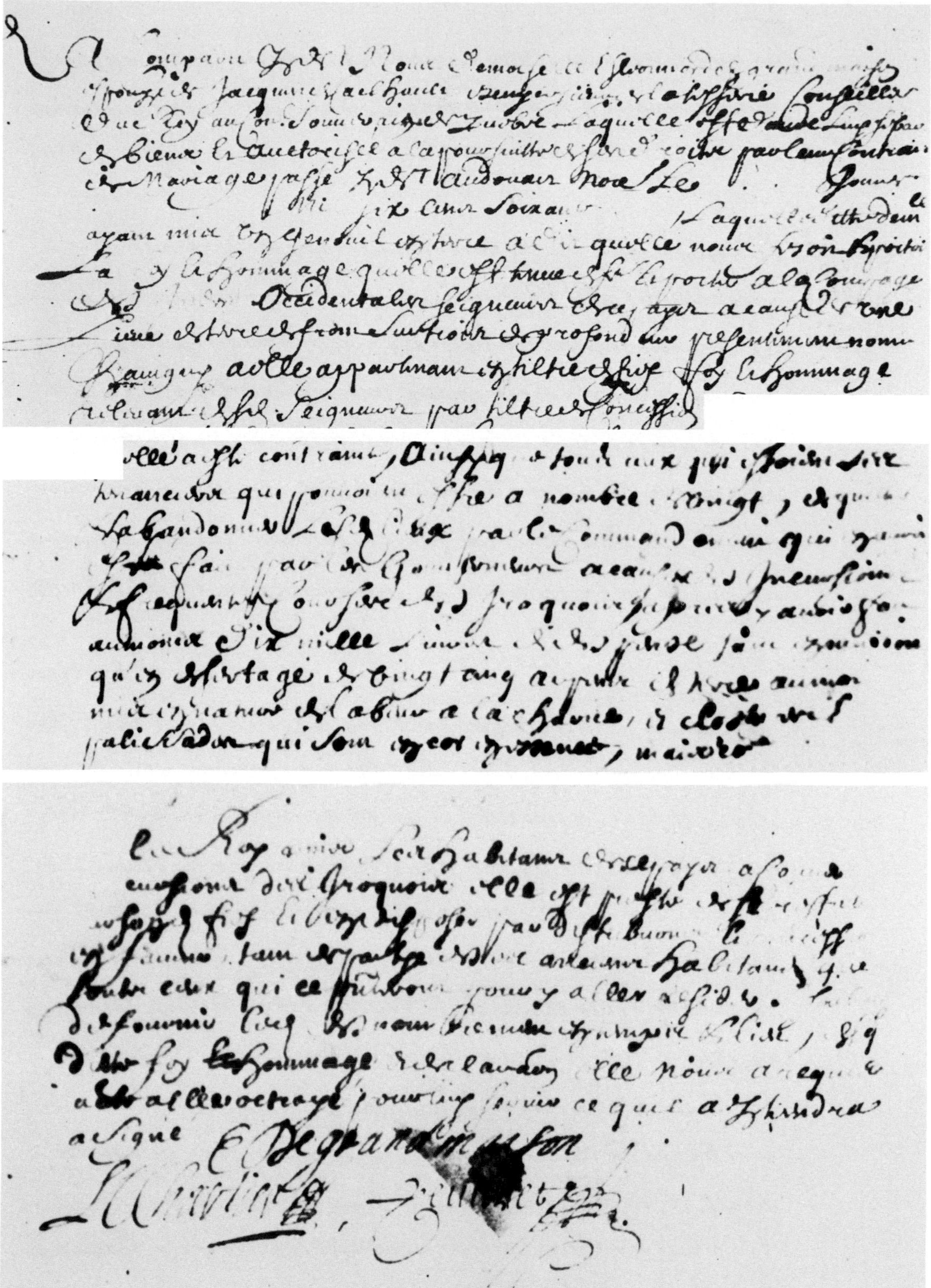

Oath of fealty and act of homage by Éléonore de Grandmaison for her fief of Chavigny, 10 December 1667.

She "has been forced, as have all those who were her tenants and who might number twenty, to leave and abandon" her domain "because of the Iroquois raids and frequent attacks." But now "the king has provided protection for the inhabitants of this country against the Iroquois raids," and "she is ready to go back to live on her fief named herein."

Archives nationales du Québec, Centre d'archives de la Capitale, Québec: Foi et hommage, cahier 1, fol. 181.

Par mes premieres lettres iay eu l'honneur de Vos.re mander le grand nombres d'habitans dela Colonie que Nous auons dans les bois aux Outaouas auec des congez & permissions, dans

Le Voyage q. ie uiens de faire, iay ueu la preuue des grands — inconueniens qu'il y a d'en laisser aler un si grand nombre, on — ne sçauroit trop tost trauailler a y aporter remede, parce que — sans doute les manéges passez tendent tous a la perte et a la — ruine entiere de la Colonie, ceux qui ont des habitations les — laissent en friche comme plusieurs que iay ueu, les gens — mariez abandonent leurs femmes et enfans qui sont a charge au public po. leur entretien ou sendebtent chez les marchands,

Cela Monseign

est uenu a un tel excez, que dez le moment que les Enfans peuuent porter un fuzil, Les Peres ne peuuent plus retenir leurs enfans, et nosent les fascher. Jugez en suitte des

maux qui peuuent suiure d'une telle maniere de uiure. Ces dereglemens Monseigneur se trouuent bien plus grands — dans les familles de ceux qui sont Gentilshommes, ou qui se sont mis sur le pied de le vouloir estre, soit par faineantise ou par uanité n'ayans aucune ressource pour subsister q. les bois, car n'estans pas acoutumez a tenir la charue la — pioche et la hache, toute leur ressource n'estant que le fuzil, il faut qu'ils passent leurs uies dans les bois, ou — ils n'ont ny Curez qui les gênent, ny Peres ny Gouuern.r qui les contraignent.

Letter from Governor General Denonville to the minister Seignelay, Québec, 13 November 1685.

According to Denonville life in the woods was leading to "the complete ruin of the colony; those who have farms let them lie fallow,...married men desert their wives and children, who are dependent upon the public for their living or get into debt to the merchants."

Archives nationales, Paris, France: Fonds des Colonies, série C^{11A}, vol. 7, fol. 88v–90.

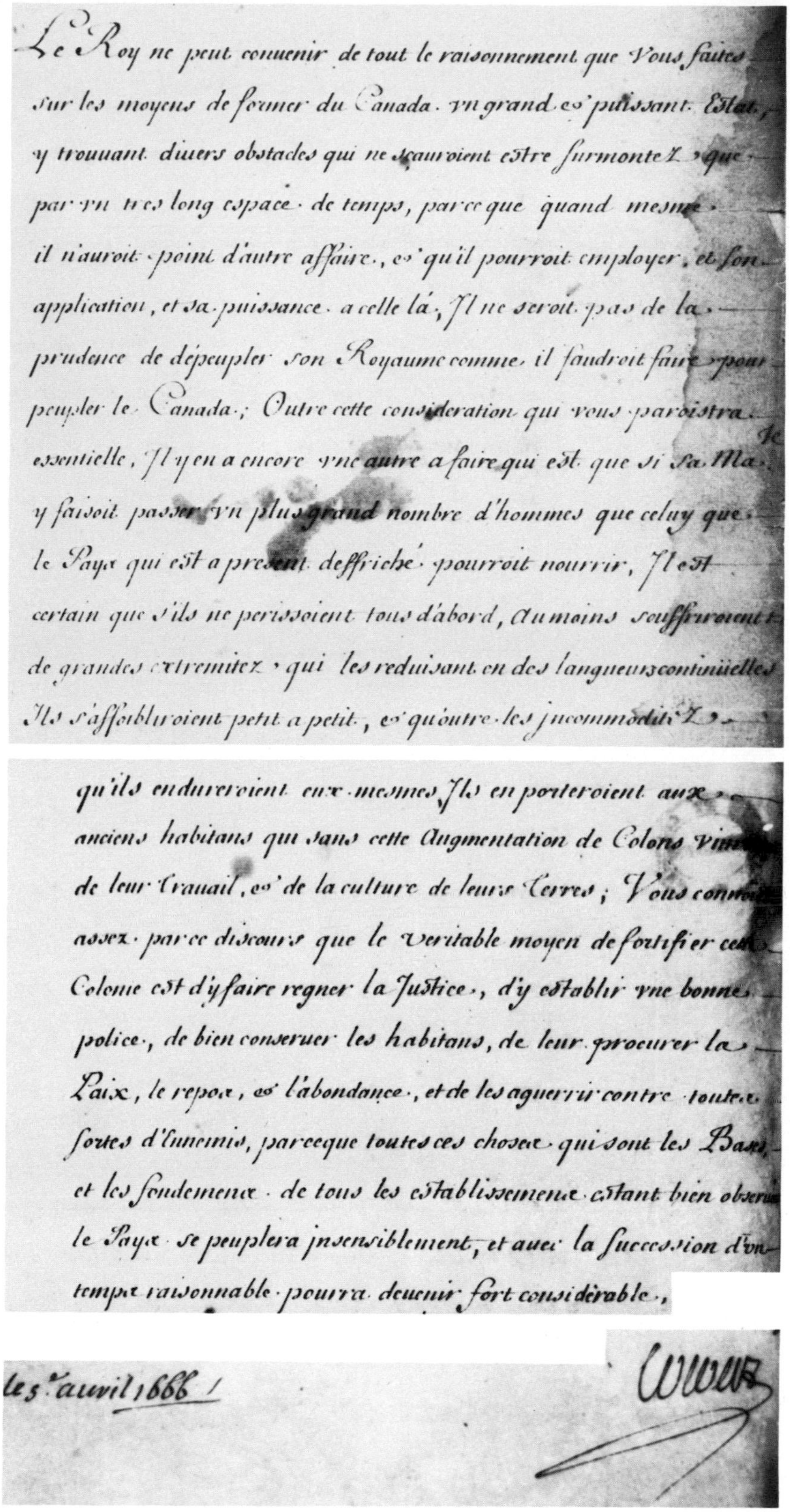
Le Roy ne peut conuenir de tout le raisonnement que Vous faites sur les moyens de former du Canada vn grand et puissant Estat, y trouuant diuers obstacles qui ne sçauroient estre surmontez que par vn tres long espace de temps, parceque quand mesme il n'auroit point d'autre affaire, et qu'il pourroit employer, et son application, et sa puissance a celle là, Il ne seroit pas de la prudence de dépeupler son Royaume comme il faudroit faire pour peupler le Canada; Outre cette consideration qui vous paroistra essentielle, Il y en a encore vne autre a faire qui est que si Sa Ma.té y faisoit passer vn plus grand nombre d'hommes que celuy que le Pays qui est a present deffriché pourroit nourrir, Il est certain que s'ils ne perissoient tous d'abord, Au moins souffriroient ils de grandes extremitez qui les reduisant en des langueurs continüelles Ils s'affoibliroient petit a petit, et qu'outre les incommoditez

qu'ils endureroient eux mesmes Ils en porteroient aux anciens habitans qui sans cette Augmentation de Colons viuent de leur Trauail, et de la culture de leurs Terres; Vous connoistrez assez par ce discours que le veritable moyen de fortifier cette Colonie est d'y faire regner la Justice, d'y establir vne bonne police, de bien conseruer les habitans, de leur procurer la Paix, le repos, et l'abondance, et de les aguerrir contre toutes sortes d'Ennemis, parceque toutes ces choses qui sont les Bases et les fondemens de tous les establissemens estant bien obseruées le Pays se peuplera insensiblement, et auec la succession d'vn temps raisonnable pourra deuenir fort considérable,

le 5e auril 1666 /

Colbert

Letter from the minister Colbert to Intendant Talon, Versailles, 5 April 1666.

The minister explained to Talon, who wanted massive immigration to make Canada into "a great and powerful State," that for the king "it would not be prudent to depopulate his kingdom as would be necessary to do in order to people Canada."

Archives nationales, Paris, France: Fonds des Colonies, série C[11A], vol. 2, fol. 199–199v, 206v.

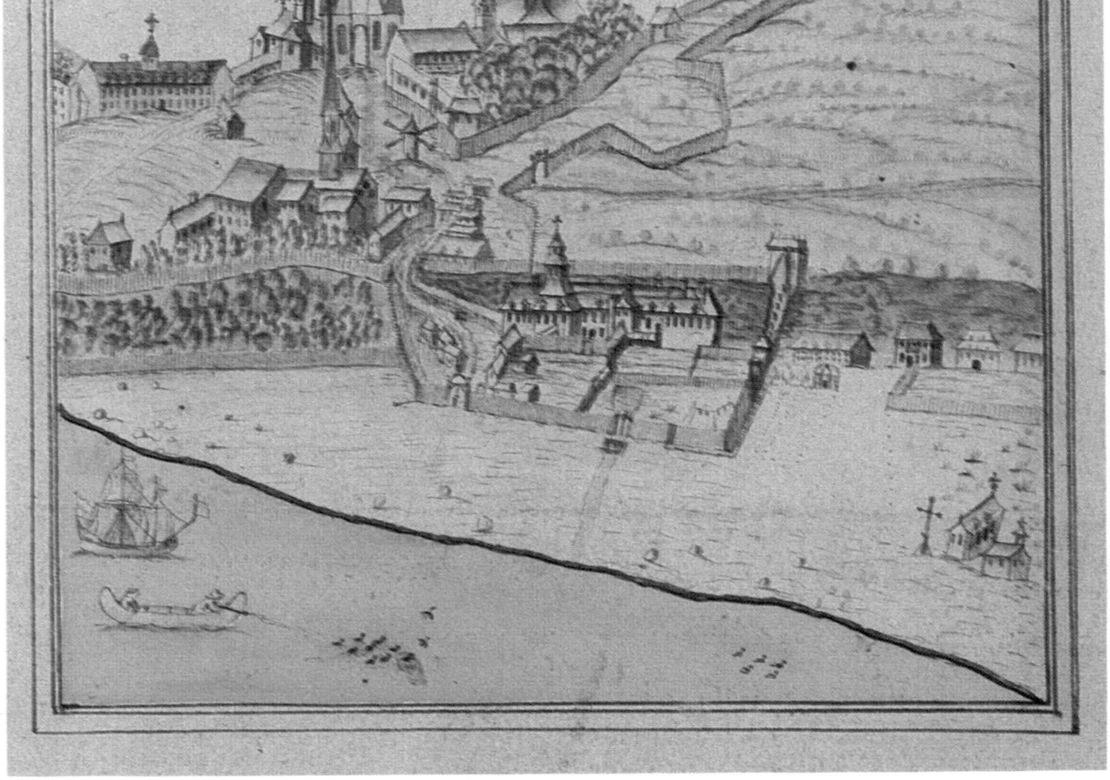

"Partie de l'Amerique Septentrionalle ou est compris la Nouvelle France..., 1699"; Jean-Baptiste-Louis Franquelin; col. ms.; 90 x 135 cm.

View of the town of Québec.

Service historique de la Marine, Vincennes, France: Vol. 4040B, no. 12 a–d.

III

Censuses and population

The censuses taken in New France during the second half of the seventeenth century generally seem to have been incomplete. The one for 1688 for Canada gives 11,249 persons, including more than 1,200 Indians settled there; that for 1686 counted 915 persons for Acadia, including 30 soldiers.

The Canadians had of course qualities and failings: in 1685 Governor Denonville wrote that they were "all big, well built and sturdy, used to living on little in times of need, robust and vigorous, but very headstrong and frivolous, and prone to dissolute living. They are witty and vivacious." Intendant Jacques de Meulles noted for his part how quickly they multiplied.

De Meulles was less enthusiastic in 1686 when he spoke of Acadia, which was so far removed from Québec that it was almost out of touch with the colony in Canada, so neglected by France that it received no help from her, and so close to the English that many Acadians had gone to settle around Boston.

In October 1685 de Meulles had visited Acadia. He had seen Port-Royal and considered that fortifications should be built for this settlement of slightly fewer than six hundred souls. It was older than Québec in a sense, but was far from having progressed as much as Québec, for which the engineer Robert de Villeneuve had just drawn up a detailed plan with a view to providing it with fortifications worthy of the name.

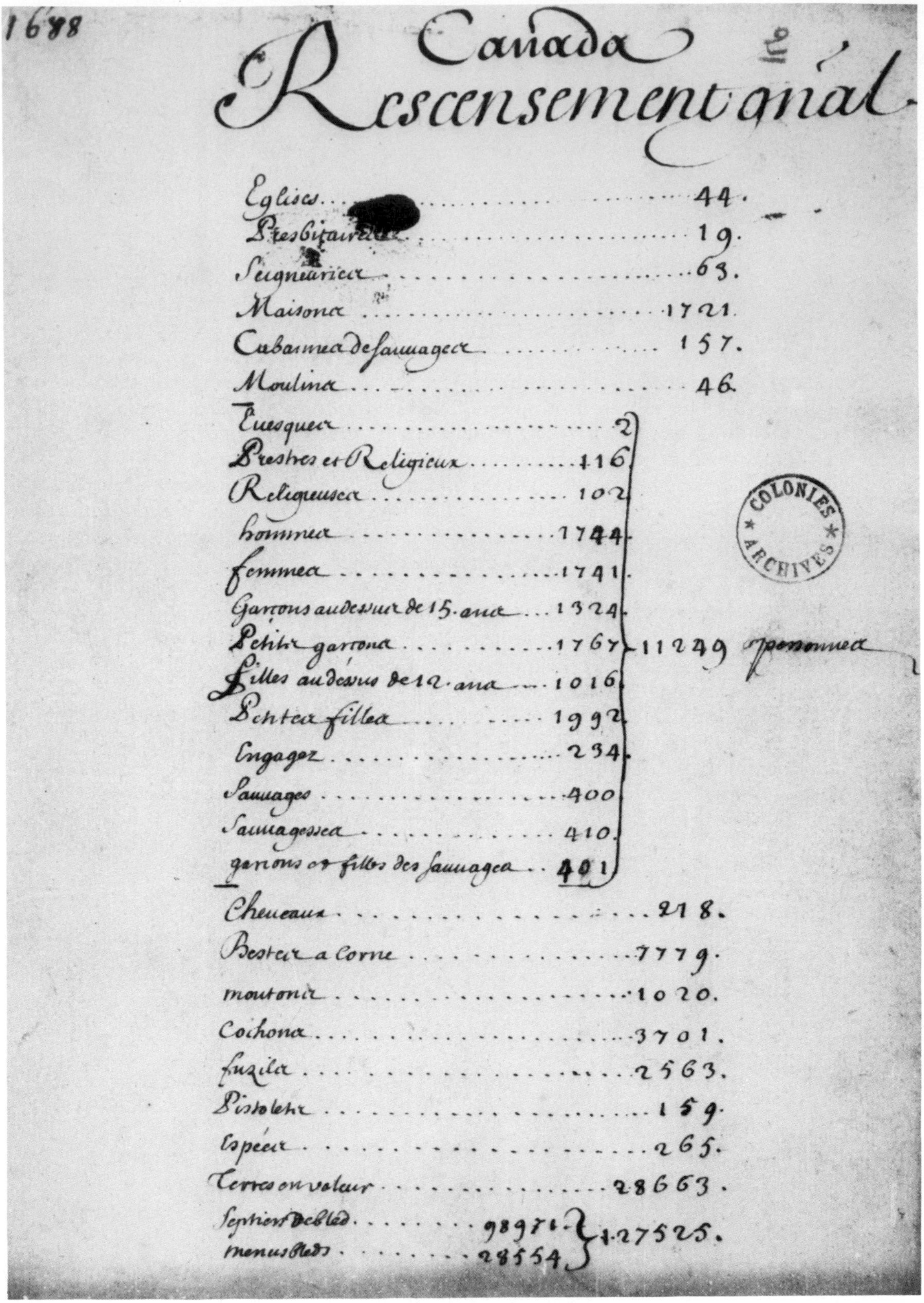

1688

Canada

Rescensement gnal

Eglises	44.	
Presbytaires	19.	
Seigneuries	63.	
Maisons	1721.	
Cabannes de sauuages	157.	
Moulins	46.	
Euesques	2	
Prestres et Religieux	116	
Religieuses	102	
hommes	1744	
femmes	1741	
Garçons au dessus de 15 ans	1324	
Petits garçons	1767	11249 personnes
Filles au dessus de 12 ans	1016	
Petites filles	1992	
Engagez	234	
Sauuages	400	
Sauuagesses	410	
garçons et filles des sauuages	401	
Cheueaux	218.	
Bestes a Corne	7779.	
moutons	1020.	
Cochons	3701.	
fuzils	2563.	
Pistolets	159.	
Espées	265.	
Terres en valeur	28663.	
Septiers de bled	98971	127525.
menus bleds	28554	

General census of Canada, 1688.

Canada counted about three thousand souls in 1663, and more than eleven thousand in 1688. The population of the colony had therefore increased notably, thanks to the efforts made by France from 1665 to 1672 to settle it, and thanks also to the high birth rate in the country.

Archives nationales, Paris, France: Section Outre-Mer, série G[1], vol. 461, p. 2.

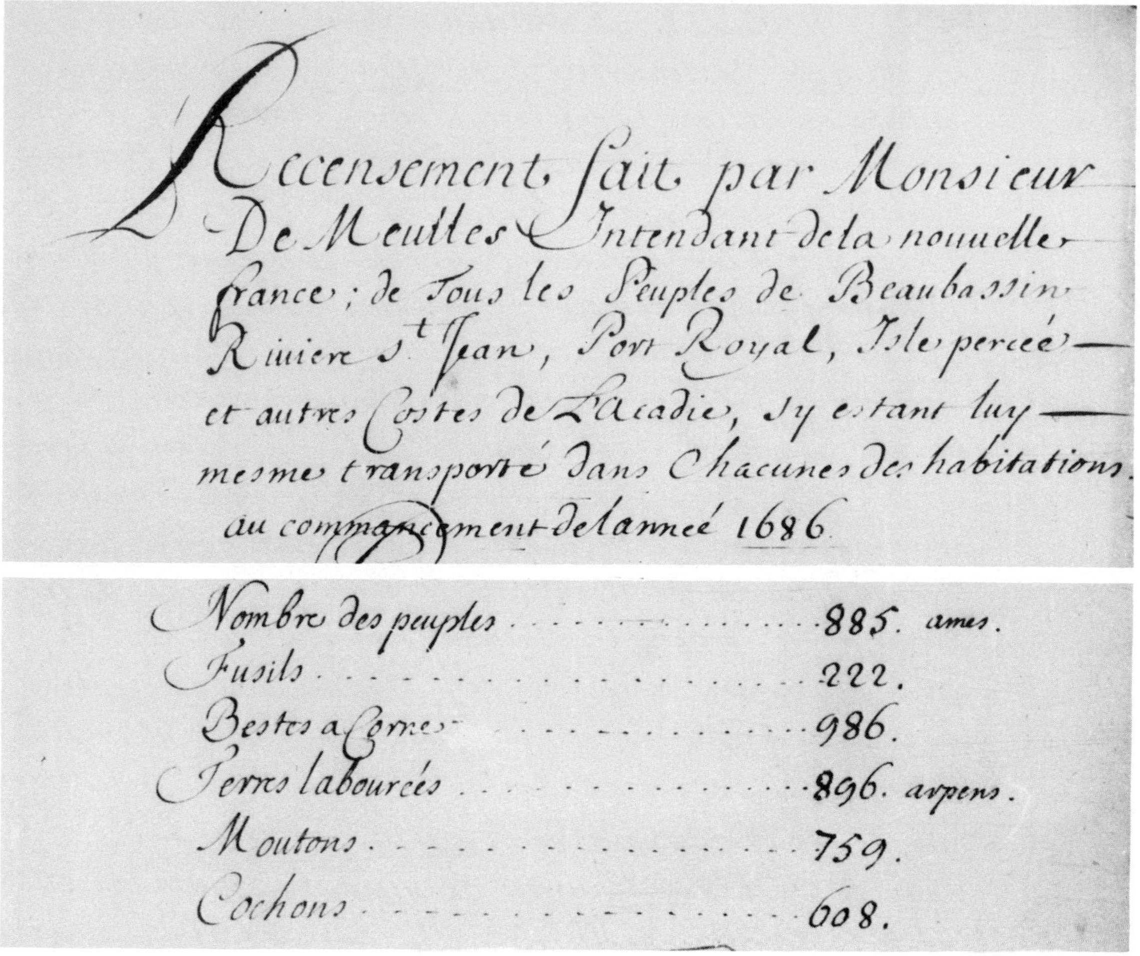

Recensement fait par Monsieur De Meulles Intendant de la nouvelle france; de Tous les Peuples de Beaubassin Riuiere St Jean, Port Royal, Isle percée et autres Costes de L'Acadie, S'y estant luy mesme transporté dans Chacunes des habitations au commancement de l'année 1686.

Nombre des peuples	885. ames.
Fusils	222.
Bestes a Cornes	986.
Terres labourées	896. arpens.
Moutons	759.
Cochons	608.

Summary of the census of Acadia in 1686.

Fewer than a thousand French people were living in this colony, which was neglected by France.

Archives nationales, Paris, France: Section Outre-Mer, série G^1, vol. 466, no 10.

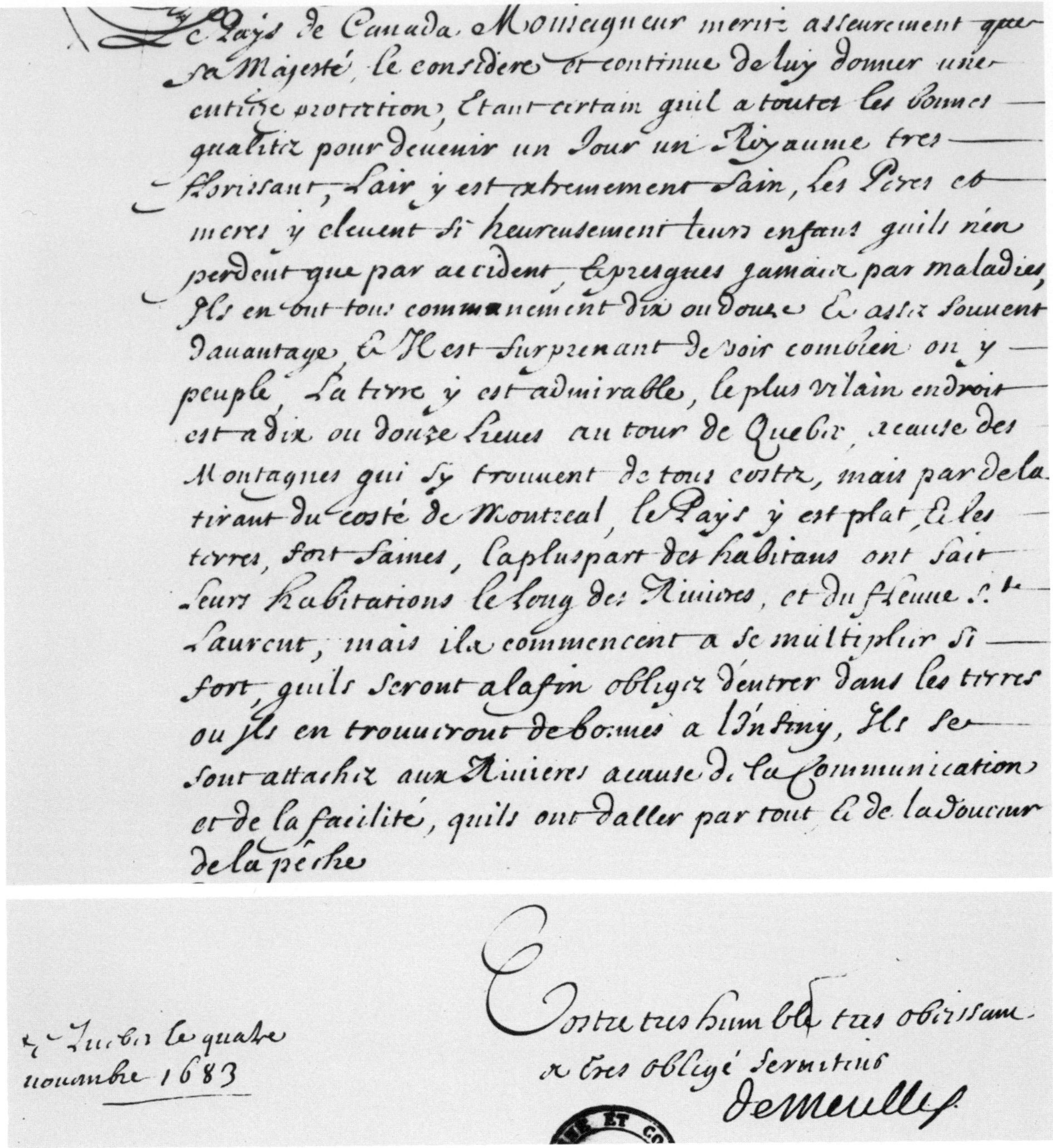

Le Pays de Canada Monseigneur merite assurement que
sa Majesté le considere et continue de luy donner une
entière protection, Estant certain quil a toutes les bonnes
qualitez pour devenir un Jour un Royaume tres
florissant, Lair y est extremement sain, les Peres et
meres y elevent si heureusement leurs enfans quils n'en
perdent que par accident, et presques jamais par maladies,
Ils en ont tous communement dix ou douze Et assez souvent
davantage, Et Il est surprenant de voir combien on y
peuple, La terre y est admirable, le plus vilain endroit
est a dix ou douze lieues au tour de Quebec, a cause des
Montagnes qui sy trouvent de tous costez, mais par dela
tirant du costé de Montreal, le Pays y est plat, Et les
terres fort saines, la pluspart des habitans ont fait
leurs habitations le long des Rivieres, et du fleuve St
Laurent, mais ils commencent a se multiplier si
fort, quils seront alafin obligez dentrer dans les terres
ou Ils en trouveront de bonnes a l'infiny, Ils se
sont attachez aux Rivieres acause de la Communication
et de la facilité, quils ont daller par tout Et de la douceur
de la pesche

Vostre tres humble tres obeissant
et tres obligé Serviteur
deMeulles

A Quebec le quatre
novembre 1683

Letter from the intendant Jacques de Meulles to the minister Seignelay, Québec, 4 November 1683.

De Meulles expressed his astonishment at the number of children that the Canadians had: "They all have ten or twelve ordinarily and fairly often more, and it is surprising to see how much the population is growing here."

Archives nationales, Paris, France: Fonds des Colonies, série C^{11A}, vol. 6, fol. 183, 198.

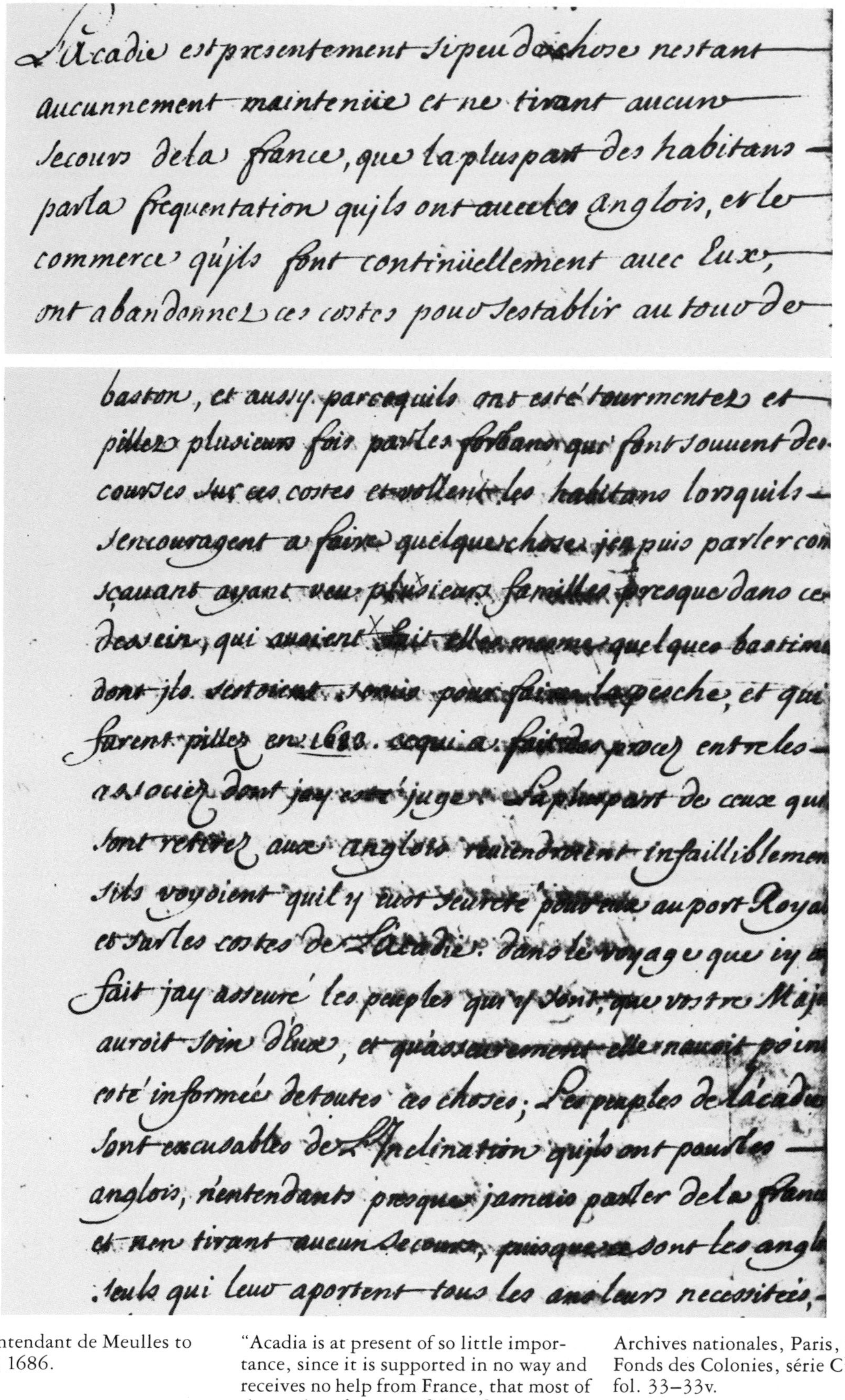
L'Acadie est presentement si peu de chose n'estant
aucunnement maintenüe et ne tirant aucun
secours de la france, que la pluspart des habitans
par la frequentation qu'ils ont avec les anglois, et le
commerce qu'ils font continüellement avec Eux,
ont abandonnez ces costes pour s'establir au tour de

baston, et aussy parcequils ont esté tourmentez et
pillez plusieurs fois par les forbans qui font souvent des
courses sur ces costes et vollent les habitans lorsquils
s'encouragent a faire quelquechose. je puis parler com
sçavant ayant veu plusieurs familles presque dans ce
dessein, qui avoient fait elles mesme quelques bastim
dont ils se servoient tenus pour faire la pesche, et qui
furent pillez en 1680. cequi a fait des procez entre les
associez dont jay esté juge. la pluspart de ceux qu
sont retirez aux anglois reviendroient infailliblemen
sils voyoient quil y eust seureté pour eux au port Roya
et sur les costes de l'acadie. dans le voyage que iy a
fait jay asseuré les peuples qui y sont, que vostre Maj
auroit soin d'eux, et qu'assurement elle n'avoit poin
esté informée de toutes ces choses; Les peuples de l'acadi
sont excusables de l'inclination quils ont pour les
anglois, n'entendants presque jamais parler de la fran
et n'en tirant aucun secours, puisque ce sont les angl
seuls qui leur aportent tous les ans leurs necessitées,

Report sent by Intendant de Meulles to King Louis XIV, 1686.

"Acadia is at present of so little importance, since it is supported in no way and receives no help from France, that most of the settlers, because of their frequent contacts with the English and the trade that they carry on continually with them, have abandoned these shores to go to live around Boston."

Archives nationales, Paris, France: Fonds des Colonies, série C^11D, vol. 2, fol. 33–33v.

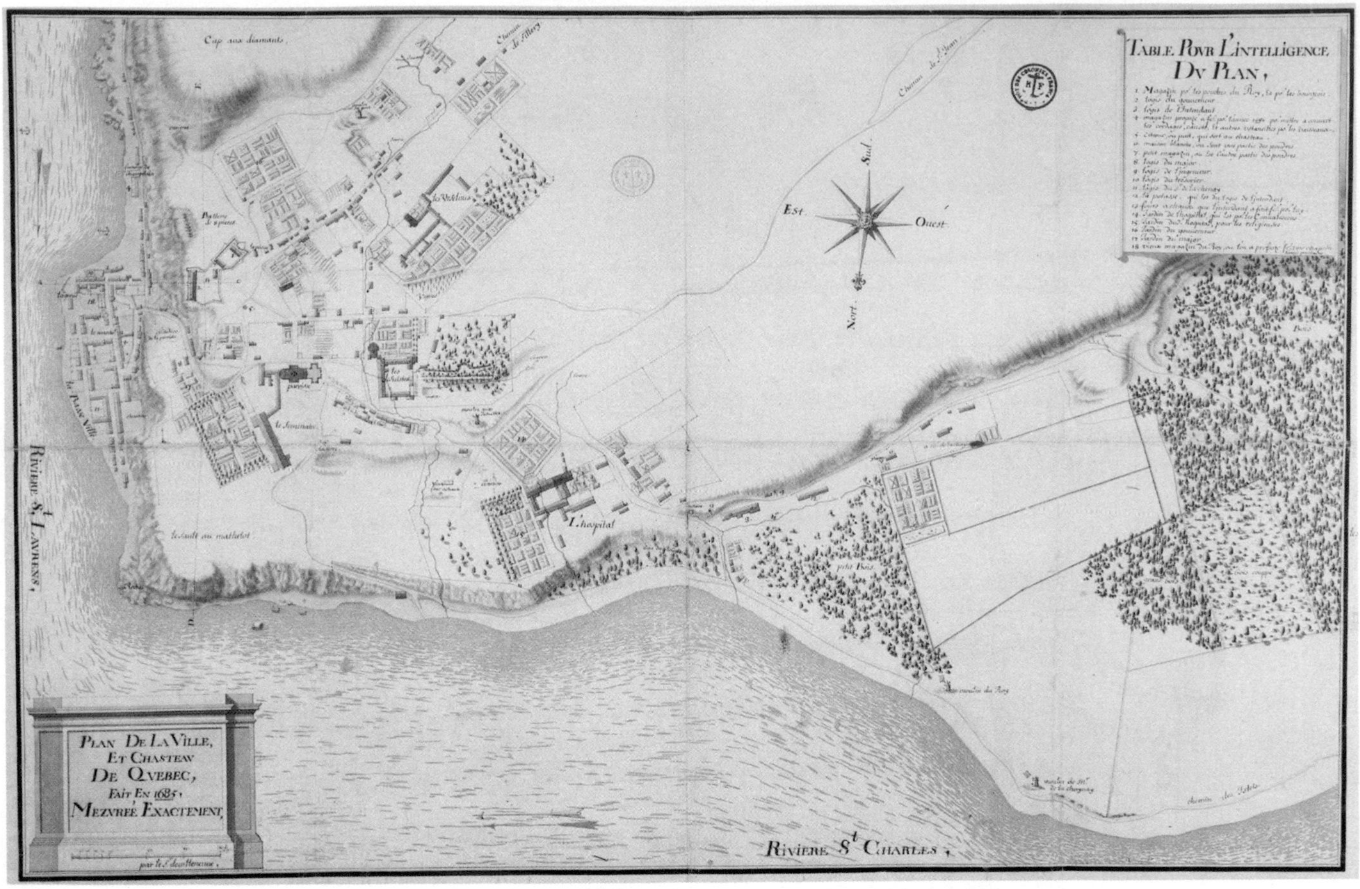

"Plan De La Ville Et Chasteau De Qvebec, Fait En 1685, Mezvrée Exactement"; [Robert] de Villeneuve; col. ms.; 70 x 47 cm.

The main buildings existing in the town of Québec in 1685. One can pick out the Château Saint-Louis, the Séminaire de Québec, the hospital (Hôtel-Dieu), the Ursuline convent, the Jesuit house, the cathedral church, and the intendant's dwelling.

Archives nationales, Paris, France: Section Outre-Mer, Dépôt des fortifications des colonies, Amérique septentrionale, 349B.

III

The native peoples

While on the subject of population one must not forget the native peoples: Eskimos (Inuit) and Indians. Before 1700 scarcely anyone but the explorers looking for a northwest passage had had any contact with the Inuit, of whom little was yet known and who had their own civilization, which was very different from that of the Indians.

As for the Indians, those in the valley of the St. Lawrence and Acadia all belonged to the Algonkian family. Being basically nomadic, they lived almost exclusively on hunting, fishing, and picking fruit, and travelled in small groups. Their shelters, made of skins or strips of bark stretched over poles, were easy to take down and carry.

The Indians belonging to the Huron-Iroquois family, who lived farther south, were on the contrary semi-sedentary; they cultivated the soil, but without neglecting hunting and fishing. Their "lodges" were of more lasting construction and were grouped inside an enclosure. Each lodge could hold several families.

The Europeans owed much to both the nomads and the sedentary Indians; would they have even survived in New France without them? In the fields of transportation, dwellings, clothing, cooking, medicine, as well as hunting, fishing, and war, the Whites borrowed more from the Indians than is generally believed. And without those indispensable informants and guides, would they have been able to explore the interior of the vast continent so rapidly?

Eskimos; F. Wiebman; line engraving; 19 x 14.3 cm. (page).

In Dionyse Settle. *Historia navigationis Martini Forbisseri angli praetoris sive capitanei, A.C. 1577....* Hamburgi: Sumptibus Joh. Naumanni & Georgi Wolffi, 1675, page frontispiece (detail).

The Eskimos' language and culture were very different from the Indians'; they lived in the Arctic regions and on the Labrador coast. Their contacts with the Europeans before 1700 were rare and generally not very friendly. They lived by hunting and fishing and travelled on water with the help of a small sealskin craft, the kayak.

National Library of Canada, Rare Books and Manuscripts Division, Ottawa.

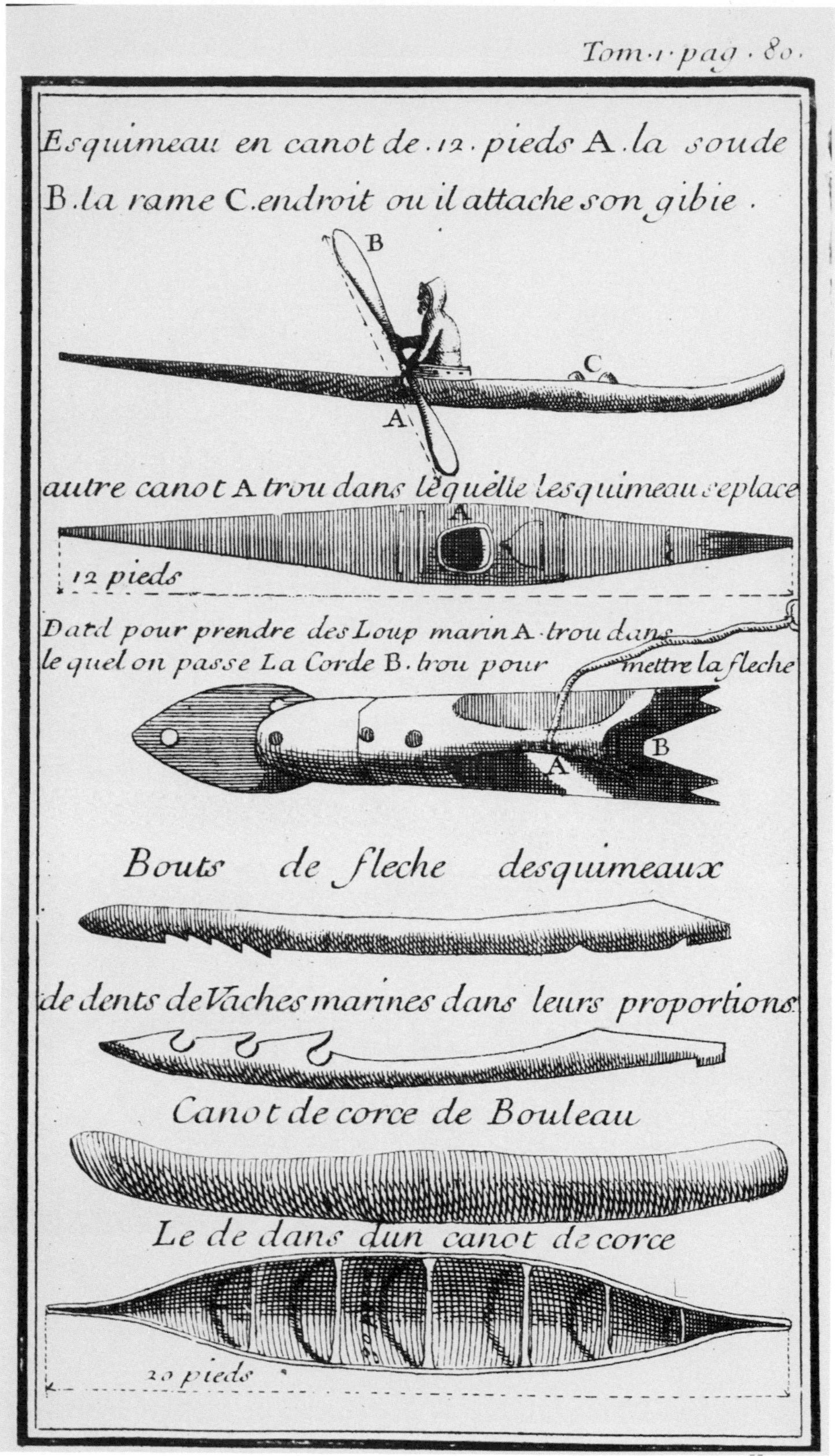

Tom. 1. pag. 80.
Esquimeau en canot de 12 pieds A. la soude
B. la rame C. endroit ou il attache son gibie.
B
C
A
autre canot A trou dans lequelle lesquimeau se place
A
12 pieds
Dard pour prendre des Loup marin A. trou dans
le quel on passe La Corde B. trou pour mettre la fleche
B
A
Bouts de fleche desquimeaux
de dents de Vaches marines dans leurs proportions
Canot de corce de Bouleau
Le de dans dun canot de corce
20 pieds

Kayak, Spear and Arrowheads; engraved by I.B. Scotin; etching; 15.6 x 8.5 cm. (page).

In Claude Charles Le Roy Bacqueville de La Potherie. *Histoire de l'Amérique septentrionale....* Paris: J.-L. Nion & F. Didot, 1722, vol. 1, p. 80.

Public Archives of Canada, Library, Ottawa (Negative no. C 113196).

"De Terra nuper inuenta"; engraved by Theodor de Bry (1528–98) or Matthaeus Merianus (1593–1650) after Le Moyne; line engraving; 15 x 18.1 cm. (image).

In Theodor de Bry ed. [America. pt. 13. Latin]. *Decima Tertia Pars Historiae Americanae....* Francofvrti ad Moenvm: Sumptibus Meriani, 1634, p. 11.

In the seventeenth century the Indians of Acadia and the valley of the St. Lawrence as far as the Great Lakes belonged to the Algonkian family, that is to say they spoke dialects that all had a common root: the Algonkian language. This linguistic group included in particular the Abenakis, Micmacs, Algonkins, Montagnais, and Ottawas. These Indians, who were essentially nomadic, lived primarily from hunting, fishing, and berry-picking.

British Library, London, England.

Indians Fishing; Louis Nicolas (1634–after 1678); brown ink and water-colour on parchment; 33.7 x 21.6 cm.

Thomas Gilcrease Institute of American History and Art, Tulsa, Oklahoma, U.S.A.

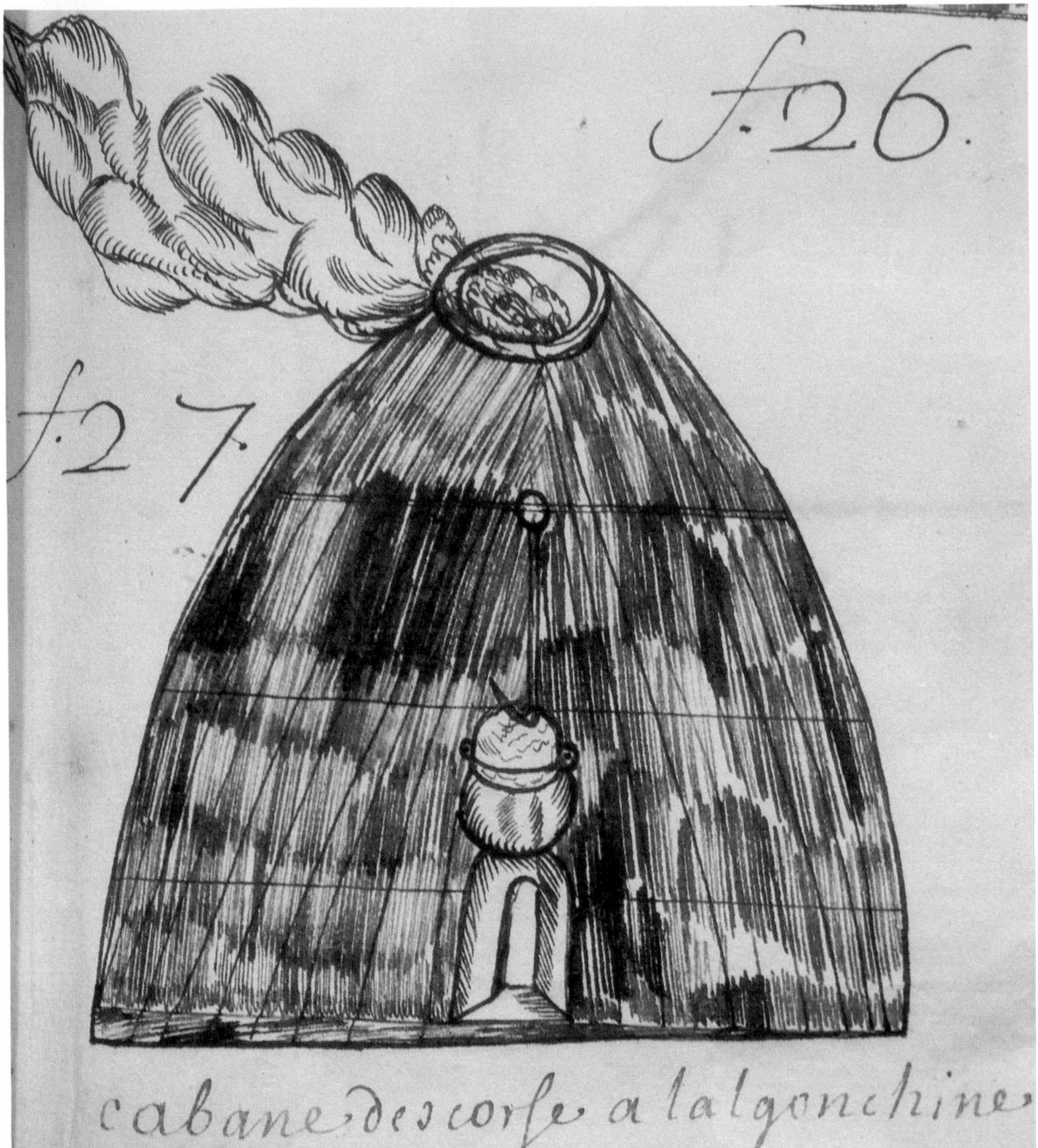

Algonkian Bark House; Louis Nicolas (1634–after 1678); brown ink on parchment; 10.2 x 9.5 cm. (detail).

Thomas Gilcrease Institute of American History and Art, Tulsa, Oklahoma, U.S.A.

Onondaga – an Iroquois Village; after a drawing by Samuel de Champlain (1567 [?] – 1635); etching; 16.1 x 14.1 cm. (plate).

In Samuel de Champlain. *Les voyages de la Novvelle France occidentale, dicte Canada....* Paris: Pierre Le-Mur, 1632, p. 259.

Several tribes speaking dialects that all had the same origin, the Iroquoian language, were connected with the Huron-Iroquois family. The two most important groups were the Hurons and the Iroquois. The first lived south of Georgian Bay (Lake Huron) and the others lived mainly south of Lake Ontario and as far as the area around Lake Erie. These Indians were semi-sedentary: they cultivated the soil, without neglecting hunting and fishing.

Public Archives of Canada, Library, Ottawa (Negative no. C 5749).

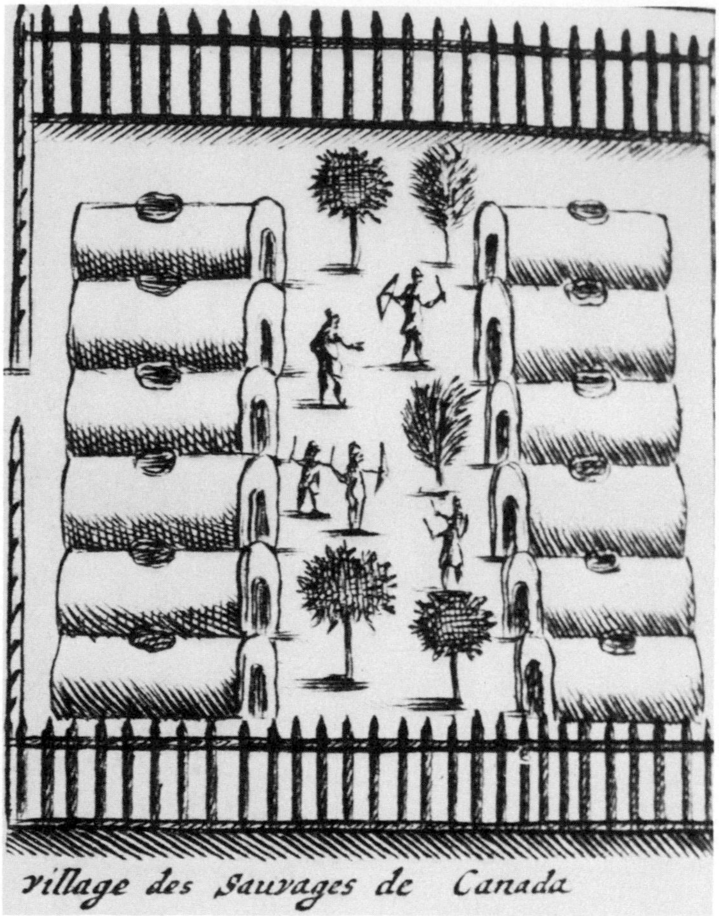

Indian Village in Canada; etching with line engraving; 16 x 9.7 cm. (page).

In Louis Armand de Lom d'Arce, baron de Lahontan. *Nouveaux voyages de mr. le baron de Lahontan, dans l'Amérique septentrionale....* La Haye: Les frères L'Honoré, 1715, vol. 2, p. 95 (detail).

Public Archives of Canada, Library, Ottawa (Negative no. C 99250).

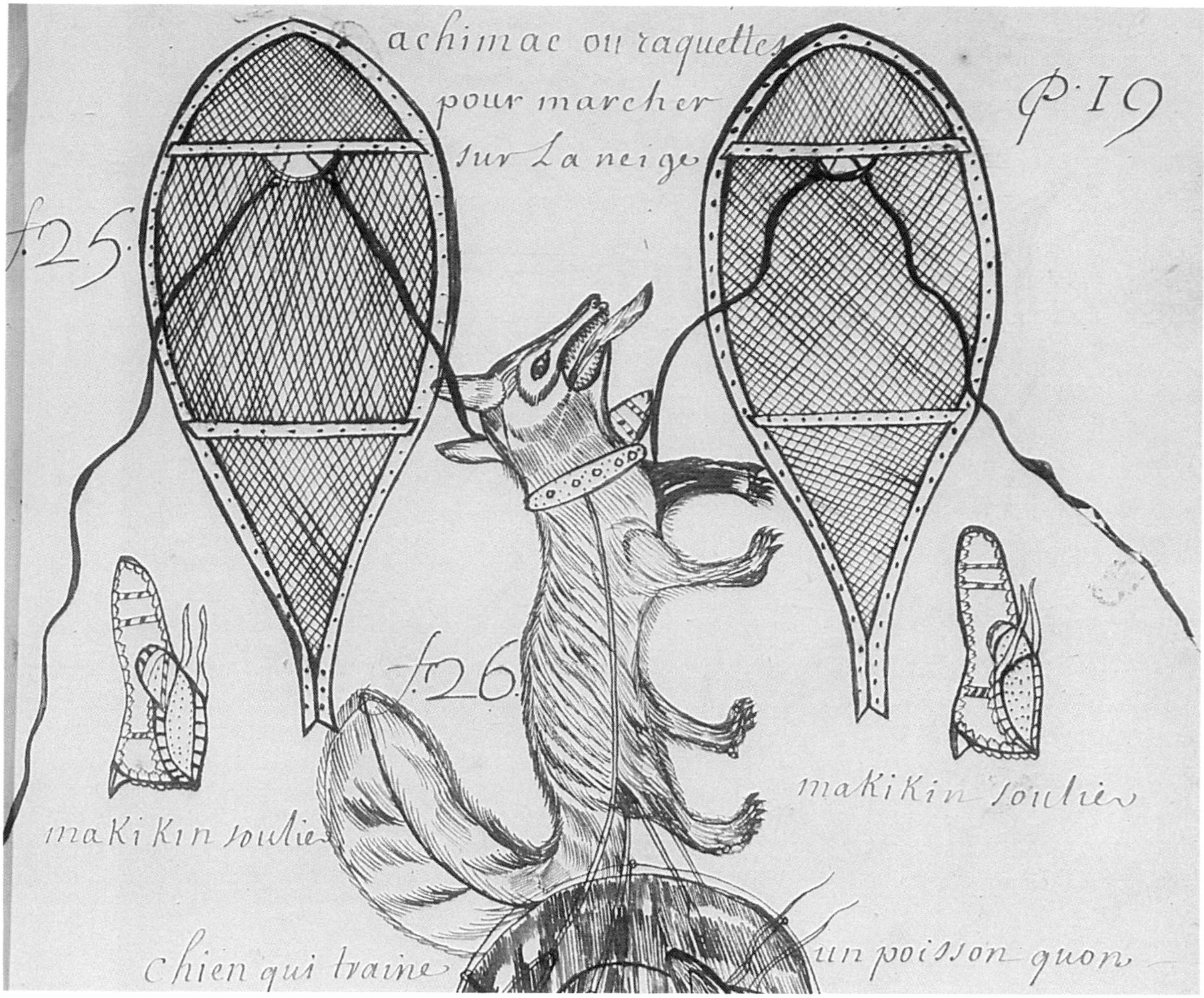

Snowshoes (detail); Louis Nicolas (1634–after 1678); brown ink on parchment; 33.7 x 21.6 cm.

Snowshoes and the canoe represent only a very small part of what the Whites borrowed from the Indians. In the fields of transportation, clothing, medicine, hunting, fishing, and war, the Indians' contribution was considerable.

Thomas Gilcrease Institute of American History and Art, Tulsa, Oklahoma, U.S.A.

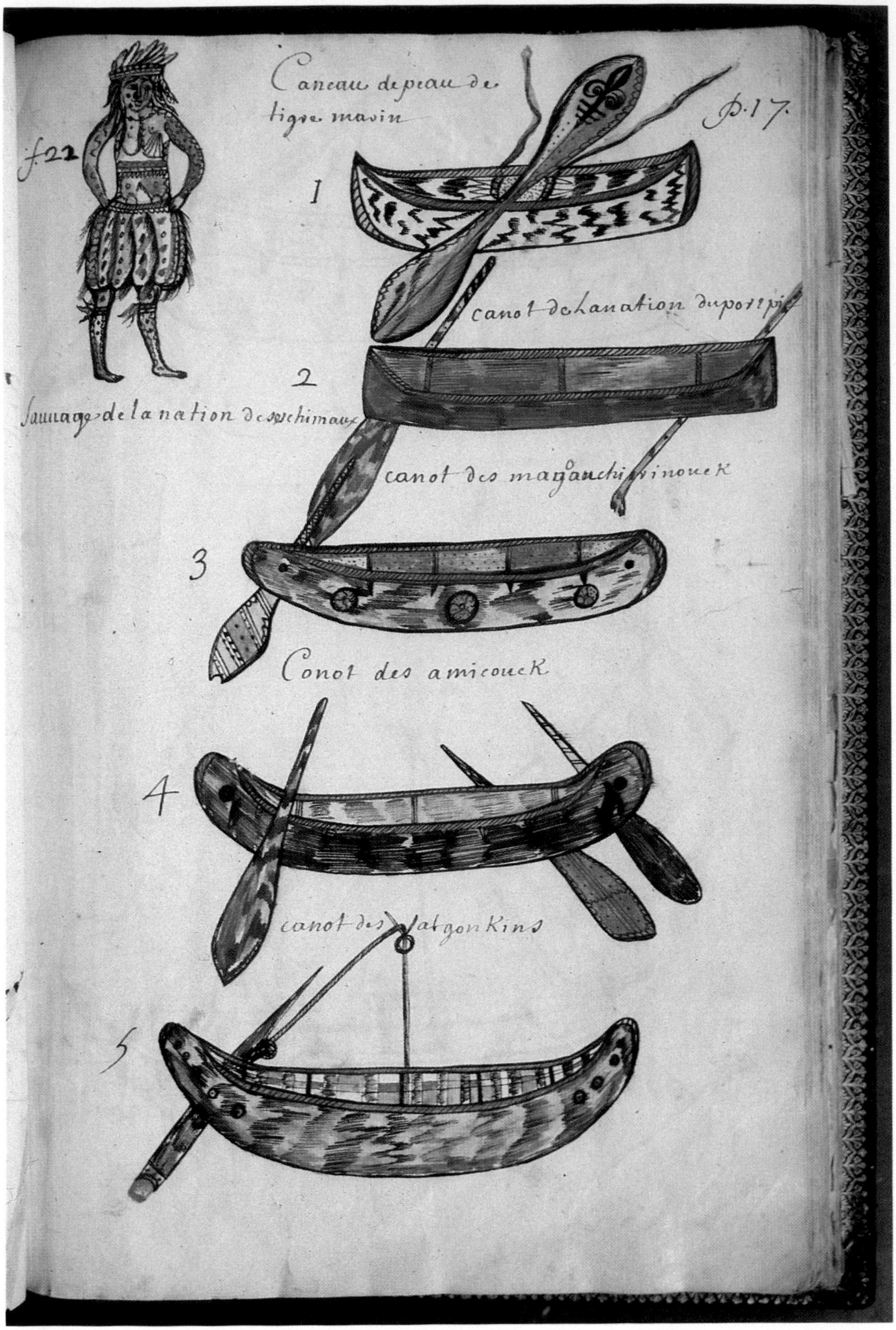

Canoes; Louis Nicolas (1634–after 1678); brown ink and watercolour on parchment; 33.7 x 21.6 cm.

Thomas Gilcrease Institute of American History and Art, Tulsa, Oklahoma, U.S.A.

IV

Government

In 1627 Cardinal Richelieu created the Compagnie des Cent-Associés, to which the king handed over New France "in full ownership, justice, and seigneury." Under the authority of Richelieu, representing the royal power, the Cent-Associés received responsibility for administering New France; Champlain commanded at Québec "in the absence of his Eminence the Cardinal."

In 1636 the king appointed the first titular governor, who was invested with military, civil, and judicial powers; only the financial administration of the colony and control of the fur trade rested with the Cent-Associés' chief clerk. In 1647 the clerk's duties were transferred to a council, which was altered in 1648; the king also entrusted this council with the enforcement of public order, which up till then had rested in great part with the governor. The governor retained his other powers, however, and even held, it seems, a right of veto on the council.

In 1651 Québec and Trois-Rivières shortly afterwards were both provided with a regular tribunal, the seneschal's court; as for Ville-Marie, it had its own seigneurial court. The seneschal's courts heard civil and criminal cases as the court of first instance, and perhaps received appeals from the seigneurial courts that were being set up in their respective districts; appeals from the seneschal's courts and the court in Montréal were brought before the governor general, who was the final judge.

In rapid succession in 1657 and 1659 the king reorganized the council set up in 1648 and conferred a great number of legislative, executive, and judicial powers upon it; in addition, beginning in 1659 appeals from the decisions of the seneschal's courts were to come before the *parlement* of Paris, except for unimportant or very urgent matters, which would continue to be heard by the governor. Moreover, the governor could no longer suspend or dismiss officers of justice, this right being reserved by the king himself. Consequently the governor, whose powers were virtually non-existent in the realm of justice and were reduced in other fields proportionately as those of the council increased, would henceforth enjoy only limited authority.

IV

The Cent-Associés handed in their resignation in 1663. Louis XIV retook possession of the colony and immediately decided to give it institutions similar to those of the French provinces, providing it with a governor, an intendant, and a parlement, the Conseil souverain. These three great institutions were going to last until the conquest in 1760. But the intendant who was appointed in 1663 did not come to Canada, and Talon did not arrive until 1665; in the intervening period the king had handed New France over to the Compagnie des Indes occidentales. These two circumstances explain the hesitations that marked the years from 1663 to about 1666. Besides, the company was dismissed in 1674; it is from that time on that the administrative structure of the colony must be examined.

As the king's personal representative and the highest ranking person in Canada, the governor general enjoyed great moral authority, which he had to use to keep New France in allegiance to the king. Military and diplomatic matters depended exclusively on him; as commander-in-chief of the armed forces he also decided on the line of conduct to be followed in dealing with the Indian tribes and the English colonies. That was the reason that he had jurisdiction over the outlying territories, appointing the fort commandants, issuing trading licences, and exercising a certain degree of authority over the missions and the missionaries. In other areas – settlement and colonization, trade and industry, general administration and religion – he had jurisdiction jointly with the intendant.

It was the intendant, however, who through the number, importance, and extent of his powers was the most powerful person in New France. Everything that did not fall under the exclusive authority of the governor and the bishop came under him or at least required his participation. He had jurisdiction over justice, police (that is to say the entire civil administration), and finances. On him depended in great part the economic, demographic, and social progress of the colony.

The governor general, the bishop, and the intendant met on the Conseil souverain, which had been created in 1663; the council, which was a court of justice above all, also included the attorney general, five – and later (in 1674) seven – councillors, and a secretary. In addition to its purely judicial attributions the council registered royal ordinances and put them into force. At first, and thereafter particularly as a result of the absence of an intendant from 1663 to 1665, it played a considerable administrative role, of which it would soon retain only some part in the general enforcement of public order.

In 1666 and 1667 the former seneschal's courts, which had disappeared with the Cent-Associés, were replaced by the new company; it set up the Provost Court of Québec and the Jurisdiction of Trois-Rivières, which after the dismissal of the Compagnie des Indes occidentales became royal courts. These courts heard civil and criminal cases in the first instance in their respective governments – Canada being divided into three governments: Québec, Trois-Rivières and Montréal – in addition to receiving appeals from the seigneurial courts in their jurisdiction. The case of Montréal, which had a seigneurial court, was different: royal justice was not established there until 1693. Appeals emanating from the courts of Québec, Trois-Rivières, and Montréal came before the Conseil souverain, which was the highest court in the colony.

In principle the governor general, the intendant, and the Conseil souverain had jurisdiction over all the French possessions in North America; in practice, because of the distances, Acadia had its own institutions in the seventeenth century and depended directly on France: it had a governor, but no intendant, and it had a court, but no Conseil souverain. In short, unlike Canada, on which it depended theoretically, it did not obtain the virtual status of a French province.

IV

Administering a trading post

In 1616 the Prince de Condé, viceroy of New France, was arrested. Taking advantage of this opportunity the Société des Marchands de Rouen et de Saint-Malo, which had been formed by Champlain in 1614, wanted to give command of Québec to François Gravé Du Pont. To thwart the partners' intrigues and obtain recognition of his rights, Champlain had recourse to the king's council of State, which issued a decree in his favour on 18 July 1619.

Since the king had ordered him to exercise justice in the "colony," Champlain appointed in 1621 the first court officers in Canada: Gilbert Courseron, lieutenant of the provost court (judge), Louis Hébert, king's attorney, and a certain Nicolas, court clerk.

Previous to these appointments Champlain did not have to render justice himself, it seems, except in 1608 in the affair concerning Jean Duval, who had fomented a plot to murder him. Constituting about him a sort of jury, Champlain heard the witnesses and received a confession from Duval, who was hanged for his crime.

After being lieutenant to lieutenants general and viceroys, in 1627 Champlain became lieutenant to Cardinal Richelieu himself and continued to exercise in a way the function of governor, without bearing the title. But the following year the Kirke brothers were threatening the post of Québec. In 1629, for lack of aid, Champlain had to surrender. For three years the English were in control of Québec.

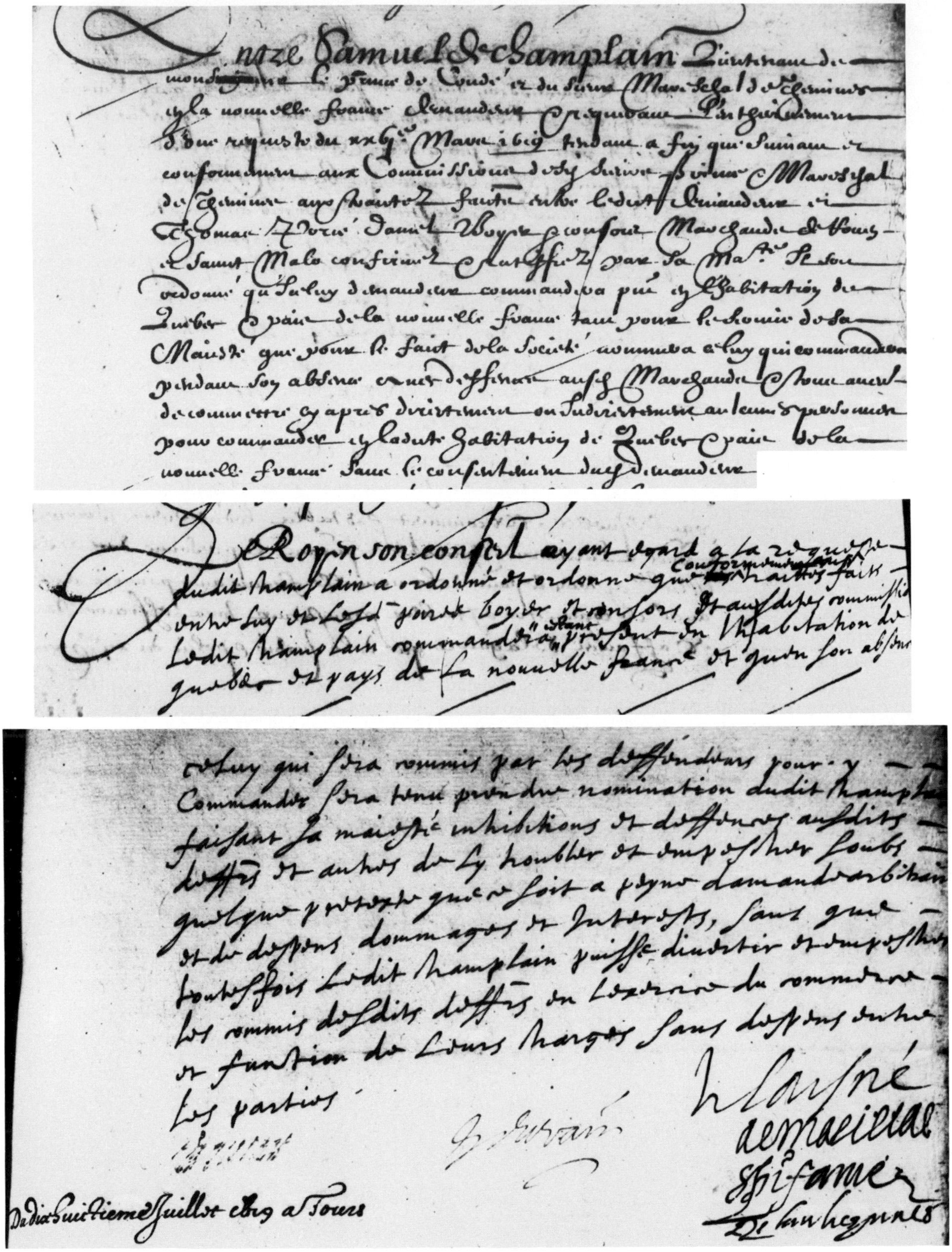

Decree by the king's council of State ordering that "the aforesaid Champlain will be in command in person in the habitation of Québec and the country of New France," Tours, 18 July 1619.

Samuel de Champlain was the guiding spirit of the colony from 1608 to 1635.

Archives nationales, Paris, France: Fonds anciens, série E, 61^{D}–62^{A}, fol. 350–351.

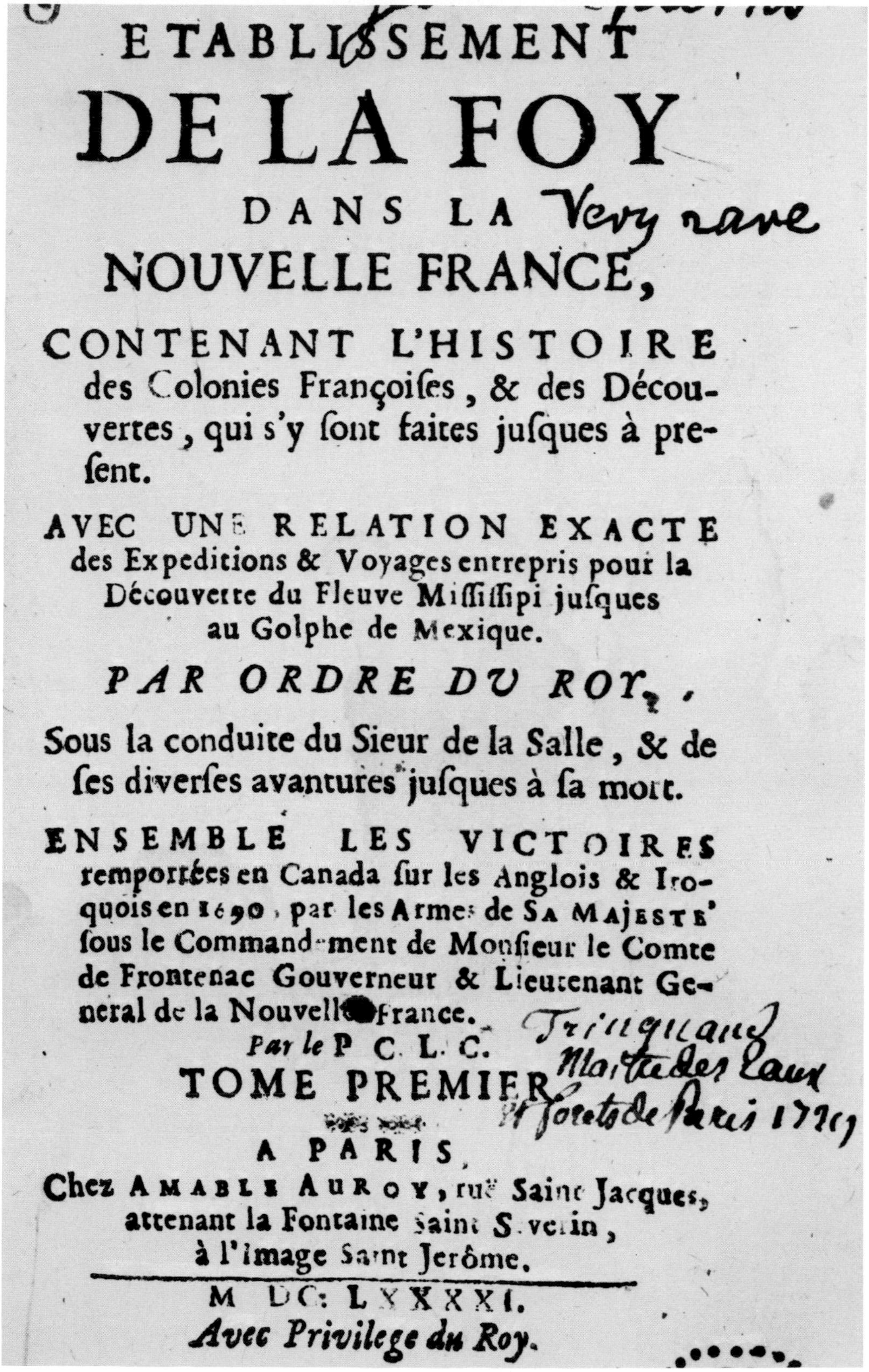

ETABLISSEMENT
DE LA FOY
DANS LA
NOUVELLE FRANCE,
CONTENANT L'HISTOIRE des Colonies Françoiſes, & des Découvertes, qui s'y ſont faites juſques à preſent.
AVEC UNE RELATION EXACTE des Expeditions & Voyages entrepris pour la Découverte du Fleuve Miſſiſſipi juſques au Golphe de Mexique.
PAR ORDRE DU ROY,
Sous la conduite du Sieur de la Salle, & de ſes diverſes avantures juſques à ſa mort.
ENSEMBLE LES VICTOIRES remportées en Canada ſur les Anglois & Iroquois en 1690. par les Armes de SA MAJESTÉ ſous le Commandement de Monſieur le Comte de Frontenac Gouverneur & Lieutenant General de la Nouvelle France.
Par le P. C. L. C.
TOME PREMIER.
A PARIS,
Chez AMABLE AUROY, ruë Saint Jacques, attenant la Fontaine Saint Severin, à l'Image Saint Jerôme.
M. DC. LXXXXI.
Avec Privilege du Roy.

Chrestien Le Clercq. *Etablissements de la foy dans la Nouvelle-France....* Paris: Chez Amable Auroy, 1691, vol. 1, title page, p. 186.

The names are mentioned here of the first officers of the law appointed in Canada: Gilbert Courseron, provost's lieutenant (judge); Louis Hébert, king's attorney; and a certain Nicolas, court clerk.

186 *Premier établiſſement de la Foi*

Nouvelle France ſous la ſignature des principaux Habitans, faiſant pour le general, leſquels pour authentiquer davantage cette delegation, ont prié le tres Reverend Pere en Dieu Denis Jamay Commiſſaire des Religieux qui ſont en ces terres d'appoſer ſon ſceau Eccleſiaſtique ce jour & an que deſſus. Signé Champlain. F. Denis Jamay Commiſſaire. F. Joſeph le Caron. Hebert Procureur du Roy. Gilbert Courſeron Lieutenant du Prevoſt. Boullé. Pierre Reye. Le Tardif I. Le Groux. P. des Portes. Nicolas Greffier de la Juriſdiction de Quebec, & Greffier de l'aſſemblée. Guers Commiſſionné de Monſeigneur le Vice-Roy & preſent en cette élection, & ſcelé en placard du Scel dudit R. P. Commiſſaire des Recollets.

Cornell University Library, Department
of Rare Books, Ithaca, New York, U.S.A.

106

Aprés que le Pont & moy, auec le Capitaine du vaiſſeau, le Chirurgiē, maiſtre, contre maiſtre, & autres mariniers euſmes ouy leurs depoſitions & confrontations, Nous aduiſames que ſe ſeroit aſſez de faire mourir ledit du Val, comme le motif de l'entreprinſe, & auſſi pour ſeruir d'exemple à ceux qui reſtoient, de ſe cōporter ſagement à l'aduenir en leur deuoir, & afin que les Eſpagnols & Baſques qui eſtoient en quantité au pays n'en fiſſent trophee: & les trois autres condamnez d'eſtre pendus, & cependant les rēmener en Frāce entre les mains du ſieur de Mons, pour leur eſtre fait plus ample iuſtice, ſelon qu'il aduiſeroit, auec toutes les informations, & la ſentence, tant dudict Iean du Val qui fut pendu & eſtranglé audit Quebecq, & ſa teſte miſe au bout d'vne pique pour eſtre plantee au lieu le plus eminent de

noſtre fort & les autres trois renuoyez en France.

Samuel de Champlain. *Les voyages dv sievr de Champlain Xaintongeois, capitaine ordinaire pour le roy, en la marine, divisez en deux livres....* Paris: Chez Jean Berjon, 1613, p. 183–184.

Champlain gives an account of the procedure used in 1608 against the locksmith Jean Duval and his accomplices, who had plotted to murder him. Duval was "hanged and strangled at the aforementioned Québec, and his head stuck on a pike at the highest point of the fort."

National Library of Canada, Rare Books and Manuscripts Division, Ottawa.

The English capture of Québec; I. van Vianen (circa 1660–after 1726); etching; 17.7 x 13.6 cm. (page).

In Louis Hennepin. *Nouveau voyage d'un pais plus grand que l'Europe avec les réflections des entreprises du Sieur de la Salle, sur les mines de St. Barbe,...* Utrecht: A. Schouten, 1698, facing p. 343.

Imaginary depiction of Québec City.

In 1629 Sir William Alexander seized Port-Royal in Acadia and David Kirke forced Champlain to surrender at Québec. New France did not remain English long, since Québec and Port-Royal were returned to France by the Treaty of Saint-Germain-en-Laye in 1632.

National Library of Canada, Rare Books and Manuscripts Division, Ottawa.

IV

The régime of the Cent-Associés

The very simple administrative machinery of the post of Québec was largely sufficient for its needs. And when the Compagnie des Cent-Associés was created, it was less to provide the "colony" with a more complex administration than to ensure settlement. That was why the clauses concerning administration in the edict creating the company were few in number and generally vague.

In reality it was the commercial structure that was strengthened between 1632 and 1647. There were no longer even any court officers in the colony. The governor exercised all the powers: military, civil, and judicial. The only thing that escaped him was the purely financial management, which was entrusted to the chief clerk of the Cent-Associés.

A council, the first important administrative structure, was set up in 1647 consisting of the governor, the Jesuit superior, and the governor of Montréal. But this council found its raison d'être much more in the management of commerce and the fur trade than in civil administration in general, since the governor retained his attributions and his paramount role in the other domains.

A court of justice, the seneschal's court, was first set up in 1651. On a plan of Québec drawn up by Jean Bourdon in 1660 can be seen the site of the seneschal's court (Upper Town) and the site of the store where the Conseil de la Nouvelle-France sat in 1647 (Lower Town).

4. Et pour aucunement recompenſer ladite Compagnie des grãds frais & aduances qu'il luy conuiendra faire pour paruenir à ladite

Peuplade, entretien, & conſeruation d'icelle, ſa Maieſté donnera à perpetuité auſdits cent Aſſociez leurs hoirs & ayans cauſe, en toute proprieté, Iuſtice & Seigneurie, le fort & habitation de Quebecq, auec tout ledit pays de la Nouuelle France, dite Canada, tant le long des coſtes depuis la Floride, que les Predeceſſeurs Roys de ſa Maieſté ont faict habiter en rangeant les coſtes de la Mer iuſqu'au cercle Arctique pour latitude, & de longitude depuis l'Iſle de terre Neufue, tirant à Loueſt iuſques au grand lac dict la Mer Douce, & au delà, que dedans les terres & le long des Riuieres qui y paſſent, & ſe deſchargent dans le fleuue appellé Sainct Laurens, autrement la grãde Riuiere de Canada, & dans tous les autres fleuues qui les portent à la Mer, terres, mines, minieres. pour ioüyr toutefois deſdites mines conformement à l'ordõnance, Ports, & Haures, Fleuues, Riuieres, Eſtangs, Iſles, Iſleaux, & generalement toute l'eſtenduë dudit pays au long & au large, & par delà, tant & ſi auant qu'ils pourront eſtendre & faire cognoiſtre le nom de ſa Maieſté, ne ſe reſeruant ſadite Maieſté que le reſſort & la foy, & hommage, qui luy ſera portée & à ſes Succeſſeurs Roys par leſdits Aſſociez, ou l'vn d'eux, auec vne Couronne d'or du poix de huict marcs à chaque mutation de Roys, & la prouiſion des officiers de la Iuſtice ſouueraine, qui luy ſeront nommez & preſentez par leſdits Aſſociez lors qu'il ſera iugé à propos d'y en eſtablir. Permettant auſdits Aſſociez faire fondre Canons & Boullets, forger toutes ſortes d'armes offenſiues & deffenſiues, faire pouldre à Canon, baſtir & fortifier places, & faire generalement eſdits lieux toutes choſes neceſſaires, ſoit pour la ſeureté dudit pays, ſoit pour la conſeruation du commerce.

Faict à Paris, ce vingt neufieſme Auril mil ſix cens vingt ſept, ſigné Armand, Card. de Richelieu, de Rocquemont, Houel, tant pour moy que leſdits du Cheſne, & Lataignant, Dablon Scindic de Dieppe, & Caſtillon.

Act creating the Compagnie de la Nouvelle-France, called Compagnie des Cent-Associés, Paris, 29 April 1627.

This company received "in full ownership, justice, and seigneury the fort and habitation of Québec, with all the aforesaid country of New France." It could "do generally in the aforesaid places everything that was necessary, either for the security of the said country or for maintaining trade."

Archives nationales, Paris, France: Fonds des Colonies, série C^{11A}, vol. 1, fol. 80v–81, 83v.

Seal of the Compagnie des Cent-Associés (1627–63). Obverse: against a background semy of fleur-de-lis, a female figure standing on waves holding a lily stalk in her left hand and a Latin cross in her right; 65 mm. (approximate diameter); ME DONAVIT LVDOVICUS DECIMUS TERTIVUS 1627. Reverse: a ship with full sail on waves; 30 mm. (diameter); IN MARI VIAE TVAE; wax.

Archives des ursulines de Québec, Québec.

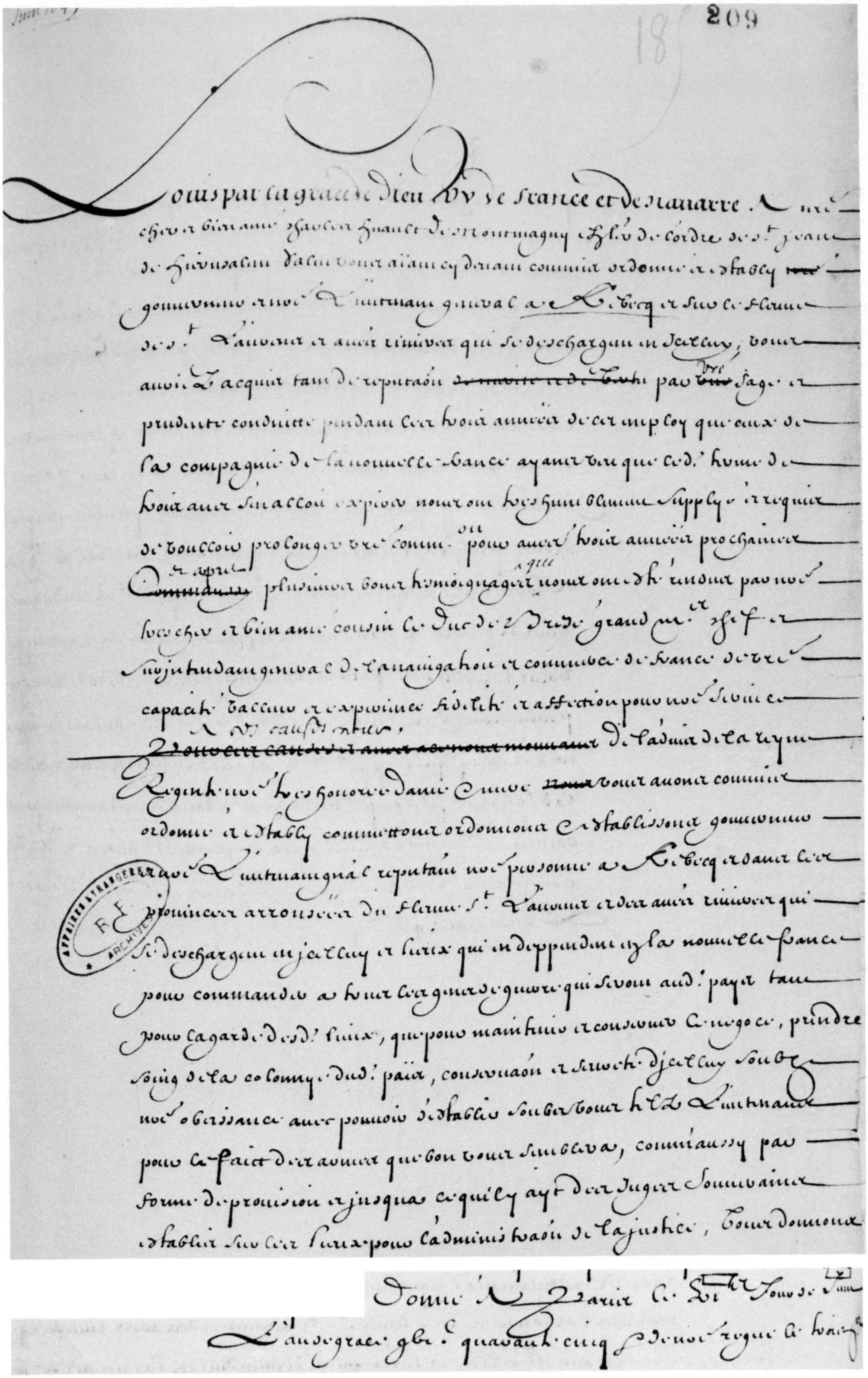
Louis par la grace de dieu Roy de France et de Navarre

Commission from King Louis XIV extending for three years Charles Huault de Montmagny's term of office as governor and lieutentant general of New France, Paris, 6 June 1645.

Montmagny was the first titular governor of New France. He held that office from 1636 to 1648.

Archives du ministère des Affaires étrangères, Paris, France: Mémoires et documents, Amérique, vol. 4, fol. 209 – 209v.

111

SA MAIESTE,
EN SONDIT CONSEIL, La Reyne Regente ſa Mere preſente, Voulant pourvoir auſdits abus, & faire viure ſes ſubiects de la Nouuelle France, en paix, vnion, bon ordre & police, A faict & ordonné le Reglement qui s'enſuit.

SCAVOIR, Qu'il ſera eſtably vn Conſeil compoſé du Gouuerneur dudit pays, & iuſqu'à ce qu'il y ayt vn Eueſque du Superieur de la Maiſon des Ieſuites qui ſera lors à Quebec, enſemble du Gouuerneur particulier de l'Iſle de Montreal: Et en l'abſence du Gouuerneur dudit pays, & du Gouuerneur particulier dudit Montreal, de leurs Lieutenans: Lequel Conſeil ſe tiendra en la Maiſon commune où eſt eſtably le Magazin de Quebec.

Que par ledit Conſeil à la pluralité des voix, ſera pourueu à la nomination du General de la flotte, des Capitaines & autres Officiers des Vaiſſeaux, des Commis & Controolleurs de la Traicte, tant dans ledit pays qu'en France.

Sera auſſi par ledit Conſeil nommé vn Secretaire qui ne pourra eſtre domeſtique d'aucun de ceux qui compoſent ledit Conſeil, pour garder les Regiſtres, Receuoir & expedier les Actes, Commiſſions & Reſultats, des Deliberations, & les deliurer à ceux qu'il appartiendra: Lequel Secretaire pourra auſſi receuoir tous autres actes & Contracts qui ſe paſſeront entre les particuliers, comme Notaires & perſonne publique, faiſant ſigner deux teſmoins auec les parties, conformement aux Ordonnances gardées en France.

Seront audit Conſeil, veuz, examinez & arreſtez tous les Comptes reglez, les gages & appoinctemens des Officiers & Commis, & generalement pourueu à tout ce qui ſera neceſſaire pour la Traicte & le bien dudit pays, ſans que leſdits Officiers & Commis puiſſent pretendre aucun profit directement ou indirectement autre que les appoinctemens qui leur ſeront accordez par ledit Conſeil, ny eſtre nourris aux deſpens du Magazin: Ce que ſa Maieſté defend tres expreſſément à l'aduenir.

Le General de lad flotte, & les Syndics des habitās de Quebec, des trois riuieres & de Montreal auront entrée & ſceance audit Conſeil, ſans voix deliberatiue, pour y repreſenter ſeulement ce qui regarde leurs charges, & l'intereſt de leurs Communautez.

Sera permis à l'aduenir à tous les habitans François dudit pays, de traicter & faire commerce de peaux & Pelteries auec les Sauuages, de leurs fruicts prouenans dudit pays ſeulement, & à la charge & non autrement, d'apporter aux magazins communs, toutes les peaux & Pelteries qu'ils auront receuës auec leſdits Sauuages, pour le prix qui leur en ſera payé, ainſi qu'il ſera reglé par ledit Conſeil, à peine de confiſcation d'icelles, & d'amende arbitraire.

Les Syndics de Quebec, des trois riuieres & de Montreal ſeront eſleus chacun par les habitans deſdits lieux, chacun an par ſcrutin, & ne pourront eſtre continuez plus de trois ans de ſuite.

Faict au Conſeil d'Eſtat du Roy, ſa Maieſté y eſtant, la Reyne Regente ſa Mere preſente, tenu à Paris le vingt-ſeptieſme iour de Mars mil ſix cens quarante ſept. Signé DE LOMENIE.

284

Royal regulation making various changes in the administration of Canada, Paris, 27 March 1647.

Creation of council to control commerce and the fur trade: "In the said Council will be seen, examined, and settled all accounts paid, the wages and allowances of the officers and clerks, and generally all that will be necessary for the fur trade and the good of the said country will be provided for."

Archives nationales, Paris, France: Fonds des Colonies, série F[3], vol. 3, fol. 233 – 234v.

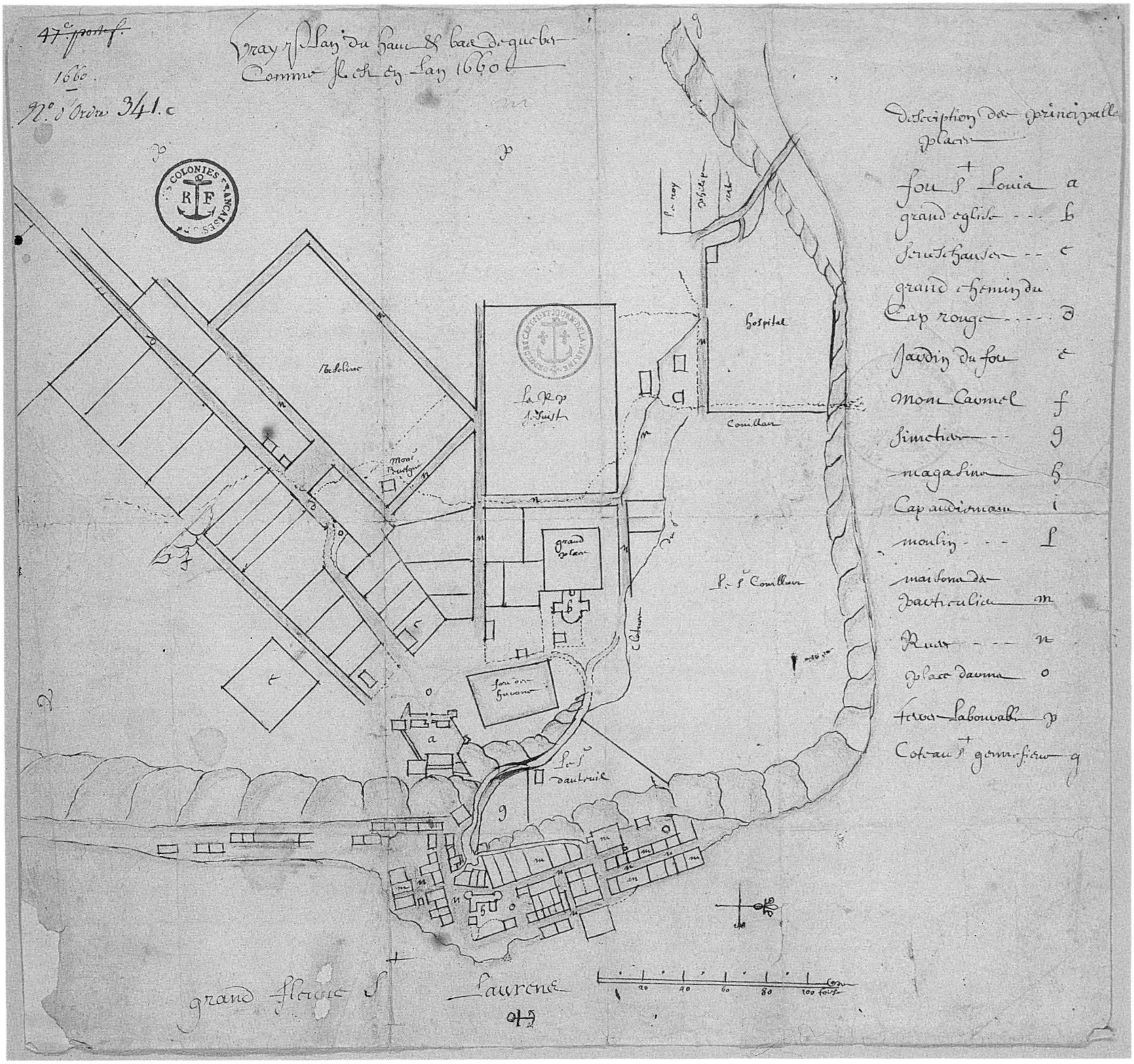

"Vray Plan du haut & bas de quebec Comme il est en l'an 1660"; [Jehan Bourdon]; ms.; 35.7 x 32 cm.

This map of Québec shows the two sections of the town: Lower Town, the centre of commerce, and Upper Town, the centre of religion and government.

Archives nationales, Paris, France: Section Outre-Mer, Dépôt des fortifications des colonies, Amérique septentrionale, 341 c.

IV

The great institutions

After the resignation of the Cent-Associés in 1663, Louis XIV made the governor his personal representative in the colony. This was a notable increase in prestige and authority, which was nevertheless accompanied by a considerable decrease in his powers, since the governor could no longer act alone except in the areas of war, diplomacy, and external relations.

Several of the governor's previous attributions devolved upon the intendant, who was responsible for the whole civil administration of the colony. The intendant also became the colony's superintendent of finances, so that even the governor was dependent upon him for financing the performance of his own duties.

The governor, the intendant, and the apostolic vicar met on the Conseil souverain, which had been set up in 1663. The council, which was above all a court of justice, was at first entrusted with a great number of administrative responsibilities, which it subsequently shed gradually, to become around 1700 almost nothing but a final court of appeal.

But in 1664 the king and Colbert created the Compagnie des Indes occidentales and granted it New France "in complete seigneury, property, and justice." The competition which developed between the king's and the company's representatives was one of the factors that led to revocation of the company's charter in 1674.

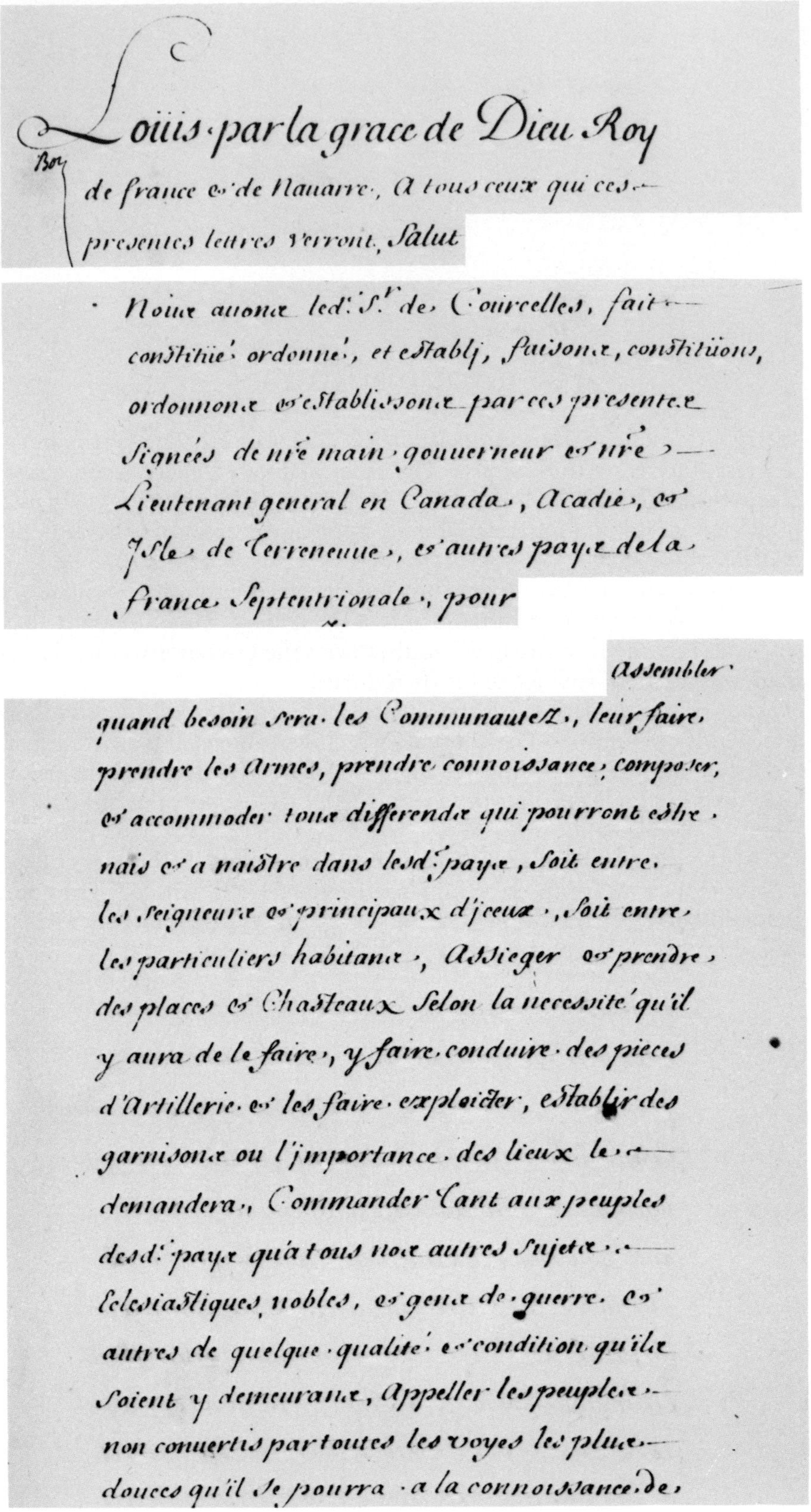
Roy

Louis par la grace de Dieu Roy de france et de Navarre, A tous ceux qui ces presentes lettres verront, Salut

Nous avons ledt. Sr. de Courcelles, fait constitüé ordonné, et estably, faisons, constitüons, ordonnons et establissons par ces presentes signées de nre main, gouverneur et nre Lieutenant general en Canada, Acadie, et Isle de Terreneuve, et autres pays de la france Septentrionale, pour

assembler quand besoin sera les Communautez, leur faire prendre les armes, prendre connoissance, composer, et accommoder tous differends qui pourront estre nais et a naistre dans lesd. pays, soit entre les seigneurs et principaux d'jceux, soit entre les particuliers habitans, Assieger et prendre des places et Chasteaux selon la necessite qu'il y aura de le faire, y faire conduire des pieces d'Artillerie et les faire exploicter, establir des garnisons ou l'jmportance des lieux le demandera, Commander tant aux peuples desd. pays qu'a tous nos autres sujets Eclesiastiques, nobles, et gens de guerre et autres de quelque qualité et condition qu'ils soient y demeurans, Appeller les peuples non convertis par toutes les voyes les plus douces qu'il se pourra a la connoissance de

Commission from King Louis XIV appointing Rémy de Courcelle governor general of New France, Paris, 23 March 1665.

From 1663 on the governor general, the king's personal representative in the colony, was entrusted principally with military matters and relations with the Indians and foreign colonies.

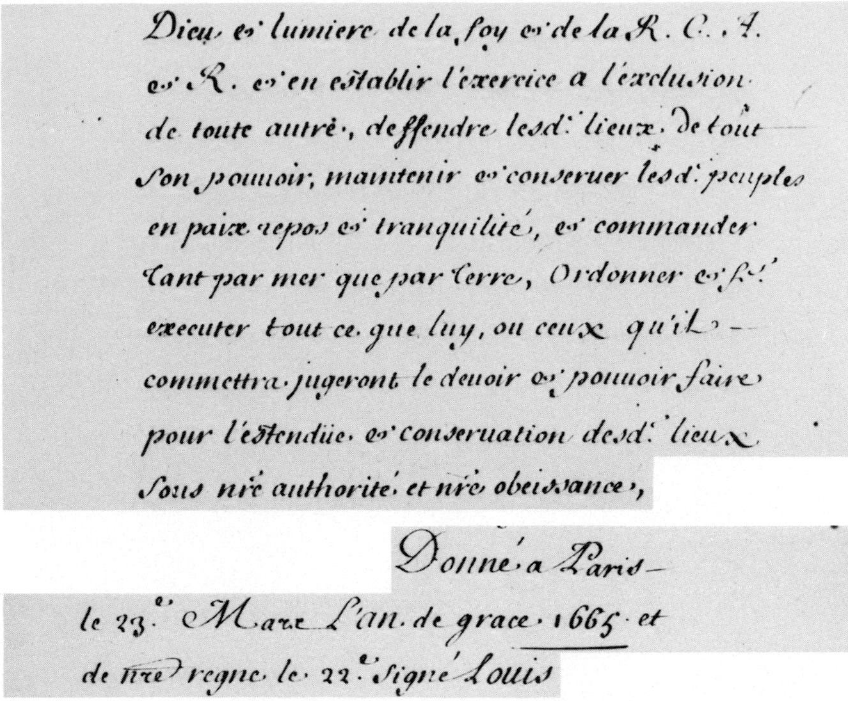
Dieu et lumiere de la foy et de la R. C. A.
et R. et en establir l'exercice a l'exclusion
de toute autre, deffendre lesd. lieux de tout
son pouvoir, maintenir et conserver lesd. peuples
en paix repos et tranquilité, et commander
tant par mer que par terre, Ordonner et fe.
executer tout ce que luy, ou ceux qu'il –
commettra jugeront le devoir et pouvoir faire
pour l'estendüe et conservation desd. lieux
sous nre authorité et nre obeissance,

Donné a Paris
le 23e Mars l'an de grace 1665 et
de nre regne le 22e signé Louis

Archives nationales, Paris, France: Fonds des Colonies, série B, vol. 1, fol. 68–69v, 71.

Portrait of Daniel de Rémy de Courcelle (1626–98); artist unknown; oil.

Courcelle was governor general of New France from 1665 to 1672.

Mr. Xavier de Rémy de Courcelles, Amiens, France.

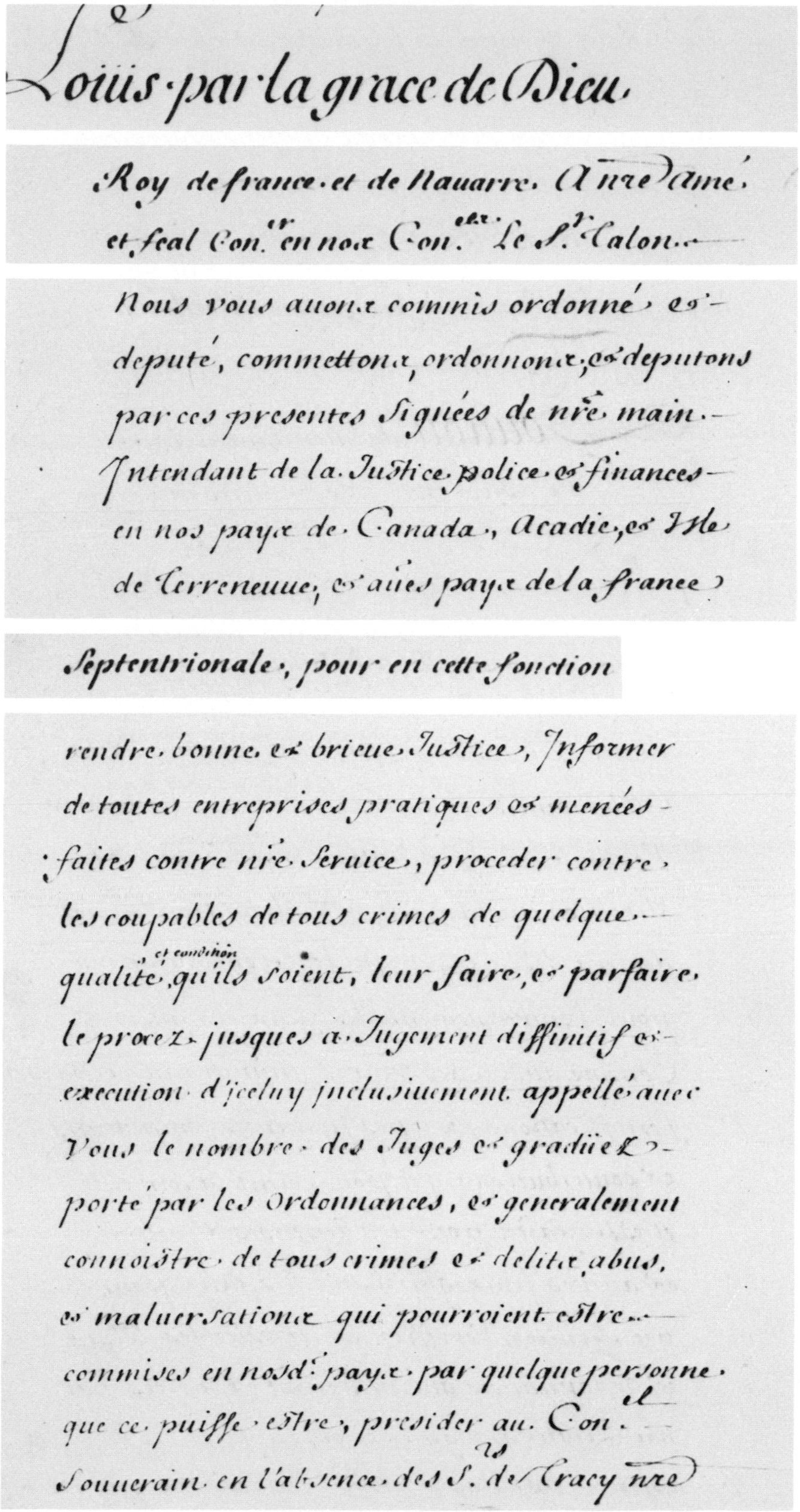

Louis par la grace de Dieu

Roy de france et de Navarre. A nre amé
et feal Con.^er^ en nore Con.^el^ Le Sr Talon

Nous vous auons commis ordonné et
deputé, commettons, ordonnons, et deputons
par ces presentes signées de nre main
Intendant de la Justice police et finances
en nos pays de Canada, Acadie, et Isle
de Terreneuue, et aües pays de la france

Septentrionale, pour en cette fonction

rendre bonne et brieue Justice, Informer
de toutes entreprises pratiques et menées
faites contre nre Seruice, proceder contre
les coupables de tous crimes de quelque
qualité et condition qu'ils soient, leur faire, et parfaire
le procez jusques a Jugement diffinitif et
execution d'iceluy inclusiuement appellé auec
Vous le nombre des Juges et graduez
porté par les Ordonnances, et generalement
connoistre de tous crimes et delitz abus,
et maluersations qui pourroient estre
commises en nosd. pays par quelque personne
que ce puisse estre, presider au Con.^el^
Souuerain en l'absence des Srs de Tracy nre

Commission from King Louis XIV appointing Jean Talon intendant of New France, Paris, 23 March 1665.

The intendant received very wide powers which allowed him to exercise effective control over finances, industry, commerce, agriculture, population, justice, and police.

Lieutenant general en l'Amerique, & de Courcelles gouuerneur & nre Lieuten.t gnal en nosd. pays de Canada, juger souuerainem.t seul en matiere Ciuile, & de tout ordonner ainsy que vous verrez estre juste & apropos,

Voulons aussy que vous ayez l'oëil & la direction, maniement & distribution de nos deniers destinez & qui le seront cy apres pour l'entretenement des gens de guerre, Comme aussy des viures, munitions, reparaons fortiffications, parties jnopinées, emprunts & contributions qui pourroient auoir esté et estre faites pour les depenses d'jcelles, & autres fraix qui y seront a faire pour nre Seruice, Veriffier & arrester les Estats & Ordonnances qui en seront expediées

Donné a Paris le 23e Jour de Mars l'an de grace 1665 & de nre regne le 22e. Signé Louis

Archives nationales, Paris, France: Fonds des Colonies, série B, vol. 1, fol. 71 – 72v, 73v.

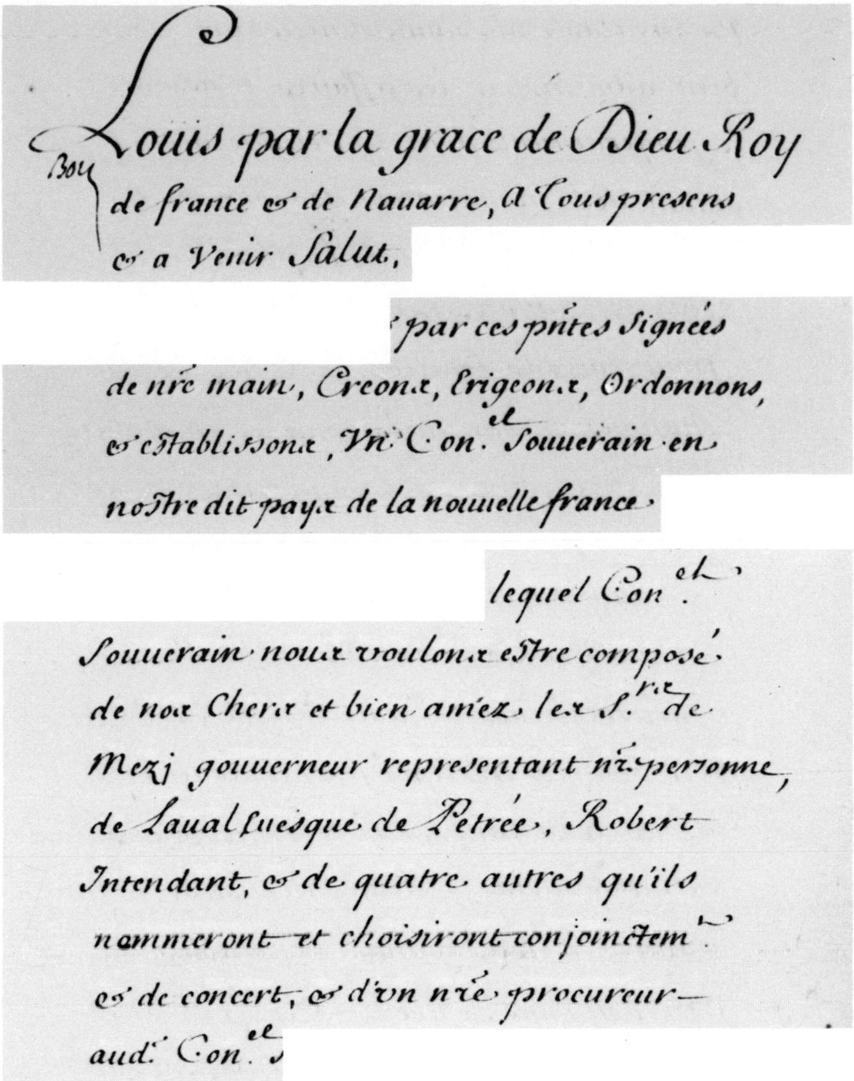
Louis par la grace de Dieu Roy
de france et de Nauarre, A Tous presens
et a Venir Salut.

par ces pntes Signées
de nre main, Creons, Erigeons, Ordonnons,
et establissons, Vn Con.el Souuerain en
nostre dit pays de la nouuelle france.

lequel Con.el
Souuerain nous voulons estre composé
de nos Chers et bien amez les S.rs de
Mezi gouuerneur representant nre personne,
de Laual Euesque de Petrée, Robert
Intendant, et de quatre autres qu'ils
nommeront et choisiront conjointem.t
et de concert, et d'vn nre procureur
aud. Con.el

Edict by King Louis XIV creating a supreme council, the Conseil souverain, at Québec, to "judge without appeal and in the last resort according to the laws and ordinances" of the kingdom of France, Paris, March 1663.

Auons en outre audit
Con.el Souuerain donné & attribüé, donnons
et attribüons le pouuoir de connoistre de
toutes causes ciuiles & Criminelles pour
juger Souuerainement & en dernier ressort
Selon les loix & Ordonnances de nre
Royaume,

Donné a
Paris au mois de Mars L'an de grace
1663, & de nre regne le 20.e Signé Loüis

Archives nationales, Paris, France: Fonds des Colonies, série B, vol. 1, fol. 60, 61–62, 63v.

Seal of the Conseil souverain; the Royal Arms of France, i.e., a shield charged with three fleur-de-lis and ensigned by the Royal Crown of France; wax; 32 mm. (oval).

Archives nationales du Québec, Centre d'archives de la Capitale, Québec.

Establishment of the Compagnie des Indes occidentales; artist unknown; medal; struck in copper; restrike circa 1870; 41.8 mm. Obverse: LUDOVICUS XIIII. REX CHRISTIANISSIMUS./I. MAVGER.F. Reverse: JUNGENDIS COMMERCIO GENTIBUS. In the exergue: SOCIETATES NEGOTIATORUM/ IN UTRAMQUE INDIAM./ M.DC.LXIV.

Public Archives of Canada, Picture Division, Ottawa (Negatives nos. C 14811 obverse, C 14855 reverse).

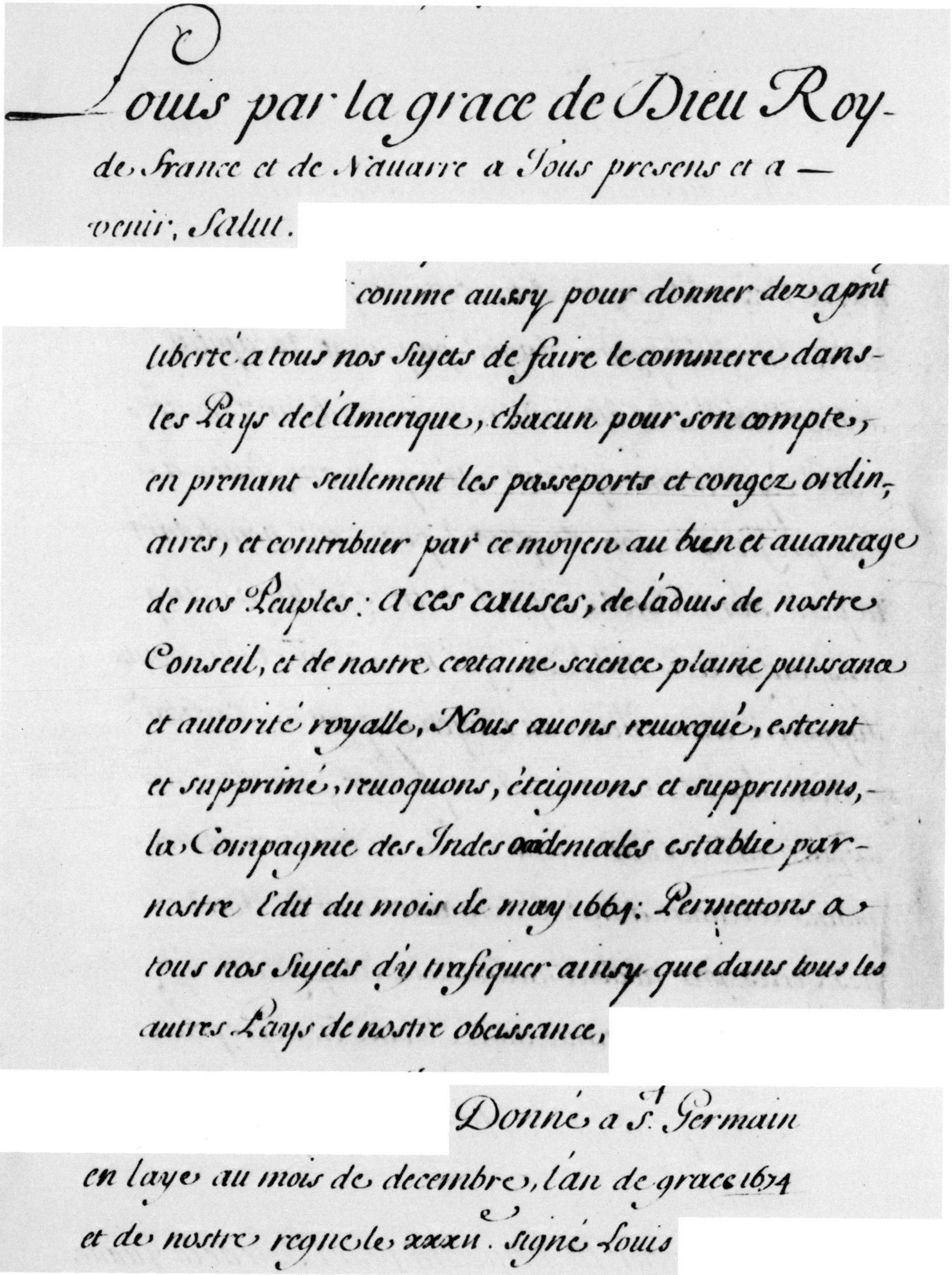

Louis par la grace de Dieu Roy
de France et de Navarre a Tous presens et a —
venir, Salut.

comme aussy pour donner dez aprsnt
liberté a tous nos Sujets de faire le commerce dans-
les Pays de l'Amerique, chacun pour son compte,
en prenant seulement les passeports et congez ordinaires, et contribuer par ce moyen au bien et auantage
de nos Peuples: A ces causes, de l'aduis de nostre
Conseil, et de nostre certaine science plaine puissance
et autorité royalle, Nous auons reuocqué, esteint
et supprimé, reuoquons, éteignons et supprimons,-
la Compagnie des Indes occidentales establie par-
nostre Edit du mois de may 1664: Permettons a
tous nos Sujets d'y trafiquer ainsy que dans tous les
autres Pays de nostre obeissance,

Donné a St Germain
en laye au mois de decembre, l'an de grace 1674
et de nostre regne le xxxii. signé Louis

Edict by the king revoking the privilege of the Compagnie des Indes occidentales, Saint-Germain-en-Laye, December 1674.

This company, which had been formed in 1664, was the last one to be entrusted, in whole or in part, with the administration of New France.

Archives nationales, Paris, France: Fonds des Colonies, série B, vol. 6, fol. 60, 62v, 66.

IV

Politics and administration

The rivalries between the governor general and the intendant were not long in appearing; conflict was virtually permanent between these two personages, one receiving much honour and enjoying great moral authority, the other holding the purse strings and possessing nearly all the real powers. The temptation was great for the first to encroach upon the authority of the second, and for the latter to "set himself on a parallel" with the former, to borrow Colbert's expression.

New France was divided into three governments: Québec, Trois-Rivières, and Montréal. The governor and the intendant, who resided at Québec, appointed people to represent them in the other two governments: local governors, and subdelegates of the intendant (or financial commissaries) respectively. Under the responsibility of the governor or the intendant as the case might be, they worked on their authority in the same fields as their superiors.

In the area of public order (that is to say making rules and regulations in civil matters), the Conseil souverain played an important role: it adopted and promulgated regulations, such as those of 11 May 1676, for example, which were a reworking, in forty-three articles, of the council's previous decrees and the ordinances of the governors and intendants since Augustin de Saffray de Mézy and Jean Talon. Registered and posted at Québec, Montréal, and Trois-Rivières, these regulations applied to the three governments.

120

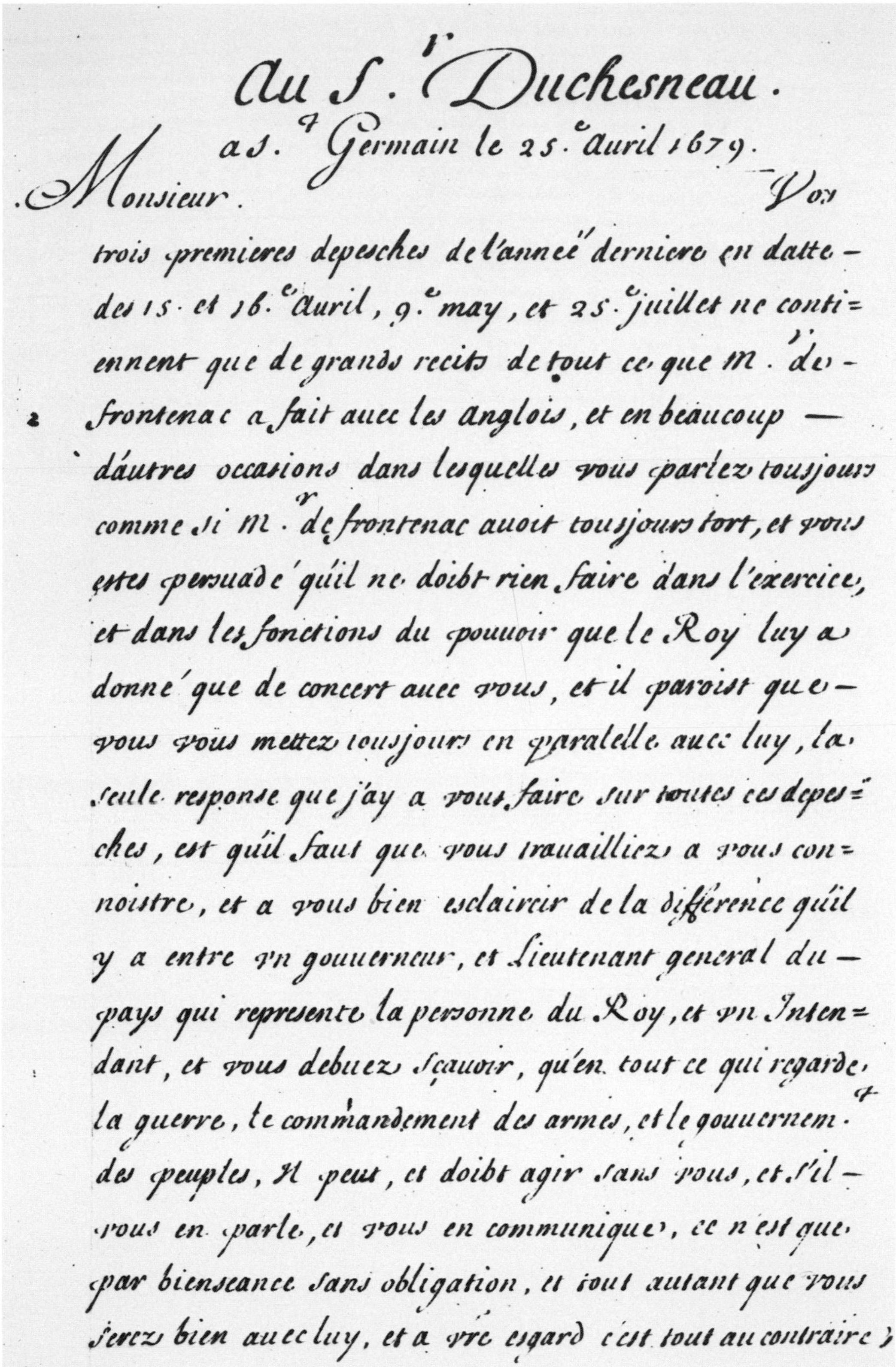

Au Sr. Duchesneau.

a St. Germain le 25e auril 1679.

Monsieur. Vos trois premieres depesches de l'année derniere en datte des 15. et 16e auril, 9e may, et 25e juillet ne contiennent que de grands recits de tout ce que Mr. de frontenac a fait auec les anglois, et en beaucoup d'autres occasions dans lesquelles vous parlez tousjours comme si Mr. de frontenac auoit tousjours tort, et vous estes persuadé qu'il ne doibt rien faire dans l'exercice, et dans les fonctions du pouuoir que le Roy luy a donné que de concert auec vous, et il paroist que vous vous mettez tousjours en paralelle auec luy, la seule response que j'ay a vous faire sur toutes ces depesches, est qu'il faut que vous trauailliez a vous connoistre, et a vous bien esclaircir de la difference qu'il y a entre vn gouuerneur, et Lieutenant general du pays qui represente la personne du Roy, et vn Intendant, et vous debuez sçauoir, qu'en tout ce qui regarde la guerre, le commandement des armes, et le gouuernemt. des peuples, il peut, et doibt agir sans vous, et s'il vous en parle, et vous en communique, ce n'est que par bienseance sans obligation, et tout autant que vous serez bien auec luy, et a vre esgard c'est tout au contraire ;

Letter from the minister Colbert to Intendant Jacques Duchesneau, Saint-Germain-en-Laye, 25 April 1679.

He blamed him for speaking "as if M. de Frontenac was always wrong," and for "always drawing a parallel" between himself and Frontenac.

Occasions for wrangling were frequent between the governor general and the intendant, whose respective jurisdictions overlapped and often were opposed in practice.

Archives nationales, Paris, France: Fonds des Colonies, série B, vol. 8, fol. 3.

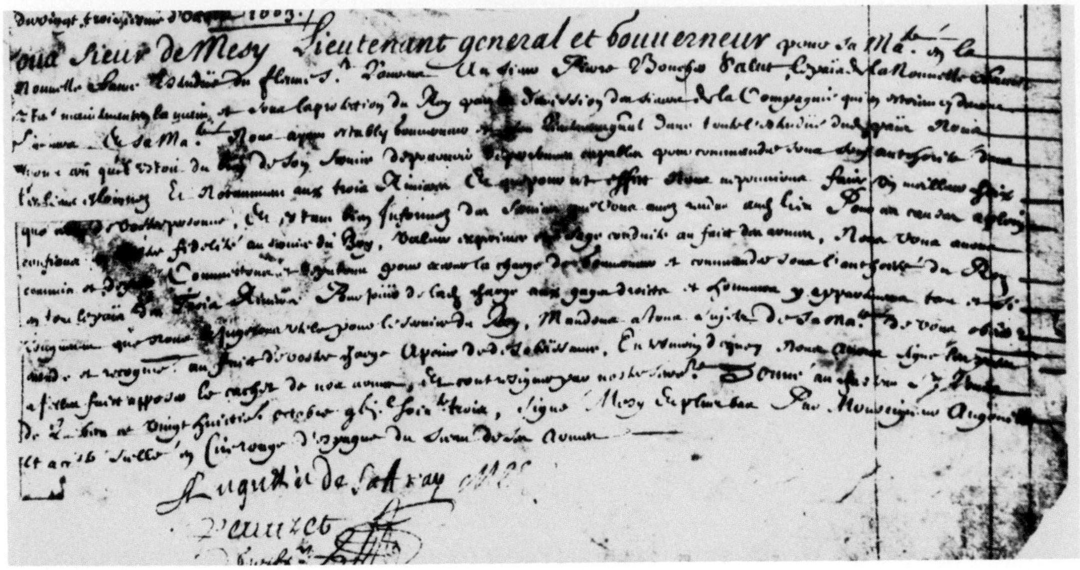

Sieur de Mesy Lieutenant general et Gouuerneur

Commission as governor of Trois-Rivières granted Pierre Boucher by Governor General Mézy, Québec, 28 October 1663.

New France was divided into three governments: Québec, Trois-Rivières, and Montréal. The governor general, who resided at Québec, had a representative, the local governor, in each of the governments of Montréal and Trois-Rivières.

Archives nationales du Québec, Centre d'archives de la Capitale, Québec: Insinuations du Conseil souverain, vol. 1, fol. 5.

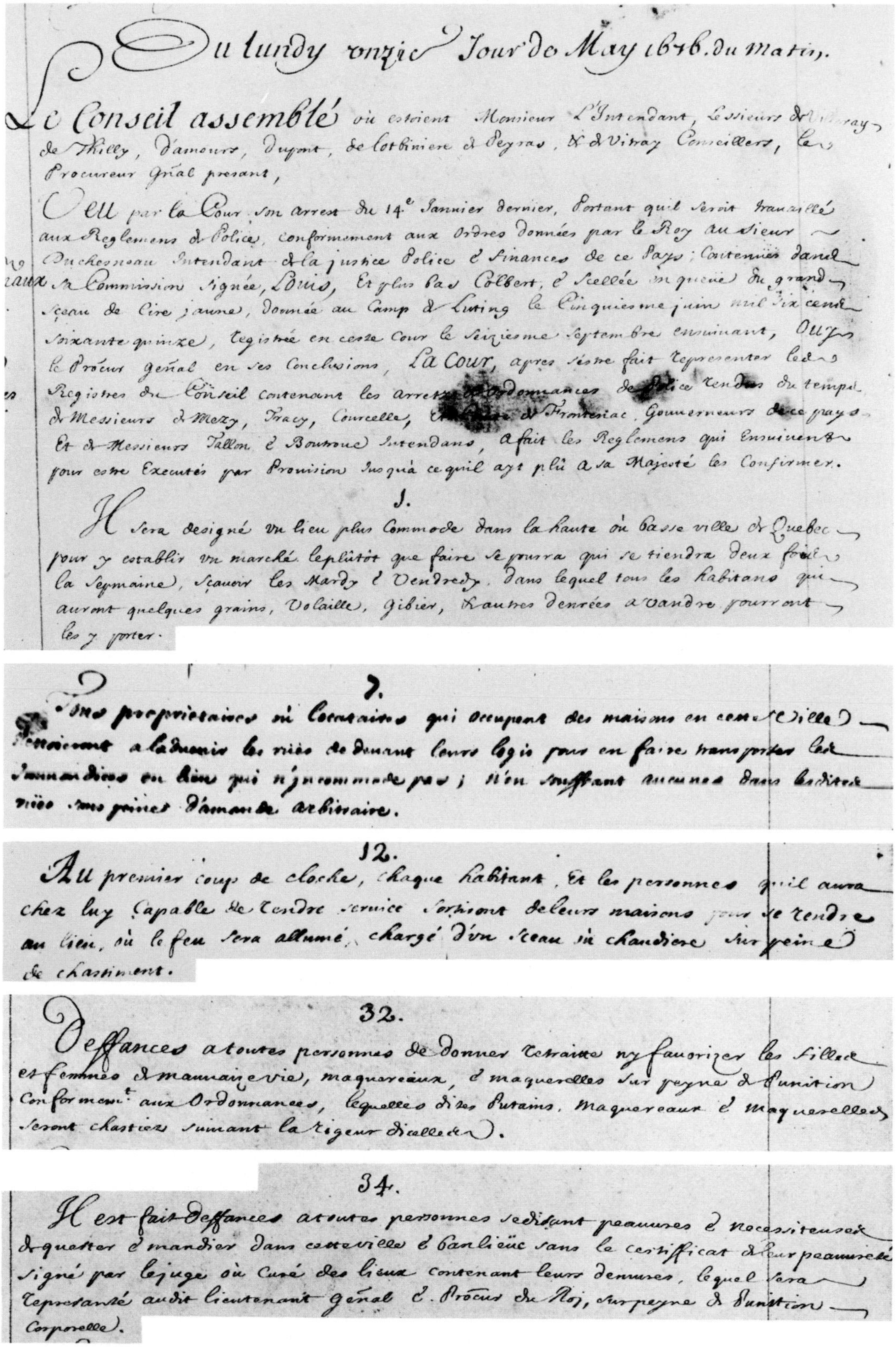

Du lundy onzie Jour de May 1676. du matin.

Le Conseil assemblé où estoient Monsieur L'Intendant, Les sieurs de Villeray, de Thilly, d'amours, dupont, de Lotbiniere de Peyras, & de Vitray Conseillers, le Procureur général present,

Veu par la Cour son arrest du 14e Janvier dernier, Portant qu'il seroit travaillé aux Reglemens de Police, conformement aux Ordres données par le Roy au sieur Duchesneau Intendant de la justice Police & finances de ce Pays; Contenües dans sa Commission signée, Louis, Et plus bas Colbert, & scellée en queüe du grand Sceau de Cire jaune, donnée au Camp de Luting le Cinquiesme juin mil six cens soixante quinze, registrée en ceste Cour le seiziesme Septembre ensuivant, Ouy le Procur général en ses Conclusions, La Cour, apres s'estre fait representer les Registres du Conseil contenant les arrests et Ordonnances de Police rendus du temps de Messieurs de Mezy, Tracy, Courcelle, et [illegible] de Frontenac Gouverneurs de ce pays Et de Messieurs Tallon & Bouteroue Intendans, a fait les Reglemens qui ensuivent pour estre Executés par Provision Jusqu'à ce qu'il ayt plû a sa Majesté les Confirmer.

1.

Il sera designé un lieu plus Commode dans la haute ou basse ville de Quebec pour y establir un marché le plustost que faire se pourra qui se tiendra deux fois la Semaine, sçavoir les Mardy & Vendredy, dans lequel tous les habitans qui auront quelques grains, Volaille, gibier, & autres denrées a vendre pourront les y porter.

7.

Tous proprietaires ou locataires qui occupent des maisons en ceste Ville nettoyeront a l'advenir les rües de devant leurs logis pour en faire transporter les immondices en lieu qui n'y incommode pas; n'en souffrant aucunes dans lesdites rües sous peine d'amande arbitraire.

12.

Au premier coup de cloche, chaque habitant, Et les personnes qu'il aura chez luy capable de rendre service sortiront de leurs maisons pour se rendre au lieu, où le feu sera allumé, chargé d'un sceau ou chaudiere sur peine de chastiment.

32.

Deffences a toutes personnes de donner retraitte ny favoriser les filles et femmes de mauvaise vie, maquereaux, & maquerelles sur peyne de punition conformement aux Ordonnances, lesquelles dites putains, maquereaux & maquerelles seront chastiez suivant la rigeur d'icelles.

34.

Il est fait deffences a toutes personnes se disant pauvres & necessiteux de quester & mandier dans ceste ville & banlieüe sans le certificat de leur pauvreté signé par le juge ou Curé des lieux contenant leurs demeures, lequel sera representé audit lieutenant général & Procur du Roy, sur peyne de punition corporelle.

Regulation issued by the Conseil souverain, Québec, 11 May 1676.

This regulation dealt particularly with trade, cleanliness in public places, protection against fire, and morality.

Archives nationales du Québec, Centre d'archives de la Capitale, Québec: Jugements et délibérations du Conseil souverain, vol. 1, fol. 270v, 271, 273.

IV

Justice

Under the régime of the Compagnie des Indes occidentales the judicial system of New France began to take form.

In 1666 and 1667 the company set up two courts of justice, one at Québec (the Provost Court of Québec), the other at Trois-Rivières (the Jurisdiction of Trois-Rivières). Since the seigneurs of Montréal had power of justice, it was not until 1693 that a jurisdiction was established there. The tribunals of the three towns heard civil and criminal cases in the first instance; those of Québec and Trois-Rivières also heard appeals coming from the seigneurial courts in their governments. Soon cases concerning maritime law came under the Provost Court of Québec, and that is the reason that it was eventually called the Provost and Admiralty Court of Québec. Appeals from the three courts came before the Conseil souverain, the highest court of appeal.

After the dismissal of the Compagnie des Indes occidentales the administration of justice was the responsibility of the intendant. Thus it was he who, following recommendations by the seigneurs, named the judges in the seigneuries that possessed a court and presented to the king, who made the appointments, the court officers of the Provost Court of Québec and of the Jurisdictions of Trois-Rivières and Montréal.

Following a tradition that began with Talon, the intendant himself rendered justice "out of charity" when small civil cases were involved.

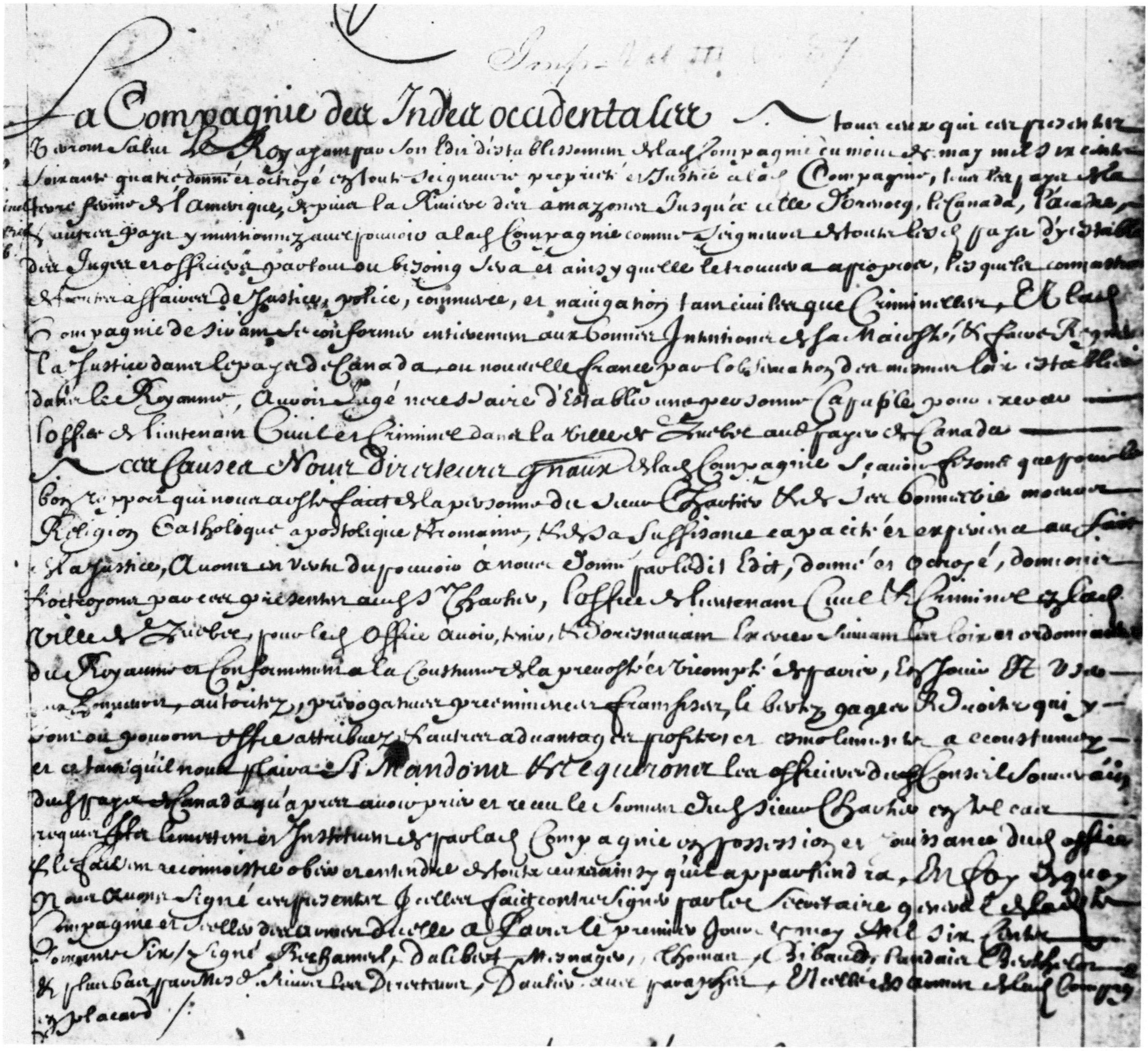
La Compagnie des Indes occidentales

Commission as lieutenant general for civil and criminal affairs of the Provost Court of Québec granted Louis-Théandre Chartier de Lotbinière, Paris, 1 May 1666.

The Provost Court of Québec and the Jurisdiction of Trois-Rivières were first of all courts of first instance. They also heard appeals from the seigneurial tribunals in their governments.

Archives nationales du Québec, Centre d'archives de la Capitale, Québec: Insinuations du Conseil souverain, vol. 1, fol. 29.

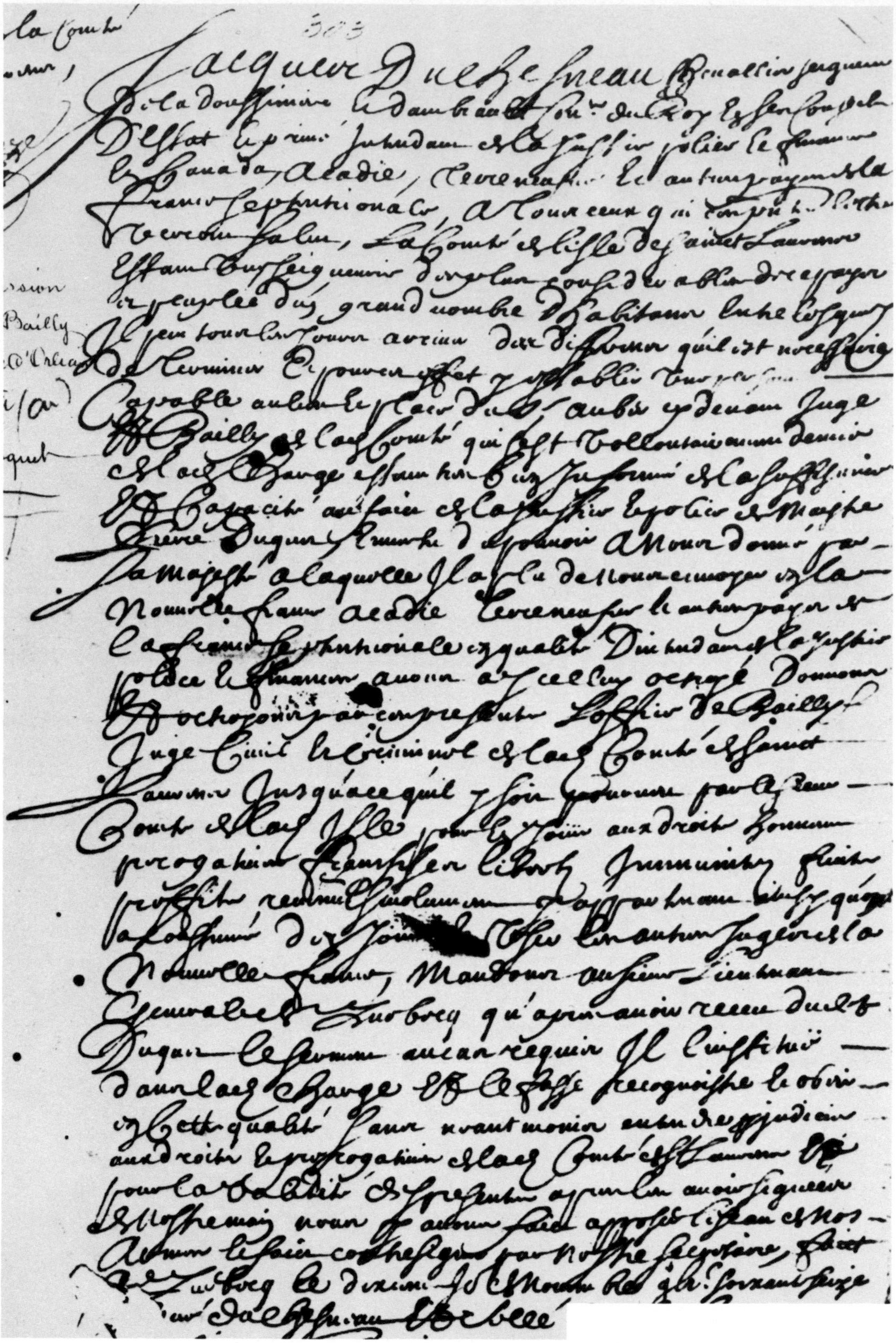

Commission from Intendant Duchesneau appointing Pierre Duquet judge and bailiff of the Île Saint-Laurent (Île d'Orléans), Québec, 10 November 1676.

"Being very well informed of the competence and ability in matters of justice and police of Maître Pierre Duquet…we have granted him, give and grant hereby the office of bailiff civil and criminal judge for the said county of Saint-Laurent."

Archives nationales du Québec, Centre d'archives de la Capitale, Québec: Insinuations de la Prévôté de Québec, vol. 1, fol. 303.

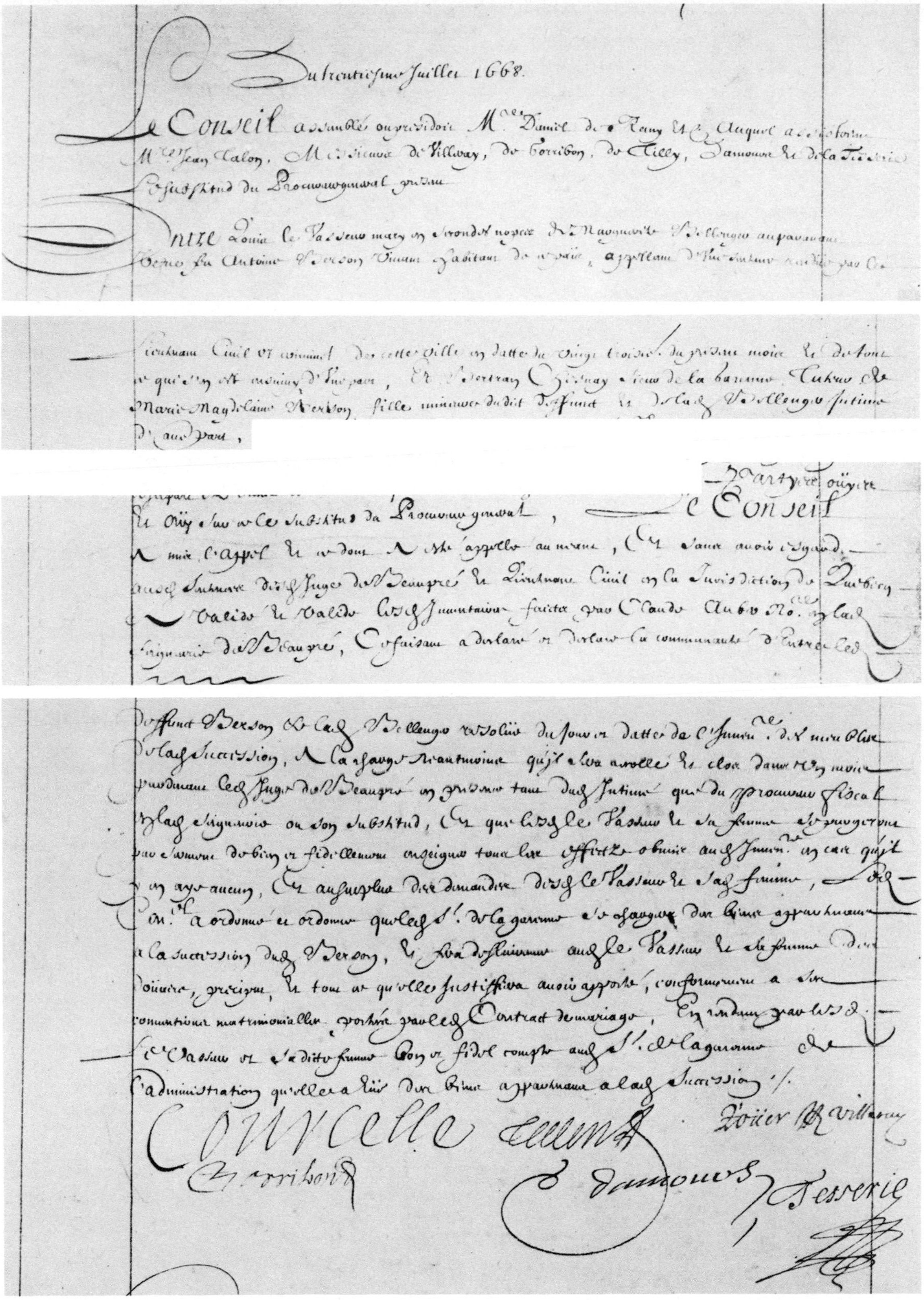
Du trentiesme Juillet 1668.

Le Conseil assemblé ou presidoit Mr. Daniel de Remy etc. Auquel assistoient Mr. Jean Talon, Mrs. Sieurs de Villeray, de Gorribon, de Tilly, Damours et de la Tesserie

Entre Louis Le Vasseur ... appellant ... et Bertrand Chesnay ... tuteur de Marie Magdelaine Berson, fille mineure dudit deffunct ...

... Le Conseil ...

Courcelle Talon Rouer Villeray Gorribon Damours Tesserie

Decision of the Conseil souverain in the lawsuit between Louis Le Vasseur, "appellant against a decision reached by the lieutenant for civil and criminal affairs of this town," and Bertrand Chesnay, guardian of Marie-Madeleine Berson, Québec, 30 July 1668.

The Conseil souverain heard appeals emanating from the lower courts of the colony.

Archives nationales du Québec, Centre d'archives de la Capitale, Québec: Jugements et délibérations du Conseil souverain, vol. 1, fol. 93–94v.

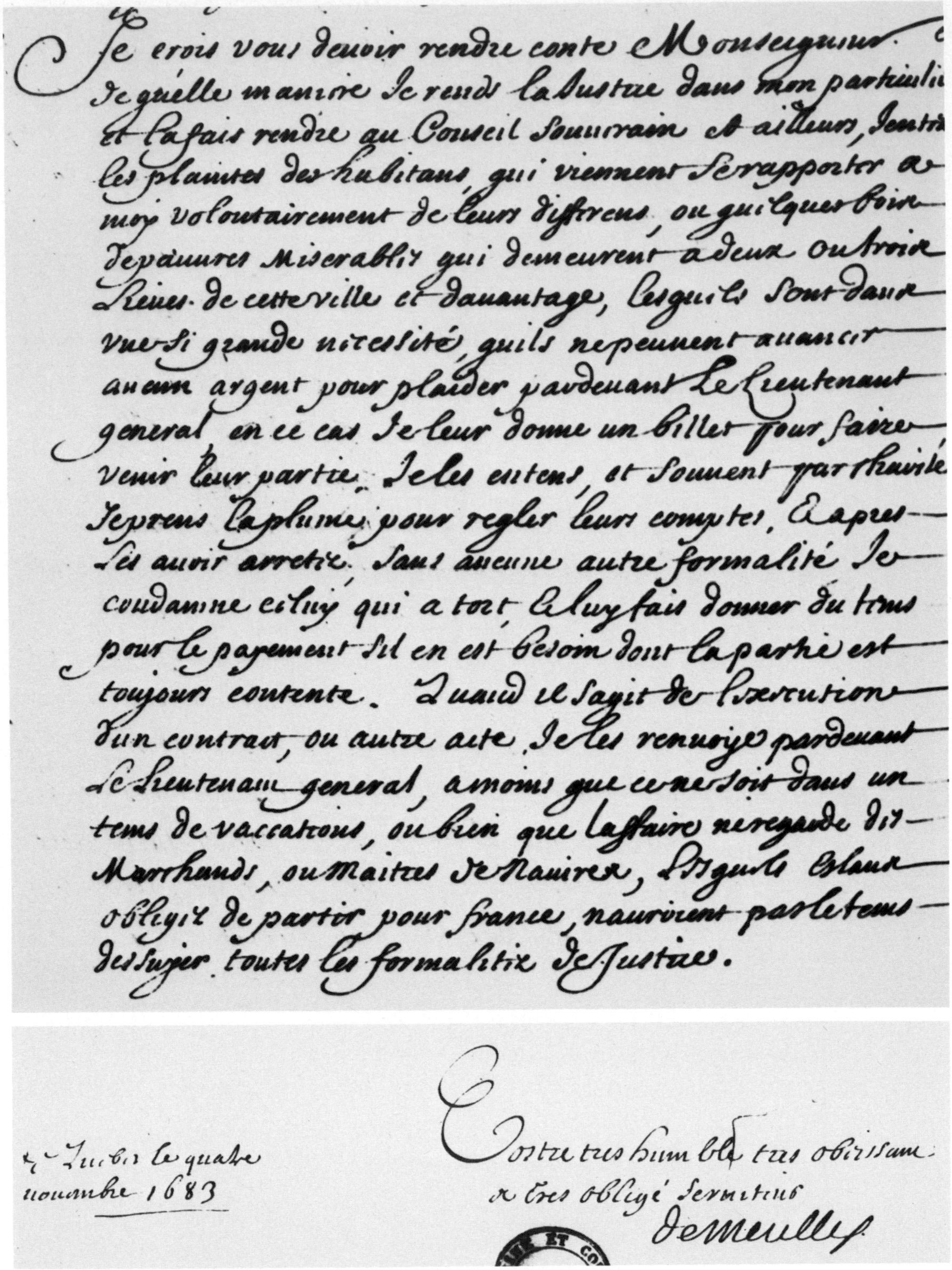

Je crois vous devoir rendre conte Monseigneur
de quelle maniere Je rends la Justice dans mon particulier
et la fais rendre au Conseil Souverain et ailleurs, Jentens
les plaintes des habitans, qui viennent se rapporter a
moy volontairement de leurs differens, ou quelquefois
de pauvres Miserables qui demeurent a deux ou trois
Lieues de cette ville et davantage, lesquels sont dans
une si grande necessité, quils ne peuvent avancer
aucun argent pour plaider pardevant Le Lieutenant
general, en ce cas Je leur donne un billet pour faire
venir leur partie. Je les entens, et souvent par lhuile
Je prens la plume pour regler leurs comptes, Et apres
les avoir arrestez. sans aucune autre formalité Je
condamne celuy qui a tort, Et luy fais donner du tems
pour le payement sil en est besoin dont la partie est
toujours contente. Quand il sagit de lexecution
dun contract, ou autre acte, Je les renvoye pardevant
Le Lieutenant general, a moins que ce ne soit dans un
tems de vaccations, ou bien que laffaire ne regarde des
Marchands, ou Maitres de Navires, lesquels estans
obligez de partir pour france, nauroient pas le tems
de subir toutes les formalitez de Justice.

a Quebec le quatre
novembre 1683

Vostre tres humble tres obeissant
et tres obligé serviteur
deMeulles

Letter from Intendant de Meulles to the minister Seignelay, Québec, 4 November 1683.

As de Meulles explains, on occasion an intendant dispensed justice himself when small civil cases were involved: "I hear the complaints of the habitants who readily come to present their differences to me, or sometimes of poor wretches" who "cannot put up any money to plead their cause before the lieutenant general."

Archives nationales, Paris, France: Fonds des Colonies, série C^{11A}, vol. 6, fol. 194v, 198.

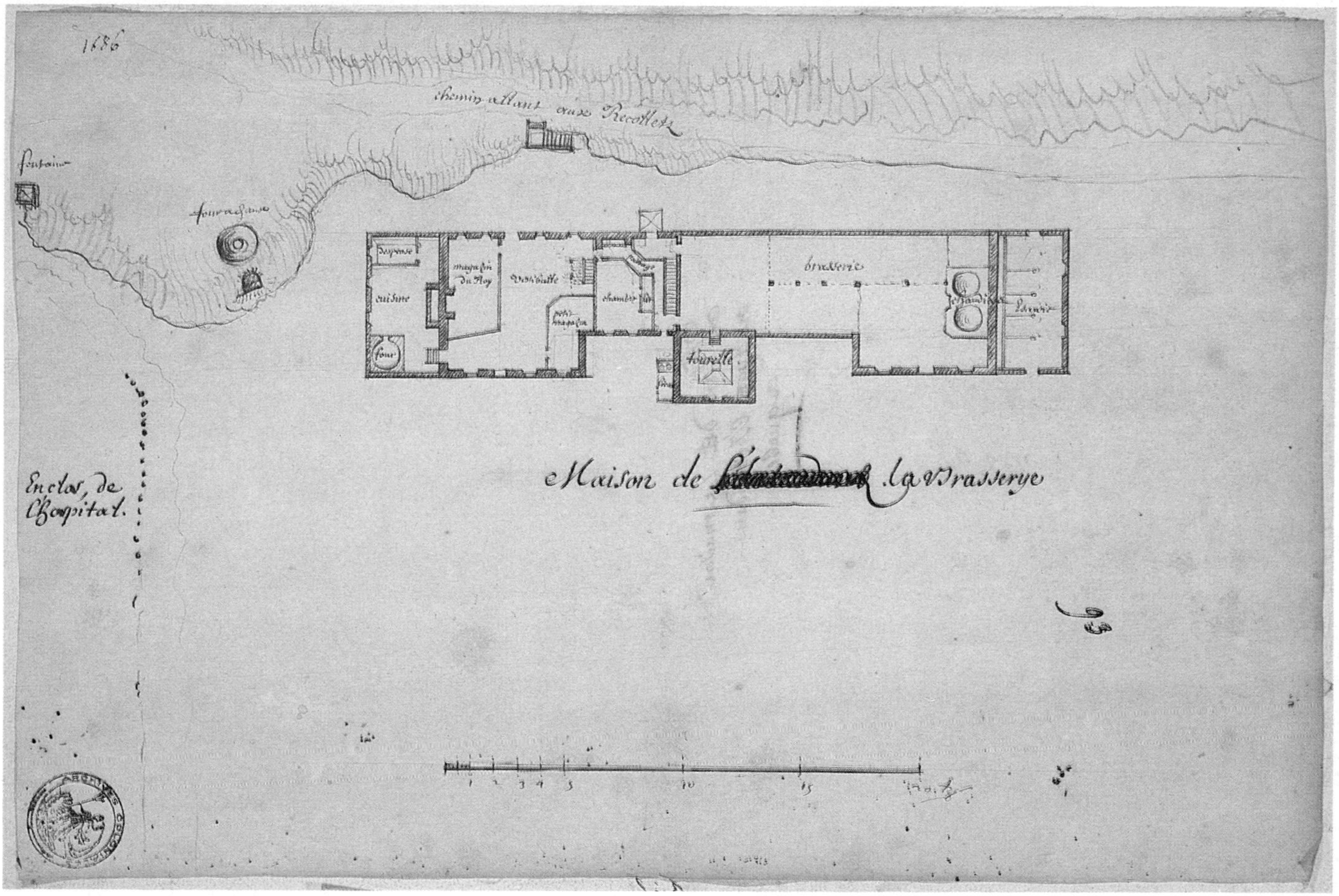

"Maison de l'intendant...la Brasserie," [1686]; anonymous; ms.; 24.5 x 36.7 cm.

Plan of the brewery that Talon had built at Québec in 1668–70. It began production in 1670 and shut down in 1675. This building, which was sold to the king in 1685, became the intendant's residence and the seat of the Conseil souverain.

Archives nationales, Paris, France: Section Outre-Mer, Atlas Colonies, vol. III, no. 93.

IV

Acadia and Newfoundland

Since 1632 two seigneurs had shared authority in Acadia: quarrels soon broke out over each one's jurisdiction. On 10 February 1638 the king wrote Charles de Menou d'Aulnay to make clear to him "the limits of the places" where he and Charles de Saint-Étienne de La Tour would have "authority to command, one and the other."

After being in the hands of the English from 1654 to 1667, Acadia got away a little from its internal quarrels upon the arrival of the first real governor in 1670. But fifteen years later the colony had scarcely made any progress. In 1687, in the hope of inspiring it with some enthusiasm, the king gave Acadia a new governor, Louis-Alexandre Des Friches de Meneval, and provided the ordinary court of Acadia with a new judge and a new king's attorney.

In Newfoundland David Kirke was the first English governor, from 1638 to 1651; then the British government sent commissioners who had the mission of putting an end to his mandate. Soon, after John Treworgie's régime, authority passed to the commandant (or "commodore") of the convoy which escorted the fishing ships every year and to the "fishing admirals" – the first ship's captains to reach a port. Administration of the French territory of Newfoundland – Plaisance (Placentia) and the southern part of the island – was carried out better; from 1655 governors succeeded one another there without interruption.

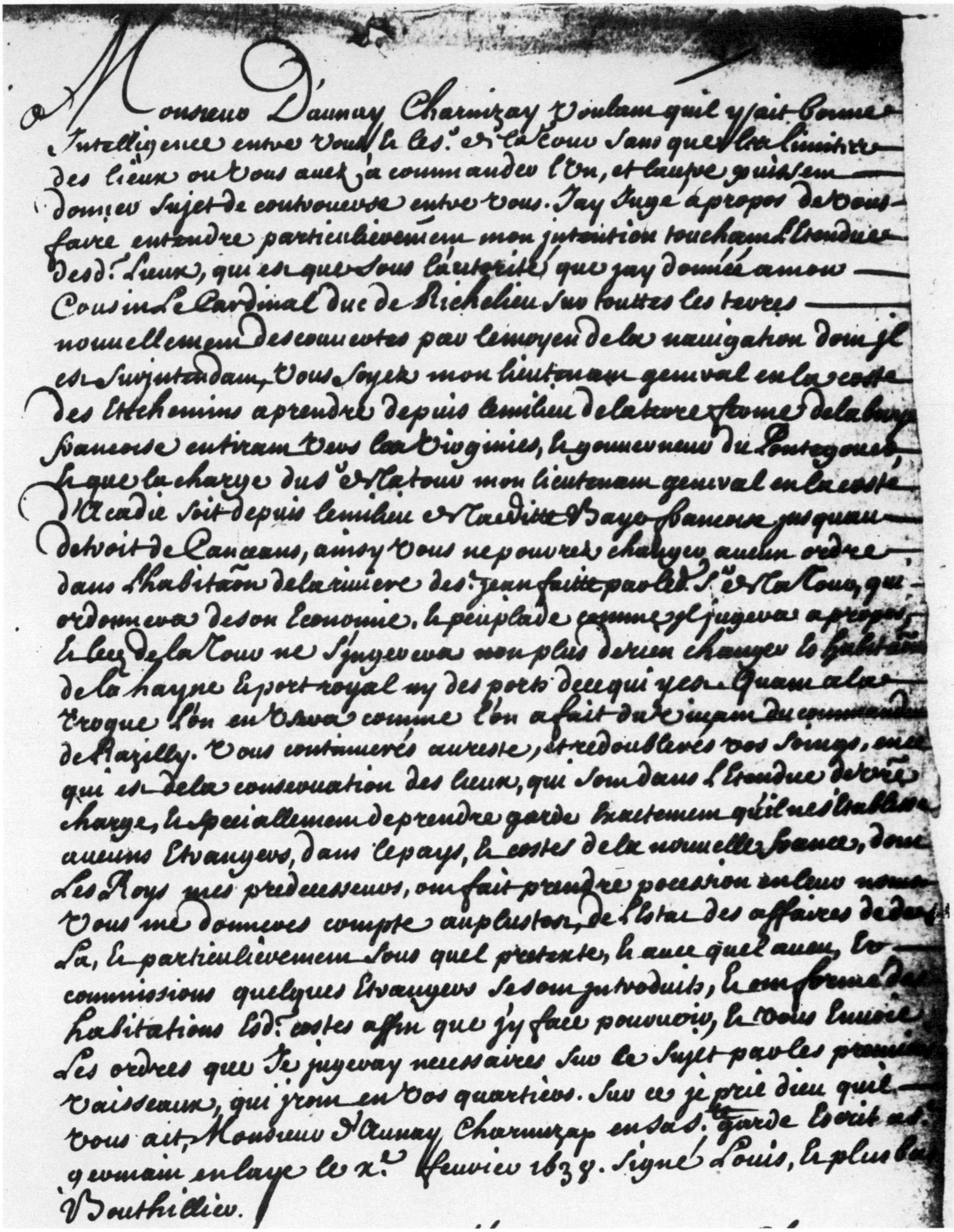

Monsieur D'aunay Charnizay voulant qu'il y ait bonne
Intelligence entre vous, le Sr. de la Tour sans que les limites
des lieux ou vous avez à commander l'un, et l'autre puissent
donner sujet de controverse entre vous. J'ay jugé à propos de vous
faire entendre particulièrement mon intention touchant l'estendue
desd. Lieux, qui est que sous l'autorité que j'ay donnée a mon
Cousin le Cardinal duc de Richelieu sur toutes les terres
nouvellement descouvertes par le moyen de la navigation dont il
est surintendant, vous soyez mon lieutenant general en la coste
des Etchemins a prendre depuis le milieu de la terre ferme de la baye
françoise en tirant vers les Virginies, et gouverneur de Pentegouet,
et que la charge dud. Sr. de la Tour mon lieutenant general en la coste
d'Acadie soit depuis le milieu de ladite Baye françoise jusqu'au
destroit de Canceaus, ainsy vous ne pourrez changer aucun ordre
dans l'habitation de la riviere de St. Jean faitte par led. Sr. de la Tour, qui
ordonnera de son economie, la peuplade comme il jugera a propos,
et led. de la Tour ne s'ingerera non plus de rien changer les habitans
de la hayne et port royal ny des ports de ce qui y est. Quant a la
troque l'on en usera comme l'on a fait du vivant du commandeur
de Razilly. Vous continuerés au reste, et redoublerés vos soings, en ce
qui est de la conservation des lieux, qui sont dans l'estendue de vostre
charge, et specialement de prendre garde exactement qu'il ne s'establisse
aucuns Etrangers dans le pays, et costes de la nouvelle france, dont
Les Roys mes predecesseurs, ont fait prendre possession en leur nom.
Vous me donnerez compte au plustost, de l'estat des affaires de de
La, et particulierement sous quel pretexte, et avec quel aveu, et
commissions quelques Etrangers se sont introduits, et ont formé des
habitations esd. costes affin que j'y face pourvoir, et vous envoie
Les ordres que je jugeray necessaires sur le sujet par les premiers
vaisseaux, qui iront en vos quartiers. Sur ce je prie dieu qu'il
vous ait, Monsieur d'Aunay Charnizay en sa Ste. garde. Escrit a St.
germain en laye le xe. fevrier 1638. signé Louis, et plus bas
Bouthillier.

Letter from Louis XIII, king of France, to Charles de Menou d'Aulnay, Saint-Germain-en-Laye, 10 February 1638.

The king was laying down the boundaries of the areas of which d'Aulnay and La Tour would have command respectively in Acadia: "I want you, d'Aulnay, to be my lieutenant general for the coast of the Etchemins from the middle of the mainland of the Baie Française [Bay of Fundy] and extending in the direction of the Virginias, and governor of Pentagouet, and that the responsibility of the Sieur de La Tour, my lieutenant general for the coast of Acadia, extend from the middle of the aforementioned Baie Française to the Strait of Canso."

Archives nationales, Paris, France: Fonds des Colonies, série C^{11D}, vol. 1, fol. 64.

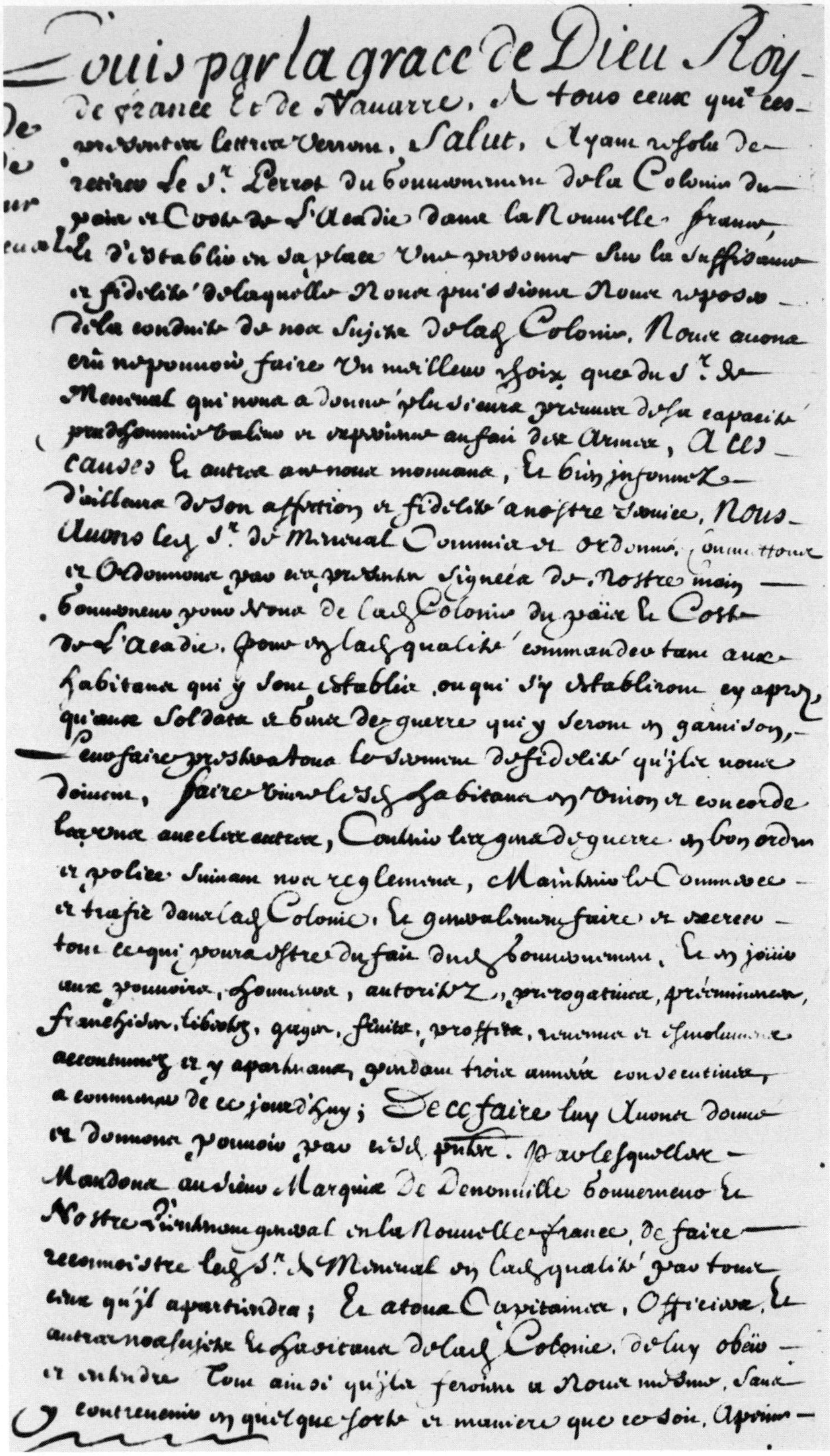

Louis par la grace de Dieu Roy
de france et de Navarre, A tous ceux qui ces
presentes lettres verront, Salut, Ayant resolu de
retirer le Sr. Perrot du gouvernement de la Colonie du
pais et Coste de l'Acadie dans la Nouvelle france,
Et d'establir en sa place une personne sur la suffisance
et fidelité de laquelle Nous puissions Nous reposer
de la conduite de nos Sujets de lad. Colonie, Nous avons
crû ne pouvoir faire un meilleur choix que du Sr. de
Meneval qui nous a donné plusieurs preuves de sa capacité
prud'hommie valeur et experience au fait des Armes, A ces
causes et autres a ce nous mouvans, Et bien informez
d'ailleurs de son affection et fidelité a nostre service, Nous
avons led. Sr. de Meneval Commis et ordonné, Commettons
et Ordonnons par ces presentes signées de Nostre main
gouverneur pour Nous de lad. Colonie du pais et Coste
de l'Acadie, pour en lad. qualité commander tant aux
habitans qui y sont establis, ou qui s'y establiront cy apres,
qu'aux Soldats et gens de guerre qui y seront en garnison,
leur faire prester a tous le serment de fidelité qu'ils nous
doivent, faire vivre lesd. habitans en union et concorde
les uns avec les autres, Contenir lesd. gens de guerre en bon ordre
et police suivant nos reglemens, Maintenir le Commerce
et trafic dans lad. Colonie, Et generalement faire et exercer
tout ce qui pourra estre du fait dud. gouvernement, Et en jouir
aux pouvoirs, honneurs, autoritez, prerogatives, préeminences,
franchises, libertez, gages, droits, proffits, revenus et emolumens
accoustumez et y appartenans, pendant trois années consecutives,
a commencer de ce jourd'huy; De ce faire luy Avons donné
et donnons pouvoir par cesd. presentes. Par lesquelles
Mandons au sieur Marquis de Denonville Gouverneur et
Nostre Lieutenant general en la Nouvelle france, de faire
reconnoistre led. Sr. de Meneval en lad. qualité par tous
ceux qu'il appartiendra; Et a tous Capitaines, Officiers, Et
autres nos sujets et habitans de lad. Colonie, de luy obeir
et entendre tant ainsi qu'ils feroient a Nous mesmes, Sans
contrevenir en quelque sorte et maniere que ce soit, Apeine —

Commission from King Louis XIV appointing Louis-Alexandre Des Friches de Meneval governor of Acadia, Versailles, 1 March 1687.

"We have appointed and established, appoint and establish the aforementioned Sieur de Meneval by these present signed by our hand governor for us of the afore[said] colony of the country and coast of Acadia."

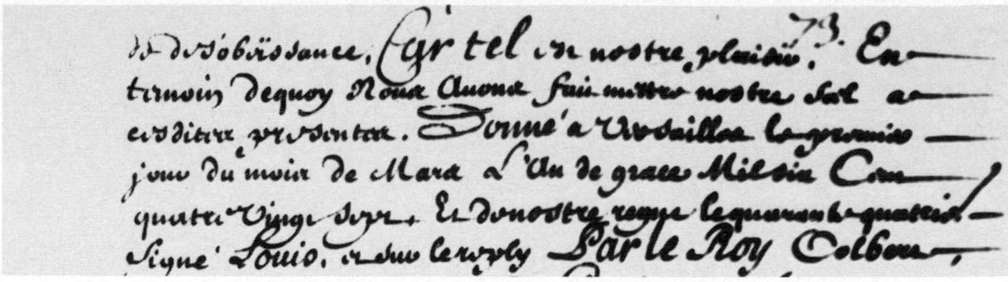
de desobeissance, Car tel est nostre plaisir. 73. En
tesmoin dequoy Nous avons fait mettre nostre scel a
cesdites presentes. Donné a Versailles le premier
jour du mois de Mars l'an de grace Mil six Cens
quatre vingt deux. Et de nostre regne le quarante quatrie-
Signé Louis, et sur le reply Par le Roy Colbert,

Archives nationales du Québec, Centre d'archives de la Capitale, Québec: Insinuations du Conseil souverain, vol. 2, fol. 72.

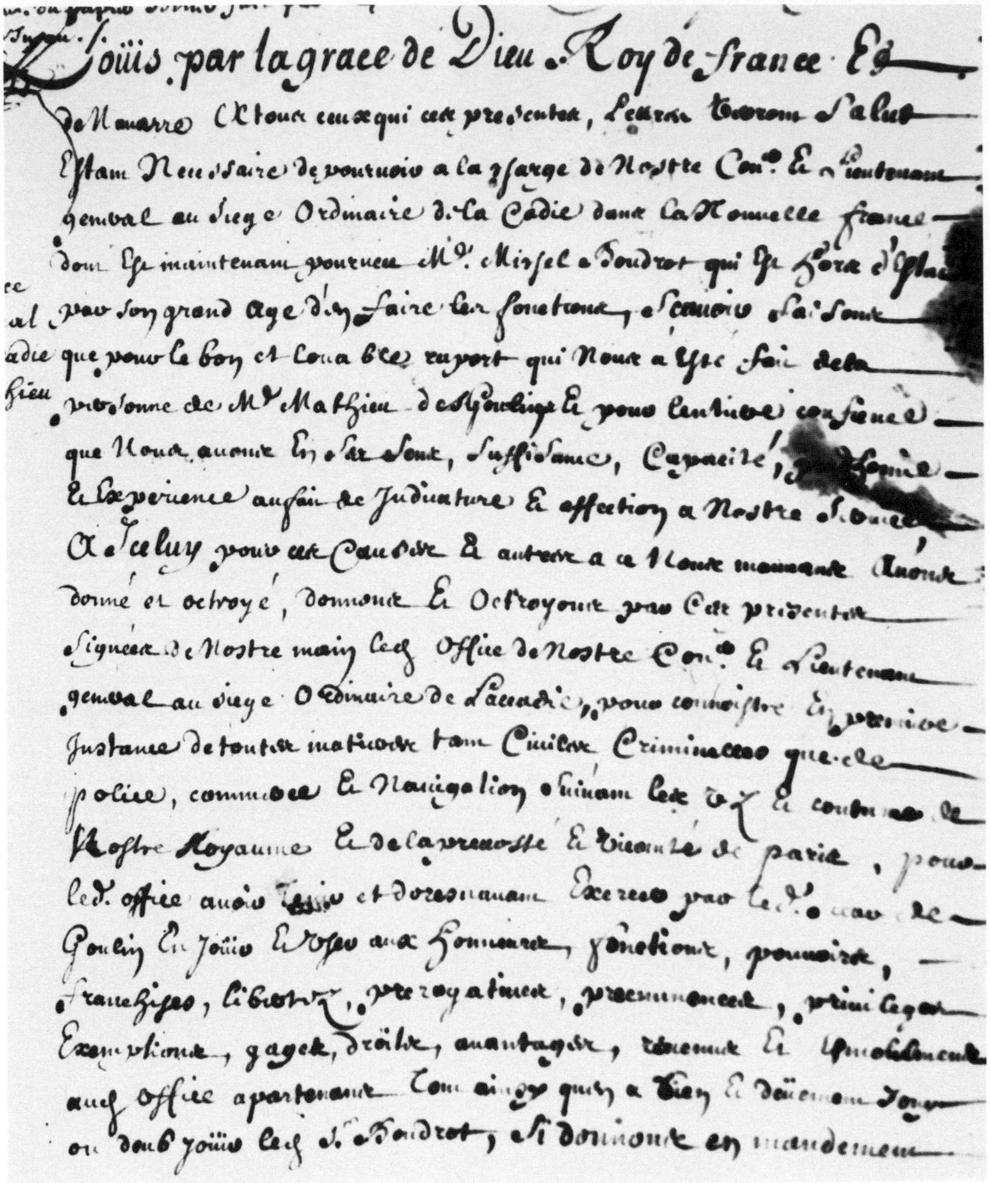

Louis par la grace de Dieu Roy de France et
de Navarre A tous ceux qui ces presentes lettres verront Salut
Estant necessaire de pourvoir a la charge de Nostre Con.er et Lieutenant
general au siege Ordinaire de la Cadie dans la Nouvelle france
dont est maintenant pourveu M.e Michel Boudrot qui est hors d'estat
par son grand age d'y faire les fonctions, et scavoir faisons
que pour le bon et louable raport qui Nous a esté fait de la
personne de M.e Mathieu de Goutin et pour l'entiere confiance
que Nous avons en ses sens, suffisance, capacité, preud'homie
et experience au fait de Judicature et affection a Nostre service
A celuy pour ces causes et autres a ce Nous mouvans Avons
donné et octroyé, donnons et octroyons par ces presentes
signées de Nostre main led. Office de Nostre Con.er et Lieutenant
general au siege Ordinaire de l'Acadie, pour connoistre en premiere
Instance de toutes matieres tant Civiles Criminelles que de
police, commerce et Navigation suivant les us et coutumes de
Nostre Royaume et de la prevosté et Vicomté de paris, pour
led. office avoir tenir et doresnavant exercer par led. S.r de
Goutin en jouir et user aux honneurs, fonctions, pouvoirs,
franchises, libertez, prerogatives, preeminences, privileges
exemptions, gages, droits, avantages, revenus et emoluments
aud. office apartenans tout ainsy qu'en a bien et deuement jouy
ou deub jouir led. S.r Boudrot, Si donnons en mandement

Commission from King Louis XIV appointing Mathieu de Goutin "lieutenant general of the ordinary court of Acadia, to hear in the first instance all matters, civil, criminal, and those pertaining to public order, trade, and navigation according to the usages and customs of our kingdom and of the Provost and Viscounty Court of Paris," Versailles, 31 March 1687.

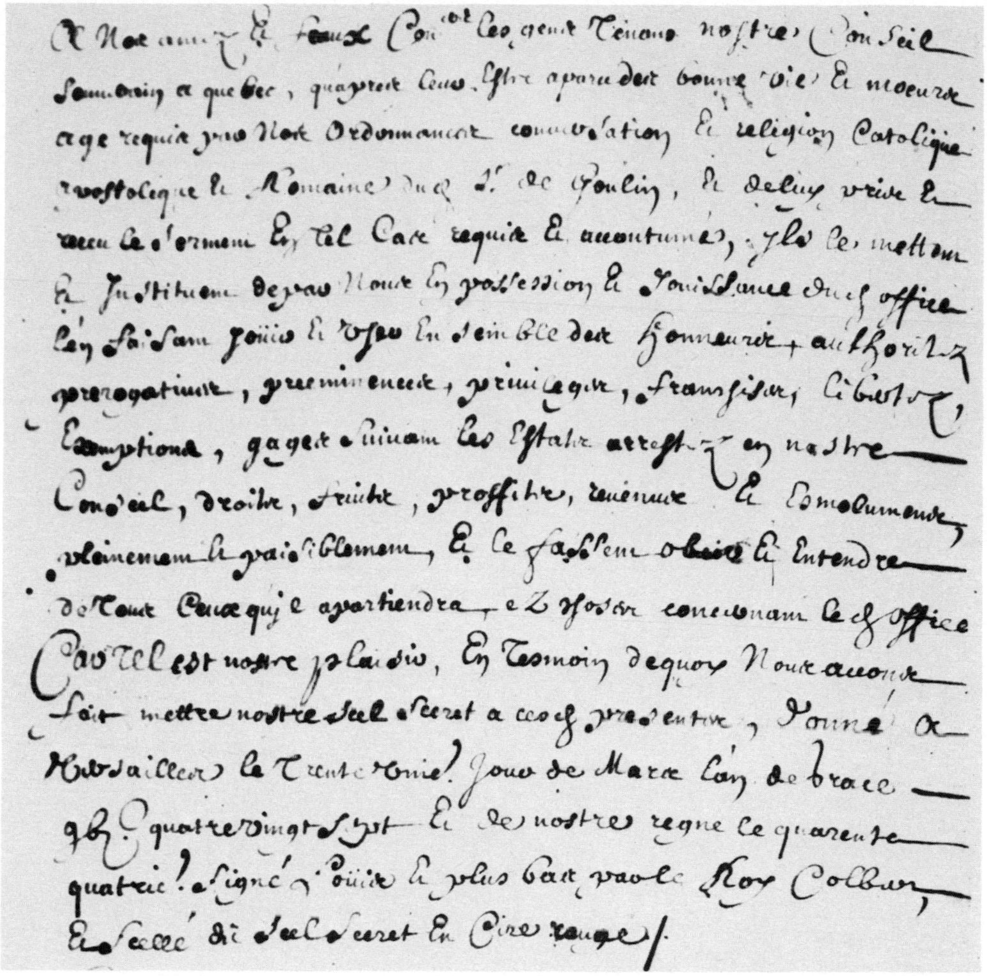
A Nos amez et feaux Con.ers les gens tenans nostre Conseil
Souverain a quebec, qu'apres leur estre aparu des bonne vie et moeurs
age requis par Nos Ordonnances conversation et religion Catolique
apostolique et Romaine dud. S.r de Joulin, et deluy pris et
receu le serment en tel cas requis et accoutumés, Ils le mettent
et Instituent de par Nous en possession et Jouissance dud. office
l'en faisant jouir et user ensemble des honneurs, authoritez
prerogatives, preeminences, privileges, franchises, libertez
Exemptions, gages suivant les Estats arrestez en nostre
Conseil, droits, fruits, proffits, revenus et Emoluments,
pleinement et paisiblement, et le fassent obeir et entendre
de tous ceux qu'il apartiendra es choses concernant led. office
Car tel est nostre plaisir, En tesmoin dequoy Nous avons
fait mettre nostre seel secret a ces d. presentes, Donné a
Versailles le trente unie. jour de Mars l'an de grace
mil six cent quatrevingt sept et de nostre regne le quarante
quatrie. Signé Louis et plus bas par le Roy Colbert,
Et scellé du seel secret en cire rouge/.

Archives nationales du Québec, Centre d'archives de la Capitale, Québec: Insinuations du Conseil souverain, vol. 2, fol. 74–74v.

Portrait of Charles de Menou d'Aulnay (circa 1604–50); artist unknown; sepia drawing; 1642; 16.8 x 13.6 cm.

Lieutenant general in Acadia from 1638 on and governor of that colony from 1647 to 1650, d'Aulnay established several settlers there and supplied them with the means to live by farming, fishing, and engaging in industry.

New Brunswick Museum, St. John.

Portrait of Sir Humphrey Gilbert (circa 1537–83); artist unknown; oil.

On 5 August 1583 Sir Humphrey Gilbert officially took possession of Newfoundland in the name of the queen of England. From 1610 on the English were the first Europeans to have permanent settlements on the island. Towards the end of the seventeenth century the English colony amounted to nearly two thousand souls, spread out in about thirty-five bays or harbours on the east coast. The principal settlements were St. John's, Renews, Ferryland, Bay Bulls and Carbonear.

Mrs. Walter Raleigh Gilbert, Compton Castle, Devon, England.

V

Wars

Probably to ensure their friendship and encourage the fur trade, Champlain had promised the Algonkins and Montagnais to help them in their war against the Iroquois. In 1609 and 1610 the allies won two victories in succession; in 1615, being badly supported by the Indians and having been wounded, Champlain had to give up the fight before winning. Peace was concluded on the Iroquois' initiative in 1624; in 1627 it was broken.

Another enemy was not long in appearing. As a result of the creation of the Virginia Company of London the question of the "boundaries" of Acadia arose. For the gentlemen of Virginia – a geographical term that designated all New England – Acadia was a threat. In 1613, after seizing two French ships in the port of Pentagouet, Samuel Argall pillaged and razed to the ground the settlements of Saint-Sauveur, Île Sainte-Croix, and Port-Royal.

Fifteen years later, at the moment when Champlain could hope that the colony was finally established, the Kirke brothers, who held letters of marque and reprisal from the authorities in London, captured the Cent-Associés' ships. After this initial success an Anglo-Scottish company was formed to trade in furs on the St. Lawrence. In 1629 Sir William Alexander seized Port-Royal with the permission of Charles I of England, while at Québec David Kirke was forcing Champlain to surrender.

Thus, even before New France was truly established in North America, the first territorial and economic rivalries, which would finally overcome her, were becoming apparent. At the same time an alliance was being formed that would become traditional: the French were siding with the Algonkins, Montagnais, and Hurons against the Iroquois.

In 1614, moreover, the Dutch in New Netherland (New York) had sealed an alliance, which was more an economic than military one, with the Iroquois tribes; the Iroquois would deliver furs to the Dutch, who would supply them with European products in exchange. As their territories were poor in furs, the Iroquois devised the scheme of diverting towards New Netherland the pelts belonging to the Hurons, who obtained them from other tribes. Lying in ambush along the rivers at the periods when the heavily-laden canoes were making their way towards the French colony, the Iroquois, attacking without warning, would massacre the canoeists, take over and send their cargo off to the Dutch trading posts.

From 1632 on the Iroquois made a practice of making raids into the colony. After 1639, having been supplied by the Dutch with harquebuses, they became much bolder. A little time before the short peace of 1645 they made ready a very daring plan: wipe out the Hurons and take their place as middlemen in the fur trade. By 1649 Huronia was already destroyed. As this victory had had the unexpected effect of strengthening the bonds between the tribes that supplied the furs and the French, the Iroquois resolved to destroy the whole French trading network. They carried the war to the allied tribes everywhere: in Acadia, at Tadoussac, at Lac Saint-Jean, on the Saint-Maurice, on the Ottawa. And once trade was almost completely paralyzed, they turned against the French themselves, to drive them out of the valley of the St. Lawrence.

They reduced the colony to dire straits. In 1660 many of the French were afraid that they would have to "leave this country." Desperate appeals to the king were finally heard: in 1665 the Carignan-Salières regiment arrived and the following year it destroyed part of the Iroquois villages. In 1667 peace was made. Now, that same year the Treaty of Breda returned Acadia to France, which had been in English hands since the capture of Port-Royal by Robert Sedgwick on 16 August 1654. New France took advantage of the peace to consolidate its positions.

The next serious action again came from the Iroquois who, being "at peace" with the French, carried the war into the territory of an allied tribe, the Illinois. Governor Antoine Le Febvre de La Barre made the situation worse by his cupidity; finally, in 1684, at Famine Cove on the southeast side of Lake Ontario, he had to accept the peace terms dictated to him by the Iroquois, who were in part won over to the English cause. In the spring of 1687 his successor, Jacques-René de Brisay de Denonville, led an expedition against the Senecas, whose country he ravaged. For a long time there was no response; then the Iroquois struck the colony hard at several points, particularly at Lachine in August 1689.

War had broken out again too with the English, who in 1685 had seized Fort Bourbon on Hudson Bay; the following year the French took three of their forts on James Bay. Then it was the war of the League of Augsburg in 1689. Frontenac, who had come back to Québec the same year, tried "to keep...the English occupied at home," to prevent them from joining the Iroquois in their attacks on the colony: in the early months of 1690 he organized raids on Corlaer (New York), Salmon Falls and Casco (Massachusetts). In the autumn, after capturing Port-Royal, Admiral Sir William Phips besieged Québec in vain with thirty-four ships. Later New England was satisfied – except for an attempt against Laprairie in 1692 – with letting the Iroquois fight. In 1696 Frontenac ravaged the Onondagas' country; this expedition put an end to the warlike activity of the Five Nations, who signed the "Peace of Montréal" in 1701.

In 1694 Pierre Le Moyne d'Iberville had seized the main English post on Hudson Bay, Fort Nelson. In 1696 he captured Fort Pemaquid in Acadia, at the mouth of the Kennebec River. Also in that year, in a mad dash, he captured St. John's in Newfoundland and all except two of the English settlements on the island. Back on Hudson Bay the following year, he won, with the *Pélican*, a naval battle against three English ships and forced the commandant of Fort Nelson, which had been taken back from the French in 1696, to surrender. Now, in September 1697 the Treaty of Ryswick, which put an end to hostilities, annulled the conquests on both sides and returned the situation in America to what it had been before the war.

V

The first clashes

Accompanied by his Indian allies Champlain first won two victories against the Iroquois: in 1609, at the south end of Lake Champlain he frightened the enemy by killing two of their chiefs with one harquebus shot; in 1610, on the Richelieu River, he had an even easier success – the last of that kind – against an enemy who was, however, well entrenched in a small fort made of "strong trees."

During this time the English were landing in New England. On 2 July 1613 Samuel Argall, of the Virginia Company of London, seized two French ships, one of which was the *Jonas*, at anchor in the port of Pentagouet; several Frenchmen were killed and others were taken prisoner. In the same year, on the order of the council of Virginia, Argall returned to destroy the French settlements in Acadia.

The English soon took the war to the St. Lawrence. In 1628 the Kirke brothers seized Tadoussac, then captured the Cent-Associés' fleet, which was coming to supply Québec. As they lacked the prime necessities, Champlain and Gravé Du Pont had to surrender the following year, on 19 July. Since Acadia was again in English hands, New France became English.

Having become French again after the peace of 1632, Acadia soon went through a real civil war. In 1643 there was even the spectacle of Charles de La Tour making an attack on Port-Royal at the head of a troop of Frenchmen and some thirty English mercenaries from Boston.

Iroquois Defeat at Lake Champlain (1609); after a drawing by Samuel de Champlain (1567 [?]–1635); etching; 14.9 x 24.4 cm. (plate).

In Samuel de Champlain. *Les voyages dv sievr de Champlain Xaintongeois, capitaine ordinaire pour le roy, en la marine, divisez en deux livres....* Paris: Chez Jean Berjon, 1613, facing p. 232.

The people who supplied the French with furs (Algonkins, Montagnais, etc.) were enemies of the Iroquois. To retain their friendship Champlain had no choice: he had to take part in their wars against the Iroquois. In 1609 and 1610 he was involved in two skirmishes with the Iroquois, the first one at Lake Champlain, the other at the entry to the Richelieu.

National Library of Canada, Rare Books and Manuscripts Division, Ottawa.

Champlain's Second Victory on the Richelieu River (1610); after a drawing by Samuel de Champlain (1567 [?]–1635); etching; 16.1 x 24 cm. (plate).

In Samuel de Champlain. *Les voyages dv sievr de Champlain Xaintongeois, capitaine ordinaire pour le roy, en la marine, divisez en deux livres....* Paris: Chez Jean Berjon, 1613, facing p. 255.

National Library of Canada, Rare Books and Manuscripts Division, Ottawa.

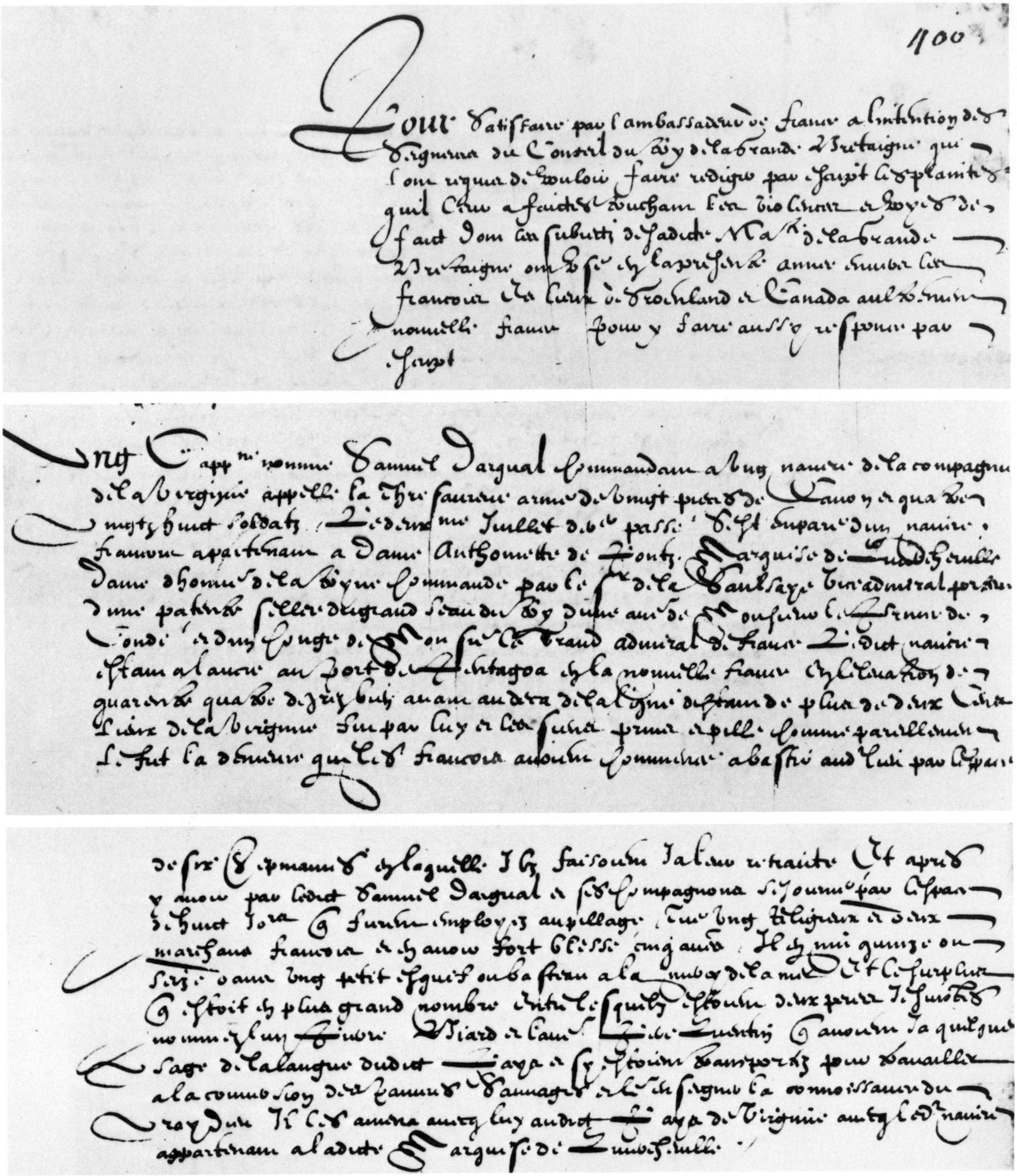

Memoir sent to the Council of England by Samuel Spifame, the French ambassador, 28 December 1613.

"A captain named Samuel Argall commanding a ship of the Virginia Company called the *Trésorerie*...on 2 July last seized a French ship belonging to Dame Antoinette de Pons, Marquise de Guercheville...the said ship being at anchor in the port of Pentagouet...was taken and plundered by him and his men as was the dwelling that the French had begun to build at the aforementioned place."

Bibliothèque nationale, Département des manuscrits, Paris, France: Fonds français, vol. 15987, fol. 400–401.

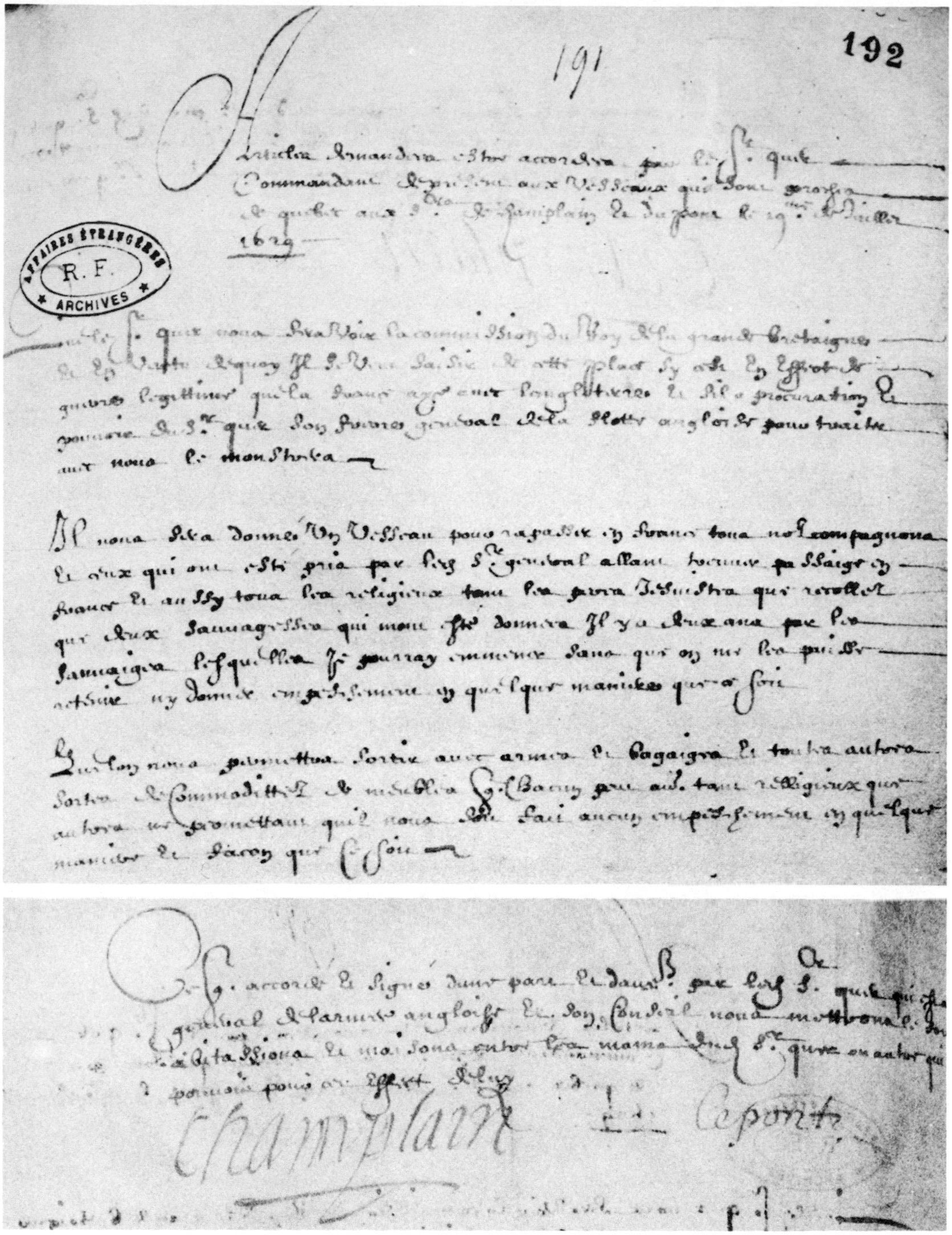
191

192

AFFAIRES ÉTRANGÈRES
R. F.
ARCHIVES

Champlain

Le pont

Terms requested of Kirke by Champlain and Gravé Du Pont for the surrender of Québec, Québec, 19 July 1629.

"A vessel will be given us to carry all our companions back to France. . . . we will be allowed to go out with arms and baggage and all other kinds of personal effects and belongings that each one may have."

Québec and Port-Royal were returned to France by the Treaty of Saint-Germain-en-Laye in 1632.

Archives du ministère des Affaires étrangères, Paris, France: Correspondance politique, Angleterre, vol. 43. fol. 192–192v.

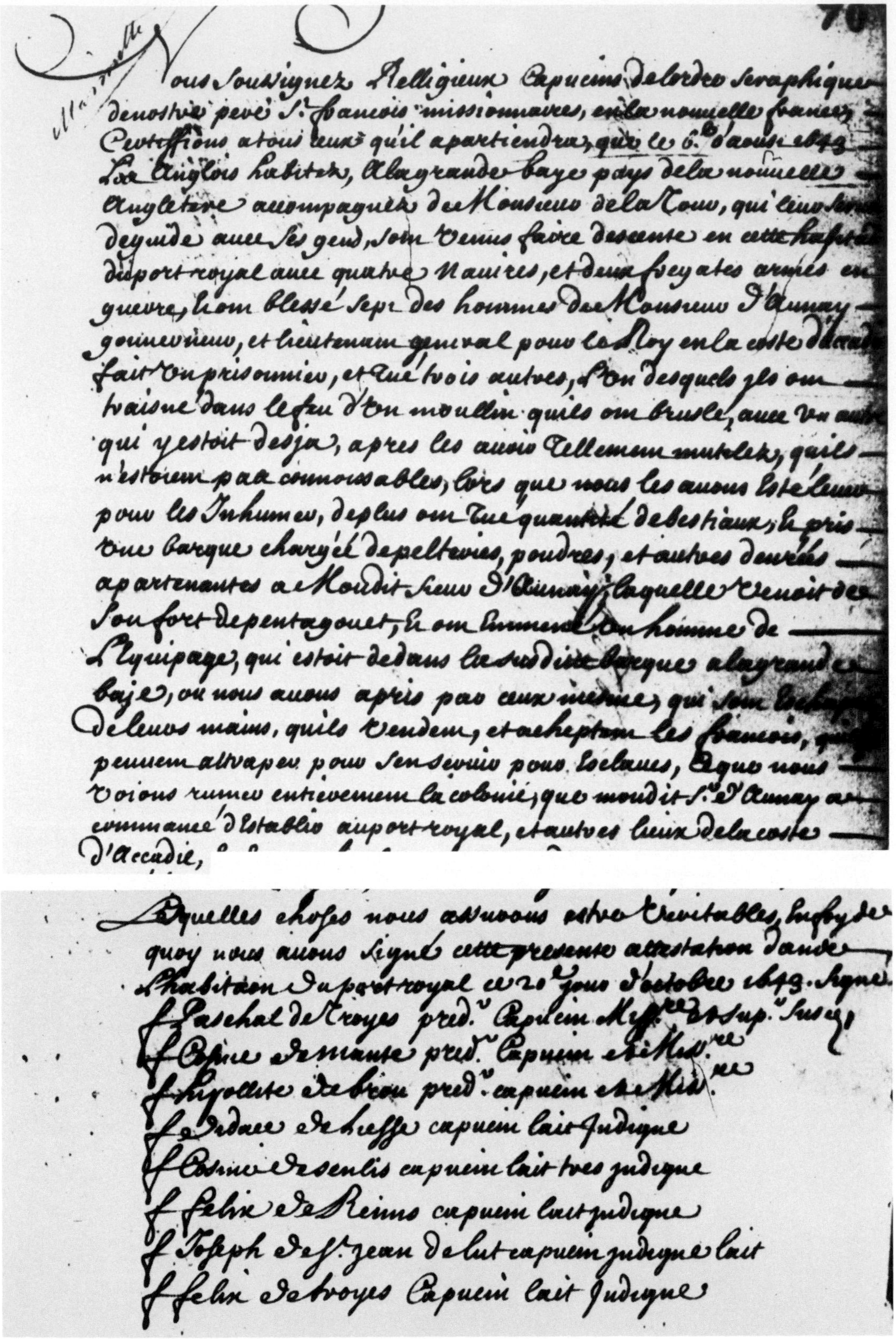

70

Nous soubsignez Relligieux Capucins de lordre seraphique de nostre pere S. francois missionnaires en la nouvelle france Certiffions a tous ceux quil apartiendra que le 6e d'aoust 1643 Les Anglois habitez a la grande baye pays de la nouvelle Angleterre accompagnez de Monsieur de la Tour, qui leur a ayde avec ses gens, sont venus faire descente en cette habitation du port royal avec quatre navires, et deux fregates armées en guerre, l'on blessé sept des hommes de Monsieur d'Aunay gouverneur, et lieutenant general pour le Roy en la coste d'Acadie fait un prisonnier, et tué trois autres, l'un desquels ils ont traisné dans le feu d'un moullin quils ont bruslé, avec un autre qui y estoit desja, apres les avoir tellement mutilez, quils n'estoient pas connoissables, lors que nous les avons osté leur pour les Inhumer, de plus ont tué quantité de bestiaux, le pris une barque chargée de pelteries, poudres, et autres denrées apartenantes a Mondit sieur d'Aunay, laquelle venoit de son fort de pentagouet, et ont emmené un homme de l'equipage, qui estoit dedans la susditte barque a la grand baye, ou nous avons apris par ceux mesme, qui sont [illegible] de leurs mains, quils vendent, et acheptent les francois, qu'ils peuvent attraper pour s'en servir pour esclaves, ce que nous voions ruiner entierement la colonie, que mondit S. d'Aunay a commancé d'establir au port royal, et autres lieux de la coste d'Accadie, [illegible]

Lesquelles choses nous asseurons estre veritables, en foy de quoy nous avons signé cette presente attestation dans l'habitation du port royal ce 20e jour d'octobre 1643. Signé

f Paschal de Troyes pred.r Capucin Miss.re et sup.r susd.

f Cosme de Mante pred.r Capucin et Miss.re

f Hypollite de [illegible] pred.r capucin et Miss.re

f Ignace de [illegible] capucin lait indigne

f Cosme de Senlis capucin lait tres indigne

f felix de Reims capucin lait indigne

f Joseph de S. Jean de lut capucin indigne lait

f felix de troyes Capucin lait indigne

Account of Charles de Saint-Étienne de La Tour's raid on Port-Royal signed by the Capuchins, Port-Royal, 20 October 1643.

On 6 August La Tour and his men, accompanied by some thirty English mercenaries from Boston, "came to raid this settlement of Port-Royal with four ships and two armed frigates, and wounded seven of Monsieur d'Aulnay's men...killed three others...in addition killed a number of animals, and took a bark loaded with pelts, powder, and other goods."

The rivalry between La Tour and d'Aulnay, the king's two lieutenants in Acadia, showed up on several occasions.

Archives nationales, Paris, France: Fonds des Colonies, série C^{11D}, vol. 1, fol. 70–70v.

V

The first Iroquois war

In 1643 war was raging with the Iroquois. The Jesuit Isaac Jogues, who was a prisoner of the Mohawks, thought that he could guess the Iroquois' immediate aim: "to take all the Hurons if possible, put to death the chiefs along with a large part of the tribe, and with the others make one nation and one country."

A certain number of Hurons did in fact give themselves up to the Iroquois and were incorporated into one or another of the Five Nations; but the greater part perished during the invasion of Huronia, to the point that in 1650 the Jesuit Ragueneau announced the ruin of this tribe, that previously had been flourishing and had been feared.

After eliminating or dispersing, to all intents and purposes, the Indians who were allied to the French, the Iroquois attacked the very heart of the colony. During these campaigns people had to live crowded together in "réduits" (small forts). In 1654 the inhabitants at Cap-Rouge formed a "community" to protect themselves better against the Iroquois, everyone taking an engagement before a notary to respect a certain number of rules so as to "present a solid front" to the enemy.

In 1660 an unprecedented disaster took place: sixteen young men from Montréal, with Adam Dollard Des Ormeaux at their head, fought against hundreds of Iroquois at the Long-Sault. Despite the support of forty Hurons and four Algonkins, they all perished with their leader after a desperate struggle that lasted more than a week.

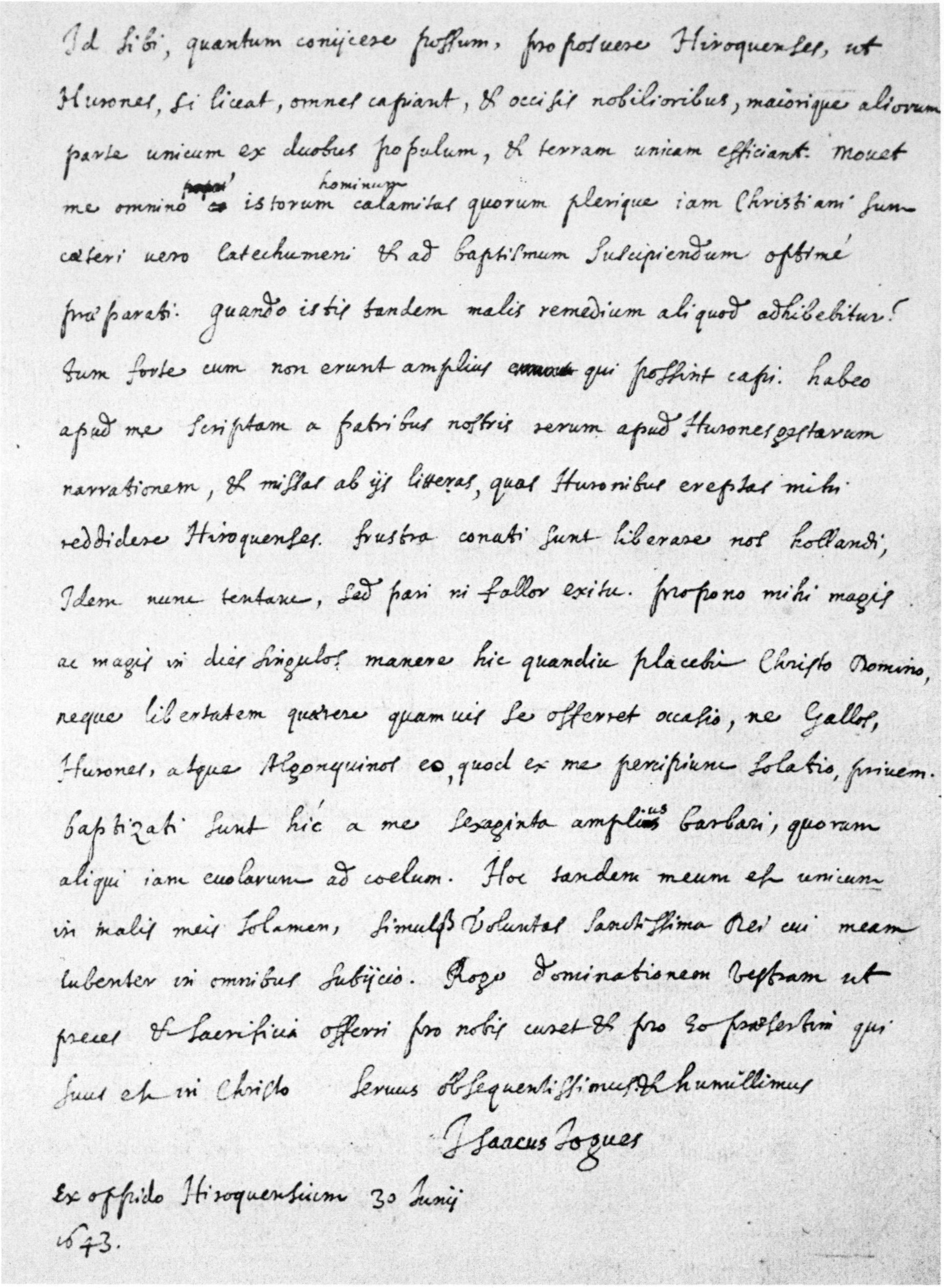
Id sibi, quantum conijcere possum, proposuere Hiroquenses, ut
Hurones, si liceat, omnes capiant, & occisis nobilioribus, maiorique aliorum
parte unicum ex duobus populum, & terram unicam efficiant. Movet
me omnino istorum hominum calamitas quorum plerique iam Christiani sunt
cæteri vero catechumeni & ad baptismum suscipiendum optime
præparati. quando istis tandem malis remedium aliquod adhibebitur?
tum forte cum non erunt amplius qui possint capi. habeo
apud me scriptam a patribus nostris rerum apud Hurones gestarum
narrationem, & missas ab ijs litteras, quas Huronibus ereptas mihi
reddidere Hiroquenses. frustra conati sunt liberare nos hollandi;
Idem nunc tentare, sed pari ni fallor exitu. propono mihi magis
ac magis in dies singulos manere hic quandiu placebit Christo Domino,
neque libertatem quærere quamvis se offerret occasio, ne Gallos,
Hurones, atque Algonquinos eo, quod ex me percipiunt solatio, priuem.
baptizati sunt hic a me sexaginta amplius barbari, quorum
aliqui iam euolarunt ad coelum. Hoc tandem meum est unicum
in malis meis solamen, simulque voluntas sanctissima Dei cui meam
lubenter in omnibus subijcio. Rogo Dominationem vestram ut
preces & sacrificia offerri pro nobis curet & pro eo præsertim qui
sum et in Christo servus obsequentissimus & humillimus
Isaacus Jogues
Ex oppido Hiroquensium 30 Junij
1643.

Letter from Isaac Jogues, a Jesuit missionary, to Governor Montmagny, Iroquois Village, 30 June 1643.

According to Father Jogues "The Iroquois plan...is to take all the Hurons if possible, put to death the chiefs along with a large part of the tribe, and with the others to make one nation and one country."

Competition in the trade in pelts was at the time very intense between the Iroquois, who supplied New Netherland (New York), and the Hurons, who supplied the French.

Archivum Romanum Societatis Iesu, Rome, Italy: Gallia, 109, fol. 379v.

1

RELATION

DE CE QVI S'EST PASSE' EN LA MISSION DES PERES DE LA COMPAGNIE de IESVS, aux Hurons, païs de la Nouuelle France, depuis l'Esté de l'année 1649. iusqu'à l'Esté de l'année 1650.

Au R. P. CLAVDE DE LINGENDES, Prouincial de la Compagnie de IESVS en la Prouince de France.

MON R. PERE,

PAX CHRISTI.

Ce n'est plus du païs des Hurons, que j'addresse à vostre Reuerence la Relation de ce qui s'y est passé. Cette pauure Eglise naissante

A

Paul Ragueneau. *Relation de ce qvi s'est passé en la mission des pères de la Compagnie de Iesvs, aux Hurõs, & aux païs plus bas de la Nouuelle France, depuis l'esté de l'année 1649 jusques à l'esté de l'année 1650.* Paris: Chez Sébastien Cramoisy et Gabriel Cramoisy, 1651, pp. 1–2.

The Jesuit Ragueneau announced that the Iroquois had been successful in destroying the Huron nation: "The number of dead exceeds that of those who have survived the destruction of their homeland."

qui parut il y a Vn an, toute couuerte de ſon ſang, opprimée ſous la cruauté des Iroquois, ennemis du nom de Dieu & de la Foy; a du depuis continué plus que iamais dans ſes ſouffrances: La plus grande part de nos bons Neophytes, & quelques-Vns de leurs Paſteurs ont ſuiuy le chemin des premiers, au milieu des feux & des flammes, & maintenant ſont dans le Ciel de compagnie. Vne famine eſpouuentable qui a regné partout, y a mis la deſolation. Nous comptons plus de trois mille baptizez cette derniere année: mais le nombre des morts eſt plus grand que de ceux qui ont ſurueſcu à la ruine de leur Patrie. Les choſes eſtant reduites à l'extremité, nous nous ſommes Veus obligez de quitter enfin Vne place qui n'eſtoit plus tenable, pour en ſauuer au moins les reſtes. Ce fut le dixieſme iour du mois de Iuin dernier, que nous ſortiſmes de ces terres de Promiſsion, qui eſtoient noſtre Paradis, & où la mort nous euſt eſté mille fois plus douce, que ne ſera la Vie en quelque lieu que nous puiſsions eſtre. Mais il faut ſuiure Dieu, & il faut aimer ſes conduites, quelques oppoſées qu'elles paroiſſent à nos deſirs, à nos plus ſaintes eſperances, & aux plus tendres amours de noſtre cœur. En Vn mot, nous ſommes deſcendus à Kebec, auec

Public Archives of Canada, Library, Ottawa (Negatives nos. C 113476 and C 113477).

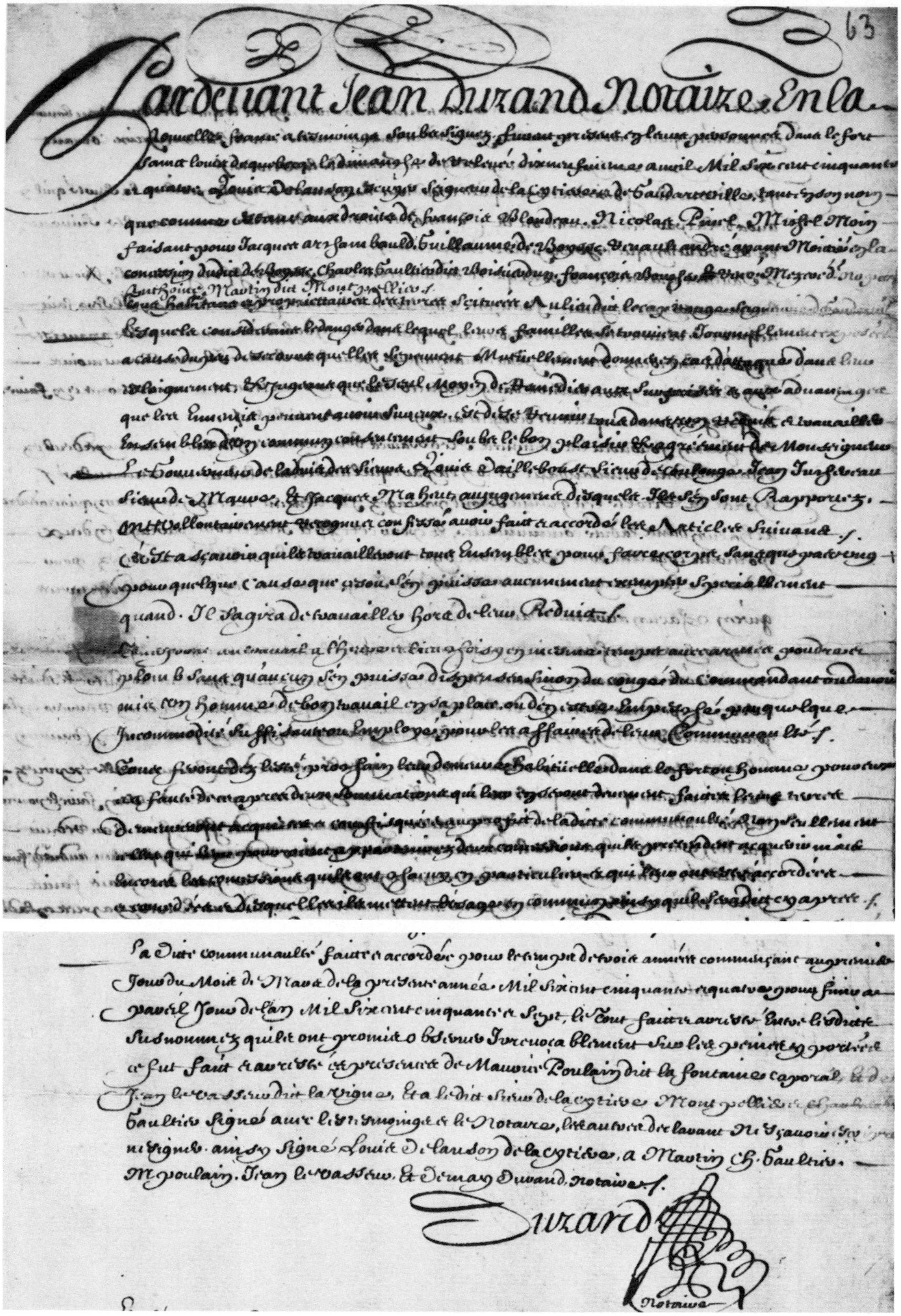

Pardevant Jean Durand Notaire En la

Durand Notaire

Formation of a community by the settlers of Cap-Rouge to protect themselves against the Iroquois, 19 April 1654.

"They will all work together to form a body...always at work at the time and place chosen, bringing with them arms, powder, shot.... Beginning next summer they will all make their habitual residence in the fort...their lands will be acquired and confiscated on behalf of the aforementioned community."

Public Archives of Canada, Ottawa: Cap-Rouge, MG 18, H 35.

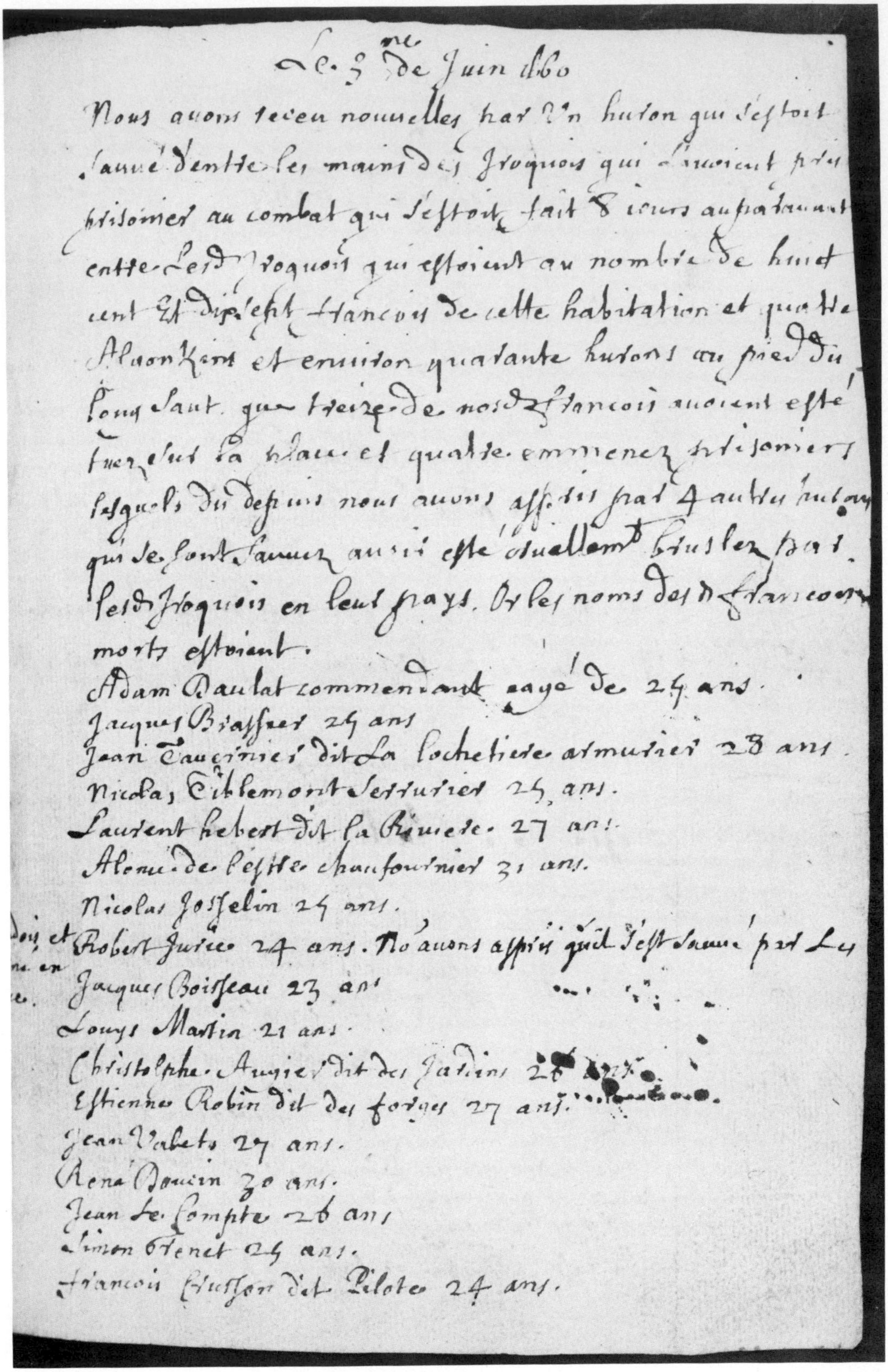

Le 3me de Juin 1660

Nous avons receu nouvelles par un huron qui s'estoit sauvé d'entre les mains des Iroquois qui l'avoient pris prisonier au combat qui s'estoit fait 8 iours auparavant entre lesd Iroquois qui estoient au nombre de huict cent Et dix sept françois de cette habitation et quatre Algonkins et environ quarante hurons au pied du long saut que treize de nosd françois avoient esté tuez sur la place et quatre emmenez prisoniers lesquels du depuis nous avons appris par 4 autres hurons qui se sont sauvez aussi estre actuellement brulez par lesd Iroquois en leur pays. Or les noms desd françois morts estoient.

Adam Daulat commendant agé de 25 ans.
Jacques Brassier 25 ans
Jean Tavernier dit La lochetiere armurier 28 ans.
Nicolas Tiblemont serrurier 25 ans.
Laurent hebert dit la Riviere 27 ans.
Alonié de lestre chaufournier 31 ans.
Nicolas Josselin 25 ans.
Robert Jurée 24 ans. No avons appris qu'il s'est sauvé par les
Jacques Boisseau 23 ans
Louys Martin 21 ans.
Christofle Augier dit des Jardins 26 ans.
Estienne Robin dit des forges 27 ans.
Jean Valets 27 ans.
René Doussin 30 ans.
Jean Le Compte 26 ans
Simon Grenet 25 ans.
François Crusson dit Pilote 24 ans.

Death certificate for Dollard Des Ormeaux and his companions, Montréal, 3 June 1660.

In it is mentioned the recent battle between the "Iroquois who were eight hundred in number and seventeen Frenchmen from this settlement and four Algonkins and about forty Hurons, at the bottom of the Long-Sault, that thirteen of our aforementioned Frenchmen were killed on the spot and four taken away as prisoners."

These young Montréalers put the Iroquois off from their plan to invade the colony that year.

Paroisse Notre-Dame, Montréal: Registres paroissiaux.

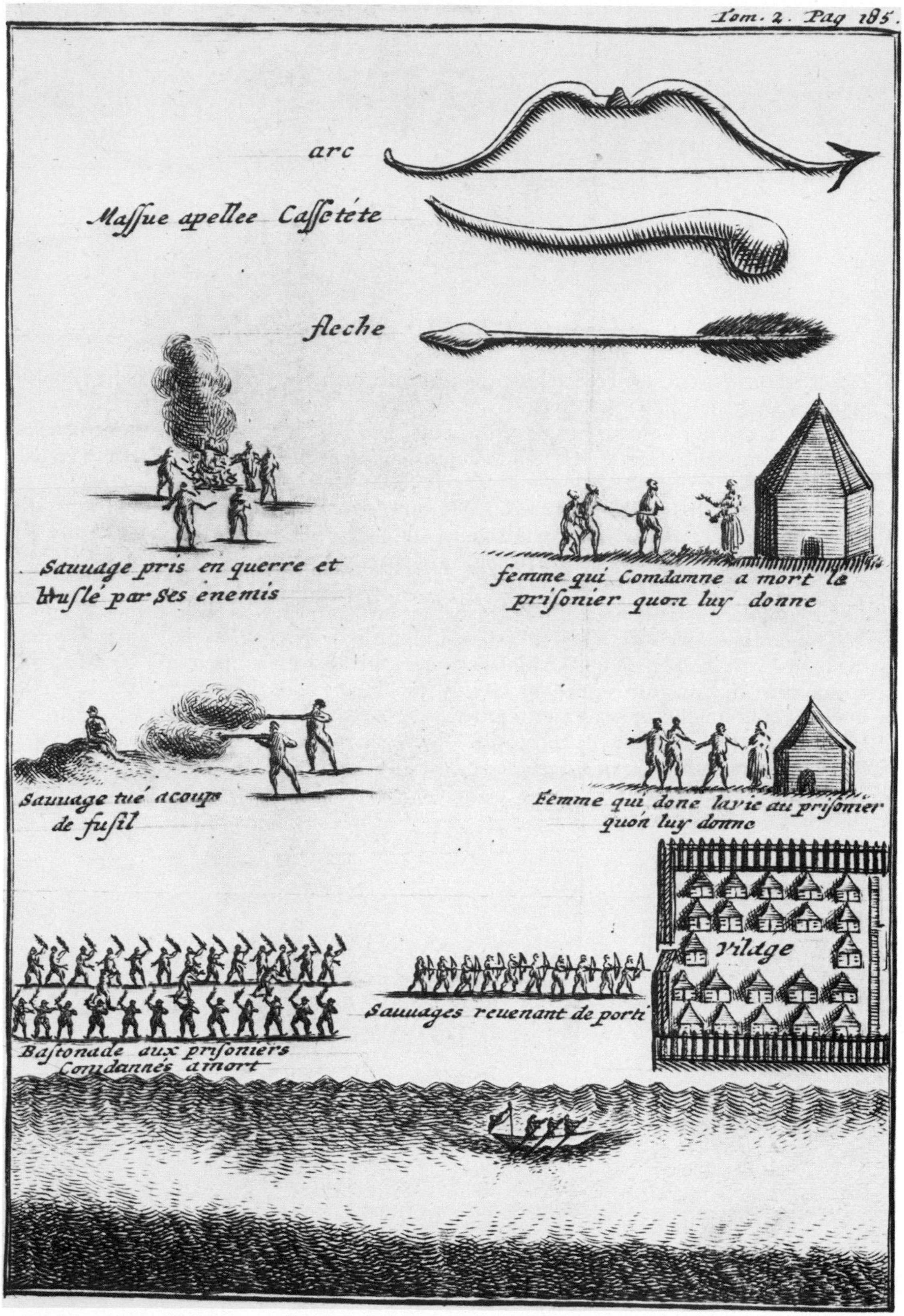

Indian War Methods; etching with line engraving; 16.4 x 11.6 cm. (page).

In Louis Armand de Lom d'Arce, baron de Lahontan. *Voyages du baron de La Hontan dans l'Amérique septentrionale....* 2e éd. rev., corr. et augm. La Haye: C. Delo, 1706, p. 185.

"The fate of a prisoner [among the Indians] is not always the same; either he is condemned to be burned, or he becomes a slave, or he is adopted." If he was adopted, he replaced a dead son or husband and was considered a full member of the clan and a child of the tribe.

Public Archives of Canada, Library, Ottawa (Negative no. C 99243).

V

From war to peace

The Iroquois war and the French losses had reached such proportions that many people believed that the colony was finished: in all circles people were seriously wondering whether it was not necessary to return to France. At this critical point, immediately after the Long-Sault disaster, the Jesuit Paul Le Jeune launched a moving appeal to Louis XIV.

Father Le Jeune's appeal, the steps taken by Bishop Laval and Pierre Boucher, the report by persons sent specially to the colony, all convinced Louis XIV of the necessity of destroying the Iroquois nations. This task was entrusted to Monsieur de Tracy and the Carignan-Salières regiment, which landed at Québec in 1665.

The Iroquois nations were not destroyed; nevertheless they received a good lesson. The Onondagas, who were better disposed towards the French, signed a peace with them on 13 December 1666. The Mohawks and Oneidas were more reticent but had to follow suit; they in turn signed on 10 July 1667. For more than twenty years, New France would finally enjoy a slight respite.

The year 1667 also saw the conclusion of peace in Europe with the Treaty of Breda. Now, as Acadia was once more occupied by the English (since 1654) the terms X and XI of the treaty returned it to France, which was not able, however, to take possession of it completely and officially until 1669.

AV ROY.

SIRE,

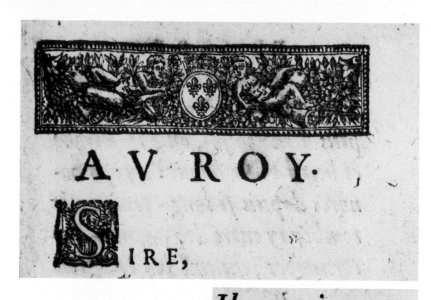

Il y a enuiron vn an, que ſes enfans vos ſuiets, habitans de ce nouueau Monde, firent entendre l'extremité du danger où ils eſtoient; mais le mal-heur du temps n'ayant pas permis qu'ils fuſſent ſecourus, le Ciel & la terre ont marqué par leurs prodiges, les cruautez & les feux que ces ennemis de Dieu, & de V. M. leur ont fait ſouffrir depuis ce temps-là. Ces perfides rauiront vn fleuron de voſtre Couronne, ſi voſtre main puiſſante n'agit auec voſtre parole. Si vous conſultez le Ciel, il

Paul Le Jeune. *Relation de ce qvi s'est passé de plvs remarqvable avx Missions des Pères de la Compagnie de Iesus, en la Novvelle France, és années 1660 & 1661....* Paris: Chez Sébastien Cramoisy, 1662.

Father Le Jeune made a moving appeal to King Louis XIV, asking him to come to the aid of his Canadian colony, which was being threatened by the Iroquois raids: "These perfidious people will rob your crown of one of one of its jewels if your powerful hand does not act...your salvation is perhaps wrapped up with the salvation of so many peoples which will be lost if they are not succoured by Your Majesty's attentions."

vous dira que voſtre ſalut eſt peut-eſtre enfermé dans le ſalut de tant de Peuples, qui ſeront perdus, s'ils ne ſont ſecourus par les ſoins de V. M. Si vous conſiderez le nom François, vous ſçaurez, SIRE, que vous eſtes un grand Roy, qui faiſant trembler l'Europe, ne doit pas eſtre meſprisé dans l'Amerique.

Bibliothèque de la ville de Montréal, Salle Gagnon, Montréal.

The Reverend Father Paul Le Jeune of the Society of Jesus (1591–1664); René Lochon (1636–75); line engraving; 1665; 36.8 x 27 cm. (page).

Father Le Jeune, who was superior of the Jesuits of Québec from 1632 to 1639, was also the author of the first eleven *Relations* of the Jesuits of New France. These annual reports informed the European reader of what was going on in Canada. They inspired many generous actions (alms) and many undertakings which were beneficial to the colony: the establishment of the Ursulines and Religious Hospitallers, the founding of Montréal, etc.

Public Archives of Canada, Picture Division, Ottawa (Negative no. C 21404).

145

Nous avons apris ces nouvelles depuis quelques jours, & l'on nous aſſure de plus que toute l'armée eſt en bonne ſanté; que Monſieur le Gouverneur conduit l'avant-garde, & Monſieur de Chamblay tient l'arriere garde. Monſieur de Saliere eſt le Colonel du Regiment, & Monſieur de Tracy comme Generaliſſime commande à tout le corps. Nos nouveaux Chrêtiens Sauvages ſuivent l'armée Françoiſe avec tous nos jeunes François-Canadois qui ſont tres-vaillans, & qui courent dans les bois comme des Sauvages. Nous ne ſçaurions avoir de nouvelles du combat de plus de quinze jours: Cependant toute cette nouvelle Egliſe eſt en prieres, & l'on fait l'oraiſon de quarante heures, qui continuë dans les quatre Egliſes tour à tour, parceque du bon ou du mauvais ſuccez de cette guerre depend le bien & le mal de tout le païs. Voici la troiſieme fois que nos François ſont allez en leur païs depuis le mois de Fevrier, au grand étonnement des Anglois & des Hiroquois méme, qui ne peuvent comprendre comme ils ont ſeulement oſé entreprendre ce voiage. Monſieur de Tracy n'eſt parti d'ici avec le gros de l'armée, que le jour de l'Exaltation de ſainte Croix, & l'on tient qu'ils ſont arrivez là aprés un mois de chemin. Je vous dirai plus au long des nouvelles de cette expedition aprés leur retour, ou ſi-tôt que nous en aurons apris par des voies certaines. Pour le preſent je vous prie de trouver bon que je finiſſe pour prendre un peu de repos étant fort fatiguée du grand nombre de lettres que j'ay écrites: Il ne m'en reſte pas plus de quarante à écrire, que j'eſpere envoier par le dernier vaiſſeau. Ne ceſſez point de prier pour nous.

De Quebec le 16. Octobre 1666.

Mère Marie de l'Incarnation. *Lettres de la vénérable mère Marie de l'Incarnation première supérieure des Ursulines de la Nouvelle France, divisées en deux parties.* Paris: Chez Louis Billaine, 1681, p. 610.

Marie de l'Incarnation told her son that a third expedition had just been carried out in the year 1666 with the aim of destroying the Iroquois: "This is the third time that our Frenchmen have gone into their country since the month of February."

Public Archives of Canada, Library, Ottawa (Negative no. C 113057).

TROISIESME PAIX

ACCORDE'E PAR L'EMPEREUR de France, aux Iroquois de la Nation d'Onnontague.

Le treiziéme Decembre 1666.

ARTICLES de la Paix demandée par ſix Ambaſſadeurs Iroquois, Garakontie, Ahonnonh8araton, Gatiennonties, Hotre8ti, Ha8endaientak, Te Gannontie, de la Nation d'Onnontague, tant au nom de ladite Nation, qu'en celuy des deux Superieures, Goio8en, Tſonnont8an : Enſemble par Achinnhara, de la Nation d'Onnei8t ; les intereſts de laquelle il a ſtipulé, aprés s'eſtre joint auſdits Ambaſſadeurs : Et accordez au nom & de la part du Roy Tres-Chreſtien, par Meſſire Alexandre de Prouville, Chevalier, Seigneur de Tracy, Conſeiller du Roy en ſes Conſeils, Lieutenant General des Armées de Sa Majeſté, & dans les Iſles & Terre Ferme de l'Amerique Meridionale & Septentrionale, tant par Mer que par Terre, de ce ſuffiſamment autoriſé en vertu du Pouvoir à luy donné par les Lettres Patentes de Sa Majeſté, en datte du   en la preſence & aſſiſté de Meſſire Daniel de Courcelle, Conſeiller du Roy en ſes Conſeils, Lieutenant General des Armées de Sa Majeſté, & Gouverneur de l'Acadie, Iſle de Terre Neuve & de Canada ; & de Meſſire Jean Talon, auſſi Conſeiller de Sa Majeſté, & Intendant de Juſtice, Police & Finances de la Nouvelle France.

VII.

Que ſur l'aſſeurance donnée au nom des quatre Nations, qu'il ne ſera fait aucun acte d'hoſtilité ſur les François Al-

"Troisième paix accordée par l'empereur de France aux Iroquois de la nation d'Onnontague, le treizième décembre 1666."

In *Traitez de paix conclus entre S.M. le roy de France et les Indiens du Canada....* Paris: Sébastien Mabre-Cramoisy, 1667, pp. 6, 10, 11.

Third peace granted by the emperor of France to the Iroquois of the Onondaga nation, 13 December 1666.

"On the assurance given in the name of the four [Iroquois] nations that no hostile act will be committed against the French, Algonkins and Hurons, the hatchet of the aforementioned French, Algonkins, and Hurons will be hung up with regard respectively to the aforementioned Iroquois nations until the ambassadors return with ratification of the present treaty."

~ 146 ~

gonquins & Hurons, la Hache deſdits François Algonquins & Hurons, demeurera reſpectivement ſuſpenduë à l'égard deſdites Nations Iroquoiſes, juſqu'au retour des Ambaſſadeurs avec la Ratification du preſent Traité. Bien entendu que comme il y a des Onnei8teronnons & Gaigneigronnons en parti de Chaſſe & de Guerre; Si, qu'à Dieu ne plaiſe, ils attaquoient ou par hazard, ou par malice les François Algonquins ou Hurons, il ſera permis à ceux-cy de repouſſer la force par la force, & d'avoir recours aux Armes pour mettre leurs vies en ſeureté, ſans que pour la mort ou défaite deſdits partis, on puiſſe imputer leur juſte reſiſtance à infraction de Traité.

IX.

Que pour le preſent Traité demeure ſeure, ferme & inviolable, & qu'il ſoit accompli en tous les points & articles y contenus, traitez, accordez & ſtipulez, entre Meſſire Alexandre de Prouville, en preſence & aſſiſté comme deſſus, & les ſix Ambaſſadeurs cy-deſſus nommez, il ſera reſpectivement ſigné de part & d'autre, pour demeurer autentique & y avoir recours en cas de beſoin; Aprés que lecture en aura eſté faite en Langue Iroquoiſe, & que dans quatre Lunes la Ratification en ſera apportée de la part des quatre Nations

Public Archives of Canada, Library, Ottawa (Negatives nos. C 113472, C 113473, and C 113482).

147

X.

Le cy-devant nommé Seigneur le Roy de la Grande Bretagne, reſtituera auſſi & rendra au cy-deſſus nommé Seigneur le Roy Tres Chreſtien, ou à ceux qui auront charge & mandement de ſa part, ſcellé en bonne forme du grand Sceau de France, le Pays appellé l'Acadie, ſitué dans l'Amerique Septentrionale, dont le Roy Tres-Chrétien a autrefois joüy. Et pour executer cette reſtitution, le ſuſnommé Roy de la Grande Bretagne, incontinent aprés la ratification de la preſente Alliance, fournira au ſuſnommé Roy Tres-Chreſtien, tous les actes & mandemens expediez deuëment & en bonne forme, neceſſaires à cet effet, ou les fera fournir à ceux de ſes Miniſtres & Officiers, qui ſeront par luy deleguez.

XI.

Si quelques-uns des Habitans du Pays appellé l'Acadie, preferent de ſe ſoumettre pour l'avenir à la domination du Roy d'Angleterre, ils auront la liberté d'en ſortir pendant l'eſpace d'un an, à compter du jour que la reſtitution de ce Pays ſera faite; & de vendre & aliener leurs fonds, champs & terres, eſclaves & en general tous leurs biens, meubles & immeubles, ou en diſpoſer autrement à leur diſcretion & volonté: Et ceux qui auront contracté avec eux ſeront tenus & obligez par l'autorité du Sereniſſime Roy Tres-Chreſtien, d'accomplir & executer leurs pactions & conventions. Que s'ils aiment mieux emporter avec eux leur argent comptant, meubles, uſtanciles & emmener leurs eſclaves, & generalement tous leurs biens meubles; ils le pourront faire entierement ſans aucun empêchement ou trouble.

Traitté de paix entre les couronnes de France et d'Angleterre, conclu à Breda le 31 juillet 1667. Paris: Imprimerie de Frederic Leonard, 1689, pp. 5–6.

By this treaty Acadia, which had been under English occupation since 1654, was returned to France.

Public Archives of Canada, Library, Ottawa (Negatives nos. C 113469 and C 113479).

V

A precarious peace

Through experience people knew how precarious peace with the Iroquois was; and more and more they were feeling the threat coming from the English colonies in New England. It is not astonishing, therefore, that in 1669 the king ordered the governor to form militia companies in the colony, all the more so because since the Carignan regiment had been disbanded there was no longer any corps of army troops in the country.

The same anxieties soon drove the authorities to increase the number of forts in the distant regions despite the king's wishes to the contrary. In 1673 Frontenac carried out one of Talon's projects and laid the foundations on Lake Ontario of the Fort Katarakouy (or Frontenac), which was intended to contain the Iroquois within their territories to the south.

These forts – or posts – played both a military and an economic role, as is seen with a map by Jaillot in 1685 that bears several entries such as the following: "The Sieur Duluth's post to prevent the Assiniboins and other Indians from going down to Hudson Bay."

Economic rivalries were a potential source of conflict; the question of the respective frontiers of New France and the English colonies was another – and not only in Acadia. For example, did the Iroquois country belong to New France or New England? And of what ruler were the Iroquois subjects? One serious question, among many others.

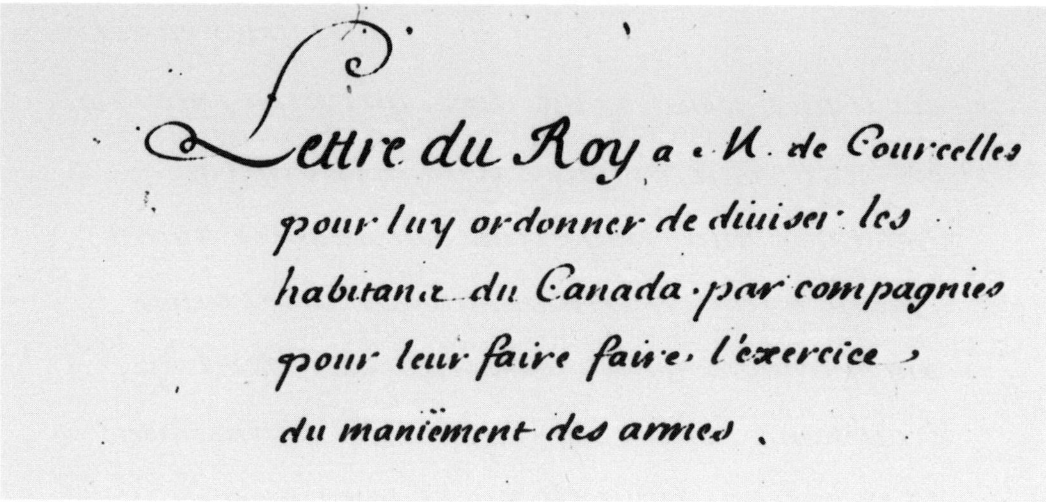
Lettre du Roy a M. de Courcelles
pour luy ordonner de diuiser les
habitans du Canada par compagnies
pour leur faire faire l'exercice
du maniement des armes.

Letter from King Louis XIV to Governor General Courcelle, Paris, 3 April 1669.

The king is asking him to create a Canadian militia: "My intention is that you should divide all my subjects living in the aforesaid country by companies taking into consideration their proximity, ...that you should appoint captains, lieutenants, and ensigns to command them, ...that you should give orders for them to assemble once a month for arms drill."

Je vous escris
ces lignes pour vous dire que mon intention
est que vous diuisiez tous mes sujets
habitans aud. pays par compagnies ayant
esgard a leur proximité, qu'apres les auoir
ainsy diuisez, vous establissiez des Cap.nes
Lieutenans, et enseignes pour les commander;
qu'en cas que tous ceux qui composeront
lesd. Compagnies puissent s'assembler auec
facilité et s'en retourner chez eux en un
jour, vous donniez les ordres qu'ils
s'assemblent une fois chacun mois pour faire
l'exercice du maniement des armes, et en cas
qu'ils soient trop esloignez, vous subdiuisiez
les Compagnies par escoüades de 40. ou 50.
hommes, et que vous leur fassiez faire
l'exercice une fois le mois, ainsy qu'il est
dit cy dessus, et a l'esgard des Compagnies
entieres, vous les fassiez assembler une fois
ou deux l'Année.

Que vous preniez soin qu'ils soient tous
bien armez, et qu'ils ayent tousjours la
poudre, plomb, et mesches necessaires pour
pouuoir se seruir de leurs armes dans les

occasions.

Que vous visitiez souvent les escoüades et Compagnies, et leur fassiez faire l'exercice en vre presence.

Qu'autant qu'il sera possible vous puissiez assembler une fois l'année le plus grand nombre desdts habitans qu'il se pourra pour leur faire faire pareillement l'exercice en corps, en observant toutes fois de ne leur pas faire faire de trop grandes marches, laissant a vre prudence d'assembler seulement tous ceux qui pourront le faire et s'en retourner en deux jours de temps, afin qu'un plus grand temps ne consomme celuy qu'ils doivent employer a leur commerce, et a la Culture de leurs Terres,

Escrit a Paris le troisiesme avril 1669. Signé LOUIS et plus bas Colbert.

Archives nationales, Paris, France: Fonds des Colonies, série B, vol. 1, fol. 115v–117.

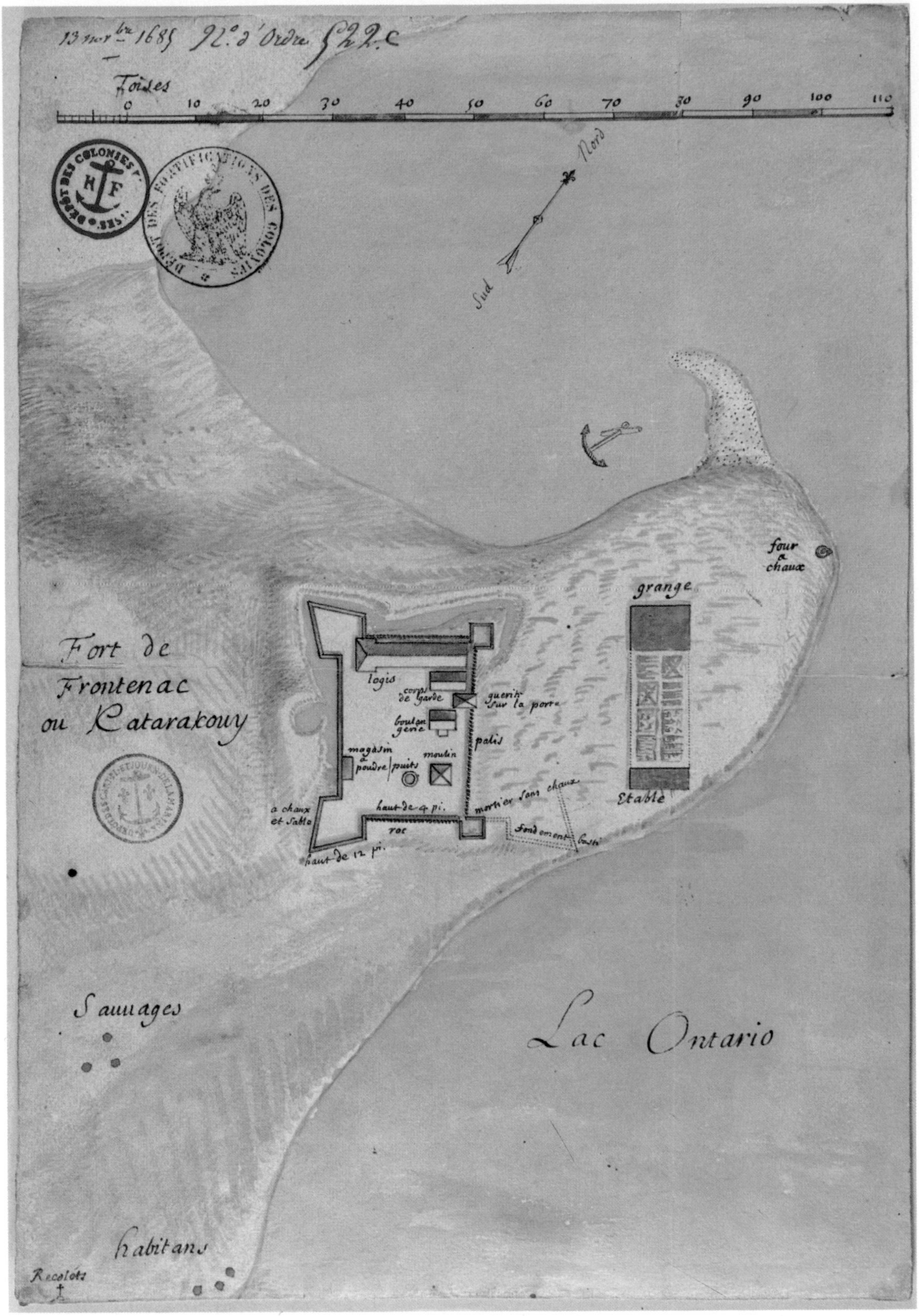

«Fort de Frontenac ou Katarakouy», envoyée par M. Denonville, 13 novembre 1685; anonymous; col.ms.; 23.2 x 33.1 cm.

In 1673 Frontenac had this fort built on the north shore of Lake Ontario, on the site of the present-day city of Kingston, with an aim to containing the Iroquois within their territories to the south, keeping an eye on what they were doing, and holding them in check. In founding this fort he also wanted to further the French fur trade, to the detriment of that of the English and Dutch.

Archives nationales, Paris, France: Section Outre-Mer, Dépôt des fortifications des colonies, Amérique septentrionale, 522 c.

[Plan de la situation du fort de Richelieu, 1665]; [Jean Talon]; ms.; 30.4 x 19.1 cm.

This fort was built in 1665 at the mouth of the Richelieu River by the company of the Carignan Regiment commanded by Pierre de Saurel. The Iroquois had to be prevented from going along this river to attack the settlements in the valley of the St. Lawrence.

Archives nationales, Paris, France: Section Outre-Mer, Dépôt des fortifications des colonies, Amérique septentrionale, 492 c.

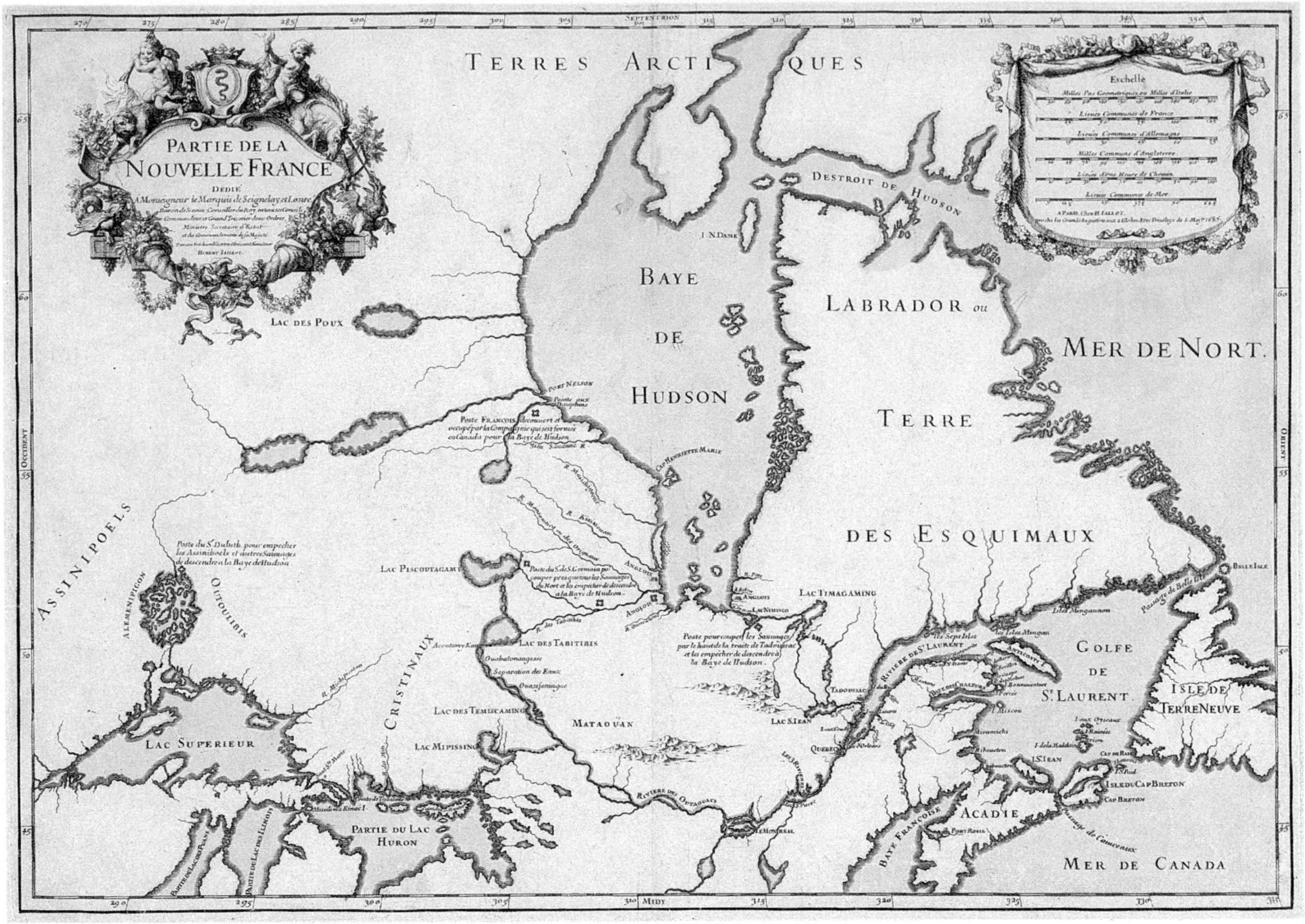

Partie de la Nouvelle France..., Paris, 1685; Hubert Jaillot; map printed from copperplate, hand col.; 45.3 x 64.8 cm.

On this map are mentioned three posts that were designed to prevent the Indians from taking their pelts to the English on Hudson Bay. One of these trading factories, which had been established in the Lake Superior region by the coureur des bois Dulhut, cost the Hudson's Bay Company a great deal of trade.

Public Archives of Canada, National Map Collection, Ottawa (NMC 6349).

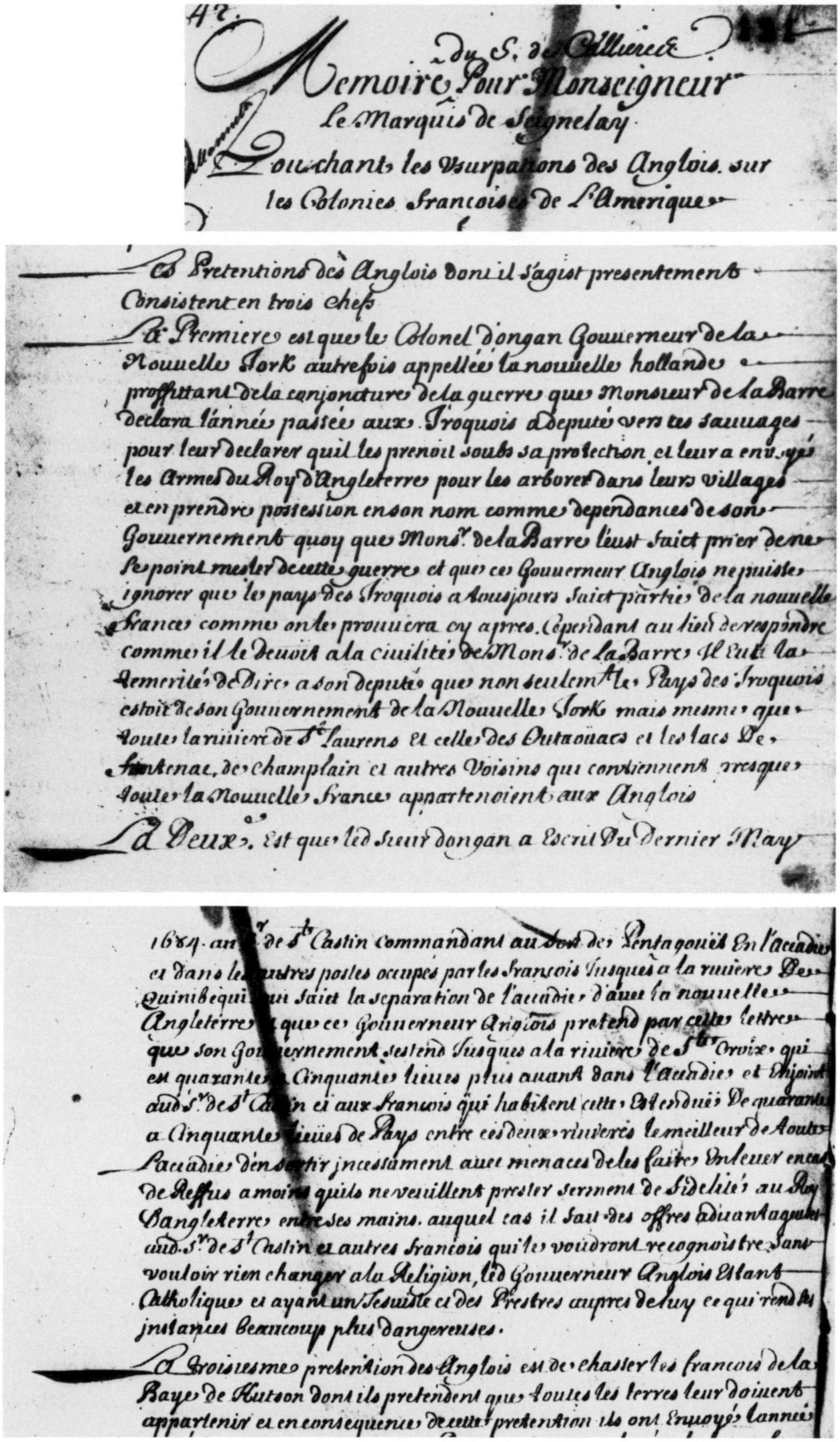

42.

du S. de Callieres

Memoire Pour Monseigneur
le Marquis de Seignelay
Touchant les Usurpations des Anglois sur
les Colonies Francoises de l'Amerique

Les Pretentions des Anglois dont il s'agist presentement
Consistent en trois chefs
La Premiere est que le Colonel dongan Gouverneur de la
Nouvelle York autrefois appellée la nouvelle hollande
proffitant de la conjoncture de la guerre que Monsieur de la Barre
declara l'année passée aux Iroquois a deputé vers ces sauvages
pour leur declarer quil les prenoit soubs sa protection et leur a envoyé
les Armes du Roy d'Angleterre pour les arborer dans leurs villages
et en prendre possession en son nom comme dependances de son
Gouvernement quoy que Monsr. de la Barre l'eust faict prier de ne
se point mesler de cette guerre et que ce Gouverneur Anglois ne puisse
ignorer que le pays des Iroquois a tousjours faict partie de la nouvelle
France comme on le prouvera cy apres. Cependant au lieu de respondre
comme il le devoit a la civilité de Mons. de la Barre Il eut la
temerité de dire a son deputé que non seulemt. le Pays des Iroquois
estoit de son Gouvernement de la Nouvelle York mais mesme que
toute la riviere de St Laurens et celle des Outaouacs et les lacs de
frontenac, de champlain et autres Voisins qui contiennent presque
toute la Nouvelle France appartenoient aux Anglois
La Deuxe. est que led Sieur dongan a Escrit du dernier May

1684 au Sr de St Castin commandant au fort de Pentagouët En l'Acadie
et dans les autres postes occupés par les françois jusques a la riviere de
Quinibequi qui faict la separation de l'acadie d'avec la nouvelle
Angleterre que ce Gouverneur Anglois pretend par cette lettre
que son Gouvernement sestend jusques a la riviere de Ste Croix qui
est quarante a cinquante lieues plus avant dans l'acadie et enjoint
audt. Sr de St Castin et aux francois qui habitent cette Estendue de quarante
a cinquante lieues de Pays entre ces deux rivieres le meilleur de toute
l'acadie d'en sortir incessament avec menaces de les faire enlever en cas
de Reffus a moins quils ne veuillent prester serment de fidelité au Roy
d'Angleterre entre ses mains. auquel cas il fait des offres advantageuses
audt. Sr de St Castin et autres francois qui le voudront recognoistre sans
vouloir rien changer a la Religion, led Gouverneur Anglois Estant
Catholique et ayant un Jesuiste et des Prestres aupres de luy ce qui rend ses
instances beaucoup plus dangereuses.
La troisiesme pretention des Anglois est de chasser les francois de la
Baye de Hutson dont ils pretendent que toutes les terres leur doivent
appartenir et en consequence de cette pretention ils ont Envoyés l'année

Memoir from Callière, governor of Montréal, to the minister Seignelay, concerning the territorial claims of the English, February 1685.

The governor of New York had declared that "the Iroquois country was under his administration." He also asserted "that his government extends to the Rivière de Sainte-Croix" in Acadia. Finally, "the third of the English pretensions is to chase the French from Hudson Bay, of which they claim all the lands must belong to them."

Archives nationales, Paris, France: Fonds des Colonies, série C^{11E}, vol. 1, fol. 121–121v.

V

The second Iroquois war

As they were officially at peace with New France, the Iroquois had turned their arms against an allied nation, the Illinois; in addition they were suspected of wanting to re-open hostilities with the French at the instigation of the English. On 10 October 1682, during an assembly called together by the governor, it was decided to conduct a punitive expedition into the Iroquois country.

The reason for the Iroquois' restlessness was still the same: "to know who will be in control of the trade in beaver skins to the south and southwest," wrote Governor Le Febvre de La Barre in 1683. He added: "Whatever treaty is made with them, as the cause will still be there they will not fail to take advantage of the slightest occasions to seize control of the tribes and the posts."

In the summer of 1684 La Barre set out from Montréal with a thousand men and stopped at Famine Cove on Lake Ontario (or Lake Frontenac). There an Iroquois mission and in particular an Onondaga chief with the nickname "Grande Gueule" or "Grangula" ("Big Mouth") met him and forced him to accept humiliating conditions for peace.

In an attempt to heighten French prestige, Denonville led an expedition in 1687 against the Senecas; the Iroquois responded by increasing their raids. In the night of 4 to 5 August 1689, fifteen hundred Iroquois massacred twenty-four habitants of Lachine; of the some fifty prisoners whom they took there, forty-two are believed to have been put to death.

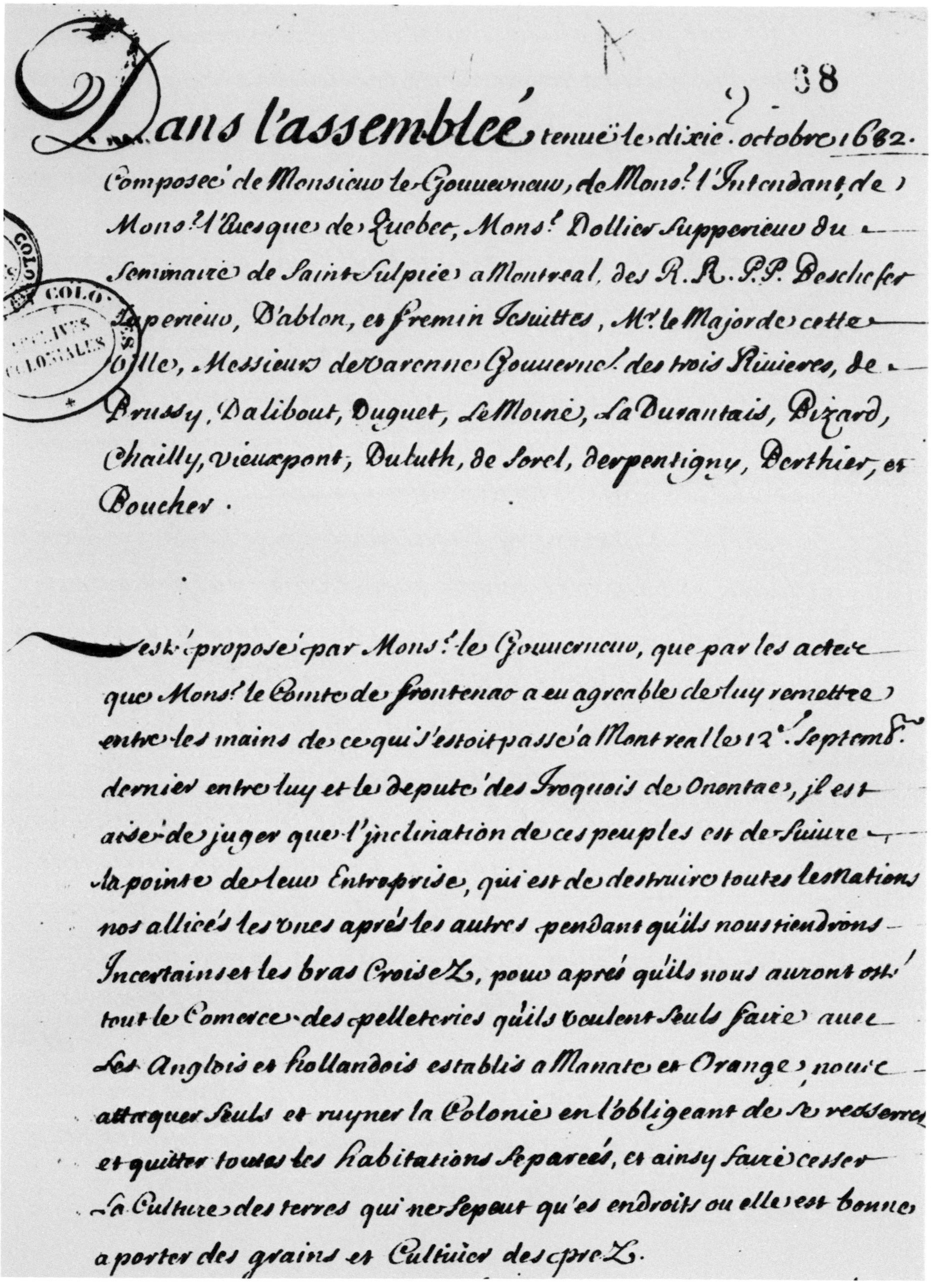

38

Dans l'assemblée tenuë le dixie. octobre 1682.

Composée de Monsieur le Gouverneur, de Mons.r l'Intendant, de Mons.r l'Evesque de Quebec, Mons.r Dollier supperieur du Seminaire de Saint Sulpice a Montreal, des R.R.P.P. Deschefer Superieur, D'ablon, et fremin Jesuittes, M.r le Major de cette Ville, Messieurs de Varenne Gouvern.r des trois Rivieres, de Brussy, Dalibout, Duguet, Le Moine, La Durantais, Bizard, Chailly, vieuxpont, Duluth, de Sorel, de repentigny, Berthier, et Boucher.

Il est proposé par Mons.r le Gouverneur, que par les actes que Mons.r le Comte de frontenac a eu agreable de luy remettre entre les mains de ce qui s'estoit passé a Montreal le 12.e Septemb.re dernier entre luy et le deputé des Iroquois de Onontae, il est aisé de juger que l'inclination de ces peuples est de suivre la pointe de leur Entreprise, qui est de destruire toutes les Nations nos alliée les unes aprés les autres pendant qu'ils nous tiendrons Incertains et les bras Croisez, pour aprés qu'ils nous auront osté tout le Comerce des pelleteries qu'ils veulent seuls faire avec Les Anglois et hollandois establis a Manate et Orange, nous attaquer seuls et ruyner la Colonie en l'obligeant de se resserrer et quitter toutes les habitations separées, et ainsy faire cesser la Culture des terres qui ne se peut qu'es endroits ou elle est bonne a porter des grains et Cultiver des prez.

Minutes of a meeting called by Governor La Barre to discuss the Iroquois peril, Québec, 10 October 1682.

Consideration was given to sending "a thousand good men under arms" against the Iroquois, who wish to "destroy all the [allied Indian] nations," after which they will "take all the trade in pelts away [from the French]...attack [them] when they are alone and destroy the colony."

Ils ont jugé plus apropos de differer et nous amuser,
tandis qu'ils attaqueroient ces Nations; Et qu'a cet effet
ayant Commancé l'annee derniere a attaquer Les
Illinois, ils auroient eu un si grand auantage sur eux

qu'outre trois ou quatre Cens morts, Ils leurs auroient prise
Neuf Cens prisonniers, ainsi que cette annee marchant
auec un Corps de Douze Cens hommes bien armez &
bons soldats, il n'y auoit point a douter qu'ils ne les
destruisissent entierement, Et qu'a leur retour ils n'attaquas=
sent Les Miamis et les Kiskakons et par leur defaitte ne
se rendissent maitres de Missilimachina et des Lacs erie
et huron, et baye des puans, et par la ne nous priuassent
de tout le Comerce que l'on tire de ce pays en destruisant
en mesme tems toutes les missions Chrestiennes qui sont
Establies chez les Nations, Et qu'ainsy il falloit faire les
derniers efforts pour Empescher qu'ils ne ruinassent les
Nations comme ils ont fait cy deuant les Alkonquins,
Les Andastez, Les Loups, Les Abenaquis et autres dont
Nous auons les restes ès habitations ~~nations~~ de Sillery, de Laurette
du Lac Champlin et autres repandues parmy nous. Que
pour parvenir a cet Effet il falloit Considerer l'Etat de
la Colonie et les moyens de s'en seruir le plus Utilement
Contre les Ennemis: que pour la Colonie nous pouuions
mettre ensemble mil bons hommes portans les Armes & a-
bitutez a l'usage des Canots comme les Iroquois;

Archives nationales, Paris, France: Fonds des Colonies, série C^{11A}, vol. 6, fol. 68–69.

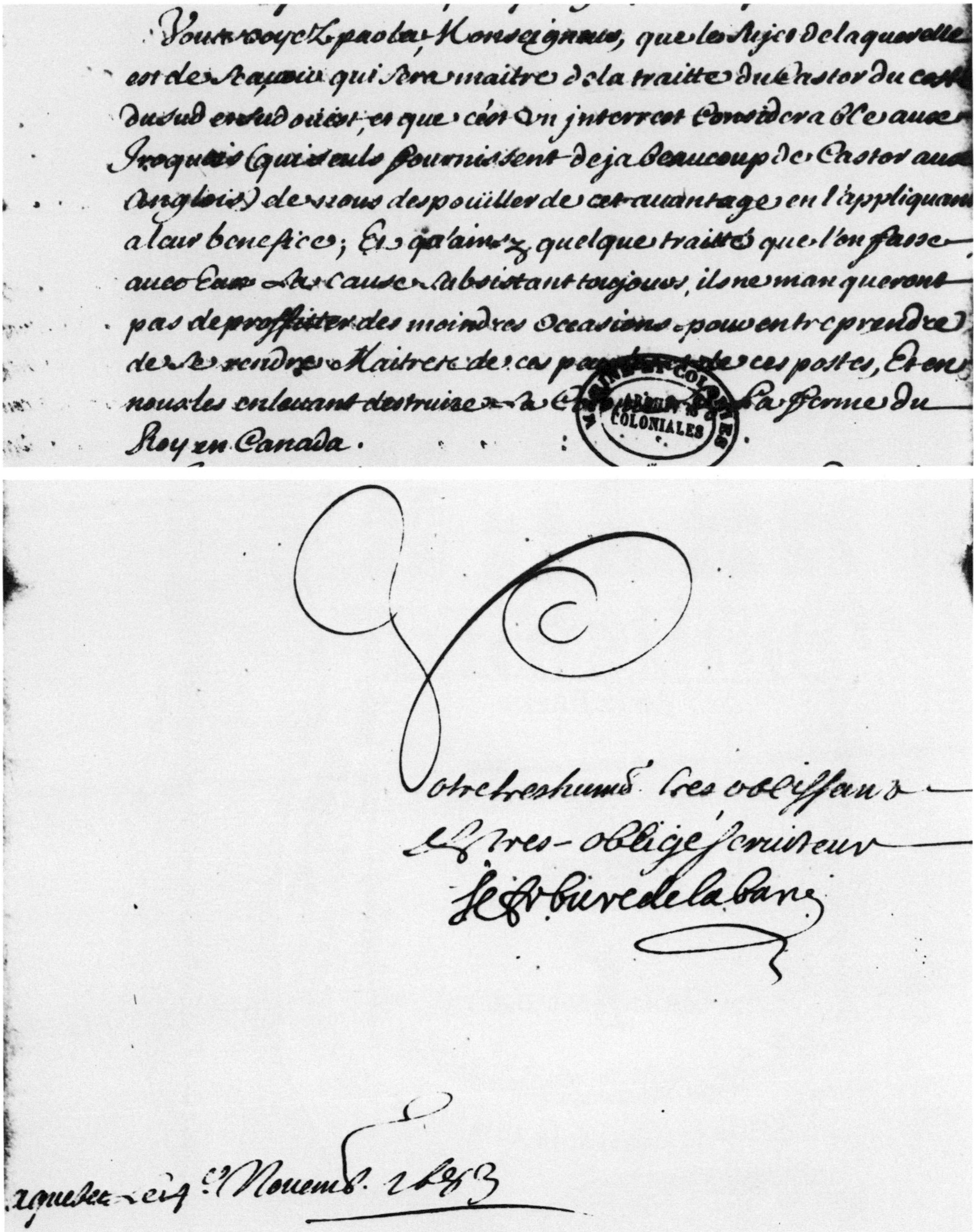
Vous voyez par la, Monseigneur, que le sujet de la querelle est de scavoir qui sera maitre de la traitte du castor du costé du sud et sud ouest, et que c'est un interest considerable aux Iroquois (qui seuls fournissent deja beaucoup de Castor aux Anglois) de nous despouiller de cet avantage en l'appliquant a leur benefice; Et qu'ainsy quelque traittés que l'on fasse avec Eux, la cause subsistant toujours, ils ne manqueront pas de proffitter des moindres occasions pour entreprendre de se rendre Maitres de ces pays et de ces postes, Et en nous les enlevant destruire [illegible] la ferme du Roy en Canada.

Votre tres humble tres obeissant et tres obligé serviteur

Lefebvre de la barre

a quebec ce 4e Novembre 1683

Letter from Governor General La Barre to the minister Seignelay, Québec, 4 November 1683.

"The cause of the quarrel [between the French and the Iroquois] is the question of who will be master of the trade in beaver in the south and southwest."

Archives nationales, Paris, France: Fonds des Colonies, série C^{11A}, vol. 6, fol. 135, 144v.

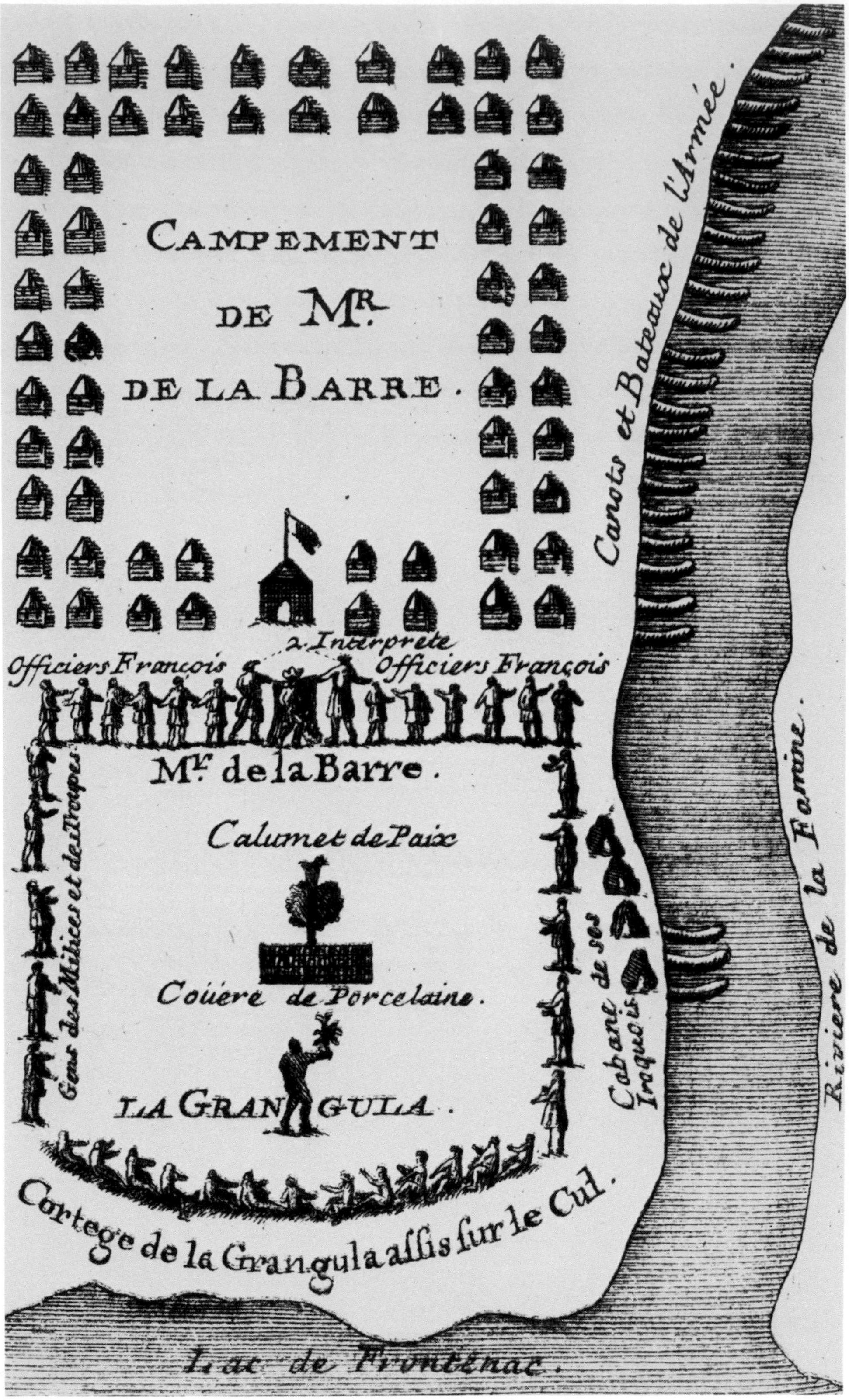

De La Barre's Encampment; etching; 17 x 9.8 cm. (page).

In Louis Armand de Lom d'Arce, baron de Lahontan. *Nouveaux voyages de mr. le baron de Lahontan, dans l'Amérique septentrionale....* La Haye: Les frères L'Honoré, 1715, vol. 1, p. 47.

On 5 September 1684, at Anse de la Famine (Famine Cove) on Lake Ontario, Governor General La Barre entered into negotiations with an Iroquois embassy led by an Onondaga chief known as Grande Gueule (or Grangula) – "Big Mouth." Because his army was short of provisions and decimated by illness, La Barre was not able to impose his will upon the Iroquois and was forced to accept humiliating peace terms.

Public Archives of Canada, Library, Ottawa (Negative no. C 113195).

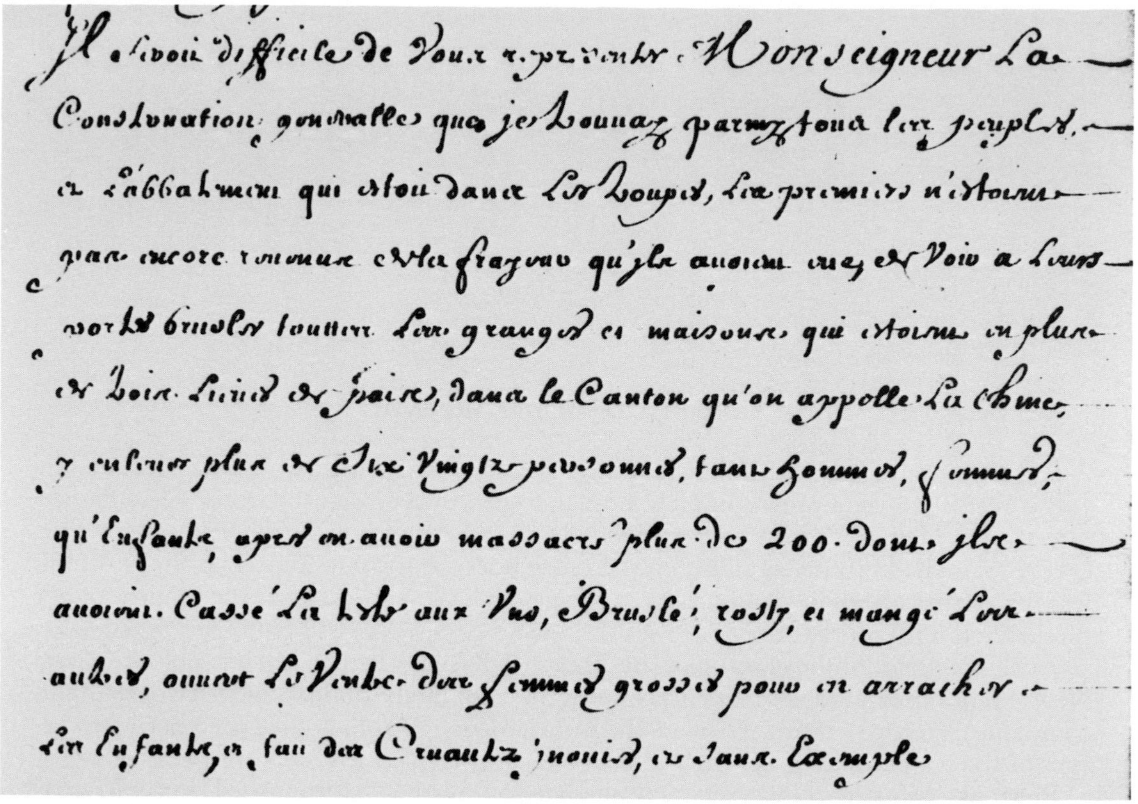

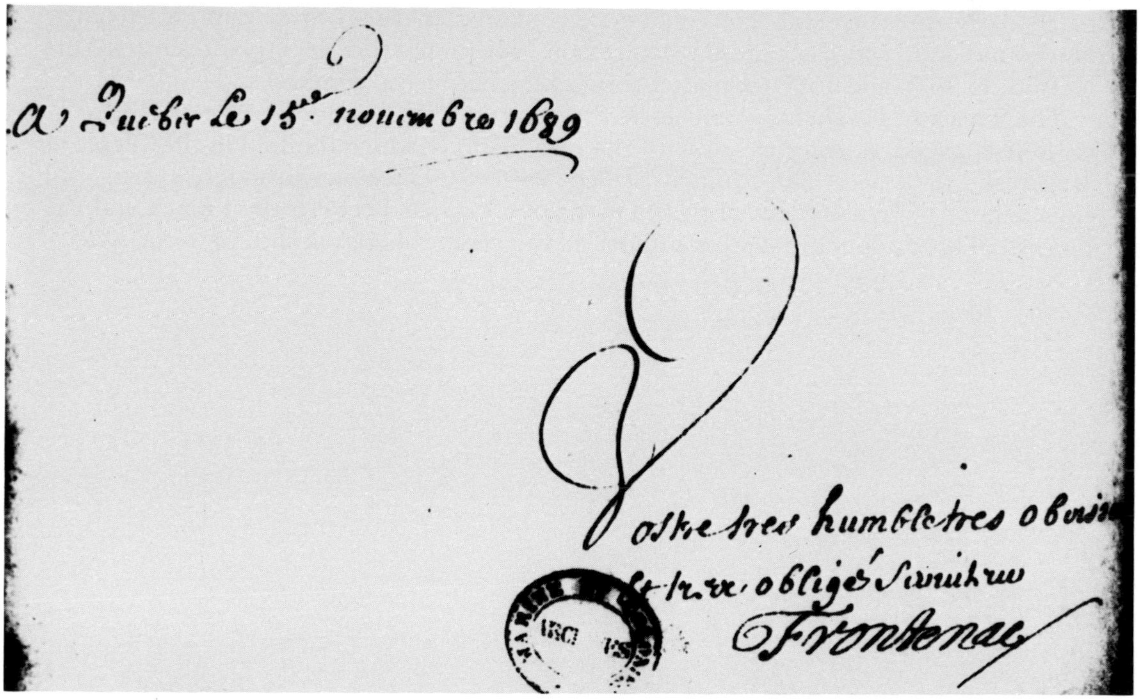

Letter from Governor General Frontenac to the minister Seignelay, Québec, 15 November 1689.

In the night of 4–5 August, at Lachine, the Iroquois were said to have burned "all the barns and houses... [carried off] more than one hundred and twenty people, men, women, and children, after massacring some...and committed unbelievable and unexampled cruelties."

Archives nationales, Paris, France: Fonds des Colonies, série C^{11A}, vol. 10, fol. 219, 224v.

V

The inter-colonial war

A new European war, called the war of the League of Augsburg, which was declared in 1689, furnished the English in New England with the occasion to attack New France directly. In May 1690 Phips seized Port-Royal, in Acadia; in October he was before Québec, and had Frontenac summoned to surrender the town to him. The old governor was not of that mind: he would reply to the general, he said, through the mouths of his cannon and with musket fire.

At the moment of the signing of the Treaty of Ryswick, which put an end to the war, New France had under arms 1,376 officers and men, divided into twenty-eight companies; on top of that there were the militiamen – all able-bodied men between the ages of sixteen and sixty – and the allied Indians.

Pierre Le Moyne d'Iberville, a Canadian by birth, distinguished himself very particularly in this war by conquering, one after the other, part of Acadia, Newfoundland, and the Hudson Bay region, where he twice took possession of Fort Nelson, in 1694 and 1697 (the latter time after a hard naval combat).

The Treaty of Ryswick did not settle the question of the Iroquois country. Hector de Callière engaged in negotiations with the Five Nations, which resulted in the "Peace of Montreal" in 1701. The Iroquois sided with the French, although taking the engagement to remain neutral in the event of a conflict between the French and the English. This diplomatic success authorized the greatest hopes in the economic field.

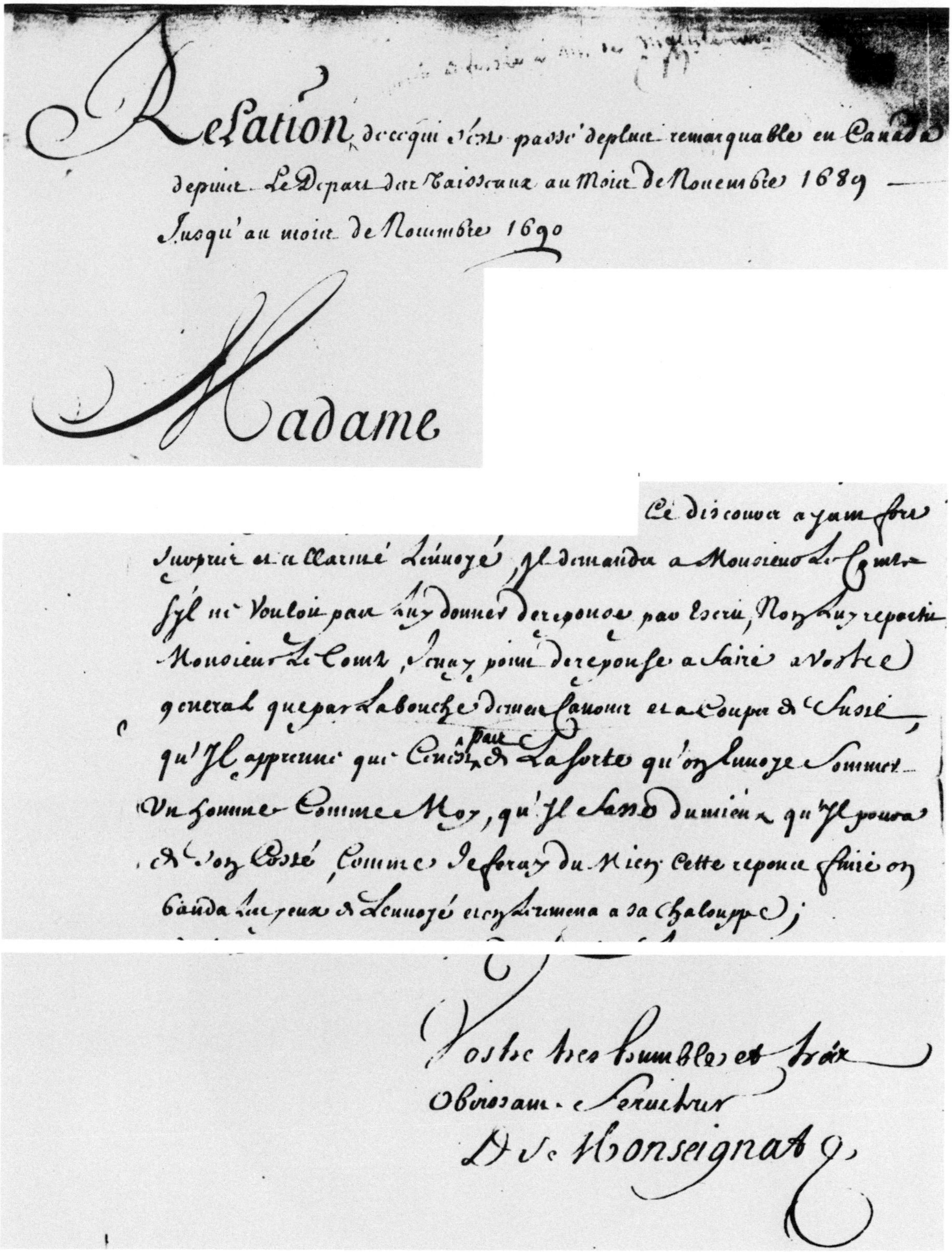

Relation de ce qui s'est passé de plus remarquable en Canada depuis le Depart des Vaisseaux au Mois de Novembre 1689 — Jusqu'au mois de Novembre 1690

Madame

Ce discours ayant fort surpris et allarmé l'envoyé, il demanda a Monsieur le Comte s'il ne vouloit pas luy donner de reponse par escrit, Non luy repartit Monsieur le Comte, je n'ay point de reponse a faire a vostre general que par la bouche de mes canons et a coups de fusils, qu'il apprenne que ce n'est pas de la sorte qu'on envoye sommer un homme comme moy, qu'il fasse du mieux qu'il pourra de son costé, comme je feray du mien, cette reponse finie on banda les yeux de l'envoyé et on le remena a sa chaloupe;

Vostre tres humble et tres Obeissant Serviteur
De Monseignat

"Account of the most remarkable things that happened in Canada…from November 1689 to the month of November 1690," by Charles de Monseignat.

Monseignat quoted Frontenac's famous response to the emissary of Admiral Phips, who called upon him to surrender Québec: "I have no reply to make to your general other than from the mouths of my cannons and muskets."

Archives nationales, Paris, France: Fonds des Colonies, Série C^{11A}, vol. 11, fol. 5, 34, 40.

KEBECA LIBERATA; Jean Mauger (1648–1722); medal; struck in bronze; restrike; 41 mm. Obverse: LUDOVICUS XIIII. REX CHRISTIANISS./I. MAVGER. F. Reverse: FRANCIA IN NOVO ORBE VICTRIX. In the exergue: KEBECA LIBERATA/M.DC.XC.

This medal was struck to commemorate the victory over Admiral Sir William Phips's troops, who laid siege to Québec in 1690.

Public Archives of Canada, Picture Division, Ottawa (Negatives nos. C 115686 obverse, C 115685 reverse).

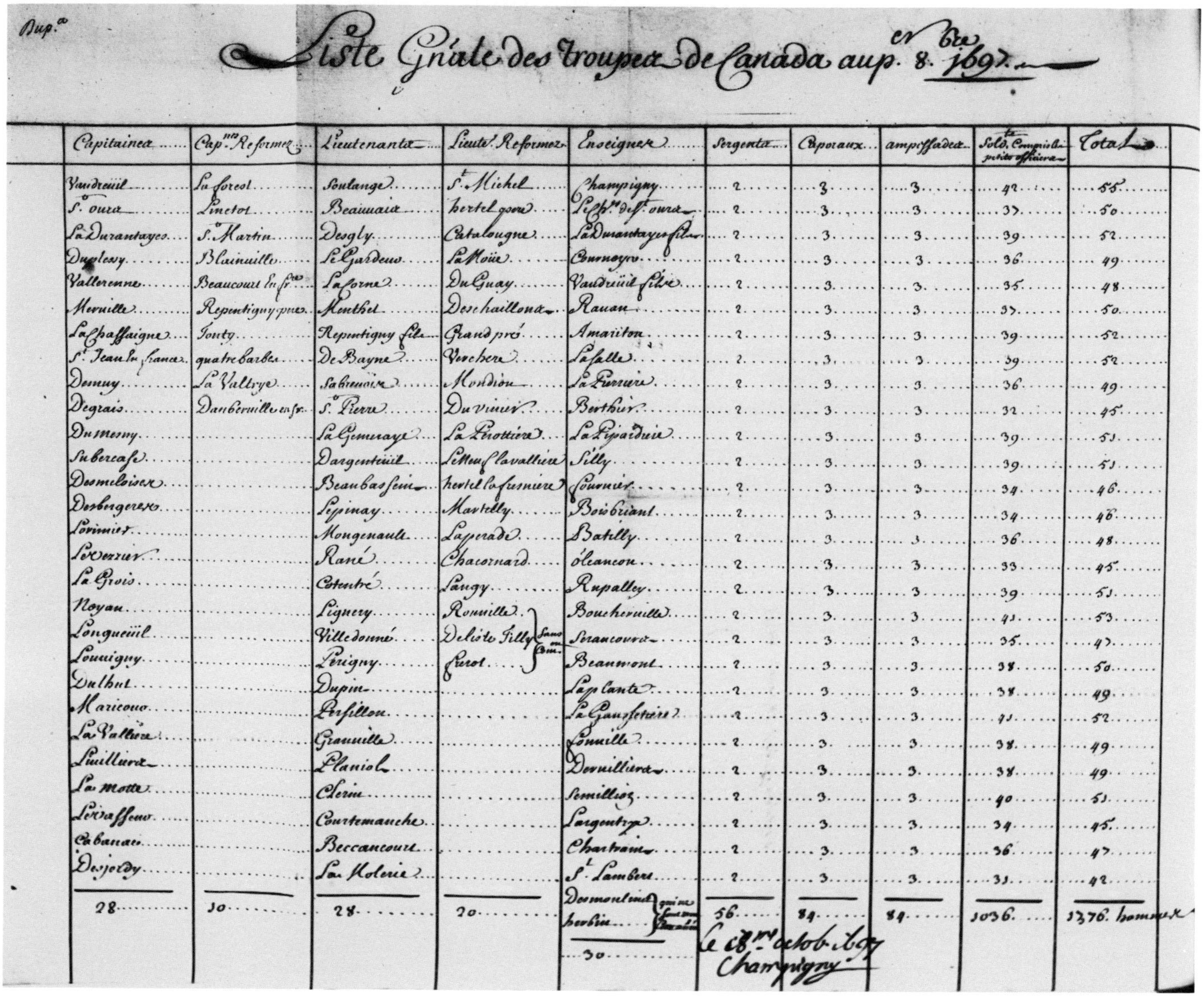

Bup.on

Liste Gnale des troupes de Canada au pr. 8bre 1697.

Capitaines	Capnes Reformez	Lieutenants	Lieute. Reformez	Enseignes	Sergents	Caporaux	anspessades	Soldats Compris les petits officiers	Total
Vaudreüil	La forest	Soulange	St. Michel	Champigny	2	3	3	42	55
St. Ours	Linctot	Beauvais	hertel pere	Le Chr. de St. Ours	2	3	3	37	50
La Durantayes	St. Martin	Desgly	Catalougne	La Durantayes fils	2	3	3	39	52
Duplessy	Blainville	Le Gardeur	La Noüe	Cournoyer	2	3	3	36	49
Vallerenne	Beaucourt Ing. fr.	La Corne	Du Guay	Vaudreüil fils	2	3	3	35	48
Merville	Repentigny pere	Menthel	Deschaillons	Rauan	2	3	3	37	50
La Chassaigne	Tonty	Repentigny fils	Grand pré	Amariton	2	3	3	39	52
St. Jean la france	quatrebarbes	De Bayne	Verchere	La Salle	2	3	3	39	52
Demuy	La Valtrye	Sabrevoix	Mondion	La Pierriere	2	3	3	36	49
Degrais	Dauberville en fr.	St. Pierre	Du Vivier	Berthier	2	3	3	32	45
Du Mesny		La Gemeraye	La Perottiere	La Pipardiere	2	3	3	39	51
Subercase		Dargenteüil	Leneuf Lavalliere	Silly	2	3	3	39	51
Desmeloises		Beaubassin	hertel la fresniere	Fournier	2	3	3	34	46
Desbergeres		Lepinay	Martelly	Boisbriant	2	3	3	34	46
Lorimier		Mongenault	Laperade	Batilly	2	3	3	36	48
Le Verrier		Rané	Chacornard	Oleancon	2	3	3	33	45
La Grois		Cotentré	Langy	Rupalley	2	3	3	39	51
Noyan		Lignery	Rouville } sans Com.	Boucherville	2	3	3	41	53
Longueüil		Villedonné	Delisle Silly }	Serancourt	2	3	3	35	47
Louvigny		Périgny	Ferot }	Beaumont	2	3	3	38	50
Dulhut		Dupin		Laplante	2	3	3	38	49
Maricour		Persillon		La Gauzeterie	2	3	3	41	52
La Vallière		Granville		Lonville	2	3	3	38	49
Duilliers		Planiol		Dervilliers	2	3	3	38	49
La Motte		Clerin		Semilliez	2	3	3	40	51
Levasseur		Courtemanche		Largentry	2	3	3	34	45
Cabanac		Beccancourt		Chartrain	2	3	3	36	47
Desjordy		La Nolerie		St. Lambert	2	3	3	31	42
28	10	28	20	Desmoulins, Herbin } quinze sans Com. — 30	56	84	84	1036	1376 hommes

Le 18me octob. 1697
Champigny

General roll of the troops in Canada as of 1 October 1697.

At that time New France had 1,376 officers and men under arms, without counting the Canadian militiamen and the Indian allies who took part in military operations.

Archives nationales, Paris, France: Fonds des Colonies, série D[2C], vol. 47.

160

Bombardment and Capture of Fort Nelson; engraved by I.B. Scotin; etching; 15.4 x 26.1 cm. (page).

In Claude Charles Le Roy Bacqueville de La Potherie. *Histoire de l'Amérique septentrionale....* Paris: J. – L. Nion & F. Didot, 1722, vol. 1, p. 105.

On 5 September 1697 the Canadian Pierre Le Moyne d'Iberville, on board the *Pelican*, won a brilliant victory over three English ships, the *Hampshire*, *Dering* and *Hudson Bay*, which disposed of much superior forces. Some days later he captured Fort Nelson, which was considered the best English post on Hudson Bay.

Public Archives of Canada, Library, Ottawa (Negative no. C 113194).

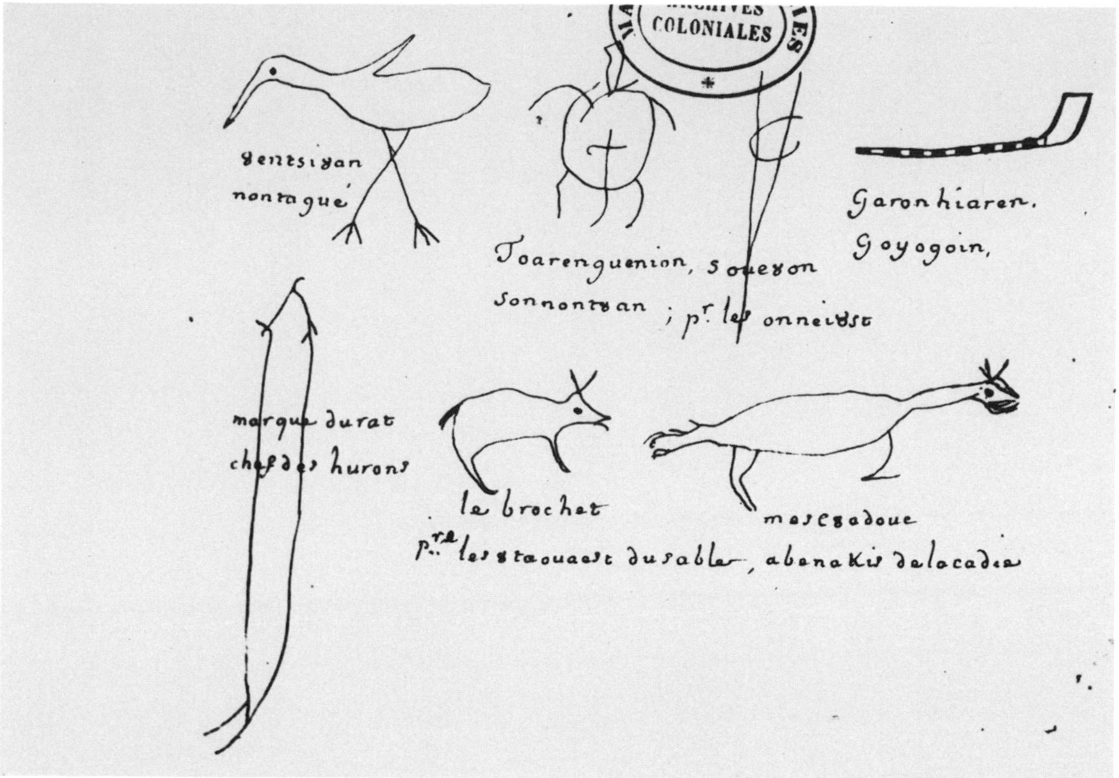

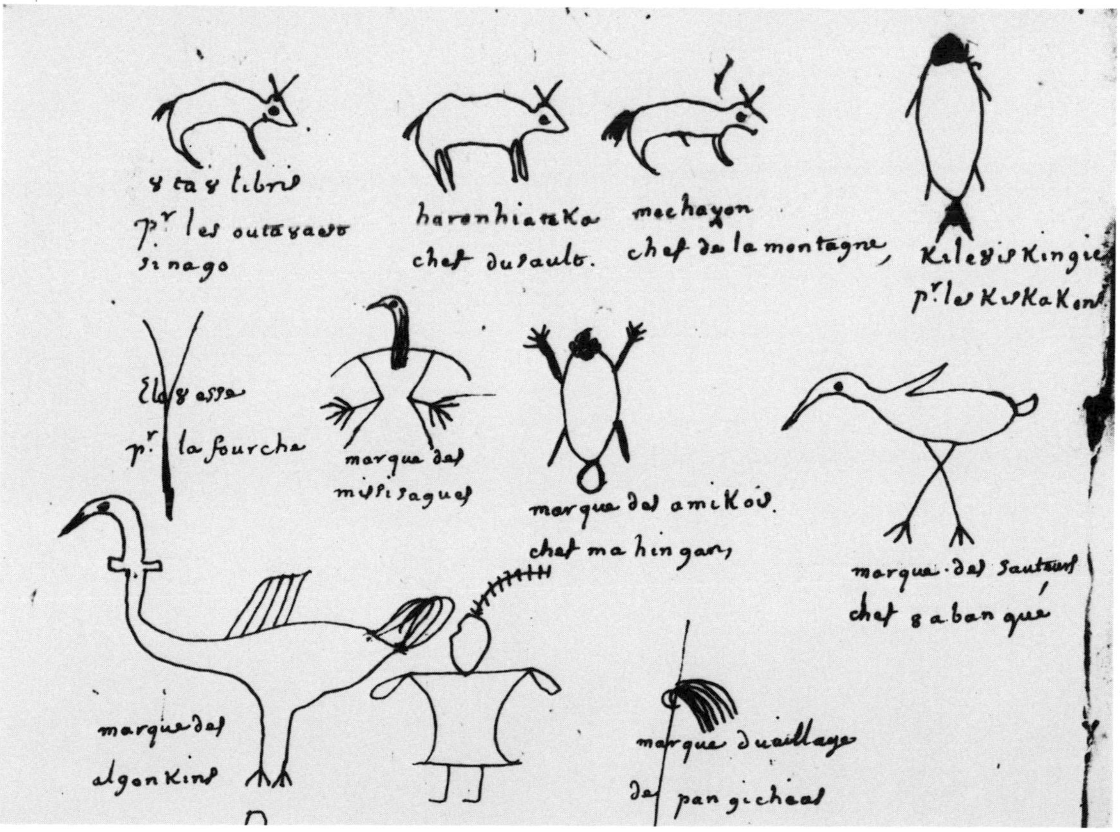

Indian chiefs' signatures on the peace treaty concluded with the Iroquois, Montréal, 4 August 1701.

Each one signed by drawing the totemic animal representing his tribe.

Archives nationales, Paris, France: Fonds des Colonies, série C[11A], vol. 19, fol. 43–43v.

VI

Economy

Officially it was the search for a trade route to Asia that prompted voyages of discovery in America, and particularly in North America; in reality, it is possible that Breton fishermen had frequented the banks of Newfoundland since the middle of the fifteenth century. Whether they were discoverers or fishermen, they were impelled by economic motives.

For a long time cod appeared as the great source of wealth of North America; then on top of that came the furs, trade in which expanded incredibly. The cod fisheries led England to occupy more and more, in actual fact, the island of Newfoundland. The trade in pelts prompted France to settle in the valley of the St. Lawrence and from there to explore and occupy the greater part of the North American continent. Acadia, which was at the meeting-point between the colony of Canada and Newfoundland, had a part in both economies, dividing itself between the fur trade and fishing.

From Champlain to Talon, the colony along the St. Lawrence depended exclusively on the fur trade, the monopoly of which was granted in succession to several companies in return for the promise to establish settlers. Now, the companies saw the settlers as potential competitors, with the result that until 1629 Quebec remained more or less a trading factory. The Compagnie de la Nouvelle-France, which was set up in 1627, aroused hopes, but it was almost ruined from the beginning by the loss of Roquemont's fleet in 1628. And then, at the beginning of the 1640s the Iroquois war put the partners in a desperate situation. The Communauté des Habitants took advantage of the situation to obtain the grant of the monopoly to the fur trade in return for the promise to support the country financially. Under the Cent-Associés the fur trade had been open, except that the habitants had to sell their furs to the company's stores; from then on it was forbidden.

From 1608 to about 1640 the fur trade had been fairly profitable; it dropped greatly as a result of the Iroquois war and the destruction of Huronia. Except in the occasional year the Indians could not go down to Québec or Trois-Rivières any longer to deliver the pelts. Consequently, the colony was languishing. In 1663 the Cent-Associés resigned; despite the creation of the Compagnie des Indes occidentales in 1664, the king and his representatives took the situation into hand.

When Jean Talon arrived in 1665, the colony possessed no industry; even agriculture, according to Pierre Boucher, was limited almost entirely to the growing of wheat. The intendant created various "manufactories," which he conceived as an outlet for agriculture on one hand and as an incentive to export on the other. First he brought in large numbers of farm animals; with the wool from the sheep and the hides from the cattle he had clothes and shoes made. He encouraged the growing of hemp, barley, and hops, the production of tar, and the development of the forests. The wood and tar were used for building ships in the shipbuilding yard that he established on the banks of the Saint-Charles, and the hemp served to make the rigging needed for the sails. With the hops and barley he made beer in the "king's brewery" that he had built near the shipbuilding yard; surplus agricultural products, wood (boards, planks, stave wood), and beer were soon exported to the West Indies on ships built at Québec. Talon also exported fish. Nevertheless, if in 1666 he had thought of fixed fisheries, which seemed even more profitable to him than roving fisheries, Talon did not have time to truly give shape to the idea, which would have allowed settling people on the coasts of Canada and Acadia who would have practised fishing in summer and hunting in winter. Despite prospecting for all kinds of mines that he had carried out, he was not successful in discovering any that could be exploited with the means of the time.

Talon left in 1672 at the time that Louis XIV was engaged in a European war and he was not replaced until 1675. During that period the impetus that he had imparted to the colony slowed down and in many cases was completely lost. Once more furs were almost the sole item in the Canadian economy; for lack of outlets agriculture stagnated; the export trade was reduced, other than pelts, to exporting wood; the brewery was quickly shut down and shipbuilding given up almost completely. The very stability that Talon had begun to give the colony was lost, following a major change that took place in fur-trading techniques. Formerly the Indians brought their furs to the colony's stores; from the end of the 1660s the French had to go to get the pelts themselves, obtaining them from ever more distant tribes. This marked the beginning of the life in the woods, with all its drawbacks. It was forbidden on several occasions; a system of congés (licences) distributed by the governor was put into effect, but taking to life in the woods was never brought under control.

And then competition from the English, to the west and the north, became more severe. In 1670 the Hudson's Bay Company was founded; its Canadian counterpart from 1682 on was the Compagnie du Nord. Commercial rivalries on Hudson Bay took on the aspect of a regular war, in which d'Iberville distinguished himself, until the Treaty of Ryswick. One could already feel that, being too dependent on the fur trade and lacking an industrial base, New France would not be able to resist her rivals indefinitely. Acadia was already threatened more directly since it was closer to the New England colonies and was in addition very sparsely populated. A company was formed in 1682 to set up fixed fisheries, but it disappeared in 1710.

In 1700 New France was far from having realized in the economic field the hopes that Champlain and Talon had placed in her.

VI

A source of wealth: cod

Very soon after Columbus had discovered America, and perhaps even before then, European ships went to the Newfoundland banks every year to fish for cod; very soon it became customary to clean the fish and dry it on "stages" on the shore.

Jean Denys from Honfleur, who travelled to the "New-Found Lands" in 1506, was the first French sailor whose name is known to us for having made the voyage; we also know that two years later Thomas Aubert from Dieppe made the same voyage on board a ship called *La Pensée,* and that he was the first person to bring some Indians back to France.

Except for the sketchy drawings that decorate old maps we have no plans of sixteenth century Newfoundland fishing boats; a single drawing, superimposed on a page of a handwritten treatise on hydrography, gives us a fairly good idea of the ships that travelled to the "New-Found Lands" towards 1550.

In 1610, in view of the fact that subjects of his realm had been frequenting the coasts and the ports of Newfoundland for fifty years and more, the king of England granted a charter to the London and Bristol Company and allowed it to settle the territory that was regularly visited by the English, in order to facilitate the development of the fisheries, along with other resources.

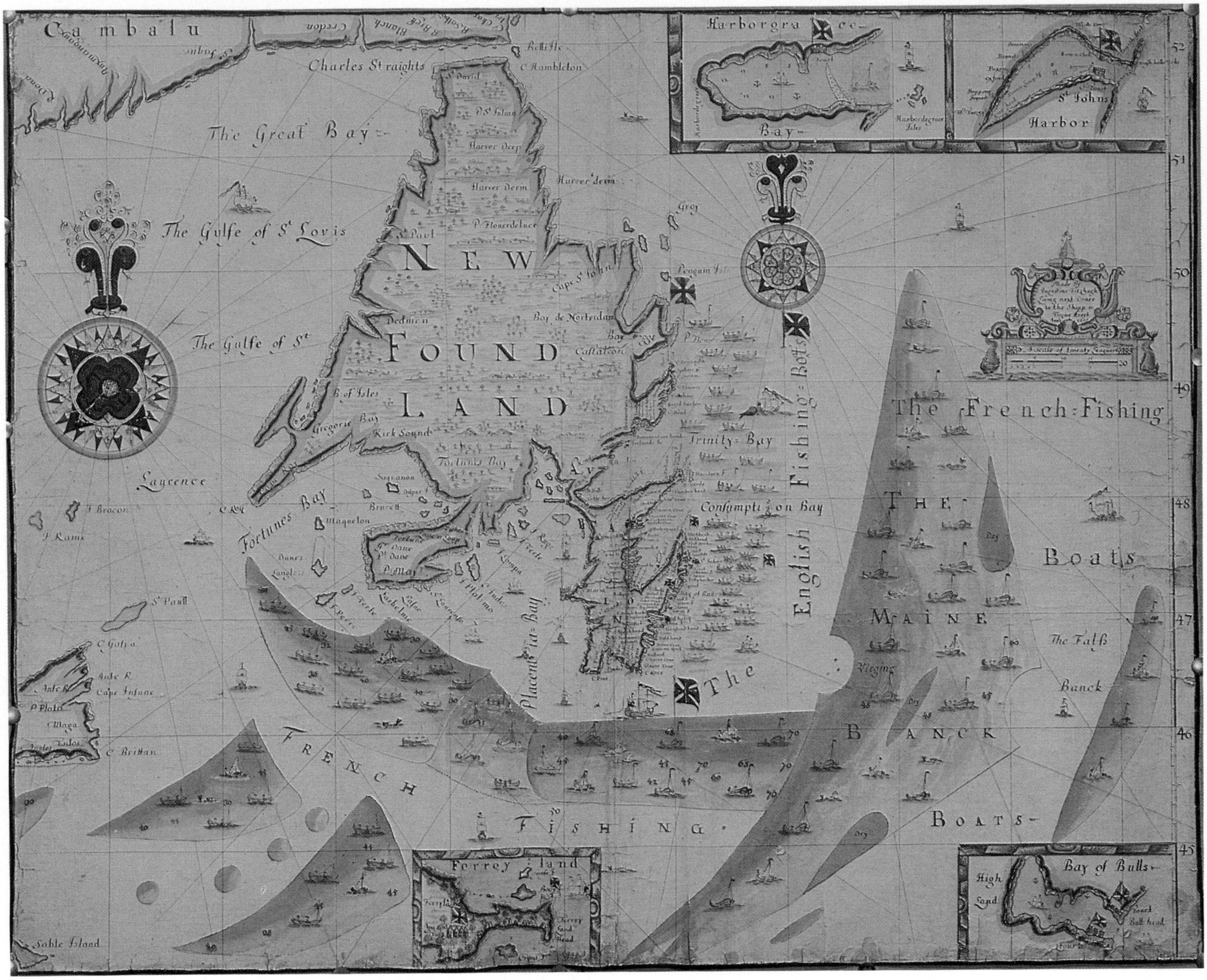

[The Newfoundland coastline and surrounding fishing banks]; Augustine Fitzhughe; col. ms.; 39.5 x 49.5 cm.

This map indicates the places in Newfoundland where the English and the French carried on fishing. The English occupied the east coast of the island, where they dried the cod (dried cod); the French salted the cod (simply salted) in mid-ocean, on the banks located primarily to the south and the southeast of the island.

British Library, London, England: Add. Ms. 5414, art. 30, nos. 13–16.

DISCORSO D'VN GRAN CAPITANO

di mare Franceſe del luoco di Dieppa ſopra le nauigationi fatte alla terra nuoua dell'Indie occidentali, chiamata la nuoua Francia, da gradi 40 fino a gradi 47 ſotto il polo artico, & ſopra la terra del Braſil, Guinea, Iſola di San Lorenzo, & quella di Summatra, fino alle quali hanno nauigato le Carauelle & naui Franceſe.

Di quelli che hanno diſcoperta la terra nuoua.

Detta terra è ſtata ſcoperta da 35 anni in quà, cioè quella parte che corre leuante & ponente p li Brettoni & Normandi, per la qual cauſa è chiamata queſta terra il capo delli Brettoni. L'altra parte che corre tramontana & mezzo dì, è ſtata ſcoperta per li Portogheſi dopo il Capo di Ras fino al Capo di buona viſta, il che contiene circa 70 leghe, & il reſtante è ſtato ſcoperto fin al golfo delli caſtelli, & piu oltra per detti Brettoni & Normandi. & ſono circa 33 anni che vn nauilio d'Onfleur, del quale era Capitano Giouanni Dioniſio, & il Pilotto Gamarto di Roano primamente v'andò, & nell'anno 1508 vn nauilio di Dieppa detto la Penſee, ilquale era gia di Giouan Ango padre del Monſignor lo Capitano & Viſconte di Dieppa v'andò, ſendo maeſtro ouer patron di detta naue maeſtro Thomaſo Aubert, & fu il primo che conduſſe qui le genti del detto paeſe. F

Giovanni Battista Ramvsio. *Terzo volvme delle navigationi et viaggi*.... Venetia: Nella stamperia de Givnti, 1565. leaf 423 rv.

Mention is made of the fact that Jean Denys and Thomas Aubert were among the first French sailors to make fishing voyages to Newfoundland at the beginning of the sixteenth century: "It was about 33 years ago that a ship from Honfleur, whose captain was Jean Denys [from Honfleur] and whose pilot was Gamarto from Rouen, was the first to go there [in 1506], and in 1508 a ship from Dieppe called *La Pensée* went there... Thomas Aubert being the master or captain of the said ship."

Public Archives of Canada, Library, Ottawa (Negatives nos. C 113343 and C 113347).

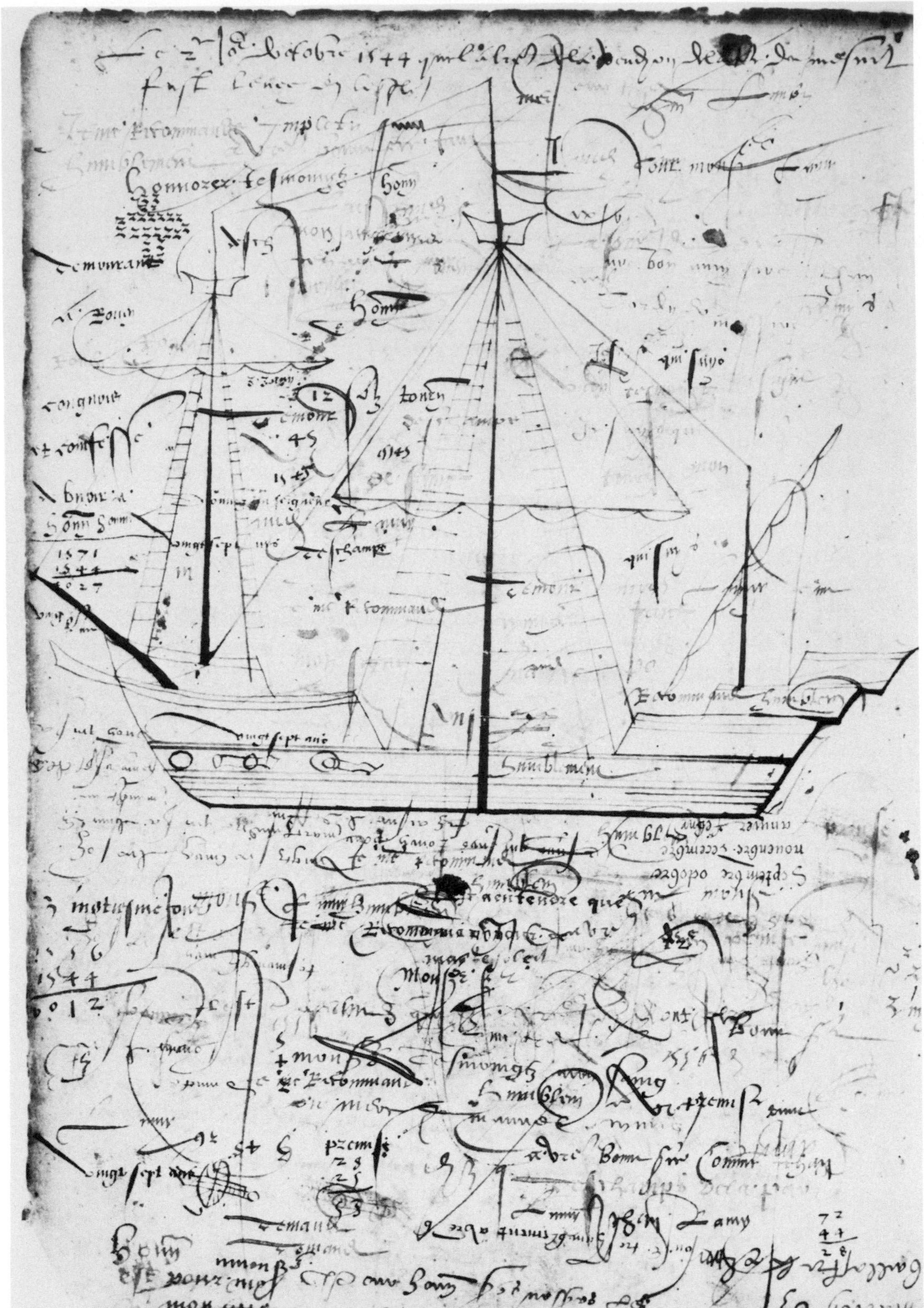

Sketch of a merchant ship from Normandy, around 1550.

Bibliothèque nationale, Départment des manuscrits, Paris, France: Fonds français, vol. 24269, fol. 55v.

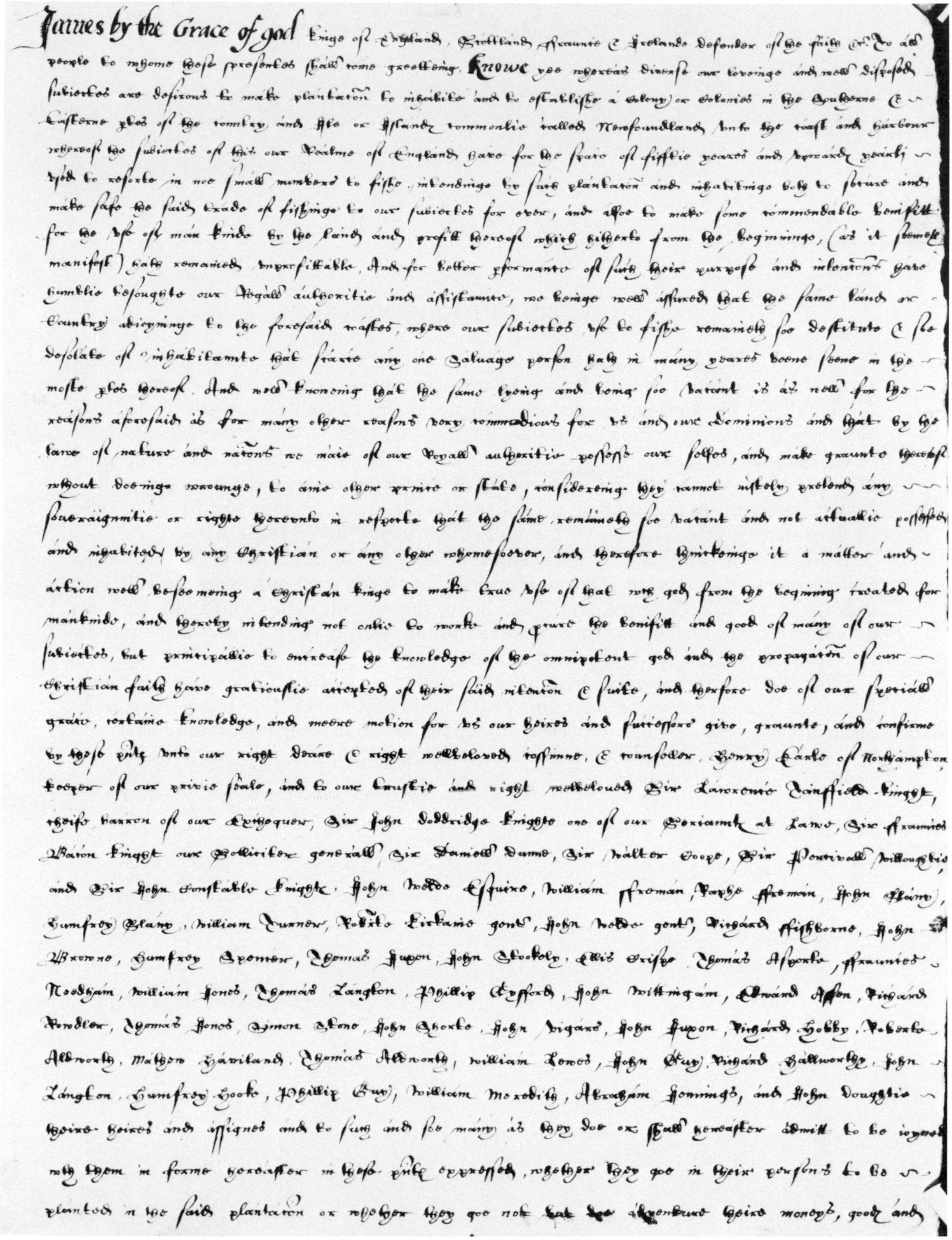

James by the Grace of god Kinge of England, Scotland, ffraunce & Ireland defender of the faith &c. To all people to whome these presentes shall come greetinge. Knowe yee that whereas divers our lovinge and well disposed subiectes are desirous to make plantacon to inhabite and to establishe a Colony or Colonies in the Southerne & Easterne ptes of the Country and Ile or Iland commonlie called Newfoundland, unto the coast and harbour whereof the subiectes of this our Realme of England have for the space of fiftie yeares and upwardes yearli used to resorte in noe small number to fishe, intendinge by such plantacon and inhabitinge both to secure and make safe the said trade of fishinge to our subiectes for ever, and alsoe to make some commendable benifitt for the use of mankinde by the landes and profitt thereof which hitherto from the beginninge, (as it seemeth manifest) hath remained unprofitable. And for better pformance of such their purpose and intencons have humblie besought our Royall authoritie and assistance, wee beinge well assured that the same landes or Country adioyninge to the foresaid coastes, where our subiectes use to fishe remaineth soe destitute & soe desolate of inhabitantes that scarce any one Salvage person hath in many yeares beene seene in the moste ptes thereof. And well knowing that the same lyeing and being soe vacant is as well for the reasons aforesaid as for many other reasons very commodious for us and our Dominions and that by the lawe of nature and nacons we maie of our Royall authoritie possesse our selves, and make graunte thereof without doeinge wronge, to anie other prince or state, consideringe they cannot iustlie pretend any soveraignitie or righte thereunto in respecte that the same remaineth soe vacant and not actuallie possessed and inhabited by any Christian or any other whomesoever, and therefore thinkinge it a matter and action well beseeming a Christian kinge to make true use of that which god from the beginning created for mankinde, and thereby intending not onlie to worke and procure the benifitt and good of many of our subiectes, but principallie to encrease the knowledge of the omnipotent god and the propagacon of our Christian faith have graciouslie accepted of their said intencon & suite, and therefore doe of our speciall grace, certaine knowledge, and meere motion for us our heires and successors give, graunte, and confirme by these pnts unto our right deare & right welbeloved cosinne, & counsellor, Henry Earle of Northampton keeper of our privie seale, and to our trustie and right welbeloved Sir Laurence Tanfield knight, chiefe baron of our Exchequer, Sir John Doddridge knighte one of our Seriantes at Lawe, Sir ffrancis Bacon knight our Sollicitor generall, Sir Daniell Dunne, Sir Walter Cope, Sir Percivall Willoughbie, and Sir John Constable knighte, John Welde Esquire, William ffreman, Raphe ffreman, John Slany, Humfrey Slany, William Turner, Roberte Kirkame gent, John Welde gent, Richard ffishborne, John Browne, Humfrey Spooner, Thomas Juxon, John Stokeley, Ellis Crispe, Thomas Alporte, ffrauncis Needham, William Jones, Thomas Langton, Phillip Gyfforde, John Wittingham, Edward Allen, Richard Fowler, Thomas Jones, Simon Stone, John Shorte, John Vigars, John Juxon, Richard Hobby, Roberte Aldworth, Mathew Haviland, Thomas Aldworth, William Lewes, John Guy, Richard Hallworthy, John Langton, Humfrey Hooke, Phillip Guy, William Meredith, Abraham Jennings, and John Doughtie their heires and assignes and to such and soe many as they doe or shall hereafter admitt to be ioyned with them in forme hereafter in these pnts expressed, whether they goe in their persons to be planted in the said plantacon or whether they goe not but doe adventure their monyes, goods and

Charter granted by the king of England, James I, to the London and Bristol Company for the colonization of Newfoundland, 2 May 1610.

This company established a colony at Cupids (Cuper's Cove), in Conception Bay, which soon counted more than sixty settlers.

British Library, Department of Manuscripts, London, England: Harleian Mss., 589.

VI

The era of monopolies

It very nearly became customary in France to grant companies the monopoly of the fur trade and of commerce in New France in return for the obligation to set up and maintain settlers there. The Compagnie de Montmorency obtained such a monopoly in 1620; in 1627 it was replaced by the Compagnie des Cent-Associés.

In 1645 the latter company surrendered the monopoly of the fur trade (except at Miscou and in Acadia) to the Communauté des Habitants de la Nouvelle-France, which undertook in return to pay off all the colony's public expenses, thus acquiring the right to administer it in accordance with a budget that it established itself.

Being in a way an offshoot of the Compagnie des Cent-Associés, the Communauté des Habitants was dissolved in 1663, at the same time as the company. Now, the following year Louis XIV and Colbert founded another company, called the Compagnie des Indes occidentales, to which it once more granted the monopoly of the fur trade and commerce in return for the obligation to run the country.

From the time he was appointed intendant, Talon considered the fact that the colony had been placed under the administrative authority of the Compagnie des Indes occidentales unfavourable to its development; besides, this company, whose charter was revoked in 1674, was the last one to be entrusted, in whole or in part, with the running of New France.

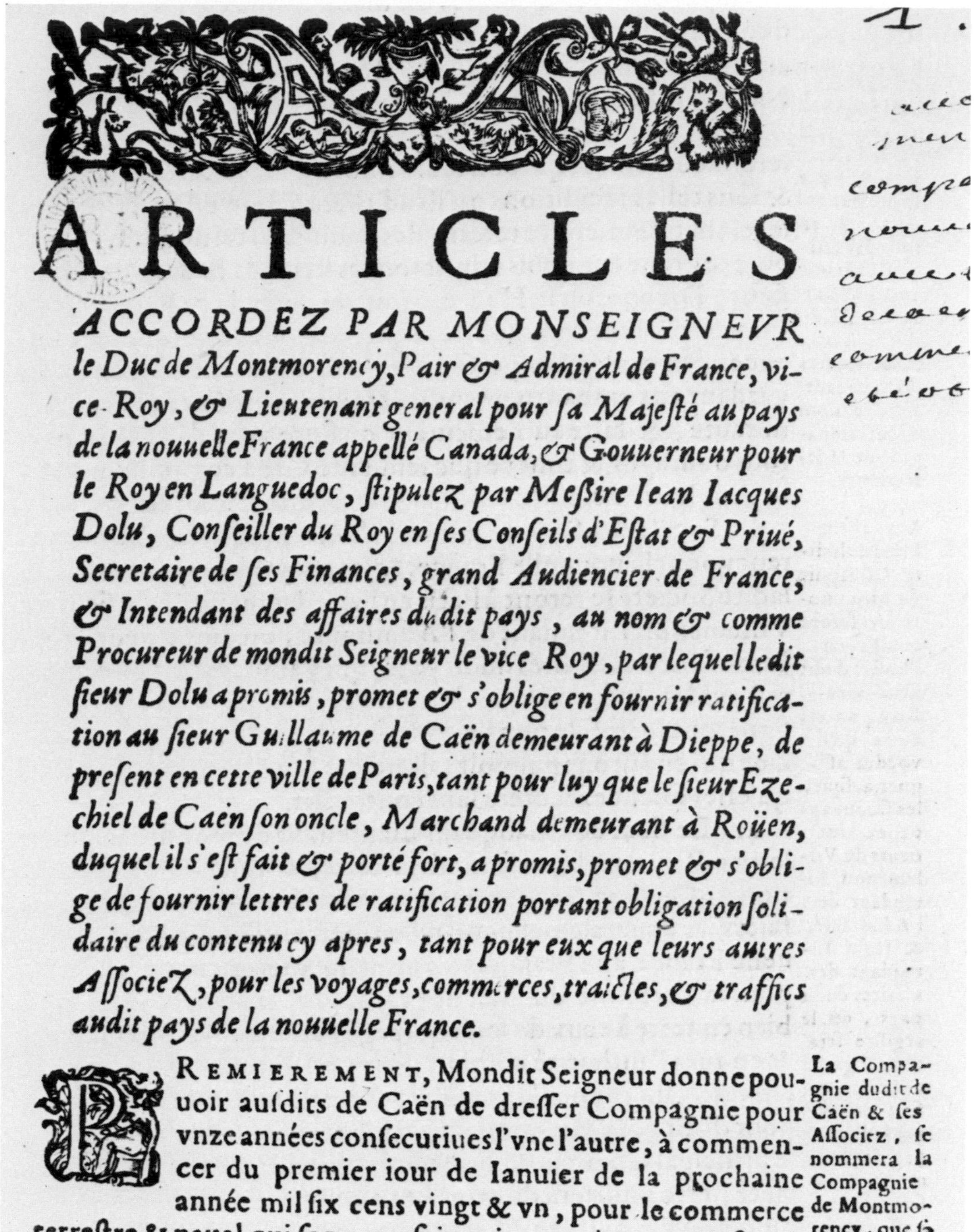

ARTICLES

ACCORDEZ PAR MONSEIGNEVR le Duc de Montmorency, Pair & Admiral de France, vice-Roy, & Lieutenant general pour sa Majesté au pays de la nouuelle France appellé Canada, & Gouuerneur pour le Roy en Languedoc, stipulez par Meßire Iean Iacques Dolu, Conseiller du Roy en ses Conseils d'Estat & Priué, Secretaire de ses Finances, grand Audiencier de France, & Intendant des affaires dudit pays, au nom & comme Procureur de mondit Seigneur le vice Roy, par lequel ledit sieur Dolu a promis, promet & s'oblige en fournir ratification au sieur Guillaume de Caën demeurant à Dieppe, de present en cette ville de Paris, tant pour luy que le sieur Ezechiel de Caën son oncle, Marchand demeurant à Roüen, duquel il s'est fait & porté fort, a promis, promet & s'oblige de fournir lettres de ratification portant obligation solidaire du contenu cy apres, tant pour eux que leurs autres Associez, pour les voyages, commerces, traictes, & traffics audit pays de la nouuelle France.

PREMIEREMENT, Mondit Seigneur donne pouuoir ausdits de Caën de dresser Compagnie pour vnze années consecutiues l'vne l'autre, à commencer du premier iour de Ianuier de la prochaine année mil six cens vingt & vn, pour le commerce terrestre & naual qui se pourra faire, tirer, traitter ou trafiquer

La Compagnie dudit de Caën & ses Associez, se nommera la Compagnie de Montmorency, que sa Majesté pour

A

"Articles granted by Monseigneur the Duc de Montmorency", viceroy of New France, to Guillaume de Caen and his partners for the creation of the Compagnie de Montmorency, Paris, 8 November 1620.

Up until 1674 France entrusted the upkeep of New France to trading companies, which in return received a monopoly of trade and commerce in the colony.

dudit pays, en quelque ſorte ou maniere que ce ſoit, en l'eſtenduë du gouuernement dudit Seigneur vice-Roy audit pays, & autant qu'il ſe pourra eſtendre, dont leur a eſté baillé coppie collationnée du pouuoir.

9. Leſdits de Caën ou leurdite Societé ſera tenuë de nourrir ſix Peres Recollets à l'ordinaire, & comme les ouuriers, compris deux qui ſeront ſouuent aux deſcouuertures dans le pays parmy les Sauuages.

10. Iceux de Caën & leurs Aſſociez pendant ledit temps de vnze années, paſſeront, nourriront, & entretiendront ſix familles ſur leſdits lieux, chacune deſquelles ſera composée de trois perſonnes, & ne ſeront leſdits de Caën ny ſeſdits Aſſociez tenus d'y en mener plus grand nombre pour les nourrir à leurs deſpens, & en cas du retour ou de mort d'aucunes deſdites familles, leſdits de Caën en paſſeront d'autres en leur lieu & place iuſques à pareil nombre pour le tenir remply, & où plus grand nombre ſe preſenteroit pour aller audit pays, & y faire habitation, ſeront leſdits de Caën & leur Societé tenus les paſſer auec leur equipage, & nourrir pour & à raiſon de trente ſix liures pour teſte, iuſques à huict iours apres leur arriuée & debarquement à Quebec.

11. Aucun de quelque qualité qu'il ſoit, ne pourra traitter directement ou indirectement d'aucunes ſortes de pelleterie, ny faire aucun traffic ny commerce que pour ſon vſage audit pays, ou pour leſdits de Caën ou leur Societé, & par l'ordre d'icelle, à peine de confiſcation applicable à ladite Societé.

22. Promet mondit Seigneur pendant ledit temps de vnze années, de ne bailler aucun paſſeport ou permiſſion à autres perſonnes qu'auſdits de Caën, pour les voyages & commerces ſuſdits en tout ou partie deſdits lieux cy deſſus,

Faict & arreſté double entre nous ſouſſignez eſdits noms à Paris, le huictieſme iour de Nouembre, mil ſix cens vingt. Dolu, de Caën, ainſi ſignez.

Bibliothèque nationale, Département des manuscrits, Paris, France: Fonds français, vol. 16738, fol. 148–148c.

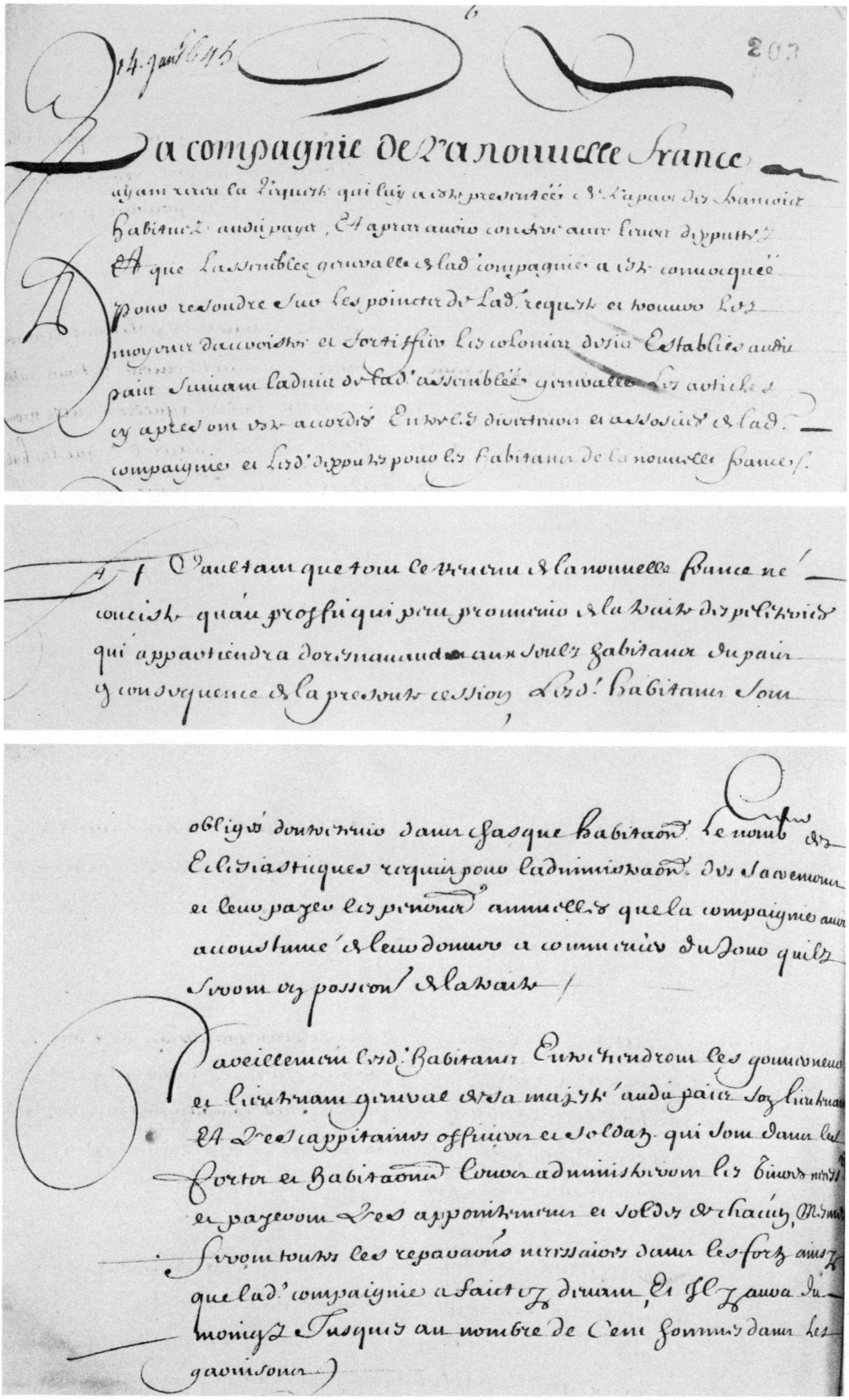
14. janv. 1645

La compagnie de la nouvelle France ayant receu la requeste qui luy a esté presentée de la part des habitans dudit pays, et apres avoir conferé avec leurs deputez et que l'assemblée generalle de lad. compagnie a esté convoquée pour resoudre sur les poinctz de lad. requeste et trouver les moyens d'accroistre et fortiffier les colonies desja establies audit pais suivant l'advis de lad. assemblée generalle les articles cy apres ont esté accordés entre les directeurs et associés de lad. compagnie et lesd. deputez pour les habitans de la nouvelle france.

Dautant que tout le revenu de la nouvelle france ne consiste qu'au proffit qui peut provenir de la traitte des pelleteries qui appartiendra doresnavant aux seulz habitans du pais en consequence de la presente cession, lesd. habitans sont obligés d'entretenir dans chasque habitation le nombre des ecclesiastiques requis pour l'administration des sacremens et leur payer les pensions annuelles que la compagnie avoit accoustumé de leur donner [illegible] quilz seront en possession de la traitte.

Pareillement lesd. habitans entretiendront les gouverneurs et lieutenant general de sa majesté audit pais, son lieutenant et les cappitaines officiers et soldatz qui sont dans les fortz et habitations, leur administreront les vivres [illegible] et payeront les appointemens et soldes de chacun, [illegible] feront toutes les reparations necessaires dans les fortz ainsi que lad. compagnie a faict cy devant, et il y aura du moings jusques au nombre de cent hommes dans les garnisons.

Agreement by which the Compagnie des Cent-Associés handed the monopoly of the fur trade over to the Communauté des Habitants de la Nouvelle-France, which in return undertook to pay off the colony's administrative expenses, 14 January 1645.

"The trade in pelts... will henceforth belong solely to the inhabitants of the country," who will be obliged "to maintain in each settlement the number of ecclesiastics needed..., the captains, officers, and soldiers..., will pay the salaries and pay of each of them, and will also carry out all the repairs required in the forts."

Archives du ministère des Affaires étrangères, Paris. France: Mémoires et documents, Amérique, vol. 4, fol. 203, 204–204v.

Portrait of Armand-Jean Du Plessis, Cardinal de Richelieu (1585–1642); Philippe de Champaigne (1602–74); oil; 259.7 x 177.8 cm.

In order to set up a colonial empire in America, Richelieu founded the Compagnie des Cent-Associés in 1627 and imposed upon it the obligation to establish four thousand settlers in New France within fifteen years.

Reproduced by courtesy of the Trustees, National Gallery, London, England.

Portrait of Jean-Baptiste Colbert (1619–83); Claude Lefebvre (1632–75); oil; 1663; 1.38 x 1.13 m.

From 1663 to 1683 the minister Colbert had several measures adopted which were aimed at promoting the development of New France.

Musée du Louvre, Paris, France. Photo: Musées Nationaux, Paris.

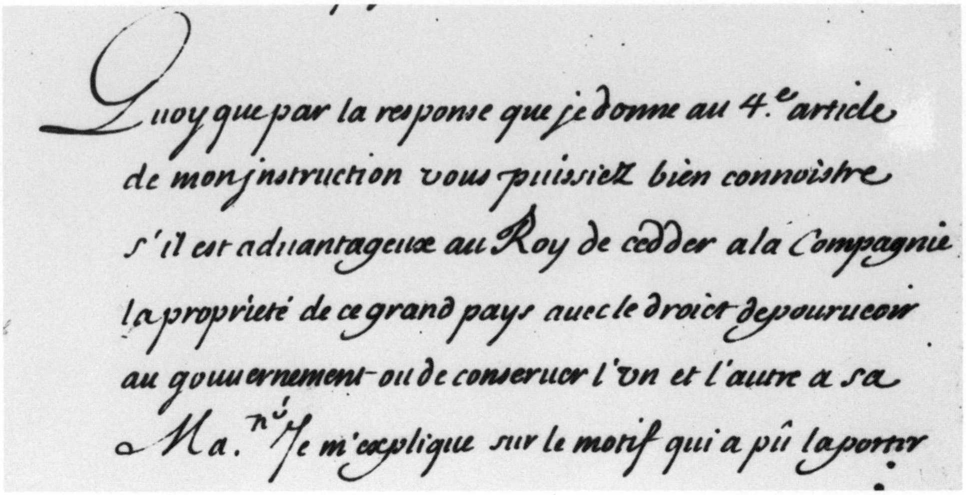

Quoyque par la response que je donne au 4.e article
de mon instruction vous puissiez bien connoistre
s'il est aduantageux au Roy de cedder a la Compagnie
la proprieté de ce grand pays auec le droict de pouruceoir
au gouuernement ou de conseruer l'un et l'autre a sa
Ma.té Je m'explique sur le motif qui a pû la porter

Letter from Intendant Talon to the minister Colbert, Québec, 4 October 1665.

In Talon's opinion Canada could not be made into "a very important State" if the king left "in other hands than his own the seigneury and ownership of the lands" and the colony's trade. If the king allowed the Compagnie des Indes occidentales to retain such powers, it would "probably make a great deal of profit by skimming the fat off the country and...it will be a serious obstacle to its settlement."

a faire cette cession a lad.^e Compagnie et je dis que
s'il a esté d'augmenter ses profits pour luy donner
dautant plus de moyens de soustenir ses premieres
despenses, augmenter le nombre de ses vaisseaux
et faire vn grand commerce vtil a son estat sans au[...]
pour objet l'estendue des habitations de ce pays et la
multiplication de ses colons il est a mon sens plus vtil
au Roy de laisser a lad.^e Comp.^e cette proprieté sans
aucune reserue. Mais si Elle a regardé ce pays com[...]
vn beau plan dans lequel on peut former vn grand
Royaume et fonder vne monarchie ou du moins vn
Estat fort considerable Je ne puis me persuader qu'Ell[e]
reussisse dans son dessein laissant en d'autres mains q[ue]
siennes La seigneurie, la proprieté des terres, la nommina[tion]
aux cures et j'adjoust mesme le commerce qui fait
l'ame de l'Establissement qu'elle pretend. Ce que j'ay
veu jusques icy depuis mon arriuée m'a bien persu[adé]
ce que j'auance, puisque depuis que les Agens de la
Comp.^e ont fait entendre qu'Elle ne souffriroit auc[une]
liberté de Commerce, non seulement aux francois q[ui]
auoient coustume de passer en ce pays pour le trans[port]
des marchandises de france Mais mesme aux p[...]
habitans du Canada jusques a leur disputer le dr[oit]

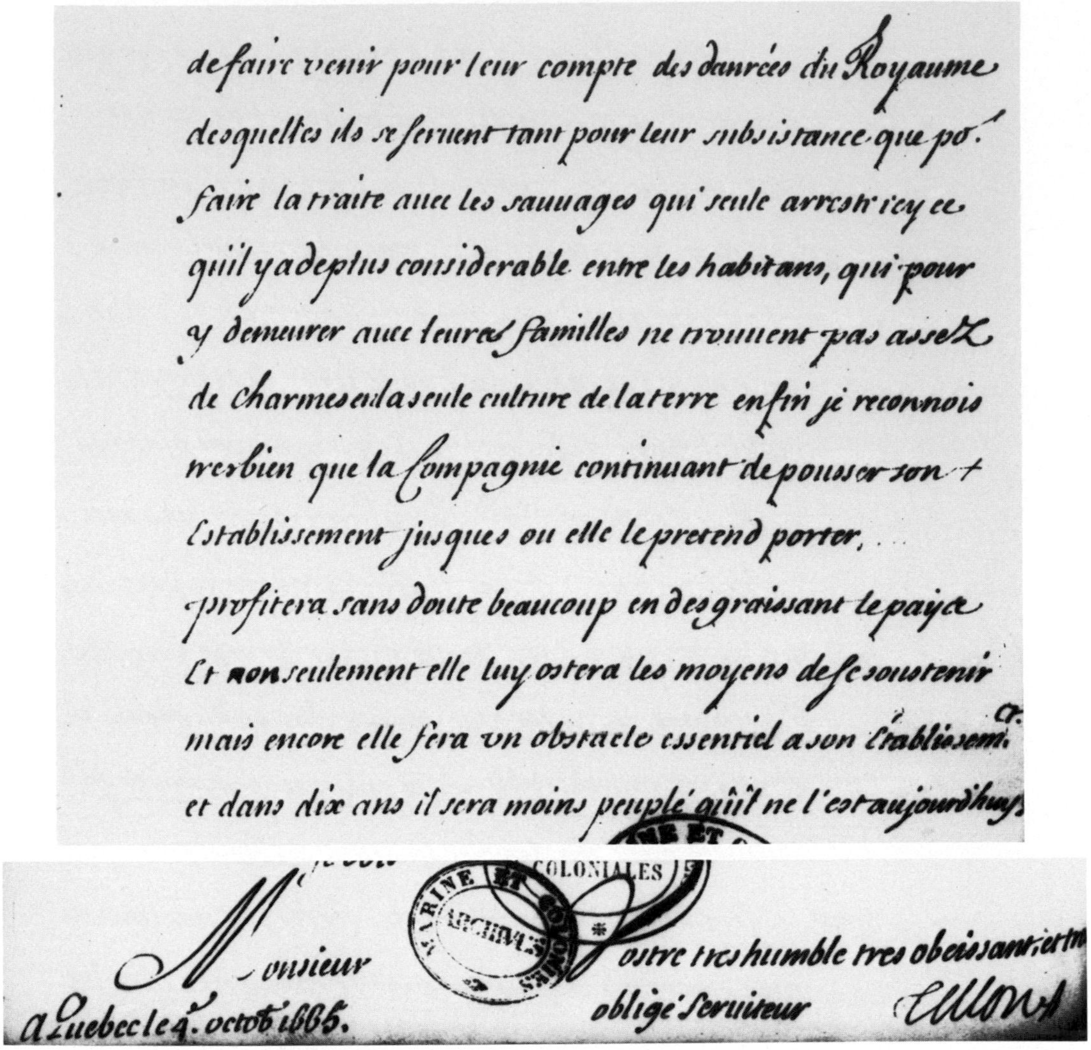

de faire venir pour leur compte des denrées du Royaume
desquelles ils se servent tant pour leur subsistance que po.
faire la traite avec les sauvages qui seule arreste icy ce
quil y a de plus considerable entre les habitans, qui pour
y demeurer avec leurs familles ne trouvent pas assez
de charmes en la seule culture de la terre enfin je reconnois
tres bien que la Compagnie continuant de pousser son
Establissement jusques ou elle le pretend porter,
profitera sans doute beaucoup en desgraissant le paiys
Et non seulement elle luy ostera les moyens de se soustenir
mais encore elle sera un obstacle essentiel a son Establissement
et dans dix ans il sera moins peuplé quil ne l'est aujourd'huy

Monsieur
Vostre tres humble tres obeissant et tr
obligé Serviteur
Talon
a Quebec le 4. octob. 1665.

Archives nationales, Paris, France: Fonds des Colonies, série C^{11A}, vol. 2, fol. 146–147, 153v.

VI

Another source of wealth: furs

Fishermen had acquired imperceptibly the habit of bringing furs back to France; then companies were created with this trade as their aim. Soon they sought to obtain the monopoly of trade with the Indians, in return for the promise, which was often badly kept, to establish settlers in New France. Furs, particularly beaver and moose, sold well in Europe; they were obtained from the Indians in exchange for knives, axes, cooking pots, glass beads.

For a long time the first settlers were not permitted to trade in furs with the Indians. In 1656 they were given such permission for a year, because they had no other means of subsistence, as furs were the sole resource of the colony.

Under Talon the fur trade became free again, but private individuals could only sell their furs to the company's agent. After the company disappeared, the *Conseil du Roi* farmed out to a tradesman, Jean Oudiette, the dues (or taxes), including those on beaver and moose hides, that were levied in Canada; consequently he alone was authorized to buy Canadian beaver and to resell it in Europe.

Shortly after 1685 a statement was prepared, year by year, of the "beaver pelts that have come from Canada from 1675 until 1685," that is to say during "all the time that Oudiette held the tax farm."

Beavers Building a Dam; etching with line engraving; 19.9 x 14.6 cm. (plate).

In François Du Creux. *Historiae canadensis, sev Novae-Franciae libri decem, ad annum vsque Christi MDCLVI.* Parisiis: S. Cramoisy et S. Mabre-Cramoisy, 1664, p. 51.

In the seventeenth century furs, especially beaver and moose, were almost the only resource being exploited in New France. They were obtained from the Indians in return for knives, axes, cooking pots, and glass beads. They were then sold in Europe.

Public Archives of Canada, Library, Ottawa (Negative no. C 99220).

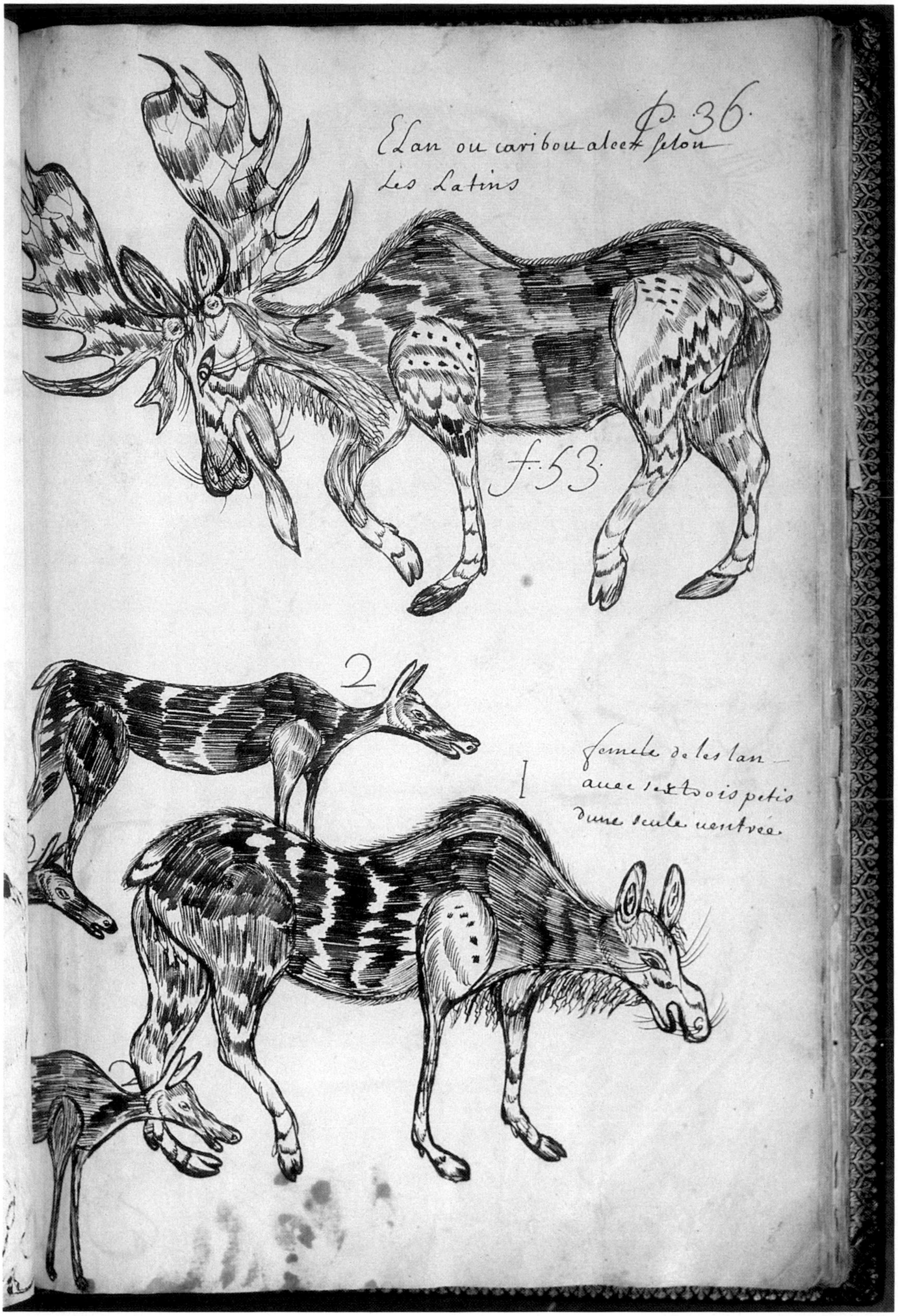

Caribou; Louis Nicolas (1634–after 1678); brown ink on parchment; 15.2 x 20.9 cm. (detail).

Thomas Gilcrease Institute of American History and Art, Tulsa, Oklahoma, U.S.A.

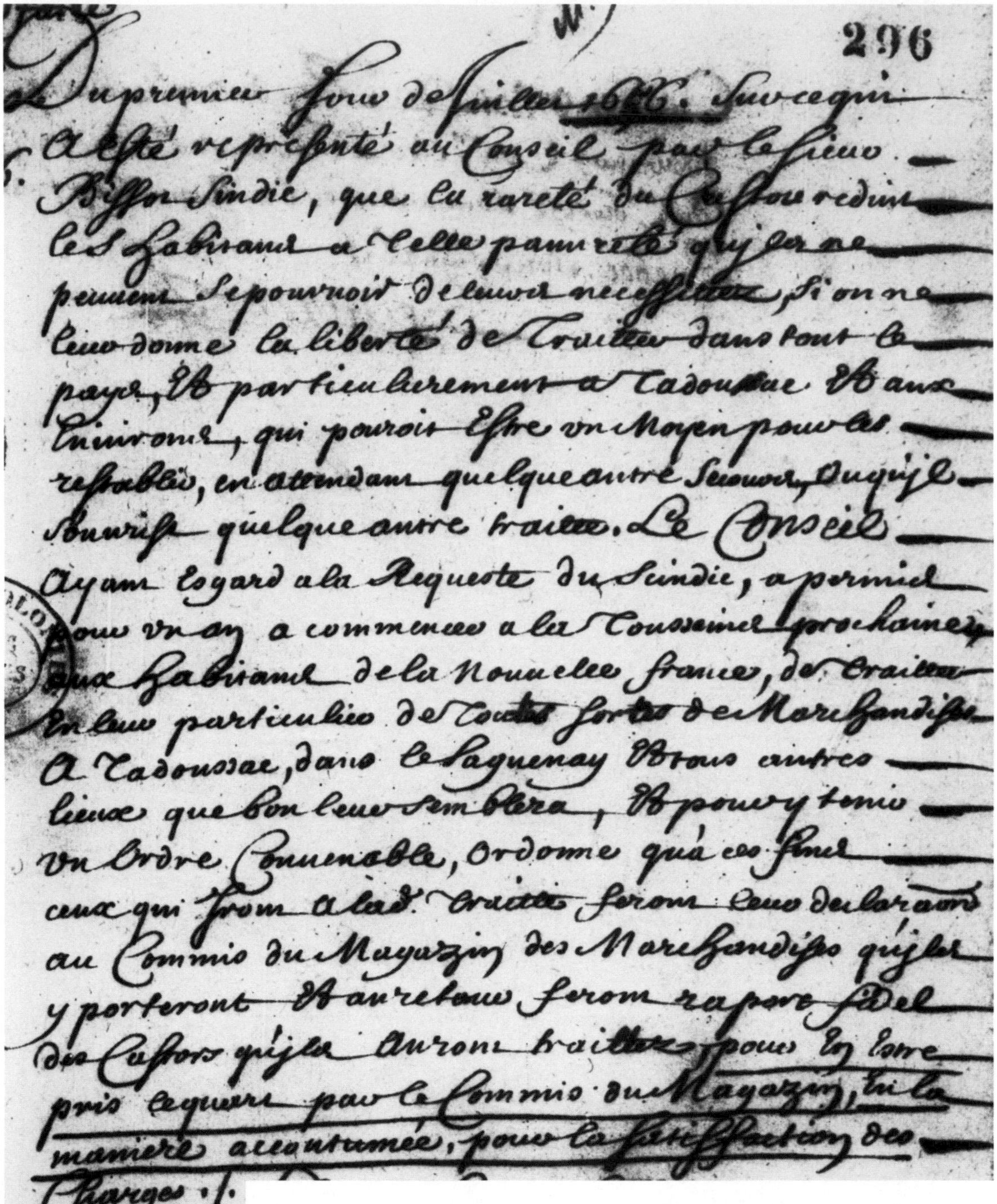
296

Du premier Jour de Juillet 1656. Sur ce qui
A esté représenté au Conseil par le Sieur
Bisson Sindic, que la rareté du Castor reduit
les habitans a telle pauvreté qu'ils ne
peuvent se pourvoir de leurs necessitez, si on ne
leur donne la liberté de Traitter dans tout le
pays, Et particulierement a Tadoussac Et aux
Environs, qui pourroit Estre un Moyen pour les
restablir, en attendant quelque autre Secours, ou qu'il
survint quelque autre traitte. Le Conseil
Ayant Egard a la Requeste du Sindic, a permis
pour un an a commencer a la Toussainct prochaine
aux habitans de la Nouvelle france, de Traitter
En leur particulier de toutes sortes de Marchandises
A Tadoussac, dans le Saguenay Et tous autres
lieux que bon leur semblera, Et pour y tenir
un Ordre Convenable, Ordonne qu'a ces fins
ceux qui Iront a lad. traitte feront leur declaration
au Commis du Magazin des Marchandises qu'ils
y porteront Et au retour feront rapport fidel
des Castors qu'ils auront traittez pour Estre
pris et requis par le Commis du Magazin en la
maniere accoustumée, pour la satisfaction des
Charges. /.

Decree by the Conseil de la Nouvelle-France allowing the settlers to engage in the fur trade wherever they wished "for a year," Québec, 1 July 1656.

The colony had been receiving few furs since the Iroquois raids had eliminated certain suppliers (the Hurons) and spread panic among the others. For that reason it was decided to allow the settlers to go themselves to look for pelts in distant regions.

Archives nationales, Paris, France: Fonds des Colonies, série C^{11A}, vol. 1, fol. 296.

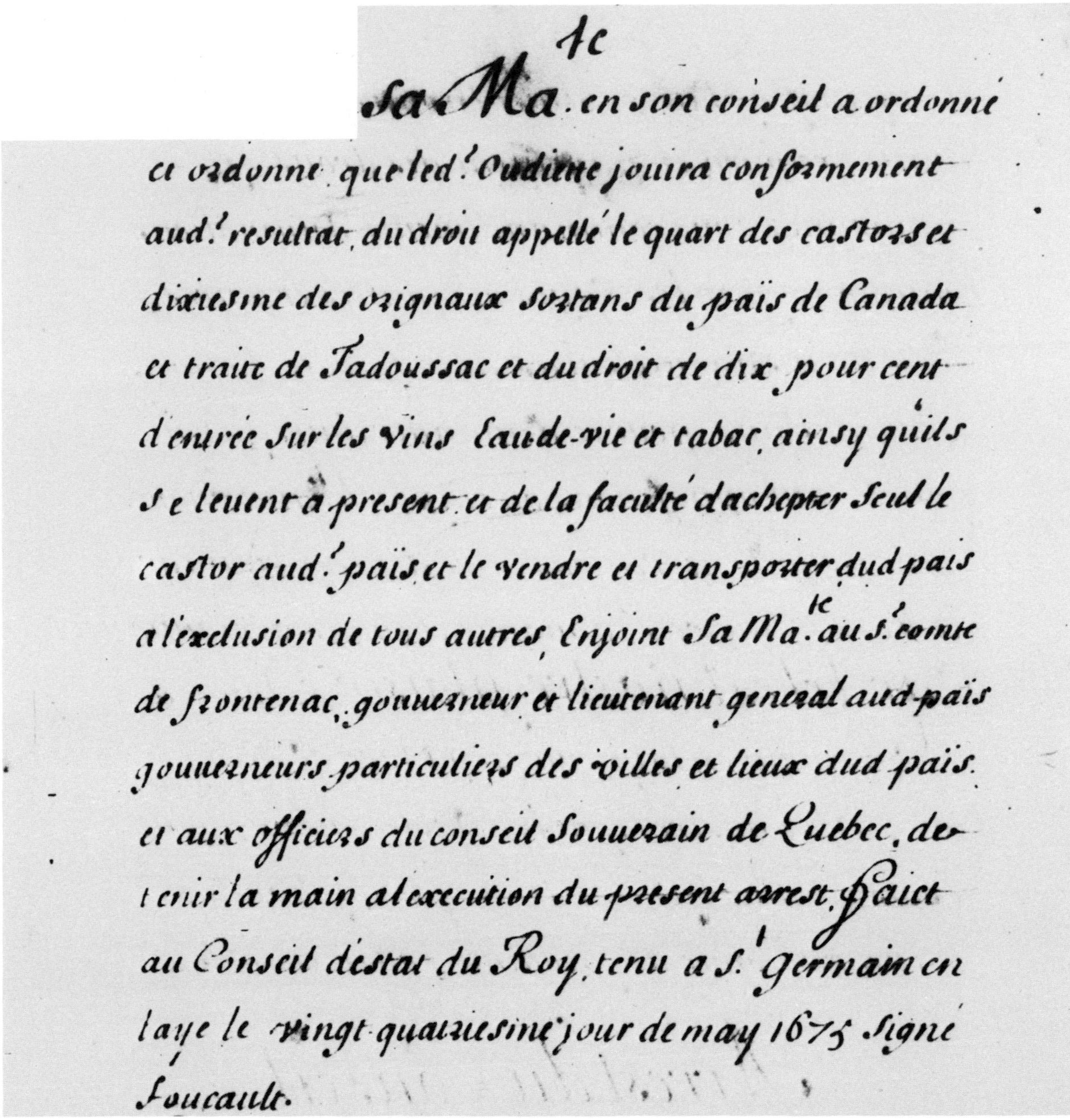

Sa Ma.te en son conseil a ordonné
et ordonne que led.t Oudiette jouira conformement
aud.t resultat, du droit appellé le quart des castors et
dixiesme des orignaux sortans du païs de Canada
et traitte de Tadoussac et du droit de dix pour cent
d'entrée sur les vins eau de vie et tabac, ainsy quils
se leuent a present. et de la faculté dachepter seul le
castor aud.t païs et le vendre et transporter dud païs
a l'exclusion de tous autres, Enjoint Sa Ma.te au S.r comte
de Frontenac, gouuerneur et lieutenant general aud païs
gouuerneurs particuliers des villes et lieux dud païs.
et aux officiers du conseil souuerain de Quebec, de
tenir la main a lexecution du present arrest, Faict
au Conseil destat du Roy, tenu a S.t Germain en
laye le vingt quatriesme jour de may 1675 Signé
Foucault.

Decree by the king's council of State declaring that the Sieur Jean Oudiette would enjoy "the right to the levy called the quarter on beaver and the tenth on moose skins leaving the country of Canada and the Tadoussac trade and the levy of ten per cent on wines, spirits, and tobacco entering the country, as they are raised at present, and the option to be sole buyer of beaver in the aforementioned country and to sell it and transport it from the aforementioned country to the exclusion of all others," Saint-Germain-en-Laye, 24 May 1675.

Archives nationales, Paris, France: Fonds des Colonies, série B, vol. 6, fol. 156–156v.

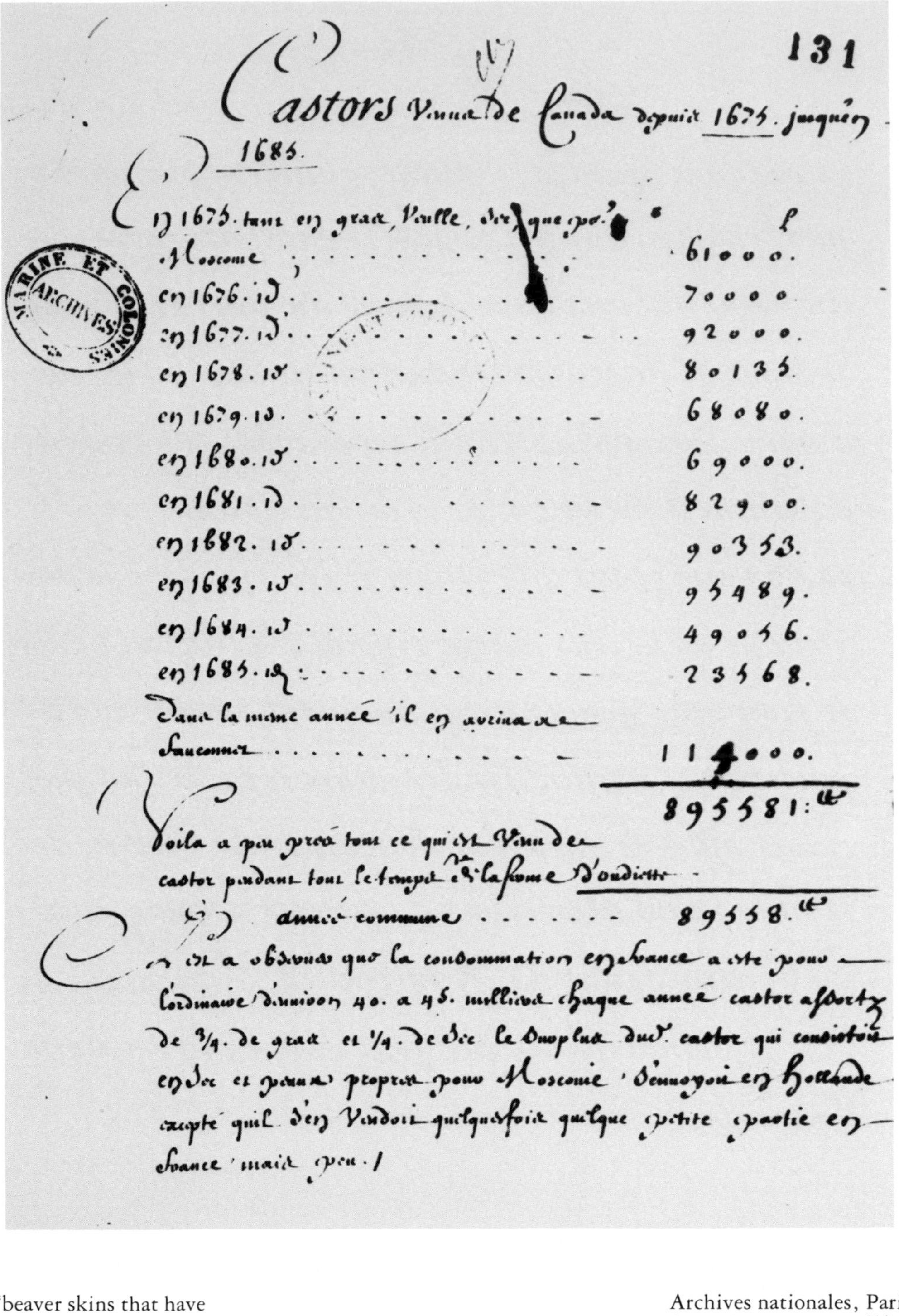

131

Castors venus de Canada depuis 1675 jusques en 1685.

En 1675 tant en gras, veulle, sec que pour Moscovie	61000.
en 1676 id	70000
en 1677 id	92000.
en 1678 id	80135.
en 1679 id	68080.
en 1680 id	69000.
en 1681 id	82900.
en 1682 id	90353.
en 1683 id	95489.
en 1684 id	49056.
en 1685 id	23568.
dans la mesme année il en a venu de Fauconnet	114000.
	895581 lt

Voila a peu prés tout ce qui est venu de castor pendant tout le temps de la ferme d'Oudiette

de année commune .... 89558 lt

Est a observer que la consommation en france a esté pour l'ordinaire d'environ 40 a 45 milliers chaque année castor assortz de 3/4 de gras et 1/4 de sec le surplus dud. castor qui consistoit en sec et peaux propres pour Moscovie s'envoyoit en hollande excepté quil s'en vendoit quelquefois quelque petite partie en france mais peu.

Statement of the "beaver skins that have come from Canada from 1675 to 1685," that is to say "during the whole period of Oudiette's tax farm."

Archives nationales, Paris, France: Fonds des Colonies, Série C[11A], vol. 7, fol. 131.

VI

Agriculture and trade

Intendant Talon was struck with the fertility of the soil in Canada, which seemed to him also to be very suitable for raising "country animals"; and after appraising the situation carefully, he thought that he could affirm that "in fifteen years" the colony would have "enough surplus" to supply the West Indies.

Talon did not wait that long; in 1668 he sent to the West Indies a ship that had been built in Canada and was loaded with peas, fish and boards. The intendant was also counting on the brewery that he had installed at Québec and that would consume annually twelve thousand bushels of Canadian grain and export two thousand casks of beer to the West Indies.

But once Talon was gone, agriculture remained a subsistence one, fettered moreover by the departure of men for the woods. Internal trade developed slowly. Perhaps it was under too tight control: the authorities set the number of bakers, butchers, and other shopkeepers; it also set the number of their apprentices and even the price of goods. And then there was not enough currency in the colony; beaver, even wheat, were used as barter. Soon, while awaiting the annual funds intended to meet the public expenditures, the intendant had to have recourse to a "playing-card-money" (playing cards to which a certain value was attached), refundable when the king's ship arrived.

176

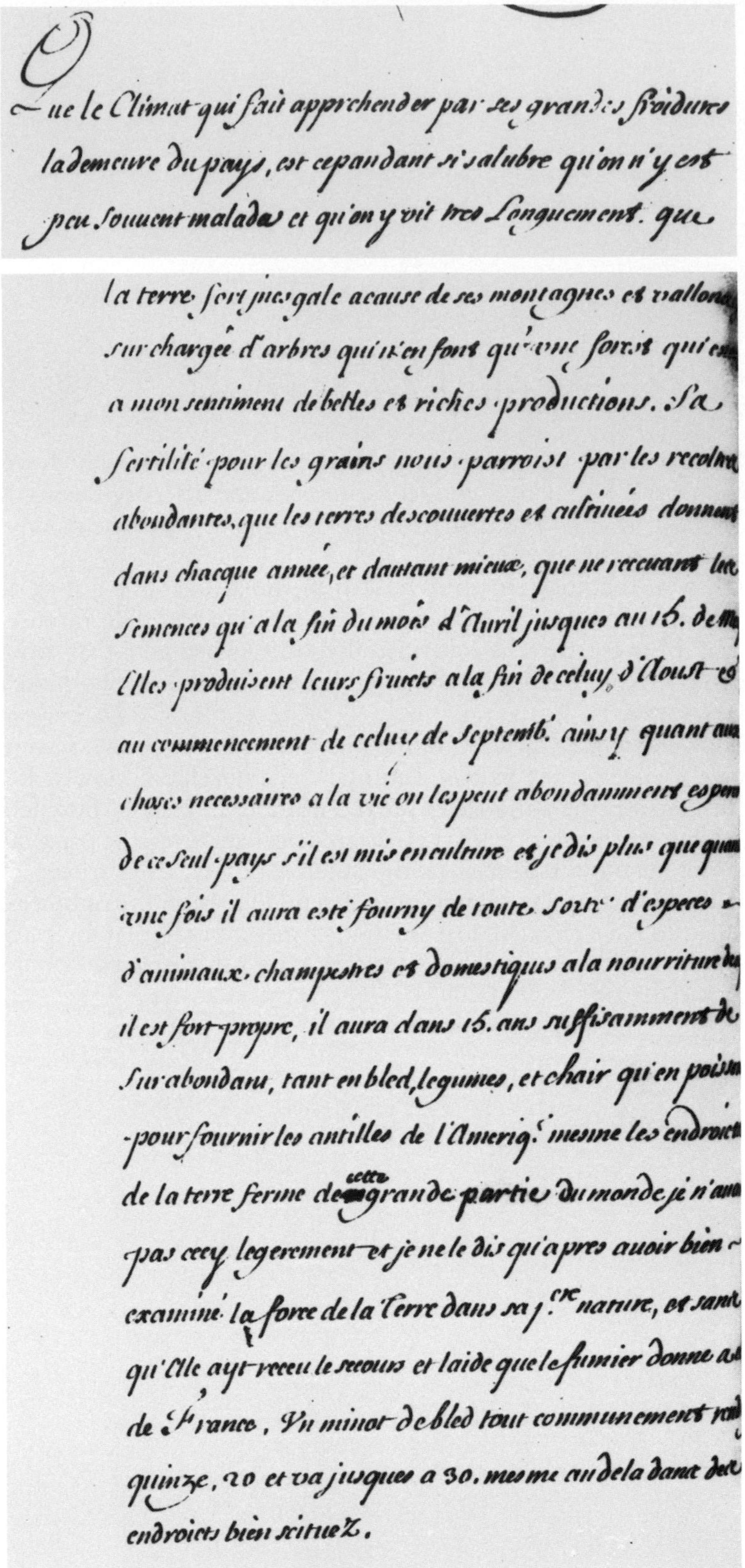

Que le Climat qui faict apprehender par ses grandes froidures
la demeure du pays, est cependant si salubre qu'on n'y est
peu souuent malade et qu'on y vit tres longuement. que
la terre fort inegale acause de ses montagnes et vallons
surchargée d'arbres qui n'en font qu'une forest qui en
a mon sentiment de belles et riches productions. Sa
fertilité pour les grains nous parroist par les recoltes
abondantes, que les terres descouuertes et cultiuées donnent
dans chacque année, et dautant mieux, que ne receuant les
semences qu'a la fin du mois d'Auril jusques au 15. de May
elles produisent leurs fruicts a la fin de celuy d'Aoust et
au commencement de celuy de Septemb. ainsy quant aux
choses necessaires a la vie on les peut abondamment esperer
de ce seul pays s'il est mis en culture et je dis plus que quand
une fois il aura esté fourny de toute sorte d'especes
d'animaux champestres et domestiques a la nourriture desquels
il est fort propre, il aura dans 15. ans suffisamment de
surabondant, tant en bled, legumes, et chair qu'en poisson
pour fournir les antilles de l'Ameriq. mesme les endroicts
de la terre ferme de cette grande partie du monde, je n'auance
pas cecy legerement et je ne le dis qu'apres auoir bien
examiné la force de la terre dans sa 1.re nature, et sans
qu'elle ayt receu le secours et l'aide que le fumier donne a celle
de France. Un minot de bled tout communement rend
quinze, 20 et va jusques a 30. mesme au dela dans des
endroicts bien scituez.

Letter from Intendant Talon to the minister Colbert, Québec, 4 October 1665.

Talon spoke highly of the excellent quality of the Canadian soil: "Its fertility for grain is apparent to us because of the abundant crops that the lands that have been cleared and cultivated bear each year." This colony could have "a sufficient surplus in fifteen years, in wheat, vegetables, meat, and fish, to supply the West Indies."

Archives nationales, Paris, France: Fonds des Colonies, série C[11A], vol. 2, fol. 144–144v.

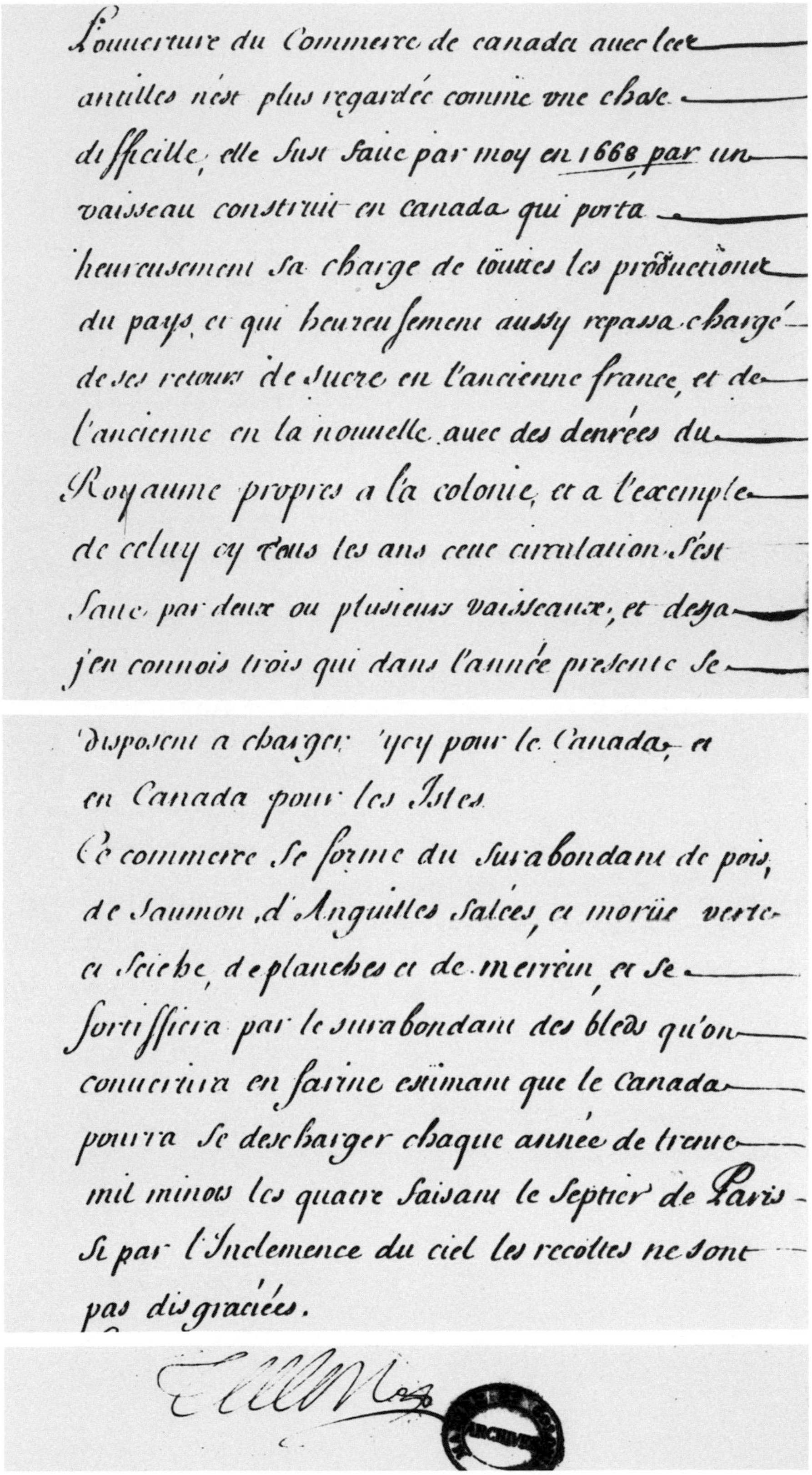

L'ouverture du Commerce de canada avec les
antilles n'est plus regardée comme une chose
difficille, elle fust faite par moy en 1668 par un
vaisseau construit en canada qui porta
heureusement sa charge de toutes les productions
du pays, et qui heureusement aussy repassa chargé
de ses retours de sucre en l'ancienne france, et de
l'ancienne en la nouvelle avec des denrées du
Royaume propres a la colonie, et a l'exemple
de celuy cy tous les ans cette circulation s'est
faite par deux ou plusieurs vaisseaux, et desja
j'en connois trois qui dans l'année presente se
disposent a charger icy pour le Canada, et
en Canada pour les Isles.
Ce commerce se forme du surabondant de pois,
de saumon, d'Anguilles salées, et morüe verte
et seiche, de planches et de merrein, et se
fortiffiera par le surabondant des bleds qu'on
convertira en farine estimant que le Canada
pourra se descharger chaque année de trente
mil minots les quatre faisant le Septier de Paris
si par l'Inclemence du ciel les recoltes ne sont
pas disgraciées.

Memoir on Canada from Intendant Talon, 1673.

Talon recalled "the opening" of Canadian trade with the West Indies: "It was done by me in 1668 with a vessel built in Canada that fortunately carried to its destination its cargo of all the products of the country...every year this traffic was carried on by two or several vessels.... This trade is made up of the surplus of peas, salmon, salted eel, both salt and dried cod, boards and stave wood."

Archives nationales, Paris, France: Fonds des Colonies, série C11A, vol. 4, fol. 36, 36v, 43v.

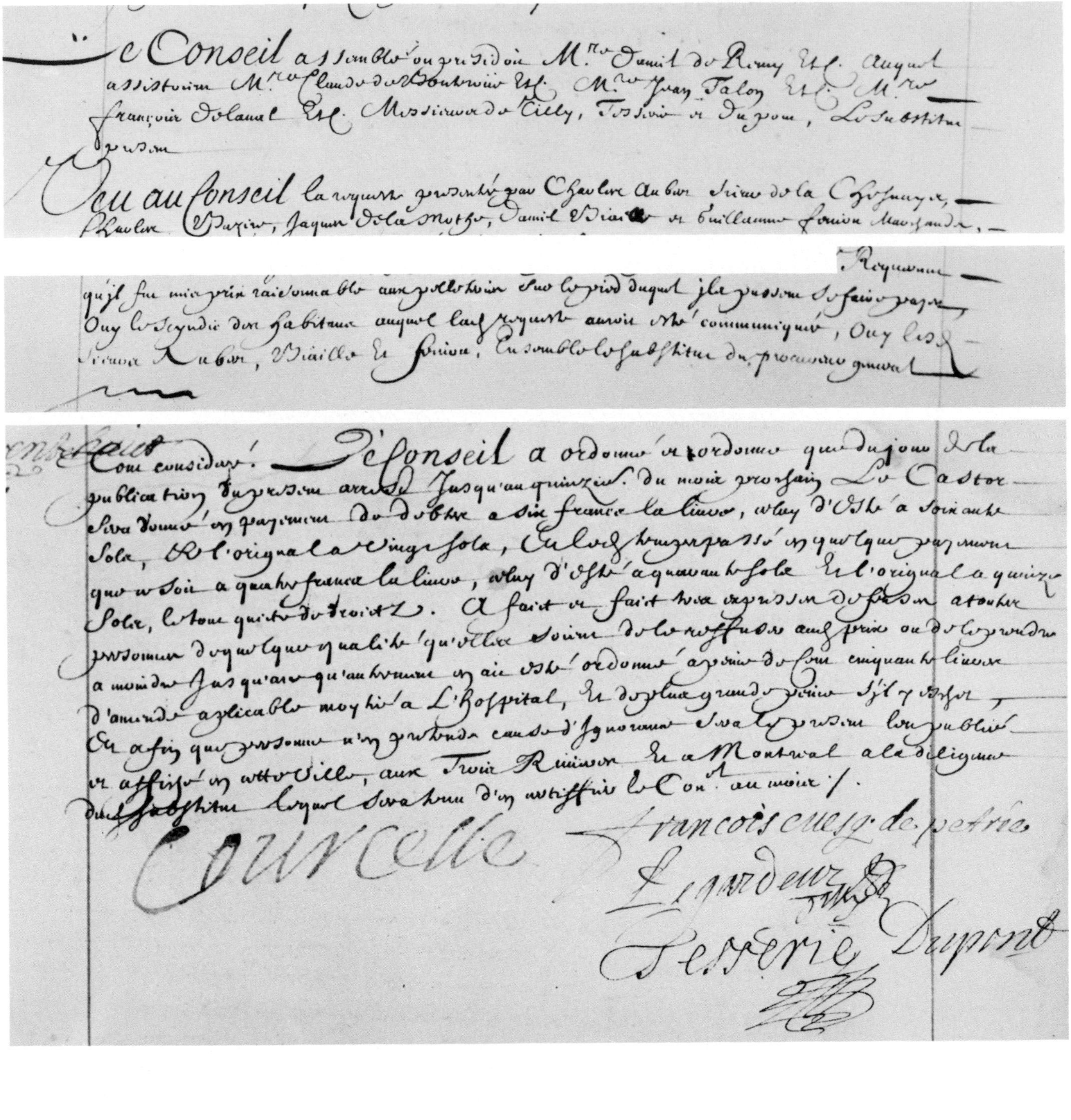
Le Conseil assemblé ou presidoit Mre Daniel de Remy Esc. auquel assistoient Mre Claude de Bouteroue Esc. Mre Jean Talon Esc. Mre François de Laval Esc. Messieurs de Tilly, Tesserie et Dupont, Le substitut present

Veu au Conseil la requeste presentée par Charles Aubert sieur de la Chesnaye, Charles Bazire, Jacques de la Mothe, Daniel Biaille et Guillaume Feniou Marchands, …

… Requerans qu'il fut mis prix raisonnable aux pelleteries sur le pied duquel ils pussent se faire payer, Ouy le Syndic des habitans auquel lad. requeste auroit esté communiquée, Ouy les sieurs Aubert, Biaille et Feniou, ensemble le substitut du procureur general

Tout considéré. Le Conseil a ordonné et ordonne que du jour de la publication du present arrest jusqu'au quinzie. du mois prochain Le Castor sera donné en payement de debtes a six francs la livre, celuy d'esté a soixante sols, et l'orignal a vingt sols, et ledit temps passé en quelque payement que ce soit a quatre francs la livre, celuy d'esté a quarante sols et l'orignal a quinze sols, le tout quitte de [illegible]. A fait et fait tres expresses deffenses a toutes personnes de quelque qualité qu'elles soient de le refuser aud. prix ou de le prendre a moindre jusqu'a ce qu'autrement en ait esté ordonné a peine de cent cinquante livres d'amende aplicable moytié a L'Hospital, et de plus grande peine s'il y eschet, Et afin que personne n'en pretende cause d'ignorance sera le present publié et affiché en cette ville, aux Trois Rivieres et a Montreal a la diligence du substitut lequel sera tenu d'en certiffier le Con. au mois.

Courcelle   François evesq. de petrée
Legardeur
Tesserie   Dupont

Decree from the Conseil souverain setting the price of pelts delivered by debtors to their creditors to pay off their debts, Québec, 15 September 1670.

Because there was not enough currency in the colony, beaver and moose hides were used as barter.

Archives nationales du Québec, Centre d'archives de la Capitale, Québec: Jugements et délibérations du Conseil souverain, fol. 137v–138.

Playing card used as money (detail); copy attributed to Henri Beau (1863–1949); watercolour and Indian ink; 43.2 x 44.8 cm.

From 1684 on, when they were short of funds the intendants had to have recourse to playing-card money (a playing card on which a certain amount was inscribed), refundable when the funds from the king arrived. This money benefitted the colony's internal trade, which lacked currency.

Public Archives of Canada, Picture Division, Ottawa (Negative no. C 17059).

VI

Industry

Talon was the first person in New France to take an interest in industry. He created several "manufactories" for making wool products, coarse muslin, leather, and shoes, for example. Six years after his arrival he could write that with what was produced in Canada he had "what is necessary to dress oneself from head to foot."

Talon's activity was very well coordinated. The brewery would permit the growing of hops on a commercial level; the beer would supply the West Indies trade. This trade would be carried on by means of ships built in the colony and the shipbuilding yards would be an excellent outlet for Canadian wood, hemp, and tar, development of which he encouraged. Moreover, all the surpluses, whether of grain, wood, or fish, would themselves be exported to the West Indies.

Mines interested the intendant; coal, copper, lead, iron would all be sources of wealth for the colony. Tackle for the ships, indeed the cannons that were needed, could be made in Canada itself, and the surpluses, of coal for example, would be exported.

For lack of encouragement and manpower, or because of the high costs of development, most of the industries launched by Talon disappeared or stagnated soon after he left. And in 1704 the king announced that the colonies must not compete with industries in the kingdom but rather limit their aims to sending it raw materials.

Portrait of Jean Talon (circa 1626–94); Claude François (Brother Luc) (1614–85); oil; circa 1671; 72.7 x 59.3 cm.

From 1665 to 1672 Intendant Talon endeavoured to develop New France in all possible fields of activity: territorial expansion, population growth, creation of industry, land utilization, extension of trade, etc.

Monastère des augustines de l'Hôtel-Dieu de Québec, Québec.

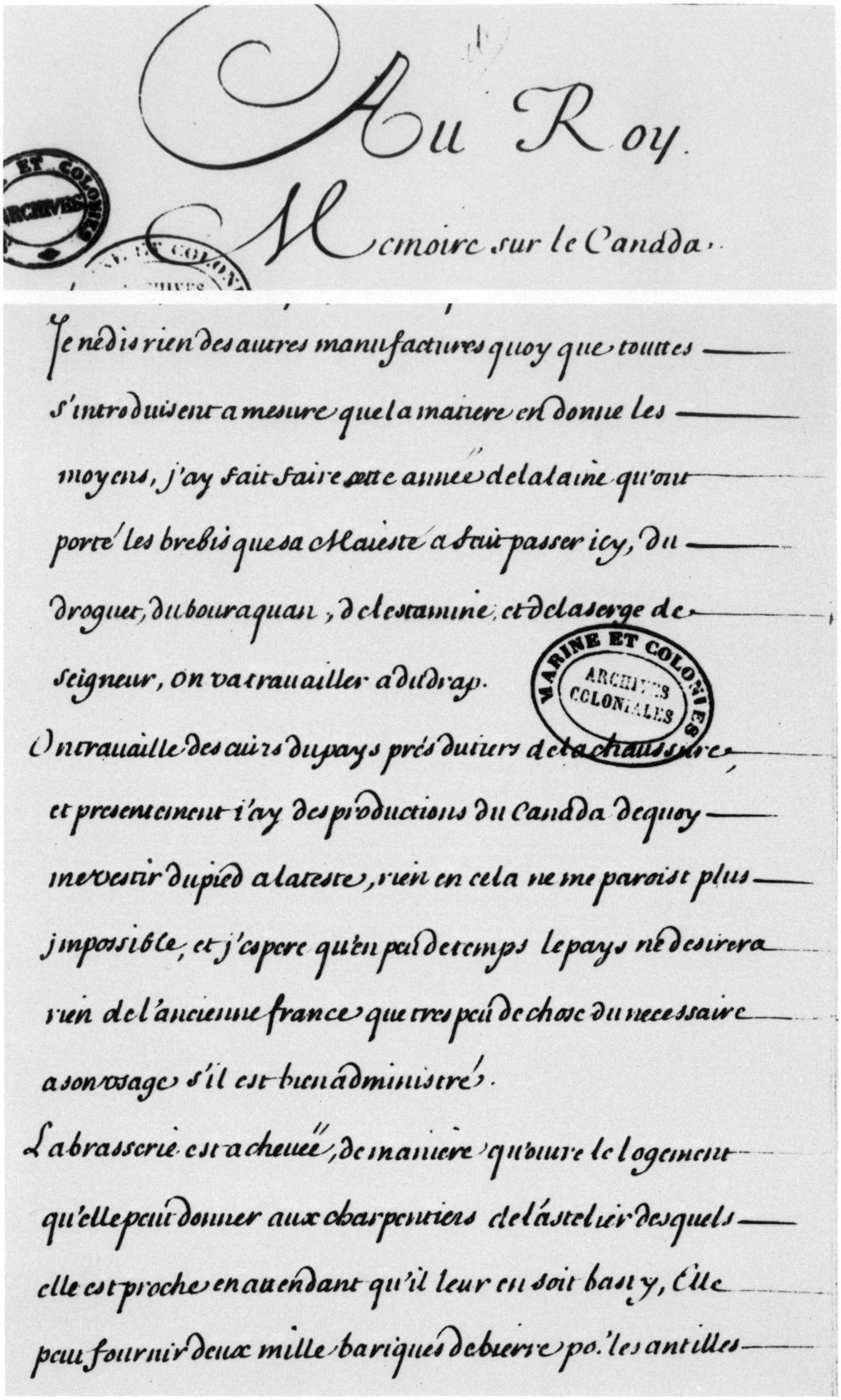
Au Roy.

Memoire sur le Canada.

Je ne dis rien des autres manufactures quoy que toutes s'introduisent a mesure que la matiere en donne les moyens, j'ay fait faire cette année de la laine qu'ont porté les brebis que sa Majesté a fait passer icy, du droguet, du bouracan, de l'estamine, et de la serge de seigneur, on va travailler au drap.

On travaille des cuirs du pays prés du tiers de la chaussure, et presentement j'ay des productions du Canada dequoy me vestir du pied a la teste, rien en cela ne me paroist plus jmpossible, et j'espere qu'en peu de temps le pays ne desirera rien de l'ancienne france que tres peu de chose du necessaire a son usage s'il est bien administré.

La brasserie est achevée, de maniere qu'outre le logement qu'elle peut donner aux charpentiers de l'astelier desquels elle est proche en attendant qu'il leur en soit basty, Elle peut fournir deux mille bariques de bierre po.r les antilles

Memoir on Canada from Intendant Talon, Québec, 2 November 1671.

Talon mentioned some "manufactories" which were beginning to be set up, thanks to his good offices: "This year I have some wool products made..., drugget, coarse camlet, coarse muslin, and serge.... Native hides are being worked, nearly a third of the shoes, and at the present time I have from Canadian products what I need to dress myself from head to toe.... The brewery is finished, ...it can supply two thousand barrels of beer for the West Indies."

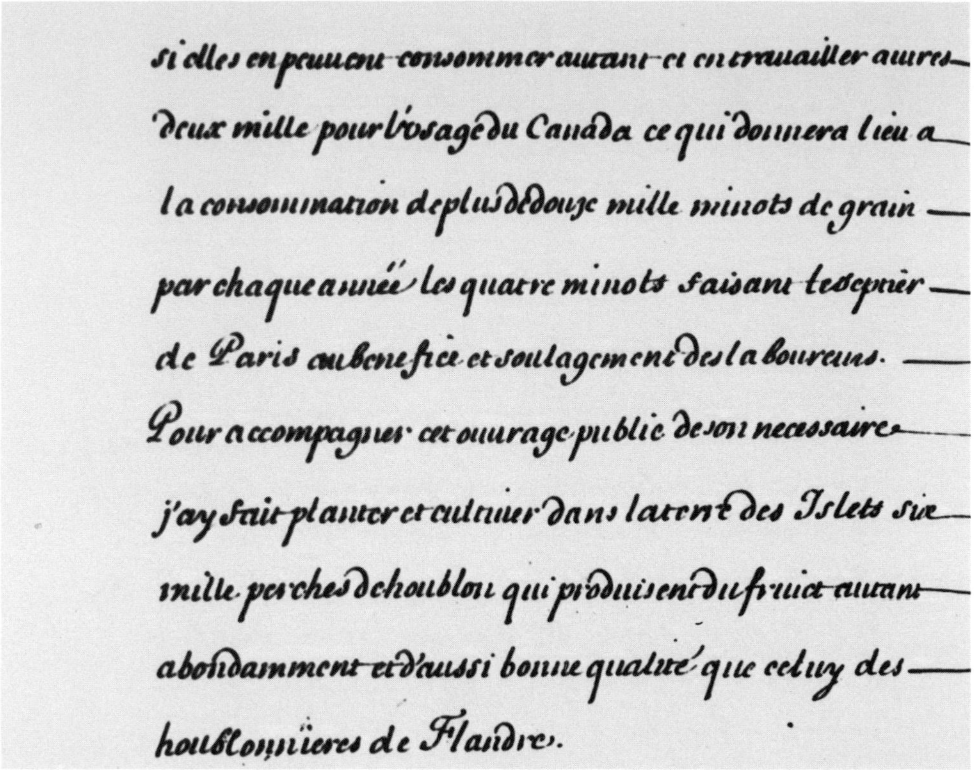
si elles en peuvent consommer autant et en travailler autres
deux mille pour l'usage du Canada ce qui donnera lieu a
la consommation de plus de douze mille minots de grain
par chaque année les quatre minots faisant le septier
de Paris au benefice et soulagement des laboureurs.
Pour accompagner cet ouvrage public de son necessaire
j'ay fait planter et cultiver dans la terre des Islets six
mille perches de houblon qui produisent du fruict autant
abondamment et d'aussi bonne qualité que celuy des
houblonnieres de Flandre.

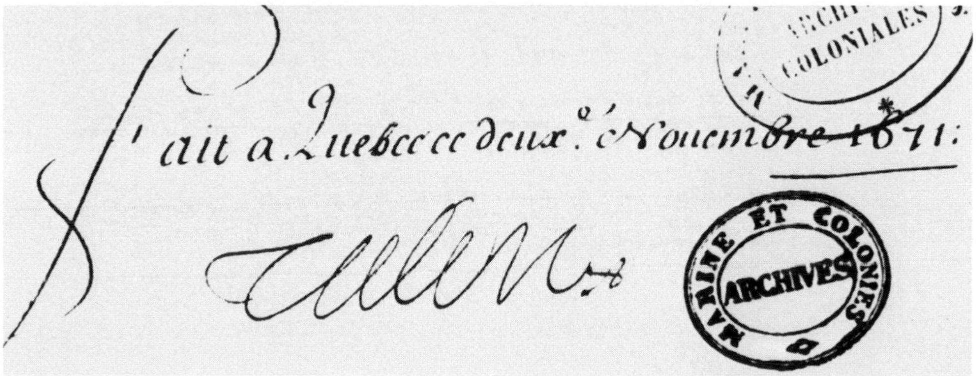
Fait a Quebec ce deuxe. Novembre 1671.
Talon

Archives nationales, Paris, France: Fonds des Colonies, série C^{11A}, vol. 3, fol. 159, 167–167v, 171v.

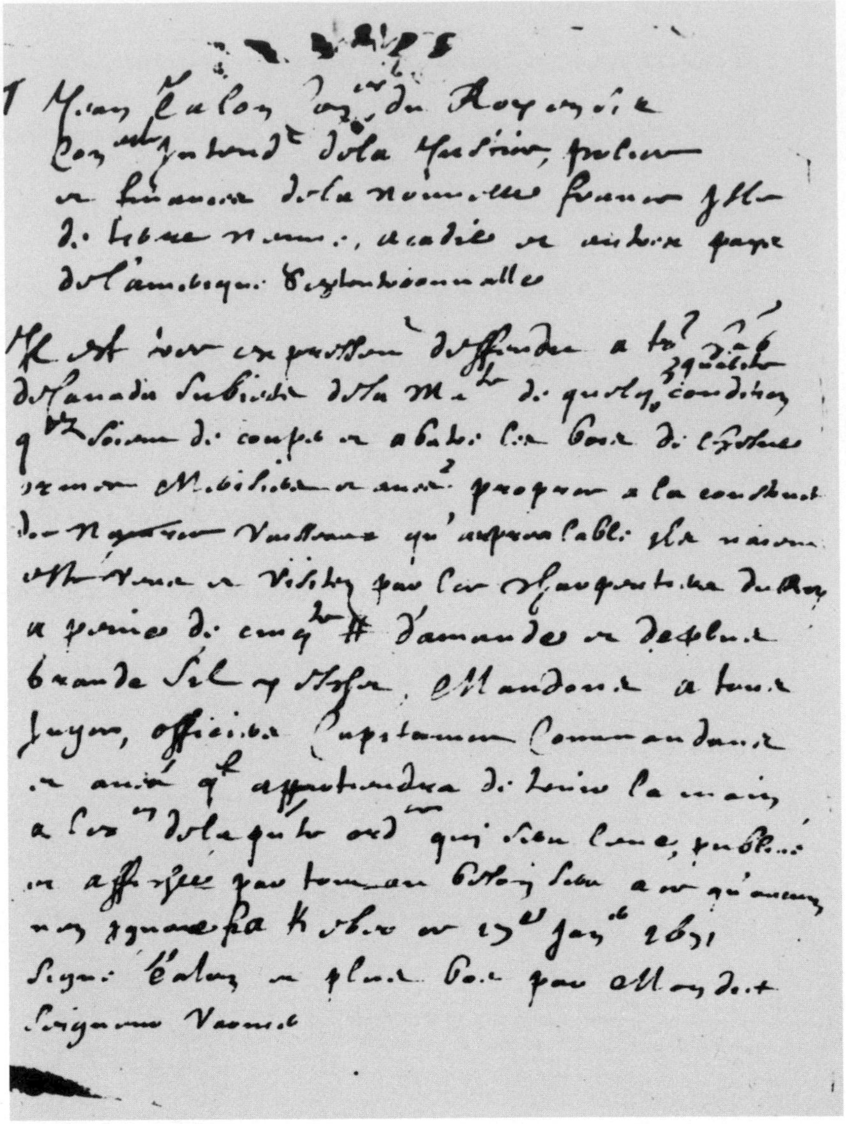

Ordinance by Intendant Talon forbidding anyone "to cut or fell woods of oaks, ash, or wild cherry or others suitable for building ships until they have been seen and inspected by the king's carpenters," Québec, 13 January 1671.

These woods could be used in the ship-building yards set up by Talon on the Saint-Charles River and in the king's yards in France.

Archives nationales du Québec, Centre d'archives de la Capitale, Québec: Ordonnances, carton intitulé "Papiers divers."

Je ne suis pas assez hardy pour promettre le succez de la
recherche qu'on fait des mines, Mais ie suis assez conuaincu
qu'il y en a en Canada de cuiure de fer et de plomb, ce pais

est si vaste qu'il est mal aisé de tomber juste sur l'endroit
qui les couure, Cependant ie m'appercois qu'on en a tous les
ans de nouuelles connoissances par l'application qu'on donne
a en faire la recherche, par une espreuue faite dans un creuset
d'une matiere tirée du lac champlain i'ay reconnu que dans
ses bords il a du plomb.

Le cuiure que i'enuoye tiré du lac superieur et de la riuiere
Nantaouagan fait connoistre qu'il y a quelque mine ou
quelque bord de fleuue qui produit de cette matiere la plus pure
qu'on puisse desirer.

Je ne parle plus des mines de fer puisque l'espreuue s'en doit
faire en france, je dis seullement que durant l'absence du
s^r. de la potardiere i'ay fait trauailler a luy preparer de

Memoir on Canada from Intendant Talon, Québec, 2 November 1671.

Talon was "not bold enough to promise success in the search that is being made for mines," since searching in previous years had not yet produced any certain results. Being however "fairly well convinced that there are copper, iron, and lead [mines] in Canada," he informed the minister of searches that appeared promising.

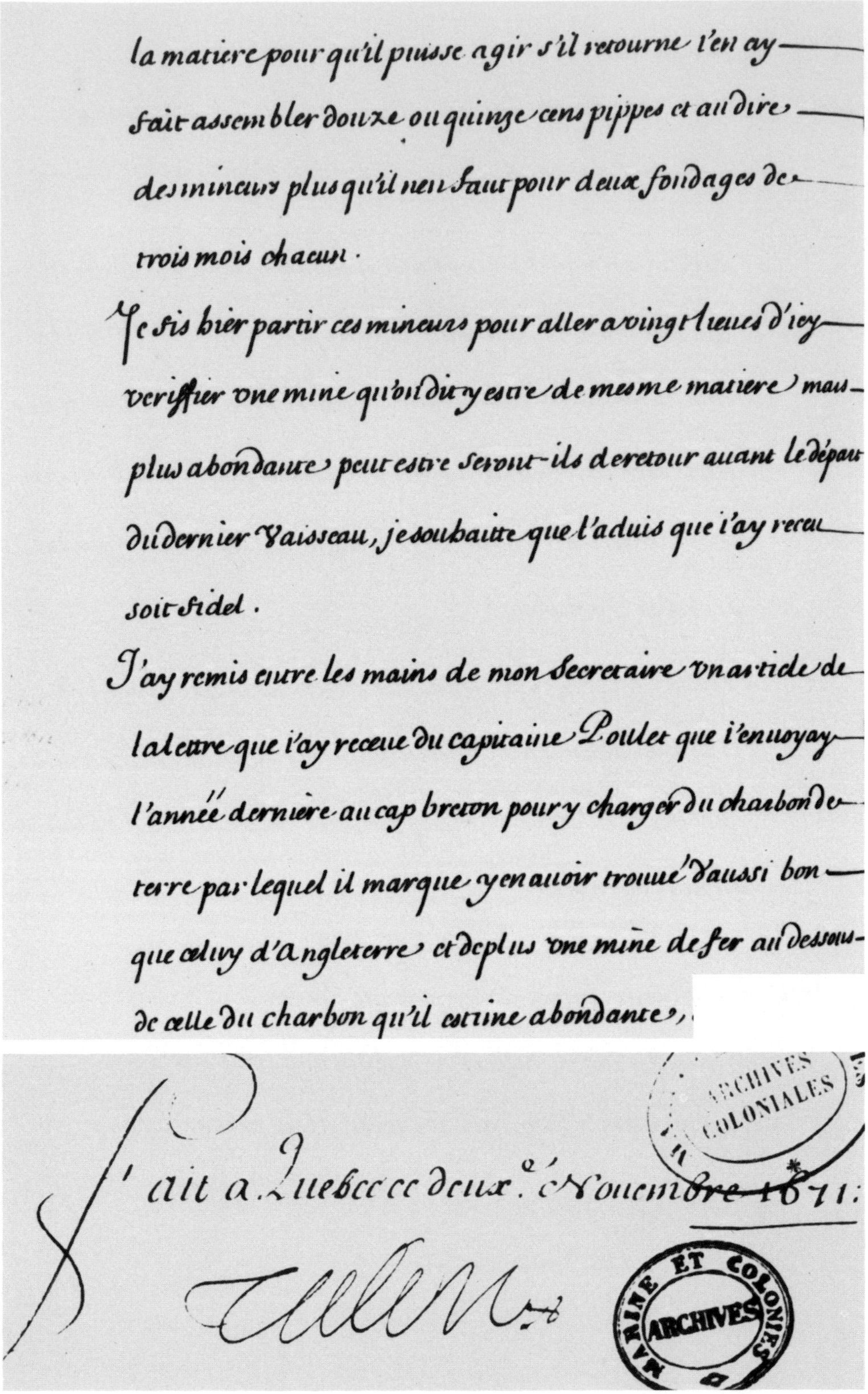
la matiere pour qu'il puisse agir s'il retourne i'en ay fait assembler douze ou quinze cens pippes et au dire des mineurs plus qu'il n'en faut pour deux fondages de trois mois chacun.

Je fis hier partir ces mineurs pour aller a vingt lieues d'icy verifier vne mine qu'on dit y estre de mesme matiere mais plus abondante peut estre seront-ils de retour auant le départ du dernier Vaisseau, je souhaitte que l'aduis que i'ay receu soit fidel.

J'ay remis entre les mains de mon Secretaire vn article de la lettre que i'ay receue du capitaine Poullet que i'enuoyay l'année derniere au cap breton pour y charger du charbon de terre par lequel il marque y en auoir trouué d'aussi bon que celuy d'Angleterre et de plus vne mine de fer au dessous de celle du charbon qu'il estime abondante.

Fait a Quebec ce deuxe Nouembre 1671.

Talon

Archives nationales, Paris, France: Fonds des Colonies, série C^{11A}, vol. 3, fol. 163–164v, 171v.

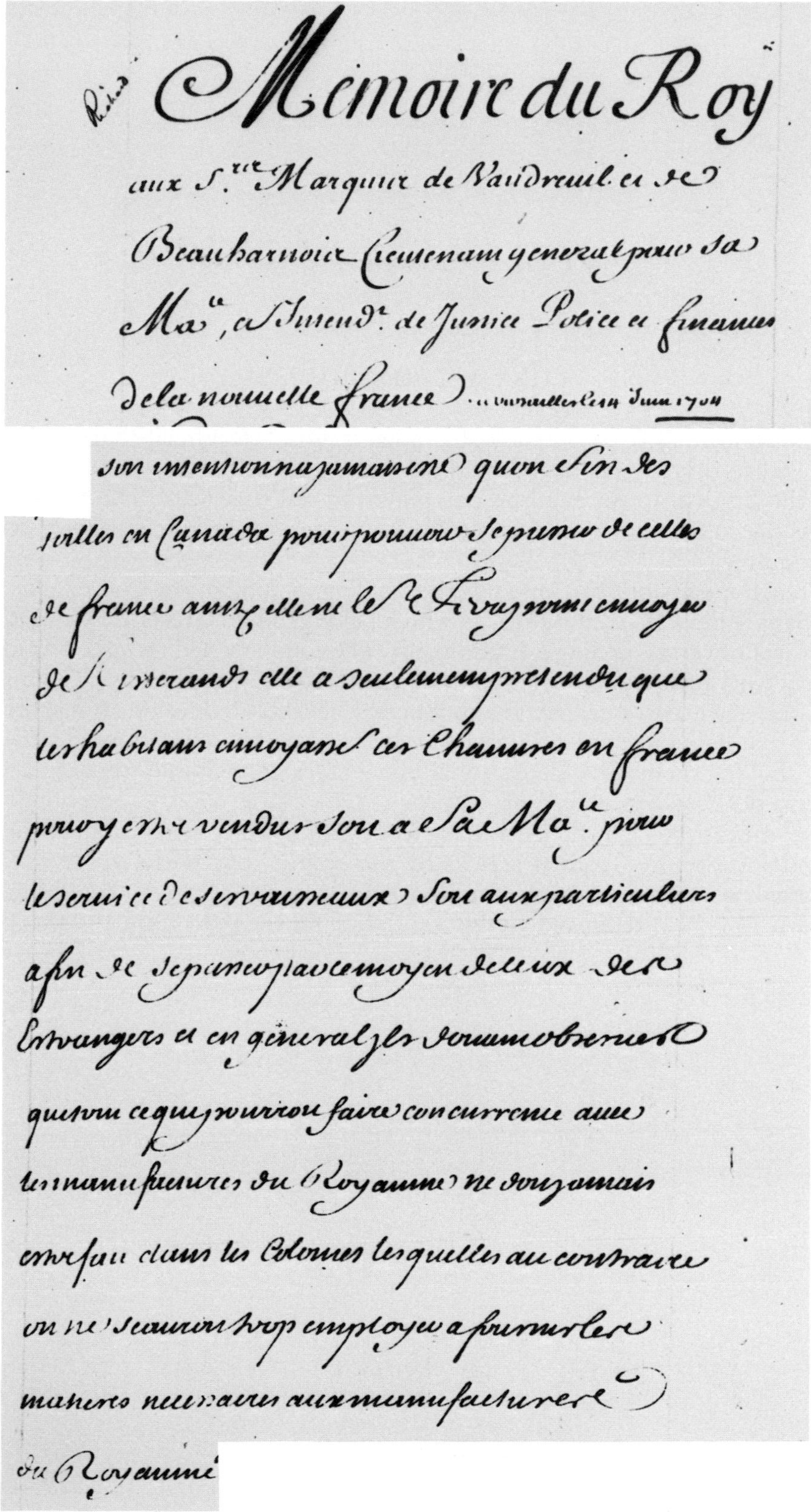
Memoire du Roy

aux Srs Marquis de Vaudreuil et de
Beauharnois Lieutenant general pour Sa
Maté, et Intendt de Justice Police et finances
de la nouvelle france ... Versailles le 14 Juin 1704

Son intention n'a jamais esté qu'on fit des
toilles en Canada pour pouvoir se passer de celles
de france ainsy elle ne le Sr [illegible] envoye
de [illegible] tisserands elle a seulement pretendu que
les habitans envoyant ces chanvres en france
pouvoyent y vendre soit a Sa Maté pour
le service de ses vaisseaux soit aux particuliers
afin de se procurer par ce moyen de ceux des
Etrangers et en general ils doivent observer
que tout ce qui pourroit faire concurrence avec
les manufactures du Royaume ne doit jamais
estre fait dans les Colonies lesquelles au contraire
on ne scauroit trop employer a fournir les
matieres necessaires aux manufactures
du Royaume

Memoir from King Louis XIV sent to Governor General Vaudreuil and Intendant Beauharnois, Versailles, 14 June 1704.

"Anything that could compete with the manufactories in the kingdom must never be made in the colonies, which on the contrary could not be used too much to supply the materials necessary to the manufactories in the kingdom."

This declaration by the king shows that the French authorities of the period subordinated the economic progress of the colonies to that of France.

Archives nationales, Paris, France: Fonds des Colonies, série B, vol. 25, fol. 112v, 118.

New companies

In 1670 the Hudson's Bay Company of London received its official charter. The French in New France quickly realized that there was a risk of the northern tribes turning towards the English in the Hudson Bay region to sell their furs. The threat was very serious, as the colony in the valley of the St. Lawrence was almost exclusively dependent on that resource.

The French merchants' response was the creation in 1682 of the Compagnie du Nord (or Compagnie de la Baie du Nord), to which belonged Des Groseilliers and Radisson, who later went over to the English side again. The company had to wage war in the bay until the Treaty of Ryswick, when it merged with the Compagnie de la Colonie.

The Compagnie de l'Acadie was also founded in 1682 to develop an inshore fishery, like those that Talon had ardently wished to see set up. The king granted a tract to the partners and let them have commercial advantages comparable for example to the twenty-five per cent levy on beaver.

In the meantime the English were continuing with their annual fishing at Newfoundland despite frequent attacks by the French, and without the island really being settled and organized. Interesting statistics have been preserved on the number of ships and size of the catches and on the population for the years from 1698 to 1705.

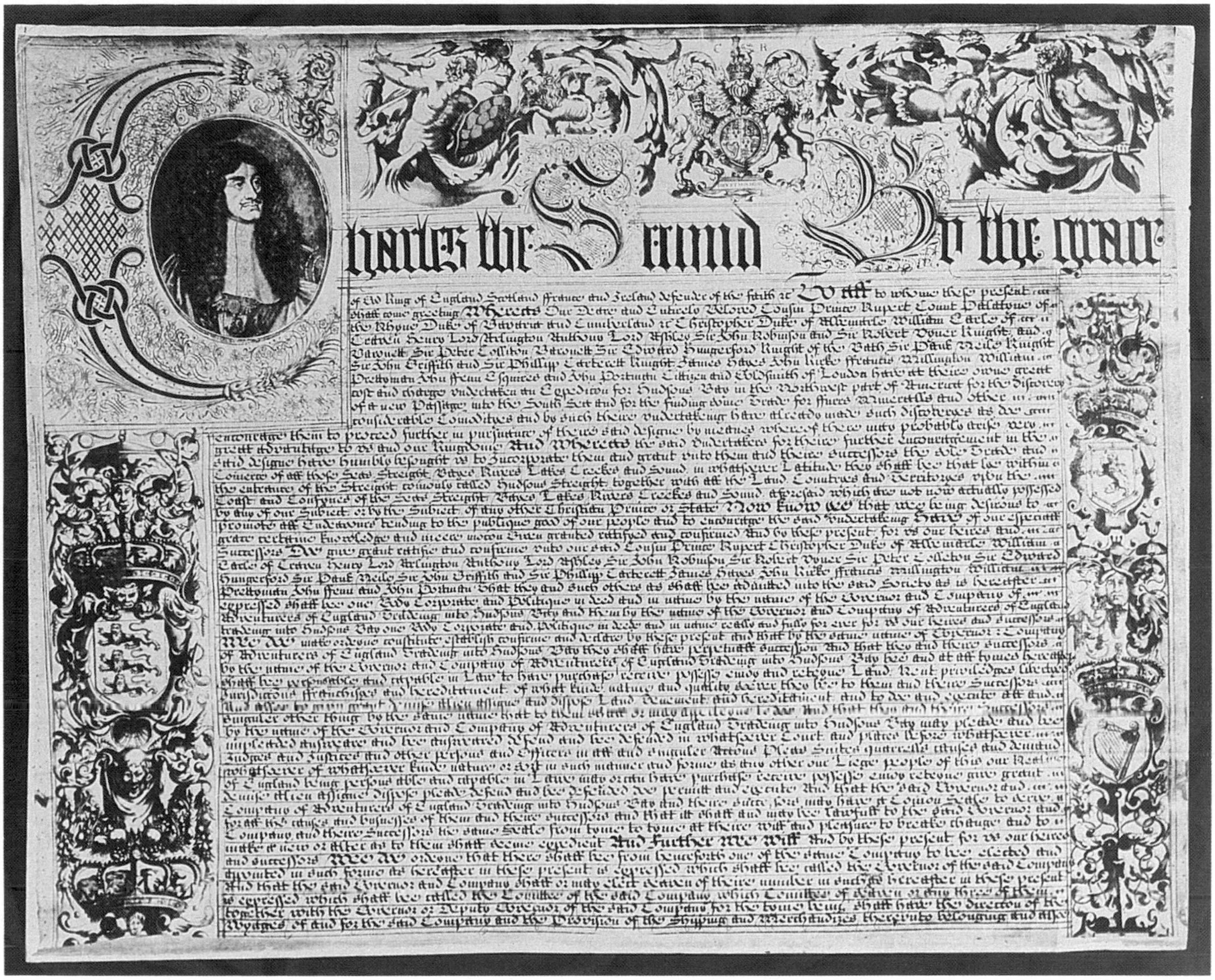

Charter granted the Hudson's Bay Company by the king of England, Charles II, Westminster, 2 May 1670.

This fur-trading company set up posts in the regions of James Bay and Hudson Bay. It was in competition continually with the French traders in the valley of the St. Lawrence.

Hudson's Bay Company, Winnipeg.

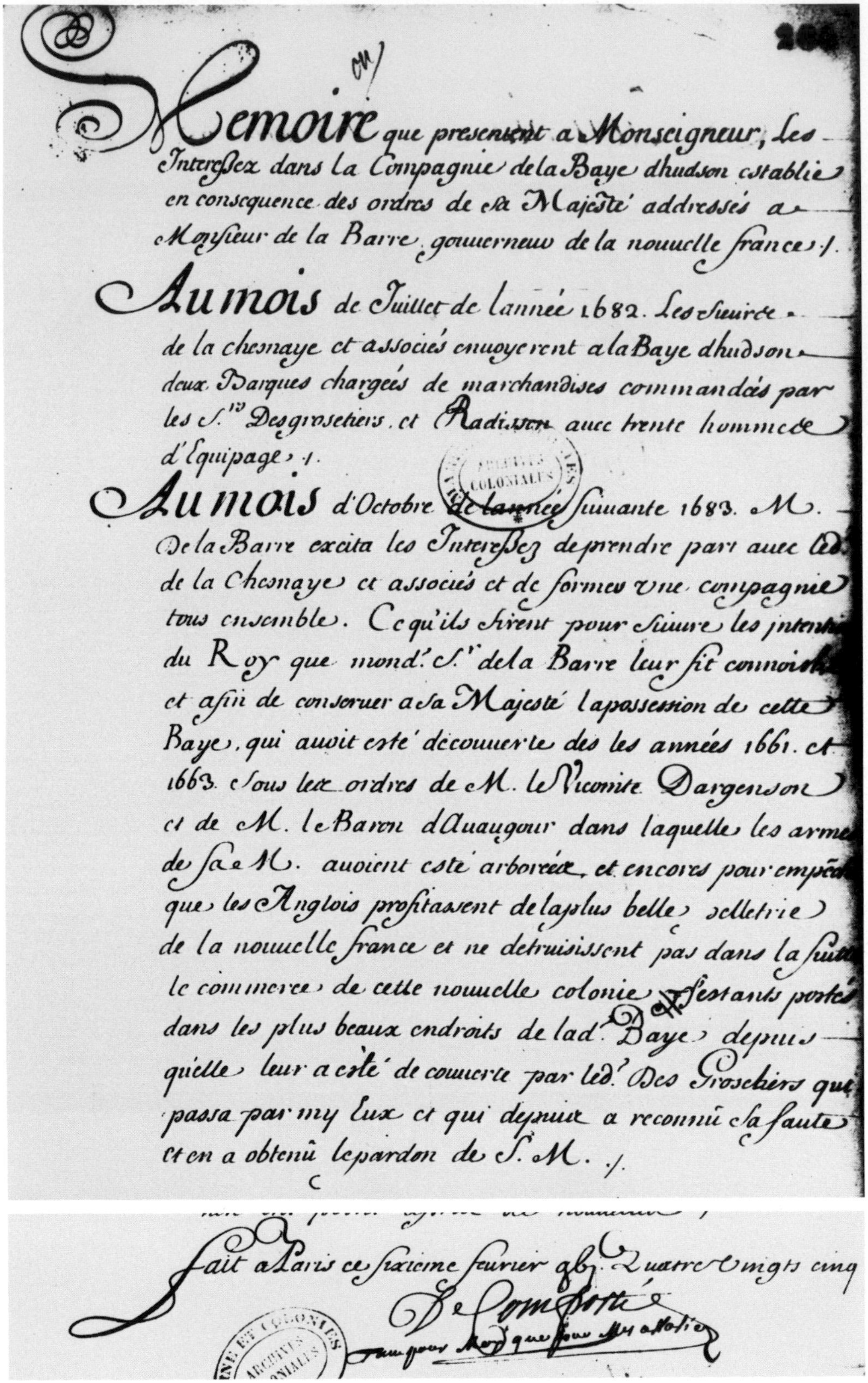

Memoire que presentent a Monseigneur, les Interessez dans la Compagnie de la Baye dhudson establie en consequence des ordres de sa Majesté addressés a Monsieur de la Barre, gouverneur de la nouvelle france./

Au mois de Juillet de lannée 1682. Les sieurs de la chesnaye et associés envoyerent a la Baye dhudson deux Barques chargées de marchandises commandées par les Srs Desgroseliers. et Radisson avec trente hommes d'Equipage./

Au mois d'Octobre de lannée suivante 1683. M. De la Barre excita les Interessez de prendre part avec lesd. de la Chesnaye et associés et de former une compagnie tous ensemble. Ce qu'ils firent pour suivre les intentions du Roy que mond. Sr de la Barre leur fit connoistre et affin de conserver a sa Majesté la possession de cette Baye, qui avoit esté decouverte dès les années 1661. et 1663. sous les ordres de M. le Vicomte Dargenson et de M. le Baron dAvaugour dans laquelle les armes de sa M. avoient esté arborées, et encores pour empescher que les Anglois profitassent de la plus belle pelleterie de la nouvelle france et ne detruisissent pas dans la suitte le commerce de cette nouvelle colonie s'estants portés dans les plus beaux endroits de lad. Baye depuis qu'elle leur a esté decouverte par led. Des Groseliers qui passa parmy Eux et qui depuis a reconnu sa faute et en a obtenu le pardon de S. M./

Fait a Paris ce sixieme fevrier [illegible] Quatre Vingts cinq

De Comporté

tant pour moy que pour mes associés

Memoir sent to the minister Seignelay by the members of the Compagnie du Nord, Paris, 6 February 1685.

They explained that their company had been formed "to prevent the English from benefitting from the finest pelts in New France...since they have gone into the best spots in the aforementioned bay" (Hudson Bay).

They therefore wanted to prevent the Hudson's Bay Company from taking over all the fur trade with the northern Indian tribes.

Archives nationales, Paris, France: Fonds des Colonies, série C11A, vol. 7, fol. 260, 261v.

3 mars 1684. Double 17

Extrait des Regiſtres du Conſeil d'Eſtat.

LE ROY Ayant par ſon Arreſt du dernier Février 1682. concedé aux Sieurs Bergier, Gaultier, Boucher & autres, leurs hoirs, ſucceſſeurs & ayant cauſe, les Terres qu'ils trouveroient propres le long de la Coſte de l'Acadie & de la Riviere de S. Jean, pour y faire l'eſtabliſſement d'une Peſche ſedentaire dans l'eſtenduë de ſix lieuës aux environs de l'habitation qu'ils feroient, deſquelles Terres ſa Majeſté leur fait don, en cas qu'elles n'ayent point eſté concedées depuis la revocation de la Compagnie d'Occident; & la réunion qui en a eſté faite au Domaine de ſa Majeſté par l'Edit du mois de Decembre 1674. & qu'elles ne fuſſent pas actuellement poſſedées par des Sujets de ſa Majeſté, meſme ſans tiltre; à la charge de payer à ſa Majeſté une redevance d'un marc d'argent par chacun an, & de faire l'eſtabliſſement d'une Peſche ſedentaire dans un an, ſinon & à faute de ce faire dans ledit an, ledit don demeureroit nul: Moyennant quoy ſa Majeſté leur permet de negocier aux Iſles Françoiſes de l'Amerique & en la Nouvelle France, du Poiſſon & Huille de leur Peſche, Bois à baſtir, & autres Marchandiſes du Païs. Voulant de plus ſa Majeſté, qu'ils jouïſſent des meſmes Exemptions de Droits de toutes les Marchandiſes & Vivres qu'ils envoyeront à ladite Coſte, dont jouïſſent les Negocians François qui trafiquent auſdites Iſles, ſuivant & conformément aux Arreſts du Conſeil des quatre Juin & vingt-cinquiéme Novembre 1671. & autres donnez en conſequence, & qu'à cet effet toutes Lettres neceſſaires ſeroient expediées. Et depuis leſdits Supplians ayant expoſé à ſa Majeſté qu'en conſequence dudit Arreſt de Conceſſion du dernier Février 1682. ils auroient formé leur Eſtabliſſement quatre mois aprés dans un lieu deſert & inhabité nommé Chadabouctou, à cinq lieuës du Cap de Campſeaux coſte de l'Acadie, où ils auroient fait des Baſtimens & un Fort pour mettre trente hommes à couvert & hors d'inſulte, avec toutes ſortes d'Armes & munitions; ce qui auroit augmenté conſiderablement en l'année derniere 1683. comme ils eſperent l'augmenter toutes les années: Mais ils ſe ſeroient aperçeus en faiſant leur Peſche, que cette Conceſſion n'avoit pas aſſez d'eſtenduë,

Decree from the king's council of State granting various privileges to the Compagnie des Pêches sédentaires de l'Acadie, Versailles, 3 March 1684.

This company, formed in 1682 by the Sieurs Bergier, Gautier, and their partners, owned an establishment at Chedabucto at that time.

Archives nationales, Paris, France: Fonds des Colonies, série C^{11D}, vol. 1, fol. 179.

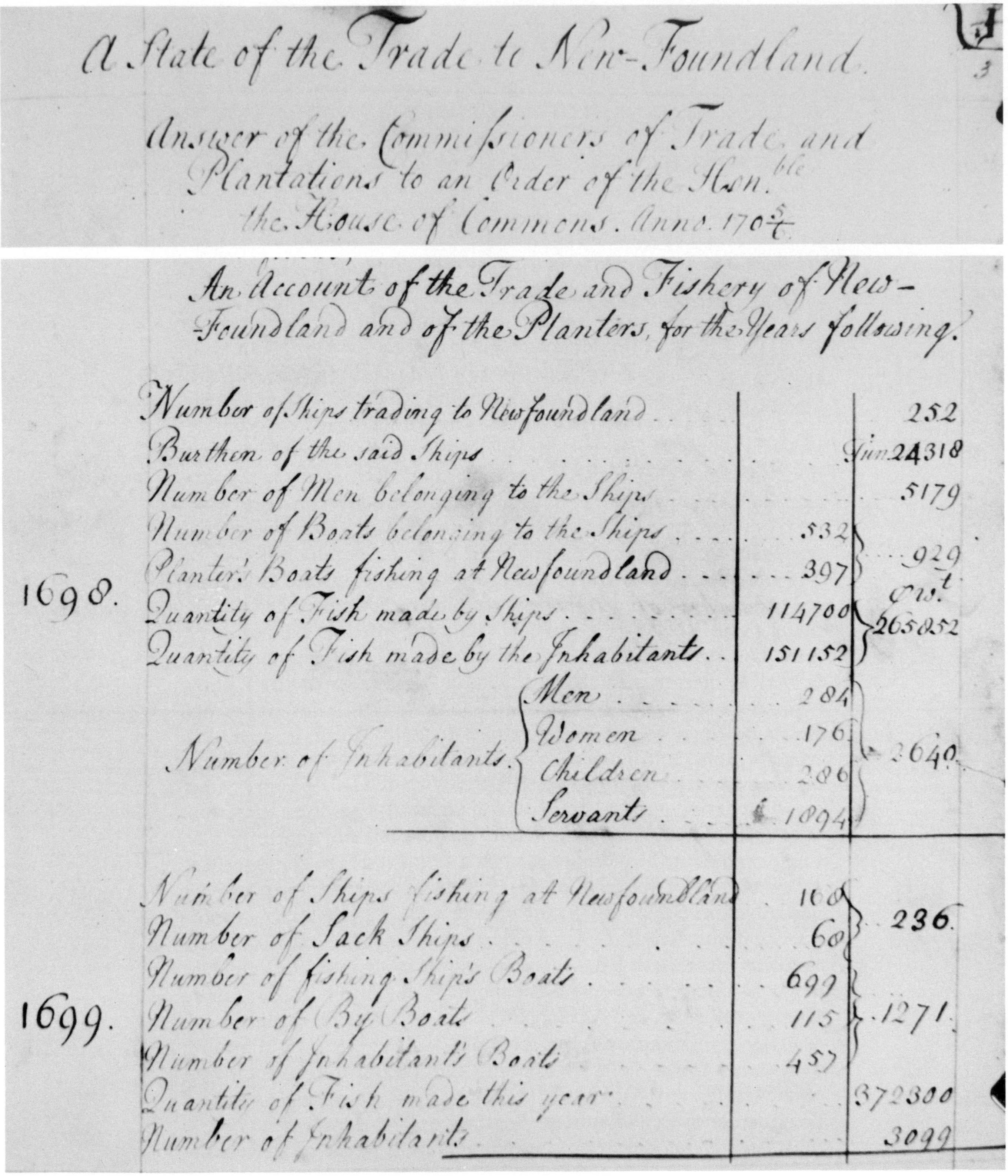

A State of the Trade to New-Foundland.

Answer of the Commissioners of Trade and Plantations to an Order of the Hon.ble the House of Commons. Anno. 170 5/6

An Account of the Trade and Fishery of New-Foundland and of the Planters, for the Years following.

1698.	Number of Ships trading to Newfoundland			252
	Burthen of the said Ships			Tun. 24318
	Number of Men belonging to the Ships			5179
	Number of Boats belonging to the Ships		532	929
	Planter's Boats fishing at Newfoundland		397	
	Quantity of Fish made by Ships		114700	C.w.t 265852
	Quantity of Fish made by the Inhabitants		151152	
	Number of Inhabitants	Men	284	2640
		Women	176	
		Children	286	
		Servants	1894	
1699.	Number of Ships fishing at Newfoundland		166	236
	Number of Sack Ships		60	
	Number of fishing Ship's Boats		699	1271
	Number of By Boats		115	
	Number of Inhabitant's Boats		457	
	Quantity of Fish made this year			372300
	Number of Inhabitants			3099

Statement of English trade (fishing) on Newfoundland for the years 1698 and 1699.

The English had several establishments (Saint John, Carbonear, Bonavista, etc.) along the east coast of Newfoundland, whilst the French occupied Plaisance on the south shore of the island.

British Library, Department of Manuscripts, London, England: Egerton Mss., 921, fol. 3

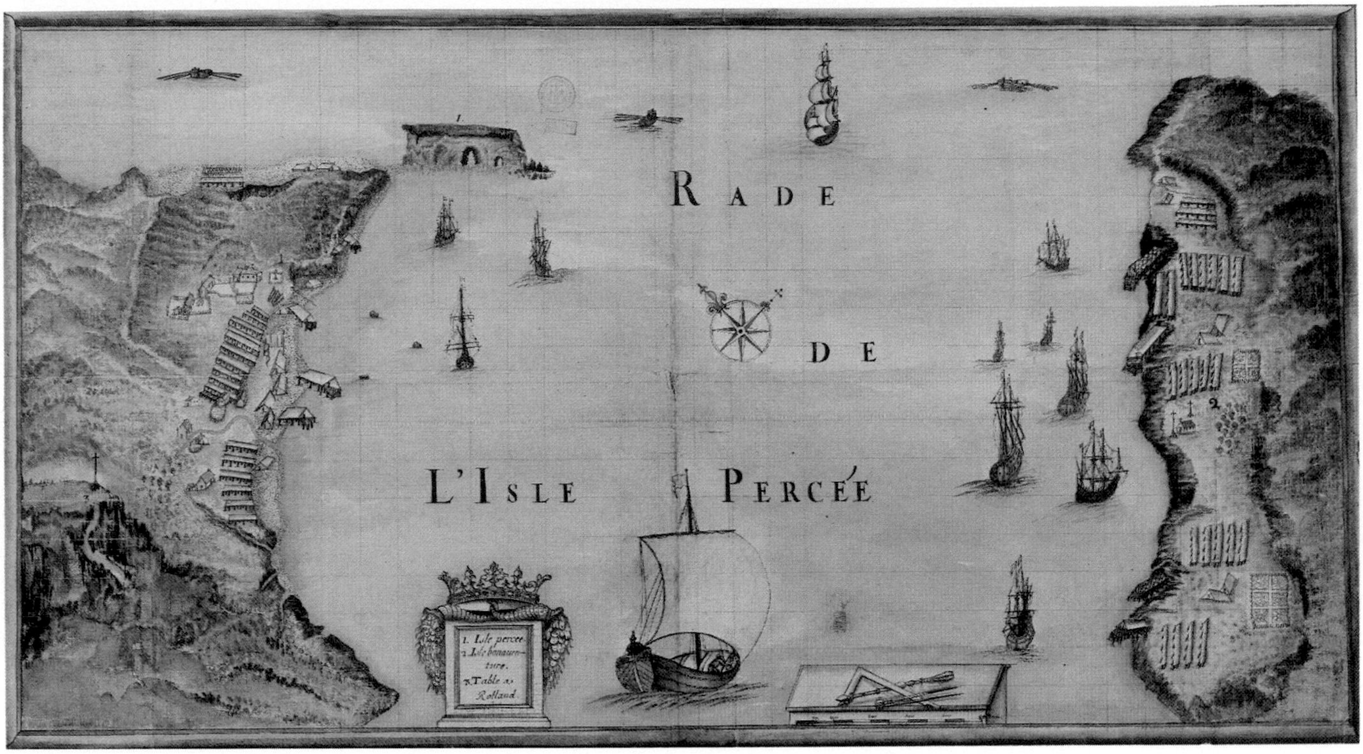

"Rade de L'Isle Percée," sent by Intendant de Meulles, 1686; anonymous; col. ms.; approx. 25 x 14 cm.

At Île Percée, near the Gaspé Peninsula, inshore fishing was carried on not only by the ships that came from France, but also by Canadians. In the 1680s Denys de Bonaventure ran a considerable fishing enterprise there, which had been set up by his father, Denys de La Ronde.

Bibliothèque nationale, Département des cartes et plans, Paris, France: Service hydrographique, portefeuille 125-5-1.

VII

Society and Culture

Society in New France took a certain time, as was normal, to acquire its distinctive characteristics. In the period from 1632 to 1665 some two thousand immigrants, of rather different social backgrounds, provinces and professions, had come to Canada. Pioneers, woodcutters, farmers, craftsmen, day labourers, and soldiers made up most of the population, along with a few score more well-to-do persons – at least apparently so: clerks, merchants, and seigneurs, who gave a certain impetus to life in the colony. Little by little these groups got over their differences and learned to live in harmony, so that towards 1665 they formed what can be called a society.

In twenty years this society had endowed itself with rudimentary administrative institutions. It had seen a certain commercial élite come into existence around the Communauté des Habitants. At Québec it disposed of a hospital, a boys' college, and a convent for the girls; at Montréal primary teaching was provided, and the Hôtel-Dieu took care of the sick and wounded. The seigneurial system provided a method of settlement and at the same time a social structure that was propitious to the population's advancement. To be sure, people still lived a little too much withdrawn into themselves, within a purely subsistence economy where nothing was exported except furs – and even that commerce was above all in the hands of the clerks of the Communauté des Habitants until 1663, and after that of the Compagnie des Indes occidentales. In many places people were still at the stage of clearing land and planting their first crops.

Between 1665 and 1672 Canadian society changed greatly. Thanks to the immigration of a large number of filles du roi in particular, but also of entire families, the number of households increased. Then hundreds of officers and men of the Carignan-Salières regiment settled in Canada; in the year 1672 alone Intendant Talon made grants of forty-six seigneuries. Marie de l'Incarnation noted at that period the changes happening in the colony where the social customs were less uniform than a short time before, and the population less submissive. It was at this time also that going off to live in the woods began to become widespread, and this developed a spirit of independence in the settlers and brought about disorders that had been unknown up till that time.

VII

Certain permanent traits of character appeared, particularly in the Canadians: pride, often to the point of arrogance; a spirit of independence that went as far as the rejection of authority; a passion for adventure leading to the giving up of living in society. In all that must be recognized the influence – and even the ascendancy – of the Indians on a great number of young men, who adopted their free and apparently carefree way of life.

The fur trade, coming on top of the Iroquois war, hindered the progress of agriculture by inciting young men to abandon the soil for life in the woods and distant voyages. Prohibitions, menaces, promises of amnesty were of no avail; the coureurs des bois no longer wanted to return to the colony. On the contrary, they thrust farther and farther to the south, the west, and the north. In the meantime manpower was cruelly lacking in the colony; workmen and day labourers were scarce and cost a great deal. This penury, together with the stagnation of agriculture and the absence of agricultural surpluses, prevented the setting up of "manufactories." The fur trade hardly brought any wealth to the colony, as more than half the profits went off to France. Consequently the tradespeople, with a few exceptions, were poor, as were moreover the owners of seigneuries. Only the habitants who remained faithful to the land succeeded in enjoying a certain well-being, albeit a purely relative one.

The secular clergy, among whom the proportion of Canadian-born priests was slowly increasing, had difficulty subsisting, since the tithes did not bring in enough; every year the king had to pay a gratuity to the "poor parishes." The nobles in the country, who were few in number and whose numbers it was hoped around the 1680s would not increase any more, were poor and idle, according to the declarations of the authorities. The seigneurs, many of whom claimed to belong to the nobility, often lived beyond their means, like country-gentlemen as it were, more interested in hunting and fishing than in exploiting their domains and as a result, poor and in debt. If we leave the fur trade aside, the only resource left these nobles or so-called gentlemen was an officer's commission in the colonial regular troops (after 1683) or else a commission as an officer of the law; but the army and the public service did not pay well, and if they had, the marked propensity on the part of those people to live on a scale above their real station would have left them just as poor as they were.

Over and above their arrogance, their independent spirit, their taste for a carefree life, however, these men – seigneurs (nobles or commoners) and copyholders – were lacking neither in courage, nor in skill, nor in physical strength. They were redoubtable soldiers, experienced in fighting from ambush, capable of astonishing exploits and of suffering all sorts of hardships. In addition they were light-hearted, sociable, and very courteous. We may wonder whether the governors and intendants in the last twenty years of the century did not exaggerate slightly faults that doubtless did exist in the colony by insisting upon them and generalizing a little more than was necessary.

Doubtless, too, men of that stamp and an uncommonly adventurous spirit were needed to live in New France and to build up there an organized society in spite of all the adverse conditions. In this regard all the essential bases were laid in the seventeenth century; by about 1700 the indispensable institutions were in place, the population was living in a setting and a way of life that had become familiar, and already letters, arts, and sciences had made a modest appearance on the banks of the St. Lawrence.

VII

The governing classes

In Canada as in France at the same period people belonged, according to their political and social condition, to one of the following three estates: the clergy, the nobility, or the people. In its turn the French clergy included the upper and lower clergy. If certain ecclesiastics in the colony came from the aristocracy, they nonetheless shared the pioneers' harsh life of poverty.

The colonial nobility consisted of only a few families, but included a certain number of so-called noblemen. All the same, all those real or alleged noblemen were "poor beggars" and often idlers. Too proud to work the land, they had no other resource but "the woods," where their sons engaged in the fur trade.

It was among the seigneurs – the great majority of whom were commoners – that were to be found the greatest number of those who aspired to live in the colony as the gentry in France lived on its estates. All that could ensue from that for them was running into debt, poverty, and a disorderly life.

The members of the Conseil souverain and other officers of justice, of whatever social origin, enjoyed unquestionable prestige. Although they were very poorly remunerated and although they were generally not very learned, they were in fact entitled to a certain number of marks of honour. Consequently those posts were very much sought after.

190

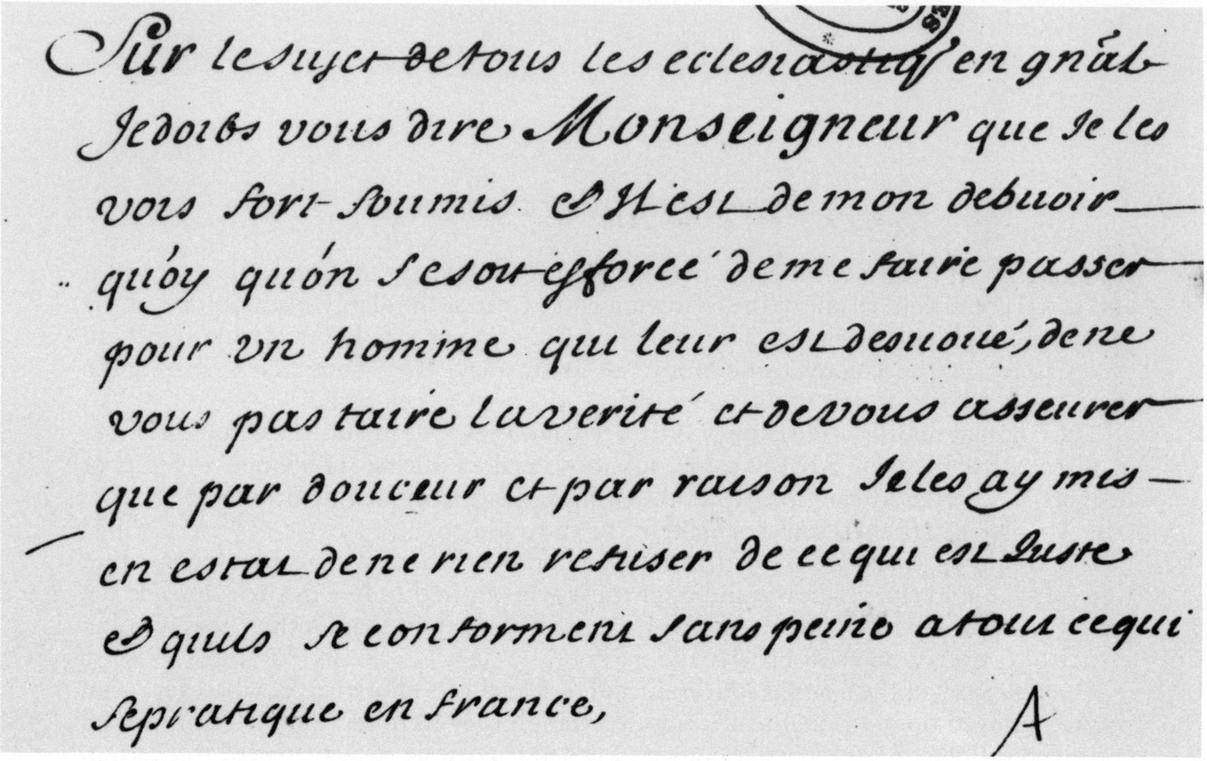
Sur le sujet de tous les ecclesiastiques en gnal
Je doibs vous dire Monseigneur que je les
vois fort soumis et il est de mon debuoir
quoy quon se soit efforcé de me faire passer
pour un homme qui leur est devoué, de ne
vous pas taire la verité et de vous asseurer
que par douceur et par raison je les ay mis
en estat de ne rien refuser de ce qui est juste
et quils se conforment sans peine a tout ce qui
se pratique en france,
A

Letter from Intendant Duchesneau to the minister Colbert, Québec, 10 November 1679.

Duchesneau expressed a favourable opinion of the clergy in the colony: "On the subject of all the ecclesiastics in general, I must tell you, Monseigneur, that I find them very submissive...and that they conform without difficulty to all that is practised in France."

Archives nationales, Paris, France: Fonds des Colonies, série C^{11A}, vol. 5, fol. 50.

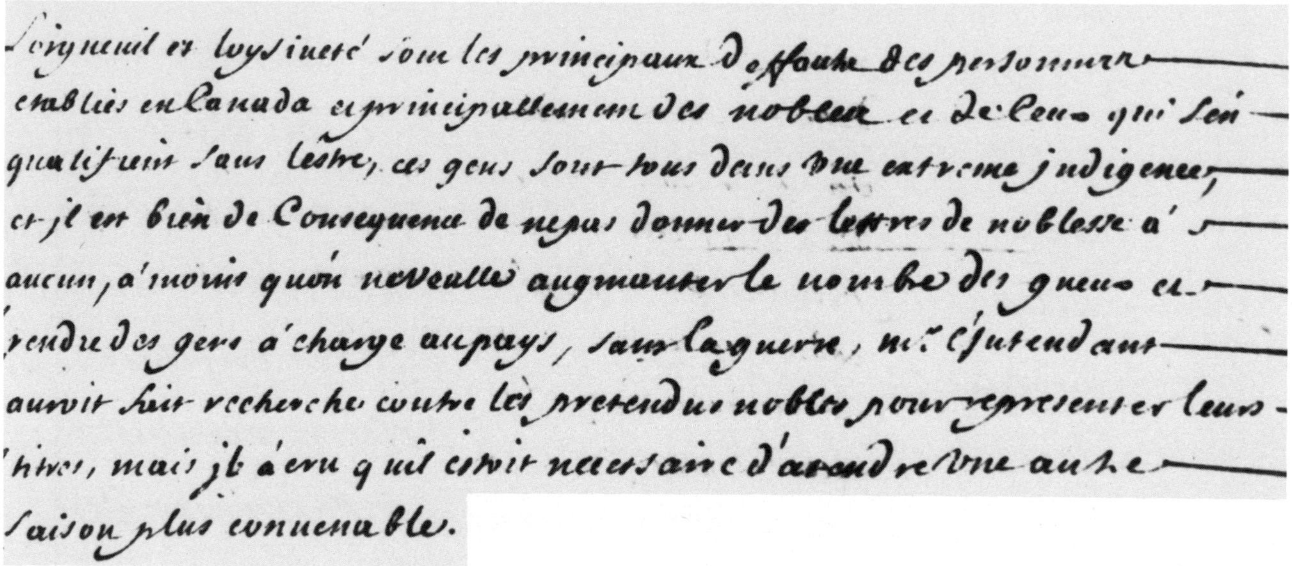

Orgueil et loysiveté sont les principaux deffauts des personnes
establies en Canada et principallement des nobles et de ceux qui s'en
qualiffient sans lestre, ces gens sont tous dans vne extreme indigence,
et il est bien de Consequence de ne pas donner des lettres de noblesse a
aucun, a moins quon ne veuille augmenter le nombre des gueux et
rendre des gens a charge au pays, sans la guerre, mr. l'Intendant
auroit fait recherche contre les pretendus nobles pour representer leurs
tiltres, mais il a cru quil estoit necessaire d'attendre vne autre
saison plus convenable.

"Information report on Canada" by Intendant Champigny, Québec, 10 May 1691.

Champigny did not have a high opinion of the Canadian nobility: "Pride and idleness are the main defects in the people who have settled in Canada, and principally of the nobles and those who call themselves thus without being nobles, those people are all in a state of extreme poverty."

Archives nationales, Paris, France: Fonds des Colonies, série C^{11A}, vol. 11, fol. 265v.

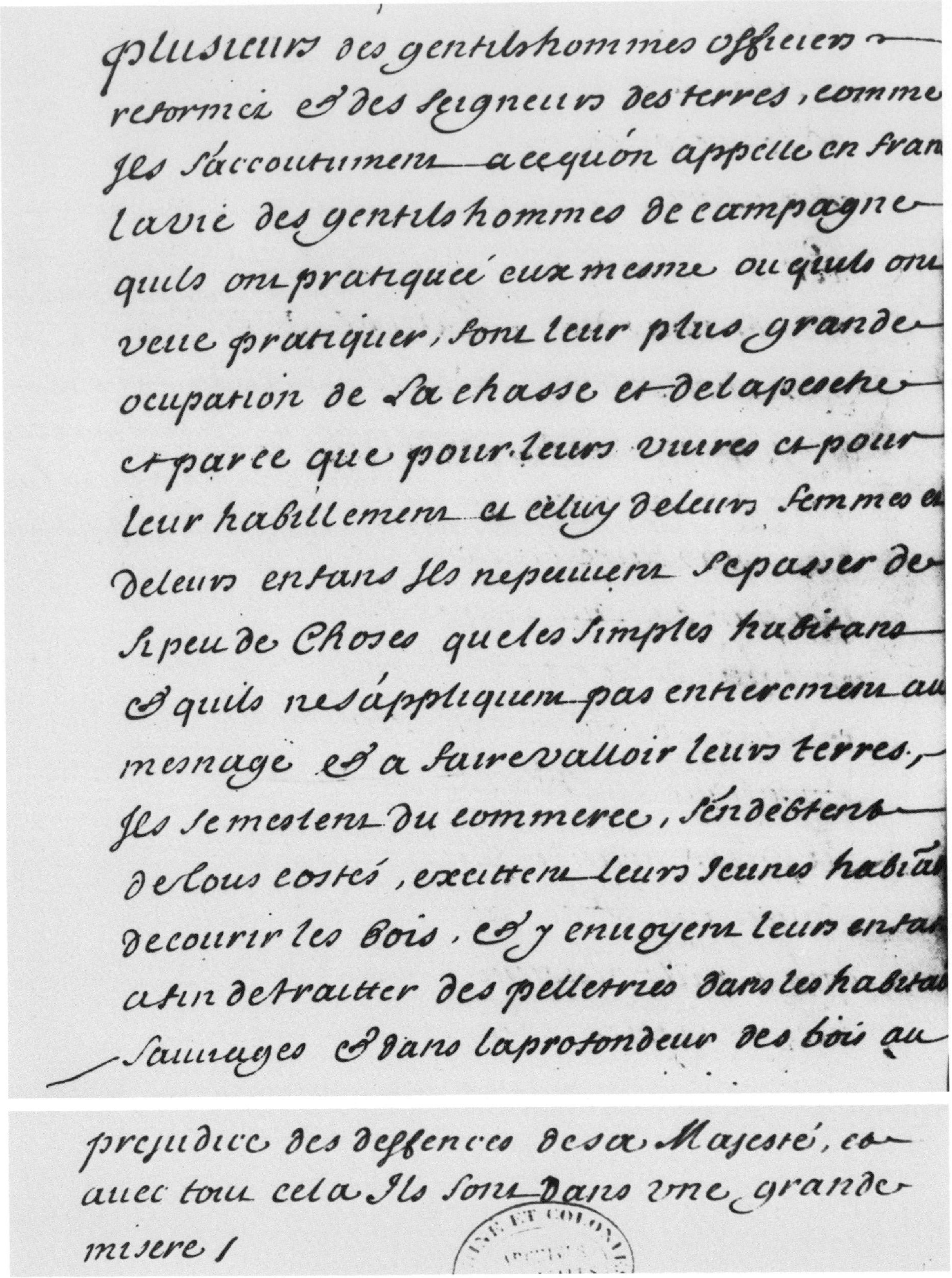

plusieurs des gentilshommes officiers
reformez & des seigneurs des terres, comme
Ils s'accoutument a ce qu'on appelle en Fran[ce]
la vie des gentilshommes de campagne
qu'ils ont pratiquée eux mesme ou qu'ils ont
veue pratiquer, sont leur plus grande
occupation de la chasse et de la pesche
et parce que pour leurs vivres et pour
leur habillement et celuy de leurs femmes et
de leurs enfans Ils ne peuvent se passer de
si peu de choses que les simples habitans
& qu'ils ne s'appliquent pas entierement au
mesnage & a faire valloir leurs terres,
Ils se meslent du commerce, s'endebtent
de tous costés, excittent leurs jeunes habita[ns]
de courir les bois, & y envoyent leurs enfa[ns]
afin de traitter des pelleteries dans les habita[tions]
sauvages & dans la profondeur des bois au
prejudice des deffences de sa Majesté, et
avec tout cela Ils sont dans une grande
misere !

Letter from Intendant Duchesneau to the minister Colbert, Québec, 10 November 1679.

Duchesneau described the idle and wretched life of certain Canadian gentlemen and seigneurs: "As they were accustomed to what is called in France the life of country gentlemen…, [they] make hunting and fishing their greatest occupation…and since they do not apply themselves entirely to their families and to exploiting their lands, they get mixed up in trade, make debts on all sides, incite their young settlers to become coureurs des bois and send their children into the woods…and with all that they are in great poverty."

Archives nationales, Paris, France: Fonds des Colonies, série C^{11A}, vol. 5, fol. 50v–51.

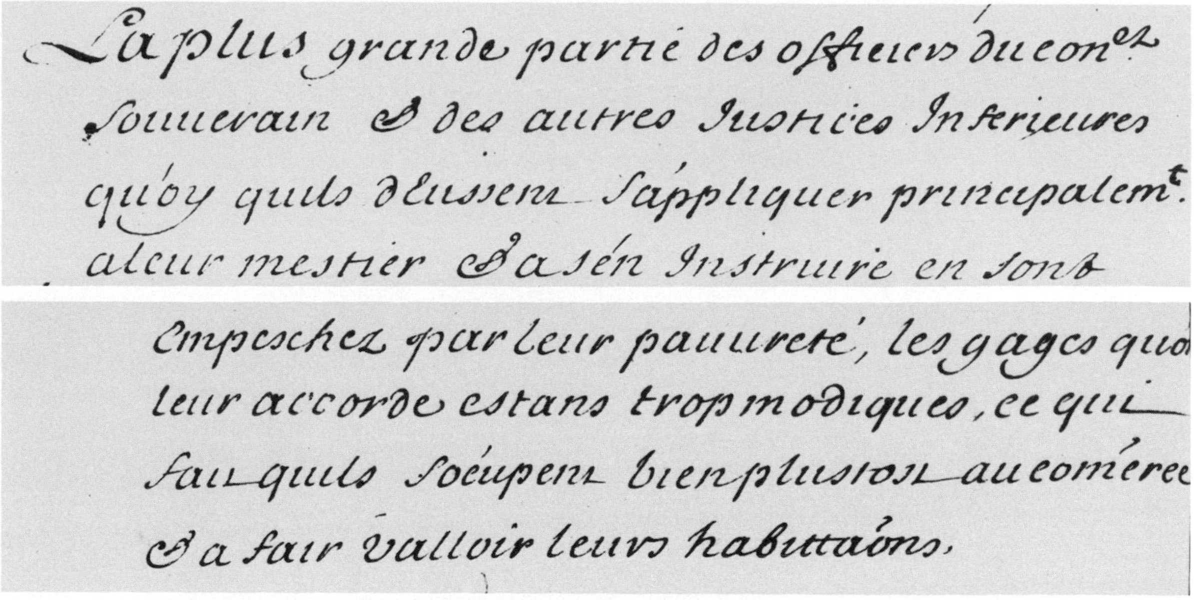
La plus grande partie des officiers du con.el
Souverain & des autres Justices Inferieures
quoy quils deussent s'appliquer principalem.t
a leur mestier & a s'en Instruire en sont
Empeschez par leur pauvreté, les gages quo
leur accorde estans trop modiques, ce qui
fait quils s'ocupent bien plustost au comerce
& a fair valloir leurs habitaons.

Letter from Intendant Duchesneau to the minister Colbert, Québec, 10 November 1679.

According to Duchesneau, the officers of the law (judges) in the colony were too badly paid to be able "to apply themselves principally to their profession and to learn more about it...with the result that they concern themselves much more with trade and with developing their settlements."

Archives nationales, Paris, France: Fonds des Colonies, série C^{11A}, vol. 5, fol. 50–50v.

194

The Armorial Bearings of Charles Le Moyne de Longueuil; watercolour on parchment; arms: azure, three roses Or; on a chief cousu Gules, a crescent Argent between two mullets of the same; helmet: silver, affronty; mantling: of the colours; crest: a savage issuant proper holding in his sinister hand an arrow sable; supporters: two savages proper, each vested with a loin-cloth Gules and holding in his sinister hand an arrow sable.

Charles Le Moyne, Robert Giffard, Pierre Boucher and other eminent persons received letters patent of nobility because they had rendered valuable service to the colony.

Archives of the Le Moyne de Sérigny family, Bordeaux, France.

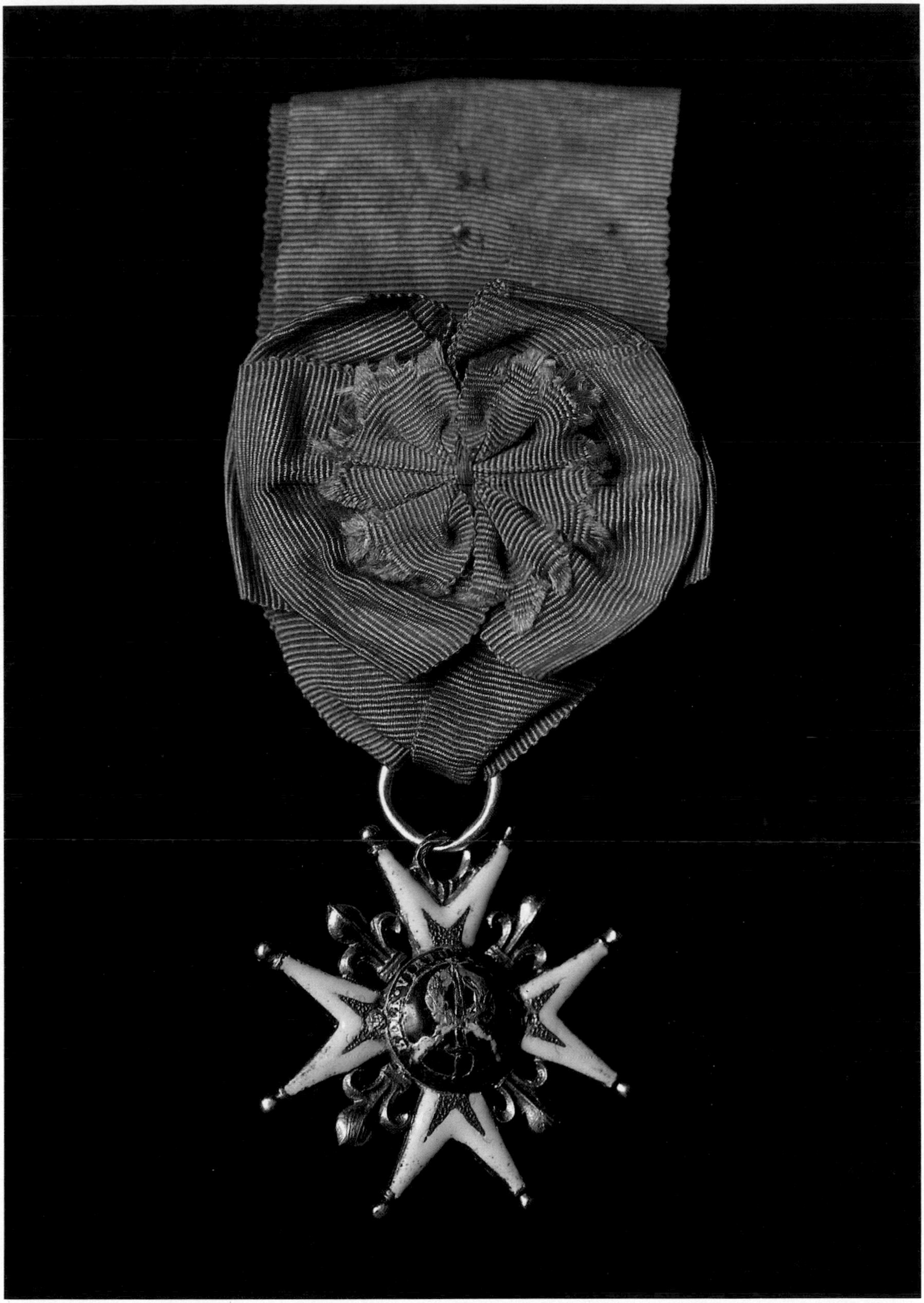

Cross of a Knight of the Royal Military Order of Saint-Louis; obverse; enamel and gold; 4 cm.; LUDOVICUS MAGNUS INSTITUIT 1693.

This cross was awarded to officers whose "valour, merit, and services rendered" had earned them the honour of being named members of the order by the king. This honour was bestowed upon several officers from Canada.

Musée national de la Légion d'honneur et des ordres de chevalerie, Paris, France.

The people

In spite of appearances the merchants in the colony were poor, except for four or five who had "some wealth," according to one intendant's testimony. If many of them lived on a grand scale and dressed opulently – as did their wives and children too – most often they were heavily in debt.

In reality, truly comfortable circumstances were most often found among the ordinary settlers who cultivated their land diligently. Towards the end of the century there were still "poor people" among the habitants, but they were generally those who did not put any effort into working their land but preferred the life of the coureurs des bois.

As for workers, there were too few of them in the colony. People even spoke of "an extreme need for workers and labourers." As well as being scarce, they were very costly, so that a masonry job could cost five times as much at Québec as it did in France.

The Canadian habitants were proud and in no way resembled "peasants." Freedom-loving, they were brave, strong, and hardy; if they excelled in fighting from ambush, they also had all that was needed to succeed as coureurs des bois. Going off to live in the woods was often disastrous for them, however. After a few years many became unfit for any other work, and in particular for working the land.

Ex-voto of Madame Denis Riverin and her Four Children; attributed to Michel Dessailliant dit Richeterre (active circa 1700–23); oil; 1703; 47.6 x 55.2 cm.

The tradesman Riverin's family is richly dressed in this picture. This was not an exception in New France, since many Canadians liked to wear fine clothes, even if few of them had the means to do so. Many pieces of material and articles of clothing were therefore imported from Europe so that people could dress fashionably.

Musée Historial, Sainte-Anne-de-Beaupré.

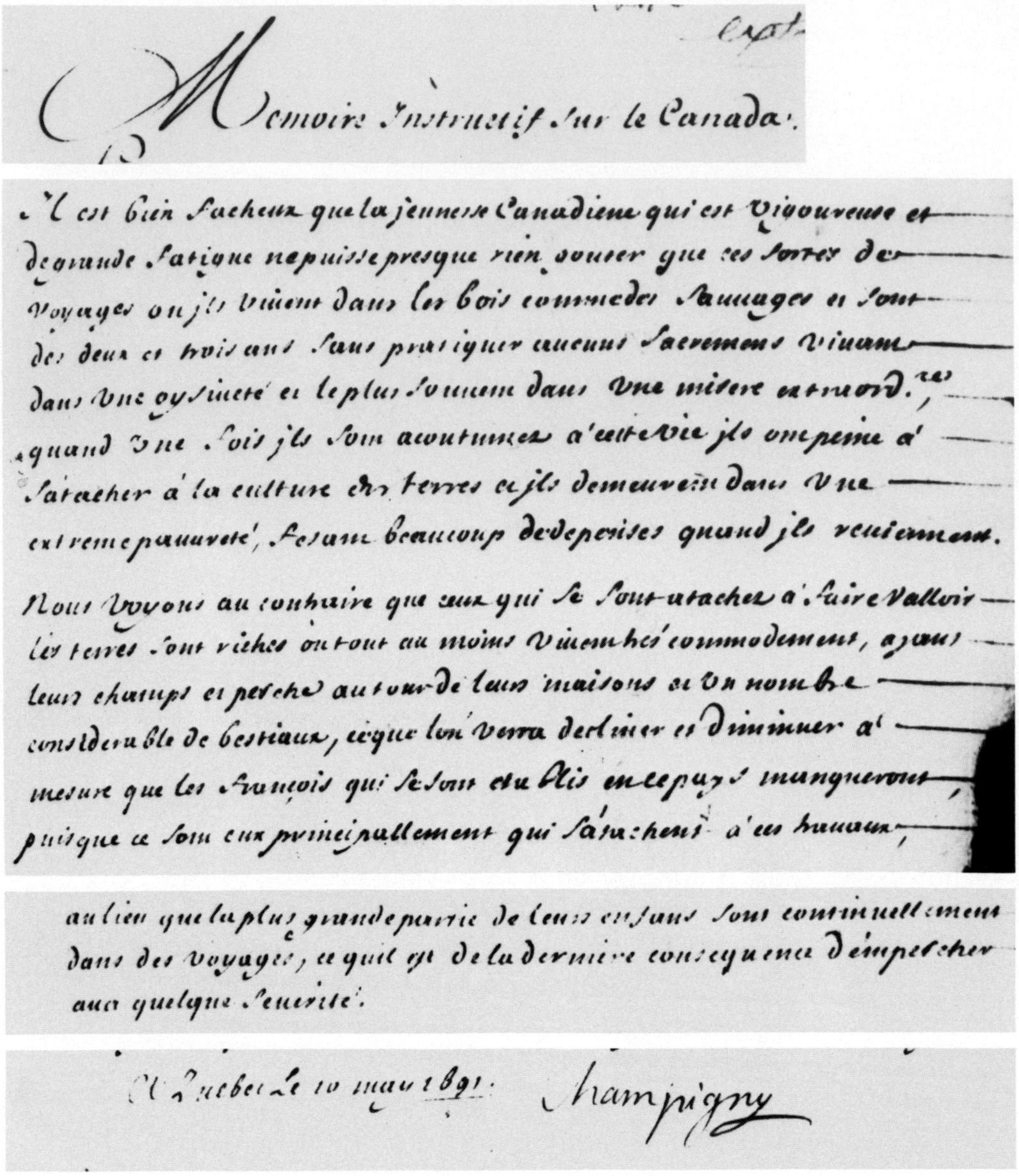

Memoire Instructif sur le Canada.

Il est bien facheux que la jeunesse Canadienne qui est vigoureuse et de grande fatigue ne puisse presque rien souffrir que ces sortes de voyages ou ils vivent dans les bois comme des sauvages et sont des deux et trois ans sans pratiquer aucuns sacremens vivant dans une oysiveté et le plus souvent dans une misere extraord.res, quand une fois ils sont acoutumez a cette vie ils ont peine a s'atacher a la culture des terres et ils demeurent dans une extreme pauvreté, fesant beaucoup de depenses quand ils reviennent.

Nous voyons au contraire que ceux qui se sont atachez a faire valloir les terres sont riches ou tout au moins vivent tres commodement, ayant leurs champs et pesche autour de leurs maisons et un nombre considerable de bestiaux, ce que l'on verra decliner et diminuer a mesure que les françois qui se sont etablis en ce pays manqueront, puisque ce sont eux principallement qui s'atachent a ces travaux,

au lieu que la plus grande partie de leurs enfans sont continuellement dans des voyages, ce quil est de la derniere consequence d'empescher avec quelque severité.

A Quebec le 10 may 1691. Champigny

"Information report on Canada" by Intendant Champigny, Québec, 10 May 1691.

According to Champigny the Canadians who became coureurs des bois "lived in extraordinary idleness and most often in extraordinary poverty," whilst "those who have applied themselves to cultivating the land are rich or at least live very comfortably."

Archives nationales, Paris, France: Fonds des Colonies, série C^{11A}, vol. 11, fol. 262–262v, 268.

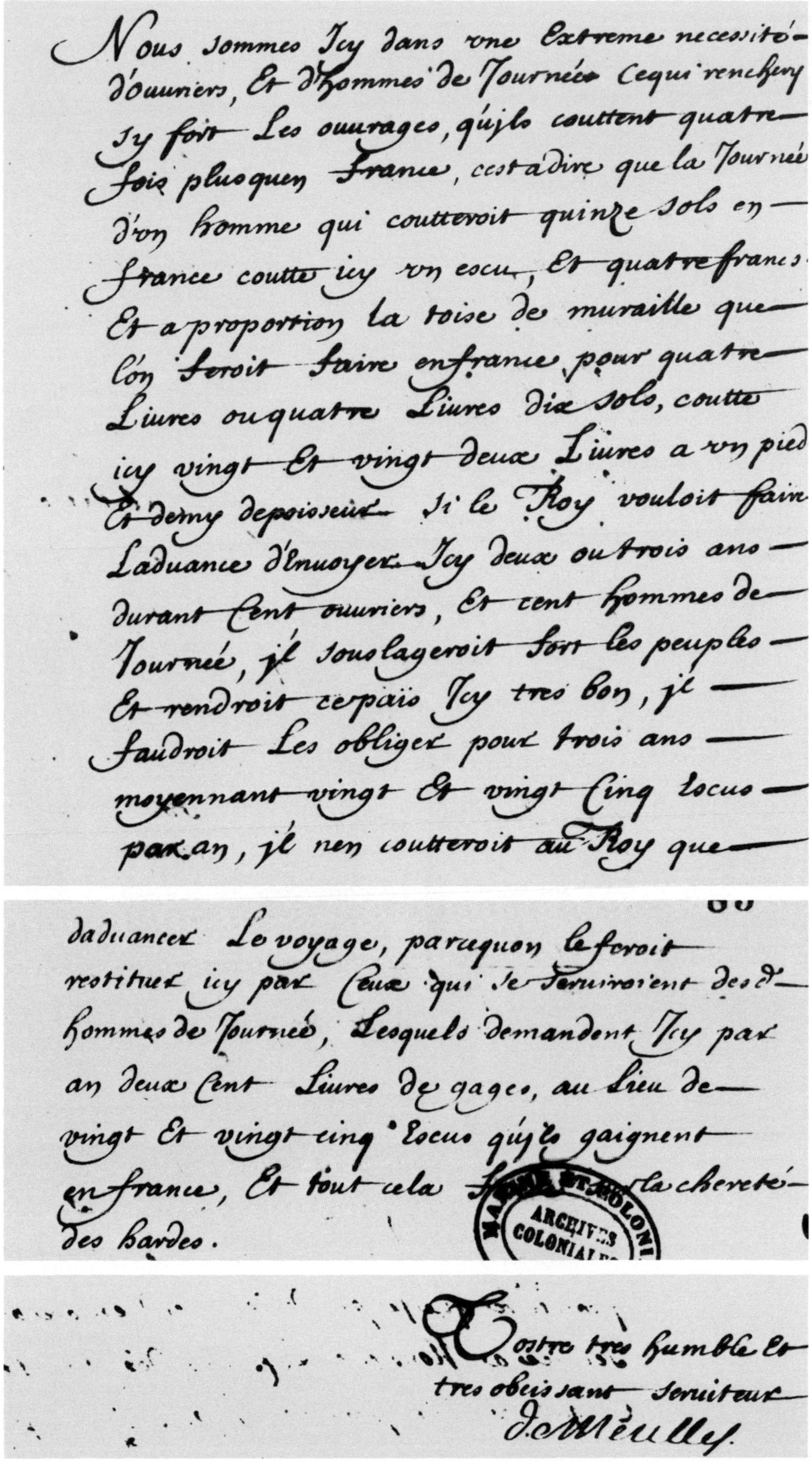
Nous sommes Icy dans une Extreme necessité
d'ouuriers, Et d'hommes de Journée Cequi renchery
Icy fort Les ouurages, qu'ils couttent quatre
fois plusqu'en France, cest a dire que la Journée
d'un homme qui coutteroit quinze sols en
France coutte icy un escu, Et quatre francs.
Et a proportion la toise de muraille que
l'on feroit faire en france pour quatre
Livres ou quatre Livres dix sols, coutte
icy vingt Et vingt deux Livres a un pied
Et demy depoisseur. si le Roy vouloit faire
Laduance d'Enuoyer Icy deux ou trois ans
durant Cent ouuriers, Et cent hommes de
Journée, il soulageroit fort les peuples
Et rendroit ce pais Icy tres bon, il
faudroit Les obliger pour trois ans
moyennant vingt Et vingt Cinq Escus
par an, il nen coutteroit au Roy que

daduancer Le voyage, parcequon le feroit
restituer icy par Ceux qui se seruiroient des
hommes de Journée, Lesquels demandent Icy par
an deux Cent Livres de gages, au lieu de
vingt Et vingt cinq Escus qu'ils gaignent
en france, Et tout cela [illegible] la chereté
des hardes.

Vostre tres humble Et
tres obeissant Seruiteur
deMeulles.

Letter from Intendant de Meulles to the minister Colbert, Québec, 12 November 1682.

De Meulles deplored the lack of manpower in Canada: "We have an extreme shortage of workmen here, and of day labourers, which raises the cost of products so much, that they cost four times more than in France."

Archives nationales, Paris, France: Fonds des Colonies, série C^{11A}, vol. 6, fol. 81, 84v, 85, 92v.

Canadiens en Raquette allant en guerre sur la nege

Canadians Going to War on Snowshoe; engraved by I.B. Scotin; etching; 15.6 x 8.4 cm. (page).

In Claude Charles Le Roy Bacqueville de La Potherie. *Histoire de l'Amérique septentrionale....* Paris: J.–L. Nion & F. Didot, 1722, vol. 1, p. 51.

According to La Potherie the Canadians had "on several occasions given sure tokens of their loyalty" to the king by taking part in military operations against the Iroquois and the English. "Cold, rain, snow, hunger and thirst" were sometimes more difficult obstacles to overcome than were the enemy forces. Commenting upon the success of d'Iberville's military expedition in Hudson Bay in 1697, this French observer wrote: "You had to be a Canadian, or have the heart of a Canadian, to have carried out such an undertaking successfully."

Public Archives of Canada, Library, Ottawa (Negative no. C 113193).

VII

Education

The Jesuit college, which had been founded at Québec in 1635, was the only institution of secondary education in New France. It developed rapidly. On 2 July 1666 two Canadians, Louis Jolliet and Pierre Francheville, defended the first "thesis in philosophy" there, in the presence of Bishop Laval, the governor and the intendant. The latter argued well at it, probably in Latin, and the two pupils replied, very well too, on all fields of logic.

The Jesuits also did primary teaching; at Montréal in 1658 Marguerite Bourgeoys welcomed the first children of school age, and also in that year she recruited some of her companions to help her. Little by little she laid the foundations of the Congrégation de Notre-Dame, the schools of which multiplied in the colony.

Bishop Laval's Petit Séminaire, which was founded in 1668, took in pupils who were intending to enter the priesthood; they took their classes at the Jesuit college and boarded at the seminary. Later Bishop Laval founded another institution, which was for teaching arts and crafts.

The Ursulines had been at Québec since 1639. Besides the usual school subjects they taught the young girls to keep house, but also to keep themselves busy, both agreeably and usefully, thanks to needlework, for example, in which they themselves excelled.

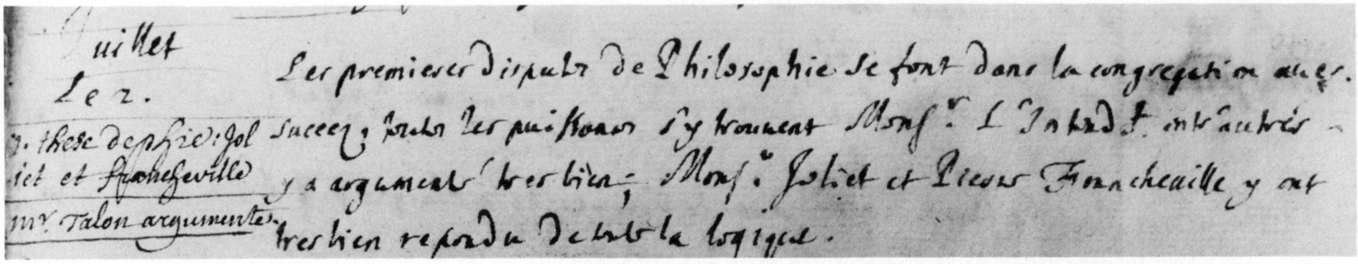
Juillet
Le 2.
1. these de phie: Jolliet et Francheville
mr. Talon argumente

Les premieres disputes de Philosophie se font dans la congregation avec succez; toutes les puissances s'y trouvent Monsr. l'Intendt. entr'autres y a argumenté tres bien; Monsr. Jolliet et Pierre Francheville y ont tres bien repondu de toute la logique.

Extract from the *Journal des Jésuites* concerning the first thesis in philosophy defended at the Jesuit College, 2 July 1666.

"The first philosophical debates are being conducted successfully in the congregation. All the powers are present; Monsieur the Intendant, among others, made a strong argument; Monsieur Jolliet and Pierre Francheville replied very well, upon the whole subject of logic."

Archives du Séminaire de Québec, Québec: Journal des Jésuites, MS–48, p. 177.

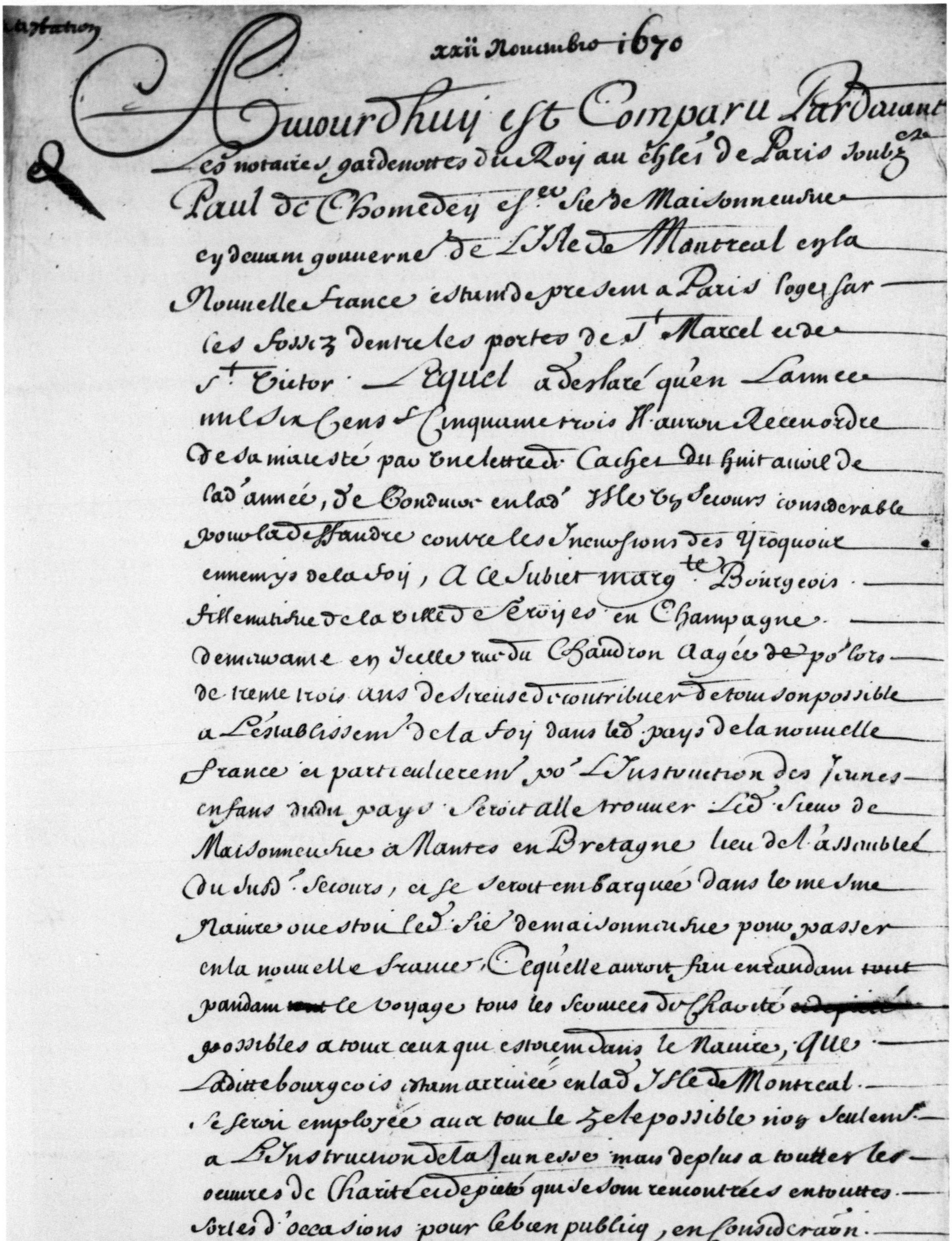

xxii Novembre 1670

Aujourdhuy est Comparu Pardevant
les notaires gardenottes du Roy au chlet de Paris soubz[signez]
Paul de Chomedey escuyer Sieur de Maisonneufve
cy devant gouverneur de l'Isle de Montreal en la
Nouvelle France estant de present a Paris logé sur
les fossez d'entre les portes de St Marcel et de
St Victor — Lequel a declaré qu'en l'annee
mil six cens cinquante trois il auroit receu ordre
de sa maiesté par une lettre de cachet du huit avril de
lad. année, de conduire en lad. Isle un secours considerable
pour la deffandre contre les incursions des Yroquois
ennemys de la foy, a ce subiet Margte Bourgeois
fille majeure de la ville de Troyes en Champagne
demeurante en icelle rue du Chaudron aagée de po. lors
de trente trois ans desireuse de contribuer de tout son possible
a l'establissemt de la foy dans led. pays de la nouvelle
France et particulierement po. l'instruction des jeunes
enfans dudit pays seroit allé trouver led. sieur de
Maisonneufve a Nantes en Bretagne lieu de l'assemblée
du susd. secours, et se seroit embarquée dans le mesme
navire ou estoit led. Sr de maisonneufve pour passer
en la nouvelle France, laquelle auroit fait en randant tout
pandant le voyage tous les services de charité
possibles a tous ceux qui estoient dans le navire, que
ladite bourgeois estant arrivée en lad. Isle de Montreal
se seroit employée avec tout le zele possible non seulemt
a l'instruction de la jeunesse mais de plus a toutes les
oeuvres de charité et de pieté qui se sont rencontrées en toutes
sortes d'occasions pour le bien publiq, en consideraon

Declaration by Chomedey de Maisonneuve in favour of Marguerite Bourgeoys, Paris, 22 November 1670.

Maisonneuve affirmed that she had "exerted herself with all possible zeal not only to teaching the young, but in addition to all the works of charity and piety that occurred on all sorts of occasions for the common good."

Little by little Marguerite Bourgeoys laid the foundations of the Congrégation de Notre-Dame, a community which devoted itself mainly to educating young girls.

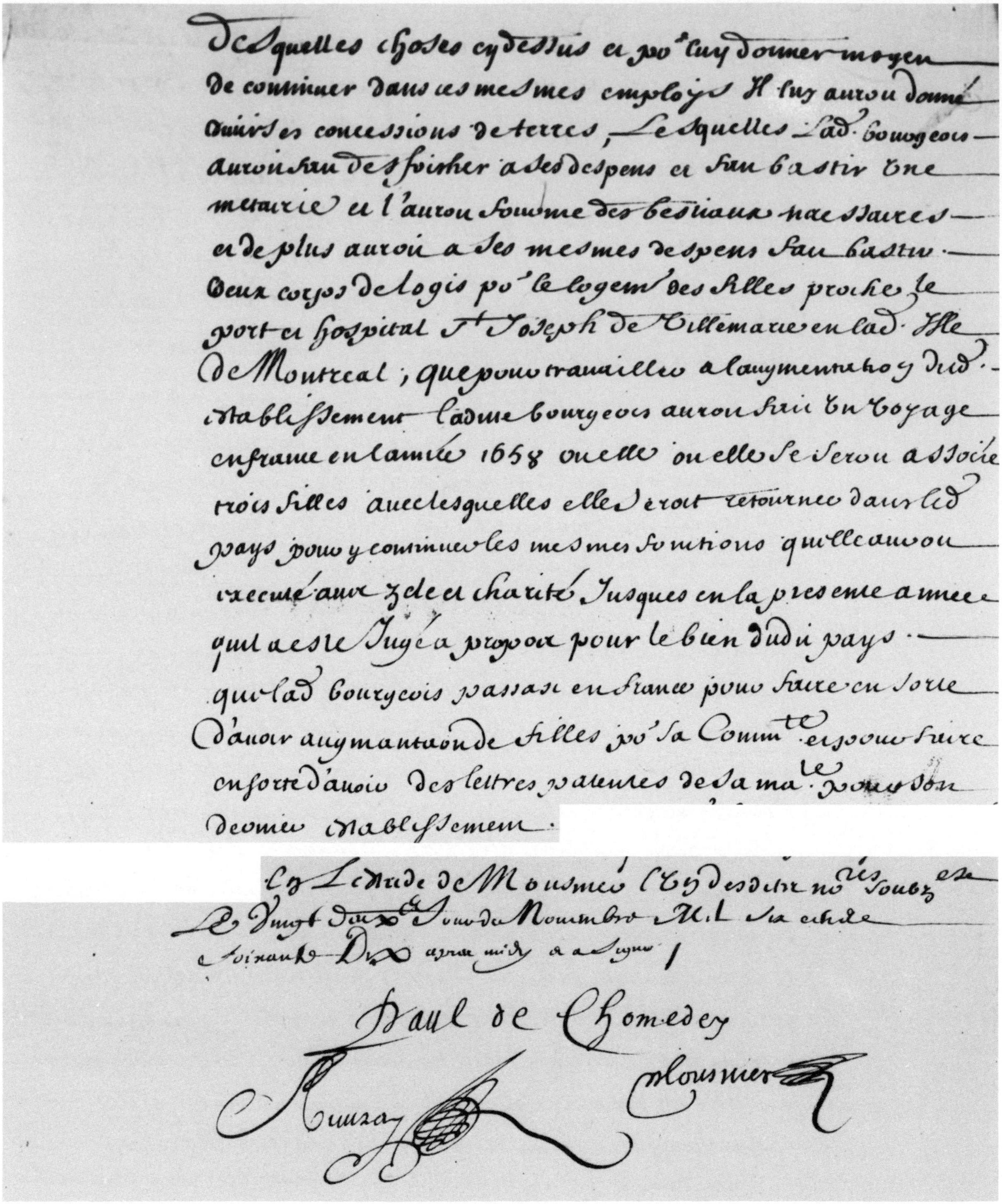

desquelles choses cy dessus et po^r luy donner moyen
de continuer dans ces mesmes employs Il luy auroit donné
divers concessions de terres, lesquelles lad. bourgeois
auroit faict defricher a ses despens et fait bastir une
metairie et l'auroit fournie des bestiaux necessaires
et de plus auroit a ses mesmes despens fait bastir
deux corps de logis po^r le logem^t des filles proche le
fort et hospital St Joseph de Villemarie en lad. Isle
de Montreal ; que pour travailler a l'augmentation dud.
establissement lad. bourgeois auroit faict un voyage
en france en l'année 1658 ou elle ou elle se seroit associé
trois filles avec lesquelles elle seroit retournee dans led.
pays pour y continuer les mesmes fonctions qu'elle avoit
exercé avec zele et charité jusques en la presente année
qu'il a esté jugé a propos pour le bien dud. pays
que lad. bourgeois passast en france pour faire en sorte
d'avoir augmentation de filles po^r sa Comm^té et pour faire
en sorte d'avoir des lettres patentes de sa ma^té pour son
dernier establissement.

Ce fait Leu et lecture de Mousnier cy dessus no^res soubz^és
le vingt deux^e jour de Novembre Mil six cent
soixante dix apres midy et a signé

Paul de Chomedey

Rimbault Mousnier

Archives nationales, Paris, France:
Minutier central des notaires, Étude
CXII, 134 (Mousnier).

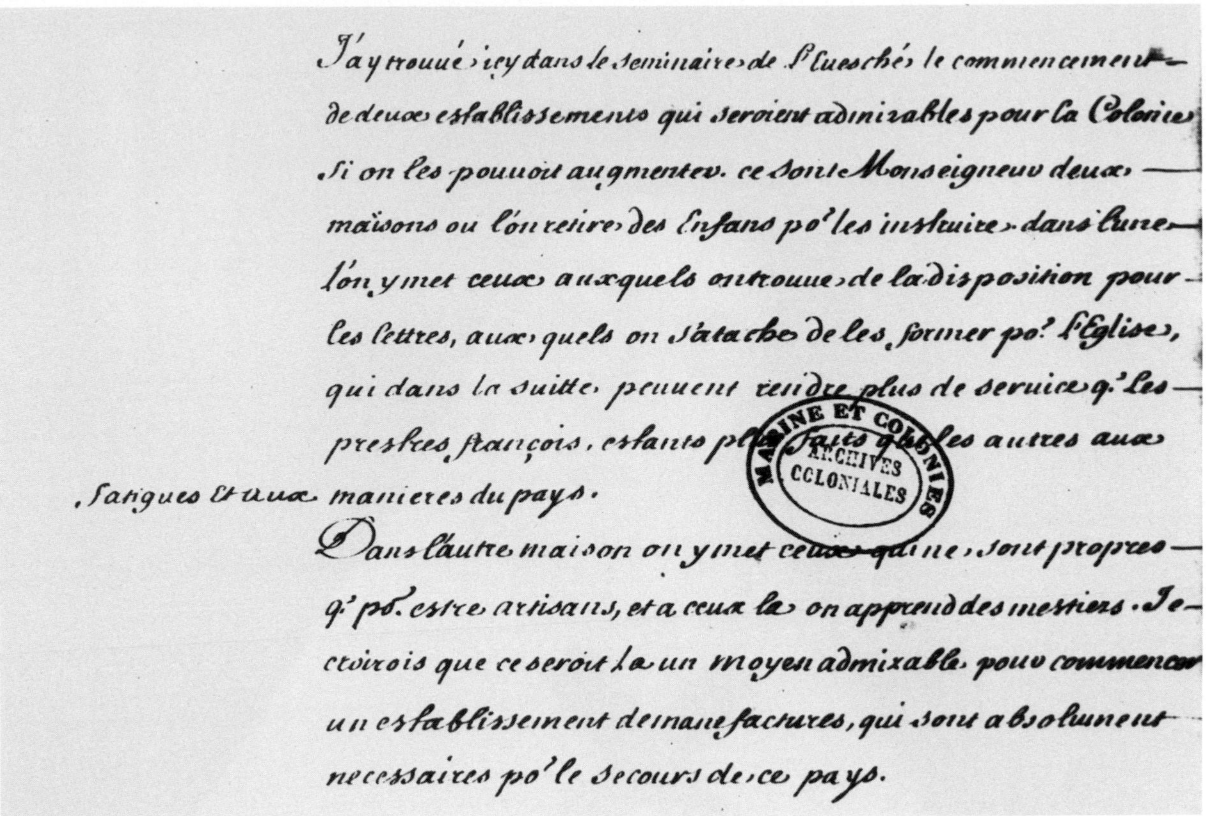

J'ay trouvé icy dans le seminaire de Mr l'Evesché le commencement
de deux establissements qui seroient admirables pour la Colonie
si on les pouvoit augmenter. ce sont Monseigneur deux
maisons ou l'on retire des Enfans po.r les instruire. dans l'une
l'on y met ceux auxquels on trouve de la disposition pour
les Lettres, auxquels on s'atache de les former po.r l'Eglise,
qui dans la suitte peuvent rendre plus de service q.e les
prestres françois, estants plus faits que les autres aux
fatigues et aux manieres du pays.
Dans l'autre maison on y met ceux qui ne sont propres
q.e po.r estre artisans, et a ceux la on apprend des mestiers. Je
croirois que ce seroit la un moyen admirable pour commencer
un establissement de manufactures, qui sont absolument
necessaires po.r le secours de ce pays.

MARINE ET COLONIES
ARCHIVES COLONIALES

Letter from Governor General Denonville to the minister Seignelay, Québec, 13 November 1685.

Denonville spoke about two schools run by the Séminaire de Québec: "In one are put those in whom is discerned some disposition for the humanities, for whom efforts are made to train them for the Church. . . . In the other house are put those who are only apt to be artisans, and they are taught trades."

Archives nationales, Paris, France: Fonds des Colonies, série C^{11A}, vol. 7, fol. 93, 106v.

Portrait of Mother Marie de l'Incarnation (1599–1672); attributed to Hugues Pommier (circa 1637–86); oil; 1672; 100 x 77 cm.

Marie de l'Incarnation was the first superior of the Ursulines of New France, a religious community that was dedicated to educating young French and Indian girls. Her *Lettres*, published in 1681, teem with information about the events, habits, and customs of the period.

Archives des ursulines de Québec, Québec.

VII

A developing civilization

As harsh as life might be in Canada, when they knew how to read, the settlers sometimes owned some books, most often devotional works. Some who were better educated, such as Jean Nicollet, owned a small and more varied library: literature, geography, history were represented in it. Another man even owned some books in Latin.

The colony also had its painters. The most famous in the seventeenth century was without doubt Brother Luc, a Recollet, who left a fairly large body of works, including portraits of Bishop Laval and Intendant Talon. Perhaps more engaging is the figure of a very talented Canadian, Abbé Jean Guyon, to whom we owe a fine portrait of Mother Juchereau de Saint-Ignace, a nun hospitaller.

Not even music was absent from Canada: in February 1661 the use of an organ in the church of Québec is mentioned – the oldest one known in North America; and in 1667 the Sieur Chartier de Lotbinière gave the first ball to be seen in the colony at Québec.

On the science side, other than teaching mathematics and in the final years of the century, hydrography, everything remained to be done. But a man was getting ready to enter upon the scene who would be the first "scientist" in New France: Michel Sarrazin, a remarkable doctor and naturalist, who began the scientific tradition in Canada.

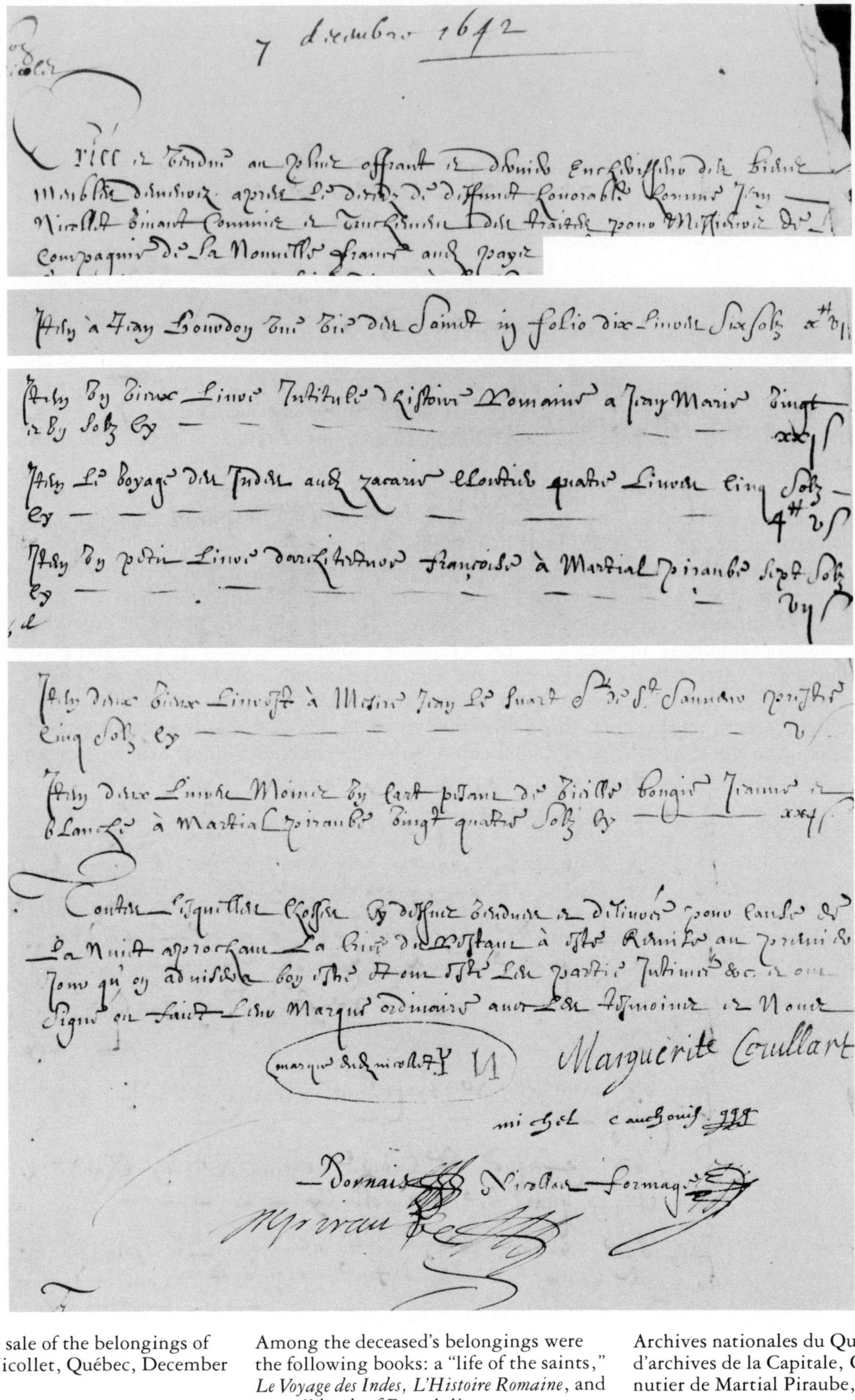
7 décembre 1642

Marguerite Couillart

michel cauchois

Minutes of the sale of the belongings of the late Jean Nicollet, Québec, December 1642.

Among the deceased's belongings were the following books: a "life of the saints," *Le Voyage des Indes, L'Histoire Romaine*, and a small book of French literature.

The settlers who could read sometimes owned a few books.

Archives nationales du Québec, Centre d'archives de la Capitale, Québec: Minutier de Martial Piraube, pièce 44.

Portrait of Mother Juchereau de Saint-Ignace (1650–1723); attributed to Jean Guyon (1659–87); oil; circa 1684; 68.5 x 56.1 cm.

This portrait of the superior of the Religious Hospitallers of the Hôtel-Dieu de Québec was done by Abbé Jean Guyon, one of the earliest Canadian painters. This artist also did watercolours of "elements of Laurentian flora."

Monastère des augustines de l'Hôtel-Dieu de Québec, Québec.

Sister of Charity Tending to Our Lord as a Sick Man; Claude François (Brother Luc) (1614–85); oil; 1670 or 1671; 99.6 x 140.3 cm.

Brother Luc, of the Recollet order, spent fifteen months at Québec in 1670–71. He painted several pictures for churches in New France and some religious communities in the colony. He also did a few portraits, including those of Bishop Laval and Intendant Talon.

Monastère des augustines de l'Hôtel-Dieu de Québec, Québec.

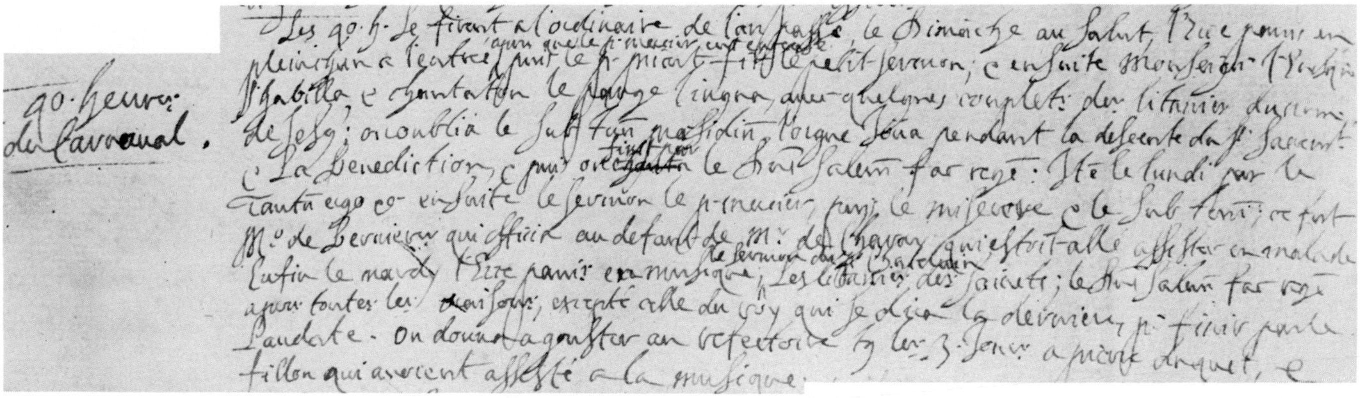

Extract from the *Journal des Jésuites*: first mention of an organ in the church at Québec, February 1661.

"The forty hours were celebrated as usual last year: on Sunday...the organ played during the reposition of the Blessed Sacrament and the Benediction."

Archives du Séminaire de Québec, Québec: Journal des Jésuites, MS-48, p. 154.

208

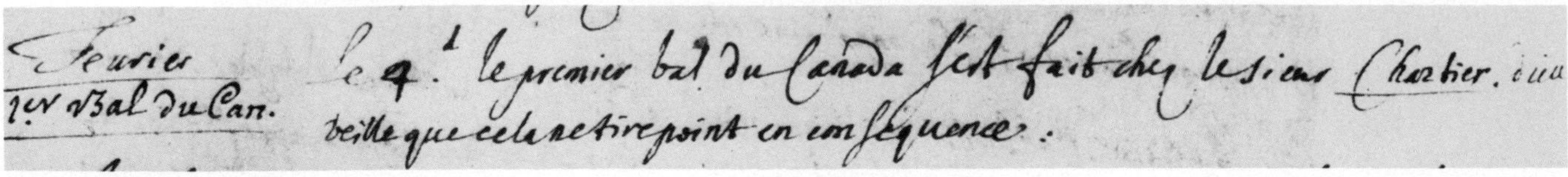
Feurier
1er Bal du Can.
Le 4. le premier bal du Canada s'est fait chez le sieur Chartier. Dieu veille que cela ne tire point en consequence.

Extract from the *Journal des Jésuites* mentioning the first ball in Canada, 4 February 1667.

"On the 4th the first ball in Canada was held in the home of the Sieur Chartier."

Archives du Séminaire de Québec, Québec: Journal des Jésuites, MS-48, p. 182.

~ 209 ~

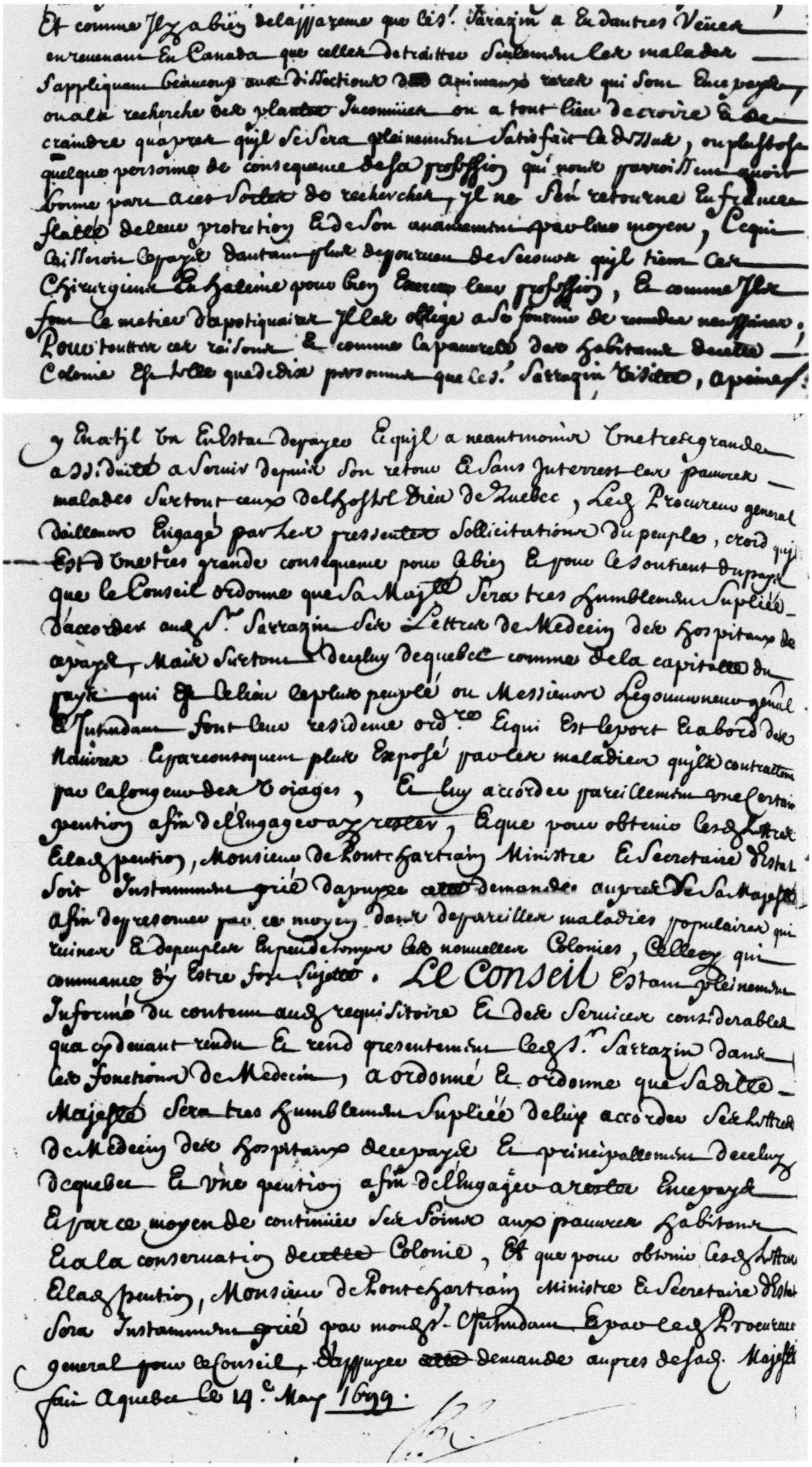
Et comme Il a esté [illegible] de la [illegible] que led. Sarazin a eu d'autres veues
en revenant en Canada que celles de traitter seulement les malades
s'appliquant beaucoup aux dissections des animaux rares qui sont en ce pays
ou a la recherche des plantes inconnues on a tout lieu de croire et de
craindre qu'apres qu'il se sera pleinement satisfait la dessus, ou plustost
quelque personne de consequence de sa profession qui nous paroist en avoir
donne part a ces sortes de recherches, il ne s'en retourne en France
flatté de leur protection et de son avancement par leur moyen, ce qui
osteroit ce pays d'autant plus de secours qu'il tient ces
chirurgiens en haleine pour bien exercer leur profession, et comme il a
fait le metier d'apotiquaire il les a obligé a se fournir de remedes necessaires;
Pour toutes ces raisons et comme la pauvreté des habitans de cette
colonie est telle que de dix personnes que led. Sarazin visite, a peine

y en a t il un en estat de payer et qu'il a neantmoins une tres grande
assiduité a servir depuis son retour et sans interest les pauvres
malades surtout ceux de l'hostel Dieu de Quebec, led. Procureur general
d'ailleurs engagé par les pressentes sollicitations du peuple, croid qu'il
est d'une tres grande consequence pour le bien et pour le soutient du pays
que le Conseil ordonne que Sa Majesté sera tres humblement suppliée
d'accorder aud. Sr. Sarrazin des lettres de Medecin des hospitaux de
ce pays, mais surtout de celuy de Quebec comme de la capitalle du
pays qui est le lieu le plus peuplé ou Messieurs le Gouverneur general
et Intendant font leur residence ordre. et qui est le port et abord des
navires et par consequent plus exposé par les maladies qu'ils contractent
par la longueur des voiages, et luy accorder pareillement une certaine
pention afin de l'engager a y rester, et que pour obtenir lesd. lettres
et lad. pention, Monsieur de Pontchartrain Ministre et Secretaire d'Estat
soit instamment prié d'appuyer cette demande auprez de Sa Majesté
afin de preserver par ce moyen dans de pareilles maladies populaires qui
ruinent et depeuplent en peu de temps les nouvelles colonies, celle cy qui
commance d'y estre fort sujette. Le Conseil estant pleinement
informé du contenu aud. requisitoire et des services considerables
qu'a cy devant rendu et rend presentement led. Sr. Sarrazin dans
les fonctions de Medecin, a ordonné et ordonne que Sad.
Majesté sera tres humblement suppliée de luy accorder ses lettres
de Medecin des hospitaux de ce pays et principallement de celuy
de Quebec et une pention afin de l'engager a rester en ce pays
et par ce moyen de continuer ses soins aux pauvres habitans
et a la conservation de cette colonie, et que pour obtenir lesd. lettres
et lad. pention, Monsieur de Pontchartrain Ministre et Secretaire d'Estat
sera instamment prié par monsr. l'Intendant et par led. Procureur
general pour ce Conseil, d'appuyer cette demande auprès de Sa Majesté
fait a Quebec le 14e May 1699.

Deliberations of the Conseil souverain concerning the surgeon Michel Sarrazin, Québec, 14 May 1699.

It is stated that in addition to displaying "great assiduity since his return in serving disinterestedly the needy poor," Sarrazin devoted "a great deal of time to dissecting the rare animals which are found in this country or to seeking out unknown plants."

Michel Sarrazin was the first great Canadian scientist.

Archives nationales du Québec, Centre d'archives de la Capitale, Québec: Jugements et délibérations du Conseil souverain, vol. 9, pp. 271–272.

VII

The theatre

Under the heading of cultural activities in the colony one must not forget the theatre. The first performance – a play written for the occasion by Marc Lescarbot – was given at Port-Royal on 14 November 1606. It was the *Théâtre de Neptune en la Nouvelle-France.*

At Québec a tragi-comedy was presented in 1640 to celebrate the birth of the Dauphin. Then in 1651 and 1652 two of Corneille's plays, *Le Cid* and *Héraclius,* were performed. In 1658 a short play written for the occasion, in French and in Indian languages, was presented to celebrate the governor's arrival: *La reception de Mgr le vicomte d'Argenson.*

The settlers were also very fond of other entertainments; for a time a bonfire was lit every year on the eve of the feast of St. Joseph, the patron saint of Canada, and every year on the evening of 23 June the traditional bonfires for the feast of St. John were lit at Québec, Trois-Rivières, and probably at Montréal.

While we are on the matter of shows, Governor Frontenac's plan to stage Molière's *Tartuffe* gave rise at the end of the century to what has been called the *Tartuffe* affair, a series of comical events in which, for example, Bishop Saint-Vallier could be seen handing a hundred pistoles to Frontenac to dissuade him from having the play presented.

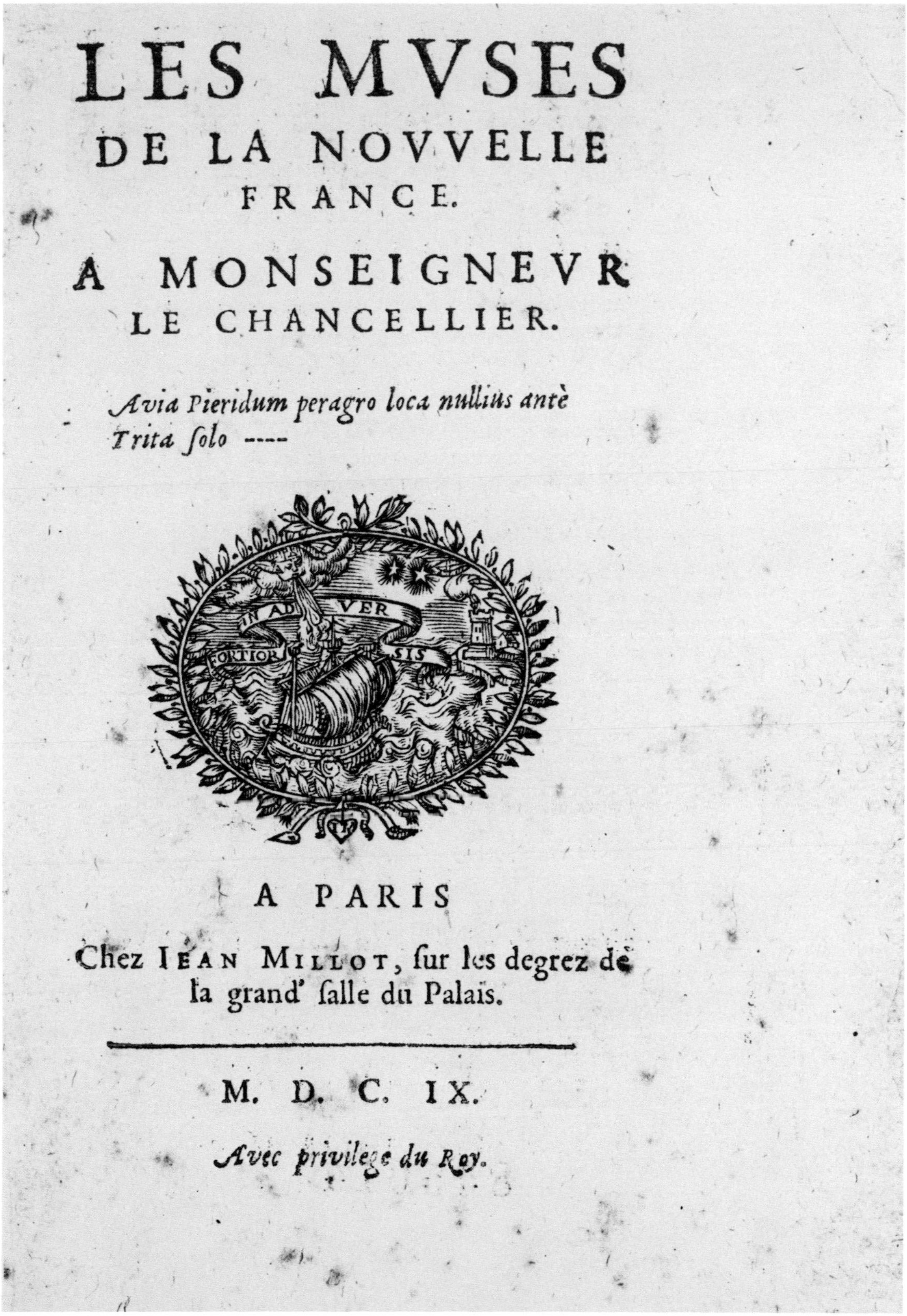

LES MVSES
DE LA NOVVELLE
FRANCE.

A MONSEIGNEVR
LE CHANCELLIER.

Avia Pieridum peragro loca nullius antè
Trita solo ----

A PARIS
Chez IEAN MILLOT, sur les degrez de
la grand' salle du Palais.

M. D. C. IX.

Avec privilege du Roy.

Marc Lescarbot. *Les mvses de la Novvelle France. A Monseignevr le chancellier.* Paris: Chez Iean Millot..., 1609, title page, pp. 11, 17.

"Le théâtre de Neptune en la Nouvelle-France," a play written for the occasion by Marc Lescarbot, was presented at Port-Royal on 14 November 1606. It was the first theatrical performance in North America.

LE THEATRE DE NEPTVNE EN LA NOVVELLE-FRANCE

Repreſenté ſur les flots du Port Royal le quatorziéme de Novembre mille ſix cens ſix, au retour du Sieur de Poutrincourt du païs des Armouchiquois.

Neptune commence revetu d'vn voile de couleur bleuë, & de brodequins, ayant la chevelure & la barbe longues & chenuës, tenant ſon Trident en main, aſſis ſur ſon chariot paré de ſes couleurs : ledit chariot trainé ſur les ondes par ſix Tritons juſques à l'abord de la chaloupe où s'eſtoit mis ledit Sieur de Poutrincourt & ſes gens ſortant de la barque pour venir à terre. Lors ladite chaloupe accrochée, Neptune commence ainſi.

NEPTVNE.

ARRETE, Sagamos, * *arréte toy ici,*
Et écoutes vn Dieu qui a de toy ſouci.
Si tu ne me conois, Saturne fut mon pere,
Ie ſuis de Iupiter & de Pluton le frere.

*C'eſt vn mot de Sauvage, qui ſignifie Capitaine.

DEVXIEME SAVVAGE.

Le deuziéme Sauvage tenant ſon arc & ſa fleche en main, donne pour ſon preſent des peaux de Caſtors, diſant:

Voici la main, l'arc, & la fleche
Qui ont fait la mortele breche
En l'animal de qui la peau
Pourra ſervir d'vn bon manteau
(Grand Sagamos*) à ta hauteſſe.*
Reçoy donc de ma petiteſſe
Cette offrande qu'à ta grandeur
I'offre du meilleur de mon cœur.

Bibliothèque de la ville de Montréal, Salle Gagnon, Montréal.

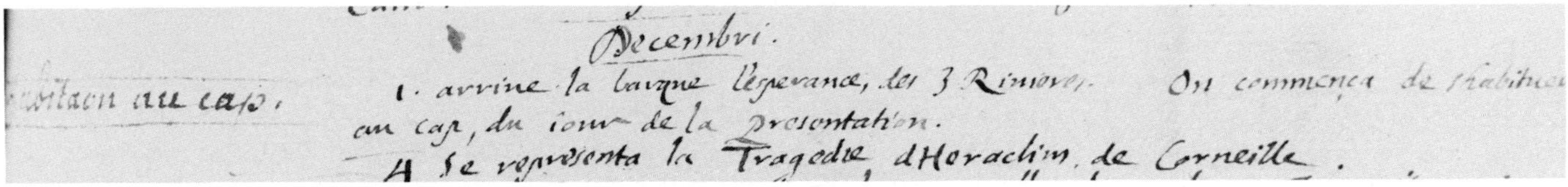

…itacion au cap.

Decembre.

1. arrive la barque lesperance, des 3 Rivieres. On commence de s'habituer au cap, du iour de la presentation.

4 se representa la Tragedie d'Heraclius, de Corneille.

Extract from the *Journal des Jésuites* making mention of the performance of Corneille's tragedy *Héraclius*, 4 December 1651.

"On the 4th Corneille's tragedy *Héraclius* was performed."

Archives du Séminaire de Québec, Québec: Journal des Jésuites, MS-48.

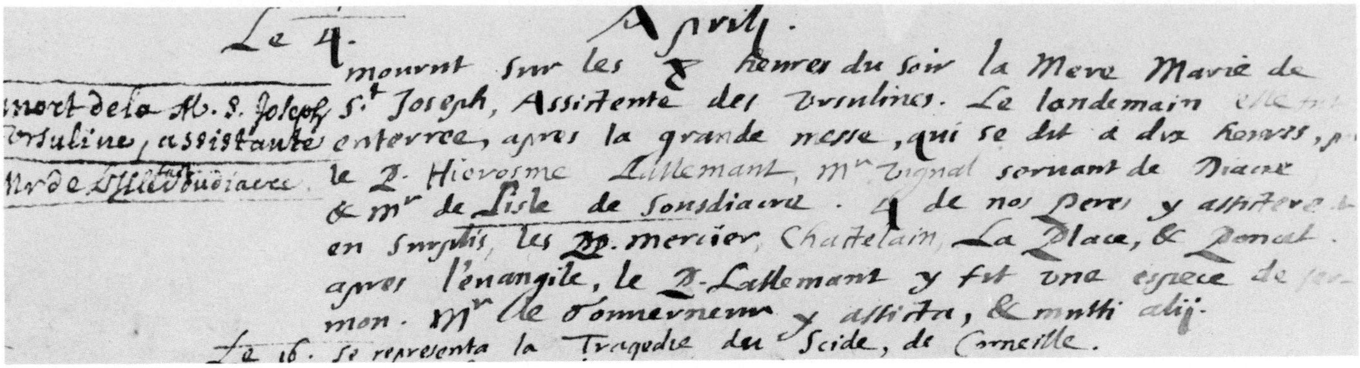

Le 4. Avril.

mort de la M. S. Joseph Ursuline, assistante

mourut sur les 8 heures du soir la Mere Marie de St Joseph, Assistente des Ursulines. Le landemain elle fut enterree, apres la grande messe, qui se dit a dix heures, p... le P. Hierosme Lallemant, Mr Vignal servant de Diacre & Mr de Lisle de Soudiacre. 4 de nos peres y assisterent en Surplis, les PP. mercier, Chastelain, La Place, & Poncet. apres l'evangile, le P. Lallemant y fit une espece de sermon. Mr le Gouverneur y assista, & multi alij.

Le 16. se representa la Tragedie du Scide, de Corneille.

Extract from the *Journal des Jésuites* mentioning the performance of Corneille's *Le Cid,* 16 April 1652.

"On the 16th Corneille's tragedy *Le Cid* was performed."

Archives du Séminaire de Québec, Québec: Journal des Jésuites, MS-48.

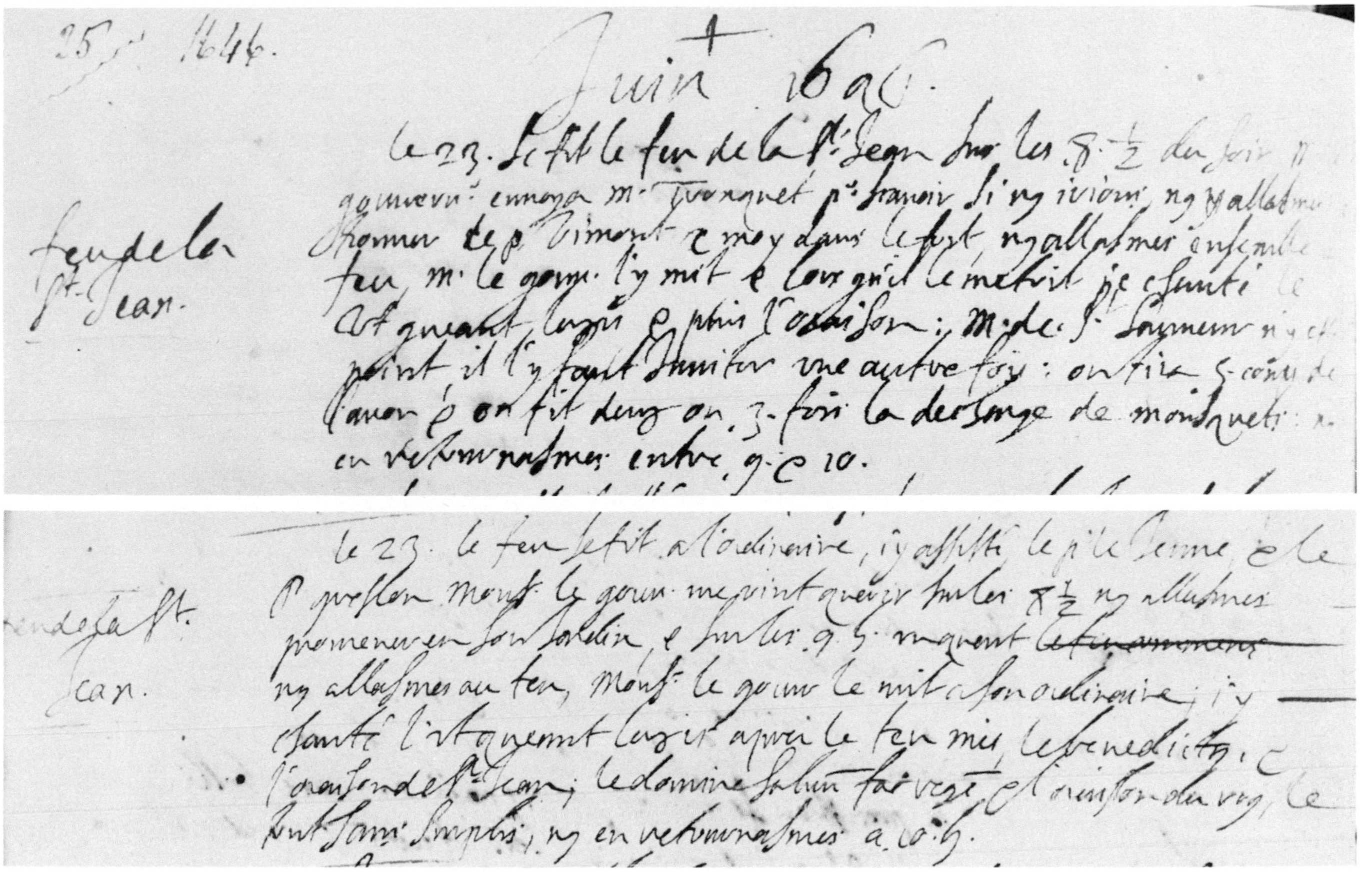

Extracts from the *Journal des Jésuites* concerning the bonfires for the feast of St. John, 23 June 1646 and 23 June 1648.

"On the 23rd the bonfire for the feast of St. John was held at half past eight in the evening. ... The governor lit it. ... Five cannon shots were fired, and muskets were fired two or three times."

This bonfire was lit every year on the evening of 23 June.

Archives du Séminaire de Québec, Québec: Journal des Jésuites, MS-48, pp. 25, 62.

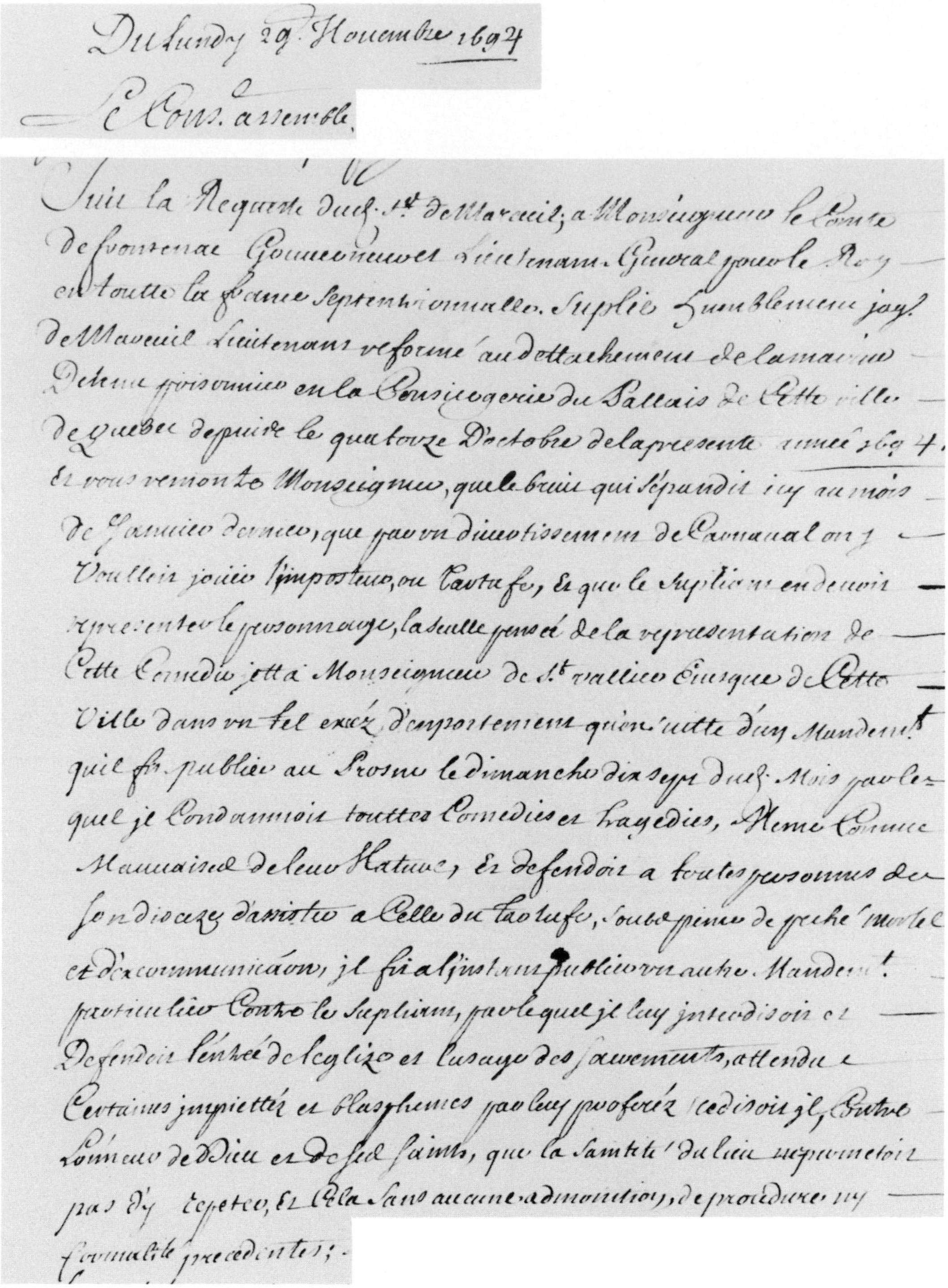

Du Lundy 29e Novembre 1694

Le Cons.e assemblé.

Veu la Requeste dud. S.r de Mareuil, a Monseigneur le Comte de Frontenac Gouverneur et Lieutenant General pour le Roy en toutte la france Septentrionnalle. Suplie humblement jacq.s de Mareuil Lieutenant reformé au detachement de la marine Detenu prisonnier en la Conciergerie du Pallais de cette ville de Quebec depuis le quatorze D'octobre de la presente année 1694. Et vous remonstre Monseigneur, que le bruit qui se repandit icy au mois de Janvier dernier, que par un divertissement de Carnaval on y vouloit jouer l'imposture, ou Tartufe, et que le Supliant en devoit representer le personnage, la seulle pensée de la representation de cette Comedie jetta Monseigneur de St vallier Evesque de cette Ville dans un tel excez d'emportement qu'on vitte deux Mandem.ts qu'il fit publier au Prosne le dimanche dix sept dud. Mois par lez quel il Condamnoit touttes Comedies et tragedies, Meme Comme Mauvaise de leur Nature, et defendoit a toutes personnes de son dioceze d'assister a celle du tartufe, soubz peine de peché mortel et d'excommunication, il fit a l'instant publier un autre Mandem.t particulier Contre le Supliant, par lequel il luy interdisoit et Defendoit l'entrée de l'eglize et l'usage des sacrements, attendu certaines impietéz et blasphemes par luy proferez (ce disoit il) Contre l'honneur de Dieu et de ses saints, que la sainteté du lieu ne permettoit pas d'y repeter, et cela sans aucune admonition, de procedure ny formalitéz precedentes;

Deliberations of the Conseil souverain on the affair of Molière's *Tartuffe,* Québec, 29 November 1694.

The officer Mareuil was complaining of two pastorals from the bishop of Québec, one of which "forbade him to enter the church or take communion," the other which "condemned all comedies and tragedies as being bad by their nature, and forbade everyone in his diocese to attend *Tartuffe,* on pain of mortal sin and excommunication."

Archives nationales du Québec, Centre d'archives de la Capitale, Québec: Jugements et délibérations du Conseil souverain, vol. 10, fol. 64–65.

VII

Charitable institutions

According to the authorities of New France, the Hôtel-Dieu de Québec was an absolutely indispensable institution: settlers who were ill, wounded soldiers, and travellers who too often landed at Québec suffering from contagious maladies after two or three months aboard ship were taken care of there.

The Hôtel-Dieu de Montréal rendered settlers and soldiers the same services as did that of Québec. The two institutions, which were often overwhelmed by the number of patients, were among the poorest in the colony; governors and intendants begged the king to come to their aid.

At the end of the century there were many people in need; people could be seen begging all over the place. In 1688 the Conseil souverain created in each of the three towns in the colony an office of the needy which had the task of coming to the aid of those who were truly poor, so as to make idlers get themselves into a position to provide for their own keep.

But an institution was needed that could take in poor people who were suffering from chronic illnesses and old people without support. In 1693 Bishop Saint-Vallier founded the Hôpital-Général de Québec to help them; one year later the bishop also contributed to the founding of a similar institution in Montréal, which was placed under the direction of the Brothers Hospitallers of the Cross and of St. Joseph (frères hospitaliers de la Croix ou de Saint-Joseph, ou frères Charon).

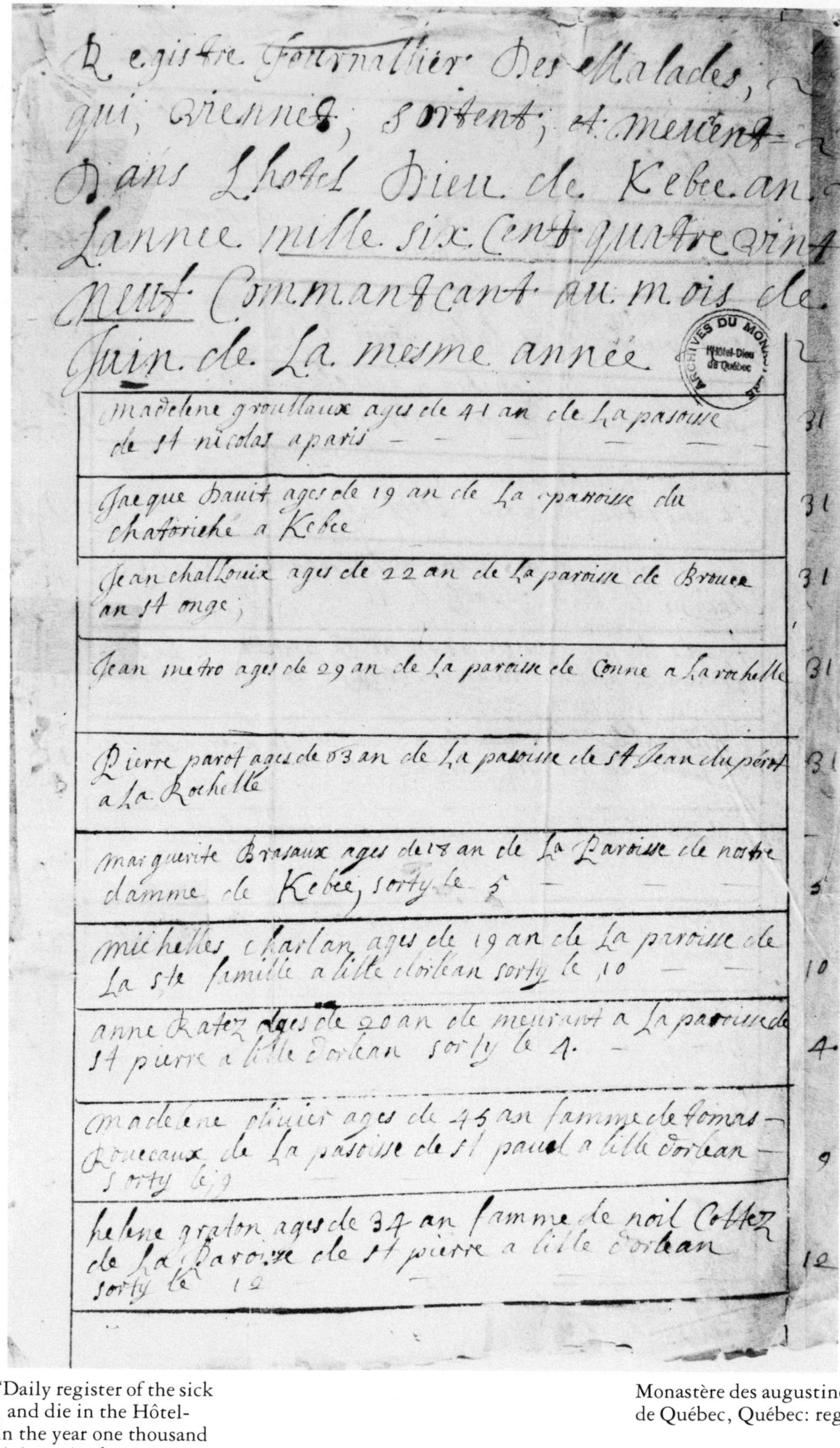

Registre Journallier Des Malades, qui viennent, sortent, et meurent Dans Lhotel Dieu de Kebec an Lannee mille six Cent quatre vin neuf Commancant au mois de Juin de La mesme année

madelene groullaux ages de 41 an de La parouse de st nicolas a paris	31
Jacque Davit ages de 19 an de La paroisse du chatoriche a Kebec	31
Jean challouix ages de 22 an de La paroisse de Brouce an st onge;	31
Jean metro ages de 29 an de La paroisse de Conne a La rochelle	31
Pierre parot ages de 53 an de La pasoisse de st Jean du pérot a La Rochelle	31
marguerite Brasaux ages de 18 an de La Paroisse de notre damme de Kebec, sorty le 5	5
michelles charlan ages de 19 an de La paroisse de La ste famille a lille dorlean sorty le 10	10
anne Ratez ages de 20 an de meurant a La paroisse de st pierre a lille dorlean sorty le 4.	4.
madelene olivier ages de 45 an famme de tomas Rousseaux de La pasoisse de st paul a lille dorlean sorty le 9	9
heline graton ages de 34 an famme de noil Cottez de La Paroisse de st pierre a lille dorlean sorty le 12	12

First page of the "Daily register of the sick who come, leave, and die in the Hôtel-Dieu de Québec in the year one thousand six hundred and eighty-nine beginning in the month of June of the same year."

Monastère des augustines de l'Hôtel-Dieu de Québec, Québec: registre des malades.

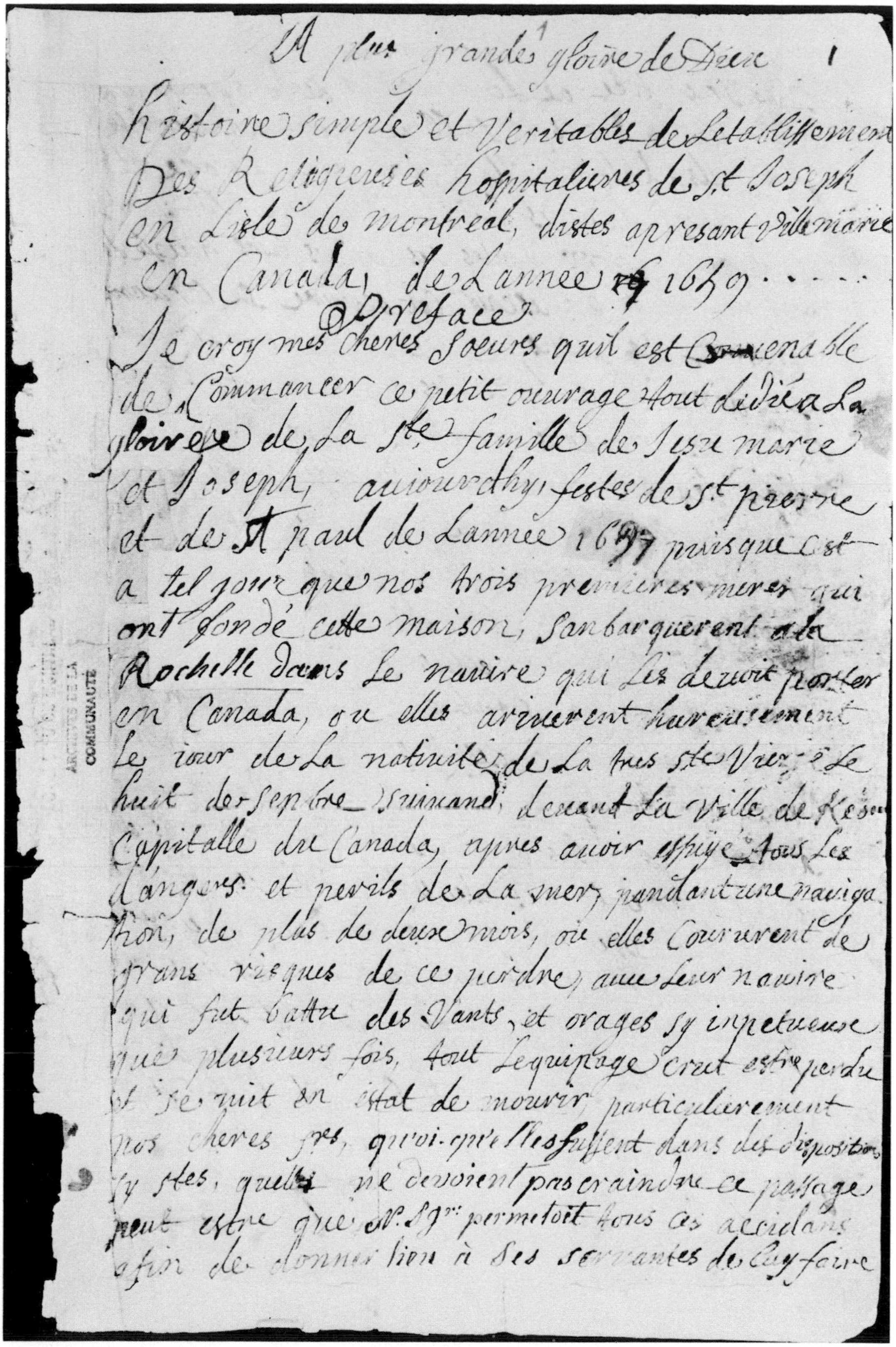

A plus grande gloire de Dieu 1

histoire simple et veritables de Letablissement
Des Religieuses hospitalieres de St Joseph
en Lisle de montreal, distes apresant ville marie
en Canada, de Lannee 1659 . . . .

Preface

Je croy mes cheres Soeurs quil est convenable
de Commancer ce petit ouvrage tout dedie a La
gloire de La Ste famille de Jesu marie
et Joseph, aujourdhuy festes de St pierre
et de St paul de Lannee 1697 puisque cest
a tel jour que nos trois premieres meres qui
ont fondé cette maison, sanbarquerent a La
Rochelle dans Le navire qui Les devoit porter
en Canada, ou elles arriverent heureusement
Le jour de La nativité de La tres Ste Vierge Le
huit de septembre suivant devant La ville de Kebec
Capitalle du Canada, apres avoir essuyé tous Les
dangers et perils de La mer, pandant une naviga
tion, de plus de deux mois, ou elles coururent de
grans risques de ce perdre, avec Leur navire
qui fut battu des vants, et orages sy impetueuse
que plusieurs fois, tout Lequipage crut estre perdu
et se mit en estat de mourir particulierement
nos cheres Srs, quoi quelles fussent dans des dispositions
sy stes, quelles ne devoient pas craindre ce passage
peut estre que Mr Sgr permetoit tous ces accidans
afin de donner lieu a ses servantes de luy faire

"Simple and true history of the establishment of the Nuns Hospitallers of St. Joseph on Montréal Island, now called Ville-Marie, in Canada, in the year 1659," by Sister Marie Morin, 1697–1725.

Marie Morin was the first nun of Canadian origin. In her history she recounts the arrival of the first nuns hospitallers who established themselves in the Hôtel-Dieu de Montréal, a hospital that had been founded by Jeanne Mance.

Religieuses hospitalières de Saint-Joseph, Montréal.

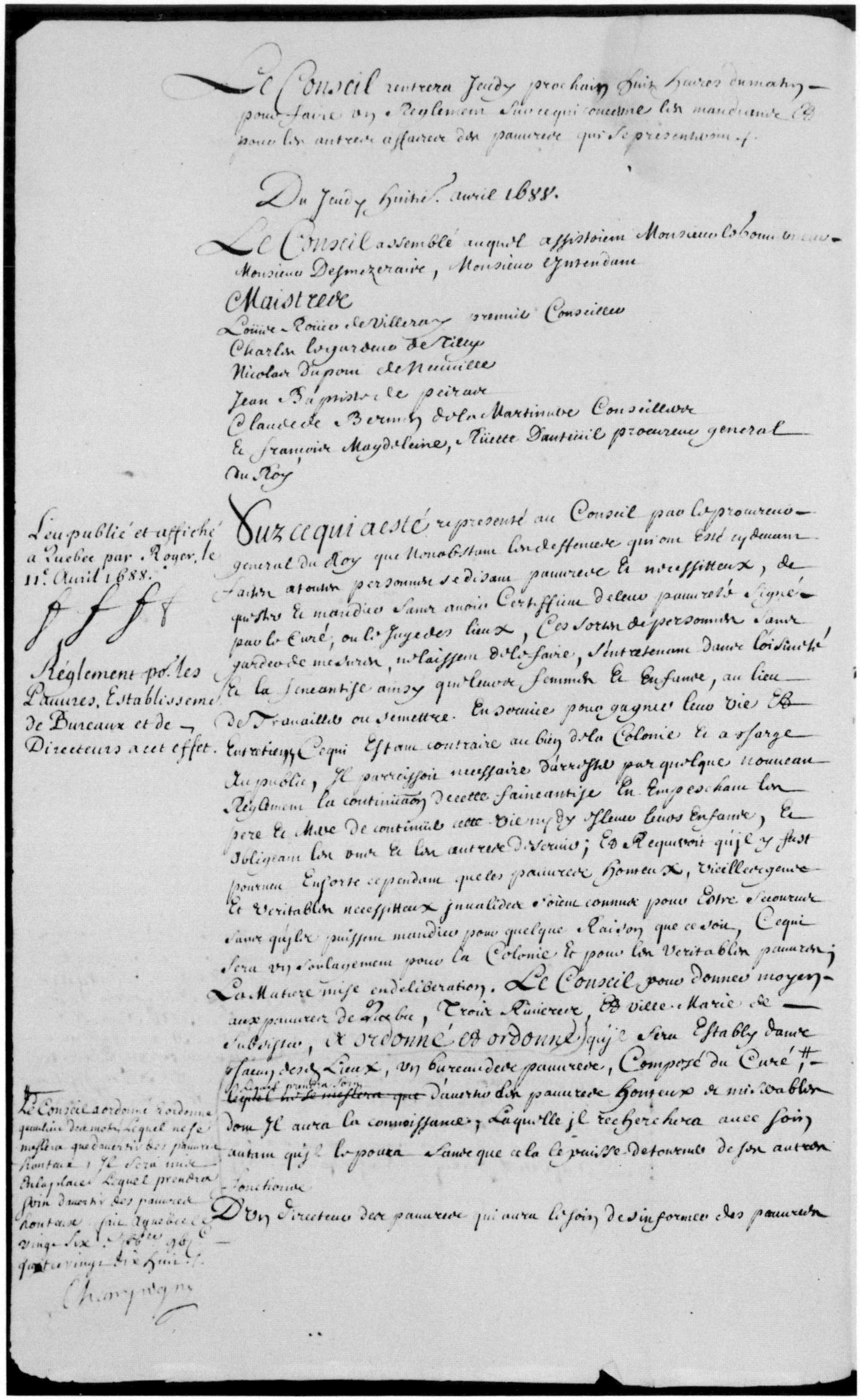
Le Conseil rentrera Jeudy prochain huit heures du matin pour faire un reglement sur ce qui concerne les mandiants et pour les autres affaires des pauvres qui se presenteront.

Du Jeudy huitie. avril 1688.

Le Conseil assemblé auquel assistoient Monsieur le Gouverneur, Monsieur Desmezeraire, Monsieur l'Intendant

Maistres
Louis Rouer de Villeray premier Conseiller
Charles Legardeur de Tilly
Nicolas Dupont de Neuville
Jean Baptiste de peiras
Claude de Bermen de la Martiniere Conseiller
Et François Magdeleine Ruette Dauteuil procureur general du Roy

Leu publié et affiché a Quebec par Roger, le 11e Avril 1688.

Réglement po. les Pauvres, Establissement de Bureaux et de Directeurs a cet effet.

Sur ce qui a esté representé au Conseil par le procureur general du Roy que nonobstant les deffenses qui ont esté cy devant faites a toutes personnes se disant pauvres et necessiteux, de quester et mandier sans avoir certificat de leur pauvreté signé par le Curé, ou les Juges des lieux, Ces sortes de personnes sans garder de mesures, ne laissent de le faire, s'entretenant dans l'oisiveté et la faineantise ainsy que leurs femmes et enfants, au lieu de travailler ou se mettre en service pour gagner leur vie et entretien, Ce qui estant contraire au bien de la Colonie et a charge au public, il paroissoit necessaire d'arrester par quelque nouveau Reglement la continuation de cette faineantise en empeschant les pere et mere de continuer cette vie ny d'y eslever leurs enfants, et obligeant les uns et les autres de servir; Et requeroit qu'il y fust pourveu en sorte cependant que les pauvres honteux, vieilles gens et veritables necessiteux invalides soient connus pour estre secourus sans qu'ils puissent mandier pour quelque raison que ce soit, Ce qui sera un soulagement pour la Colonie et pour les veritables pauvres; La matiere mise en deliberation. Le Conseil pour donner moyen aux pauvres de Quebec, Trois Rivieres et Ville Marie de subsister, a ordonné et ordonne qu'il sera estably dans chacun desd. Lieux, un bureau des pauvres, Composé du Curé, d'un [illegible] des pauvres honteux et miserables dont il aura la connoissance, Laquelle il recherchera avec soin autant qu'il le poura sans que cela le puisse detourner de ses autres fonctions

D'un Directeur des pauvres qui aura le soin de s'informer des pauvres

Champigny

Decree by the Conseil souverain for setting up offices of the needy in the towns, Québec, 8 April 1688.

"To give the poor in Québec, Trois-Rivières, and Ville-Marie the means to subsist, the council has ordered and orders that an office of the needy will be set up in each of the aforementioned places."

Archives nationales du Québec, Centre d'archives de la Capitale, Québec: Jugements et délibérations du Conseil souverain, vol. 7, fol. 8.

Portrait of Bishop Jean-Baptiste de La Croix de Chevrières de Saint-Vallier (1653–1727); artist unknown; oil; circa 1699; 80.4 x 64.4 cm.

Bishop Saint-Vallier directed the diocese of Québec from 1688 to 1727.

Monastère des augustines de l'Hôpital-Général de Québec, Québec.

VII

The Indians

The Indians were completely adapted to their natural environment. In the northern regions, which were not suited to agriculture but were rich with game, they had adopted a nomadic existence; farther south, for just the opposite reasons they had adopted a semi-sedentary way of life – thanks especially to the growing of corn. Moreover, there was a regular north-south exchange of products.

Whether they were nomadic or semi-sedentary, the Indians had an organized political life: like the Huron or Iroquois tribes, the Algonkin band had its chiefs and held councils. Wonderful orators were to be heard at these occasions who compelled the admiration of the most cultured white men. The Indians were also excellent diplomats; they treated with the neighbouring tribes and concluded agreements with them that were guaranteed by the exchange of beaded necklaces and belts (wampum). These pieces of beadwork took the place of archives, since through the arrangement and colour of the beads they conveyed a precise meaning.

On the cultural side, the Indians had a particular devotion to the dead: the Hurons for example periodically celebrated the feast of the dead. In other respects they knew how to enjoy themselves; they liked to play and even played certain games, some of which have remained with us. They also like to sing, dance, and feast. They were not sad people at all, and particularly they were not as miserable as the French sometimes thought.

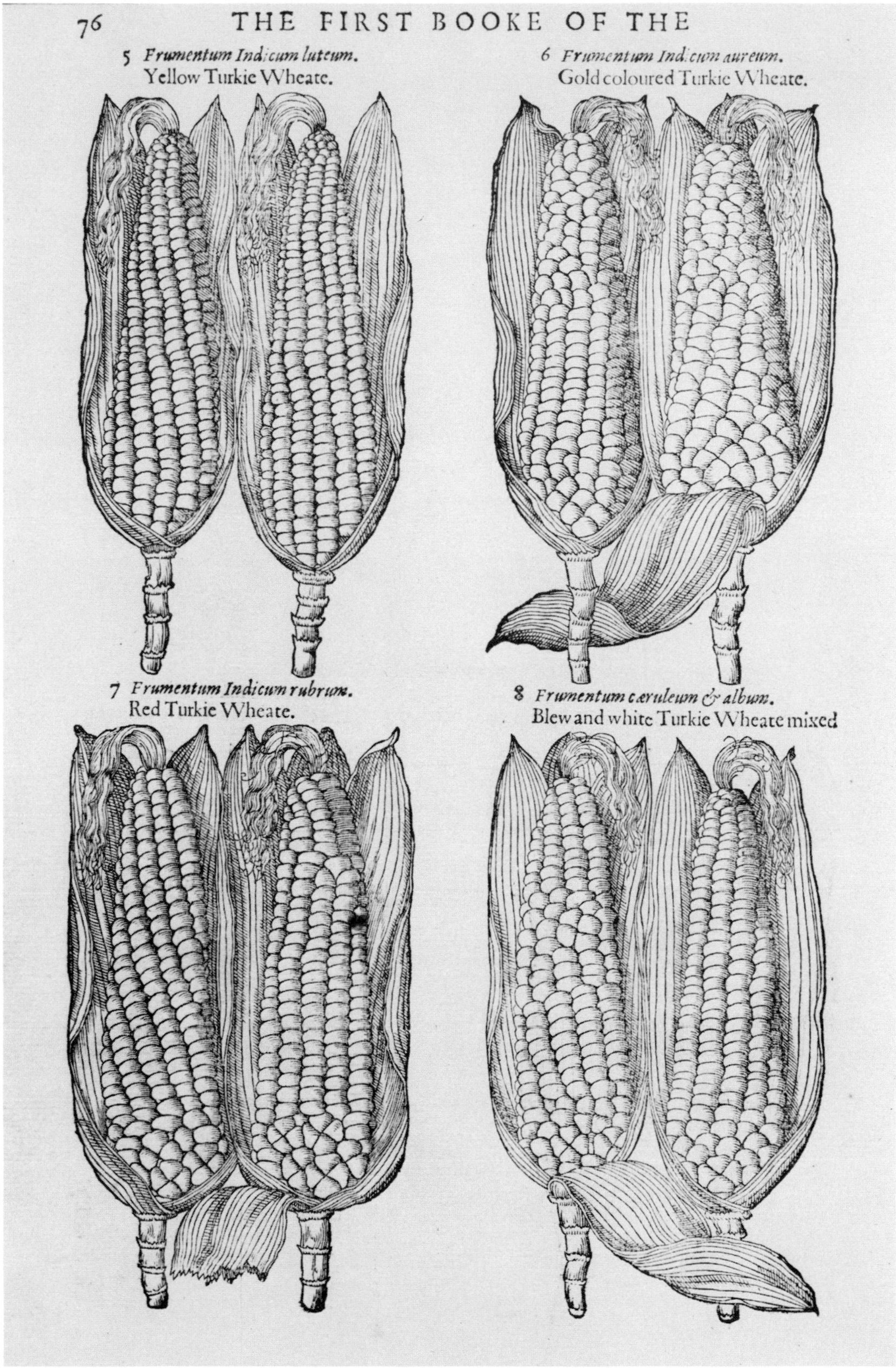

'Turkie Wheate"; woodcut, 29.5 x 21 cm. (page).

In John Gerard. *The herball; or, General historie of plantes.* London: J. Norton, 1597, p. 76.

The semi-sedentary Indians such as the Hurons and Iroquois grew pumpkins, corn, beans, and some other vegetables. They made a kind of bread with ground corn, or again, they prepared a gruel called "sagamité" to which they added pieces of meat and fish and beans.

McGill University, Osler Library, Montréal.

220

Grinding Corn; after a drawing by Samuel de Champlain (1567 [?]–1635); etching; 13.8 x 8.4 cm. (plate).

In Samuel de Champlain. *Les voyages de la Novvelle France occidentale, dicte Canada....* Paris: Pierre Le-Mur, 1632, p. 291.

Public Archives of Canada, Library, Ottawa (Negative no. C 113065).

p. 5
Capitaine de La Nation
des Illinois, Il est armé de sa pipe, et de son dard.
f 9.

Tribal Chief; Louis Nicolas (1634–after 1678); brown ink on parchment; 33.7 x 21.6 cm.

The Illinois occupied "the valleys of the Mississippi and its tributaries (Illinois River, etc.) on the east bank." They were among the main suppliers of furs to the French.

Thomas Gilcrease Institute of American History and Art, Tulsa, Oklahoma, U.S.A.

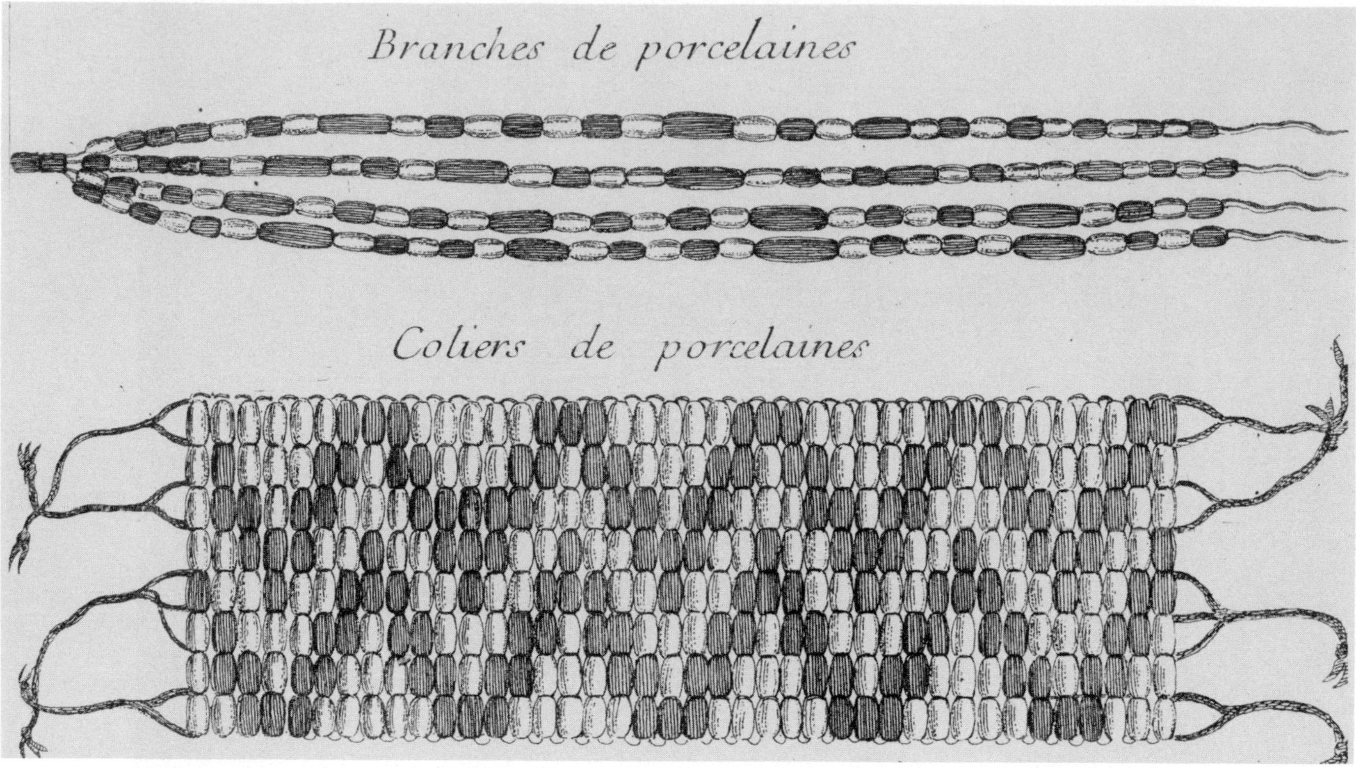

Wampum; engraved by I. B. Scotin; etching; 8.3 x 15.6 cm. (page).

In Claude Charles Le Roy Bacqueville de La Potherie. *Histoire de l'Amérique septentrionale....* Paris: J.-L. Nion & F. Didot, 1722, vol. 1, p. 334.

These sticks and strings (wampum) served as jewellery and money among the Indians. They were used regularly to transact business and conclude an agreement. For example, negotiations and treaties with other tribes were regularly conducted with exchanges of wampum. They had then a precise meaning (peace, war, friendship) according to the arrangement and colours of the beads.

Public Archives of Canada, Library, Ottawa (Negative no. C 10891).

223

Ces preſens conſiſtoient en trente mille grains de pourcelaine qu'ils avoient reduits à dix-ſept colliers qu'ils portoient partie ſur eux, & partie dans un petit ſac placé tout auprés deux. Tous étant aſſemblez & chacun aiant pris ſa place, le Grand Hiroquois (je le nomme ainſi, parce qu'il étoit d'une grande & haute taille) ſe leva, & regarda premierement le Soleil, puis aiant jetté les yeux ſur toute la compagnie, il prit un collier de Pourcelaine en ſa main, & commença ſa harangue d'une voix forte en ces termes: Onontiò, prête l'oreille à mes paroles, je ſuis la bouche de tout mon païs: Tu entend tous les Hiroquois, quand tu m'entend parler. Mon cœur n'a rien de mauvais, je n'ay que de bonnes intentions. Nous avons en nôtre païs des chanſons de guerre en grand nombre, mais nous les avons toutes jettées par terre, & nous n'avons plus aujourd'hui que des chans de rejouïſſance. Là deſſus il ſe mit à chanter, & ſes compatriotes lui répondoient. Il ſe promenoit en cette grande place, comme un acteur ſur un theatre en faiſant mille geſtes. Il regardoit le Ciel, il enviſageoit le Soleil, & il ſe frottoit les bras comme s'il en eut voulu faire ſortir la vigueur qui les anime dans les combats.

Alors il commença à exprimer ces peines, mais d'une maniere ſi naturelle, qu'il n'y a point de Comedien en France qui exprime ſi naïvement les choſes, que ce Sauvage faiſoit celles qu'il vouloit dire. Il avoit un bâton à la main qu'il mettoit ſur ſa tête pour repreſenter comme ce priſonnier portoit ſon pacquet. Il le portoit en ſuite d'un bout de la place à l'autre, pour exprimer ce qu'il avoit fait dans les ſauts & dans les courans d'eaux où étant arrivé il lui avoit fallu tranſporter ſon bagage piece à piece. Il alloit & venoit repreſentant les tours & retours de cet homme. Il feignoit heurter contre une pierre, puis il chanceloit comme dans un chemin boüeux & gliſſant. Comme s'il eut été ſeul dans un Canot, il ramoit d'un côté, & comme ſi ſon petit bâteau eut voulu tourner il ramoit de l'autre pour le redreſſer. Prenant un peu de repos il reculloit autant qu'il avoit avancé: il perdoit courage, puis il reprenoit ſes forces. En un mot, il ne ſe peut rien voir de mieux exprimé que cette action dont les mouvemens étoient accompagnez de paroles qui diſoient ce qu'il repreſentoit.

Voila ce qui ſe paſſa en cette aſſemblée, où l'on n'a peu recueillir que quelques pieces detachées de la harangue de l'Hiroquois, par la bouche de l'interprete qui n'avoit que par des intervalles la liberté de parler; mais tous conviennent que ce Sauvage étoit fort eloquent, & tres-bon acteur pour un homme qui n'a d'autre étude que ce que la nature lui a apris ſans regles & ſans preceptes. La concluſion fut que les Hiroquois, les Algonquins, les Montagnez, les Hurons, & les François danſeroient tous enſemble, & qu'ils paſſeroient la journée dans l'allegreſſe.

Mère Marie de l'Incarnation. *Lettres de la vénérable mère Marie de l'Incarnation première supérieure des Ursulines de la Nouvelle France, divisées en deux parties.* Paris: Chez Louis Billaine, 1681, pp. 396–397, 400.

Marie de l'Incarnation spoke highly of the eloquence of the Iroquois chief Kiotseaeton: "He was walking about this great place, making a thousand gestures like an actor on a stage.... Then he began to express his griefs, but in such a natural manner that there is no actor in France who expresses things so naïvely...everyone agrees that this Indian is very eloquent, and a very good actor."

Public Archives of Canada, Library, Ottawa (Negatives nos. C 113831, C 113832 and C 113835).

Ball Players; engraved by Theodor de Bry (1528–98) after Le Moyne; engraving; 15.2 x 21.2 cm. (plate).

In Theodore de Bry. [America- pt. 2. German]. *Der ander Theyl der newlich erfundenen Landtschafft Americae. ...* Francoforti ad Moenum: Typis I Wecheli, Sumptibus verso Theodori de Bry, 1591. Plate XXXVI.

The Indians knew how to amuse themselves: they liked to sing, dance, feast, practice certain sports, and gamble.

Public Archives of Canada, Library, Ottawa (Negative no. C 114192).

VIII

Religion

For the first time since Cartier, Catholic priests practised their ministry in New France at Port-Royal in 1604. The first one to play a missionary role there was Abbé Jessé Fléché, who baptized twenty-one Micmacs at Port-Royal on 24 June 1610. He was followed in 1611 by the Jesuits Pierre Biard and Énemond Massé, whose mission came to an end with Argall's attack. Later on some Recollets from Aquitaine made two short stays in Acadia.

In 1615 four Recollets from Paris arrived at Québec. While ministering to the French and keeping up a "seminary" to teach the Indians, the Recollets devoted themselves to missionary work. In 1615–16 the Huron mission was founded; in 1618–19 the mission at Tadoussac was inaugurated. In 1623 Father Joseph Le Caron again lived with the Montagnais; the following year he went up to the Huron country with two fellow religious. In the course of their apostolic work the Recollets had made a dictionary of the Huron language and two Montagnais and Algonkin dictionaries.

In 1625 three Jesuit fathers and two lay brothers came to join the Recollets at Québec. One of them, Father Jean de Brébeuf, displayed great activity. In 1625–26 he followed a group of Montagnais during the winter; in 1626 he left for the Huron country with Father Anne de Nouë. They were called back urgently in 1629, at the time of the surrender of Québec: the Recollets and Jesuits all returned to France.

After the treaty of 1632, Jesuits and Capuchins shared the mission of New France: the Capuchins carried on their work in Acadia, and the Jesuits spread out from their base in Québec – to which place the Recollets did not return until 1670 – to the whole of the continent. The Capuchins devoted themselves particularly to ministering to the French; while serving the settlers at the same time, the Jesuits displayed an intense zeal for converting the Indians. For about thirty years the mission absorbed, as it were, the colony, which received various institutions whose primary objectives were of a missionary nature.

VIII

It was Father Paul Le Jeune, the superior of the Jesuits (1632–39), who really launched missionary work in New France. To learn their language he first went with the Indians on their winter hunt. This experience suggested to him various means of carrying on the apostolate: have the nomads adopt a sedentary existence (hence the village at Sillery which was founded in 1637); care for and keep sick or elderly Indians (hence the founding of the Hôtel-Dieu de Québec in 1639); teach young Indians (hence the founding of the Ursuline "seminary" in 1639 and to some extent the founding of the Jesuit college in 1635). Through his annual *Relations* Father Le Jeune, helped by a few confrères from France, was also in a way responsible for the missionary enterprise of Ville-Marie and of the foundations (Hôtel-Dieu and Congrégation de Notre-Dame) to which it gave rise.

The missions themselves were rapidly organized. Soon there were Jesuits everywhere that there were nomads living: Algonkins, Montagnais, Attikamegues, Ottawas, etc. And in 1634 Father Brébeuf had re-opened the Huron mission. The missionaries suffered from the living conditions, the climate, the Indians' hostility. Conversions were slow in coming, particularly among the Hurons. Finally they were converted in large numbers, a few years before the destruction of their country, which was marked by the martyrdom of several Jesuits. Nevertheless, taking advantage of peaceful periods or periods of calm, missionaries went shortly afterwards to establish themselves in the heart of the Iroquois country.

At that time the Jesuit superior was still the top ecclesiastical authority in Canada, and the colony's parishes, which were still in an embryonic state, were served by Jesuits. In 1659 Bishop François Laval, the vicar apostolic in New France, arrived. The Canadian Church was finally going to be able to get itself organized from more regular bases. Secular priests, French or Canadian, gradually took over responsibility for the parishes. In 1663 during a voyage to Paris Bishop Laval set up the Séminaire de Québec, which was both a theological seminary and a community of secular priests who constituted the "clergy of this new Church." In 1668 Bishop Laval founded a petit séminaire to train future priests. In 1663 he had also instituted tithing, for the clergy's upkeep. However, Bishop Laval, a simple vicar apostolic, felt that his authority was contested; therefore he wanted to be named titular bishop of Québec, which title he obtained in 1674. From that time on the Canadian Church was no longer solely a mission church: now it was incorporated into the colony rather than embracing it, in a way, as formerly.

The bishop of Québec set up several parishes canonically and provided them with priests, most often from the secular clergy; for the parish services he sometimes used the Recollets, who had returned to Québec in 1670; he entrusted the Jesuits with looking after the missions and the Sulpicians with carrying on the ministry on Montréal Island. The missions made headway, but they were generally located near the forts and trading posts: the missionaries were less isolated and their flocks were in more direct contact with the traders, which the Jesuits deplored. All the same, in the colony, which in 1688 counted thirty-five parishes, there was not much reason to complain about the settlers, who were faithful to their religious duties even though "abuses," such as those denounced by Bishop Saint-Vallier, Bishop Laval's successor after his resignation in 1684, tended to become more numerous as the population increased. Nevertheless, thanks to its institutions and the force of character of its first bishop, the Canadian Church enjoyed, just before the end of the seventeenth century, an enviable situation. Internal difficulties emerged, however, under Bishop Saint-Vallier, particularly over the Séminaire de Québec.

VIII

The first missionaries

If he was not the first priest to land in New France, Abbé Jessé Fléché was the first who can be called a missionary. On 24 June 1610 he baptized the old Micmac chief Membertou and twenty members of his family at Port-Royal. In 1611 the Jesuits Pierre Biard and Énemond Massé succeeded Abbé Fléché, who had returned to France, at Port-Royal.

Québec was behind Port-Royal in this respect and did not receive its first missionaries, some Recollets from Paris, until 1615. We are well acquainted with their work, thanks especially to one of them, Gabriel Sagard, who put it down in two works, his *Histoire du Canada* and *Le grand voyage dv pays des Hurons*, which were published in 1632 and 1636 respectively.

In 1625 three Jesuit fathers and two lay brothers arrived to assist the Recollets of Québec. Father Charles Lalemant, who was the superior of the group, published a letter to his brother in 1627 in which he describes the morals of the Indians, of whom he did not yet see much other than the negative aspects.

The white men's first reaction was to consider the Indians as people without any religion and without morals, which, as was discovered later, was not absolutely correct. Father Jean de Brébeuf, for example, described in 1636 the feast of the dead, which was celebrated among the Hurons every twelve years. In it he saw correctly "a fairly clear sign of hope [on the part of these Indians] of a future life."

LA
CONVERSION
DES SAVVAGES
QVI ONT ESTE' BA-
PTIZE'S EN LA NOVVELLE
France, cette annee 1610.

AVEC VN BREF RECIT
du voyage du Sieur DE
POVTRINCOVRT.

A PARIS,

Chez IEAN MILLOT, tenant sa boutique sur
les degrez de la grand' Salle du Palais.

Avec Privilege du Roy.

Marc Lescarbot. *La conversion des savvages qvi ont esté baptizés en la Novvelle France, cette année 1610*.... Paris: Chez I. Millot, [1610], title page, p. 21.

Lescarbot mentions in this text the first baptisms that had been solemnly held in New France: "Membertou [a Micmac chief] is today, by the grace of God, a Christian, with all his family, having been baptized and twenty others after him, last St. John's day, 24 June" at Port-Royal.

roger ſon dæmon (qu'il appelle *Aou-
tem*) afin d'auoir nouvelle de quelque
choſe future, ou abſente: car chaque
village, ou compagnie de Sauvages,
ayant vn *Aoutmoin*, c'eſt à dire Devin,
qui fait cet office, Membertou eſt celui
qui de grande ancienneté à prattiqué
cela entre ceux parmi leſquels il a con-
verſé. Si bien qu'il eſt en credit pardeſ-
ſus tous les autres Sagamos du païs, aiāt
dés ſa jeuneſſe eſté grand Capitaine, &
parmi cela exercé l'office de Devin &
de Medecin, qui ſont les trois choſes
plus efficaces à obliger les hommes, & à
ſe rendre neceſſaire en ceſte vie humai-
ne. Or ce Membertou aujourd'huy par
la grace de Dieu eſt Chrétien avec toute ſa famille, aiant eſté baptizé, & vingt
autres apres lui, le jour ſainct Iehan dernier 24. Iuin. I'en ay lettres dudit Sieur
de Poutrincourt en datte du vnzieme
jour de Iuillet enſuivant. Ledit Membertou a eſté nommé du nom de nôtre
feu bon Roy HENRY IIII. & ſon fils
ainé du nom de Monſeigneur le Dauphin aujourd'huy nôtre Roy LOVIS
XIII. que Dieu benie. Et ainſi conſe-
quemment la femme de Membertou a

New York Public Library, Rare Books and Manuscripts Division, Astor, Lenox and Tilden Foundations, New York, New York, U.S.A.

Gabriel Sagard. *Le grand voyage dv pays des Hurons*.... Paris: Chez Denys Moreau, 1632. Cover.

In his works Brother Sagard brought out the apostolic activity of the Recollets, who in the course of the years 1615–29 set up missions in Huronia (1615–16) and among the Montagnais at Tadoussac (1618–19), while ministering at the same time to the French.

Public Archives of Canada, Library, Ottawa (Negative no. C 113480).

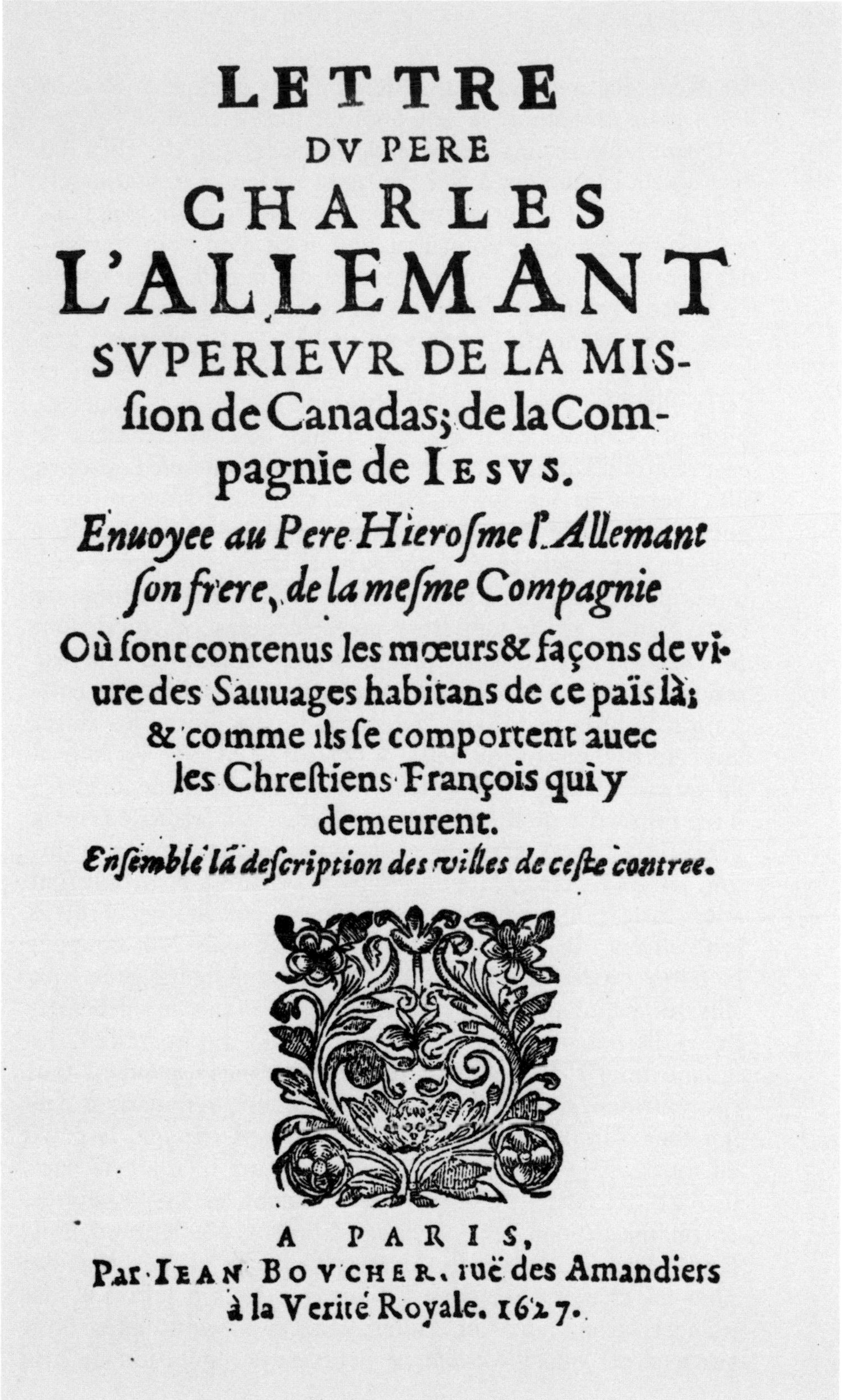

LETTRE
DV PERE
CHARLES
L'ALLEMANT
SVPERIEVR DE LA MIS-
ſion de Canadas; de la Com-
pagnie de IESVS.
Enuoyee au Pere Hieroſme l'Allemant ſon frere, de la meſme Compagnie
Où ſont contenus les mœurs & façons de vi-
ure des Sauuages habitans de ce païs là;
& comme ils ſe comportent auec
les Chreſtiens François qui y
demeurent.
Enſemble la deſcription des villes de ceſte contree.

A PARIS,
Par IEAN BOVCHER, ruë des Amandiers
à la Verité Royale. 1627.

Charles Lalemant. *Lettre dv pere Charles L'Allemant svperievr de la mission de Canadas, de la Compagnie de Iesvs.* ... Paris: Iean Bovcher, 1627, title page, p. 6.

The Jesuits arrived in Canada in 1625. Their superior, Father Lalemant, could scarcely see anything but the negative aspects of the Indians' customs: "They have no concern other than to fill their stomachs...the vices of the flesh are very frequent among them...they are very dirty in their eating and in their lodges...."

6

ſtre Reuerēce me fera plaiſir de conſulter quelqu'vn de nos Peres pour en ſçauoir la reſolution & me l'eſcrire.

Quant aux façons de faire des Sauuages, c'eſt aſſez de dire qu'elles ſont tout à fait ſauuages. Depuis le matin iuſques au ſoir, ils n'ont autre ſoucy que de remplir leur ventre. Ils ne viennent point nous voir ſi ce n'eſt pour demander à manger, & ſi vous ne leur en donnez ils teſmoignent du meſcontentement. Ils ſont de vrais gueux ſ'il en fut iamais, & neantmoins ſuperbes au poſſible. Ils eſtiment que les François n'ont point d'eſprit au prix d'eux; les vices de la chair ſont fort frequēts chez eux ; tel qui y eſpouſera pluſieurs femmes qu'il quittera quand bon luy ſemblera & en prendra d'autres. Il y en a icy vn qui a eſpouſé ſa propre fille, mais tous les autres Sauuages s'en ſont trouuez indignez ; de netteté chez eux il ne s'en parle point, ils ſont fort ſales en leur manger & dans leurs cabanes, ont force vermine qu'ils mangent quand ils l'ont priſe. La couſtume de cette Nation eſt de tuër leurs peres & meres lors qu'ils ſont ſi vieux qu'ils ne peuuēt plus marcher, penſans en cela leur rendre de bons ſeruices ; car autrement ils ſeroient contraints de mourir de faim, ne pouuans plus ſuiure les autres lors qu'ils changent de lieu; & comme ie fis dire vn iour à vn qu'on luy en feroit autant lors qu'il ſeroit deuenu vieil ; il me reſpondit qu'il ſ'y attendoit bien. La façon de faire la guerre auec leurs ennemis c'eſt pour l'ordinaire par trahiſon, les allans eſpier lors qu'ils ſont à l'eſcart ; & s'ils ne ſont aſſez forts pour emmener priſonniers ceux ou celuy qu'ils rencontrent, ils tirent des fleches deſſus, puis leur couppēt la teſte, qu'ils emportent pour monſtrer à leurs gens, que s'ils les peuuent emmener priſonniers iuſques en leurs cabanes ils leur font endurer des cruautez nompareilles, les faiſant mourir à petit feu : & choſe eſtrange ! pendant tous ces tourmens, le patient chante touſiours, reſputans à deſhonneur ſ'ils crient & s'ils ſe plaignent Apres que le patiēt eſt mort, ils le mangent, & ny a ſi petit qui n'en ait ſa part, ils font des feſtins auſquels ils ſe conuient les vns les autres, & meſme ils conuient quelques François de leur cognoiſſance, & en ces feſtins ils donnent à chacun ſa part dans des plats ou eſcuelles d'eſcorce & lors que ce ſont feſtins à tout manger, il ne faut rien laiſſer, autrement vous eſtes obligez à payer quelque choſe, & perdriez la reputation de bra-

Public Archives of Canada, Library, Ottawa (Negatives nos. C 113056 and C 113061).

Huron Burial Ceremony; after a drawing by Samuel de Champlain (1567 [?]-1635); etching; 13.8 x 8.2 cm. (plate).

In Samuel de Champlain. *Les voyages de la Novvelle France occidentale, dicte Canada....* Paris: Pierre Le-Mur, 1632, p. 304.

Champlain described the feast of the dead, which was celebrated every twelve years among the Hurons: they exhumed "all the bones of the dead, ...feasted and danced continually during the ten days that the festival lasted, ...they contracted a new bond of friendship among themselves, saying that the bones of their relatives and friends are there to be put all together, ...they dig a big pit measuring sixty square feet in which they put the said bones with necklaces and chains of beads, hatchets, cooking pots, sword blades, knives, and other small things."

Public Archives of Canada, Library, Ottawa (Negative no. C 113747).

VIII

The era of the martyrs

After they had returned to Québec in 1632, the Jesuits launched headlong into the missionary adventure. Now, the bands that frequently visited the region of Québec were nomadic. Father Paul Le Jeune decided to go with them on their winter hunts. For him the winter of 1633–34 was a constant martyrdom.

Their apostolic zeal rapidly impelled the missionaries towards the western tribes: the Hurons, the Neutrals, the Ottawas, etc. The beginnings were very arduous and progress was very slow; then there was a breakthrough, with all the tribes showing themselves to be favourably disposed towards Christianity, as Marie de l'Incarnation testified in 1641.

Nowhere had the successes been greater than in Huronia, the most splendid of the Indian churches in New France. Father François-Joseph Bressani, who had been horribly mutilated after being taken prisoner by the Iroquois, was affected to that church for eight years. The map that he made in 1657 is a sort of résumé of the history of that mission, which ended in fire and blood, with the martyrdom of several Jesuits and the killing of numerous Hurons, who were massacred by the Iroquois.

Of the Jesuits, Jean de Brébeuf and Gabriel Lalemant were particularly cruelly tortured. A witness has described in an especially moving letter their sufferings and their superhuman courage.

229

Relation de la Nouuelle France,

Eſtans arriuez au lieu où nous deuions camper, les femmes alloient couper les perches pour dreſſer la cabane, les hommes vuidoient la neige, comme ie l'ay plus amplement déduit au Chapitre precedent : or il falloit trauailler à ce baſtiment, ou bien trembler de froid trois groſſes heures ſur la neige en attendant qu'il fut fait, ie mettois par fois la main à l'œuure pour m'échauffer, mais i'eſtois pour l'ordinaire tellement glacé que le feu ſeul me pouuoit dégeler ; les Sauuages en eſtoient eſtonnez car ils ſuoient ſoubs le trauail, leur témoignant quelquefois que i'auois grād

froid, ils me diſoient, donne tes mains que nous voyons ſi tu dis vray, & les trouuans toutes glacées, touchez de compaſſion ils me donnoient leurs mitaines échauffées, & prenoient les miennes toutes froides : iuſque là que mō hoſte apres auoir experimenté cecy pluſieurs fois, me dit *Nicanis* n'hyuerne plus auec les Sauuages, car ils te tuëront ; il vouloit dire, comme ie penſe, que ie tōberois malade & que ne pouuant eſtre traiſné auec le bagage, qu'on me feroit mourir, ie me mis à rire, & luy reparty qu'il me vouloit épouuenter.

La cabane eſtant faite, ou ſur la nuit, ou vn peu deuant, on parloit de diſner & de ſouper tout enſemble : car ſortant le matin apres auoir mangé vn petit morceau, il falloit auoir patience qu'on fut arriué & que l'hoſtellerie fuſt faite pour y loger, & pour y manger, mais le pis eſtoit que ce iour là nos gens n'allans point ordinairement à la chaſſe, c'eſtoit pour nous vn iour de ieuſne auſſi bien qu'vn iour de trauail.

Paul Le Jeune. *Relation de ce qvi s'est passé en la Nouvelle France, en l'année 1634.* Paris: Chez Sébastien Cramoisy, 1635, pp. 246–247.

Father Le Jeune, who accompanied a group of Montagnais during their winter hunt (1633–34), revealed just how painful their nomadic life was for him: "I was ordinarily so chilled that only the fire could thaw me out. . . ."

Library of Parliament, Ottawa.

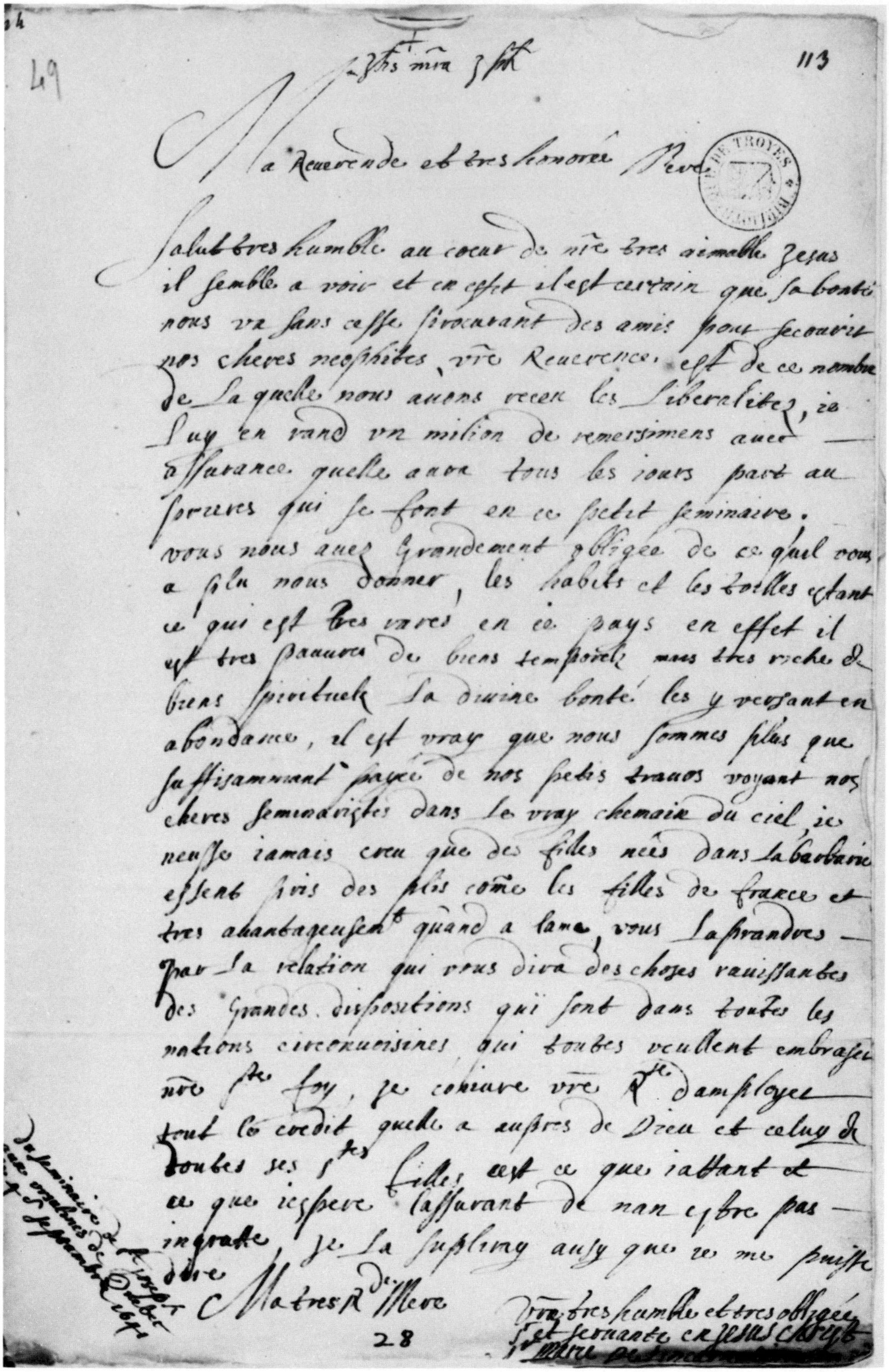

Letter from Marie de l'Incarnation to the Reverend Mother Catherine-Agnès de Saint-Paul, abbess of Port-Royal, Québec, 4 September 1641.

Marie de l'Incarnation testified to the favourable dispositions of many Indians towards Christianity. "You will learn of it from the account which will tell you wonderful things about the great dispositions which exist in all the surrounding tribes who all want to embrace our holy faith."

Bibliothèque municipale, Troyes, France: Manuscrit 2196, fol. 113.

Novae Franciae Accurata Delineatio 1657, [Rome]; F.G. Bressani; Map printed from copperplate, 52.7 x 77.8 cm.

This map, which is attributed to the Jesuit François-Joseph Bressani, depicts the Huron missions on Lake Huron and the martyrdom endured by certain missionaries who had fallen into the hands of the Iroquois. This missionary witnessed the destruction by the Iroquois of the Huron missions.

Bibliothèque nationale, Départment des cartes et plans, Paris, France: Ge DD 2987 B(8580).

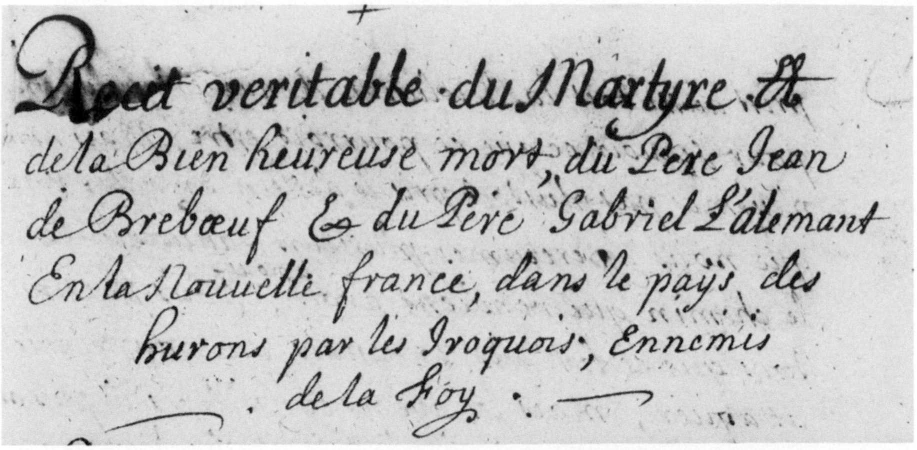
Recit veritable du Martyre et
de la Bien heureuse mort, du Pere Jean
de Brebœuf & du Pere Gabriel Lalemant
En la Nouvelle france, dans le pays des
hurons par les Iroquois, Ennemis
de la Foy.

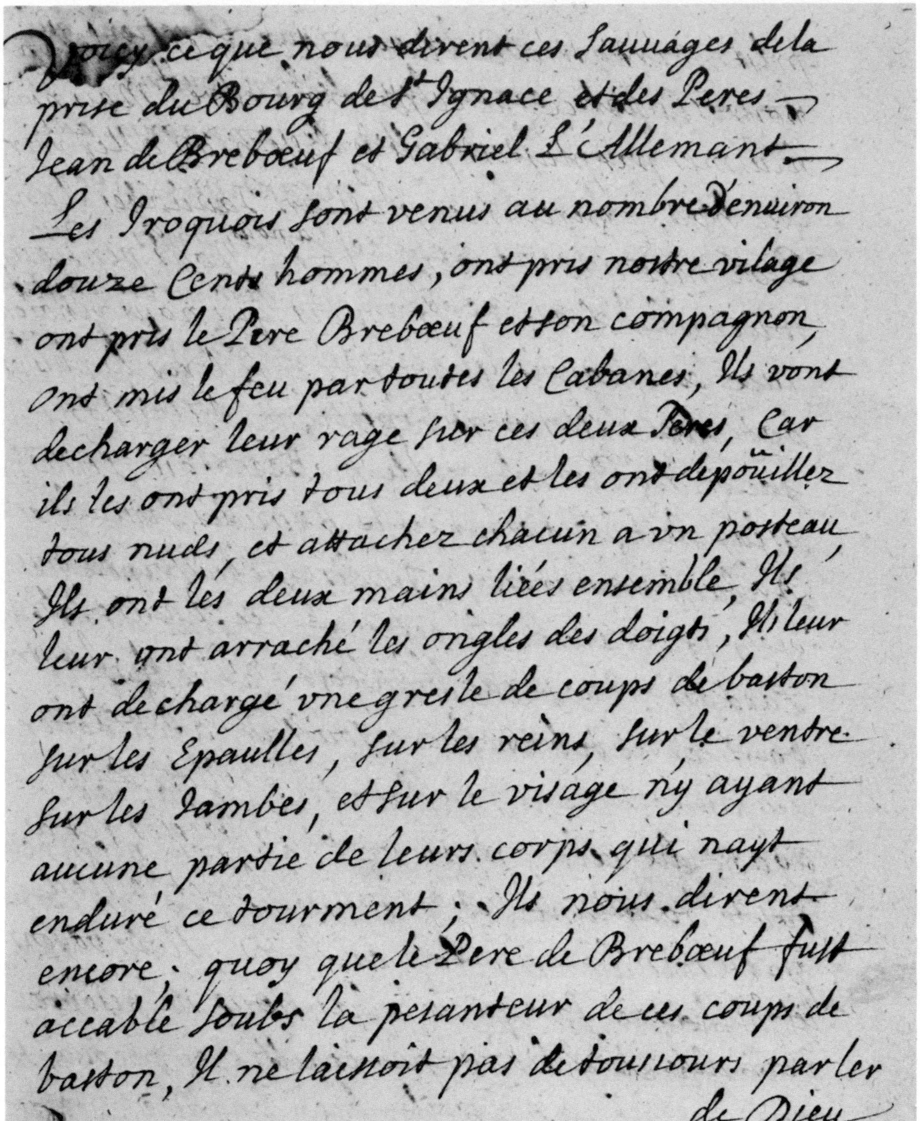
Voicy ce que nous dirent ces Sauvages de la
prise du Bourg de St Ignace et des Peres
Jean de Breboeuf et Gabriel L'Allemant.
Les Iroquois sont venus au nombre d'environ
douze Cents hommes, ont pris nostre vilage
ont pris le Pere Brebœuf et son compagnon,
ont mis le feu par toutes les Cabanes, Ils vont
decharger leur rage sur ces deux Peres, Car
ils les ont pris tous deux et les ont depoüillez
tous nuds, et attachez chacun a vn posteau
Ils ont les deux mains liées ensemble, Ils
leur ont arraché les ongles des doigts, Ils leur
ont dechargé vne greile de coups de baston
sur les Epaulles, sur les reins, sur le ventre
sur les Jambes, et sur le visage n'y ayant
aucune partie de leurs corps qui nayt
enduré ce tourment. Ils nous dirent
encore quoy que le Pere de Brebœuf fust
accablé soubs la pesanteur de ces coups de
baston, Il ne laissoit pas de tousiours parler
de Dieu

Account of the martyrdom of the Jesuits Jean de Brébeuf and Gabriel Lalemant at the hands of the Iroquois in 1649, written by Brother Christophe Regnault, around 1678.

Despite his sufferings Father Brébeuf "did not cease speaking of God and encouraging all the new Christians, who were captives as he was, to endure their sufferings, in order to die well so that they might go with him to paradise."

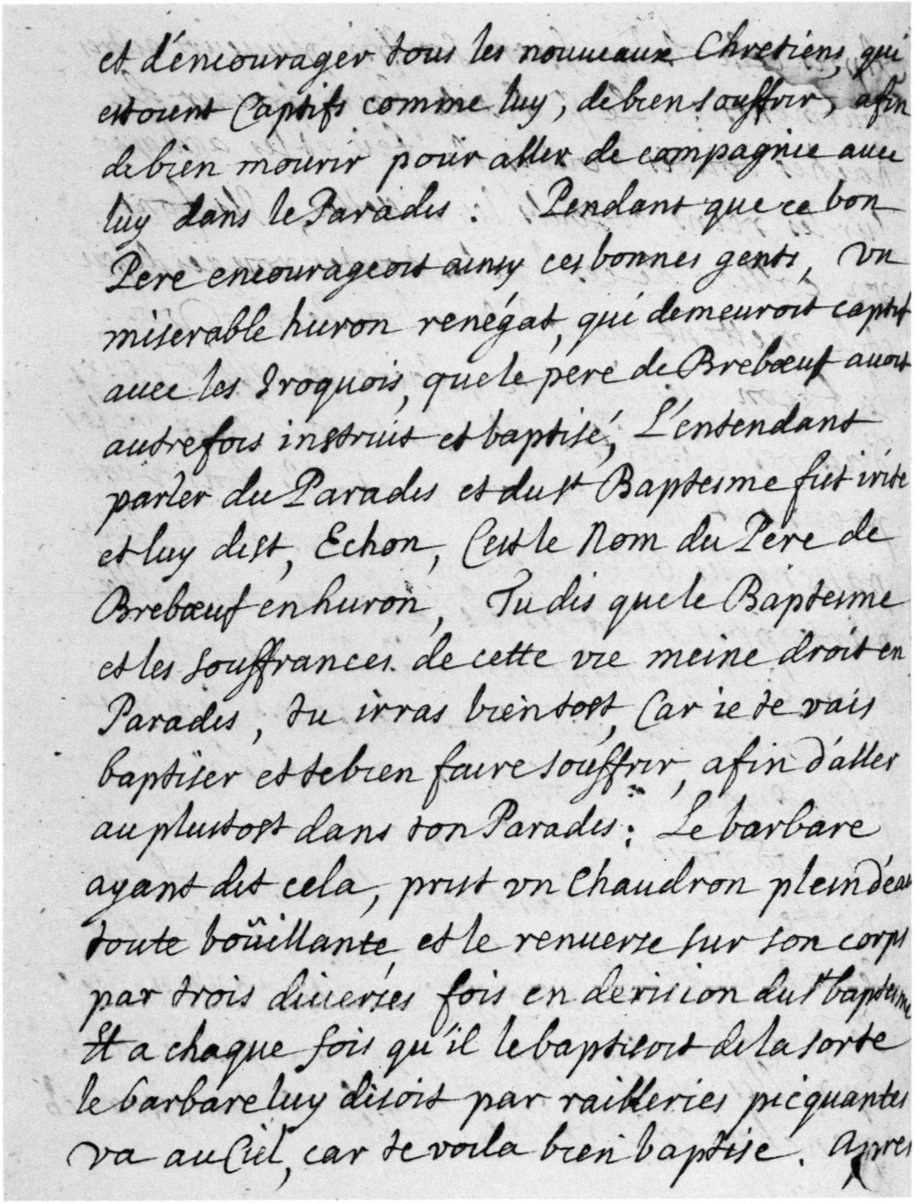
et d'encourager tous les nouveaux Chretiens qui
estoient Captifs comme luy, de bien souffrir, afin
de bien mourir pour aller de compagnie avec
luy dans le Paradis : Pendant que ce bon
Pere encourageoit ainsy ces bonnes gents, vn
miserable huron renegat, qui demeuroit captif
avec les Iroquois, que le pere de Brebœuf avoit
autrefois instruit et baptisé, L'entendant
parler du Paradis et dud.t Bapteime fist irrite
et luy dist, Echon, C'est le Nom du Pere de
Brebœuf en huron, Tu dis que le Bapteime
et les souffrances de cette vie meine droit en
Paradis, tu irras bientost, Car ie te vais
baptiser et te bien faire souffrir, afin d'aller
au plustost dans ton Paradis : Le barbare
ayant dit cela, prist vn Chaudron plein d'eau
toute bouillante et le renverse sur son corps
par trois diverses fois en derision du baptesme
Et a chaque fois qu'il le baptisoit de la sorte
le barbare luy disoit par railleries picquantes
va au Ciel, car te voila bien baptisé. Apres

Christophe Regnaut Coadiuteur
frere aux Jesuites ... 1678 Compagnon des peres brebeuf
et lallemand deffuncts

Public Archives of Canada, Ottawa:
Christophe Regnault, MG 18, E 10,
fol. 1–3, 7.

VIII

Religious foundations

Having noticed that the nomadic Indians put to death those among them who because of age, illness, or wounds, could no longer follow the band, Father Le Jeune wished that a hospital might be founded where those Indians would be cared for, kept, and converted. Responding to his appeal, three nuns hospitallers came across the ocean to Québec in 1639 to found a Hôtel-Dieu there.

In the same year, three Ursulines also landed at Québec. They came on the invitation of Father Le Jeune to set up a seminary or boarding school to teach young Indian girls along with young French girls.

At the same time when the Hospitallers and Ursulines were settling in at Québec, another great missionary project was being elaborated among a group of French people whose only aim was to convert the Indians. This project began to be achieved with the founding of Ville-Marie in 1642. Without delay Jeanne Mance opened a hospital there; in 1658 Marguerite Bourgeoys began teaching there, while laying the groundwork for the Congrégation de Notre-Dame. In 1657 the Sulpicians and in 1659 the Hospitallers of Saint-Joseph came to take charge respectively of the parish and the Hôtel-Dieu at Ville-Marie.

These foundations had been preceded at Sillery in 1637 by the founding of a village for the Indians: it was thought that their conversion would be easier and perseverance in their faith would be ensured if they became sedentary and engaged in farming like the French.

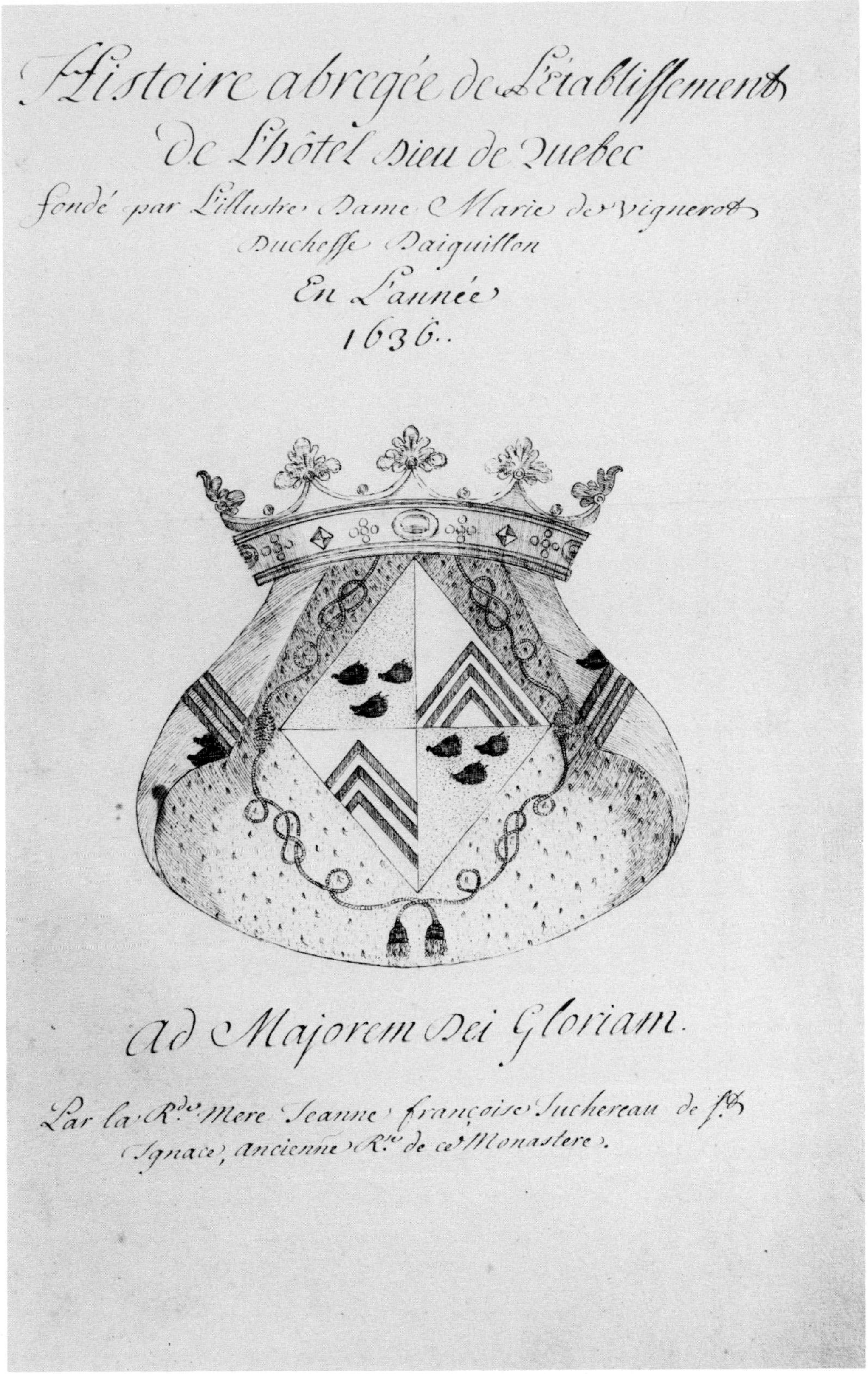

Histoire abregée de L'établissement
de L'hôtel Dieu de Quebec
fondé par L'illustre Dame Marie de Vignerot
Duchesse Daiguillon
En L'année
1636.

Ad Majorem Dei Gloriam.

Par la Rde Mere Jeanne françoise Juchereau de St
Ignace, ancienne Rre de ce Monastere.

"Short history of the creation of the Hôtel-Dieu de Québec," recounted by Mother Jeanne-Françoise Juchereau de La Ferté, called Mother Saint-Ignace, and Mother Marie-Andrée Regnard Duplessis, called Mother Sainte-Hélène, 1716–22.

It was the Duchesse d'Aiguillon who assured the founding of this hospital through the numerous steps that she took and through her financial aid.

On 2 February 1639 the Augustines of the Hôtel-Dieu de Dieppe chose "Reverend Mother Marie Guenet de Saint-Ignace to be the superior, Mother Anne Le Cointre de Saint-Bernard, and Mother Marie Forestier de Saint-Bonaventure-de-Jésus to accompany her, and to come together to found and establish the convent and the Hôtel-Dieu de Québec."

Il y avoit plusieurs années que l'on souhaitoit vn hôpital en canada non seulement pour secourir le peu de françois qui l'habitoient; mais beaucoup plus pour soulager les sauuages qui étoient sujets a de grandes maladies, et qui n'auoient au=cun moyen d'addoucir la misere dont ils étoient accablez,

Les plus considerables habitants du païs en écriuirent aussy en france aux personnes de qualité et de pieté auec qui ils auoient quelque liaison, et en europe ceux qui s'interressoient pour le bien du canada parlerent si efficacement de l'auantage que cette Colonie en retireroit, qu'en l'année 1636 Madame la Duchesse Daiguillon prit la résolution d'en faire la fondation, elle étoit niece de Monseigneur le cardinal de Richelieu qui voulut participer a cette bonne oeuure, et qui nous honora jusqu'à sa mort de sa singuliere protection.

Cette vertueuse Dame s'addressa a nos reuerendes Meres les Religieuses hospitalieres de Dieppe qui étoient nouuellement reformées, c'est a dire qu'elles auoient pris depuis peu vn habit et vne maniere de vie reguliere, s'obligeant a la clôture qu'elles n'auoient point gardée jusqu'alors. Elles accepterent auec joye la proposition, et promirent de fournir des sujets propres a établir vn hôtel Dieu dans la nouuelle france, Madame la Duchesse Daiguillon donna pour lors quinze cents liures de reuenu a prendre sur les coches et carosses de soissons,

le 2e de feurier de l'année 1639. les Religieuses de la misericorde de Jesus de l'hôtel Dieu de Dieppe, capitulairement assemblées, firent l'élection de trois d'entr'elles, sçauoir la Reuerende mere Marie Guenet de St Ignace pour être superieure, la mere Anne le Cointre de St Bernard, et la mere Marie forestier de St Bonnauenture de Jesus pour l'accompagner, et venir ensemble fonder et établir ce conuent et hôtel Dieu de Quebec en la nouuelle france.

Monastère des augustines de l'Hôtel-Dieu de Québec, Québec.

234

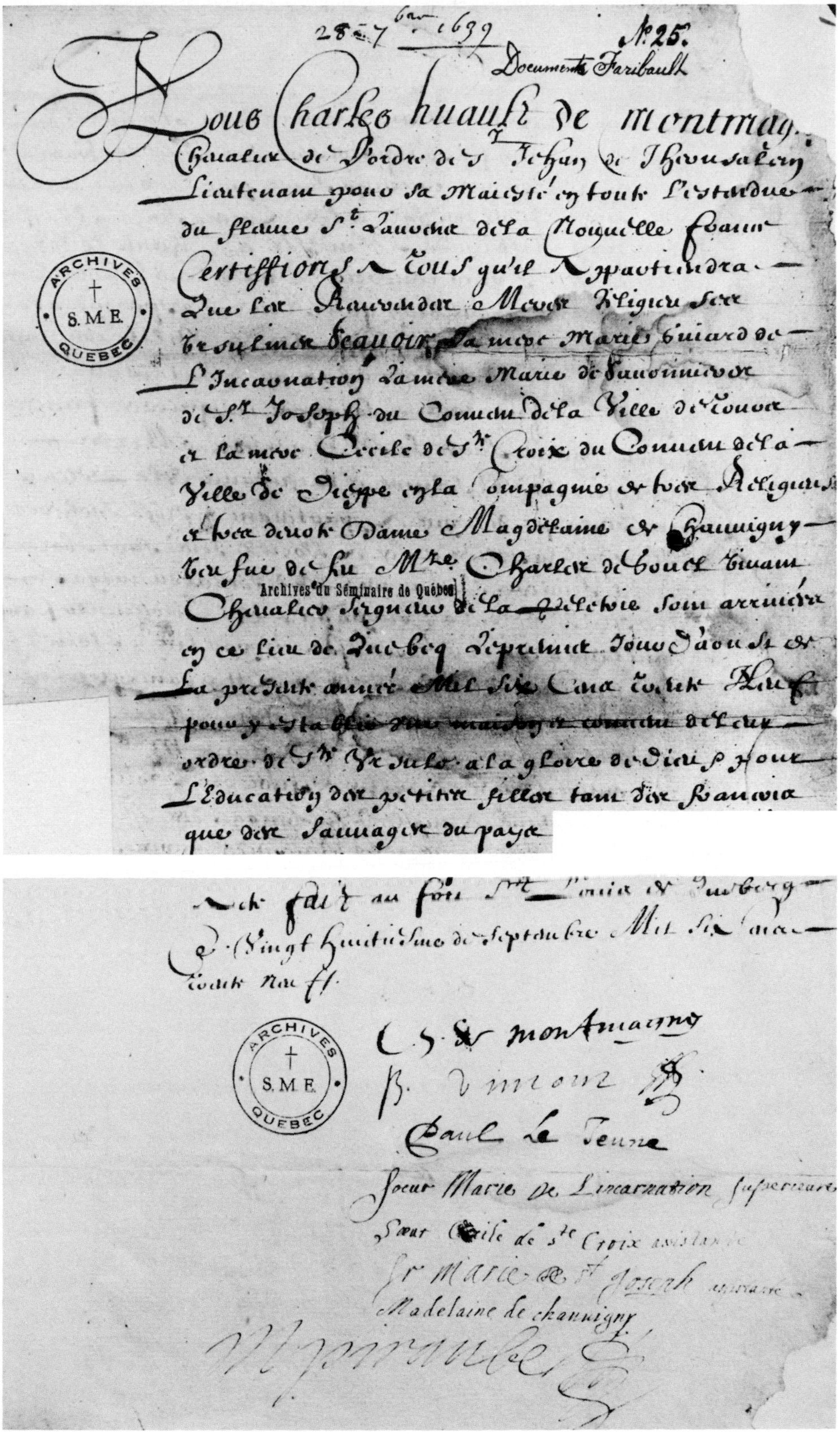

Account of the arrival of the Ursulines at Québec prepared by Governor Montmagny, Québec, 28 September 1639.

"The reverend mothers of the Ursuline order, that is to say Mother Marie Guyart de l'Incarnation, Mother Marie de Savonnières de Saint-Joseph, from the convent in the city of Tours, and Mother Cécile de Sainte-Croix...arrived here in Québec on the first day of August of the present year 1639, to create a house and convent here...and to educate the girls, both the French ones and the native Indians."

Archives du Séminaire de Québec, Québec: Documents Faribault, no 25.

Portrait of Marguerite Bourgeoys (1620–1700); Pierre Le Ber (1669–1707); oil; 1700; 62.3 x 49.5 cm.

Marguerite Bourgeoys founded the Congrégation de Notre-Dame in Canada, a religious community dedicated to educating young girls.

Archives des Soeurs de la Congrégation de Notre-Dame, Montréal.

RELATION
DE CE QVI S'EST PASSÉ
EN LA
NOVVELLE FRANCE
EN L'ANNÉE 1638.
Enuoyée au
R. PERE PROVINCIAL
de la Compagnie de IESVS
en la Prouince de France.
Par le P. PAVL LE IEVNE de la mesme Compagnie, Superieur de la Residence de Kébec.

A PARIS,
Chez SEBASTIEN CRAMOISY Imprimeur
ordinaire du Roy, ruë sainct Iacques,
aux Cicognes.
M. DC. XXXVIII.
AVEC PRIVILEGE DV ROY.

Paul Le Jeune. *Relation de ce qvi s'est passé en la Novvelle France en l'année 1638....* Paris: Chez Sébastien Cramoisy, 1638, title page, pp. 41–42.

Father Le Jeune announced the founding of the Indian village at Sillery, which was intended to lead the Indians to become sedentary so that it would be easier to convert them. "One of the most powerful means that we can have to bring them to Jesus Christ is to bring them to live in a sort of large village, in a word to help them to clear and cultivate the ground and to build homes for themselves."

De quelques Sauuages errans deuenus ſedentaires.

CE Chapitre donnera de la conſolation à V. R. & à toutes les perſonnes qui prennent plaiſir de voir regner IESVS-CHRIST dans nos grands bois; Car il nous met dans vne grande eſperance de la conuerſion des Sauuages, ſi tant eſt qu'on les puiſſe ſecourir à la façon que ie le vay deduire.

L'vn des plus puiſſans moyens que nous puiſſions auoir pour les amener à IESVS-CHRIST, c'eſt de les reduire dans vne eſpece de Bourgade, en vn mot de les aider à defricher & cultiuer la terre, & à ſe baſtir. Comme nous cherchions touſiours quelque ſecours pour faire cette entrepriſe, arriue qu'vne perſonne de vertu de voſtre France bien cognuë au Ciel & en la terre, & dont le nom ne peut ſortir de ma plume ſans luy deplaire, me donna aduis d'vn deſſein qu'il auoit de ſeruir Noſtre Seigneur en ces contrées. Il gage à cét effet quelques artiſans & quelques hommes de trauail pour commencer vn baſtiment, & pour defricher quelques terres, m'aſſurant dans ſes lettres qu'il n'auoit point d'autre but en ce trauail que la plus grande gloire de Dieu: Nous miſmes ſes ouuriers dans vn bel endroit nommé à preſent la reſidence S. Ioſeph, vne bonne lieuë au deſſus de Kebek ſur le grand fleuue. Monſieur Gand auoit pris ce lieu pour ſoy, mais il le conſacra volontiers à vn ſi bon deſſein. Les affaires eſtant en cette diſpoſition, nous mandaſmes à ce bon Seigneur, qu'il feroit vn grand ſacrifice à Dieu s'il vouloit appliquer le trauail de ſes hommes à ſecourir les Sauuages. Il falloit attendre vne année pour auoir reſponſe. Cependant il arriue que demandans à vn Sauuage ſes enfans pour les mettre au Seminaire, il nous reſpondit; c'eſt trop peu de vous dõner mes enfans, prenez le pere & la mere & toute la famille, & logez-nous aupres de voſtre demeure, afin que nous puiſſions entendre voſtre doctrine, & croire en celuy qui a tout fait.

Public Archives of Canada, Library, Ottawa (Negatives nos. C 113485 to C 113486 and C 113488).

VIII

Organizing the Church

In 1657 circumstances seemed favourable for setting up a bishopric in Canada. For various reasons, however, the candidate chosen to occupy the see of Québec, François de Laval, was named vicar apostolic of New France, with the title of bishop of Petraea, rather than titular bishop of Québec. His bulls were signed at Rome on 3 June 1658.

On 26 March 1663, while in Paris, Bishop Laval made a start at organizing the Canadian Church by creating the Séminaire de Québec, an institution that, if it was to play the role of a theological seminary for training future priests, was also "to act as a clergy for this new Church" by bringing together and supporting the secular priests responsible for the various diocesan ministries.

In organizing his Church Bishop Laval, who had become bishop of Québec in 1674, did not fail to found religious brotherhoods and sisterhoods, such as the Confrérie de Sainte-Anne, for which he drew up the regulations himself in 1678.

In 1699 Intendant Jean Bochart de Champigny remarked upon the "particular inclination" that Bishop Saint-Vallier, Bishop Laval's successor, had "for creating new Communities." He had, in fact, founded the Hôpital-Général de Québec in 1693 and an Ursuline convent at Trois-Rivières in 1697. The foundresses of these two institutions were drawn from the Hôtel-Dieu and the Ursuline convent in Québec respectively.

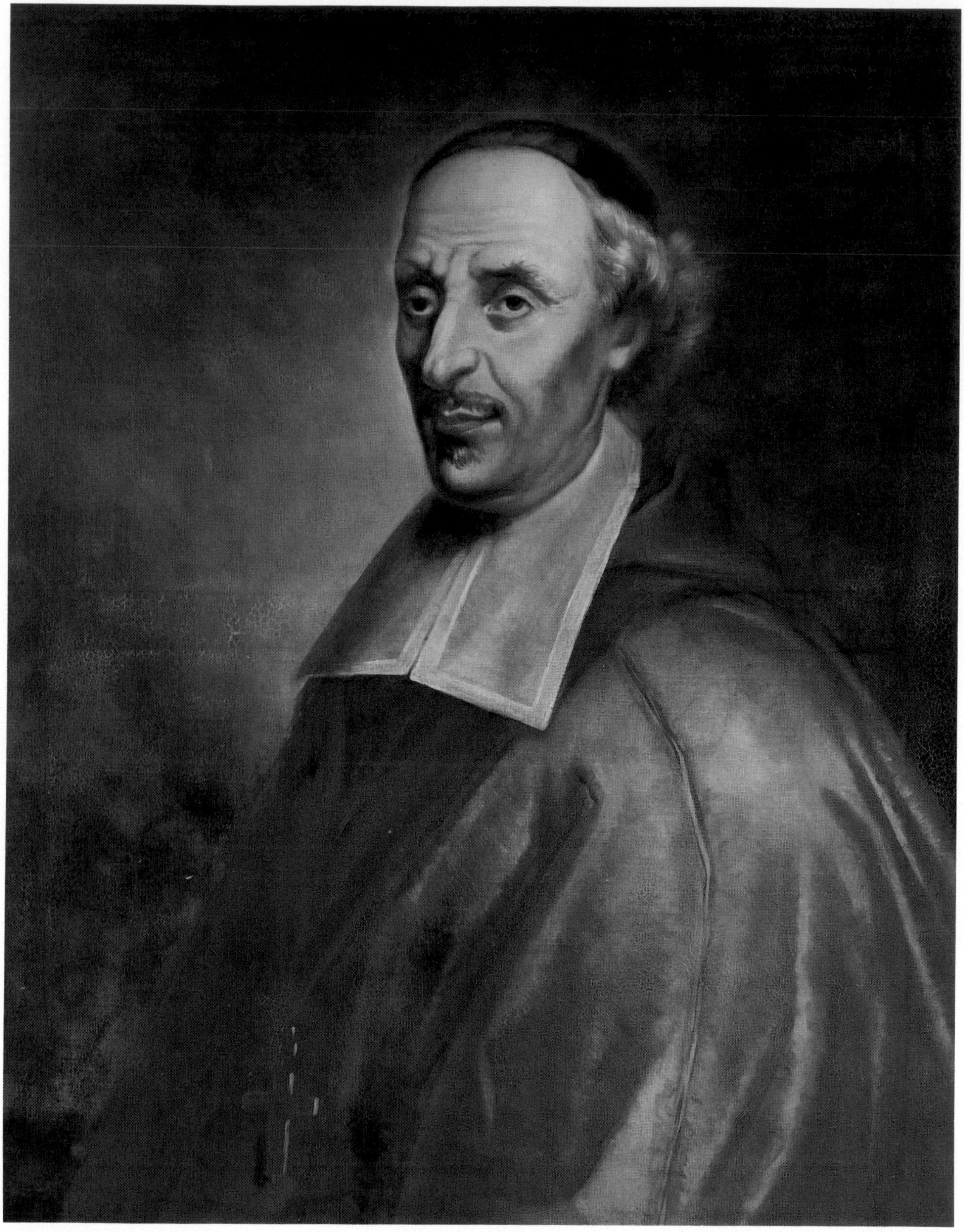

Portrait of Bishop François de Laval (1623–1708); attributed to Claude François (Brother Luc) (1614–85); oil; circa 1672; 86.4 x 71.1 cm.

Bishop Laval was the first bishop of New France; he directed the diocese of Québec from 1659 to 1684.

Musée du Séminaire de Québec, Québec.

Bull from Pope Alexander VII appointing François de Laval apostolic vicar in Canada, Rome, 3 June 1658.

This bull would allow Bishop Laval to exercise the functions of bishop until his appointment as titular bishop of Québec in 1674.

Archives de l'archidiocèse de Québec, Québec. Photo: musée du Québec.

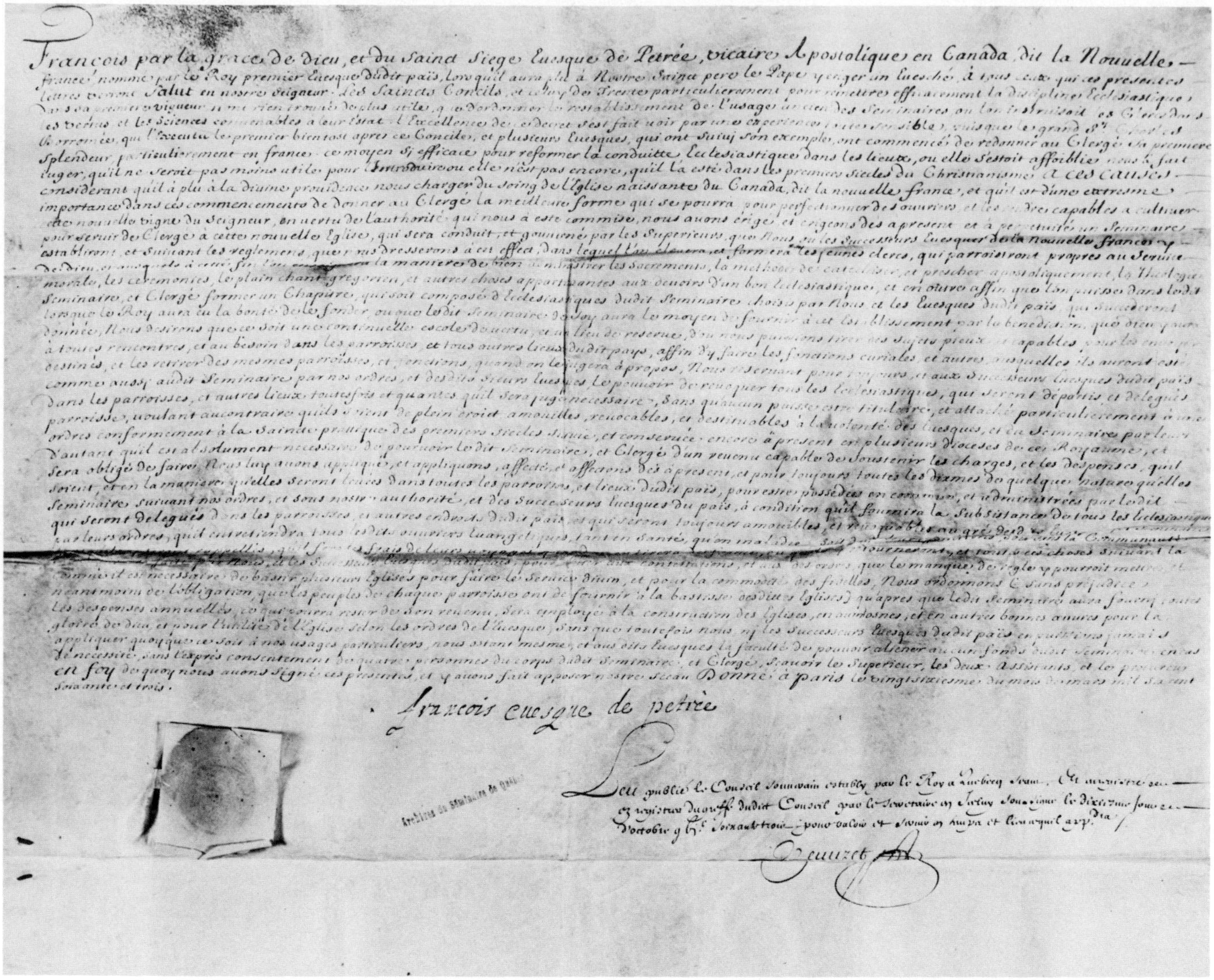
Francois par la grace de dieu, et du Saint Siege Evesque de Petrée, vicaire Apostolique en Canada dit la Nouvelle

Francois evesque de petrée

Pastoral letter from Bishop Laval creating the Séminaire de Québec, Paris, 26 March 1663.

This seminary would train "young clerics who will appear suited for the service of God and who will be taught to this end how to administer the sacraments properly, how to catechize and to preach apostolically, moral theology, the ceremonies, Gregorian plain song, and other things that form part of the duties of a good ecclesiastic."

Archives du Séminaire de Québec, Québec: Polygraphie 9, n° 1.

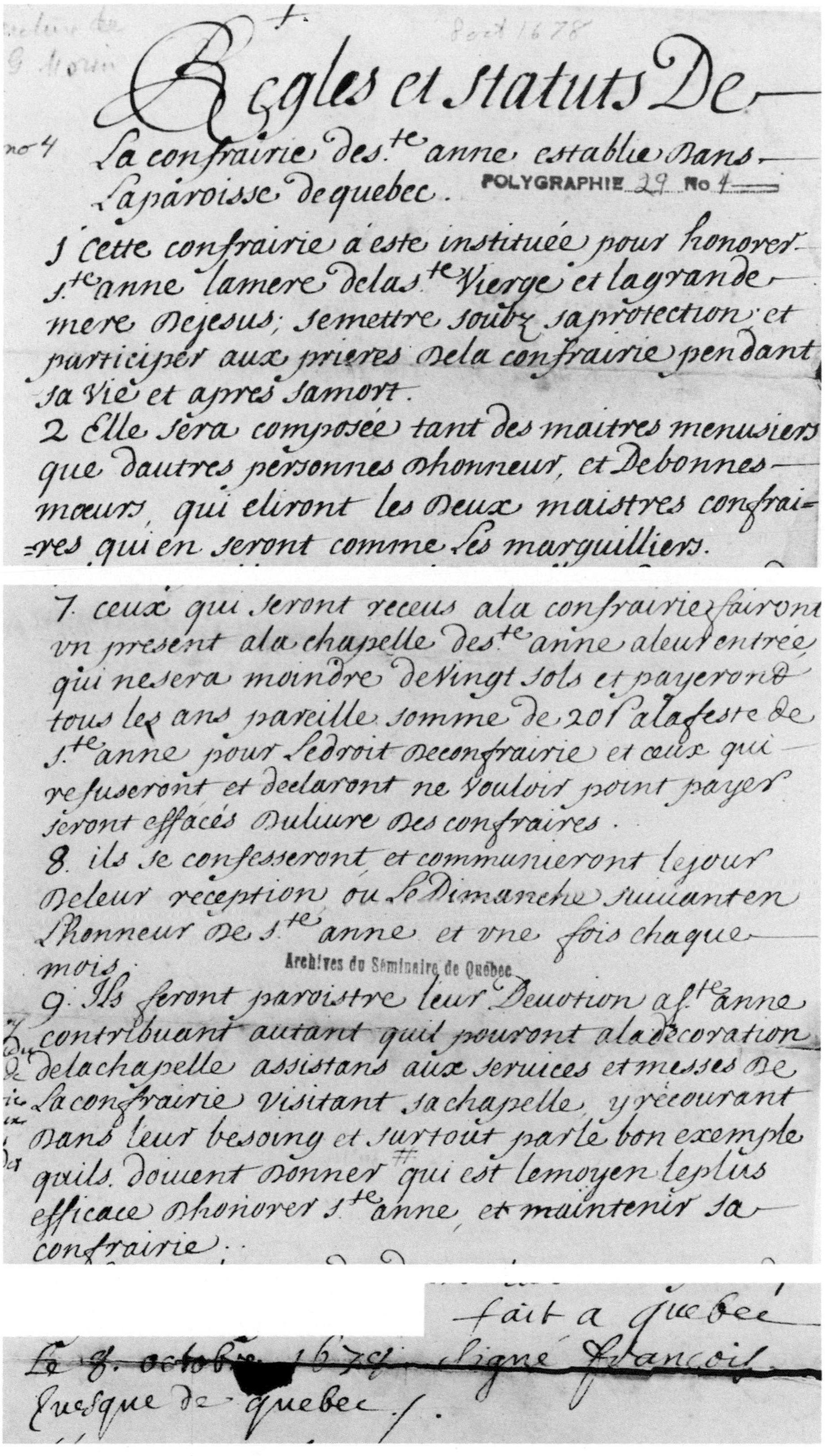

Regles et statuts De

La confrairie de s.te anne establie dans
la paroisse de quebec.

POLYGRAPHIE 29 No 4

1 Cette confrairie a este instituée pour honorer
s.te anne la mere de la s.te Vierge et la grande
mere de jesus; se mettre soubz sa protection et
participer aux prieres de la confrairie pendant
sa vie et apres sa mort.

2 Elle sera composée tant des maitres menusiers
que dautres personnes dhonneur, et de bonnes
moeurs, qui eliront les deux maistres confraires qui en seront comme les marguilliers.

7. ceux qui seront receus a la confrairie feront
vn present a la chapelle de s.te anne a leur entrée
qui ne sera moindre de vingt sols et payeront
tous les ans pareille somme de 20 l a la feste de
s.te anne pour le droit de confrairie et ceux qui
refuseront et declaront ne vouloir point payer
seront effacés du liure des confraires.

8. ils se confesseront et communieront le jour
de leur reception ou le Dimanche suiuant en
lhonneur de s.te anne et vne fois chaque
mois.

Archives du Séminaire de Québec

9. Ils feront paroistre leur deuotion a s.te anne
contribuant autant quil pouront a la decoration
de la chapelle assistans aux seruices et messes de
la confrairie visitant sa chapelle y recourant
dans leur besoing et surtout par le bon exemple
quils doiuent donner qui est le moyen le plus
efficace dhonorer s.te anne, et maintenir sa
confrairie.

fait a quebec
Le 8. octobre 1678. signé françois
Euesque de quebec.

"Rule and statutes of the Confrérie de Sainte-Anne created in the parish of Québec," Québec, 8 October 1678.

"This brotherhood has been instituted to honour St. Anne the mother of the Virgin Mary and the grandmother of Jesus. … It will be composed of the master carpenters and other persons of honour and of good moral character."

Archives du Séminaire de Québec, Québec: Polygraphie 29, n° 4.

241

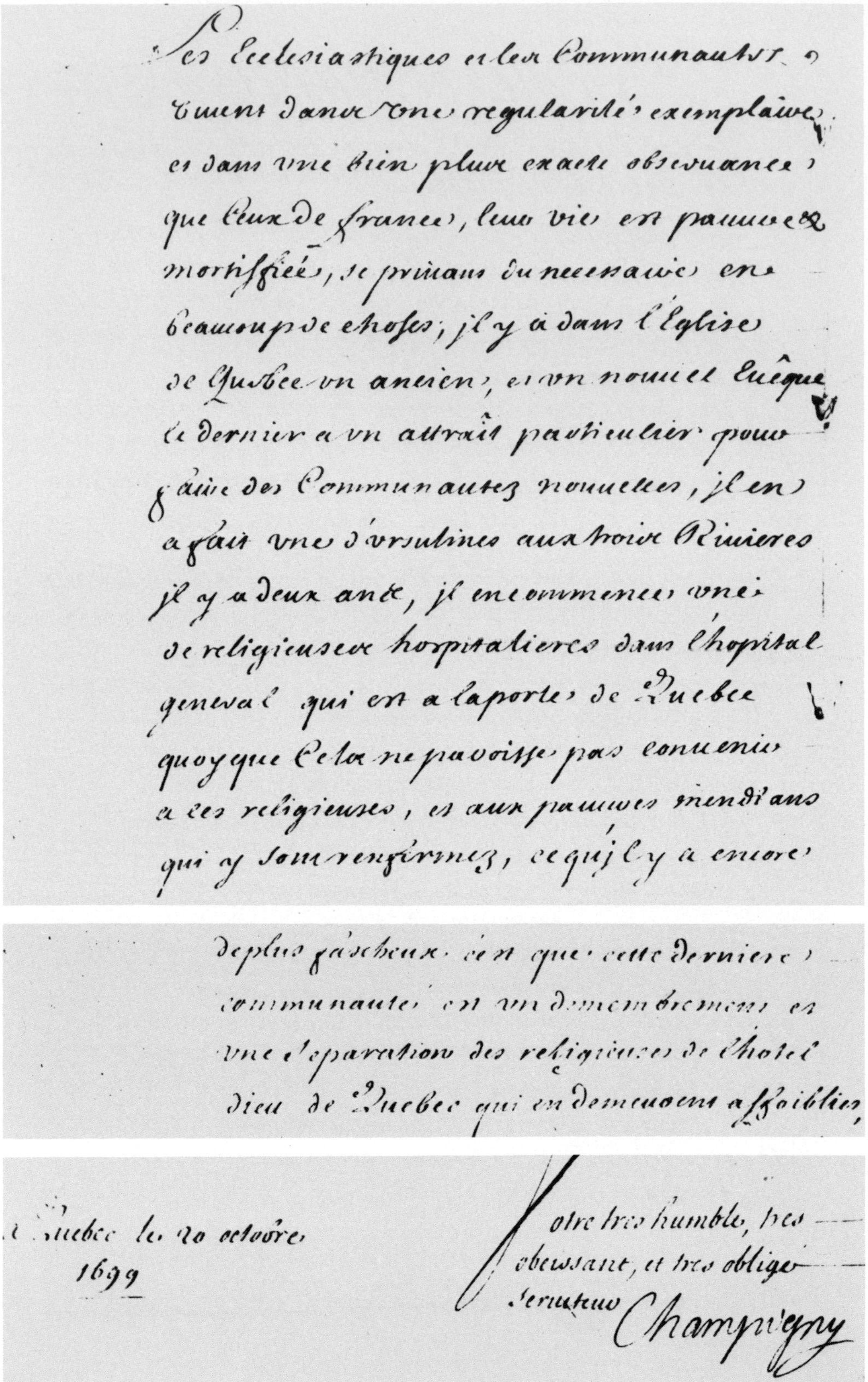

Les Ecclesiastiques et les Communautez
vivent dans une regularité exemplaire
et dans une bien plus exacte observance
que ceux de france, leur vie est pauvre &
mortiffiée, se privans du necessaire en
beaucoup de choses; il y a dans l'Eglise
de Quebec un ancien, et un nouvel Evêque
le dernier a un attraît particulier pour
faire des Communautez nouvelles, il en
a fait une d'ursulines aux trois Rivieres
il y a deux ans, il en commence une
de religieuses hospitalieres dans l'hopital
general qui est a la porte de Quebec
quoyque cela ne paroisse pas convenir
a ces religieuses, et aux pauvres mendians
qui y sont renfermez, ce qu'il y a encore

de plus fascheux c'est que cette derniere
communauté est un demembrement et
une separation des religieuses de l'hotel
dieu de Quebec qui en demeurent affoiblies,

A Quebec le 20 octobre
1699

Votre tres humble, tres
obeissant, et tres obligé
Serviteur Champigny

Letter from Intendant Champigny to the minister Pontchartrain, Québec, 20 October 1699.

Champigny mentioned that Bishop Saint-Vallier "has a particular inclination for creating new communities, he created one of Ursulines at Trois-Rivières two years ago, he is beginning one of Religious Hospitallers in the Hôpital-Général at the gate of Québec."

This bishop founded the Hôpital-Général de Québec and contributed to the founding of a similar institution in Montréal intended for poor people who were chronically ill and old people without means of support.

Archives nationales, Paris, France: Fonds des Colonies, série C^{11A}, vol. 17, fol. 67v – 68, 75.

VIII

Church and State

In the seventeenth century it was normal to entrust responsibilities within State bodies to high-ranking ecclesiastics. Thus, in creating the Conseil souverain in 1663 the king appointed Bishop Laval to it.

If the respective jurisdictions of the Church and the State were in general well defined, questions involving both of them, such as selling spirits to the Indians, were sources of conflict between the civil and religious authorities. Despite the opposition of the representatives of the civil authority, and for considerations of morality, Bishop Laval conducted a bitter fight against the traffickers in spirits.

The king helped the Canadian Church as best he could, but often according to his own ideas or by trying to bring into the colony ways of doing things that were current in France. In 1679, for example, he set regulations for the payment of tithes in Canada and in so doing upset the practice that had been followed up till then.

The king wanted the bishop to create as many parishes as possible whose incumbents would be irremovable; Bishop Laval considered that in view of the slender amounts that the tithes brought in and the small number of heads of families, very few parishes could provide a living for a parish priest and that consequently the system of officiating priests was the only one that suited the state of the colony.

Minutes of the first sitting of the Conseil souverain, Québec, 18 September 1663.

The signature of Bishop Laval, who was a member of the Conseil, appears here.

Archives nationales du Québec, Centre d'archives de la Capitale, Québec: Jugements et délibérations du Conseil souverain, vol. 1, fol. 1.

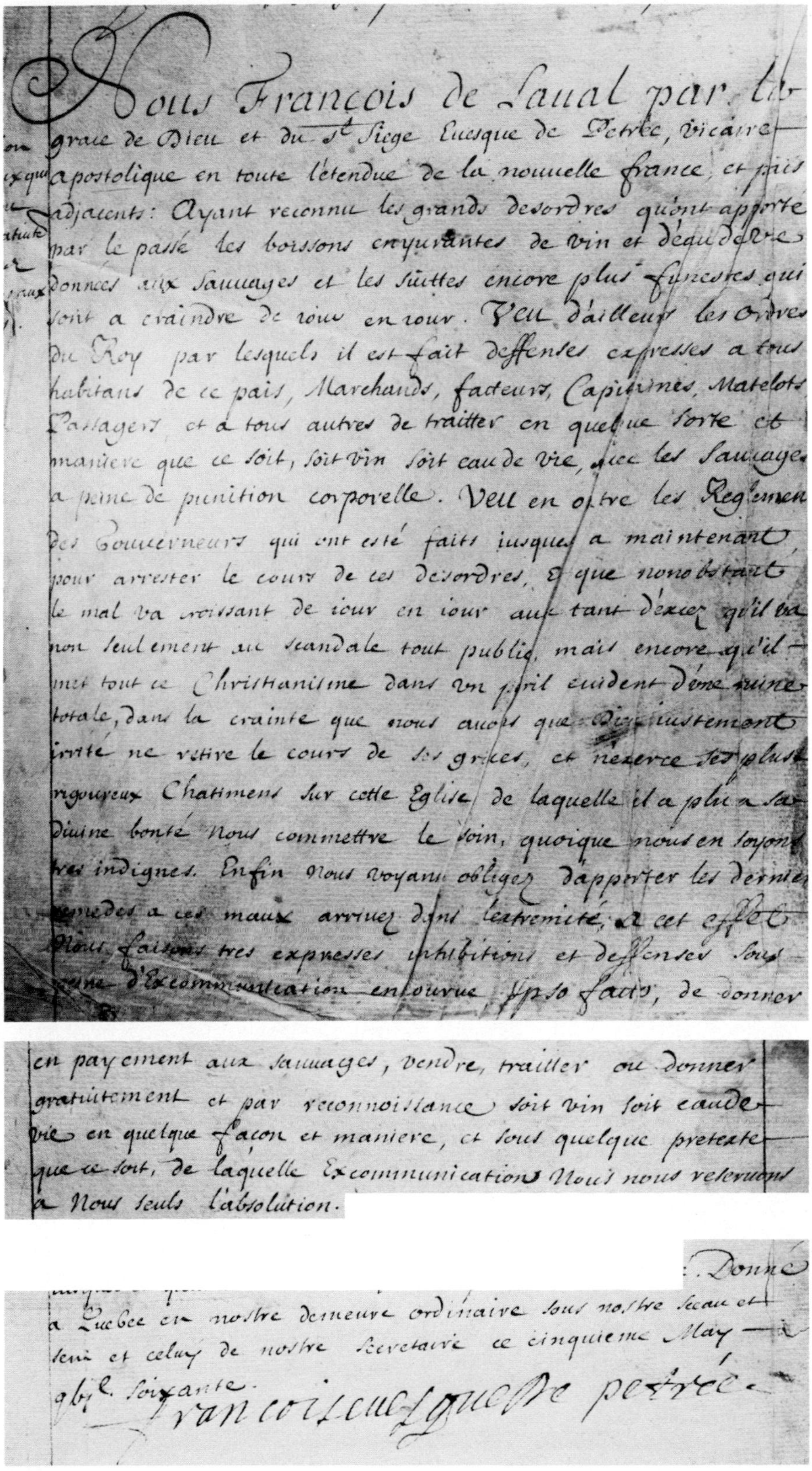

Nous François de Laval par la grace de Dieu et du S.t Siege Evesque de Petrée, Vicaire apostolique en toute l'étendue de la nouvelle france, et pais adjacents: Ayant reconnu les grands desordres qu'ont apporté par le passé les boissons enyvrantes de vin et d'eau de vie données aux Sauvages et les suittes encore plus funestes qui sont a craindre de iour en iour. Veu d'ailleurs les Ordres du Roy par lesquels il est fait deffenses expresses a tous habitans de ce pais, Marchands, facteurs, Capitaines, Matelots Passagers, et a tous autres de traitter en quelque sorte et maniere que ce soit, soit vin soit eau de vie, avec les Sauvages a peine de punition corporelle. Veu en outre les Reglemens des Gouverneurs qui ont esté faits iusques a maintenant, pour arrester le cours de ces desordres, et que nonobstant le mal va croissant de iour en iour au tant d'excez qu'il va non seulement au scandale tout public, mais encore qu'il met tout ce Christianisme dans un peril euident d'une ruine totale, dans la crainte que nous avons que Dieu iustement irrité ne retire le cours de ses graces, et n'exerce ses plus rigoureux Chatimens sur cette Eglise de laquelle il a plu a sa diuine bonté Nous commettre le soin, quoique nous en soyons tres indignes. Enfin Nous voyans obligez d'apporter les derniers remedes a ces maux arrivez dans l'extremité, A cet effet Nous faisons tres expresses inhibitions et deffenses sous peine d'Excommunication encourue ipso facto, de donner en payement aux Sauvages, vendre, traitter ou donner gratuitement et par reconnoissance soit vin soit eau de vie en quelque facon et maniere, et sous quelque pretexte que ce soit, de laquelle Excommunication Nous nous reservons a Nous seuls l'absolution.

: Donné a Quebec en nostre demeure ordinaire sous nostre seau et seing et celuy de nostre Secretaire ce cinquieme May [illegible] soixante.

François Evesque de Petrée.

Pastoral letter from Bishop Laval, which expressly prohibits and forbids under pain of excommunication incurred *ipso facto*, giving in payment to the Indians, selling, trading, or giving for nothing and through gratitude either wine or spirits in any manner whatever, and under any pretext whatsoever," Québec, 5 May 1660.

Archives de l'archidiocèse de Québec, Québec.

Repudiation of Alcohol; Father Claude Chauchetière (1645–1709); brown ink; 20 x 15.7 cm.; from the manuscript "Narration annuelle de la mission du Sault depuis sa fondation jusques à l'an 1686" (1667–86).

The religious authorities in the colony were opposed to the sale of spirits to the Indians. Intoxicating beverages caused various disorders among the Indians and were a major obstacle to establishing and maintaining the Christian faith among them. On the other hand the civil authorities generally tended to tolerate this traffic, which seemed to favour the fur trade, the main source of wealth in the colony.

Archives départementales de la Gironde, Bordeaux, France.

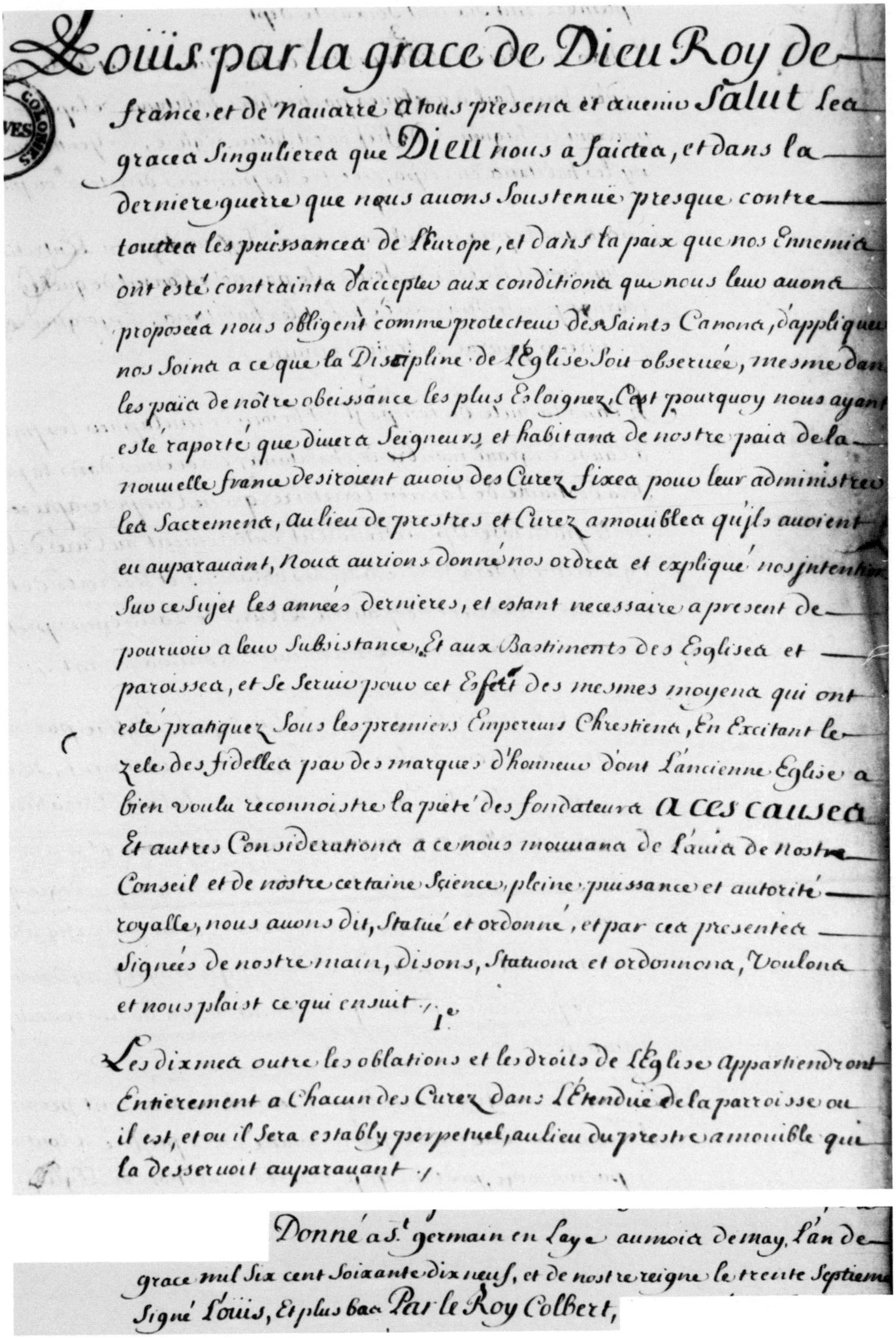

Louis par la grace de Dieu Roy de France et de Navarre A tous presens et advenir Salut Les graces Singulieres que Dieu nous a faictes, et dans la derniere guerre que nous avons Soustenue presque contre toutes les puissances de l'Europe, et dans la paix que nos Ennemis ont esté contraints d'accepter aux conditions que nous leur avons proposées nous obligent comme protecteur des Saints Canons, d'appliquer nos Soins a ce que la Discipline de l'Eglise Soit observée, mesme dans les pais de nostre obeissance les plus Esloignez, C'est pourquoy nous ayant esté raporté que divers Seigneurs et habitans de nostre pais de la nouvelle france desiroient avoir des Curez fixes pour leur administrer les Sacremens, au lieu de prestres et Curez amovibles qu'ils avoient eu auparavant, Nous aurions donné nos ordres et expliqué nos intentions Sur ce Sujet les années dernieres, et estant necessaire a present de pourvoir a leur Subsistance, Et aux Bastiments des Eglises et paroisses, et Se Servir pour cet Effet des mesmes moyens qui ont esté pratiquez Sous les premiers Empereurs Chrestiens, En Excitant le zele des fidelles par des marques d'honneur dont l'ancienne Eglise a bien voulu reconnoistre la pieté des fondateurs A ces causes Et autres Considerations a ce nous mouvans de l'avis de nostre Conseil et de nostre certaine Science, pleine puissance et autorité royalle, nous avons dit, Statué et ordonné, et par ces presentes Signées de nostre main, disons, Statuons et ordonnons, Voulons et nous plaist ce qui ensuit.

1e

Les dixmes outre les oblations et les droits de l'Eglise appartiendront Entierement a Chacun des Curez dans l'Estendue de la parroisse ou il est, et ou il Sera estably perpetuel, au lieu du prestre amovible qui la desservoit auparavant.

Donné a St. germain en Laye au mois de may, l'an de grace mil Six cent Soixante dix neuf, et de nostre reigne le trente Septieme Signé Louis, Et plus bas Par le Roy Colbert,

Letters patent from King Louis XIV in the form of an edict concerning tithes in Canada, Saint-Germain-en-Laye, May 1679.

Having learned that many Canadians "wanted to have regular parish priests to administer the sacraments to them, instead of movable priests and parish priests whom they had had before," the king decided that henceforth tithes "will belong entirely to each of the parish priests throughout the parish where he is, and where he will be fixed in perpetuity, instead of the movable priest who served them before."

In this way, the king imposed upon the bishop the obligation to create fixed parish charges.

Archives nationales, Paris, France: Fonds des Colonies, série F^{5A}, vol. 3, fol. 63, 64.

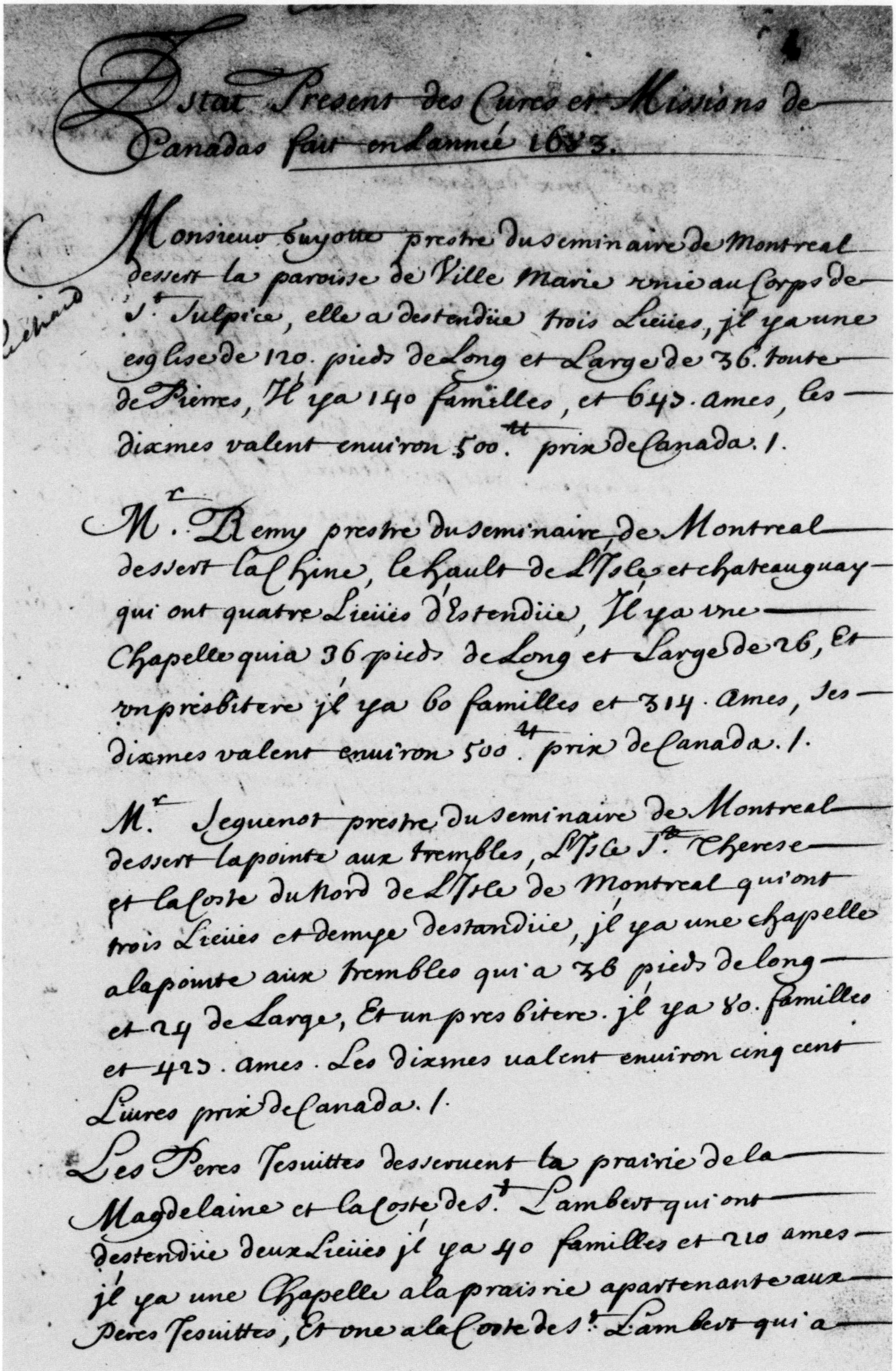

Estat Present des Cures et Missions de Canadas fait en l'année 1683.

Monsieur Guyotte prestre du seminaire de Montreal dessert la paroisse de Ville Marie unie au Corps de St. Sulpice, elle a destendüe trois Lieües, jl y a une eglise de 120. pieds de Long et Large de 36. toute de Pierres, Il y a 140 famelles, et 643. ames, les dixmes valent environ 500.tt prix de Canada. 1.

Mr. Remy prestre du seminaire de Montreal dessert la Chine, le hault de L'Isle et chateauguay qui ont quatre Lieües d'Estendüe, Il y a une Chapelle qui a 36 pieds de Long et Large de 26, Et un presbitere jl y a 60 familles et 314. ames, les dixmes valent environ 500.tt prix de Canada. 1.

Mr. Seguenot prestre du seminaire de Montreal dessert la pointe aux trembles, L'Isle Ste. Therese et la Coste du Nord de L'Isle de Montreal qui ont trois Lieües et demye destandüe, jl y a une chapelle a la pointe aux trembles qui a 38 pieds de long et 24 de Large, Et un presbitere. jl y a 80. familles et 423. ames. Les dixmes valent environ cinq cent Livres prix de Canada. 1.

Les Peres Jesuittes desservent la prairie de la Magdelaine et la Coste de St. Lambert qui ont destendüe deux Lieües jl y a 40 familles et 210 ames jl y a une Chapelle a la prairie apartenante aux Peres Jesuittes, Et une a la Coste de St. Lambert qui a

Present state of parish charges and missions in Canada, 1683.

In view of the slenderness of the tithes and the small number of heads of families, very few parishes could supply a living for a parish priest. Certain priests had therefore to serve more than one parish.

Archives nationales, Paris, France: Fonds des Colonies, série F^{5A}, vol. 3, fol. 4.

VIII

Spiritual life

In the first half of the seventeenth century a current of mysticism went across France, which also had an effect upon the colony, through the agency of several persons, monks and nuns, priests and laymen, who lived in it. Among them Mother Catherine de Saint-Augustin, of the Hôtel-Dieu de Québec, has an important place.

At that period the settlers themselves, with a few exceptions, led an orderly life and in general displayed great piety. Several devotions were in honour in the colony, such as the devotion to Sainte Anne, of which the church Sainte-Anne-du-Petit-Cap (Sainte-Anne-de-Beaupré) was already the centre. Important personnages and ordinary people went there on pilgrimage and left ex-votos, often as the result of a promise made in a moment of danger.

Just as did the Indians at Lorette those at La Montagne in Montréal came in for praise from the authorities for their religious behaviour. The Iroquois at La Montagne profited not only from the zeal of the Sulpicians, who were in charge of the mission, but also from the devotion of Marguerite Bourgeoys's nuns, who were beginning moreover, to spread about everywhere in the colony.

Nonetheless there were "abuses" in the country, and they became more and more numerous, it seems, as the years went by. Bishop Saint-Vallier made it his duty to denounce them.

7. Avant que nous parlions du détail de la Vie de cette vertueuſe Religieuſe, en voicy comme un abregé dans une lettre que Monſeigneur l'Evéque de Petrée écrivit à la Reverende Mere Marie de S. Auguſtin, Fondatrice & Superieure des Religieuſes Hoſpitalieres de Bayeux, apres la mort de celle dont la Vie eſt icy décrite.

Ma chere Mere, il y a grand ſujet de benir Dieu de la conduite qu'il a tenuë ſur nôtre Sœur Catherine de ſaint Auguſtin : c'étoit une ame qu'il s'étoit choiſie pour luy communiquer des graces tres-grandes & tres-particulieres : ſa ſainteté ſera mieux connuë dans le Ciel qu'en cette vie; car aſſeurément elle eſt extraordinaire. Elle a beaucoup fait, & beaucoup ſouffert avec une fidelité inviolable, & un courage qui étoit audeſſus du commun. Sa charité pour le prochain étoit capable de tout embraſſer pour difficile qu'il fût. Je n'ay pas beſoin des choſes extraordinaires qui ſe ſont paſſées en elle pour étre convaincu de ſa ſainteté ; ſes veritables vertus me la font parfaitement connoître. L'on envoye au R. Pere Ragueneau les remarques que l'on a faites de ce que l'on a pû connoître des graces & des vertus qui ont paru davantage en elle. Vous aurez ſans doute bien de la conſolation de voir ce que l'on en a recüeilly. Dieu a fait une faveur bien particuliere à nos Hoſpitalieres de Quebec, & méme à tout le Canada, lors qu'il y a envoyé cette Ame qui luy étoit ſi chere. A Quebec, le 10. Octobre 1669.

Ma chere Mere,

Vôtre tres-humble & tres-obeïſſant ſerviteur FRANCOIS,
Evéque de Petrée.

Paul Ragueneau. *La vie de la mère Catherine de Saint-Avgvstin, religieuse Hospitalière de la Misericorde de Québec en la Nouvelle-France.* Paris: Chez Florentin Lambert, 1671, pp. 7–8.

Bishop Laval spoke in praise of the late Mother Catherine de Saint-Augustin, religious of the Hôtel-Dieu de Québec, considered to be a saint: "I have no need of the extraordinary things which took place within her in order to be convinced of her saintliness; her real virtues make it perfectly known to me."

National Library of Canada, Rare Books and Manuscripts Division, Ottawa.

Ex-voto of Pierre Le Moyne d'Iberville (1661–1706); artist unknown; oil; 1698–1700; 76.2 x 56.5 cm.

In 1658 a chapel in honour of St. Anne was built at Côte de Beaupré. Seven years later Marie de l'Incarnation wrote her son that miracles were taking place there: "You can see paralytics walk there, the blind receive sight, and people sick with any sort of malady recover their health." Common people and even important persons such as d'Iberville would go there on pilgrimage and leave ex-votos as a mark of gratitude.

Musée Historial, Sainte-Anne-de-Beaupré.

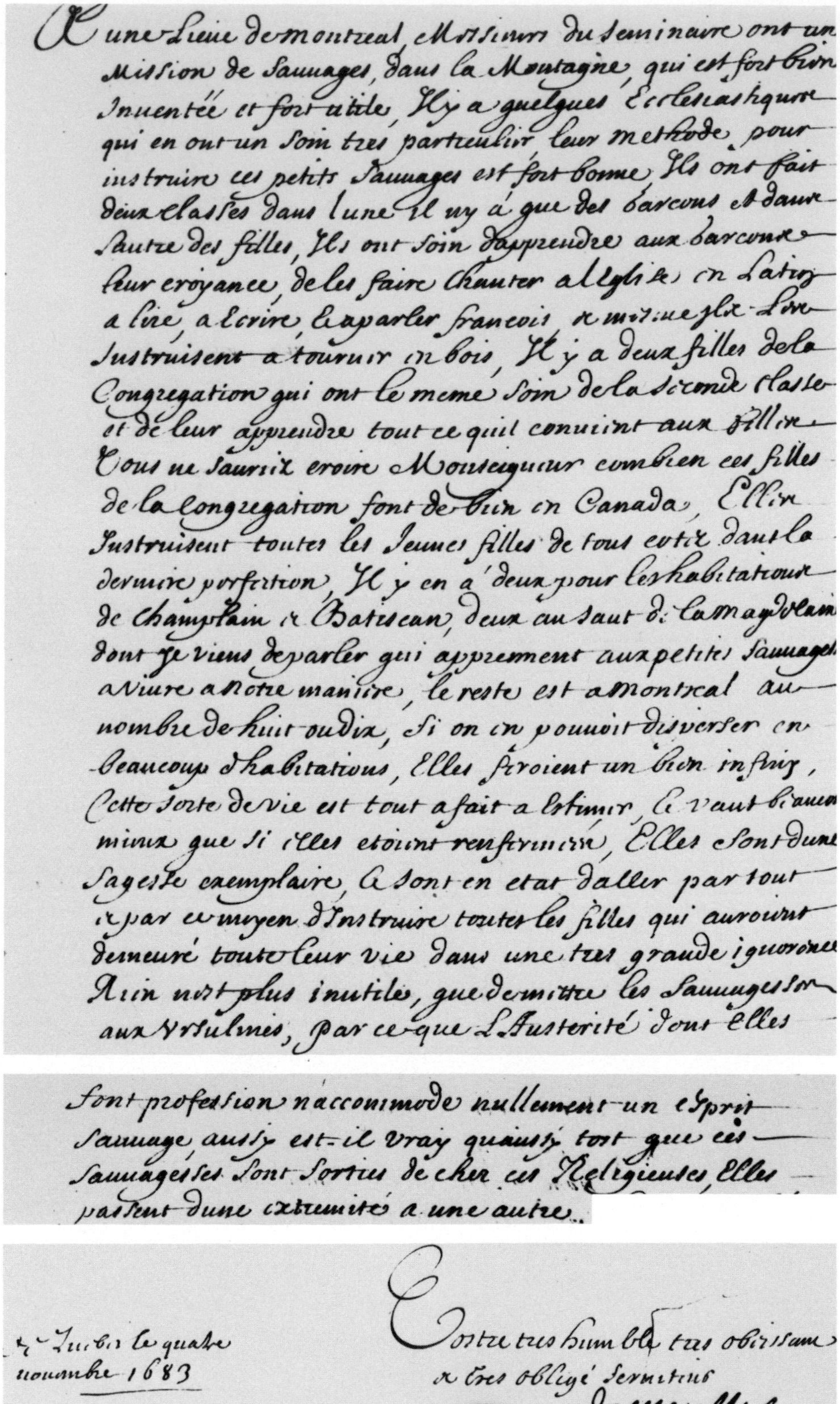

A une Lieue de montreal, Messieurs du seminaire ont un
Mission de Sauuages, dans la Montagne, qui est fort bien
Inuentée et fort utile, Il y a quelques Ecclesiastiques
qui en ont un Soin tres particulier leur methode, pour
instruire ces petits Sauuages est fort bonne, Ils ont fait
deux classes dans lune il ny a que des garcons et dans
lautre des filles, Ils ont soin dapprendre aux garcons
leur croyance, de les faire chanter a leglise en Latin
a lire, a lecrire, et a parler francois et mesme ils les
Instruisent a tourner en bois, Il y a deux filles de la
Congregation qui ont le meme soin de la seconde classe
et de leur apprendre tout ce quil conuient aux filles
Vous ne sauriez croire Monseigneur combien ces filles
de la Congregation font de bien en Canada, Elles
Instruisent toutes les Jeunes filles de tous cotez dans la
derniere perfection, Il y en a deux pour les habitations
de Champlain et Batiscan, deux au Saut de la Magdelaine
dont je viens de parler qui apprennent aux petites Sauuagesses
a viure a notre maniere, le reste est a Montreal au
nombre de huit ou dix, si on en pouuoit disperser en
beaucoup d'habitations, Elles feroient un bien infiny,
Cette sorte de vie est tout a fait a estimer, et vaut beaucoup
mieux que si elles etoient renfermées, Elles sont dune
sagesse exemplaire, et sont en etat daller par tout
et par ce moyen d'instruire toutes les filles qui auroient
demeuré toute leur vie dans une tres grande ignorance
Rien nest plus inutile, que de mettre les Sauuagesses
aux Vrsulines, par ce que L'Austerité dont elles

font profession naccommode nullement un esprit
sauuage aussy est il vray quaussy tost que ces
Sauuagesses sont sorties de chez ces Religieuses, Elles
passent dune extremité a une autre.

A Quebec le quatre
nouembre 1683

Vostre tres humble tres obeissant
et tres obligé seruiteur
de Meulles

Letter from Intendant de Meulles to the minister Seignelay, Québec, 4 November 1683.

The Sulpicians' mission at La Montagne (Montréal) seemed to be very successful: the little Indians were learning "their faith" there, as well as learning to "sing in Latin at church, to read, to write, and to speak French."

The same was true for the schools of the sisters of the Congrégation de Notre-Dame: "They are teaching all the young girls from all sides with utter perfection."

Archives nationales, Paris, France: Fonds des Colonies, série C^{11A}, vol. 6, fol. 193v–194, 198.

3. Nous deffendons tres-expreſſement aux filles & aux vevues, d'avoir la gorge, les épaules, ou la tête découvertes lorſqu'elles ſe preſentent au Sacrement de Mariage: enjoignons aux Curez & autres Prêtres de noſtre Diocéſe de ne les y point recevoir en cet eſtat, & de tenir auſſi exactement la main à ce que nous leur avons déja cy-devant ordonné de ne point admettre les filles & les femmes aux Sacremens de Penitence & d'Euchariſtie, ou à l'offrande, & aux queſtes qui ſe font dans les Egliſes, ſi elles oſoient s'y preſenter avec une pareille indecence, & immodeſtie; comme eſtant une choſe indigne de la profeſſion du chriſtianiſme, & encore plus de la ſainteté de nos Temples & condamnée pour cette effet dans la ſainte Ecriture par le ſaint Eſprit, dans les Ecrits des ſaints Peres & Docteurs, & dans les Conſtitutions de l'Egliſe.

5. Nous avons eſté ſenſiblement touchez dans les viſites que Nous avons faites dans les Paroiſſes de la campagne, d'apprendre l'abus qui s'eſt gliſſé parmis pluſieurs de ſortir du Prône & de l'exhortation qui ſe fait aux jours de Fêtes & Dimanches à la Meſſe Paroiſſiale, ſans neceſſité, & pour aller cauſer dans les maiſons pendant le Sermon; cette coûtume qui s'eſt introduite en divers endroits de ce Diocéſe eſt une marque évidente d'indevotion & d'irreligion qui tourne au mépris de la parole de Dieu

7. Et parce que nous avons eſté informez qu'il ſe faiſoit en divers lieux des aſſemblées de danſes & autres divertiſſemens aux jours de Fêtes & Dimanches, & quelquefois même pendant le Service divin, ce qui eſt deffendu par les Ordonnances du Roy & par les Loix de la Police ſeculiere, Nous exhortons & conjurons pour l'amour de Notre-Seigneur, & pour l'honneur de la Religion tous les fidelles de noſtre Diocéſe, de s'abſtenir à l'avenir de ces ſortes de choſes dans leſdits jours, & pour ce qui eſt des danſes & autres recreations dangeureuſes qui ſe pratiquent entre perſonnes de different ſexe, comme l'experience fait voir qu'elles ſont à la pluſpart des occaſions prochaines d'un grand nombre de pechez conſiderables, Nous exhortons les Curez, Confeſſeurs, & autres qui ont ſoin des Ames de les en détourner pâr toutes les voyes les plus efficaces qu'ils pouront trouver.

8. Nous avons auſſi apris avec bien de la douleur qu'un grand nombre de perſonnes ſur tout de jeunes hommes & de garçons ſe donnent la liberté de proferer en toutes rencontres des paroles déshonnêtes, ou a double entente, ce qui cauſant dans les mœurs une corruption qu'on ne peut aſſez deplorer, nous voulons que les Paſteurs & Confeſſeurs uſent de tous les moyens qu'ils jugeront propres pour déraciner cette licence empeſtée; qu'ils ſe comportent à l'endroit des perſonnes habituées à ces infames diſcours, comme envers les impudiques d'habitude & même ſcandaleux, & qu'ils ne leur accordent l'abſolution, qu'aprés qu'ils auront des preuves ſuffiſantes de leur contrition par le retranchement de ces paroles impures pendant un temps raiſonnable.

9. Ayant remarqué que nonobſtant l'exactitude que nous avions apporté à faire connoître aux peuples l'obligation qu'ils ont de payer les diſmes, pluſieurs perſonnes neanmoins s'en diſpenſent; ce qui peut provenir de la facilité que les Curez ont de les abſoudre, ſous pretexte de la crainre qu'ils ont de paroître intereſſez. Nous voulans remedier à ce mal, déclarons que le payement des diſmes étant d'une étroite obligation par les Loix naturelles, divines, Eccleſiaſtiques, & civiles; les peuples ne peuvent manquer à ce devoir ſans ſe rendre coupables de larcin, ou de retention du bien d'autrui, qui tient même du ſacrilége, comme eſtant un bien ſacré & Eccleſiaſtique, & qu'ainſi les Curez & autres Confeſſeurs de ce Diocéſe ne peuvent en conſcience admettre aux Sacremens leſdites perſonnes, c'eſt pourquoi nous leurs enjoignons de ne les y point recevoir, lorſque par leur faute, ils n'auront pas payé les dixmes, ou qui ne les auront point payez fidellement, ſoit en retenant une partie de ce qui eſt deu, ſoit en donnant ce qui eſt de plus mauvais.

Mgr Jean-Baptiste de La Croix de Chevrières de Saint-Vallier. *Ordonnance de Monseigneur l'évesque de Québec pour remédier à différens abus.* Paris: Urbain Coustelier, 1691, pp. 2–3.

Among the abuses denounced by the bishop, let us mention the immodest dress of certain women when at church, the "impure words" that several persons "take the liberty of uttering on every occasion," and "the dances and other dangerous forms of recreation which are practised between persons of different sex."

Public Archives of Canada, Library, Ottawa (Negatives nos. C 113059 and C 113060).

Index